WORLD OF SPORTS INDOOR

WORLD OF SPORTS INDOOR

(In Two Volumes)

(Volume - 1)

Anil Taneja

KALPAZ

World of Sports Indoor

Rs. 1500 (Set)
Rs. 750 each Volume

ISBN: 978-81-7835-765-2 (Set)
ISBN: 978-81-7835-766-9 (Vol.1)

Published in 2009 in India by
Kalpaz Publications
C - 30, Satyawati Nagar,
Delhi - 110052
E-mail: kalpaz@hotmail.com
Phone: 9212729499

Printed at: Singhal Print Media, Delhi

Contents

Preface

Sports has a very significant role to play in the growth and development of mind and body. Indian history of sports dates back to the Vedic times when physical exercises were considered to be a mandatory part of religious rituals. Sports can be classified into two main categories: outdoor and indoor. In India outdoor sporting activities have a greater mass appeal as compared to indoor ones. Cricket is far and away the most popular sport in India. Apart from cricket, India has a worldwide identity in field hockey, chess, lawn tennis, table tennis, formula one racing, badminton, billiards and snooker and to some extent, in football. Relatively recent originzation to the world of virtual intelligence has sparked off a wave of crazy fanaticism particularly among the younger generation.

The whole idea of indoor sports is to give people a healthy and professionally managed environment to enjoy playing throughout the year. In indoor games, it hardly matters if a person is young or old or a serious high grade player. Today, there are a wide variety of games that can be played in indoor stadiums. Indoor games are becoming popular by the day not only for the kids but also for the teens and grown-ups. This book is intended to make readers aware of the rules and regulations of various sports played all over the world, apart from this to make the topic more interesting and knowledge orientation historical facts and records are also been mentioned in the respective sports topics.

However there is no dearth of books and literature on the topic but this book has its own unique and distinctive style of presentation and assimilation of facts in distinguished manner. I am confident enough that the readers will find it interesting to go through the pages of the book. Every possible effort has been made to bring out the book with appropriate correctness but still a few errors are likely to be remained there. Comments and suggestions of the readers are always heartily welcome.

Introduction

Sport is activity that is ruled by a set of regulations or customs and frequently employed in competitively. Sports ordinarily refer to actions where the physical capabilities of the competitor are the sole or primary causal factor of the outcome, but the term is also used to include actions such as mind sports and motor sports where mental keenness or equipment quality are main components. Sport is ordinarily defined as an organized, competitive and skilful physical activity requiring dedication and fair play. Sports differ from games based on levels of organization and profit. Accurate records are kept and updated, while failures and achievements are widely announced in sport news.

There are many views from which sport can be referred to. Thus, very much some binary divisions are stressed, such as: professional — amateur, mass — top-level, active — passive/spectator, men — women, sports - play. Sport has had and continues to have an enormous affect on society and its members. Studies conducted in the 1970s, 1980s, and 1990s disclosed that at least two-thirds of people regarded themselves to be a sport fan. The reason that most people identify themselves as being sports fans though some others have no interest at all in sport can be explicated through sport socialization process.

Families that are highly involved as sports fans in general have a high percentage of children that become socialised into the sport fan role. Though they are well cognisant of the values, notions, attitudes, and norms of the sport fan culture, they are not encouraged to enlist in the activity by any comprehended benefits. Similarly, some individuals who are only indifferently socialized in the sport fan role may become highly concerned fans because they are powerfully prompted by several specific factors. There are dozens of motives, but researchers and theorists have distinguished the following as being the most common: group affiliation, family, aesthetic, self-esteem, economic, eustress, escape, and entertainment.

Sport followers and sport watching can help fulfil the human need for social interaction by providing a sense of belonging. The fact that most spectators consume sport as a fellow member of a social group proposes that fans do indeed use sport to satisfy social interaction needs. Some historians, notably Bernard Lewis, claim that team sports are primarily an invention of Western cultures.

The orthodox teams sports, according to these authors, springs from Europe, primarily England. This ignores some of the ancient games of cooperation from Central America and the Indian subcontinent. The Industrial Revolution and mass production added increased leisure which allowed increases in spectator sports, less elitism in sports, and greater accessibility. With the advent of mass media and global communication, professionalism became prevalent in sports. This further sports popularity in general. Perhaps in a reaction to the demands of contemporary life, there have been developments in sport that are best described as post-modern. For thousands of years people have invented indoor games and sports to amuse themselves when confined within a house or other building. Often these are played in social or family situations, or when darkness or bad weather prevent people from moving outside.

Such amusements have been developed throughout the world. Some, especially those for young children, are largely a matter of luck. Others require a great deal of skill on the part of the players. Perhaps the most famous indoor game is basket ball, which was created as an active sport to be played in the winter time. Many different kinds of board games are played throughout the world, and many of them have been popular for hundreds of years. A few board games are decided by chance or luck alone, but most require some amount of skill on the part of the players.

Luck plays little or no part in games of skill, the outcome is decided by the players' ability to make the most advantageous moves available. Such games are often 'war' games, which involve capturing an opponent's pieces. The most popular of all such games today is chess. Chess is a game of great skill that calls for the ability to plan moves and recognize threats several steps ahead. Each player has an 'army' of 16 pieces with which to fight a battle. There are six different kinds of piece – king, queen, bishop, knight, rook and pawn – and each has its own special way of moving about the board. If a player moves onto a square occupied by an opposing piece, that piece is captured and removed from the board. The object of the game is to trap (checkmate) the enemy king by putting it in a position where it cannot escape capture.

Various indoor games, including billiards, snooker and pool, are played on a large, flat, cloth-covered table with six pockets. In these games, each of the two players tries to pot the balls (knock them into the pockets) by striking them with a cue-ball, which is hit with the tip of a stick called a cue.

In snooker there are 22 balls: 1 cue-ball, 15 reds and 6 colours. A player must first pot one of the red balls (scoring 1 point) and then one of the colours, which are worth between 2 points (yellow) and 7 (black). The colour ball is put back on the table, and the player tries to put another red. The turn or break continues until the player fails to score or plays a foul shot. When the entire red are have gone, the colours are potted in sequence from yellow to black, which marks the end of the game or frame. The winner of the frame is the player with the most points. Most professional matches are decided over a fixed number of frames.

1

Badminton

Badminton is an indoor sport in which the contestants bat a shuttlecock to and fro over a net without admitting the shuttlecock to reach the ground. The aim of the sport is to hit the shuttlecock to the floor on the other side of the net, so that the shot cannot be picked up and returned. Only the serving player can score a point. Badminton singles is played by two opponents and doubles by teams of two individuals.

The badminton owes its starting and development in India, to the English army officers. The game assumed broad popularity in India. Its original rules were printed in Karachi, which was then a part of India, in 1877. Indian badminton developed, with the first main sport in Britain, where the first main international badminton competition started in 1899 under the name at present famous as the All England Championships. The badminton was put on organizational basis in India, in the 1920's. All India Tournaments started to be established in the middle of the thirties.

The Badminton Association of England was constituted in 1893 with rules and regulations founded on those drawn up at Karachi. From England it spread to Denmark and U.S.A. The International Badminton Federation was establishedin 1934. The two chief matches of badminton are the Thomas Cup for men and the Uber Cup for women.

Davinder Mohan, Amrit Dewan, Nandu Natekar, Prakash Nath etc. were some of the famous Indian badminton players. Nandu Natekar was the first Indian to win a title abroad - the Men's singles in the Selangor International Tournament in Kuala Lumpur in 1956. Prakash Padukone was among the world's notable player of badminton.

HISTORY

Its origins date back all over two thousand years, to 500 years before the birth of Christ and a sport called 'Ti Jian Zi' which was played in Ancient China.It was played by kicking something alike to the modern day shuttlecock, without the utilization the of rackets.

By the time of the birth of Christ, the sport 'Battledore and Shuttlecock' was being played in China, Japan and Greece. A badminton racket was a simple bat, and the intention of the sport was to hit the shuttlecock back and forward as numerous times as possible.It is unclear where the roots of the shuttlecock lie, though it is possible that the cork base was used to store feath, and then first thrown and then hit when it was found that it flew well.

By the 16th Century Battledore had developed into a children's sport and over the following century got famous with the upper classes in Europe. In land Europe it was called by its French name 'jeu de volant'.

By the mid nineteenth century a sport known'poona' had formulated in India that more closely corresponded modern-day badminton. British Army officers who were placed in India started picking up the sport, memorializing some fundamental principles and were responsible bringing it back to England.All over the same time the Duke of Beauford started innovating it to the noble and royal society at his estate in Gloucestershire, England.This estate was called Badminton House.It is advised that here the thought of putting a string among the players was born, along with trying to hit the shuttlecock away from your antagonist.

Inside a few years the Bath Badminton Club had been organized and the rules and regulations as they are at present started to be formulated. And the sport had a new name – Badminton. Clubs started appearing all round the country over the following few years and in 1893 there was a meeting of 14 of the most outstanding in Southsea in Hampshire. Soon after that meeting, the original national badminton association was established and the original set of principles were formalised. As the game went from the genteel matter that it had been to a more competitory one, the original competitions took place right at the end of that century, with the first international 'All England' tournament happening in 1899.

One of the early legend of the sport was the English tennis star Kitty Godfree who was badminton champion three times in the 1920s. As other national badminton associations started seeming and the sport received popularity all over the world, in 1934 the International Badminton Federation (IBF) was established.The real members were England, Wales, Ireland, Scotland, Denmark, Holland, Canada, New Zealand and France.India linked up as an affiliate in 1936, with Australia and United States not long after that.

The American Badminton Association had already been established in 1936 and the game had been famous there since 1878 when the 'Badminton Club of New York' was established.

As the popularity raised, the first major IBF tournament was the men's team championship, the Thomas Cup, in 1949, called after the first IBF President, Sir George Thomas. It was primitively going to be in 1939 but had to be held over due to the war.The first ladies team championship was in 1956 when the US won the Uber Cup.As more competitions were being deemed, badminton turned a manifestation game at the 1972 Munich Olympic Games.The first World Badminton Championships, including singles events were held in 1977.

Over the following decade the game extended to be prevailed by Asians, most notably China's top women Li Lingwei and Han Aiping. Morten Frost of Denmark was one exception, winning over seventy international titles throughout the 1980s.By then badminton had turn a professional game, with the IBF laying down the World Grand Prix Circuit and prize money commencing to improve.Badminton came back as an exhibition game in the 1988 Seoul Olympics and was given full medal status at the 1992 Barcelona

Then, international concern in the game in real started taking off as sponsor money and TV coverage began increasing and the world turned attracted to the speed and excitement of the sport.Mixed doubles was brought in at the 1996 Atlanta Games. Badminton at present has the glory of being the fastest racket game (the fastest smash was clocked at 260 kilometres per hour by Great Britain's Simon Archer) as well as one of the most widely played sports all around the world, and is developing in popularity all the time.

THE GAME

Court

The court is rectangular and separated into halves by a net. Courts are always labeled for both singles and doubles play, even though the laws allow a court to be marked for singles only. The doubles court is broader than the singles court, but both are the similar length. The exception, which often leads confusion to newer players, is that the doubles court has a shorter serve-length dimension.

The full breadth of the court is 6.1 metres (twenty ft), and in singles this breadth is cut down to 5.18 metres (seventeen ft). The entire length of the court is 13.4 metres (forty-four ft). The service courts are marked by a centre line separating the breadth of the court, by a short service line at a distance of 1.98 metres (6.5 ft) from the net, and by the outer side and back boundaries. In doubles, the service court is also labeled by a long service line, which is 0.78 metres (2 ft 6 inch) from the back boundary.

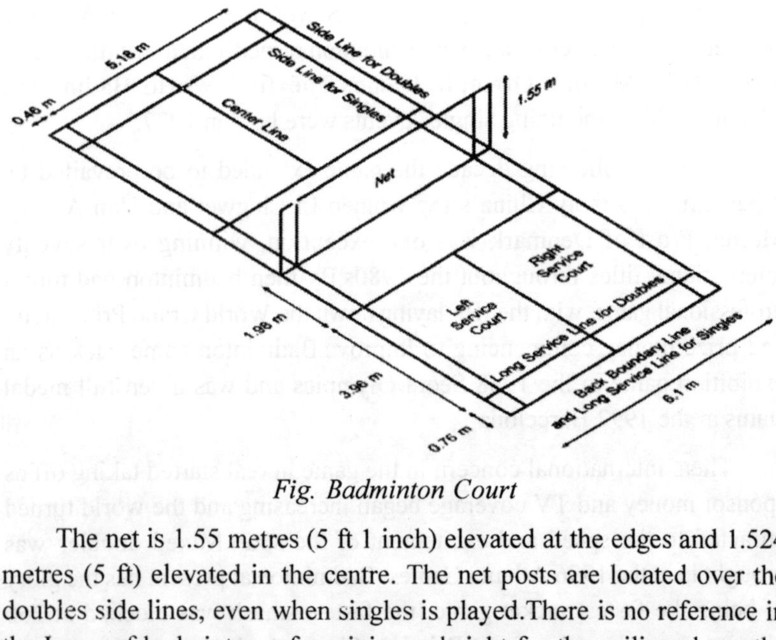

Fig. Badminton Court

The net is 1.55 metres (5 ft 1 inch) elevated at the edges and 1.524 metres (5 ft) elevated in the centre. The net posts are located over the doubles side lines, even when singles is played.There is no reference in the Laws of badminton, of a minimum height for the ceiling above the court. However, a badminton court will not be desirable if the ceiling is likely to be strike on a high serve.

Equipments

Rackets: Badminton rackets are light, with top quality rackets weighing from 79 and 91 grams including the strings. They are composed of many dissimslar materials ranging from carbon fibre composite to solid steel, which may be augmented by a variety of materials. Carbon fibre has an excellent strength to weight ratio, is stiff, and gives excellent kinetic energy transfer. Before the adoption of carbon fibre composite, rackets were made of light metals such as aluminium. Earlier still, rackets were made of wood. Cheap rackets are still often made of metal, but wooden rackets are no longer manufactured for the ordinary market, due to their excessive mass and cost.

Fig. Racket

There is a broad variety of racquet designs, even though the racquet size and shape are limited by the Laws. Dissimslar rackets have playing characteristics that appeal to dissimslar players.

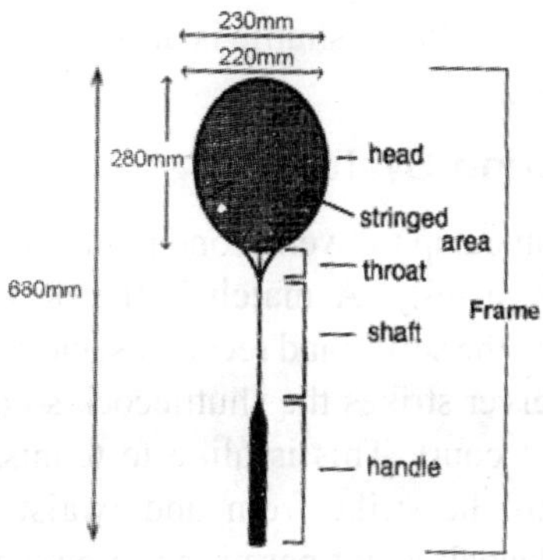

Fig: Dimensions of Badminton Racket

The traditional oval head shape is still available, but an isometric head shape is increasingly common in new rackets.

Shuttlecock: A shuttlecock is a high-drag projectile, with an exposed conical shape: the cone is established from sixteen overlapping goose feathers planted into a rounded cork base. The cork is covered up with thin leather or synthetic material.

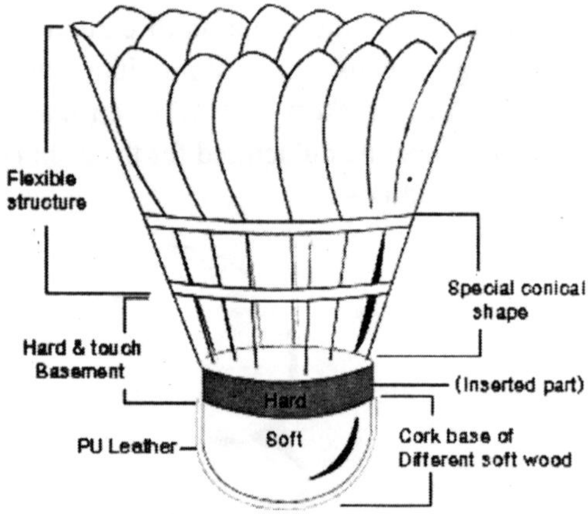

Fig. Shuttlecock

Shuttles with a plastic or nylon skirt are frequently used by recreational players to cut down their costs as feathered shuttles break up easily. These nylon shuttles may be developed with a cork made of a hard sponge rather of natural cork.

Moreover, nylon shuttlecocks come in three varieties, every variety for a dissimslar range of temperatures. These 3 varieties are as green (slow speed), blue (middle speed), and red (fast speed). The colours, and hence speeds, are pointed by colour strips fastened all over the cork. In colder temperatures, a slower shuttle is utilized, and in hotter climates, a faster one is chosen.

Service and Scoring System

Each game is played up to twenty-one points, with players making a point when they win a rally. A match is the best of 3 games.At the commence of the rally, the server and receiver stand in diagonally opposite service courts The server strikes the shuttlecock so that it would land in the receiver's service court. This is alike to tennis, leaving out that a badminton serve must be strike from underwaist in underhand form (upwards), the shuttlecock is not permitted to bounce, and in tennis the players stand outside their service courts.

When the serving side misses a rally, the serve goes on to their antagonists. In singles, the server stands in his right service court when his score is even, and in his left service court when his score is odd.In doubles, if the serving side succeeds a rally, the similar player extends to serve, but he alters service courts so that he serves to each antagonist in turn. If the antagonists succeed the rally and their new score is even, the player in the right service court serves; if odd, the player in the left service court serves. The players' service courts are decided by their positions at the start of the previous rally, not by where they were standing at the end of the rally. A result of this system is that, each time a side regains the service, the server will be the player who did not serve final time.

Strategy

To succeed in badminton, players must require to employ a broad variety of strokes in the right situations. These range from powerful jumping smashes to delicate tumbling net returns. Often rallies cease with a smash, but setting up the smash requires subtler strokes. For instance, a net shot can force the antagonist to lift the shuttlecock, which gives an chance to smash. If the net shot is tight and tumbling, then the antagonist's lift will not reach the back of the court, which makes the subsequent smash much harder to return.

Deception is also crucial. Expert players make the preparation for many dissimslar strokes look identical, and utilize slicing to deceive their antagonists about the speed or direction of the stroke. If an opposer tries to predict the stroke, he may move in the wrong direction and may be ineffective to change his body momentum in time to reach the shuttlecock.

Doubles: Both pairs will try to win and maintain the attack, smashing downwards when possible. When possible, a pair will adopt an ideal attacking formation with one player hitting down from the rearcourt, and his partner in the midcourt intercepting all smash returns except the lift. If the rearcourt attacker plays a dropshot, his partner will move into the forecourt to endanger the net reply.

If a pair cannot hit downwards, they will utilize flat strokes in an attempt to gain the attack. If a pair is forced to lift or clear the shuttlecock, then they must oppose: they will adopt a side-by-side position in the rear midcourt, to cover the full width of their court against the antagonists' smashes. In doubles, players in general smash to the middle ground among two players in order to take advantage of confusion and clashes.

At eminent levels of play, the backhand serve has become famous to the level that forehand serves at most never appear in professional sports. The straight low serve is utilized most often, in an attempt to preclude the antagonists winning the attack immediately. Flick serves are utlized to preclude the antagonist from anticipating the low serve and attacking it decisively.At eminent levels of play, doubles rallies are super fast. Men's doubles is the chippiest form of badminton, with a high symmetry of powerful jump smashes.

Singles: The singles court is broader than the doubles court, but the similar length, with the exclusion that a serve in the single can arrive at the end of the court while a serve in the doubles could not. Since one person demands to cover the entire court, singles tactics are grounded on drawing the antagonist to move as far as possible; this means that singles strokes are usually directed to the corners of the court.

Players exploit the length of the court by combining lifts and clears with dropshots and netshots. Smashing is less spectacular in singles than in doubles as players are rarely in the ideal position to carry out a smash, and smashing often leaves the smasher vulnerable if the smash is came back.

In singles, players will often begin the rally with a forehand eminent serve. Low serves are also used often, either forehand or backhand. Flick serves are less common, and drive serves are rare.At high levels of play, singles requires extraordinary fitness. Singles is a sport of patient positional maneuvering, unlike the all-out aggression of doubles.

Mixed Doubles: In mixed doubles, both mates try to preserve an attacking formation with the woman at the front and the man at the back. This is because the male players are considerably stronger, and can hence develop more powerful smashes. As a result, mixed doubles involves greater tactical consciousness and subtler positional play. Clever opposers will try to reverse the ideal position, by forcing the woman towards the back or the man towards the front. In order to defend against this danger, mixed players must be careful and systematic in their shot selection.

At eminent levels of play, the establishments will in general be more flexible: the top women players are capable of playing powerfully from the rear court, and will jubilantly do so if required. When the chance arises, still, the pair will switch back to the standard mixed attacking position, with the woman in front.

Faults

Players succeed a rally by striking the shuttlecock over the net and onto the floor inside the boundaries of their antagonists' court. Players also succeed a rally if their antagonists invest a fault. The most common fault in badminton is when the players fail to counter back the shuttlecock so that it passes over the net and lands inside their antagonists' court, but there are besides other ways that players may be faulted. Various faults pertain specific to service.

A serving player shall be faulted if the shuttlecock is over his waist at point of contact, or if his racket's head is not heading downwards at the moment of impact. This peculiar law was altered in 2006, previously, the server's racket had to be directing downwards to the level that the racket head was below the hand holding the racket; and now, any angle beneath the horizontal is satisfactory.

Neither the server nor the receiver may raise a foot till the shuttlecock has been hit by the server. The server must also primarily hit the base (cork) of the shuttlecock, even though he may later on also hit the feathers as part of the similar stroke. This law was brought in to ban an extremely effective service style known as the S-serve or Sidek serve, which permitted the server to make the shuttlecock spin chaotically in flight.Each side may only hit the shuttlecock one time before it goes back over the net; but throughout a single stroke movement, a player may contact a shuttlecock twice.A player may not, nevertheless, hit the shuttlecock once and then hit it with a new movement, nor may he persuade and sling the shuttlecock on his racket.

Lets

If a let is yelled, the rally is blocked and replayed with no alteration to the score. Lets may take place due to some unexpected disturbance such as a shuttlecock setting down on court or in small halls the shuttle may touch an overhead rail which can be classed as a let.If the receiver is not prepare when the service is delivered, a let shall be called; yet if the receiver makes any attempt to return the shuttlecock, he shall be judged to have been ready.There is no let if the shuttlecock strikes the tape.

MAJOR TOURNAMENTS

Olympics

Badminton had its introduction at the 1992 Summer Olympics and has been contended in four Olympiads. fifty dissimslar nations have came out in the Olympic badminton contests, with nineteen appearing all four times. It is ruled by the Badminton World Federation.

Four events were deemed, with singles and doubles events for both men and women. Four medals were granted in each event, including two bronzes. The following Olympiad, Atlanta 1996, had 5 events with the addition of mixed doubles. There was also now a playoff among the two semi-final losers to determine the sole winner of the bronze medal. That layout has been utilized for the 2000 and 2004 Summer Olympics.The Badminton World Federation's ranking list is used to decide qualification for the Olympic tournament. For singles, 29 contenders are choosen. For doubles, nineteen pairs are picked out.

The universal method of selection is by ranking, though the selection process blocks once all qualification positions are filled. All players or pairs from the top sixteen places on that list qualify, though each National Olympic Committee can send a utmost of three players/pairs. Players and pairs through the sixty-fourth place on that ranking qualify, with the caveat that each NOC can send only two players/pairs from that portion of the list. Players and pairs placed below that only qualify if they are the most eminent ranked competitor from their nation.

Olympic badminton comprises of a single-elimination tournament. Each match is acted to the best of three games. Games are to twenty-one points. Rally scoring is utilized, meaning a player does not demand to be serving to score. A player must succeed by two points or be the first player to thirty points.

Thomas Cup

The Thomas Cup, sometimes known as the World Men's Team Championships, is an international badminton competition between teams presenting member nations of the Badminton World Federation (BWF), the game's global organization. The championships have been carried on every two years since the 1982 tournament, improved from being conducted every three years since the first tournament deemed in 1948-1949.

The last phase of the tournament requires twelve teams contending at venues inside the host nation. The last phase of the tournament is also often known as the Thomas & Uber Cup, because it is played concurrently with the women's championships, the Uber Cup (organized since 1956-1957), as a joint extravaganza held at the similar general time and similar venue commencing in 1984. However, this unification will exist for final time in the 2008 tournament, as the BWF has already announced that each championship will be held separately once again commencing in 2010.

Of the twenty-five Thomas Cup tournaments deemed since 1948-1949, only three nations have won the title. Indonesia is the most prosperous squad, having won the tournament 13 times. The present cup holder, China, which did not commences to contend until the 1981-1982 series, follows Indonesia with seven titles, while Malaysia has won five titles. Thomas Cup and, to a lesser extent, Uber Cup are likely the world's "biggest" regularly held badminton events in terms of player and fan interest, trumping main tournaments for individual competitors such as the revered All-England Championships, the BWF World Championships, and even the badminton competitions at the Olympic Games.The 2008 Thomas Cup was contended in Jakarta, Indonesia.

The Thomas Cup contest was the idea of Sir George Alan Thomas, a extremely successful English badminton player of the early 1900's, who was inspired by tennis's Davis Cup and football's (soccer's) World Cup, first held in 1930. His idea was well welcomed at the general meeting of the International Badminton Federation (now Badminton World Federation) in 1939.In the similar year, Sir George introduced the Thomas Cup, formally known as The International Badminton Championship Challenge Cup, developed by Atkin Bros of London at a cost of US$40,000. The Cup stands 28 inches high and 16 inches at its widest, and consists of three parts: a plinth (pedestal), a bowl, and a lid with player figure.

The first tournament was primitively planned for 1941-1942 (badminton seasons in the northern hemisphere traditionally ran from the autumn of one calendar year to the spring of the following), but was retarded when World War II exploded all over the continents. Sir George's dream was finally realized in 1948-1949 when ten national teams took part in the first Thomas Cup competition. Three qualifying zones were laid down: Pan America, Europe, and the Pacific; though Malaya (now Malaysia) was the only Pacific zone participant. In a layout that would last until 1984, all ties (matches among nations) would consist of nine individual matches; the victorious nation needing to win at least five of these contests. The top two singles player on each side faced up both of the top two players on the other side, accounting for four matches. A fifth singles match was held among the third ranked singles players on each squad. At last, two doubles pairings on each side played both of the doubles pairings on the other side, accounting for four more matches. Each tie was usually contended over two days, four matches on the first day and five on the following.The United States and Denmark won their respective zone qualifications and thus joined Malaya for the inter-zone ties.

The inter-zone ties were starded in the United Kingdom. As the tournament utilized a knockout (single elimination) system, instead of than a round-robin system, one country, Denmark, was given a bye in the first round. Malaya overcame the USA 6–3 in an extremely competitive match played in Glasgow, Scotland (curiously, none of the players on either side had ever seen any of the players on the other side play before). Of note, this tie marked the first of only three ever matches among the USA's Dave Freeman and Malaya's Wong Peng Soon the two E singles players of the early post-war period. In the last round deemed in Preston, England, Malaya beat Denmark 8–1 and turned the first nation to win a Thomas Cup.

The old knockout zone qualification system in which each tie was played at a different venue and time was ruled out. Instead, common qualifying venues brought many teams together to contend in group round-robin ties followed by playoffs among group leaders. As few as one or as many as three teams from a given venue (depending upon the previously assessed strength of its field) would qualify for the final phase of the competition which until 2004 was limited to eight teams. The number of qualifying venues prior to 2004 varied among two and four and their sites basically reflected the long existent loci of badminton strength in the Far East and (to a lesser extent) in Europe.

The European qualifying venue normally hosted the greatest number of teams and to streamline play and produce more competitive ties, a two tiered system was finally instituted there. Weaker badminton nations played-off in groups for the right to contest with the stronger national teams. To have an easier road to the inter-zone competition strong Asian teams sometimes contended outside of their "natural" qualification venue. Rising power South Korea, for instance, won qualifications deemed in North America in 1986 and in 1988.

BWF World Championships

The BWF World Championships (officially known as IBF World Championships, also called as the World Badminton Championships) is a tournament organised by the Badminton World Federation (BWF) to crown the topmost badminton players in the world.

The tournament began in 1977 and was deemed once every 3 years till 1983. Nonetheless, the IBF faced trouble in hosting the first two events as the World Badminton Federation (which afterwards merged with the IBF to form one badminton federation) hosted the similar tournament a year after the IBF World Championships with the similar aims.

Started in 1985, the tournament turned bi-annual and played once every two years until 2005. Commencing 2006, the tournament was altered to an yearly event on the BWF calendar with the aim to give more chances for the players to be crowned as official "World Champions".Nonetheless, the tournament will not be held once every four years to give way to the Olympic Games.

From 1977 up to 2001, the medals were normally divided amongst five countries chiefly China, Korea, Denmark, Indonesia, and Malaysia. Nonetheless, in 2003, the winners let in seven countries and in 2005 the medal board contained a record high of ten countries.Tony Gunawan holds the distinction of gaining a gold medal in Men's Doubles, representing two dissimslar countries, 2001 partnering with Halim Haryanto for Indonesia and in 2005 partnering with Howard Bach to give the United States its first medal in the competition.

The 2005 edition also brought new faces in the mixed doubles event which had been prevailed by China and Korea since 1997. With the retirement of opposing champions and two time winners Kim Dong-moon/Ra Kyung-min (Korea), Nova Widianto/Lilyana Natsir won Indonesia's first mixed doubles gold since 1980 when Christian Hadinata/ Imelda Wijuno won it last for Indonesia.

China has been the most prosperous in the World Championships after its inception in 1977. They were the only country ever to attain a shutout of the medals which they did in 1987 in Beijing. They are complied by Indonesia and Korea with Denmark being the leading European country in the winners list.

ADMINISTRATIVE BODIES

Badminton World Federation

The Badminton World Federation (BWF) is the international organization for the game of badminton. Established in 1934 as the International Badminton Federation with 9 member nations (Canada, Denmark, England, France, Ireland, Netherlands, New Zealand, Scotland and Wales), the BWF has later expanded to achieve international identification. On September 24, 2006, at the Extraordinary General

Meeting in Madrid, it was determined to adopt the new name Badminton World Federation (BWF).

Its head office has been situated in Cheltenham, UK since its founding, but on October 1, 2005, it is now situated in Kuala Lumpur. Its present president is Kang Young Joong.The BWF on regular basis organizes six main international badminton events.The BWF adds special honours onto players, umpires, sponsors and other individuals for their accomplishment in badminton or for their contributions to badminton.

FAMOUS PLAYERS

David G. Freeman

Dr. David G. Freeman (6 September 1920 – 28 June 2001) was an American badminton player from California who was an icon in the game's history.

From early in 1939, at the age of eighteen, through his final tournament match fourteen years later on, Freeman was unconquered in singles competition. Displaying his characteristic quickness, agility, and shot-making precision, Freeman gained the honoured All-England Championship on his only try (1949) and stays the sole American to win the men's singles here. Afterwards apparently retiring from badminton in 1950 to focus on a career in neurosurgery, Freeman made a brief comeback in 1953 succeeding the four tournaments that he entered including the U.S. National Championship. He is the only American born male to be induced into both the U.S. and World Badminton Halls of Fame.

Rexy Mainaky

Rexy Ronald Mainaky (born March 9, 1968 in Ternate) is a men's doubles badminton player of Indonesia who is simply calledas Rexy.

He is a previous world champion and Olympic champion in the men's doubles with his partner, Ricky Subagdja. Collectively with Ricky, they gained the gold medal at the 1996 Summer Olympics in Atlanta, United States. In 1995, they were crowned world champions after succeeding the finals against Denmark's J.H.Christensen/Thomas Lund in the Badminton World Championships in Lausanne.They are amongst the fastest playing men's doubles pair the world till yet, ill-famed for their killer jumping smashes.Now, he is the men's doubles coach of Malaysia. Prior to this, he was coaching for England

Prakash Padukone

Prakash Padukone (born June 10, 1955) is a eminent badminton player from Karnataka, India. Prakash was inducted into the sport at a tender age by his father Ramesh Padukone, Secretary of the Mysore Badminton Association for many years.

Padukone's 1st official tournament was the Karnataka state junior championship in 1962. Though he lost in the very first round, two years afterwards he managed to gain the state junior title. He altered his playing style into a more aggressive style in 1971, and gained the Indian national junior title in 1972. He also won the senior title the similar year. He won the Indian national title consecutively for the following seven years, until 1979. In 1975, he joined the Union Bank of India as a probationary officer where he extended till 1986.

In 1978, he won his 1st major international title, that of the Commonwealth Games. Wins at the London Masters' Open, the Denmark Open and the Swedish Open. He gained the desired All England Open title in 1980 with a victory over Indonesian rival Liem Swie King. He passed much of his international career training in Denmark, and produced close friendships with European players such as Morten Frost.

Prakash presently lives in Bangalore with wife Ujjala and two daughters, and runs the Prakash Padukone Badminton Academy. He was granted the Arjuna award in 1972 and the Padma Shri in 1982.After his retirement in 1991, he was the chairman of the Badminton Association of India for a short while. He was the coach of the Indian national badminton squad in 1993 and 1996.

He in recent times had his biography published at the 2006 nationals. The book, Touchplay, is composed by Dev Sukumar.Prakash is also the father of model and actress, Deepika Padukone.

Aparna Popat

Aparna Popat (born on January 18, 1978 in Mumbai, Maharashtra) is an Indian female badminton player, rated amongst the finest badminton players in the world. As a Badminton player she is known for her elegant movements on the court, deft volleys and immense concentration. Aparna studied at the J.B.Petit School in Mumbai, and her Pre university from Mount Carmel Collge, Bangalore. Aparna also reserves a Bachelors degree in Commerce from the Mumbai University.

Aparna took up the game of badminton at the age of 8 and by the time she was 13, succeeding National level and State level tournaments turned a habit. While in Mumbai, she was coached by Anil Pradhan for 10 years. As a kid while she was playing in a garden, Mr. Anil Pradhan examined a spark in the girl and drew close her parents. True to his allegiance he made a champion of her.

He has also to his credit three national champions—Jyothi Sanghi, Radhika Bose. Radhika Bose was his first student who turned a national champion. Under his able guidance, she developed the skill demanded to face many challenges of the sport. After that, she shifted to Prakash Padukone's Badminton Academy in Bangalore in 1994 to extend her capability. Aparna considers Prakash as her role model.

The 5' 3" tall young girl gained the gold medal at the SAARC championships and a bronze medal at the Prince Junior Badminton Invitation Tournament, Hong Kong in 1996. She was the runner-up in the World Junior Championship at Denmark in 1996. She also gained the Women's Singles in the French Open, Paris in 1998 and a silver at the Commonwealth Games at Kuala Lumpur in the similar year. She gained a bronze at the Manchester Commonwealth Games in 2002. She also presented the country in the Sydney Olympic Games 2000 and was India's sole badminton interpreter at the 2004 Olympic Games, overcoming Michelle Edwards of South Africa in the first round but losing to Mia Audina of the Netherlands in the round of 16. She is employed with the Indian Oil Corporation. She is presently ranked 56th in the world.

REFERENCES

Badminton Association of England. *Know the Game Badminton.* New York, Sport-Shelf (distributors), Box 634, 1956.

Davidson, Kenneth R., and Lealand R. Gustavson : *Winning Badminton.* New York, Ronald Press Co., 1964.

Davidson, Kenneth R., and Lenore C. Smith: *Badminton.* New York, Sterling Publishing Co., 1961.

Davidson, Kenneth R., and Lenore C. Smith (consultants): *Badminton, Instructor's Guide*. Chicago, The Athletic Institute, 1950.

Davis, Dorothy (ed.): *Selected Tennis-Badminton Articles.* Washington, D.C., American Association for Health, Physical Education, and Recreation, 1963.

Devlin, J. Frank, and Rex Lardner: *Sports Illustrated Book of Badminton.* Philadelphia, J. B. Lippincott Co., 1967.

Friedrich, John, and Abbie Rutledge: *Beginning Badminton*. Belmont, Wadsworth Publishing Co., Inc., 1962

Grant, Doug: *Badminton, the International Textbook of the Game*. Montreal, Graphic Publishing Co., 1950.

Radford, Noel: *Badminton*. London, Pitman Publishing Corp., 1954.

Rogers, Wynn: *Advanced Badminton*. Dubuque, William C. Brown Co. Publishers, 1969.

Tennis-Badminton Guide. Washington, D.C., Division for Girls and Women's Sports, American Association for Health, Physical Education, and Recreation. Published biennially.

Varner, Margaret: *Badminton*. Dubuque, William C. Brown Co. Publishers, 1966.

2

Bowling

Bowling is a game in which player's effort to mark points by rolling a bowling ball along a flat surface either into objects called pins or to get close to a target ball. There are numerous forms of bowling, with the most former dating back to ancient Egypt, while other illustrates where bowling was first seen can be followed to ancient Finland and Yemen, and much later in 300 A.D. in Germany.

HISTORY

Throughout the 3d and 4th centuries, game was a religious ceremony for deciding absence of sin. German parishioners had to roll or throw an object at a pin or kegel (derivation of the word kegler for bowler) to keep off executing an act of penance.

The most former known legislation versus bowling dates to 14th Century England. The game had turn so famous that people were neglecting the archery practice necessary for national defense throughout the 100 Year War (a misnomer, since it actually lasted from 1337 to 1453). Both King Edward III who reigned from 1327-1377 and King Richard II (1377-1399) banned the sport. From Europe to America, bowling has been banned during the world for the "evil it leashes on society."

A life size diorama at The International Bowling Museum and Hall of Fame presents Martin Luther bowling on the single lane at the side of his home. A pamphlet from the Museum states that Luther, an avid bowler, "once preached a sermon which, if put into bowling vernacular, proclaimed we all strive for perfection in life. But if we roll a gutterball, all is not lost." Dutch Colonists brought bowling to America in the 17th century. The sport consisted of nine pins set in a triangle. It was on regular basis played in an area of New York City still known as "Bowling Green".

In 1841, Connecticut banned "bowling at the game of ninepins" because of widespread gambling. Other states followed suit. It is popularly conceived that at present's game of tenpins was devised to circumvent the laws against the game of ninepins. An outdoor sport for most of its history, indoor bowling turned famous in the mid-nineteenth century after the introduction of indoor lanes in New York in 1840.

THE GAME

There are many types of bowling versions played all over the world.these include the following mentioned below:

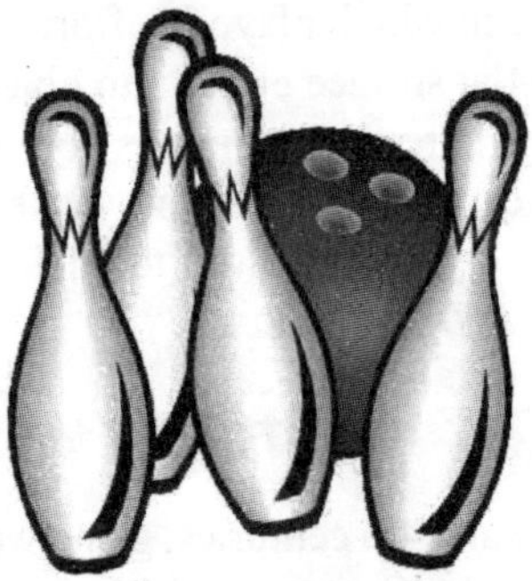

Fig. Pins & Ball

- Ten-pin bowling: In the United States, tenpins is the better known form of bowling, which in both amateur and professional variants, is also played all over the world, making it one of the most prominent participation activities. The balls have two or more drilled holes in which to insert fingers for gripping the ball.
- Candlepin bowling: Acted in eastern Canada and in New England, a version of ten-pin bowling, with "double-ended" pins that are the tallest in any bowling game.
- Duckpin bowling: Commonly determined in the mid-Atlantic and southern New England states and eastern Canada, is another version of ten-pin bowling demanding small, squat pins, sometimes with rubber at their widest points (rubber band duckpin bowling). The functionary small pin is about 9 3/8 inches (24 cm) high and 4 1/8 inches (10 cm) in diameter at its widest part. It weighs no more than 1 pound 8½ ounces (700g). The normalduckpin ball has no finger holes. The maximal diameter

is 5 inches (13 cm). For duckpins and candlepins, the maximum weight of the ball is 4 pounds 12 oz (1.7 kg).

- Five-pin bowling: Played in Canada.
- Nine-pin skittles: Played in Europe.
- Bumper bowling: Ten-pin bowling acted with the addition of barriers to the channels, making "gutter balls" nearly not possible, famous with children's parties.
- Power Wheelchair Bowling: Recent betterments have made it possible for people who are critically disabled to bowl alongside able bodied players through use of a ramp that accompanies the wheelchair. This game is sanctioned by the United States Bowling Congress

Ten-pin Bowling

Ten-pin bowling is a competitory game in which a player (the "bowler") rolls a bowling ball down a wooden or synthetic (polyurethane) lane with the aim of making points by knocking down as many pins as possible.

Fig. Correct Position

The 41.5-inch (105 cm) broad, 60-foot (18 m) lane is bordered along its length by "gutters"—semicircular channels planned to collect errant balls which also pose an obstacle to advance bowlers, as a straight ball cannot be rolled on a regulation lane at the angle needed to consistently carry (knock down) all ten pins for a strike. Most practiced bowlers will roll a more difficult-to-control hook ball to overcome this. There is a foul line at the end of the lane closest to the bowler: if any part of a bowler's body reaches the lane side of this line after the ball is delivered (rolled), it is called a foul and no pins knocked over by that delivery are scored.

(The bowler is permitted a shot at a new rack of ten pins if he fouled on the first roll of a frame.) Behind the foul line is an "approach" approximately 15 feet (5 m) long utilized to gain speed and leverage on the ball before delivering it. 60 feet (18 m) from the foul line, where the lane terminates, it is connected to a roughly 24-inch (61 cm), 41.5-inch (105 cm) broad surface of durable and impact-resistant material called the "pin deck" where each rack of pins is set.

The bowler is permitted ten frames in which to knock down pins, with each frame being composed of up to two rolls. The tenth frame may be compiled of up to three rolls: the bonus roll(s) complying a strike or spare in the tenth (sometimes referred to as the eleventh and twelfth frames) are fill ball used only to calculate the score of the mark rolled in the tenth. Bowling hans a unparalleled scoring system that is notoriously bewildering to newcomers who attempt to score a sport with multiple marks (strikes and spares). Bowling scores incline to be unintuitive: if a bowler was to knock down 9 pins with his first shot but miss his spare every frame, he would have a score of 90; if the similar bowler were to make all of his spares and knock down 9 with the bonus ball, he would have a score of 190. If he were to hold all ten pins with each shot and strike with each of his bonus balls in the tenth frame, he would have shot a perfect game of 300.

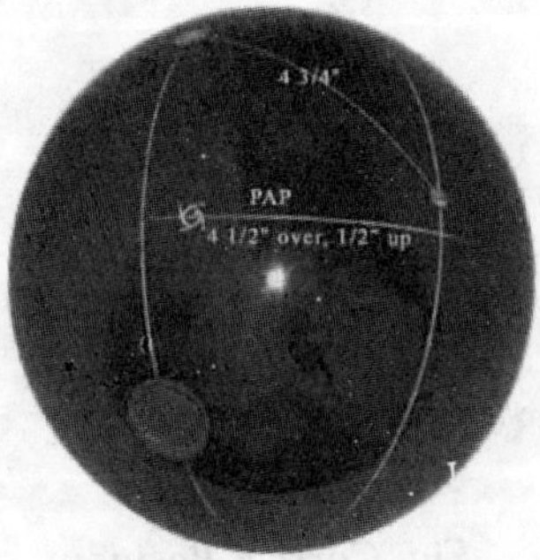

Fig. Ball

Since being locomoted to the United States from Europe, ten-pin bowling (thought to be came down from the game of skittles) has risen in popularity as its technology has bettered. The game is most famous in the United Kingdom and the United States. Both nations preserve national regulatory establishments that govern the game's rules and regulations and conduct and many of those countries' topmost players take part in tournaments on both the national and international stage. Because of the ascend in popularity, many companies are now creating bowling balls and apparel for professionals as well as for recreational bowlers. Bowling has also become more prevalent in the media in recent years, with the extended popularity of bowling publications and the appearance of films centred all over the culture of the game. However, the game extends to face challenges in garnering mainstream coverage of the athletic aspects of the sport.

Candlepin Bowling

Candlepin bowling is a version of bowling that is played chiefly in various New England states, and in the Canadian Maritime provinces of New Brunswick, Prince Edward Island, and Nova Scotia.Candlepin Bowling pins are determined as 15 /4 inches (400 mm) in height, have indistinguishable ends, and are almost 3 inches (76 mm) in diameter at the center.

Fig. Different Position

Each lane comprises of an approach area 14'-16' long for the player to bowl from, and then the lane proper, a maple surface approximately 41" broad, bounded on either side by a "channel", or trough. The lane is isolated from approach area by a foul line, which must not be intersected by players. At the far end of the lane, about 60' away, are the pins (60' from the foul line to the center of the headpin or pin #1), placed by a machine called a pinsetter which resides space both above and behind the pins. Backside the pins is a slightly depressed area for pins and balls to fall into, and a curtain behind this to gently stop the pins and balls from going any further. In general there is seating behind the approach area for teammates and spectators, and containing a small table to hold scorepads.

Candlepin pins are 15.75" (400 mm) tall, have a cylindric shape which tapers evenly toward each end (and hence having no distinct "top" or "bottom" end, unlike a tenpin), giving them an overall appearing somewhat like that of a candle. The ten candlepins are automatically set by machine into a triangle with four pins in the back row, then three, two, and finally one in the front, at the center of the lane. Numering of the candlepins is exactly the similar as in tenpin bowling, with the frontmost central pin being the number 1 pin, the two instantly behind and beside it being numbered two and three, and so on, to the rightmost rear corner pin being the number ten pin. it As in ten-pin bowling, due to the spacing of the pins (12", or 30.5 cm, center to center), it is not possible for the ball to strike every one. However, while in ten-pin a well-placed ball (normally among the front pin and one of its nearest neighbors) may knock down all ten pins from the chain reaction of pin hitting pin (a strike), in candlepin the smaller thickness of the pins makes throwing a strike extremely difficult. In general, a forcefully thrown ball striking near the center of the pins will outcome in many pins being knocked down, but not all. In order to count, the pin must be turned over entirely; in unlucky circumstances, a pin may wobble furiously, or, even more frustratingly, be "kicked" to the side by various inches, yet come to rest upright, thus not being marked (and not be reset to its original position for any throws that stay, though it may of course still be knocked over by subsequent balls).

Moreover, there is a line 10 feet (3.05 m) down the lane from the foul line; this is the lob line, and the ball must first reach the lane at a point on the bowler's side of it. Trespass of this rule makes up a lob and any pins knocked down by such a ball do not count, and such pins are not reset if the lobbed ball was not the third and final shot for that player in that box.Also, a third line, centered on two feet in front of the head pin (number-1 pin) spot is the dead wood line, which determines the maximal forward limit that any dead wood can occupy and still be legally playable. This lane specification fundamentally results in the presence of 'three' foul lines, more than in any other bowling game.

A game of candlepin bowling, frequently called a string in New England, is separated into ten rounds, each of these rounds being most normally referred to as a box, rather than a "frame" as in ten-pin bowling. In each normal box, a player is given up to three chances to knock down as many pins as possible. In the final box, three balls are rolled no matter of the pincount, meaning three strikes can be marked in the 10th frame.

In each of the first nine boxes, play moves as follows: The first player bowls their first ball at the pins. Whatsoever pins are knocked down are counted and scored. Then the player rolls a second and a third ball at any left over targets. In the event that all ten pins were knocked down with the first ball (a 'strike'), the player receives ten points plus the count on the following two rolls, the pins are cleared, a new set placed, and play passes to the following competitor. If all ten pins were knocked down with two balls (a 'spare'), the player receives 10 points plus the count of the following ball, pins are cleared and reset, and play passes to the following competitor. If all three balls are required to knock all the pins down, the score for that frame is simply 10.In the tenth box, play is alike, exclude that a player scoring a strike is allowed two additional balls, scoring a spare makes one additional ball. Three balls are rolled in the tenth frame irrespective.

Duckpin Bowling

In duckpin bowling, players undertake to knock over bowling pins with a bowling ball. The balls used in duckpin bowling are importantly smaller than those used in ten-pin bowling, and weigh one and two kilograms. Bowlers repeated throw or roll the ball down a lane in an effort to knock the bowling pins over. The pins, like the balls, are smaller than their ten-pin equivalents, and it is hence harder to knock them all down with a single throw. The pins are ordered in a triangular fashion identical to that used in ten-pin bowling. The game is played in bowling alleys, which have various lanes, allowing multiple groups of bowlers to play at the same time. The lanes are long rectangular wooden surfaces bounded on either side by gutters. Bowlers eject the ball from behind the foul line, which represents to a small edge of the rectangle, in an attempt to hit the pins which are positioned on the far end of the lane.

Fig. Bowling Positions

Duckpin bowling has patterns similar to, but slightly dissimslar from, ten-pin bowling. All over the course of ten frames, bowlers try to knock down pins as rapidly as possible. Bowlers have three balls per frame, rather of two as in ten-pin bowling, to use in overturning a set of ten pins. If a bowler knocks down all ten pins with their first cast on a frame, it is scored as a strike. If all the pins are pushed down inside the first two throws of a frame, the bowler has made a spare. If all the pins are knocked down by the third ball of the frame, the bowler gets ten points. In the case of a strike, the bowler gets ten points plus the total number of pins knocked down with the following two balls thrown, for a total of up to 30 points. In the case of a spare, the bowler gets 10 points plus the total number of pins knocked down with the following ball, for a total of up to 20 points. A bowlers' final score is the sum of the points they earned in each of the ten frames. The maximum possible score is 300 points, which is attained by throwing 12 strikes in a row. Professional bowlers normally score all over 140-150 points.

In the 1930s a version called Rubberband Duckpin Bowling was formed in the Baltimore-Washington area. The pins are encircled with hard rubber bands to enhance action and scoring. Rubber band duckpin is the only variant of duckpin played in Quebec. There have been numerous perfect games bowled in rubber band duckpin, admitting the largest duckpin prize ever given out on TV in 1994 $50,000 Cdn. Afterwards it is easier to knock down pins in rubber band duckpin, in this variant, the normals of play are identical to those of standard 10 pin bowling.

Five-pin Bowling

Five-pin bowling is a bowling version which is only played in Canada, where most bowling alleys offer it, either alone or in compounding with ten-pin bowling. It was devised all over 1909 by Thomas F. Ryan in Toronto, Ontario, at his Toronto Bowling Club, in answer to customers who complained that the ten-pin game was too strenuous. He cut five tenpins down to about 75% of their size, and used hand-sized hard rubber balls, thus inventing the original version of five-pin bowling.

The world's first trackball devised by Tom Cranston, Fred Longstaff and Kenyon Taylor working at the Royal Canadian Navy's DATAR project in 1952. It used a standard Canadian five-pin bowling ball.

The balls in five-pin are small enough to fit in the hand and hence have no holes. At the end of the lane there are five pins formatted in a V. In size they are midway among duckpins and ten-pins, and they have a heavy rubber band all over their centers to make them move farther when struck. The center pin is worth five points if knocked down, those on either side, three each, and the outermost pins, two each, giving a total of 15 in each frame.

In each frame, each player gets three seeks to bang all five pins over. Knocking all five pins down with the first ball is a strike, worth 15 points, which intends the score attained by the player's first two balls of the following frame or frames are added to his or her score for the strike. They are also, of course, counted in their own figures, so in effect they count double. A player who takes two balls to knock all the pins down gets a spare, which entails the first ball of the following frame counts double. When a bowler bowls two strikes in succession, inside a game, the bowler has scored a "double".

The count in the frame where the first strike was bowled is left blank until the bowler makes his or her first delivery of the following frame. When a double has been bowled, the count for the first strike is 30 points plus the value of the pins bowled down with the first ball of the frame following the second strike. When a bowler bowls three strikes in taking over, inside a game, the bowler has marked a "triple" (also called a "turkey"). In scoring three successive strikes, the bowler is accredited with 45 points in the frame where the first strike was bowled. As in ten-pin, if either of these happen in the final frame, the player gets to take on one or two shots at a re-racked set of pins immediately. A perfect score is 450, which is likely attained less often than perfect tenpin scores are, because of the greater chance in five-pin for splits (arrangements of the left over pins in which there are spaces large enough for a ball to pass through without touching a pin).

Until 1967, an eastern Canadian bowler was demanded to knock down the left corner ("counter") pin to score any points, while a western bowler was needed to knock down the right corner pin. The values of the pins were altered in the similar year to the present values.

Skittles

Skittles is an old European target game, a form of bowling, from which Ten-pin bowling, Duckpin bowling, and Candlepin bowling in the United States, and Five-pin bowling in Canada are went down. In the United Kingdom the sport stays a very famous pub game in England and Wales, though it tends to be found in particular regions, not nationwide. It is possibly most common in the south west counties of Bristol, Cornwall, Devon, Dorset, Somerset, Wiltshire and Gloucestershire. It is also famous in Worcestershire and South Wales. It is very famous in Germany, Austria and Switzerland. In Australia, other varieties of bowling are more famous, but the similar sport of Kegel, based on German nine-pin games, is famous in some areas.

Playing and Scoring

Playing rules and regulations are in real quite straight forward. You roll a ball down the lane to try and knock down the pins which are located at the far end. That is the key idea of the sport. In tenpin bowling, which is the standard sport played in the United States, the lane will be sixty feet long and have gutters running down every side. Once the ball rolls into the gutter it does not come out and will not hit any pins.

At the players end of the lane there is a foul line. No part of the player's body must reach or cross this line. If it does, then the delivery is a foul and no score will outcome from the throw. Behind this foul line there is fifteen feet of approach lane for the bowler to use for a lead up to bowling. At the opposite end of this approach you will find the pin deck where the pins are set in a triangular format commencing with one pin at the front. Even though bowling rules and regulations seem very straight forward the scoring system does it's best to confuse things.

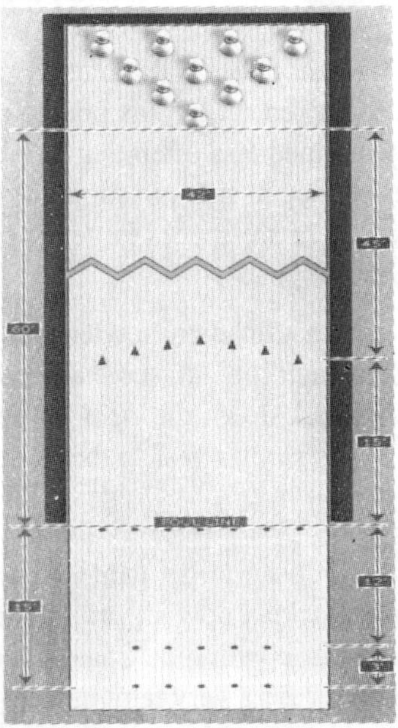

Fig. Bowling Alley

Every game will comprise of ten frames with two rolls in every frame. The tenth frame, still, may comprise of three rolls if a strike is scored. A "strike" is claimed when all ten pins are pushed down with one roll. If some pins remain after the first roll, these are got rid of and a second roll takes place. A "spare" is scored if the left over pins are knocked down on the second roll. Bowling rules and regulations specify that a bowling ball must be no more than 2.25 feet in circumference but there is no ruling concerning the weight of a ball and this will vary as per the preferences of the player.

Scoring a game of bowling is quite perplexed for those who are not used to the system. Unless a player scores a strike or a spare, he will score one point for every of the pins that he knocks down in total in his two rolls. If a strike is scored, the total of the following two rolls will also be added to the 10 points already scored.

If a strike is scored in that following roll then it too will accumulate the score from the following roll and pass it onto the previous one. This means that one roll could score up to 30 points; ten for its own ten pins and twenty from the successive roll. The maximum for a perfect game is 300. If a spare is scored, then the player will once again obtain a bonus from the following roll, but this time only one roll will count.

Bowling patterns are simple enough to let anyone enjoy the sport. The comfort at the end of the lane will normally calculate your score for you as you go along so that you do not have to worry too much about the technicalities of scoring. This clears bowling a great pastime and one which is still very famous within families and people of all ages

MAJOR TOURNAMENTS

Weber Cup

The Weber Cup, called after bowling legend Dick Weber, is the Ten-pin bowling equivalent of Golf's Ryder Cup. It comprises of two teams, Team Europe and Team USA contending over three days in a series of singles, doubles and team (baker) matches.The Weber Cup is the yearly Europe vs USA ten-pin bowling championships and is presently broadcast live from start to finish on Sky Sports in the UK and in many other international channels all over the world. It normally takes place in October each year.

For the first seven events, from 2000 to 2006, thirty-five matches were played. Every match worth one point. The first squad to eighteen points won the tournament.From 2007, the tournament was cut down slightly to thirty-three matches, once again every match is worth one point so the first squad to seventeen will win.All matches are acted in a single lane arena, with banked spectators on both sides, which are particularly constructed for the event.

World Tenpin Masters

The World Tenpin Masters is a yearly Ten-pin bowling tournament. It comprises of a single lane bordered by banked seating on both sides to give the event the kind of high-pressure atmosphere that makes the Masters the world's leading televised bowling tournament.The event is telecasted by Matchroom Sport Television and will be later on broadcast as 15 x 1 hour programmes both at home on Sky Sports and all over the world.

It is 2nd to and commences where the Weber Cup left off. It features 16 of the world's topmost bowlers, representing twelve dissimslar countries, going head-to-head in a straight knockout format. Every match is played over two games with the bowler with the most eminent aggregate (highest total pinfall) over the two games deciding the winner and proceeding.

It stands following to the Weber Cup and AMF World Cup as one of the world's largest annual international sports Ten-pin bowling championships in terms of number of taking part nations.The 2008 World Tenpin Masters was deemed at the Barnsley Metrodome from April 18 to April 20 and had 16 of the top male and female bowlers from all over the world.

ADMINISTRATIVE BODIES

Professional Bowlers Association

The Professional Bowlers Association (PBA) also called as the Lumber Liquidators PBA Tour for sponsorship grounds was established in Syracuse, New York and is presently based in Seattle, Washington. It is the main sanctioning body for the game of professional ten-pin bowling in the U.S.A.. Its season runs from September to April every year, and is televised exclusively by ESPN.

Prior to the PBA's inception, bowling was telecast on television periodically commencing in the early 1950s. NBC commenced with an early 1950s special telecast entitled Championship Bowling . Regular bowling shows, including Make That Spare and Jackpot Bowling with Milton Berle started airing nationally.

At the similar time, there was a want to start a professional bowling class in the United States; an effort led by Eddie Elias, a sports agent grounded in Akron, Ohio. Throughout the 1958 ABC (American Bowling Congress) tournament in Syracuse New York, sixty men, admitting Don Carter, Frank Esposito, Buzz Fazio, Dick Weber, Carmen Salvino, Billy

Welu, Steve Nagy, Harry Smith, Ray Bluth, Dick Hoover and Junie McMahon accompanied a presentation by Elias. After listening to his proposal, thirty-three of the men donated $1,650 each to start the organization, which was integrated in 1958, and headquartered in Akron.

Competition commenced in 1959 with three tournaments. Lou Campi gained the first event (the Empire State Open), and Dick Weber gained the other two (Paramus Eastern Open and the Dayton Open). Weber would turn the first "face" of the PBA in the former years, as he gained eleven of the first twenty events held.

Elias would also lead the effort to give the PBA a permanent home on television, which it would find on ABC Sports by 1965. Mated with the extended support of its charter members, as well as sponsorships by the Ford Motor Company, Coca-Cola (which sponsored eleven tournaments in 1963 alone), True Value Hardware and Firestone Tire, the PBA experienced growth in its tournament schedules and prize funds.

Schedules arrived at a plateau of thirty-five tournaments per year in the 1980s. The 1965 Tournament of Champions was the first to offer $100,000 in prize money; the 1982 event sported a $200,000 purse, and the 1987 U.S. Open, sponsored by Seagram distillery, offered a $500,000 prize fund as well as the first $100,000 first-place prize in PBA history.

By the 1980s, True Value pledged $100,000 to any roller of a perfect game on national television (enhansed to a $200,000 sum throughout its own True Value Open). Prior to this, the PBA would award a televised 300 game with $10,000 and a new Ford automobile. Moreover, in the early 1990s the Miller Brewing Company offered $1 million to any bowler who could win all three of its tournaments in a given season.At present, total PBA tournament prize money exceeds $9 million (2007); versus approximately $1 million annually in the 1970s.As television exposure increased for the PBA, it spun off a Seniors Tour in 1981, with Bill Beach succeeding the first seniors' championship that year.

Elias extended to be involved in the PBA till his death in 1998. Finally, the PBA was bought in March 2000 by former Microsoft executives Chris Peters (Chairman), Rob Glaser, and Mike Slade. The organization's corporate headquarters were transfered to Seattle, Washington. Together with CEO Steve Miller, a former Nike executive, this group is extensively recognized for delivering the PBA from the brink of extinction. Fred Schreyer presently serves as the PBA's CEO/President, and Commissioner; after assuming the post from Miller in 2005.

The PBA supervises the PBA Tour, the PBA Senior Tour, and the PBA Regional Tour (a sort of minor-league circuit). The PBA Regional Tour comprises of seven regions: Central, East, Midwest, Northwest, South, Southwest, and West. The PBA currently has almost 4,300 members universal.

In force October 1, 2008, the PBA commences a three-year sponsorship deal with Lumber Liquidators, causing the American hardwood flooring retailer the tour's title sponsor through the 2010-11 season. Denny's, the title sponsor from 2005-08, stays a PBA sponsor, and will extend to be the title sponsor of the Denny's Dick Weber Open tour stop.

FAMOUS PLAYERS

Dick Weber

Dick Weber (December 23, 1929 - February 13, 2005) was a notable bowling professional and an establishing member of the Professional Bowlers Association (PBA). Weber was recognized not only as a bowling superstar, but was also a bowling pioneer and one of the game's most famous players.

Weber motivated to Florissant, Missouri, in 1955 to form a soon-to-be legendary bowling squad called the Budweisers (after the famous American beer brand). Members of the Budweisers included Ray Bluth, Don Carter, Tom Hennessey and Pat Patterson.

Weber turned a founding member of the Professional Bowlers Association, which he subsequently prevailed. In 1959, Weber won his first PBA title. He won ten of the first 22 PBA tournaments held and throughout his career went on to win 30 PBA Tour events and six PBA Senior Tour events (amassing a total of 36 PBA titles in both categories). He was PBA Player of the Year in 1965, and made BPAA National Bowler of the Year honours three times (in 1961, 1963 and 1965). His 30 regular tour wins place him in sixth-place on the all-time PBA wins list. In 1999 he turned one of five people to knock down over 100,000 pins in the USBC tournament. In 2002, Weber also turned the first player to win at least one PBA title in six consecutive decades.

Weber was also known as an unofficial ambassador of his game and rarely passed up an chance to promote the game of bowling. One promotion had him bowling the highest (altitude) game ever in "Operation AstroBowl," which was held on a Boeing 707 on January 7th, 1964. This was a joint campaign for American Airlines' Cargo Service. The aircraft used was an all cargo Boeing 707 with a single AMF lane installed in the main cargo hold. The flight was from New York to Washington's Dulles Airport. Weber also appeared various times on David Letterman's Late Show. He normally bowled into strange items as requested by viewers. A lane was establish outside the studio and Weber would roll a ball into things like TV sets or eggs.

Dick Weber is a member of the United States Bowling Congress Hall of Fame and both he and his son, Pete Weber, are members of the PBA Hall of Fame. In 1999 Dick Weber was induced into the St. Louis Walk of Fame.The Weber Cup, referred after Dick, is a Ryder Cup-style event that pits European and American ten-pin bowlers against one another. It is deemed annually in England.

On April 17, 2006, the inaugural Dick Weber Tribute was curbed St. Louis. Coordinated by Bill McCorkle, the event pulled many of bowling's top luminaries. The event was attended by over twenty members of the Weber household, symbolizing four generations, as well as over fifty professional bowlers, admitting champions and members of the Hall of Fame. The highlight of the evening came when Pete Weber delivered a moving tribute. Many in the audience had never seen this side of him before.

A documentary on the life and fame of Dick Weber was published on March 23, 2007, by Live Technologies, Inc. and Bill McCorkle. It comprises of interviews with many present and former professional bowlers, household, and sportscasters as well as footage dealing Weber's 60-year history as a professional athlete.Dick Weber died of a sudden of respiratory failure on February 13, 2005. He is lasted by wife Juanita, 3 sons, and 1 daughter.

Walter Ray Williams

Walter Ray Williams, Jr. born on October 6, 1959 in Eureka, California) is one of the top-ranking professional ten-pin bowlers in account. He presently holds the record for all-time PBA career titles (forty-four) and total PBA earnings (over $4,000,000 through 2007-08). He starred in the ten-pin bowling sports documentary A League of Ordinary Gentlemen. He is also a six-time world champion in the game of horseshoes.

Williams is a six-time PBA Player of the Year (1986, '93, '96, '97, '98, 2003) and the all-time leading money winner on the PBA Tour. He was the first bowler in history to surpass $2 million in career earnings, attaining this in 1997. With his win in the 2003 U.S. Open, he also turned the first $3 million career winner; with his 42nd title (2006's Dydo Japan Cup) he turned the first $4 million career winner. Williams also has the highest monetary winnings in a single season, with $419,700 throughout his 2002-03 season. He has also gained six World Horseshoe Pitching titles. He was invited to pitch horseshoes at the White House with President George H. W. Bush in 1989. He completed second in the 2005 World Horseshoe Pitching Championships.

On September 24, 2006, Williams overshadowed Earl Anthony's career record of forty-one PBA regular tour titles with his win of the Dydo Japan Cup (and 42nd PBA tour title) over Pete Weber in a 289-236 single game pinfall. Williams has been acknowledged as "Deadeye" because of his accuracy in both bowling and horseshoes. He is known for having the record highest season spare and single-pin conversion percentage, as well as the second best strike percentage and match play average. He also holds records for number of television appearances, most television appearances in a season, most consecutive television appearances, most major titles in a season, most games bowled in one season, highest pinfall in a nine game series (2004), and most 300 games in a tournament. Upon achieving the 2007 Motor City Classic, he has now won a PBA tour title in a record 15 consecutive seasons, surpassing Earl Anthony's 1970-1983 run.

In August 2008 Walter Ray joined team USA to participate in that year's FIQ World Men's Championships in Thailand. For the first time professionals were permitted to contend in this truly international event with over 330 participants from 56 countries. Walter Ray was the most successful bowler, achieving 4 medals: Gold in Masters, Gold in Singles, Gold in Team and a Bronze medal in Trios.

Even though Pete Weber is known as the poster-boy of the PBA to the general public, Williams, in bowling circles, might be the most respected and famous player on tour. This is because of his cool, confident demeanor, and his unparalleled success for the last 15 years.He is a member of the USBC and PBA Halls of Fame, a member of the World Horseshoe Pitching Hall of Fame, and was a two-time past president of the Professional Bowlers Association.

In the 2007-08 season, at age 48, Walter Ray established the second-highest average in PBA history for a single season — 228.43. Only Norm Duke's 2006-07 mark of 228.47 is higher. Through the 2007-08 season, he has bowled 75 career 300 games in PBA competition.

REFERENCES

American Bowling Congress: *Bowler's Manual.* Milwaukee, Wisconsin, American Bowling Congress, 1968.

Bowling-Fencing-Golf Guide. Washington, D.C., Division for Girls' and Women's Sports, American Association for Health, Physical Education and Recreation. Published biennially.

Barnes, Mildred J. and others: *Sports Activities for Girls and Women.* New York, AppletonCentury-Crofts, Division of Meredith Publishing Company, 1966.

Broer, Marion R.: *Efficiency of Human Movement.* Second Edition. Philadelphia, W. B. Saunders Company, 1966.

Forslund, Ellen: *Bowling for Women.* New York, Ronald Press Company, 1964.

Kidwell, Kathro and Paul Smith Jr.: *Bowling Analyzed.* Dubuque, Iowa, William C. Brown Company, Inc., 1960.

McKee, Mary Ellen: "The Mechanics of Bowling". *Bowling-Fencing-Golf Guide*, June 1956-June 1958. Washington, D.C., Division for Girls' and Women's Sports, American Association for Health, Physical Education and Recreation, 1956, pp. 13-58.

McMahon, Junie and Murray Goodman: *Modern Bowling Techniques.* New York, Ronald Press Company, 1958.

Miller, Donna Mae and Katherine L. Ley: *Individual and Team Sports for Women.* Englewood Cliffs, N.J., Prentice-Hall, Inc., 1955.

National Bowling Council: *The Guide to Teaching Bowling.* Washington, D.C., National Bowling Council, 1967.

Vannier, Maryhelen and Hally Beth Poindexter: *Individnal and Team Sports for Girls and Women.* Second Edition. Philadelphia, W. B. Saunders Company, 1968.

Vannier, Maryhelen and Hally Beth Poindexter: *Physical Activities for College Women.* Second Edition Philadelphia, W. B. Saunders Company, 1969.

3

Basketball

Basketball is a team game in which two teams of five active players each effort to score points against one another by propelling a ball through a ten feet (3 m) high hoop (the goal) beneath organized rules. Basketball is one of the most famous and extensively viewed sports in the world.

Points are scored by hitting the ball through the basket above; the squad with more points at the end of the game wins. The ball can be progressed on the court by bouncing it (dribbling) or passing it among teammates. Riotous physical contact (fouls) is not permitted and there are limitations on how the ball can be handled (violations).

Through time, basketball has formulated to demand common techniques of shooting, passing and dribbling, besides players' positions, and offensive and defensive structures. Normally, the tallest members of a squad will play center or one of two forward positions, while shorter players or those who own the topmost ball handling skills and speed, play the safeguard positions. While competitive basketball is cautiously regulated, many variations of basketball have arose for casual play. In some countries, basketball is also a famous spectator game.

While competitive basketball is chiefly an indoor game, played on a basketball court, less structured variations have become exceedingly famous as an outdoor game within both inner city and rural groups.

HISTORY

In early December 1891, Dr. James Naismith, a Canadian physical education professor from McGill University of Montréal and instructor at YMCA Training School (at present, Springfield College) in Springfield, Massachusetts, USA, sought a energetic indoor sport to keep his students engaged and at proper levels of fitness throughout the long New England winters. After refusing other ideas as either too rough or poorly suited to walled-in gymnasiums, he wrote the fundamental rules and regulations and nailed a peach basket onto a 10-foot (3.05 m) elevated track.

In contrast with modern basketball nets, this peach basket held its bottom, and balls had to be recovered manually after each "basket" or point scored; this proved ineffective, nonetheless, so a hole was drilled into the bottom of the basket, allowing the balls to be poked out with a long dowel each time.

The peach baskets were used until 1906 when they were finally substituted by metal hoops with backboards. A advance change was soon made, so the ball simply passed through, paving the way for the sport we know at present. A soccer ball was used to shoot goals. Every time a person got the ball in the basket, his squad would earn a point. Whichsoever squad got the most points won the game.

Naismith's handwritten diaries, observed by his granddaughter in early 2006, show that he was anxious about the new game he had invented, which contained rules from a children's sport called "Duck on a Rock", as many had betrayed before it. Naismith called the new sport 'Basket Ball'.

The first prescribed sport was played in the YMCA gymnasium on January 20, 1892 with nine players and the game finished at 1-0 and the shot was made from 25 feet (7.6 m), on a court just half the size of a present-day Streetball or National Basketball Association (NBA) court. "Basket ball", the name suggested by one of Naismith's students, was famous from the commencing. By 1897-1898 teams of five turned standard.

Women's basketball started out in 1892 at Smith College when Senda Berenson, a physical education teacher, altered Naismith's rules for women. Concisely after she was employed at Smith, she went to Naismith to acquire more about the sport. Spell-bound by the new game and the values it could teach, she formed the first women's collegiate basketball game on March 21, 1893, when her Smith freshmen and sophomores played against one another.

Her rules were first published in 1899 and two years later Berenson turned the editor of A.G. Spalding's first Women's Basketball Guide, which further spread her version of basketball for women.

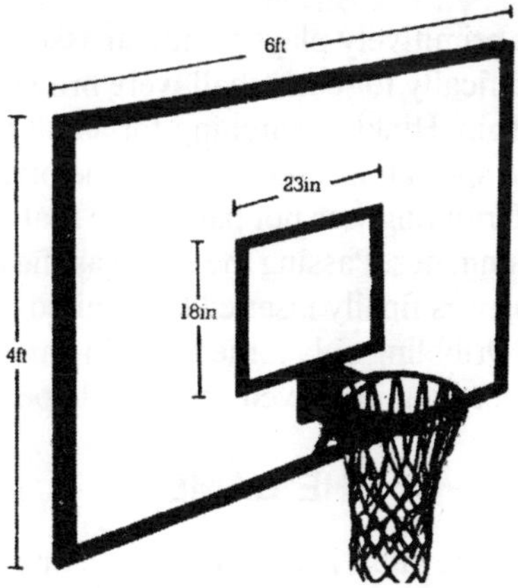

Fig. Dimensions of Basket

Basketball's early disciples were dispatched to YMCAs during the United States, and it rapidly spread through the USA and Canada. By 1895, it was well established at various women's high schools. While the YMCA was responsible initially formulating and disseminating the sport, within a decade it admonished the new game, as rough play and rowdy crowds started to detract from the YMCA's primary mission. Nonetheless, other amateur sports clubs, colleges, and professional clubs rapidly filled the void. In the years before World War I, the Amateur Athletic Union and the Intercollegiate Athletic Association of the United States (forerunner of the NCAA) vied for control over the rules and regulations for the sport. The 1st pro league, the National Basketball League, was established in 1898 to assist players from exploitation and to promote a less rough sport. This league only lasted 5 years.

By the 1950s, basketball had turn a main college game, thus paving the way for a development of interest in professional basketball. In 1959, a basketball Hall of Fame was instituted in Springfield, Massachusetts. Its rosters comprise the names of great players, coaches, referees and people who have contributed significantly to the growth of the sport.

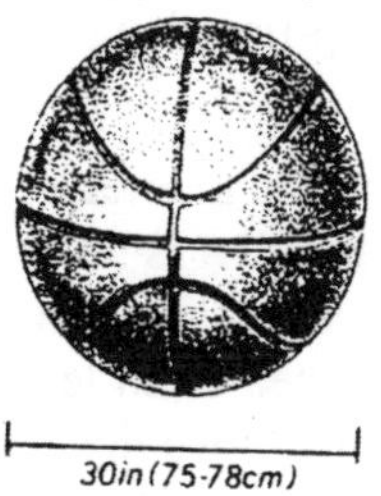

Fig. Dimensions of Basketball

Basketball was primitively played with an association football. The first balls made specifically for basketball were brown, and it was only in the late 1950s that Tony Hinkle, searching for a ball that would be more visible to players and spectators alike, inserted the orange ball that is now in common utilize. Dribbling was not part of the real sport except for the "bounce pass" to teammates. Passing the ball was the chief means of ball movement. Dribbling was finally inserted but limited by the asymmetrical shape of early balls. Dribbling only turned a main part of the sport all over the 1950s as manufacturing improved the ball shape.

THE GAME

The objective of the sport is to tscore one's opponents by throwing off the ball through the opponents' basket from over while precluding the opponents from causing so on their own. An effort to score in this way is called a shot. A productive shot is worth two points, or three points if it is taken from beyond the three-point arc which is 6.25 meters (20 ft 6 in) from the basket in international games and 23 ft 9 in (7.24 m) in NBA games.

Equipment

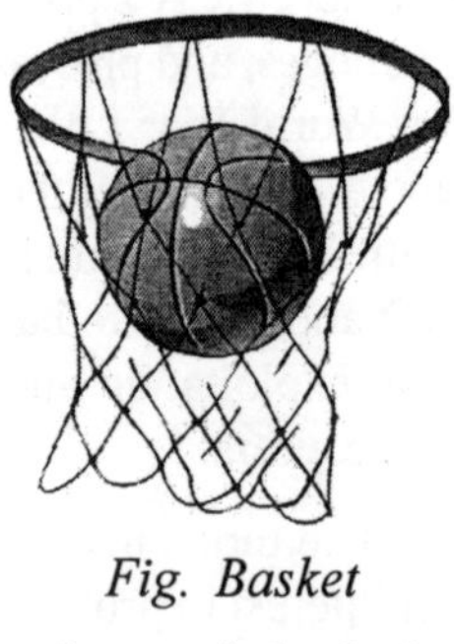

Fig. Basket

The only necessary equipment in basketball is the basketball and the court: a flat, rectangular surface with baskets at opposite ends. Competitory levels demand the use of more equipment such as clocks, score sheets, scoreboard(s), flip-flopping possession arrows, and whistle-operated stop-clock systems.

An official basketball court in international games is 28 by 15 meters (approx. 92 by 49 ft) and in the NBA is 94 by 50 feet (29 by 15 m). Most courts are built of wood. A steel basket with net and backboard string up over each end of the court. At nearly all levels of contest, the top of the rim is precisely 10 feet (3.05 m) above the court and 4 feet (1.2 m) inside the baseline. While variance is possible in the proportions of the court and backboard, it is conceived significant for the basket to be of the correct height; a rim that is off by but a few inches can have an adverse effect on shooting. There are also rules on the size a basketball should be. If women are playing, the prescribed basketball size is 28.5" in circumference (size 6) and a weight of 20 oz. For men, the prescribed ball is 29.5" in circumference (size 7) and weighs 22 oz.

Playing Regulations

Games are played in four quarters of 10 (international) or 12 minutes (NBA). College games utilize two 20 minute halves while most high school sports utilize eight minute quarters. Fifteen minutes are permitted for a half-time break, and two minutes are permitted at the other breaks. Overtime periods are five minutes long. Teams exchange baskets for the second half. The time permitted is actual playing time; the clock is stopped while the play is not active. Hence, sports in general take much longer to complete than the allotted game time, normally about two hours.

Five players from both team (out of a twelve player roster) might be on the court at a time. Substitutions are limitless but can just be done when play is ceased. Teams also have a coach, who supervises the growth and schemes of the squad, and other squad personnel such as assistant coaches, managers, statisticians, doctors and trainers.

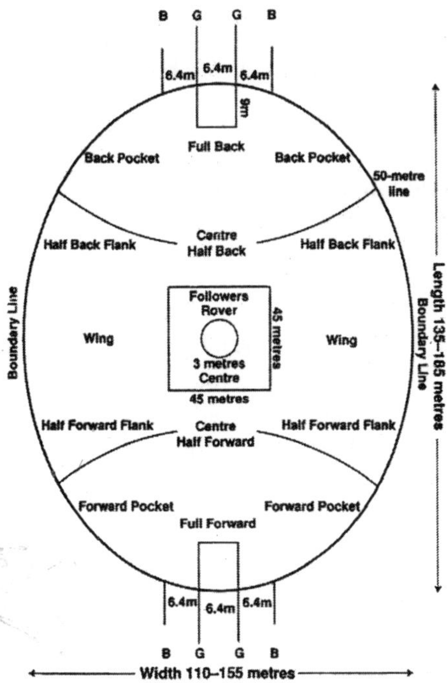

Fig. Basketball Court

For both men's and women's teams, a standard uniform comprises of a pair of shorts and a jersey with a distinctly visible number, unique among the squad, impressed on both the front and back. Players wear high-top sneakers that provide extra ankle support. Normally, squad names, players' names and, exterior of North America, sponsors are printed on the uniforms.

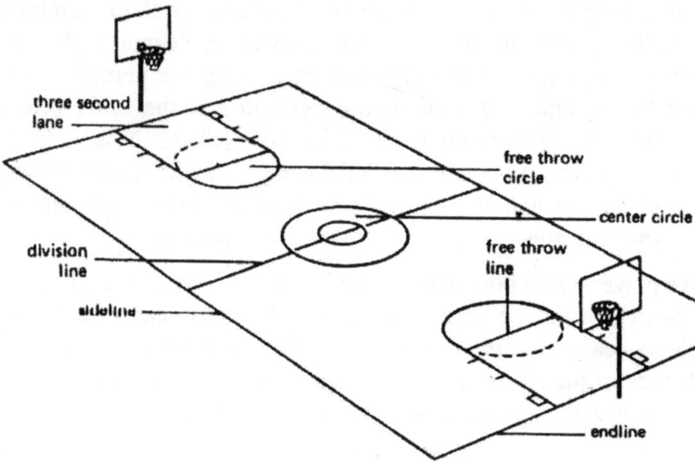

Fig. Positions of Basketball Court

A limited number of time-outs, clock stoppages requested by a coach for a short meeting with the players, are permitted. They in general last no longer than one minute unless, for televised games, a commercial break is required.

The game is assured by the officials comprising of the umpire ("crew chief" in men's college and the NBA), one or two umpires ("referees" in men's college and the NBA) and the table officials. For college, the NBA, and many high schools, there are a total of 3 referees on the court. The table officials are answerable for holding track of each teams scoring, timekeeping, individual and team fouls, player substitutions, team possession arrow, and the shot clock.

Fouls

An attempt to unfairly disadvantage an opponent through physical contact is illegal and is called a foul. These are most commonly committed by defensive players; however, they can be committed by offensive players as well. Players who are fouled either obtain the ball to pass inbounds once again, or obtain one or more free throws if they are fouled in the act of shooting, depending upon whether the shot was successful. One point is granted for making a free throw, which is attempted from a line 15 feet (4.5 m) from the basket.

The umpire may utilize discretion in calling fouls (for example, by considering whether an unfair advantage was earned), sometimes making fouls controversial calls. The calling of fouls can vary among games, leagues and even among referees.

A player or coach who demonstrates poor sportsmanship, for instance, by arguing with a umpire or by fighting with another player, can be charged with a more serious foul called a technical foul. The penalty demands free throws (which unlike a personal foul, the other squad can choose any player to shoot the free throws) and varies among leagues. Reoccurred incidents can result in disqualification. Blatant fouls with exuberant contact or that are not an attempt to play the ball are called unsporting fouls (or flagrant fouls in the NBA) and noemally will result in ejection.

If a squad exceeds a sure limit of team fouls in a given period (quarter or half) – four for NBA and international sports – the opposing squad is granted one or two free throws on all subsequent fouls for that period, the number depending upon the league. In the US college game if a squad surpasses seven fouls in the half the opposing squad is granted a one-and-one free throw (a player making the first is given a second). If a squad exceeds ten fouls in the half the opposing squad is granted two free throws on all subsequent fouls for the half. A player who, in an international game, invests five fouls (including technical fouls), or in an NBA game, commits six fouls (omitting technical fouls) is not permitted to participate for the rest of the game, and is said to have "fouled out".

After a squad has invested a specified number of fouls, it is said to be "in the penalty". On scoreboards, this is normally signified with an indicator light reading "Bonus" or "Penalty" with an enlightened directional arrow indicating that squad is to obtain free throws when fouled by the opposing squad. (Some scoreboards also show the number of fouls committed.)

The number of free throws granted increases with the number of fouls committed. Primarily, one shot is granted, but after a sure number of additional fouls are invested the opposing squad may obtain (a) one shot with a chance for a second shot if the first shot is made, called shooting "one-and-one", or (b) two shots. If a squad loses the first shot (or "front end") of a one-and-one situation, the opposing squad may recover possession of the ball and extend play. If a squad misses the first shot of a two-shot situation, the opposing squad must wait for the completion of the second shot before attempting to reclaim possession of the ball and continuing play.

If a player is fouled while undertaking a shot and the shot is unsuccessful, the player is granted a number of free throws equal to the value of the attempted shot. A player fouled while undertaking a regular two-point shot, then, receives two shots. A player fouled while undertaking a three-point shot, on the other hand, receives three shots.

If a player is fouled while undertaking a shot and the shot is successful, typically the player will be granted one additional free throw for one point. In compounding with a regular shot, this is called a "three-point play" (or more colloquially, an "and one") because of the basket made at the time of the foul (two points) and the additional free throw (one point). Four-point plays, while rare, can also occur.

Shooting

Shooting is the act of undertaking to hit points by casting the ball through the basket. While methods can vary with players and situations, the most common technique can be outlined here.

The player should be positioned facing the basket with feet about shoulder-width apart, knees slightly bent, and back straight. The player holds the ball to rest in the prevailinghand's fingertips (the shooting arm) somewhat above the head, with the other hand on the side of the ball. To aim the ball, the player's elbow should be aligned vertically, with the forearm confronting in the direction of the basket. The ball is shot by bending and stretching the knees and stretching the shooting arm to become straight; the ball rolls off the finger tips while the wrist completes a full downward flex motion. When the shooting arm is stationary for a moment after the ball released, it is known as a follow-through; it is integrated to maintain accuracy. In general, the non-shooting arm is used only to guide the shot, not to power it.

Players frequently try to put a firm backspin on the ball to deaden its affect with the rim. The ideal trajectory of the shot is somewhat arguable, but in general coaches will profess proper arch. Most players shoot right away into the basket, but shooters may utilize the backboard to redirect the ball into the basket.

The two most common shots that utilize the above depicted set up are the set shot and the jump shot. The basketball shot is taken from a standing position, with neither foot leaving the floor, normally used for free throws. The jump shot is taken while in mid-air, near the top of the jump. This allows for much greater power and range, and it also permits the player to elevate over the defender. Failure to release the ball before returning the feet to the ground is a traveling violation.

Another common shot is known as layup. This shot demands the player to be in motion towards the basket, and to "lay" the ball "up" and into the basket, normally off the backboard (the backboard-free, underhand version is called a finger roll). The most crowd-delighting, and typically highest-percentage accuracy shot is the slam dunk, in which the player jumps very high, and casts the ball downwards, straight through the hoop.

Another shot that is turning common is the "circus shot". The circus shot is a low-percent shot that is flipped, heaved, scooped, or flung toward the hoop while the shooter is off-balance, airborne, falling down, and/or facing away from the basket.

A shot that misses both the rim and the backboard entirely is concerned to as an air ball. An in particular bad shot, or one that only hits the backboard, is jocularly called a brick.

Rebounding

The aim of rebounding is to successfully gain self-possession of the basketball after a missed field goal or free throw, as it rebounds from the hoop or backboard. This plays a chief role in the sport, as most possessions end when a squad misses a shot. There are two classes of rebounds: offensive rebounds, in which the ball is recovered by the offensive side and does not alter possession, and defensive rebounds, in which the opposing squad gains possession of the loose ball. The majority of rebounds are defensive, as the squad on defense tends to be in better position to recover missed shots.

Passing

A pass is a method of moving the ball among players. Most passes are played along by a step forward to increase power and are followed up with the hands to ensure accuracy.

A staple pass is the chest pass. The ball is passed instantly from the passer's chest to the receiver's chest. A proper chest pass requires an outward snap of the thumbs to add velocity and leaves the defence little time to react.

Another type of pass is the bounce pass. Here, the passer bounces the ball crisply about two-thirds of the way from his own chest to the receiver. The ball strikes the court and bounces up toward the receiver. The bounce pass takes longer to complete than the chest pass, but it is also harder for the opposing squad to intercept (kicking the ball intentionally is a violation). Thus, players often utilize the bounce pass in crowded moments, or to pass all over a defender.

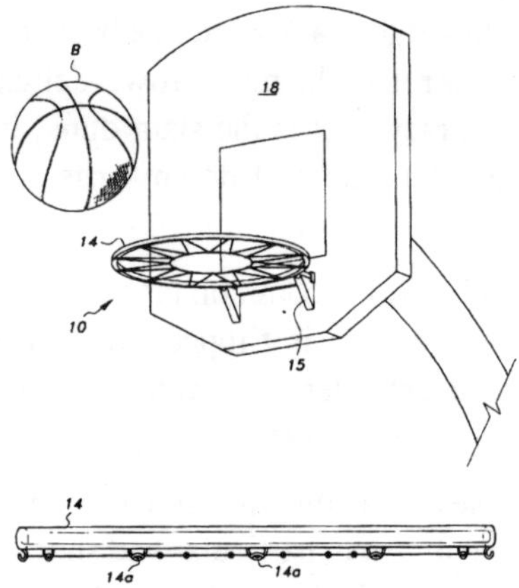

Fig. Basketball Hoop

The overhead pass is used to pass the ball over a defender. The ball is released while over the passer's head. The outlet pass occurs after a squad gets a defensive rebound. The following pass after the rebound is the outlet pass. The crucial aspect of any good pass is being not possible to intercept. Good passers can pass the ball with great accuracy and touch and know exactly where each of their teammates like to obtain the ball. A special way of doing this is passing the ball without looking at the receiving teammate. This is called a no-look pass.

Another advance style of passing is the behind-the-back pass which, as the description implies, requires throwing the ball behind the passer's back to a teammate. Even though some players can execute them effectively, many coaches discourage no-look or behind-the-back passes, conceiving them to be essentially unsound, difficult to control, and more likely to result in turnovers or violations.

Dribbling

Dribbling is the act of bouncing the ball endlessly, and is a demand for a player to take steps with the ball. To dribble, a player pushes the ball down toward the ground instead patting it; this insures greater control.

When dribbling past an opponent, the dribbler should dribble with the hand farthest from the opponent, making it harder for the defensive player to get to the ball. It is hence crucial for a player to be able to dribble competently with both hands.

Good dribblers (or "ball handlers") tend to bounce the ball low to the ground, cutting down the travel from the floor to the hand, making it harder for the defender to "steal" the ball. Moreover, good ball handlers often dribble behind their backs, among their legs, and change hands and directions of the dribble often, making a more irregular dribbling pattern that is more difficult to oppose. This is called a crossover, which is the most effective way to pass defenders while dribbling.

A experienced player can dribble without observing the ball, utilizing the dribbling motion or vision to keep track of the ball's location. with not having to focus on the ball, a player can look for teammates or scoring opportunities, as well as avoid the danger of someone stealing the ball from him/her.

MAJOR TOURNAMENTS

FIBA World Championship

The FIBA World Championship is a world basketball tournament for men's national teams deemed quadrennially by the FIBA.A analogue event for women's teams, the FIBA World Championship for Women, is also held quadrennially, in the similar year as the men's event but in a dissimslar country.

The champion squad gains the Naismith Trophy, which was first granted in the 1967 tournament.The tournament body structure is like but not identical to that of the FIFA World Cup; both of these international competitions.

FIBA World Championship for Women

The FIBA World Championship for Women also called the Basketball World Championship for Womenis a world basketball tournament for women's national teams deemed quadrennially. It is persisted the similar cycle and in the similar year as the FIBA World Championship (for Men), but in a dissimslar country.

Similar the men's event, the Women's World Championship was produced by the International Basketball Federation (FIBA). It started in 1953, three years afterward the first men's event, and was first curbed

Chile. For most of its early history, it was not curbed the similar year as the men's championship, and did not establish a consistent quadrennial cycle until 1967. After the 1983 event, FIBA altered the scheduling so that the women's tournament would be held in even-numbered non-Olympic years, a alter that had come to the men's tournament in 1970.

For 2006, the number of taking part teams will stay at 16, dissimilar the men's event, which has been extended to 24.Only 4 teams have gained titles in the account of the World Championship for Women. The United States has gained seven titles, including four of the last six. The Soviet Union gained six titles, including five in a row from 1959 to 1975. The only other countries to win have been Brazil in 1994 and Australia in 2006

ADMINISTRATIVE BODIES

International Basketball Federation

The International Basketball Federation, more usually known by the French acronym FIBA is an association of national organizations which governs international competition in basketball. Primitively known as the FederationInternationale de Basketball Amateur (hence FIBA), in 1989 it dropped the Amateur from its official name but retained the initialism, because of the beginning two letters of the word basketball.

The FIBA determines the international rules and regulations of basketball, defines the equipment and facilities needed, regulates the transfer of athletes across countries, and controls the appointment of international referees. 213 national federations are now members, formed since 1989 into five zones or "commissions": Africa, Americas, Asia, Europe, and Oceania.FIBA is a world basketball tournament for men's national teams deemed quadrennially by the International Basketball Federation (FIBA).

A parallel event for women's teams, the FIBA World Championship for Women, is also deemed quadrennially, in the similar year as the men's event but in a dissimslar country.The champion squad wins the Naismith Trophy, which was first granted in the 1967 tournament.The tournament structure is like but not indistinguishable to that of the FIFA World Cup; both of these international competitions have been acted in the similar year since 1970.

FIBA separatesthe world into five commissions, each roughly based on a continent; North and South America are under one commission.The affiliation was established in Geneva in 1932, two years after the game was formally acknowledged by the IOC. Its master name was Federation Internationale de Basketball Amateur. Eight nations were founding members: Argentina, Czechoslovakia, Greece, Italy, Latvia, Portugal, Romania, and Switzerland. Throughout the 1936 Summer Olympics held in Berlin, the Federation named James Naismith (1861-1939), the founder of basketball, as its Honourary President.

FIBA has coordinated a World Championship for men from 1950 and a World Championship for Women since 1953. Both events are now deemed every four years, flip-flopping with the Olympics.In 1989, FIBA open the door to Olympic participation by professionals such as players from the NBA in the United States. At this point, the Federation Internationale de Basketball Amateur turned the Federation Internationale de Basketball, but retained FIBA as an abbreviation.

The Federation headquarters locomoted to Munich in 1956, then came back to Geneva in 2002. Patrick Baumann is the Secretary General of FIBA.In 1991 it established FIBA Hall of Fame, the first induction ceremony was persisted September 12, 2007 throughout Euro Basket 2007.

National Basketball Association

The National Basketball Association (NBA) is North America's prime professional men's league, compiled of thirty teams; twenty-nine in the USA, and one in Canada. It is an active member of USA Basketball (USAB), which is acknowledged by the International Basketball Federation as the National Governing Body (NGB) for basketball in the United States. The NBA is one of the four major North American professional sports leagues, which also admits the National Hockey League (NHL), the National Football League (NFL), and Major League Baseball (MLB).

The league was established in New York City, on June 6, 1946 as the Basketball Association of America (BAA). The league assumed the name National Basketball Association in 1949 after immixing with the rival National Basketball League. The league's various international as well as individual squad offices are directed out of its head offices situated in the Olympic Tower at 645 Fifth Avenue in New York City. NBA Entertainment and NBA TV studios are directed out of offices situated in Secaucus, New Jersey.

The Basketball Association of America was established in 1946 by the owners of the major ice hockey arenas in the Northeast and Midwest

United States. On November 1, 1946, in Toronto, Ontario, the Toronto Huskies hosted the New York Knickerbockers which the NBA now regards as the first sport played in the league's history. Even though there had been earlier seeks at professional basketball leagues, including the American Basketball League and the National Basketball League, the BAA was the first league to attempt to play mainly in large arenas in major cities. Throughout its early years, the quality of play in the BAA was not significantly better than in competing leagues or amongst leading independent clubs such as the Harlem Globetrotters. For example the 1948 ABL finalist Baltimore Bullets locomoted to the BAA and gained its 1948 title, followed by the 1948 NBL champion Minneapolis Lakers who won the 1949 BAA title.

On August 3, 1949, the BAA agreed to mix with the NBL, expanding the National Basketball Association to seventeen franchises situated in a mix of large and small cities, as well as large arenas and smaller gymnasiums and armories. In 1950, the NBA consolidated to eleven franchises, a process that extended until 1954, when the league arrived at its smallest size of eight franchises, all of which are still in the league (the Knicks, Celtics, Warriors, Lakers, Royals/Kings, Pistons, Hawks, and Nationals/76ers).

While contracting, the league also assured its smaller city franchises move to larger cities. The Hawks shifted from "Tri-Cities" (the area now known as the Quad Cities) to Milwaukee (in 1951) and then to St. Louis (in 1955); the Royals from Rochester to Cincinnati (in 1957); and the Pistons from Fort Wayne to Detroit (in 1957). In 1960, the Lakers relocated to Los Angeles, and the Warriors moved to San Francisco, in 1963. The coming year, the Nationals left upstate New York to bring basketball back to Philadelphia, altering their nickname from "Nationals" to "76ers." This intends out of the original eight franchises, only the Knicks and Celtics have not relocated at any point.

Even though Japanese-American Wataru Misaka technically broke the NBA color barrier in the 1947-48 season when he played for the New York Knicks, 1950 is recognized as the year the NBA incorporated with the addition of African American players by various teams admitting Chuck Cooper with the Boston Celtics, Nat "Sweetwater" Clifton with the New York Knicks, and Earl Lloyd with the Washington Capitols.

Throughout this period, the Minneapolis Lakers, led by center George Mikan, won five NBA Championships and established them as the league's first dynasty. To promote shooting and discourage stalling, the league inserted the 24-second shot clock in 1954. If a squad does not seek to score a field goal (or the ball doesn't make contact with the rim) inside 24 seconds of receiving the ball, play is stopped and the ball given to its opponent.

In 1957, rookie center Bill Russell connected with the Boston Celtics, who already featured guard Bob Cousy and coach Red Auerbach, and went on to lead the club to eleven NBA titles in thirteen seasons. Center Wilt Chamberlain entered the league in 1959 and turned the prevailingindividual star of the 1960s, setting new records in scoring (100) and rebounding (55). Russell's rivalry with Chamberlain turned one of the great individual rivalries in the history of American team sports.

In 2001, an associated minor league, the National Basketball Growth League, now named the NBA Development League (or D-League) was created. Before the league was commenced, there were firm rumors that the NBA would purchase the CBA, and call it its developmental league, as the Continental Basketball Association was its "minor league" affiliate for years.

In 2004, two years after the Hornets relocation to New Orleans, the NBA came back to North Carolina as the Charlotte Bobcats were established.In 2005, the Hornets resettled to Oklahoma City for two seasons. This was required due to damage caused by Hurricane Katrina. In 2007, the Hornets came back to New Orleans.

On June 29, 2006, a new official game ball was introduced for the 2006-07 season, marking the first change to the ball in over 35 years and only the second in 60 seasons. Manufactured by Spalding, the new ball had a fresh design and new synthetic material that Spalding exacted offered a better grip, feel, and consistency than the original ball. Nevertheless, many players were vocal in their disdain for the new ball, saying that it was too sticky when dry, and too slippery when wet.

On December 11, 2006, Commissioner Stern declared that commencing January 1, 2007, the NBA would return to the traditional leather basketball in use prior to the 2006-2007 season. The alteration was influenced by frequent player complaints and confirmed hand injuries (cuts) induced by the microfiber ball. The Players' Association had filed a suit in behalf of the players against the NBA over the new ball.As of 2006, the NBA team jerseys are manufactured by Adidas, which bought the previous supplier, Reebok.

On July 19, 2007, the FBI looked into allegations that veteran NBA umpire Tim Donaghy bet on basketball games he functioned over the past two seasons and that he made calls affecting the point spread in those games.On August 15, 2007, Donaghy pleaded guilty to two federal accuses related to the investigation. Nonetheless, he could face more charges if it is determined that he intentionally miscalled individual games.

On February 19, 2008, the NBA announced that the Phoenix Suns and the Denver Nuggets will act the first outdoor game on October 11, 2008, at the Indian Wells Tennis Garden. It will be the first outdoor game in the modern era of the NBA.In June 2008, it was declared that the Seattle SuperSonics would be rendered inactive and the franchise itself would relocate to Oklahoma City. The Oklahoma City Thunder will commences playing in the 2008-2009 season. This marks the third NBA franchise to relocate in the past decade.

FAMOUS PLAYERS

Michael Jordan

Michael Jeffrey Jordan (born February 17, 1963) is a retired American professional basketball player and active businessman. His life history on the National Basketball Association (NBA) website states, "By acclamation, Michael Jordan is the most outstanding basketball player of all time." Jordan was one of the most effectively marketed athletes of his generation, and was instrumental in popularizing the NBA all over the world in the 1980s and 1990s.

After a stand-out career at the University of North Carolina, Jordan coupled with the NBA's Chicago Bulls in 1984. He rapidly came out as one of the stars of the league, nursing crowds with his prolific scoring. His leaping capability, illustrated by performing slam dunks from the free throw line at Slam Dunk Contests, earned him the nicknames "Air Jordan" and "His Airness." He also earned a repute as one of the topmost defensive players in basketball. In 1991, he won his first NBA championship with the Bulls, and followed that achievement with titles in 1992 and 1993, securing a "three-peat." Though Jordan abruptly left the NBA at the commencing of the 1993-94 NBA season to pursue a career in baseball, he rejoined the Bulls in 1995 and led them to three additional championships (1996, 1997, and 1998) as well as an NBA-record 72 regular-season wins in the 1995–96 season. Jordan retired for a second time in 1999, but he came back for two more NBA seasons in 2001 as a member of the Washington Wizards.

Jordan's individual accolades and achievements comprise five MVP honours, ten All-NBA First Team designations, nine All-Defensive First

Team honours, fourteen NBA All-Star Game appearances and three All-Star MVP, ten scoring titles, three steals titles, six NBA Finals MVP awards, and the 1988 NBA Defensive Player of the Year Honour. He deems the NBA record for highest career regular season scoring average with 30.12 points per game, as well as averaging a record 33.4 points per game in the playoffs. In 1999, he was called the greatest North American athlete of the twentieth century by ESPN, and was second to Babe Ruth on the Associated Press's list of athletes of the century. He will be entitled for induction into the Basketball Hall of Fame in 2009.

Jordan is also mentioned for his product endorsements. He fueled the success of Nike's Air Jordan sneakers, which were brought in in 1985 and remain famous at present. Jordan also starred in the 1996 feature film Space Jam. He is currently a part-owner and Managing Member of Basketball Operations of the Charlotte Bobcats in North Carolina.

Throughout his first season in the NBA, Jordan averaged 28.2 ppg on 51.5% shooting. He rapidly turned a fan favorite even in opposing arenas, and appeared on the cover of Sports Illustrated with the heading "A Star is Born" just over a month into his professional career. Jordan was also voted in as an All-Star starter by the fans in his rookie season. Controversy arose before the All-Star game when word surfaced that various veteran players, led by Isiah Thomas, were upset by the amount of attention Jordan was receiving. This led to a so called "freeze-out" on Jordan, where players declined to pass him the ball during the game. The controversy left Jordan relatively unaffected when he came back to regular season play, and he would go on to be voted Rookie of the Year.The Bulls completed the season 38–44,and lost in the first round of the playoffs in four games to the Milwaukee Bucks.

Jordan's 2nd season was cut short by a broken foot which induced him to miss sixty-four games. In spite of Jordan's injury and a 30–52 record, the Bulls made the playoffs. Jordan retrieved in time to take part in the playoffs and executed well upon his return. Against a 1985–86 Boston Celtics squad that is often considered one of the greatest in NBA history, Jordan set the still-unbroken record for points in a playoff game with 63 in Game 2.The Celtics, nevertheless, managed to sweep the series.

Jordan had retrieved completely by the 1986–87 season, and had one of the most prolific scoring seasons in NBA history. He turned the only player other than Wilt Chamberlain to score 3,000 points in a season, averaging a league high 37.1 points on 48.2% shooting.In addition, Jordan demonstrated his defensive prowess, as he turned the first player in NBA history to record 200 steals and 100 blocks in a season. In spite of Jordan's success, Magic Johnson won the league's Most Valuable Player Award. The Bulls reached 40 wins,and advanced to the playoffs for the third consecutive year. However, they were once again swept by the Celtics.

Jordan led the league in scoring once again in the 1987–88 season, averaging 35.0 ppg on 53.5% shooting and won his first league MVP award. He was also called the Defensive Player of the Year—a rarity for a guard—as he had averaged 1.6 blocks and a league high 3.16 steals per game. The Bulls completed 50–32, and made it out of the first round of the playoffs for the first time in Jordan's career, as they overcame the Cleveland Cavaliers in five games. Nevertheless, the Bulls then lost in five games to the more experienced Detroit Pistons, who were led by Isiah Thomas and a group of physical players called as the "Bad Boys".

In the 1988–89 seasons, Jordan once again led the league in scoring, averaging 32.5 ppg on 53.8% shooting from the field, along with 8 rpg and 8 assists per game (apg). The Bulls completed with a 47–35 record, and encouraged to the Eastern Conference Finals, defeating the Cleveland Cavaliers and New York Knicks along the way. The Cavaliers series admitted a career highlight for Jordan when he hit a series winning shot over Craig Ehlo in the closing moments of the determining fifth game of the series. However, the Pistons once again defeated the Bulls, this time in six games, by utilizing their "Jordan Rules" method of guarding Jordan, which consisted of double and triple teaming him each time he touched the ball.

The Bulls entered the 1989–90 seasons as a squad on the rise. With their core group of Jordan and young improving players like Scottie Pippen and Horace Grant, they were turning a more cohesive squad under the guidance of new coach Phil Jackson. Jordan averaged a league leading 33.6 ppg on 52.6% shooting, to go with 6.9 rpg and 6.3 apgin leading the Bulls to a 55–27 record. They once again advanced to the Eastern Conference Finals defeating the Bucks and Philadelphia 76ers en route. However, in spite of forcing the series to seven games, the Bulls lost to the Pistons for the third consecutive season.

Jordan played on two Olympic gold medal-winning American basketball teams. As a college player he took part, and won the gold, in the 1984 Summer Olympics. Jordan led the squad in scoring averaging out 17.1 ppg for the tournament. In the 1992 Summer Olympics he was a fellow member of the star-studded squad that admitted Magic Johnson,

Larry Bird, and David Robinson and was dubbed the "Dream Team". Playing fixed minutes due to the frequent blowouts, Jordan averaged 12.7 ppg, finishing fourth on the team in scoring. The team cruised to the gold medal, reestablishing the United States to the top of the basketball world. Jordan, Patrick Ewing, and fellow Dream Team member Chris Mullin are the only American men's basketball players to win Olympic gold as amateurs (all in 1984) and professionals.

Andrew Bogut

Andrew Michael Bogut born on November 28, 1984 is an Australian professional basketball player. He plays for the Milwaukee Bucks of the National Basketball Association.Bogut was picked out first overall by the Bucks in the 2005 NBA Draft. The 7'0", 260 lb (2.13 m, 111 kg) forward/ center was a star at the University of Utah for two years before announcing for the draft. Bogut is the first Australian to be drafted first overall.

Bogut completed a prosperous rookie season with the Bucks averaging out 9.4 ppg and 7.0 rpg. He was called to the 2005-06 All-Rookie First Team and completed third in votes for the 2006 Rookie of the Year Award. Bogut was also the only top-10 pick from the 2005 draft to start for his squad in the 2006 NBA Playoffs.

Bogut's sophomore season in the league was cut short after wricking his left foot and being put on the wounded reserve for the final 15 games. He had antecedently fought off any injury to play in 153 consecutive games.He showed improvement in his second year in the league as he averaged 12.3 points and 8.8 rebounds per game. Bogut is conceived one of the topmost passing centers in the league, having averaged 3.0 assists per game in the 2006-07 season. His per 48 minute average of 4.2 was better than a number of point-guards, of course expected to distribute the ball. In the 2007-08 NBA season the Australian center demonstrated career highs in points (14.3), rebounds (9.8), blocks (1.7), steals (0.8.) and minutes (34.9) per game.Also in the 2007/08 season Bogut commenced a career high 78 times. The low point of his second season in the NBA came when he made an obscene gesture towards a home fan after being expelled from a game for a flagrant foul against the Toronto Raptors at the Bradley Center. The move would cost him $25,000.

Bogut was a starter for the Boomers at the 2004 Athens Olympics, averaging out 14.8 points, 8.8 rebounds, and 1.2 blocked shots and shooting 58.0% from the field. He presented Australia once again in the 2006 FIBA World Championship. Australia progressed to the Round of 16, before losing to the U.S.. Bogut averaged out 12.8 points per game and 6.1 rebounds per game throughout the tournament, leading Australia in both categories. Bogut was a starter for the Boomers at the 2008 Beijing Olympics.

LeBron James

LeBron Raymone James (born December 30, 1984 in Akron, Ohio) is an American basketball player who plays for the Cleveland Cavaliers of the National Basketball Association (NBA). James, normally nicknamed "King James," was highly encouraged in the national media as a future NBA superstar while still in high school at St. Vincent - St. Mary High School, and was called Ohio's "Mr. Basketball" three times. At the age of 18, he was picked out with the first overall pick in the 2003 NBA Draft by the Cavaliers and signed an US$90 million shoe contract with Nike before his NBA debut. He has since set many youngest player records. Throughout his first season, he obtained the NBA Rookie of the Year Award and in the following four seasons received All-NBA and All-Star honours. He has led the Cavaliers to sequential playoff appearances in 2006, 2007, and 2008; in 2007, the squad progressed to the Conference Finals for the first time since 1992 and the NBA Finals for the first time in franchise history.

James is listed as a small forward, but is often classified as a point forward due to his capability to play point guard. He is a member of the United States men's national basketball squad succeeding the bronze medal at the 2004 Olympics and redeeming that result by succeeding the gold medal at the 2008 Olympics. He completed second in the league's Most Valuable Player balloting in 2006.

James has recognized himself as a legitimate triple-double threat and has averaged 27.3 points, 6.6 assists and 6.9 rebounds per game for his career.As of the 2007–08 season, he has recorded 17 triple-doubles in his career, with 14 in the regular season and 3 in the postseason. On offense, James utilizes his quickness, size, and strength to get past defenders. James is known for his particular upper body strength. When penetrating to the basket, James displays superb body control, adjusting his shot in mid-air as per the defense, permitting him to absorb contact and finish at the basket. He is also proficient at finishing all over the rim with both hands.In the 2005–06 season, he led the league in completed traditional three point plays.He is a solid rebounder who on regular basis ranks amongst the league leaders in rebounds for the small forward position.His overall skill sets and on-court play has led to many comparisons to NBA legends Oscar Robertson, Magic Johnson, and Michael Jordan.

Even though James exhibits exceptional offensive capability, he has yet to be featured on the NBA All-Defensive Team and has contended with his free throw shooting — he averaged a subpar .698 free throw percentage in the 2006-07 season.

REFERENCES

Alter, S.: *Science of Flexibility*, 2nd edn, Human Kinetics, Champaign, IL, 1996.

Alter, S.: *Sport Stretch*, Human Kinetics, Champaign, IL, 1998.

Dintiman, G. and Ward, R.:*Sport Speed*, Leisure Press, Champaign, IL, 1988.

Ellison, D.: *Performance Stretching*, Human Kinetics, Champaign, IL, 1999.

Goldberg, B. (ed.): *Sports and Exercise for Children with Chronic Health Conditions*, Human Kinetics, Champaign, IL, 1995

Newsholme, E., Leech, T. and Duester, G.: *Keep on Running*, John Wiley & Sons, Chichester, UK, 1994

Reaburn, P. and Jenkins, D.: *Training for Speed and Endurance*, Allen & Unwin, Sydney, 1996

Rowland, T.W.: *Developmental Exercise Physiology*, Human Kinetics, Champaign, IL, 1996

Sports weekly Magazine

Sports Illustrated Magazine

4

Boxing

Boxing (sometimes also known as English boxing or pugilism) is a combat game in which two participants, in general of similar weight, fight each other with their fists. Boxing is supervised by an umpire and is normally engaged in during a series of one to three-minute intervals called rounds. Victory is attained if the opponent is knocked down and unable to get up before the referee counts to ten seconds (a Knockout, or KO) or if the opponent is held too injured to continue (a Technical Knockout, or TKO). If there is no stoppage of the fight before an agreed number of rounds, a winner is determined either by the referee's decision or by judges' scorecards.

Even though fighting with fists comes naturally to people, the ancient Greeks provide us our first historical records of boxing as a game; they codified a set of rules and regulations and staged tournaments with professionals. The birth hour of boxing as a game may be its acceptance as an Olympic game as early as 688 BC. Modern boxing orginated in Europe, particularly Great Britain.

In some countries with their own fighting sports, the game is referred to as "English Boxing" (e.g. in France to contrast with French boxing). There are many dissimslar forms of boxing practiced all around the world.

HISTORY

First fighting is depicted in Sumerian relief carvings in the 3rd millennium BC, Both depictions show bare-fisted contests..In 1927 Dr. E. A. Speiser, an archaeologist, discovered a stone tablet in Baghdad, Iraq depicting two men getting ready for a prize fight. The tablet is conceived to be 7,000 years old. . Fist fighting or boxing is also described in various ancient Indian texts such as the Vedas, the ramayana, and the mahabarata. Evidence of boxing as a game was found in excavations done in Mohenjadaro and Harappa. The earliest evidence for fist fighting with a kind of gloves can be found on Minoan Crete, (c. 1500-900 BC) and on Sardinia, if we consider the boxing statues of Prama mountains (c. 2000-1000 BC).

The ancient Greeks and the Etruscans called boxing pugilism (a term now synonymous with boxing). The Greeks and Etruscans were not the first to give rules to the game, if we consider Mediterranean folks who preceded them, such as the Shardana and the Egyptians. In the Mediterranean area while clinching was strictly forbidden, there were (unlike in modern boxing) no weight classes. Fights were not isolated into rounds and had no time limit. They ended at a knockout, or at a fighter abandoning the fight, or sometimes at the death of one of the fighters. Even though gloves were used in practice, in competition fighters wrapped their hands in strips of hardened leather which protected the fist and caused unpleasant injuries for the opponent.

Homer's Iliad (ca. 675 BC) contains the first elaborated account of a box fight (Book XXIII). As per the Iliad, Mycenaean warriors included boxing amongst their competitions honouring the fallen, though it is possible that the Homeric epics reflect later Greek culture. Another Greek legend holds that the heroic ruler Theseus, said to have lived all over the 9th century BC, invented a form of boxing in which two men sat face to face and beat each other with their fists until one of them was killed. In time, the boxers started to fight while standing and wearing gloves (with spikes) and wrappings on their arms below the elbows, even though otherwise they contended naked.

Boxing was first accepted as an Olympic game in 688 BC, being called Pygme or Pygmachia. Participants trained on punching bags (called a korykos). Fighters wore leather straps (called himantes) over their hands, wrists, and sometimes breast, to protect them from injury. The straps left their fingers free. Legend had it that the Spartans were the first to box as a way to prepare for sword and shield fighting.

In ancient Rome, there were two forms of boxing both coming from Etruscan boxing. The athletic form of boxing remained famous during the Roman world. The other form of boxing was gladiatorial. Fighters were normally criminals and slaves who hoped to become champions and gain their freedom; however, free men, women and even aristocrats also fought. Finally, fist fighting turned so famous that even emperors began fighting, and the practice was promoted by Caesar Neronis. A fight among the agile Dares and the towering Entellus is described at length in the Roman national epic Aeneid (1st century BC).

In 393 A.D., the Olympics were banned by the Christian emperor Theodosius, and in 500 A.D., boxing was banned altogether by Theodoric the Great as being an insult to God because it disfigures the face, the image of God. However, this edict had little effect outside the major cities of the Eastern Empire. By this time, western Europe was no longer part of the Roman Empire. Boxing remained famous in Europe during the Middle Ages and beyond. It should be noted that wrestling, fencing and racing (both chariot and foot) were never banned by the late Romans, as they did not cause disfigurement.

THE GAME

A boxing match normally consists of a predetermined number of three-minute rounds, a total of up to 25 rounds. A minute is normally spent among every round with the fighters in their assigned corners receiving advice and attention from their coach and staff. The fight is assured by an umpire who works inside the ring to judge and control the conduct of the fighters, rule on their capability to fight safely, count knocked-down fighters, and rule on fouls. Up to three judges are normally present at ringside to score the bout and assign points to the boxers, based on punches that connect, defense, knockdowns, and other, more subjective, measures. Every fighter has an assigned corner of the ring, where his or her coach, as well as one or more "seconds" may administer to the fighter at the commencing of the fight and among rounds. Every boxer enters into the ring from their assigned corners at the commencing of each round and must cease fighting and return to their corner at the signaled end of each round.

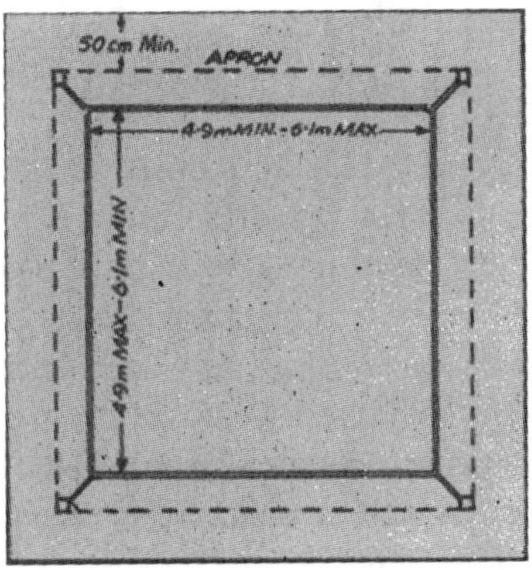

Fig. Boxing Ring

A bout in which the predetermined number of rounds passes is decided by the judges, and is said to "go the distance". The fighter with the higher score at the end of the fight is ruled the winner. With three judges, unanimous and split decisions are possible, as are draws. A boxer may win the bout before a decision is reached through a knockout; such bouts are said to have ended "inside the distance". If a fighter is knocked down throughout the fight, determined by whether the boxer touches the canvas floor of the ring with any part of their body other than the feet as a result of the opponent's punch and not a slip, as determined by the referee, the referee begins counting until the fighter returns to his or her feet and can continue. Should the referee count to ten, then the knocked-down boxer is ruled "knocked out" (whether unconscious or not) and the other boxer is ruled the winner by knockout (KO).

Fig. Dimensions of Ring

A "technical knockout" (TKO) is possible as well, and is ruled by the referee, fight doctor, or a fighter's corner if a fighter is unable to safely continue to fight, based upon injuries or being judged unable to effectively oppose themselves. Many jurisdictions and sanctioning agencies also have a "three-knockdown rule", in which three knockdowns result in a TKO. A TKO is considered a knockout in a fighter's record. A "standing eight" count rule may also be in effect, in which the referee counts no higher than eight to a boxer who regains his or her footing after a knockdown, allowing the referee time to assess if the boxer is able to continue.

Generally, boxers are prohibited from hitting below the belt, holding, tripping, forcing, biting, spitting or wrestling. The boxer's shorts are raised so the opponent is not permitted to hit to the groin area. They also are prohibited from kicking, head-butting, or hitting with any part of the arm other than the knuckles of a closed fist (including hitting with the elbow, shoulder or forearm, as well as with open gloves, the wrist, the inside, back or side of the hand). They are prohibited as well from hitting the back, back of the neck or head (called a "rabbit-punch") or the kidneys.

Fig. Various Strikes

They are prohibited from holding the ropes for support when punching, holding an opponent while punching, or ducking below the belt of their opponent. If a "clinch" — a defensive move in which a boxer wraps his or her opponents arms and holds on to create a pause — is broken by the referee, every fighter must take a full step back before punching once again (alternatively, the referee may direct the fighters to "punch out" of the clinch). When a boxer is knocked down, the other boxer must immediately cease fighting and move to the nearest neutral corner of the ring until the referee has either ruled a knockout or called for the fight to continue.

Violations of these rules may be ruled "fouls" by the referee, who may issue warnings, deduct points, or disqualify an offending boxer, causing an automatic loss, depending upon the seriousness and intentionality of the foul. An intentional foul that causes injury that prevents a fight from continuing normally causes the boxer who committed it to be disqualified. A fighter who suffers an accidental low-blow may be given up to five minutes to recover, after which they may be ruled knocked out if they are unable to continue. Accidental fouls that cause injury ending a bout may lead to a "no decision" result, or else cause the fight to go to a decision if enough rounds (normally four or more, or at least three in a four-round fight) have passed.

Equipments

Since boxing involves forceful, repetitive punching, precautions must be taken to prevent damage to bones in the hand. Most trainers do not allow boxers to train and spar without hand/wrist wraps and boxing gloves. Hand wraps are used to secure the bones in the hand, and the gloves are used to protect the hands from blunt injury, allowing boxers to throw punches with more force than if they did not utilize them. Gloves have been required in competition since the late nineteenth century, though modern boxing gloves are much heavier than those worn by early twentieth-century fighters. Prior to a bout, both boxers agree upon the weight of gloves to be used in the bout, with the understanding that lighter gloves allow heavy punchers to inflict more damage. The brand of gloves can also affect the impact of punches, so this too is normally stipulated before a bout. A mouth guard is important to protect the teeth and gums from injury, and to cushion the jaw, leadingin a decreased chance of knockout.

Fig. Boxing Gloves

Boxers practice their skills on two basic types of punching bags. A small, tear-drop-shaped "speed bag" is used to hone reflexes and repetitive punching skills, while a large cylindrical "heavy bag" filled with sand or a synthetic substitute is used to practice power punching and body blows. In addition to these distinctive pieces of equipment, boxers also utilize more general utilize training equipment to build strength, speed, and agility. Common training equipment includes free weights, rowing machines, jump rope, and medicine balls. Headgear, required in amateur boxing and used by professionals when sparring, protects against cuts, scrapes, and swelling.

Amateur Boxing

Amateur boxing is practiced at the collegiate level, at the Olympic Games and Commonwealth Games, and in many other venues sponsored by amateur boxing associations. Amateur boxing bouts are short in duration and fighters wear head protection, so this type of competition prizes point-scoring (based on number of clean punches landed) rather than physical power. Bouts comprise four rounds of two minutes in the Olympic and Commonwealth Games, and four rounds of two minutes in a national ABA (Amateur Boxing Association) bout, each with a one-minute interval among rounds.

Competitors wear protective headgear and gloves with a white strip on the the knuckle. A punch is considered a scoring punch only when the boxers connect with the white portion of the gloves. Every punch that lands on the head or torso is granted a point. An umpire monitors the fight to ensure that competitors utilize only legal blows (a belt worn over the torso represents the lower limit of punches - any boxer repeatedly landing "low blows" is disqualified). Referees also ensure that the boxers don't utilize holding tactics to prevent the opponent from swinging (if this occurs, the referee separates the opponents and orders them to continue boxing. Repeated holding can result in a boxer being penalized, or finally, disqualified). Referees will stop the bout if a boxer is seriously injured, if one boxer is significantly dominating the other or if the score is severely imbalanced. Bouts which end this way may be noted as "RSC" (referee stopped contest) with notations for an outclassed opponent (RSCO), outscored opponent (RSCOS), injury (RCSI) or head injury (RSCH).

Professional Boxing

Professional boxing, or prizefighting, emerged in the early twentieth century as boxing gradually attained legitimacy and turned a regulated, sanctioned game. Professional boxing bouts are fought for a purse which is divided amongst the fighters and promoters as determined by contract. All legal professional bouts must be sanctioned by a state athletic commission to guarantee the fighters' safety. Additionally, most high-profile bouts recieve the endorsement of a private sanctioning body, which awards championships, establishes rules, and assigns referees. Professional bouts are normally much longer than amateur bouts, and can last up to twelve rounds, though less substantial fights can be as short as four rounds. Protective headgear is not permitted, and boxers are in general permitted to take substantial punishment before a fight is halted. Professional boxing has enjoyed a much higher profile than amateur boxing during the twentieth century and beyond.

MAJOR TOURNAMENTS

Olympics

Boxing has been contested at each Summer Olympic Games since its introduction to the program at the 1904 Summer Olympics, except for the 1912 Summer Olympics in Stockholm, because Swedish law banned the game at the time. The 2008 Summer Olympics will be the final games with boxing as a male only event. Commencing with the 2012 Summer Olympics, women's boxing will be included in the programme.

The boxing competition is organized as a set of tournaments, one for every weight class. There have been from 5 and 12 Olympic weight classes over the years (presently 11), and the definition of each class has changed various times, as shown in the following table. Until 1936, weights were measured in pounds, and from 1948 onwards, weights were measured in kilograms.

World Amateur Boxing Championships

The World Amateur Boxing Championships is the highest competition for boxing amateurs, organised by world's governing body AIBA, which stands for the Association International de Boxe Amateur. The first edition of the tournament was held in Havana, Cuba, from August 17 to 30, 1974. The number of weight categories was reduced from twelve to eleven in 2003 with the removal of the light middleweight class (– 71 kg). A women's championships was first staged in 2001.

ADMINISTRATIVE BODIES

World Boxing Association

The World Boxing Association (WBA) is a boxing organization that sanctions official matches, and awards the WBA world championship title, at the professional level. It was previously known as the National Boxing Association before changing its name in 1962. It is the most former of the major organizations recognized by IBHOF which sanction world championship boxing bouts, alongside the International Boxing Federation, World Boxing Council and the World Boxing Organization.

The original sanctioning body of professional boxing, the World Boxing Association can be traced back to the original National Boxing Association, organized in 1921; the first bout recognized by the organization being the Jack Dempsey-Georges Carpentier Heavyweight Championship bout in New Jersey, USA.

The NBA was established by representatives from thirteen American states to counterbalance the influence the New York State Athletic Commission (NYSAC) wielded in the boxing world. This often meant that the NBA and the NYSAC crowned dissimslar world champions in the similar class, leading to confusion about who was the real champion.

The International Boxing Research Organization describes the early NBA in this way: "Primitively more comparable to the present American Association of Boxing Commissions than to its offspring and successor, the NBA sanctioned title bouts, published lists of outstanding challengers, withdrew titular recognition, but did not attempt to appoint its own title bout officials or otherwise impose its will on championship fights. It also did not conduct purse bids or collect 'sanctioning fees.'"

In 1962 the NBA, with the growth of boxing's popularity worldwide, changed its name to the World Boxing Association. The organization remained mainly American until 1974, however. In that year, two Panamanian boxing figures named Rodrigo Sanchez and Elias Cordova manipulated the WBA rules to give a majority of votes to nations in Latin America.

Gilberto Mendoza has been the President of the WBA since 1982. The WBA in the 1990s moved its central offices from Panama City, Panama, to Caracas, Venezuela. In January 2007 it moved its offices once again to Panama.

International Boxing Federation

The International Boxing Federation, or IBF, is one of four major organizations recognized by IBHOF which sanction world championship boxing bouts, alongside the WBA, WBC and WBO.

The IBF was preceded by the United States Boxing Association (USBA), a regional championships organization like the NABF, NABC and NABA. In 1983, at the WBA's annual convention, held in Puerto Rico that year, Bob Lee, president of the USBA, lost in his bid to become WBA president against Gilberto Mendoza. Lee and others withdrew from the convention after the election, and decided to organize a new world-level organization. At first, the new group was named the USBA-

International. They decided to base the new organization in New Jersey, where its main offices are still situated.

The IBF's first world champion was Marvin Camel, a former WBC world Cruiserweight champion who won the IBF's belt in the similar class. Throughout its first year of existence, however, the IBF remained largely obscure. But by 1984, the IBF decided to recognize Larry Holmes, Aaron Pryor, Marvin Hagler and Donald Curry, already established champions from other organizations, as IBF world champions. In Holmes' case, he relinquished his WBC title to accept the IBF's recognition. It established the IBF as the "third" sanctioning body, and a legitimate organization.

Ever since then, the IBF has been the sanctioning body of many important fights and world champions. For example, Félix Trinidad was the IBF's world Welterweight champion from 1993 to 2000, and is one of a long list of world champions who have been recognized by the IBF. The present IBF Heavyweight champion is Ukrainian Wladimir Klitschko.

The organization's reputation was seriously damaged in 1999, however, as Lee resigned as the IBF's President upon conviction on racketeering and other violations for taking bribes in exchange for high boxer rankings.Hiawatha Knight then turned the first woman president of any of the world's governing boxing bodies. In 2001, Marian Muhammad followed her as president. The organization was under federal observation from Lee's conviction through September 2004, though remaining recognized as one of boxing's "big three" sanctioning organizations.

World Boxing Organization

The World Boxing Organization (WBO) is a sanctioning organization presently recognizing professional boxing world champions. Its offices are situated in San Juan, Puerto Rico.

The WBO began after a group of Puerto Rican and Dominican businessmen broke out of the World Boxing Association's 1988 annual convention in Isla Margarita, Venezuela, claiming to be disgusted by the WBA's questionable rules and ratings systems.

The WBO's first president was Ramon Pina Acevedo of the Dominican Republic. Soon after its commencing, the WBO was staging world championship bouts all over the globe. Its first championship fight was for its vacant super middleweight title, among Thomas Hearns and James Kinchen; Hearns won by decision. In order to gain respectability, the WBO following elected former world light heavyweight champion Jose Torres of Ponce, Puerto Rico, as its president. Torres left in 1996, giving way to Puerto Rican lawyer Francisco Varcarcel as president. Varcarcel has been there since.

The WBO was made famous by boxers such as Oscar De La Hoya, Marco Antonio Barrera, Naseem Hamed, Michael Carbajal, Johnny Tapia, Harry Simon, Nigel Benn, Gerald McClellan, Joe Calzaghe, Steve Collins, Michael Moorer, Dariusz Michalczewski, Chris Eubank, Vitali Klitschko, Wladimir Klitschko and Chris Byrd in the 1990s.

The WBO twice moved Darrin Morris up in its super-middleweight rankings in 2001, in spite of the fact that he was dead. Morris was 7 at the time of his death and #5 when the WBO discovered the error. Varcarcel said "we obviously missed the fact that Darrin was dead. It is regrettable." One week after British newspaper The Independent broke the story, one of the three men ranking the boxers, Gordon Volkman, still had not heard that Morris was dead.

FAMOUS PLAYERS

Muhammad Ali

Muhammad Ali (born Cassius Marcellus Clay Jr. on January 17, 1942) is a retired American boxer and former three-time World Heavyweight Champion. To date, he stays the only man to have won the linear heavyweight championship three times (the linear title is recognized by tracing an - almost - unbroken lineage of titleholders going back over 100 years, with nearly each champion defeating the previous titleholder in the ring). Ali was also the winner of an Olympic Light-heavyweight gold medal. In 1999, Ali was crowned "Sportsman of the Century" by Sports Illustrated and the BBC.

Cassius Marcellus Clay, Jr., was born in Louisville, Kentucky. He was named after his father, Cassius Marcellus Clay Sr., who was named for the nineteenth century abolitionist and politician Cassius Clay. Ali changed his name after joining the Nation of Islam in 1964, subsequently converted to Sunni Islam in 1975 and then Sufism.

Ali was known for his fighting style, which he described as "Float like a butterfly, sting like a bee". During his career Ali made a name for himself with great handspeed, as well as swift feet and taunting tactics. While Ali was renowned for his fast, sharp out-fighting style, he also had a great chin, and displayed great courage and an capability to take a punch during his career.

Clay was first directed toward boxing by Louisville police officer, Joe E. Martin, who encountered the then twelve-year-old Cassius Clay fuming over the fact that his bicycle had been stolen. However, without Martin knowing, Clay also started training with Fred Stoner at another gym. In this way, he could continue making $4 a week on Tomorrow's Champions, a TV show that Martin hosted, while benefiting from the coaching of the more-experienced Stoner, who extended working with Clay during his amateur career.

Clay's last amateur loss was to Kent Green of Chicago, who could say he was the last person to defeat the champion until Ali lost to Joe Frazier in 1971 as a pro. Under Stoner's guidance, Cassius Clay went on to win six Kentucky Golden Gloves titles, two national Golden Gloves titles, an Amateur Athletic Union National Title, and the Light Heavyweight gold medal in the 1960 Summer Olympics in Rome. Clay's record was 100 wins, with five losses, when he ended his amateur career.

Ali states (in his 1975 autobiography) that he threw his Olympic gold medal into the Ohio River after being declined service at a 'whites-only' restaurant, and fighting with a white gang. Whether this is true is still debated, even though he was given a replacement medal throughout the opening ceremony of the 1996 Olympics in Atlanta, where he lit the torch to start the games.

After his Olympic triumph, Clay came back to Louisville to commences his professional career. There, on October 29, 1960, he won his first professional fight, a six-round decision over Tunney Hunsaker, who was the police chief of Fayetteville, West Virginia.

Standing tall, at 6-ft, 3-in (1.91 m), Clay had a highly unorthodox style for a heavyweight boxer. Rather than the normal style of carrying the hands high to oppose the face, he instead relied on foot speed and quickness to avoid punches and held his hands low.

From 1960 to 1963, the young fighter amassed a record of 19-0, with 15 knockouts. He defeated boxers such as Tony Esperti, Jim Robinson, Donnie Fleeman, Alonzo Johnson, George Logan, Willi Besmanoff, Lamar Clark (who had won his previous 40 bouts by knockout), Doug Jones and Henry Cooper.

Clay built a reputation by correctly predicting the round in which he would "finish" various opponents, and by boasting before his triumphs. Clay admitted he adopted the latter practice from "Gorgeous" George Wagner, a famous professional wrestling champion in the Los Angeles area who drew thousands of fans. Often referred to as "the man you loved to hate," George could incite the crowd with a few heated remarks, and Ali followed suit.

Amongst Clay's victims were Sonny Banks (who knocked him down throughout the bout), Alejandro Lavorante, and the aged Archie Moore (a boxing legend who had fought over 200 previous fights, and who had been Clay's trainer prior to Angelo Dundee). Clay had considered continuing utilizing Moore as a trainer following the bout, but Moore had insisted that the cocky "Louisville Lip" perform training camp chores such as sweeping and dishwashing. He also considered having his idol, Sugar Ray Robinson, as a manager, but instead hired Dundee.

Clay first met Dundee when the latter was in Louisville with light heavyweight champ Willie Pastrano. The teenaged Golden Glove winner traveled downtown to the fighter's hotel, called Dundee from the house phone, and was asked up to their room. He took advantage of the chance to query Dundee (who was working with, or had, champions Sugar Ramos and Carmen Basilio) about what his fighters ate, how long they slept, how much roadwork (jogging) they did, and how long they sparred.

Following his bout with Moore, Clay won a disputed 10-round decision over Doug Jones in a matchup that was named "Fight of the Year" for 1963. Clay's following fight was against Henry Cooper, who knocked Clay down with a left hook near the end of the fourth round. The fight was stopped in the fifth due to deep cuts over Cooper's eyes.

In spite of these close calls, Clay turned the top contender for Sonny Liston's title. In spite of his impressive record, however, he was not widely expected to defeat the champ. The fight was scheduled for February 25, 1964 in Miami, Florida, but was nearly canceled when the promoter, Bill Faversham, heard that Clay had been seen all over Miami and in other cities with the controversial Malcolm X. At the time, The Nation of Islam — of which Malcolm X was a member — was portrayed as a "hate group" by most of the media. Because of this, news of this association was perceived as a potential gate-killer to a bout where, given Liston's overwhelming status as the favorite to win (7-1 odds), had Clay's colorful persona and nonstop braggadocio as its sole appeal.

Faversham confronted Clay about his association with Malcolm X (who, at the time, was actually under suspension by the Nation as a result of controversial comments made in the wake of President Kennedy's assassination, which he called a case of "the chickens coming home to roost"). While stopping short of admitting he was a member of the Nation, Clay protested the suggested cancellation of the fight. As a compromise, Faversham asked the fighter to delay his announcement about his conversion to Islam until after the fight. The incident is described in the 1975 book The Greatest: My Own Story by Ali (with Richard Durham).

Throughout the weigh-in on the day before the bout, the ever-boastful Clay, who frequently taunted Liston throughout the buildup by dubbing him "the big ugly bear" (amongst other things), declared that he would "float like a butterfly and sting like a bee," and, summarizing his strategy for avoiding Liston's assaults, said, "Your hands can't

After achieving the championship from Liston in 1964, Clay revealed that he was a member of the Nation of Islam (often called the Black Muslims at the time) and the Nation gave Clay the name Cassius X, discarding his surname as a symbol of his ancestors' enslavement, as had been done by other Nation members. On Friday, March 6, 1964, Malcolm X took Clay on a guided tour of the United Nations building (for a second time). Malcolm X announced that Clay would be granted his "X." That similar night, Elijah Muhammad recorded a statement over the phone to be played over the radio that Clay would be renamed Muhammad (one who is worthy of praise) Ali (fourth rightly guided caliph). Only a few journalists (most notably Howard Cosell) accepted it at that time. Venerable boxing announcer Don Dunphy addressed the champion by his adopted name, as did British reporters. The adoption of this name symbolized his new identity as a member of the Nation of Islam.

Clay had discovered the Nation throughout a Golden Gloves tournament in Chicago in 1959, even writing a high school report on the organization. His school teachers at Louisville Central High were alarmed that a youngster with that much potential expressed interest in the nationalist faith. They dissuaded him from turning involved. Many sportswriters of the early 1960s described that it was Ali's brother, Rudy Clay, who converted to Islam first (estimating the date as 1962). Others wrote that Clay had been seen at Muslim rallies two years before he fought Liston. Ali's own version is that he did buy a copy of the "Muhammad Speaks" newspaper from a Muslim in Chicago, and a 45 rpm record by Minister Louis X (later Farrakhan) called "A White Man's Heaven is a Black Man's Hell."

Aligning himself with the Nation of Islam made him a lightning rod for controversy, turning the outspoken but famous champion into one of that era's most recognizable and controversial figures. Appearing at rallies with Nation of Islam leader Elijah Muhammad and declaring his allegiance to him at a time when mainstream America viewed them with suspicion — if not outright hostility — made Ali a target of outrage, as well as suspicion. Ali seemed at times to provoke such reactions, with viewpoints that wavered from support for civil rights to outright support of separatism. For example, Ali once stated, in relation to integration: "We who follow the teachings of Elijah Muhammad don't want to be forced to integrate. Integration is wrong. We don't want to live with the white man; that's all." And in relation to inter-racial marriage: "No intelligent black man or black woman in his or her right black mind wants white boys and white girls coming to their homes to marry their black sons and daughters." Indeed, Ali's religious beliefs at the time included the notion that the white man was "the devil" and that white people were not "righteous." Ali claimed that white people hated black people.

Ali converted from the Nation of Islam sect to mainstream Sunni Islam in 1975. In a 2004 autobiography, written with daughter Hana Yasmeen Ali, Muhammad Ali attributes his conversion to the shift toward Sunni Islam made by W.D. Muhammad after he earned control of the Nation of Islam upon the death of Elijah Muhammad in 1975.

There is no consensus amongst boxing experts and historians as to who is the greatest heavyweight boxer of all time. Ring Magazine, a prominent boxing magazine, named Muhammad Ali as number 1 in a 1998 ranking of greatest heavyweights from all eras. In a 1971 article, Nat Fleischer, the founder of the Ring who saw each heavyweight champion from Jim Jeffries to Joe Frazier, declined to include Ali in his all-time top ten, saying: "he does not qualify for rating with the greatest heavyweights of all time". Fleischer was writing after Ali's loss to Frazier, various years before his performance against Foreman and rematches with Frazier.

In recent times, Ali was named the second greatest fighter in boxing history by ESPN.com behind only welterweight and middleweight great Sugar Ray Robinson. In December 2007, ESPN listed its option of the greatest heavyweights of all time. Ali was second on this list also behind Joe Louis, in spite of the fact that the earlier poll placed Ali ahead of Louis.

Henry Armstrong

Henry Jackson Jr. (December 12, 1912 - October 22, 1988) was a world boxing champion who fought under the name Henry Armstrong. The son of a sharecropper and America Armstrong, an Iroquois Indian,

Henry Jr. was a boxer who not only was a member of the exclusive group of fighters that have won boxing championships in three or more dissimslar divisions(at a time when there were less weight divisions), but also has the distinction of being the only boxer to hold three world championships at the similar time. He also defended the Welterweight championship more times than any other fighter.

In 2002, Ring Magazine ranked Armstrong as the 2nd greatest fighter of the last 80 years, behind only Sugar Ray Robinson and ahead of the legendary Muhammad Ali.A native of Columbus, Mississippi, Armstrong moved as a youngster with his household to St. Louis, Missouri, where he developed his boxing skills. Armstrong passed from Vashon High School and was later inducted into the St. Louis Walk of Fame. Armstrong's two nicknames were Hurricane Henry, and Homicide' Hank.

Armstrong began out as a professional on July 28, 1931, being knocked out by Al Sorvino in three rounds. Just like Alexis Arguello, Bernard Hopkins, and Wilfredo Vazquez in the future, Armstrong was one world champion who began off on the losing end. His first win came later that year, defeating Sammy Burns by a decision in six. In 1932, Armstrong moved to Los Angeles, where he began out losing two four round decisions in a row, to Eddie Trujillo and Al Greenfield. But after that, he began a streak of 11 wins in a row, a streak which expanded to 1933, until he lost once again, to Baby Manuel. Then he went 22 straight fights without a defeat, going 17-0-5 in that span, including a win in a Sacramento rematch with Manuel, and five wins over Perfecto Lopez. After that, he moved to Mexico City, where in his first fight there, he lost to former world bantamweight champion Baby Arizmendi. He had four more fights there, going 2-2 and losing to Arizmendi in what was considered by Mexico and California a world title bout (thus Armstrong losing on his first championship try), and to Baby Casanova by a five round disqualification. He then moved back to California, where he went 8-1-1 for the following ten bouts.

In 1936, Armstrong split time campaigning among Los Angeles, Mexico City and St. Louis. Some opponents of note that year were Ritchie Fontaine, against whom he lost by decision and then won by decision in the rematch, Arizmendi, whom he finally beat by a ten round decision, former world champion Juan Zurita and former champ Mike Belloise, who also lost a decision to Armstrong.

Armstrong began out 1937 by achieving 22 bouts in a row, 21 by knockout. He beat Casanova in three, Belloise in four, Joe Rivers in three, former world champion Frankie Klick in four and former world champion Benny Bass in four. After those 22 wins in a row, the inevitable happened: Armstrong was given his first world title try, for the 126 pounds title, Featherweight world champion Petey Sarron opposing it against him at the Madison Square Garden. Armstrong turned the world's Featherweight champion knocking out Sarron in six, and closed the year with four more knockout wins.

In 1938, Armstrong began with seven more knockouts in a row, including one over future world champion Chalky Wright. The streak finally ended when Arizmendi lasted ten rounds before losing a decision to Armstrong in their fourth fight. His streak of 27 knockout wins in a row qualifies as one of the longest knockout win streaks in the history of boxing, as per Ring Magazine. After the fourth bout with Arizmendi was a bout with Fritzie Zivic's brother, Eddie Zivic, leadingin another Armstrong knockout win, and after one more bout, Armstrong, the 126 pound division world champion, challenged a fellow member of the three division champions' club, Barney Ross, then world Welterweight champion, for the title. Armstrong, 126, beat Ross, 147, by unanimous decision, adding the world Welterweight championship to his Featherweight belt. Then, he went down in weight, and challenged world Lightweight champion Lou Ambers. In a history making night, Armstrong turned the first boxer ever to have world championships in three dissimslar divisions at the similar time, by defeating Ambers on points. A few days later, he decided he couldn't make the 126 pounds weight anymore, and left the Featherweight crown vacant.

He dedicated the following two years to opposing the welterweight crown, defeating, amongst others, future world middleweight champion Ceferino Garcia, Al Manfredo and Bobby Pacho, before opposing his Lightweight belt in a rematch with Ambers, which he lost on a 15 round decision. After that, he concentrated once once again on opposing the world Welterweight title, and made eight defenses in a row, the last of which was a nine round knockout win over Puerto Rico's Pedro Montanez. Then, he tried to make history once once again by turning the first boxer to win world titles in four dissimslar categories in a rematch with Garcia, already world Middleweight champion, but the fight ended in a ten round draw, Armstrong's attempt to win a fourth division's world title being frustrated. As per boxing historian Bert Sugar, many felt Armstrong deserved the decision in this fight.

He went back to Welterweight and retained the title five more times, until Fritzie Zivic was able to avenge his brother Eddie's defeat by taking the world title away from Armstrong with a 15 round decision. With this loss, Armstrong's reign as Welterweight champion came to an end, leaving Armstrong's successful defense streak at eighteen, the most defenses by a champion ever in Welterweight history. In 1941, they boxed a rematch, this time, Zivic stopping Armstrong in 12 rounds.

1942 saw Armstrong go 13-1, including wins over world champions (Fritzie) Zivic in a ten round non title bout, Jenkins and Zurita.1943 saw him go 10-3, with wins over world champions Tippy Larkin and Sammy Angott in ten round bouts, and losses to world champions Beau Jack and Sugar Ray Robinson, also in ten round bouts.1944 saw Henry go 14-2-1 in 17 bouts, amongst those, another win over Belloise.

After achieving one fight, losing one and drawing one in 1945, Armstrong decided to retire from boxing. Apart from the ceremonies and galas that he attended afterwards, he led a relatively quiet life for the rest of his life. He turned a born-once again Christian and an ordained pastor, and he taught young, upcoming fighters how to box.

Armstrong registered an official record of 150 wins, 21 losses and 9 draws, with 100 knockout wins. His exact record, however, isn't in real known, because it is said he fought some pay fights under the nickname of Melody Jackson.Armstrong turned a member of the International Boxing Hall Of Fame.After retiring from boxing, Henry Armstrong turned a Baptist minister.On his passing in 1988, he was interred in the Rosedale Cemetery in Los Angeles, California.

Benny Leonard

Benny Leonard (April 17, 1896—April 18, 1947), born Benjamin Leiner, was an American boxer and one of the greatest lightweight fighters of all time and was named as number 8 on Ring Magazine's list of the 80 Topmost Fighters of the Last 80 Years.

The Ghetto Wizard as he was known was born and raised in the Jewish ghetto, which was then situated in the lower east side of Manhattan, New York City, on whose streets he learned to fight.Leonard was known for his speed, excellent boxing technique and capability to think fast on his feet. He also was a hard hitter, who scored 69 KOs out of his 157 wins. Leonard was defeated 11 times and was held to a draw on 5 occasions. As was common in the era in which he fought, Leonard engaged in various no-decision matches and is conceived to have fought 213 bouts.

Leonard challenged welterweight champion Jack Britton for his title on June 26, 1922. In a suspicious ending, Leonard appeared to be achieving the fight when he knocked Britton down in the 13th round. Then, in a totally uncharacteristic and unexpected move, Leonard proceeded to hit Britton while his opponent was down on one knee. The referee promptly disqualified Leonard.

Leonard is widely acknowledged as one of the greatest lightweights who ever lived. In its September 2001 issue, The Ring magazine ranked Leonard number 2 in its list of the greatest lightweights of all time.Leonard retired from boxing in 1924, undefeated, as the reigning world's lightweight champion, because his mother told him to.

He lost most of his significant fortune in the stock market crash of 1929, and embarked on an ill-advised comeback in 1931. Even though described as pudgy and slow, the balding Leonard won 23 fights, albeit against nondescript opposition, before meeting a championship caliber fighter. On October 7, 1932, his career ended when he was TKOed in 6 rounds by future champion Jimmy McLarnin.

After his boxing career was over, Leonard was a front man for National Hockey League owner Bill Dwyer of the New York Americans, who had secretly purchased the Pittsburgh Pirates of that league. Leonard was supposed to appear as if he owned the squad. The squad suffered both at the gate and on the ice. The squad moved to Philadelphia for 1930-31, and then folded.

Later, Leonard turned a famous boxing referee. After refereeing the first six bouts of the April 18, 1947, card at the St. Nicholas Arena in New York, Leonard was stricken with a massive heart attack throughout the first round of the following bout, toppled to the canvas, and died in the ring.

Leonard was inducted into the International Boxing Hall of Fame.Leonard was also inducted into the World Boxing Hall of Fame.Leonard, who was Jewish, was inducted into the National Jewish Sports Hall of Fame in 1996.Leonard was inducted into the International Jewish Sports Hall of Fame in 1979.

REFERENCES

Aaronson, Sammy and Hirshberg, Al. *As High as My Heart: The Sammy Aaronson Story*. New York: Coward-McCaim, 1957.

Bodner, Alan. *When Boxing Was a Jewish Sport*. Westport, CT, U.S.A.: Prager, 1997.

Bromberg, Lester. *Boxing's Unforgettable Fights*. New York: Ronald Press, 1962.

Butler, James. *Kings of the Ring*. London: Stanley Paul & Co., Ltd., 1936.

Carpenter, Harry. *Masters of Boxing*. New York: Dell Publishing, 1968.

Cohen, Elliot E., ed. *Commentary on the American Scene; Portraits of Jewish Life in America*. New York: Alfred A. Knopf, 1953.

Egan, Pierce. *Boxiana, Or Sketches of Ancient & Modern Pugilism*. London: Folio Society, 1976.

Engelman, Todd. *The Jews of Georgian England: 1714-1830*. Philadelphia: JPS, 1978.

Famol, Jeffrey. *Epics of the Fancy*. London: Sampson Low, Marston Co., 1928.

Roskolenko, Harry. *The Time That Was Then*. New York: Dial Press, 1971.

Ross, Barney and Abrahamson, Martin. *No Man Stands Alone: The True Story of Barney Ross*. Philadelphia: Lippincott, 1957.

Ross, Barney. *Fundamentals qf Boxing*. Chicago: Little Technical Library/Ziff-Davis Publishing Company, 1942.

5

Chess

Chess is a recreational and competitory game played among two players. Sometimes called Western chess or international chess to distinguish it from its predecessors and other chess variants, the existing form of the game emerged in Southern Europe throughout the second half of the 15th century after developing from alike, much older games of Indian and Persian origin. At present, chess is one of the world's most famous games, played by millions of people universal in clubs, online, by agreement, in tournaments and informally.

The game is played on a square chequered chessboard with 64 squares put in an eight-by-eight square. At the start, each player (one assuring the white pieces, the other assuring the black pieces) checks sixteen pieces: one king, one queen, two rooks, two knights, two bishops, and eight pawns. The objective of the game is to checkmate the opponent's king, whereby the king is under straightaway attack and there is no way to get rid of it from attack on the following move.

The custom of coordinated competitive chess began in the sixteenth century and has developed extensively. Chess at present is a distinguished game of the International Olympic Committee. The first authorized World Chess Champion, Wilhelm Steinitz, arrogated his title in 1886; Viswanathan Anand is the existing World Champion. Theoreticians have developed broad chess strategies and plans since the game's inception. Faces of art are found in chess composition.

One of the aims of early computer scientists was to produce a chess-playing machine, and at present's chess is deeply determined by the powers of existing chess programs and the capability to play other players online. In 1997, Deep Blue got the first computer to beat the reigning World Champion in a match when it defeated Garry Kasparov by a score of 3.5-2.5.

HISTORY

Chess developed in India, where its former form in the 6th century was chaturanga, which transforms as "four divisions of the military" – infantry, cavalry, elephants, and chariots, constituted respectively by pawn, knight, bishop, and rook. In Persia all over 600 the name turned shatranj and the rules were formulated further. Shatranj was taken up by the Muslim world after the Islamic conquest of Persia, with the pieces mostly holding their Persian names. In Spanish "shatranj" was rendered as ajedrez, in Portuguese as xadrez, and in Greek as zatrikion, but in the rest of Europe it was substituted by interpretations of the Persian shâh ("king").

The game arrived at Western Europe and Russia by at least three routes, the most former being in the 9th century. By the year 1000 it had spread all over Europe. Inserted into the Iberian Peninsula by the Moors in the 10th century, it was reported in a famous 13th century manuscript covering shatranj, backgammon, and dice named the Libro de los juegos.Another theory, defended by David H. Li, deals that chess arose from the game xiangqi, or at least a predecessor thereof, existing in China since the 2nd century BC.

All over 1200, patterns of shatranj commenced to be changed in southern Europe, and all over 1475, various main alterations depicted the game essentially as it is known at present. These modern rules for the fundamental moves had been followed in Italyand in Spain. Pawns earned the option of advancing two squares on their first move, while bishops and queens developed their modern abilities. This made the queen the most powerful piece; accordingly modern chess was denoted to as "Queen's Chess" or "Mad Queen Chess". These new rules rapidly spread all over Western Europe, with the exception of the rules about stalemate, which were settled in the early nineteenth century.

This was also the time when chess commenced to arise a corpus of theory. The most former preserved printed chess book, Repetición de Amores y Arte de Ajedrez (Repetition of Love and the Art of Playing Chess) by Spanish churchman Luis Ramirez de Lucena was issued in Salamanca in 1497. Lucena and afterwards masters like Portuguese Pedro Damiano, Italians Giovanni Leonardo Di Bona, Giulio Cesare Polerio and Gioachino Greco or Spanish bishop Ruy López de Segura formulated elements of openings and began to examine simple endgames.

In the eighteenth century the focus of European chess life went from the Southern European countries to France. The two most significant French masters were Francois-Andre Danican Philidor, a musician by profession, who discovered the grandness of pawns for chess strategy, and later Louis-Charles Mahé de La Bourdonnais who won a famous series of matches with the Irish master Alexander McDonnell in 1834. Centers of chess life in this period were coffee houses in big European cities like Cafe de la Regence in Paris and Simpson's Divan in London.

As the nineteenth century advanced, chess establishment developed rapidly. Many chess clubs, chess books and chess journals came out. There were correspondence matches among cities; for example the London Chess Club played in opposition to the Edinburgh Chess Club in 1824. Chess problems turned a regular part of nineteenth century newspapers; Bernhard Horwitz, Josef Kling and Samuel Loyd wrote some of the most prominentproblems. In 1843, von der Lasa published his and Bilguer's Handbuch des Schachspiels (Handbook of Chess), the first comprehensive manual of chess theory.

The first chess tournament was deemed in London in 1851 and won, astonishingly, by German Adolf Anderssen, comparatively unknown at the time. Anderssen was hailed as the heading chess master and his brilliant, energetic — but from at present's viewpoint strategically shallow — assaulting style turned typical for the time. Sparkling games like Anderssen's Immortal game or Morphy's Opera game were esteemed the highest possible summit of the chess art.

Deeper insight into the type of chess came with two younger players. American Paul Morphy, an extraordinary chess prodigy, won in opposition to all important competitors, as well as Anderssen, throughout his short chess career from 1857 and 1863. Morphy's success halted from a compounding of brilliant attacks and sound strategy; he intuitively knew how to prepare attacks. Prague-born Wilhelm Steinitz later described how to avoid helplessnesses in one's own position and how to create and exploit such weaknesses in the opponent's position. In addition to his theoretical accomplanishments, Steinitz established an significant tradition: his triumph over the heading German master Johannes Zukertort in 1886 is esteemed the first authorized World Chess Championship. Steinitz lost his crown in 1894 to a much younger German mathematician Emanuel Lasker, who preserved this title for 27 years, the longest tenure of all World Champions.

It took a portent from Cuba, José Raúl Capablanca (World champion 1921–27), who loved simple positions and endgames, to end the German-speaking dominance in chess; he was successful in tournament play for eight years until 1924. His successor was Russian-French Alexander

Alekhine, a firm attacking player, who died as the World champion in 1946, having shortly lost the title to Dutch player Max Euwe in 1935 and retrieving it two years later.

Among the world wars, chess was overturned by the new theoretical school of so-called hypermodernists like Aron Nimzowitsch and Richard Reti. They advocated commanding the center of the board with distant pieces rather than with pawns, engaging opponents to take the center with pawns which become objects of attack.

Since the end of nineteenth century, the number of yearly deemed master tournaments and matches rapidly grew. Some references state that in 1914 the title of chess grandmaster was first officially conferred by Tsar Nicholas II of Russia to Lasker, Capablanca, Alekhine, Tarrasch and Marshall, but this is a disputed claim. This tradition was extended by the World Chess Federation (FIDE), established in 1924 in Paris. In 1927, Women's World Chess Championship was laid down; the first to hold it was Czech-English master Vera Menchik.

THE GAME

Chess is played on a square board of eight rows and eight columns (called files and denoted with letters a to h) of squares. The colours of the sixty-four squares interchange and are referred to as "light squares" and "dark squares"..

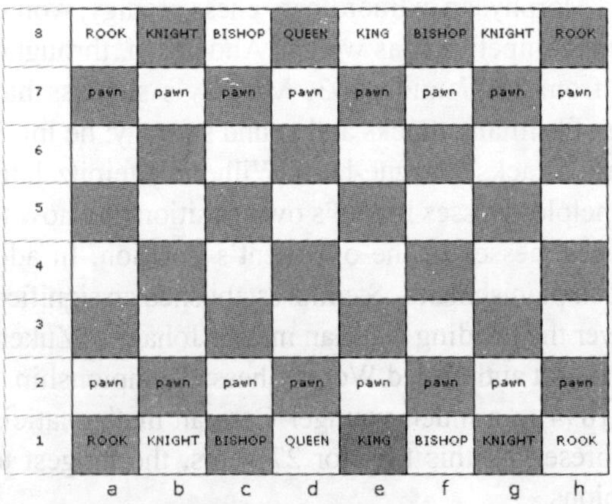

Fig. Chess Board

The pieces are separated, by convention, into white and black sets. The players are referred to as "White" and "Black" and each commences the game with sixteen pieces of the specified color. These comprise of one king, one queen, two rooks, two bishops, two knights and eight pawns. White moves first. The players alternate moving one piece at a time (with the exception of castling, when two pieces are moved simultaneously). Pieces are moved to either an untenanted square, or one occupied by an opponent's piece, capturing it and taking it from play. With one exception, all pieces capture opponent's pieces by moving to the square that the opposer's piece occupies.

Fig. Different Chess Pieces

When a king is under quick attack by one or two of the opposer's pieces, it is said to be in check. The only allowable responses to a check are to catch the checking piece, interpose a piece among the checking piece and the king, or move the king to a square where it is not under attack. Castling is not a permissible reply to a check. A move that would place the moving player's king in check is illegal. The object of the game is to checkmate the opposer; this occurs when the opponent's king is in check, and there is no way to get rid of it from attack.

Moves

Each chess piece has its uniquestyle of moving. The X's mark the squares where the piece can move if no other pieces are on the X's among the piece's initial position and finish. If there is an opposer's piece at the destination square, then moving piece can capture the opponent's piece. The only exception is the pawn which can only capture the white circles.

Special Moves: Once in every game, each king is admitted to make a special move, called as castling. Castling comprises of moving the king two squares towards a rook, then placing the rook immediately on the far side of the king. Castling is only allowable if all of the following disciplines hold.Neither of the pieces needed in the castling may have been before moved throughout the game.

Fig. Chess Pieces

There must be no pieces among the king and the rook;The king may not presently be in check, nor may the king pass through squares that are under attack by opposition pieces. As with any move, castling is banned if it would place the king in check.The king and the rook must be on the similar rank (to exclude castling with a promoted pawn, described later).

End of the Game

Chess games do not have to close in checkmate — either player may give up if the situation looks unhopeful. Games also may end in a draw (tie). A draw can take place in various situations, letting in draw by agreement, stalemate, threefold repetition of a position, the fifty move rule, or a draw by impossibleness of checkmate (normally because of insufficient material to checkmate).

Time Control: Besides daily games without exact timing, chess is also played with a time check, mainlyby club and professional players. If a player's time runs out before the game is finished, the game is automatically lost (provided his opponent has enough pieces left to deliver checkmate). The timing varies from long games played up to seven hours to shorter rapid chess games surviving normally 30 minutes or one hour per game. Even shorter is blitz chess with a time control of three to fifteen minutes for each player and bullet chess.

Strategy and Tactics

Chess strategy comprises of setting and attaining long-term aims throughout the game — for example, where to place dissimslar pieces — while tactics focus on immediate maneuver. These two parts of chess thinking cannot be completely isolated, because strategical aims are mostly attained by the means of tactics, while the tactical opportunities are established on the former strategy of play.

Because of dissimslar strategic and tactical patterns, a game of chess is normallynormally divided into three discrete phases: opening, normally the first 10 to 25 moves, when players formulate their armies and establish the stage for the coming battle; middle game, the developed phase of the game; and end game, when most of the pieces are gone and kings begin to take an dynamic part in the struggle.

Chess strategy is referred with appraisal of chess positions and with arranging aims and long-term plans for the succeeding play. Throughout the evaluation, players must allow the value of pieces on board, pawn structure, king safety, space, and control of key squares and groups of squares (for example, diagonals, open-files, and dark or light squares).

The most fundamental step in appraising a position is to calculatethe total value of pieces of both sides. The point values used for this purpose are established on experience; normally pawns are believed worth one point, knights and bishops about three points each, rooks about five points (the value difference among a rook and a bishop being known as the exchange), and queens about nine points. In the endgame, the king is in general more potent than a minor piece but less powerful than a rook, thus it is sometimes assigned a fighting value of four points. These fundamental values are then altered by other elements like position of the piece (for example, advanced pawns are normally more worthful than those on initial positions), coordination among pieces (for example, a pair of bishops normally coordinates better than the pair of a bishop and knight), or type of position (knights are in general better in closed positions with many pawns while bishops are more powerful in open positions).

Another significant factor in the evaluation of chess positions is the pawn structure (sometimes known as the pawn skeleton), or the configuration of pawns on the chessboard. Pawns being the least movableof the chess pieces, the pawn structure is comparatively static and largely determines the strategic nature of the position. Helplessnesses in the pawn structure, such as isolated, doubled or backward pawns and holes, once created, are normally permanent. Care must hence be taken to avoid them unless they are compensated by another valuable asset (for example, by the possibility to develop an attack).

In chess, tactics generally focus on short-term actions — so short-term that they can be computed in advance by a human player or by a computer. The possible depth of computation depends on the player's capability or speed of the processor. In quiet positions with many possibilities on both sides, a deep computation is not possible, while in "tactical" positions with a limited number of forced variants, it is possible to figure very long sequences of moves.

Simple one-move or two-move tactical actions — threats, changes of material, double attacks etc. — can be united into more complex variants, tactical maneuvers, often forced from one side or from both. Theoreticians described many simple tactical methods and distinctive maneuvers, for example pins, forks, skewers, discovered attacks (especially discovered checks), zwischenzugs, deflections, decoys, sacrifices, underminings, overloadings, and interferences.

A forced variant which is associated with a sacrifice and normallynormally results in a real gain is named a combination. Brilliant combinations — such as those in the Immortal game — are reported as beautiful and are admired by chess lovers. Finding a combination is also a usual type of chess puzzle directed at growth of players' skills.

MAJOR TOURNAMENTS

Chess Olympiad

The Chess Olympiad is a biyearly chess event in which teams from all over the world contend in opposition to each other. The event is organized by FIDE, which chooses the host nation.

The first Olympiad was informal. For the 1924 Olympics an attempt was made to admit chess in the Olympics Games but this flunked because of problems with discerning among amateur and professional players. While the 1924 Summer Olympics was taking place in Paris, the 1st unofficial Chess Olympiad also was held in Paris. FIDE was established on Sunday, July 20, 1924, the closing day of the 1st informal Chess Olympiad.FIDE organised the first Authorized Olympiad in 1927 which was held in London. The Olympiads were at times deemed yearly and at irregular intervals until World War II; since 1950 they have been deemed on a regular basis every two years.

Chess is a distinguished game by the International Olympic Committee with FIDE being theacceptedInternational Sports Federation for chess since June 1999.As a member of the International Olympic Committee, FIDE adheres to its rules, as well as controversially having doping tests. The aspects of chess turning an Olympic sporting event at some future date remain unclear. The naming of FIDE's team championship as the

"Chess Olympiad" is of historical origin and implies no association among this event and the Olympic Games.

Each FIDE distinguished chess association can enter a team into the Olympiad (for the UK one team for each of the four countries plus Guernsey can enter a team separately).Each team is built of up to six players, four regular players and two reserves (altered to 4+1 in Dresden 2008).Initially each teams played all the teams but as the event grow over the years this turned not possible. At first team sowing was held before the competition. Later certain drawbacks where distinguished with seeding and in 1976 a Swiss tournament system was adopted.

The trophy for achieving the men's squad is the Hamilton-Russell Cup,which was provided by the English tycoon Frederick Hamilton-Russell as a award for the 1st Olympiad (London 1927). The cup is kept by the succeeding team until the following event, when it will be consigned to the following winner. The trophy for the achieving women's team is recognized as the Vera Menchik Cup the first Women's World Chess Champion.The 2008 Olympiad is planned to be deemed in Dresden, Germany. The 2010 Olympiad is anticipated to be deemed in Khanty-Mansiysk, Russia.

World Chess Championship

The perception of a world chess champion began to emerge in the first half of the nineteenth century, and the phrase "world champion" came out in 1845. From this time onwards various players were acclaimed as world champions, but the first contest that was determined in advance as being for the world championship was the match among Steinitz and Zukertort in 1886. Until 1948 world championship subjects were matches arranged privately among the players. As a result the players also had to arrange the funding, in the form of stakes supplied by enthusiasts who wished to bet on one of the players. In the early twentieth century this was sometimes a barrier that forecloses or delayed challenges for the title.

From 1888 and 1948 various troubles that developed in match negotiations led players to try to determine agreed rules for matches, as well as the frequency of matches, how much or how little say the champion had in the considerations for a title match and what the stakes and division of the purse should be. However these attempts were unproductive in practice, as the similar issues extended to delay or prevent challenges.

The first effort by an outside organization to manage the world championship was in 1887-1889, but this experimentation was not repeated. A system for managing regular contests for the title went into operation in 1948, under the control of FIDE, and served quite smoothly until 1993. However in that year reigning champion Kasparov and challenger Short were so dissatisfied with FIDE's arrangings for their match that they establish a break-away organization. The split in the world championship extended until 2006, and the compromises needed in order to achieve re-unification have had consequences that will not vanish until 2010.

ADMINISTRATIVE BODIES

Association of Chess Professionals

The Association of Chess Professionals (ACP) is a nonprofit organisation, the closest thing in creation to a trade union for professional chess players. The association's aim is the safety of professional chess players' rights, the practice and endorsement of chess universal, in particular through the organisation of chess tournaments and other chess events.

As of March 2005, the ACP's President is French Grandmaster Joel Lautier. Its secretary is Bartlomiej Macieja, its Treasurer Almira Skripchenko, and its Deputy Treasurer Pavel Tregubov. Also on the ACP board are Igor Glek, Anna Hahn, Vladimir Kramnik, Peter Heine Nielsen and Yannick Pelletier. It has over two hundred other members, counting such outstanding players as Viswanathan Anand, Peter Leko, and Judit Polgar, but not counting Garry Kasparov. Ruslan Ponomariov and Veselin Topalov were once members, but retired in December 2004 saying "we disagree with the politics and most of the decisions of the ACP Board."

The organisation was established in 2003, the catalyst for its establishmentbeing disagreement with the European Chess Union over the selection of hotel that all participants in the 2003 European Individual Chess Championship were needed to stay in. It has since been required in a number of matters concerning to professional play.

The organisation has been equated by some to the Professional Chess Association, the body recognised by Garry Kasparov and Nigel Short as an organisation under which to play their 1993 World Championship having broken away from FIDE, the authorized leading body of chess. However, unlike the PCA, which was in competition with FIDE over the running of the world championship, the ACPprimarily stated that they "hope to work together with FIDE, as well as other international and national chess bodies". In March 2005, nevertheless, Lautier remarked that "at present FIDE avoids any contact with us, does not react to our mails, and we don't expect any positive alterations of the situation."

The ACP has been exceptionally critical of FIDE on a number of issues, counting its choice of Libya as the site for the 2004 Championships (thus putting the power of Israeli players to take part under question) and aspects concerning to the contracts with players in that championship.As well as these political behavior, the ACP has coordinated a number of online chess tournaments (open only to its members) on the Playchess server (run by Chessbase). On July 31, 2004, at a press conference deemed throughout the Dortmund tournament, Lautier declared plans for the inaugural ACP tour in which the eight ACP members who execute greatestgreatest in tournaments over the flow of a year (as decided by a points scoring system) will play in a final event (the ACP Masters) to decide the greatest player of the season .

All India Chess Federation

The All India Chess Federation (AICF) is theprimal administrative body for the game of chess in India. The AICF was established in 1951 with its headquarters in Bombay. The Chess Federation is associated to FIDE, the world body for chess. The Federation has now under its fold more than thirty affiliated state associations, sixteen special members and twenty threeacceptedacademies as its components. The AICF deserves awards for their enthusiastic efforts to promote the game in India. The Federation has played an active role in discovering new talents and ensuring quality competition in the domestic level. Such energetic organizing has paid rich dividends as India has made a name for developing precocious chess prodigies. Besides the flourishing national circuit, AICF has also played host to a number of chief world events in India like the World Junior Championships, the Commonwealth Championships and Asian Team Championships.

Apart from all these federations that cover so many outstanding chess players, women's chess in India is just all over thirty years old. The women's senior National Chess Championship was commenced in 1974. The Women's senior national championship was entirely prevailed by the Khadilkar sisters - Vasanthie, Jayshree and Rohini upto 1984. Of the ten championships deemed throughout this period, Rohini, the youngest, won five times, Jayshree won four titles, while the eldest Vasanthie won the championship in the inaugural year. Jayshree turned

India's first WIM (Woman International Master) in 1979, succeeded by Rohini and Vasanthie. Rohini also won for the first time Asian Women's Chess Championship deemed in Hyderabad in 1981 and held the title in the second edition of the Championship staged in Kuala Lumpur in 1983. However, all the three sisters bid a parting to the game and plunged in to the household business of running the newspaper.

After the epoch of the Khadilkar sisters, Bhagyashree Thipsay and Anupama Gokhale both from Maharashtra, prevailed the women's chess in the country. Both of them won the women's national chess title five times. Anupama Gokhale succeeded in the footsteps of Rohini by achieving the third and fourth Asian women's Chess Championships deemed in Dhaka in 1985 and in Hyderabad in 1987 respectively. Bhagyashree Thipsay too won the fifth Asian Women's Chess Championship curbed 1991 at Bhopal.

FAMOUS PLAYERS

Viswanathan Anand

Viswanathan Anand born on December 11, 1969 is an Indian chess grandmaster and the existing World Chess Champion.Anand won the FIDE World Chess Championship in 2000, at a time when the world title was separate. His win in the World Chess Championship 2007 has built him the unchallenged World Champion since 2007. In a 2008 article for Time Magazine, Anand showed fulfillment that the World Championship title had come back to India, the country where Chess developed. He will oppose his title in the World Chess Championship 2008 in opposition to Vladimir Kramnik in October-November 2008.

Anand has been top of the world rating list fromApril 2007, is one of four players in history to break the 2800 mark on the FIDE rating list, and has been between the top three ranked players in the world endlessly since 1997.In 2007 he was granted the second highest civilian award of India, the Padma Vibhushan. He is the first to receive of Rajiv Gandhi Khel Ratna Award in 1991-92, India's highest sporting honour.

Anand's rise in the Indian chess world was spectacular. National level success came primarily for him when he won the National Sub-Junior Chess Championship with a score of 9/9 in 1983 at the age of fourteen. He turned the youngest Indian to win the International Master Title at the age of fifteen, in 1984. At the age of sixteen he turned the national chess champion and won that title two more times. He played games at target speed. In 1987, he turned the first Indian to win the

World Junior Chess Championship. In 1988, at the age of eighteen, he turned India's first Grandmaster. He was granted Padhma Shri at the age of 18.

"Vishy", as he is sometimes called by his friends, come apart upon the upper forces of the chess scene in the early 1990s, achieving such tournaments as Reggio Emilia 1991 (ahead of Garry Kasparov and Anatoly Karpov). Playing at such a high level did not slow him down either, and he extended to play games at blitz speed.In the World Chess Championship 1993 cycle Anand qualified for his first Candidates Tournament, achieving his first match but hardly losing his quarter-final match to Anatoly Karpov.

In 1994-95 Anand and Gata Kamsky prevailed the qualifying cycles for the rival FIDE and PCA world championships. In the FIDE cycle (FIDE World Chess Championship 1996), Anand lost his quarter-final match to Kamsky after heading primarily.Kamsky went on to build championship match in opposition to Karpov.

In the 1995 PCA cycle, Anand won matches in opposition to Oleg Romanishin and Michael Adams without anyloss, then avenged his FIDE loss by defeating Gata Kamsky in the Candidates final. In 1995, he played the PCA World Chess Championship 1995 in opposition to Kasparov in New York City's World Trade Center. After an opening run of eight draws (a record for the opening of a world championship match), Anand won game nine with a mighty exchange sacrifice, but then lost four of the following five. He lost the match 10.5 - 7.5.

After various near misses, Anand won the FIDE World Chess Championship in 2000 for the first time after overcoming Alexei Shirov 3.5 - 0.5 in the final match deemed at Tehran, thereby fetching the first Indian to win that title. He lost the title when Ruslan Ponomariov won the FIDE knockout tournament in 2002.He tied for second with Peter Svidler in the FIDE World Chess Championship 2005 with 8.5 points out of 14 games, 1.5 points following the winner, Veselin Topalov.

In September 2007 Anand turned World Champion once again by achieving that year's FIDE World Championship Tournament deemed in Mexico City. He won the double round-robin tournament with a final score of 9 out of 14 points, a full point in front of joint second place finishers Vladimir Kramnik and Boris Gelfand.

In 2000, when Anand won the FIDE World Championship, there was also the competitor "Classical" World Championship, deemed by Kramnik. By 2007, the world championship had been reunified, so Anand's victory in Mexico City made him unchallenged World Chess Champion. He turned the first unchallenged champion to win the title in a tournament, rather than in matchplay, since Mikhail Botvinnik in 1948.

Anand is scheduled to oppose the title in opposition to Kramnik in a match in 2008. In October 2007, Anand told he liked the double round robin championship layout, and that the right of Kramnik to automatically challenge for the title was "ridiculous".

Anand won three sequential Advanced Chess tournaments in Leon, Spain after Garry Kasparov brought in this form of chess in 1998, and is broadlyacceptedas the world's greatest Advanced Chess player, where humans may refer a computer to aid in their computation of variations.

Anand has won the Chess Oscar in 1997, 1998, 2003, 2004, and 2007. The Chess Oscar is granted to the year's greatest player as per a world-wide poll of heading chess critics, writers, and journalists carried by the Russian chess magazine 64.

Anand's recent tournament accievements consist of the Corus chess tournament in 2006 (tied with Veselin Topalov), Dortmund in 2004, and Linares in 2007 and 2008. He has won the yearly deemed Monaco Amber Blindfold and Rapid Chess Championships in years 1994, 1997, 2003, 2005 and 2006. He is the only player to have won five titles of the Corus chess tournament. He is also the only player to win the blind and rapid sections of the Amber tournament in the similar year (and he did this twice – in 1997 and 2005).

He is the first player to have attained victories in each of the three big chess supertournaments: Corus (1998, 2003, 2004, 2006), Linares (1998, 2007, 2008), Dortmund (1996, 2000, 2004).In 2007 he won the Grenkeleasing Rapid championship, which he won for the tenth time defeating Armenian GM Levon Aronian. Incidentally, just a few days before Aronian had defeated Anand in the Chess960 final.

In March 2007, Anand won the Linares chess tournament and it was broadly conceived that he would be ranked world No.1 in the FIDE Elo rating list for April 2007. However, Anand was placed No.2 in the initial list released because the Linares result was not admitted. FIDE subsequently declarted that the Linares results would be admitted after all, making Anand number one in the April 2007 list.Anand won the Mainz 2008 Supertournament Championship by overcoming upcoming star Magnus Carlsen, making his eleventh title in that event.

Utut Adianto

Utut Adianto Wahyuwidayat is an Indonesian chess Grandmaster. As of January 1, 2006, he is Indonesia's top-ranked player of all-time with an ELO rating of 2589.

Utut Adianto studied the game of chess at the age of six. He acquired the Jakarta Junior Championship at the age of 12. In 1982, he acquired the Indonesian national championship. He was granted the GM title in 1986, fetching at the time the youngest Indonesian to do so at the age of 21 years. Since then, Susanto Megaranto has become a GM at the age of 17 years. From 1995 and 1999 Adianto coupled an prominentgroup of Grandmasters with an ELO rating over 2600.

Utut Adianto is chairman of the Indonesian Chess Association (Percasi). With Machnan R. Kamaluddin, Eka Putra Wirya and Kristiánus Liem, he established a chess school in Indonesia, which has gave rise variousnumerous national players.

Babakuli Annakov

Babakuli Annakov is the 1st Grandmaster of Turkmenistan (former Soviet Republic).He was born in 1972 and began playing chess at the age of 6, but turned seriously interested in the game at 10. The first trainer was Hakimov Shakir, who worked with him until his registration in chess boarding school in Moscow in 1985. This exclusive chess institution turned a critical point in careers of many famed chess players, such as Bareev, Morozevich, Galljamova, Yurtaev, Shipov, Alexei Kuzmin, Anna Ahsharumova, Yuri Dohojan, and numerous others.

In 1991 he entered in the chess department of the Institute of Physical Education (now Academy of Physical Culture and Sport) in Moscow. This is the exclusive academic department in the world that develops high level chess teachers. Chess section of this institute have a long and ample history with graduates such as Smyslov, Bologan, Morozevich and others.

In 1992 he turned a silver medalist of Turkmenistan Championship and won an honour of presenting my country at the World Chess Olympiad and at World Junior Championship in Buenos-Aires. He also attained many good friends at that championship with people, such as G. Veskovi and Egger. Earning his first IM norm at Ufa in 1993 was especially memorable. He had a poor start, but managed to win the left over 6 games in a row to accomplish the norm in a field of very strong players, such as A.Fedorov, V.Jandemirov, V.Golod and others. Photo finishes give important psychological confidence for the future competition. This aggregated with growing experience made conquering the left over two norms much easier.

In 1994 he enrolled a graduate program in chess department of the Institute, while staying active in chess tournaments (GM norm earned in 1997). He and the head of chess department, E.P. Linovitskii has accomplished broad work in formulating tools for chess education. Over 40 Grandmasters bestowed their ideas to the project pertaining the questions of chess strategy and tactics which were summarized in a teaching accessory for our institute. Since 1998 he turned actively occupied in teaching chess over internet.

REFERENCES

Aagaard, Jacob. *Dutch Stonewall.* London, Great Britain: Everyman Chess, 2000.

Anderson, Selby. *Center Counter Defense: The Portuguese Variation.* Wylie, TX: Pickard and Sons, 1997.

Ault, Leslie. *The Genesis of Power Chess*. Davenport, IA: Thinker's Press, 1993.

Chandler, Murray. *The Complete c3 Sicilian*. Seattle, WA: International Chess Enterprises, 1996.

Chernev, Irving, and Fred Reinfeld. *Winning Chess*. New York, NY: Fireside Chess Library, Simon and Schuster, 1975.

Christiansen, Larry, and Lou Maser, and Robert Raingruber. *The King's Gambit as White*. Davenport, IA: Thinkers' Press, 1986.

Timmer, Robert. *Castling to Win*. Seattle, WA: International Chess Enterprises, 1997.

Tirabassi, Maurizio. *Caro-Kann Defence: Advance Variation*. Bologna, Italy: s1 Editrice S.r.l., 1994.

Tisdall, Jon. *Trends in the Leningrad Dutch*. London, UK: Trends Publication, 1992.

Tykodi, Ralph J., ed. *C. J. S. Purdy's Fine Art of Chess Annotation and Other Thoughts*. Davenport, IA: Thinker's Press, 1992.

Woolum, Al. *The Chess Tactics Workbook*. N. Richland Hills, TX: Albert E. Woolum, 1997.

6

Diving

Diving relates to the sport of executing acrobatics whilst jumping or falling into water from a platform or springboard of an assured height. Diving is an internationally-accepted game that is part of the Olympic Games. In addition, unstructured and non-competitive diving is a common recreational pastime in places where swimming is famous.

While not a specially famous participant game, diving is one of the more famous Olympic sports with spectators. victorious competitors possess many of the similar characteristics as gymnasts and dancers, counting strength, flexibility, kinaesthetic judgment and air awareness.

In the recent past, the achievemnts and reputation of Greg Louganis led to American strength internationally. More in recent times, the supreme diving nation has been China, which came to fame various decades ago when the game was revolutionised by national coach Liang Boxi and after deep study of the prevailingLouganis. China has missed few world titles since. Other powers are in general those which import Chinese coaches, as well as Australia and Canada.

HISTORY

Men and women have drilled breath-hold diving for centuries. Indirect proof comes from thousand-year-old undersea artifacts found on land (e.g., mother-of-pearl ornaments), and characterizations of divers in ancient drawings. In ancient Greece breath-hold divers are known to have traced for sponges and engaged in military exploits. Of the latter, the story of Scyllis (sometimes spelled Scyllias; about 500 B.C.) is perhaps the most famed. As said by the 5th century B.C. historian Herodotus (and quoted in many modern texts).

Throughout a naval operation the Greek Scyllis was taken aboard ship as prisoner by the Persian King Xerxes I. When Scyllis educated that Xerxes was to attack a Greek flotilla, he seized a knife and jumped overboard. The Persians could not find him in the water and assumed he had drowned. Scyllis showed up at night and made his way between all the ships in Xerxes's fleet, cutting every ship loose from its moorings; he used a empty reed as snorkel to remain unseen. Then he swam nine miles (15 kilometers) to rejoin the Greeks off Cape Artemisium.

The desire to go under water has likely always lived: to hunt for food, exposed artifacts, repair ships (or sink them!), and perhaps just to notice marine life. Until humans discovered a way to breathe underwater, however, every dive was inevitably short and frantic.

Breathing through a empty reed allows the body to be underwater, but it must have become apparent right away that reeds more than two feet long do not work well; difficulty inhaling in opposition to water pressure efficiently limits snorkel length. Breathing with an air-filled bag brought under water was also tried, but it failed due to rebreathing of carbon dioxide.

In the 16th century people commenced to use diving bells provided with air from the surface, probably the first effective means of remaining under water for any time. The bell was deemed stationary a few feet from the surface, its bottom open to water and its top portion comprising of air compressed by the water pressure. A diver standing upright would have his head in the air. He could impart the bell for a minute or two to collect sponges or explore the bottom, then come back for a short while until air in the bell was no more breathable.

In 16th century England and France, full diving suits build of leather were used to depths of 60 feet. Air was pumped down from the surface with the help of manual pumps. Soon helmets were constructed of metal to hold even greater water pressure and divers went deeper. By the 1830s the surface-supplied air helmet was perfected well enough to permit broad salvage work.

Commencing in the nineteenth century, two major boulevards of investigation - one scientific, the other technologic - greatly accelerated underwater exploration. Scientific research was encouraged by the work of Paul Bert and John Scott Haldane, from France and Scotland, respectively. Their studies aided explain effects of water pressure on the body, and also define safe limits for compressed air diving. At the similar time, advancements in technology - compressed air pumps, carbon dioxide scrubbers, regulators, etc., - made it feasible for people to stay under water for long periods.

THE GAME

Equipment

Dives may be accomplished from either a springboard or a platform. The similar kinds of dives are performed from either surface-except that at times a diver will make a dive from a handstand in platform competition.

Fig. Diving

The springboard is 1 meter or 3 meters high; the length is measured from the surface of the water to the bottom of the board. In main competition, the board is 16 feet long and 20 inches broad, and is enclosed with a nonskid material.

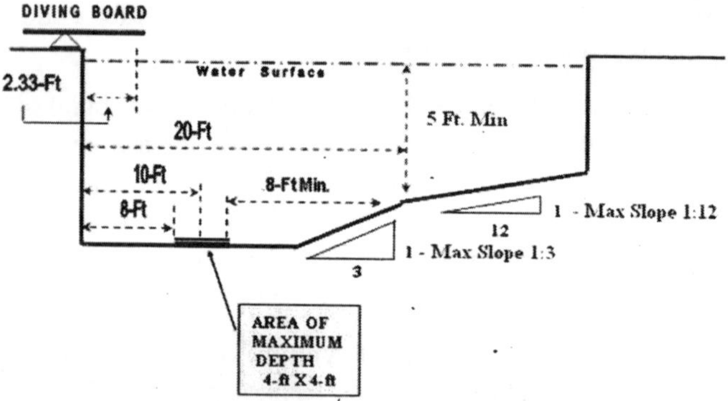

Fig. Diving Board & Pool

The board should overhang the edge of the pool by at least 5 feet and rather 6 feet. The water should be 11 to 12 feet deep.The eminent platform is 10 meters above the water surface, while the medium platform is 5 to 7 1/2 meters high. The nonskid track should be at least 20 feet long and at least 10 feet broad, and the water should be at least 16 feet deep.

Categories of Diving

All dives are divided into six categories. They are:

- Forward dives — The diver faces forward and dives forward.
- Backward dives — The diver faces backward and dives in such a manner that the body rotates out from the board.
- Reverse dives — The diver faces forward but dives so that the body circumvolves back towards the board.
- Inward dives — The diver faces backwards but dives so the body rotates towards the board.
- Twisting dives — The diver, from either beginning position, turns the body in the air before hitting the water.
- Handstand dives — These are accomplished from the platform only; the diver commences the dive from a still handstand on the edge of the platform.

Positions

Dives are more overcharacterisedas to the body positions used. There are three fundamental body positions:

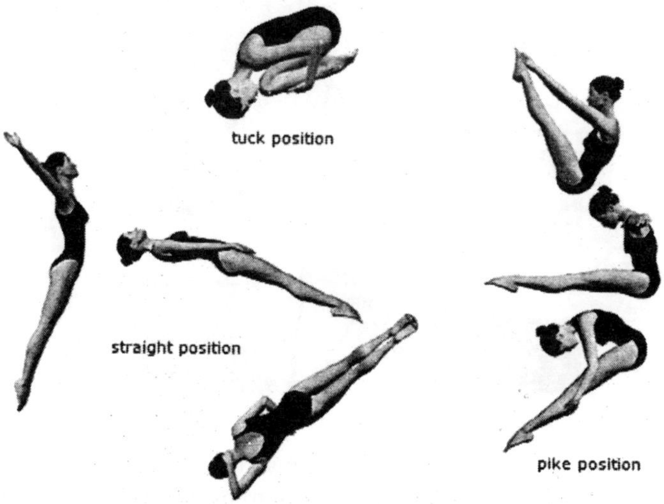

Fig. Positions

- Layout, in which the body is kept straight.
- Pike, in which the body is twisted at the waist, with the legs straight (the most familiar is the jackknife).
- Tuck, in which the body is twisted at the hips, and the knees are kept together and drawn into the chest.

There is also a so-called "free" position, for use in very perplexed dives-in effect, the diver has a choice of which position to utilize, or can utilize a amalgamation of positions.

Judging

Like gymnastics, diving is judged instinctively. Each judge rates every dive on its advance, takeoff, elevation, execution, and entry. Then a score is given, ranging from 0 to 10. In main contests there are five or seven judges; the highest and lowest scores are thrown out, and the left over scores are added. They are then multiplied by the degree of trouble for the particular dive, to give the score for that dive.

Degree of difficultness ratings range from 1.0 for very simple dives to 2.9 for very hard dives.Every diver must present a list of dives, in the episode in which they are to be performed, before the competition commences.

Fig. Player Taking Position for Diving

Each contest has a particular degree of trouble requirement that must be met. If a list doesn't meet the requirement, the diver is given a chance to amend it. If it isn't improved to meet the requirement, any dives that bring the diver out of compliance are marked as broke down.

Approach - Judging commences when a diver stands in the commencing position on the front end of the board. The dissenter should hold the body straight, head erect, with heels together and arms straight and at the sides. The advance should be smooth and straight, and should comprise of at least three steps before the hurdle.Take-off is the jump to the end of the board, known as the hurdle, is the commencing of the take-off. Both feet should hit the end of the board simultaneously; the take-off should be made lacking hesitation and should be vigorous.

Fig. Player Diving

Fig. Execution

Execution is in the passing through the air, the body should be definitely in the layout, the pike, or the tuck position (unless the dive requires somersaults mixed with twists, in which case the free position may be used).In the set up, the body should not bend at the knees or the hips; the back, nevertheless, will normally be arched. The arms should be straight, the feet together, and the toes pointed.

In the closed pike position, the legs and arms should be maintained straight, and both hands should touch the toes at the same time. The open pike position, used for some dives, requires a simple bending at the waist, to a 90-degree angle with the legs; the arms are stretched overhead, at roughly a 45-degree angle from the shoulders, with the palms twisted outward.

In the tuck, judges above all look for compactness: The diver should be rolled as tight as possible into a ball, thighs touching chest, arms locked tightly over the legs, among shin and knee.The launching should be vertical, or as about vertical as possible, with body and legs straight and toes pointed. Most launchings are made headfirst, and the arms should be straight overhead, hands touching. In the rare dives with a feet-first entry, the arms should be kept straight and close to the sides.

Balks and Failed Dives

If a diver commences the advance or press for a diver after presuming the commencing position and then stops, it is a balk. It is also a balk if the diver, while preparing for a handstand dive, loses balance and any part of the body other than the hands touches the platform.

If there's a single balk on a dive, each judge is taught by the head referee to substract 2 points from the diver's score. If there's a second balk on the similar dive, it is ruled a failed dive, which outcomes in zero points.The dive is executed out of sequence, established on the list of dives presented by the competitor.

The diver fails to execute the scheduled dive inside one minute after being warned for inducing undue delay.The diver falls off the board into the water before presuming the commencing position.On a twisting dive, the measure of twist is greater or less than declarted by 90 degrees or more.Any part of the body under the waist enters the water before the hands on a head-first dive.

Compulsory and Optional Dives

As in gymnastics and figure skating, diving tournament is broken into two parts, mandatory and nonmandatory. The springboard diver is in general needed to execute five compulsory dives, one from each of the five categories, and six optional dives. The platform diver must normally six compulsory and six optional dives.In most important meets, the mandatory dives are used as a beginninground, with the top scorers advancing to execute optional dives in the second and final round.

Mechanics of Diving

Fig. Player Diving

At the moment of take-off, two vital aspects of the dive are decided, and cannot later on be changed throughout the execution. One is the trajectory of the dive, and the other is the magnitude of the angular momentum.

The speed of rotation - and hence the entire amount of rotation - may be varied from moment to moment by altering the shape of the body, in conformity with the law of conservation of angular momentum.

The center of mass of the diver pursues a parabolic path in free-fall under the influence of gravity (disconcerning the effects of air resistance, which are negligible at the speeds demanded).

Fig. Player Twisting

Twisting: Dives with various twists and somersaults are some of the most impressive movements, as well as the most difficult to execute.

The rules state that twisting 'must not be produced manifestly on take-off'. Accordingly, divers must utilize some of the somersaulting angular momentum to generate twisting movements. The physics of twisting can be explained by looking at the components of the angular momentum vector.

As the diver imparts the board, the total angular momentum vector is horizontal, pointing immediately to the left for a forward dive for example. For twisting rotation to exist, it is essential to tilt the body sideways after takeoff, so that there is now a small component of this horizontal angular momentum vector along the body's long axis..

The tilting is done by the arms, which are extended to the sides just before the twist. When one arm is moved up and the other is acted down (like turning a big steering wheel), the body responds by tilting to the side, which then begins the twisting rotation. At the completion of the needed number of twist rotations, the arm motion is inverted (the steering wheel is turned back), which withdraws the body's tilt and blocks the twisting rotation.

An alternate elucidation is that the moving arms have precession torque on them which set the body into twisting rotation. Prompting the arms back develops opposite torque which stop the twisting rotation.

Entry

The rules and regulations state that the body should be erect, or nearly so, for entry. The arms must be alongside the body for feet-first dives and covered forwards in line for "head-first" dives. It used to be common for the hands to be interlocked with the fingers stretched towards the water, but a dissimslar technique has get favored throughout the last few decades. Now the usual practice is for one hand to grasp the other with palms down to strike the water with a flat surface (the so-called "rip entry"). This produces a vacuum among the hands, arms and head which with a vertical entry will pull down and under any splash until deep enough to have minimum effect on the surface of the water. Once a diver is completely under the water they may prefer to roll or scoop in the similar direction their dive was revolving to pull the splash away from the channel which they have just produced.

ADMINISTRATIVE BODIES

International Swimming Federation

FINA is the International Federation (IF)acceptedby the International Olympic Committee (IOC) for dealing international competition in the aquatic sports (its name translated from French is "International Swimming Federation"). It is one of variousvarious IFs which deals a given game/discipline for the IOC and/or international community. It is established in Lausanne, Switzerland.

FINA presently oversees competition in five aquatic sports: swimming, diving, synchronized swimming, water polo and open water swimming.The existing President of FINA is Mustapha Larfaoui of Algeria.

FINA was established on July 19, 1908 in Manchester Hotel in London in the long run of the 1908 Summer Olympics by the Belgian, British, Danish, Finnish, French, German, Hungarian and Swedish

Swimming Federations.The largest FINA event is the now biennial World Championships, presently deemed every odd year. It boasts events in all five aquatic disciplines, and was most in recent timeslately deemed in Melbourne, Australia, in March 2007. Prior to 2000, the event was deemed all 4 years, in the even year among Olympic (summer) Games.

The World Swimming Championship (25m), (aka "Short Course Worlds"), is a swimming-only competition, swum in 25-meter long pool. It is deemed bi-yearly, in even-numbered years, and was most latelyin recent times deemed in a make-shift pool built in the M.E.N arena, Manchester, United Kingdom in April 2008.

Amateur Swimming Association

The Amateur Swimming Association (ASA) is the English national governing body towards swimming, diving, water polo, open water, and synchronized swimming. The ASA's organization and responsibilities extend beyond with those of British Swimming, a federation of the ASA and its Scottish and Welsh siblings, which is in charge for elite swimming, as well as the Great Britain Olympic swimming, synchronized swimming, and diving teams. The ASA is in charge for recreational swimming and for the growth of the competitive sport from starter levels up to the Commonwealth Games, at which the home nations battle separately.

The ASA traces its olden times to the creation of an association of London swimming clubs in 1869. It adopted its existing name in 1886 after a clash over amateurism (a frequent source of conflict in English sport at the time). The ASA's income for the 18 months to 31 March 2006 was £11.2 million, its biggest sources of income being government grants (e.g. from Sport England) and revenue from its swimming award scheme.

MAJOR TOURNAMENTS

Olympics

Diving was first brought in in the authorized programme of the Summer Olympic Games at the 1904 Games of St. Louis and has been an Olympic sport since. It was called as "fancy diving" for the acrobatic stunts executed by divers throughout the dive (such as somersaults and twists). This field of Aquatics, along with swimming, synchronized swimming and water polo, is determined and supervised by the International Swimming Federation (FINA), the international federation (IF) for aquatic sports.

The first Olympic diving events were contended by men and comprised of a platform diving event ("fancy high diving") and also a plunge for distance event, which heralded victorious the diver who could reach the farthest underwater, while staying still after a ground-level standing dive. At the 1908 Summer Olympics, men's springboard diving was added to the programme substituting the plunge for distance, regarded as uninteresting. Women's diving debut happened at the 1912 Summer Olympics in the platform event and was elaborated to springboard diving at the 1920 Summer Olympics. A parallel platform diving event for men, called "plain high diving", was demonstrated at the Games of the V Olympiad. No acrobatic moves were permitted, only a simple straight dive off the platform.It was last contested at the 1924 Summer Olympics after which it was merged with "fancy high diving" into one competition renamed "highboard diving" (or just "high diving").

By the time of the 1996 Summer Olympics, the diving events were precisely the similar as in 1928. However, four years later in Sydney, the inclusion of a synchronized diving version for the springboard and platform events advanced the list up to eight events.

FAMOUS PLAYERS

Matthew Mitcham

Matthew Mitcham (born 2 March, 1988 in Brisbane, Queensland, Australia) is an Australian diver. He is the 2008 Olympic champion in the 10m platform, having obtained the highest single-dive score in Olympic record. He is the first Australian male to gain an Olympic gold medal in diving since Dick Eve at the 1924 Summer Olympics, and was the only openly gay male athlete at the 2008 Summer Olympics.

Mitcham earlier contended as a trampoline gymnast. He was noticed by Wang Tong Xiang, a coach at the Australian Institute of Sport Diving Program, while at the Chandler Aquatic Centre in Brisbane's suburbs, and carried on with both diving and trampolining for various years.

As a trampolinist, Mitcham presented Australia at the World Junior Championships in 1999 and 2001, succeeding the double mini-tramp event. He also contendedcontended at the Australian Youth Olympic Festival in 2003, competing sixth.

From 2002 to 2004, Mitcham was a home junior champion in diving, achieving the events in which he contendedcontended. Mitcham contended at the 2002 World Junior Diving Championships, where he positioned

11th in the 1m springboard, 5th in the 3m and 16th in the 10m platform. In 2004, he won the silver medals in the 1m, 3m synchronized, and 10m platform events at the World Junior Championships. At the 2004 Junior Nationals, he won the 1m, 3m, and 10m and 3m synchro titles. At the 2004 Olympic Trials, he rated 3rd on the 3m and 10m individual events, 2nd on the 3m and 10m synchro events, and did not qualify for the Olympic team. In 2005, Mitcham won his 1st senior national title. He contended at the Australian Olympic Youth Festival, where he won the silver medal in the 1m with a score of 508.35, and won the 3m, 10m and 3m synchro (with Scott Robertson) titles with scores of 565, 555.8, and 316.23 respectively. At the 2005 World Aquatics Championships in Montreal, he rated 12th on the 10m platform with a score of 560.73.

In 2006, Mitcham contended in the German Grand Prix event, rating 16th on the 3m and 6th on the 10m, and at the USA Grand Prix at Fort Lauderdale, placing 8th on the 3m springboard. At the Canada Cup he rated 26th on the 3m and won the bronze medal on the 10m platform. He presented Australia at the 2006 Commonwealth Games, where he contended in the 1m, 3m, and 10m events. He rated 4th in the 3m and the 3m synchro with Robertson, and 5th on the 1m and 10m events.

Taking a break from the game in 2006, he came back in 2007 and commenced to train under existing coach Chava Sobrino at the New South Wales Institute of Sport. In 2008 Mitcham won the 1m, 3m and 10m individual events at the Australian Nationals. Afterward that year he won the 2008 Diving Grand Prix event in Fort Lauderdale, Florida.

Mitcham was born in Brisbane but lives and trains in Sydney. He in public came out as gay in 2008 to the Sydney Morning Herald when they were writing Olympic hopefuls.Throughout the 2008 Beijing Olympics, he was also presented on the cover of the international gay publication The Advocate.Mitcham's partner, Lachlan Fletcher, accompanied the 2008 Summer Olympic Games as a viewer. His trip was sponsored by a grant from Johnson & Johnson's Athlete Family Support Program.

Mitcham earned media coverage as the first Australian to contend at the Olympic Games as explicitly gay at the time of his competition. Other notable gay Australian Olympians comprise Ji Wallace, who contended at the 2000 Summer Olympics and won a silver medal in the inaugural trampoline event; however, he came out after the Games.Prior to his 10m platform win, Mitcham was described to be one of only eleven openly gay athletes contending in the 2008 Beijing Olympics, out of 11,028 athletes from 204 countries. Ten of those eleven athletes were women, creating Mitcham the only openly gay man to contend in the Games.

Jan Hempel

Jan Hempel born on August 21, 1971 in Dresdenis a German diver who contended at the 1988, 1992, 1996, and the 2000 Summer Olympics, achieving two Olympic medals. Hempel won silver in 10m Platform and a bronze medal in 10m synchronized platform. He also contended on the 3m springboard, scoring "the second greatest dive of all time" in Vienna in 1993.

In 1988,Hempel laid down his Olympic debut at age 17 in Seoul. Hempel rated fifth.In 1992, Hempel came back to the Olympics in Barcelona, but once again did not medal, laying fourth.In 1996, The third time was charm, as Hempel won silver in the 10m Platform, grading 663.27. He saved his toughest dive for last. He smashed the back 1 1/2 somersault with 4 1/2 twists from the free position, earning 92.88 points. It was one of the two dives out of the 72 in the finals with a 3.6 degree of trouble.In 2000,In the inaugural men's 10m synchronized platform event, Hempel, now 29, with partner Heiko Meyer won the bronze medal at the Sydney 2000 Games, making Hempel his second medal in four Olympic appearances.

Meyer and first-time Olympian Heiko Meyer commenced training together in 1998 and gained the bronze medal at the World Championships later that year. The pair also gained the event at the 1999 European Championships.

In spite of these accomplishments, Hempel came into the 2000 Games with low prospects.. However, the team managed a solid performance on the program's most difficult dive, a back 3-1/2 somersault tuck and reverse 3-1/2 somersault tuck, scoring 78.54. extendedIn the European Diving Championships, Hempel had an renowned career achievingsilver in 1987 in Strasbourg, France, bronze in 1989 in Bonn, Germany, gold in 1993 in Sheffield, Great Britain, and silver in 1995 in Vienna, Austria.In 1997 in Seville, Spain Hempel at last won a European high board diving gold 10 years after receiving the first of three silvers on the 10-meter board.

Hempel had been carried by influenza for three days and believed pulling out of the competition. But he resolute in opposition to it and was rewarded with the gold. " Throughout the competition, he marked a rare perfect 10 mark.

After receiving the silver in 1987, 1989 and 1995 and bronze in 1993, he had ultimately added a high board gold to the European three-meter springboard gold he won in 1993.At the 2003 Arena Diving Champions Cup in Stockholm, Hempel, now 32, was identified as the man "who wrote diving history," citing the 2nd greatest dive of all time in the Diving Champions Cup 3m finals executing a back 1 1/2 somersault with 3 1/2 twists in Vienna 1993, for a tremendous 87.36 points.

Hobie Billingsley

Hobie Billingsley is an American diving champion and honouree of the International Swimming Hall of Fame. Believed one of the spotlights of his career was throughout the 1996 Summer Olympics in Atlanta, when Billingsley was honouresteemed by his nation with the chance to conduct the Judge's Oath by proclaiming, "In the name of all the judges and officials, I promise that we shall officiate in these Olympic Games with complete impartiality, respecting and abiding by the rules which govern them in the true spirit of sportsmanship."

Hobie Billingsley was Indiana University's diving coach from 1959 to 1989, throughout which time his divers won more than 100 national diving titles. His Olympic gold and bronze medalists comprise Lesley Bush, Kenneth Sitzberger, Mark Lenzi, Cynthia Potter, Win Young, and Jim Henry. Mr. Billingsley established the World Diving Coaches Association in 1968, and was inducted into the International Swimming Hall of Fame in 1983. He is believed by many to be one of the most prominentfigures in the history of diving. His legacy is held on by his former divers who are now coaches at universities, high schools, and swim clubs during the United States. Mr. Billingsley is profiled in the award-winning and broadly-televised documentary Hobie's Heroes – 25th Anniversary Edition, which describes the fights and successes of young divers training below this legendary coach.

Hobie Billingsley is one of few six diving coaches noted in the American Red Cross's Swimming and Water Safety Manual, 2004. Hobie is one of only two diving coaches with multiple mentions: he and Dick Kimball (University of Michigan) are recognized with 'opening the door for women in varsity diving programs,' and he is cited as giving to the game of diving through analysis established on principles of physical laws of motion.Pursuing retirement from university coaching, Hobie carries on to be active in the game, training divers and coaches all over the world, and is respected as a speaker on diving history, technique and ethics, and on sports generally. He has in recent times published the second edition of his Diving Illustrated, a seminal work offering elaborated technical support for coaching diving.

REFERENCES

Armbruster, David A., Sr., and Lawrence E. Morehouse : *Swimming and Diving*. 3rd ed., St. Louis, Missouri, C. V. Mosby Co., 1958.

Broer, Marion: *Efficiency of Human Movement*. Philadelphia, W. B. Saunders Co., 1966.

Counsilman, James: *The Science of Swimming*. Englewood Cliffs, New Jersey, Prentice-Hall, Inc., 1968.

Clotworthy, Robert: *Diving*. Camden, N. J., Thomas Nelson and Sons, 1962.

Curtis, Katherine Whitney: *Rhythmic Swiming*. Minneapolis, Minnesota, Burgess Publishing Co., 1942.

Downing, W. H.: *Every Boy and Girl a Swimmer*. New York, N. Y., Skiffington & Sons.

Fairbanks, Anne Ross: *Teaching Springboard Diving*. Englewood Cliffs, New Jersey, Prentice-Hall, Inc., 1963.

Goss, Gertrude: *Swimming Analyzed*. 200 West Foster Street, Melrose, Massachusetts 02176,

Goss, Gertrude: *Stunts and Synchronized Swimming*. 200 West Foster Street, Melrose, Massachusetts 02176.

Gundling, Beulah, and Peg Seller: *Aquatic Art*. 403 Iowa Theater Building, Cedar Rapids, Iowa, 1957.

Jarvis, Margaret: *Swimming for Teachers and Youth Leaders*. London, England, Faber and Faber, 1947.

Kiphuth, Robert J.: *Swimming*. New York, N. Y., A. S. Barnes & Co, 1942.

Lukens, Paul W.: *Teaching Swimming*. Minneapolis, Minnesota, Burgess Publishing Co., 1948.

Moriarty, Phillip: *Diving*. New York, N. Y., The Ronald Press, 1959.

Newman, Virginia Hunt: *Teaching an Infant to Swim*. New York, N. Y., Harcourt, Brace, 1967.

Rackham, George: *Synchronized Swimming*. London, England, Faber and Faber.

Yates, Fern, and Theresa W. Anderson: *Synchronized Swimming*. New York, N. Y., The Ronald Press, 1951.

7

Fencing

Fencing is the art of armed combat relating cutting, stabbing, or slapping bludgeoning weapons directly controlled by hand, rather than shot, thrown or positioned, of European origin. Examples comprise swords, knives, pikes, bayonets, batons, clubs, and similar weapons. In present time's common usage, "fencing" tends to denote specifically to European schools of swordsmanship and to the modern Olympic sport that has orginated out of them.

Fencing is one of the four sports which has been sported at each modern Olympic Games. Presently, three types of weapon are used in Olympic fencing;Foil, a light thrusting weapon; the logical target is restricted to the torso; double touches are not permitted.Epee, a heavy thrusting weapon; the valid target area covers the entire body; double touches are permitted.Sabre, a light cutting and thrusting weapon; the suitable target area includes nearly everything above the waist; double touches are not permitted.

HISTORY

The first manuals/handbooks on fencing are from Spain, proposing that fencing may have developed there; the Spanish term for sword skirmishes is "esgrima". Italy also has a strong historic link with fencing. The book written all over the 12th century by De Serpente brothers, or the most complete Flos Duellatorum of 1409 by Fiore de Liberi, was published in Italy at the commencing of the Renaissance. Throughout the period, many Italian masters such as Marozzo instructed their art in France and other countries, working as mercenaries and masters of defence.

In the 16th century, collections of older Fechtucher techniques were developed, some of them printed, especially by Paulus Hector Mair (in the 1540s) and by Joachim Meyer (in the 1570s).By the 16th century German fencing had formulated sportive propensities. Treatises by Paulus Hector Mair and Joachim Meyer came from the teachings of the earlier centuries inside the Liechtenauer tradition, but contributed new and distinctive characteristics. Jacob Sutor's (1612) printed fechtbuch is the last in that German tradition.

The Italian school was extended by the Dardi school, by such masters as Antonio Manciolino and Achille Marozzo. From the late 16th century, Italian rapier fencing attained significant popularity all over Europe, notably by Salvator Fabris's 1606 treatise.

Strictly, the European dueling sword is a basket and cage hilted weapon specifically used in duels from the late 17th to the nineteenth century . It developed through various forms of the rapier to the smallsword — reflecting the alterations from a cutting style of swordplay to a thrusting style ('foining').

This was a result of increasing specialization in their use on the duelling field, and the social stigma attached to carrying and utilizing swords too obviously adapted to the actual "work" of warfare. The smallsword, and the last version of the rapier, were made possible only by metallurgical advances in the seventeenth century as high toughness steels turned more readily accesible.In England, it was not uncommon for fencing masters to take on other fencing masters in a fight, often to the death, often with intervals for medical staff to dress wounds. Such spectacles were in general deemed in beargardens, particularly in the Southwark neighborhood near London.

Foil was invented in France as a training technique in the middle of the 18th century; it provided practice of fast and elegant thrust fencing with a smaller and safer weapon than an actual dueling sword. Fencers blunted its point by wrapping a foil all over the blade or fastening a knob on the point ("blossom", French fleuret). In addition to practice, some fencers took away the safety and used the sharp foil for duels. German students took up that practice and developed the Pariser ("Parisian") thrusting small sword for the Stobmensur ("thrusting mensur"). After the dress sword was abolished, the Pariser turned the only weapon for thrust fencing in German colleges and universities.

Since thrust fencing with a sharply pointed blade of any kind is quite dangerous, many students died from (especially) pierced lungs (Lungenfuchser). However, a counter movement had already began in Göttingen in the 1750s, with the invention of the Gottinger Hieber, a predecessor of the modern Korbschlager, a new weapon for cut fencing. In the following years, the Glockenschlager was invented in Eastern Germany universities, also for cut fencing.

Dueling went into sharp decline after World War I. After World War II, duelling went out of use in Europe except for very rare exceptions. Training for duels, once fashionable for males of aristocratic backgrounds (even though fencing masters such as Hope suggest that many people had only taken one or two lessons, and thus considering themselves trained), all but disappeared, along with the classes themselves. Fencing extended as a game, with tournaments and championships. However, the need to actually prepare for a duel with "sharps" vanished, changing both training and technique.

Starting with epee in the 1930s, side judges were substituted by an electrical scoring apparatus, with an audible tone and a red or green light indicating when a touch landed. Foil was electrified in the 1950s, sabre in the 1980s. The scoring box reduced the bias in judging, and permitted more accurate scoring of faster actions, lighter touches, and more touches to the back and flank than were possible with human judges.

THE GAME

A fencing bout takes place on a strip, or piste, which, as per the existing FIE regulations, should be from 1.5 and 2 meters broad and 14 meters long. There are at least three people involved: two fencers and an umpire. The referee may be assisted by two or four side-judges (also known as corner-judges).

Fig. Fensing Positions

The arrival of the electronic scoring apparatus has rendered them largely redundant. Under existing FIE rules, a fencer may ask for two side-judges (one to watch every fencer) if he thinks that the referee is failing to notice some infringement of the rules on his opponent's part (such as use of the unarmed hand, substitution of the valid target area, breaching the boundary of the piste etc.).

Equipments

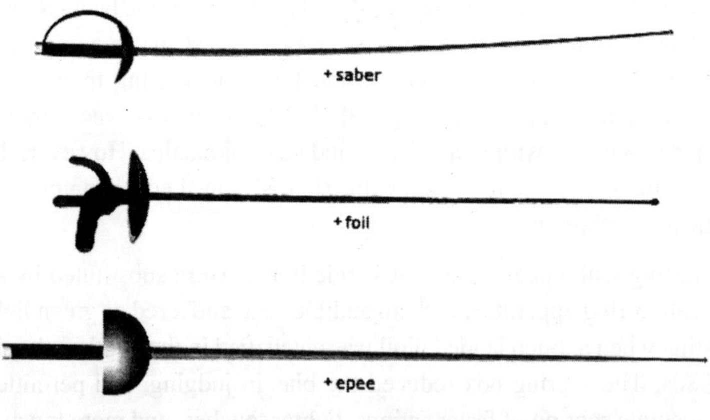

Fig.Fencing Weapons

Foil, a light thrusting weapon; the valid target is restricted to the torso; double touches are not permitted. Epee,a heavy thrusting weapon; the valid target area covers the entire body; double touches are permitted.

Sabre,a light cutting and thrusting weapon; the valid target area includes almost everything above the waist (excluding the back of the head and the hands); double touches are not permitted.

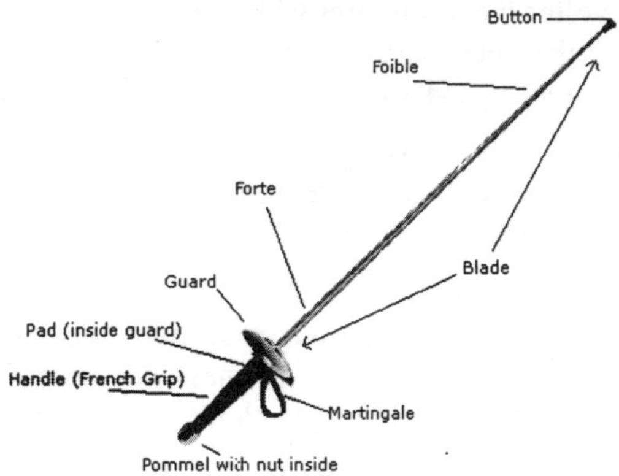

Fig.Epee Parts

Protective Clothing

The clothing which is worn in modern fencing is made of tough cotton or nylon. Kevlar was contributed to top level uniform pieces (jacket, breeches, underarm protector, lamé, and the bib of the mask) following the Smirnov incident at the 1982 World Championships in Rome. However, kevlar breaks down in chlorine and UV light, so the act of washing one's uniform and/or hanging it up in the sun to dry actually damaged the kevlar's capability to do the job.

In recent years other ballistic fabrics such as Dyneema have been developed that execute the puncture resistance function and which do not have kevlar's weakness. In fact, the FIE rules state that the entirety of the uniform (meaning FIE level clothing, as the rules are written for FIE tournaments) must be made of fabric that resists a force of 800 newtons (1600N in the mask bib). The complete fencing kit includes the following items of clothing:

Form-fitting jacket covering groin and with strap (croissard) which goes among the legs (note that in sabre fencing, jackets that are cut along the waist and exclude the groin padding are also sometimes used), a small gorget of folded fabric is also sewn in all over the collar to prevent a blade from slipping upwards towards the neck.

Under-arm protector (plastron) which goes underneath the jacket and provides double safety on the sword arm side and upper arm. It is needed to not have a seam in the armpit, which would line up with the jacket seam and provide a weak spot.

One glove for the sword arm with a gauntlet that prevents blades from going up the sleeve and causing injury, as well as protecting the hand and providing a good grip

Breeches or knickers which are a pair of short trousers. The legs are supposed to hold just below the knee.Knee-length or Thigh high socks which should cover knee and thighs.

Shoes with flat soles and reinforcement on the inside of the back foot and heel of front foot, to prevent wear from lunging.Mask, as well as a bib which protects the neck. The mask can normally support 12 kilograms of force, however FIE regulation masks can stand much more, at least 27 kg.

Plastic chest protector, mandatory for female fencers. While male versions of the chest protector are also accesible, they were, until in recent times, mainly worn by instructors, who are hit far more often throughout training than their students. Since the change of the depression timing, these are increasingly famous in foil, as the hard surface increases the likelihood of point bounce and thus a failure for a hit to register. Plastrons are still mandatory, though.

Fencing Masters will often wear a heavier protective jacket, normally reinforced by plastic foam to cushion the many hits an instructor has to endure. Sometimes in practice, masters wear a protective sleeve or a leg leather for safety of their fencing arm or leg.

Traditionally, the fencers' uniform is white in colour (black being the traditional colour for masters). This may be to some extent down to the occasional pre-electric practice of covering the point of the weapon in dye, soot, or coloured chalk in order to make it easier for the referee to decide the placing of the touches. In recent times the FIE rules have been relaxed to permit coloured uniforms (black still being reserved for the coaches). The guidelines delineating the permitted size and positioning of sponsorship logos are however still exceptionally strict.

Protocol

Very specific rules govern the behavior of fencers while contending. To commences a bout, the referee stands at the side of the piste. The fencers walk on piste fully dressed, aside from the mask. If necessary, they plug their body wires into the spools connected to the electronic scoring apparatus and test their weapons in opposition to each other, to make sure everything is functioning. They then retreat to their on-guard lines. Prior to commencing a bout, the fencers must salute first each other, then the director. Refusal to do so can result in a fencer's suspension or disqualification. They may also choose to salute the audience and/or the referee's assistants (when they are present).

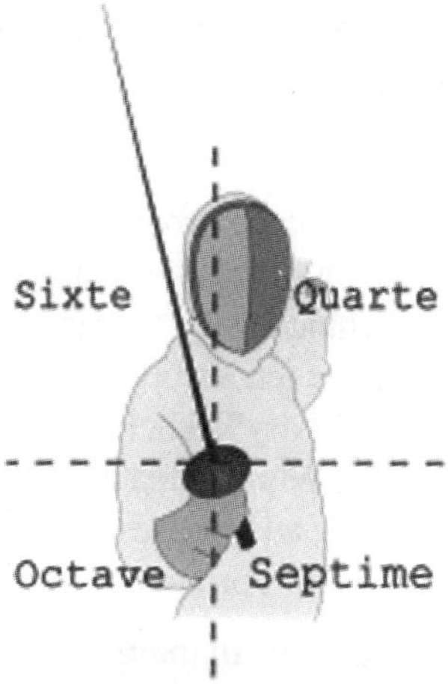

Fig. Positions

The fencers start and stop the bout at the referee's command. In general, referees interrupt the bout, whenever the electronic apparatus registers a touch (either on or off-target) or whenever one or both of the fencers break the rules of the game. Once the bout is stopped, the referee must explain his reasons for stopping it, analyze what has just happened, and grant points or penalties. If a point has been granted, then the competitors return to their on-guard lines; if not, they remain approximately where they were when the bout was interrupted. The referee will then restart the bout. This procedure is repeated until either one of the fencers has reached the needed number of points (in general, 1, 5, 10 or 15, depending upon the layout of the bout) or until the time permitted for the bout runs out.

Fencing bouts are timed: the clock is began each time the referee calls "Fence!" and stopped each time he calls "Halt!" The bout must stop after 3 minutes of fencing (or 8 touches in sabre). In 15 point bouts, a 1 minute break occurs in among the 3 minute intervals. If 9 minutes of fencing time elapse in a 15 touch bout, or 3 in a 5 touch bout, the bout is over, and the existing scores are taken as final. If the score is tied when time runs out, then the fencers go into an extra minute, at the commencing of which the referee randomly assigns "priority" to one of the fencers (in general done by coin toss). The first touch inside the extra minute wins the bout. If neither fencer makes a touch throughout the extra minute, the winner is the fencer who had "priority".

At international events and large European events as well as Opens and those similar, all refereeing is in French, which is the authorized language of international fencing.

Scoring

Prior to the introduction of electronic scoring equipment, an umpire (formerly called the president of jury) was assisted by four judges. Two judges were positioned behind every fencer, one on every side of the strip. The judges watched the fencer opposite to see if he was hit. This system is sometimes called "dry" fencing (USA) or "steam" (United Kingdom, Australia) fencing. While outdated, this practice is still extended at present throughout training and classes where the use of an electronic scoring system would be inappropriate or overly time consuming.

Electronic scoring is used in all main national and international, and most local, competitions. At Olympic level, it was first brought in to épée in 1936, to foil in 1956, and to sabre in 1988. The central unit of the scoring system is commonly known as "the box." In the simplest version both fencers' weapons are connected to the box via long retractable cables. The box normally carries a set of lights to signal when a touch has been made. (Larger peripheral lights are also often used.) In foil and sabre, because of the need to distinguish on-target hits from off-target ones, special conductive clothing and wires must be worn. This includes a lamé (a jacket with metal threads woven in), a body cord to connect the weapon to the system, a reel of retractable cable that connects to the scoring box and, in the case of sabre, a conducting mask and cuff (manchette) as the head and arms are valid target areas.

Priority Rules

Foil and sabre are governed by right of way rules, as per which the fencer who is the first to initiate an attack (by straightening the arm) receives right of way. Commonly but incorrectly it is said that the person who parries also receives right of way. Instead, the person who parries must initiate an attack to gain right of way; parrying just eliminates the antagonist's right of way and grants the defender the right to make a riposte. In the case of a double touch (both fencers landing a hit at the similar time), only the fencer who had right of way receives a point. These rules were adopted in the 18th century as part of teaching practice. Their main aim was to discourage careless tactics, which result in simultaneous hits and, in a real duel, would leave both participants dead (the least desirable outcome). In both sabre and foil, there are rules concerning what can be believed a properly executed attack or parry.

Forms of Fencing

Competitive Fencing: Russian Igor Tourchine and American Weston Kelsey fence in the second round of the Men's Individual Epee event in the 2004 Summer Olympics at the Helliniko Fencing Hall on August 17, 2004.There are many inter-related forms of competitive fencing in practice, all of which approach the activity as a game, with varying degrees of connectedness to its historic past.

Olympic fencing (or simply "fencing") refers to the fencing seen in most competitions, as well as the Olympic Games and the world cup. Competitions are carried as per rules laid down by the Fédération Internationale d'Escrime (FIE), the international governing body. These rules orginated from a set of conventions developed in Europe among mid 17th and early twentieth century with the particular aim of regulating competitive activity. The three weapons used in Olympic fencing are foil, épée, and sabre. In competition, the validity of touches is decided by the electronic scoring apparatus, so as to minimize human error and bias in refereeing.

Wheelchair fencing, an original Paralympic sport, was developed in post-World War II England. Minor modifications to the FIE rules permit disabled fencers to fence all three weapons. The most apparent change is that every fencer sits in a wheelchair fastened to a frame. Footwork is substituted by torso or arm movement, depending upon the fencer's disability. The proximity of the two fencers tends to increase the pace of bouts, which require significant skill. The weapons are identical to those used in Olympic fencing.

Other variants comprise one-hit épée (one of the five events which constitute modern pentathlon) and the various types of competitive fencing, whose rules are similar but not identical to the FIE rules. One example of this is the American Fencing League (distinct from the United States Fencing Association): the layout of competitions is dissimslar, there is no electronic scoring, and the priority rules are interpreted in a dissimslar way. In a number of countries, the accepted practice at school and university level deviates slightly from the FIE layout.

Some practitioners of fencing approach it as a Western martial art, with the aim being to train for a theoretical duel. The element of game is absent (or nearly so) from these forms of fencing, but they all share a common origin with each other and with competitive fencing.

Classical fencing is differentiated from competitive fencing as being theoretically closer to swordplay as a martial art. Those who call themselves classical fencers may advocate the use of what they see as more authentic practices, as well as little or no emphasis on sport competition. There is strong interest inside the classical fencing community in reviving the European fencing practices of the 19th and early twentieth century, when fencers were anticipated to be able to fight a duel utilizing their training. Weapons used are the standard (non-electric) foil, standard épée (often equipped with pointes d'arret), and the blunted duelling sabre. AFL fencing is often referred to as classical fencing, but this is a misnomer.

Historical fencing is a type of historical martial arts reconstruction established on surviving texts and traditions. Predictably, historical fencers study an exceptionally broad array of weapons from dissimslar regions and periods. They may work with bucklers, daggers, polearms, navajas, bludgeoning weapons, etc. One main preoccupation of historical fencers is with weapons of realistic weight, which demand a dissimslar way of manipulating them from what is the norm in modern Fencing. For example, light weapons can be manipulated through the use of the fingers (more flexibility), but more realistically-weighted weapons must be assured more through the wrist and elbow. This difference is great and can lead to drastic alterations even in the carriage of the body and footwork in combat. There is significant overlap among classical and historical fencing, especially with regard to 19th-century fencing practices.

Other Forms of Fencing: This circa 1900 painting illustrates a typical mensur bout in Heidelberg, Germany. The combatants commences the mensur from a static position, either in the "verhängte Auslage" (hanging guard) or in the "steile Auslage" (steep ward), with their swords high in the air. While neck, arms and torso are protected with thickly padded leather gear and, more in recent times mail shirts, the head normally stays uncovered except for the "Paukbrille", metal goggles to protect the eyes and nose. Dissimslar sets of rules (Comments) regulating the Mensur in dissimslar cities may admit additional protective gear for lower face, ears, or existing scars.

Finally, there are various other forms of fencing which have little in common besides history with either of the other two classifications. Academic fencing, or mensur, is a German student tradition that has become mostly extinct but is still sometimes practiced in Germany,

Switzerland and Austria as well as in Flanders and Latvia. The combat, which uses a cutting weapon known as the schläger, uses sharpened blades and takes place among members of student fraternities - "Studentenverbindungen" - in accordance with a strictly delineated set of conventions. It uses special protective gear that leaves most of the head and face, excluding the eyes, unprotected. (The special goggles are called Paukbrille.) The ultimate aim is to develop personal character, hence there is no winner or loser and flinching is not permitted. Acquiring a proper cut on the face with the sharp blade, called a Schmiss (German for "smite"), was believed a visible sign of manly courage and status as "Akademiker", or member of the professional upper class. However, tales of cuts being intentionally manipulated by sewing in horsehairs or rubbing wounds with vinegar or salt have been discredited as famous myths since the 1880s.

Stage fencing seeks to achieve maximum theatrical impact in representing a broad range of styles, as well as both modern and historical forms of fencing. Theatrical fight scenes are choreographed by a Fight Director, and fencing actions are amplified for dramatic effect and visual clarity.

Recreational roleplaying often incorporates fencing in the context of historical or fantasy themes in the Society for Creative Anachronism or live-action roleplaying games. Technique and scoring systems vary broadly from one group to the following, as do the weapons. depending upon local conventions, participants may utilize modern game fencing weapons, period weapons, or weapons invented specifically for the purpose, such as boffers.

Competition Formats

Fencing tournaments are varied in their layout, and there are both individual and team competitions. A tournament may comprise all three weapons, both individual and team, or it may be very particular, such as an Épée Challenge, with individual épée only. And, as in many sports, men and women contend separately in high-level tournaments. Mixed-gender tournaments are commonplace at lower-level events, especially those deemed by individual fencing clubs. There are two types of event, individual and team. An individual event consists of two parts: the pools, and the direct eliminations.

In the pools, fencers are divided into groups, and each fencer in a pool will have the chance to fence each other fencer once, There are normally seven fencers in a pool. If the number of fencers contending is not a multiple of seven, then there will normally be various pools of six or eight. After the pools are completed, the fencers are given a ranking, or "seed," equated to all other fencers in the tournament, established mainly on the percent of bouts they won, then established secondarily on the difference among the touches they scored and the touches they received. Once the seeds have been decided, the direct elimination round starts. Fencers are sorted in a table of some power of 2 (16, 32, 64, etc.) established on how many people are contending. Due to the fact that it is highly unlikely for the number of fencers to be exactly a power of two, the fencers with the greatest results in the pools are given byes. The winner carries on in the tournament, and loser is ruled out. Normally no one has to fence for third place (the exception is if the tournament is a qualifying tournament with limited slots for continuation). Instead, two bronze medals are given to the losers of the semi-final round.

Team competition involves teams of three fencers. A fourth fencer can be permitted on the team as an alternate, but as soon as the fourth has been subbed in, they cannot substitute once again. The modern team competition is similar to the pool round of the individual competition. The fencers from opposing teams will each fence each other once, making for a total of nine matches. Matches among teams are three minutes long, or to 5 points, and the points then carry onto the following bout, making team fencing one forty-five touch bout fought by six fencers. Unlike individual tournaments, team tournaments almost always fence for bronze.

MAJOR TOURNAMENTS

Olympics

Fencing has been contested at each Summer Olympic Games since the birth of the modern Olympic movement at the 1896 Summer Olympics in Athens. Women's foil made its Olympic debut in Paris, throughout the 1924 Olympic Games.

Commonwealth Fencing Championships

The Commonwealth Fencing Championships is one of the older sport-particular sporting events deemed in the Commonwealth of Nations, adopting the demise of fencing as an event in the Commonwealth Games. The first championships were deemed in 1974 and they have been deemed in the similar cycle as Commonwealth Games meets ever since.The first Commonwealth Fencing Championships were deemed in Ottawa, Canada in 1974.

ADMINISTRATIVE BODIES

Federation Internationale d'Escrime

Federation Internationale d'Escrime (FIE) (English: International Fencing Federation) is the international governing body dealing Olympic fencing. It was established on November 29, 1913 in Paris, France. At present, its head office is in Lausanne, Switzerland. The FIE consistsof 115 national federations, each of which isacceptedby its country's Olympic Committee as the sole representative of Olympic-style fencing in that country. The existing president of the federation is René Roch.

FAMOUS PLAYERS

Ivan Joseph Martin Osiier

Dr. Ivan Joseph Martin Osiier, (December 16, 1888 - December 23, 1965), was a Danish fencer from Copenhagen.Osier acquired a total of 25 Danish National Championships in all the three fencing weapons — foil, epee, and sabre. He acquired the Danish foil championship in 1913, 1915, 1917-19, 1923-24, and 1927-29. He was also the national epee champion in 1915-17, 1927-28, and the sabre champion in 1913, 1916-20, 1922-23, 1928-29.

He was also Scandinavian Foil title holder in 1920-21, 1923, 1927, 1929, and 1931; he was Epee Champion in 1920; and he was Sabre Champi-on in 1921, 1923, 1927, 1929, 1931, and 1933.

Osier presented Denmark in seven Olympic Games from 1908 and 1948. He boycotted the 1936 Berlin Games, to protest in opposition to the Nazis.Osier won his only Olympic medal in 1912, a silver in Individual Epee, at the Stockholm Games.Osier was one of very few athletes to obtain the Olympic Diploma of Merit.

He first contended in the 1908 London Olympics, reaching the second round in the individual épée competition (he completed 18th), while Denmark lost in the team competition to France and Great Britain.

Osiier contended in the Stockholm Olympiad in 1912 in all three fencing weapons (foil, épée, and sabre), and won the only medal of his Olympic career. In the individual épée, he completed in 2nd place to capture the silver medal by winning five of seven matches in the finals (Belgian fencer Paul Anspach won the gold medal). At Stockholm, Osiier also was ruled out in the 1st round of both the individual and team sabre competitions. In individual foil, he moved on to the semifinals before being ruled out, and completed 20th.

His following Olympic competition was held in 1920 at the Antwerp Games because the Olympics were cancelled in 1916 due to World War I. There, he contended in three events, and made the finals in all three. He completed in 4th place in the team foil event, 6th place in team sabre, and 8th in the individual foil event.

At the 1924 Paris Olympics, Osiier contended reached the finals in individual foil by winning his pool in the first 4 rounds. In the finals, he was champion in only one bout (out of six), and completed in 6th place. He also completed in 6th place in individual sabre after winning two of seven matches in the final pool (he once again won all his earlier pools). In the team events, Denmark reached the semifinals in foil before losing to Italy and Belgium, and were ruled out in the quarterfinals in epee.

At the Paris Games women's fencing made its debut, and his wife Ellen Osiier won the gold medal for Denmark at the age of 33 without losing a single bout.At the 1928 Amsterdam Olympics, Osiier contended in five fencing events (each event Denmark entered). In the individual sabre competition, he reached the semifinals. In individual foil, he won his exclusion pool, but was once again ruled out in the semifinals after finishing 5th in his pool.

Denmark was ruled out in the quarterfinals in team foil, but not because of Osiier, who won 16 of 20 bouts in the competition. In epee he got no further than the semifinals. Denmark was ruled out in the first round of the team epee, even though Osiier won five of his eight bouts.

Osiier contended in five events once again at the 1932 Los Angeles Olympics. The Danish épée team reached the semifinals before they were ruled out by the United States, in spite of Osier winning all four of his bouts (the match ended 8-8, but the U.S. had fewer touches received and hence won). He reached the finals in the team foil event, and rated 4th after Denmark lost to Italy (4-12), France (6-10), and the United States (7-9). Osier also contended in the individual foil and reached the semifinals before being ruled out. In the sabre events, Osier reached the final and rated 7th overall, while the Danish team lost to Hungary (1-11) in the first round (Osiier registered Denmark's only victory in the match).

At the age of 60, Osiier came back to Olympic competition once more, in 1948 at the London Games, 40 years after first taking part in the Olympics. He fenced in only one event, the team épée, and Denmark was ruled out in the first round, but the fact that Osiier contended at all, is a testament to one of the greatest athletes in Olympic history.

Christian d'Oriola

Christian D'Oriola (October 3, 1928 – October 29, 2007) was a famous French foil fencer named "Fencer of the 20th Century" by the FIE, the International Fencing Federation, in 2001.

Born in Perpignan(France) he was World Champion four times (1947, 1949, 1953, and 1954), and twice Olympic Champion (1952, 1956) in the foil single events. At the 1948 Olympics, at the age of 19, he gained a team gold medal and an individual silver medal in foil. At the 1952 Olympics he gained gold medals in both the team and single foil competitions, succeeding all ten bouts in the team events. In 1956, at the Olympics he once again won a gold medal in individual foil, while winning a silver medal in team foil. He was also four time team world champion (1948, 1952, 1953, 1954). Aged 42 he turned French champion in the team sabre event in 1970. He is a first cousin of the equestrian Pierre Jonquères d'Oriola. In 1972, he was granted the French Legion of Honour.

In 2001, the FIE listed the persona that made Christian d'Oriola "Fencer of the 20th Century": "The speed of his hand, his extraordinary technique, his light but devastatingly quick footwork, his instant reactions, his ingenuity and his capability to adjust perfectly from "academic" (non-electric) to electric foil—all this means that Christian d'Oriola stays a example for his successors past and present."Noting the artistic component of his fencing, the FIE stated: "Christian d'Oriola was fencing perfection was as no-one else has ever been…"

Helene Mayer

Helene Mayer (December 20, 1910 – October 15, 1953) was a world champion Olympic fencer who contended for Nazi Germany in the 1936 Summer Olympics, in spite of having being enforced to leave Germany and settle in the United States because she was Jewish. She was born in Offenbach, Germany.

Mayer was one of the top 100 female athletes of the twentieth century .Mayer was only 13 when she won the German women's foil championship in 1924. By 1930, she had won 6 German championships.

Mayer won a gold medal in fencing at the age of 17 at the 1928 Summer Olympics in Amsterdam, presenting Germany, winning 18 bouts and losing only 2.She completed 5th at the 1932 Los Angeles Olympic Games. She then stayed in the U.S. in 1933 to educate at the University of Southern California, made a certificate in social work, and fenced for the USC Fencing Club.

In 1933 she discovered that she had been ejected from the Offenbach Fencing Club as part of a Nazi purge of Jewish athletes. She had to impartfrom Germany after Hitler's rise to power, soon before World War II began, because her father was Jewish.

The Amateur Athletic Union then voted to boycott the 1936 Olympics, to be deemed in Berlin, unless Jews were permitted to take part in the German trials and contend for Germany in the Olympics. As a motion of compliance, the German Olympic Committee invited Mayer to join the national team.

She swallowed, and came back to Germany to contend in the 1936 Summer Olympics, in spite of protests from the American Jewish community and other Jewish athletes, hoping to be recognized back into German society.

She won a silver medal. Polemically, she wore a swastika and extended her right arm in the Nazi salute on the medal stand throughout the medal ceremony. This rankled many, but others elaborated that she did this to save her household. Even though her Jewish father had died in 1931, her mother and two brothers had continued to live in Germany. Mayer believed herself German and wanted to represent her country, but rumors speculated that the Nazis had threatened her household in order to get Mayer to contend. Still, she was not reaccepted into German society.

REFERENCES

Amateur Fencers League of America: *Fencing Rules and Manual.* West New York, New Jersey, Amateur Fencers League of America (33-62nd St., Zip 07093).

Barbasetti, Luigi: *The Art of the Foil.* New York, E. P. Dutton and Co., Inc., 1932.

Bernhard, Frederica and Vernon Edwards: *How To Fence*. Dubuque, Iowa, Wm. C. Brown Co., 1955.

Bower, Muriel and Torao Mori: *Fencing*. Dubuque, Iowa, Wm. C. Brown Co., 1966.

Cass, Eleanor Baldwin: *The Book of Fencing*. Boston, Lothrop, Lee and Shepard Co., 1930.

Castello, Hugo and James Castello: *Fencing*. New York, Ronald Press Co., 1962.

Crosnier, Roger: *Fencing With Foil.* New York, Ronald Press Co., 1951.

Curry, Nancy L.: *Fencing*. Pacific Palisades, California. Goodyear Publishing Company, Inc., 1969.

DeBeaumont, Charles: *Modern British Fencing*. New York, A. S. Barnes and Co., 1966.

Deladrier, Clovis: *Modern Fencing*. Annapolis, Maryland, United States Naval Institute, 1948.

Garret, Maxwell: *Fencing*. New York, Sterling Publishing Co., 1961.

Hett, G. V.: *Fencing*. London, Sir Isaac Pitman and Sons, Ltd., 1939.

Nadi, Aldo: *On Fencing*. New York, G. P. Putnam's Sons, 1943.

Palffy-Alpar, Julius: *Sword and Masque*. Philadelphia, F. A. Davis Company, 1967.

Vince, Joseph: *Fencing*. New York, Ronald Press Co., 1962.

8

Gymnastics

Gymnastics is a game demanding performance of exercises involving physical strength, nimbleness and coordination. Artistic Gymnastics is the greatest known and most famous of the gymnastics sports ruled by the Federation Internationale de Gymnastique (FIG). It normally calls for exercises on uneven bars, balance beam, floor exercise, and vault (for women), and high bar, parallel bars, still rings, floor exercise, vault, and pommel horse (for men). It orginated from exercises used by the ancient Greeks, as well as skills for mounting and dismounting a horse, and circus performance skills. Other forms of gymnastics are rhythmic gymnastics, various trampolining sports and aerobic and acrobatic gymnastics.

HISTORY

To the Ancient Greeks, physical fitness was predominant, and all Greek cities had a gymnasia, a courtyard for jumping, running, and wrestling. As the Roman Empire ascended, Greek gymnastics gave way to military training. The Romans, for example, brought in the wooden horse. In 393 AD the Emperor Theodosius banned the Olympic Games, which by then had become corrupt, and gymnastics, along with other sports declined. Afterwards, Christianity, with its medieval belief in the base nature of the human body, had a hurtful effect on gymnastics. For centuries, gymnastics was all but forgotten.

In the late eighteenth and early nineteenth centuries, however, two pioneer physical educators – Johann Friedrich GutsMuth (1759 – 1839) and Friedrich Ludwig Jahn (1778 – 1852) - produced exercises for boys and young men on apparatus they planned that finally led to what is believed modern gymnastics. Particularly, Jahn crafted early models of the horizontal bar, the parallel bars (from a horizontal ladder with the rungs taken out), and the vaulting horse.

By the end of the nineteenth century, men's gymnastics competition was famous enough to be admitted in the first "modern" Olympic Games in 1896. on the other hand, from then on until the early 1950s, both national and international competitions required a changing variety of exercises gathered under the rubric gymnastics that would seem strange to today's audiences: synchronized team floor calisthenics, rope climbing, high jumping, running, horizontal ladder, etc. Throughout the 1920s, women organized and participated in gymnastics events, and the first women's Olympic competition – primitive, for it involved only synchronized calisthenics - was deemed at the 1928 Games in Amsterdam.

By the 1954, Olympic Games apparatus and events for both men and women had been standardized in modern layout, and uniform grading structures (as well as a point system from 1 to 10) had been sanctioned upon. At this time, Soviet gymnasts amazed the world with highly disciplined and difficult performances, setting a precedent that continues to inspire.

The new medium of television helped publicize and initiate a modern age of gymnastics. Both men's and women's gymnastics now attract significant international interest, and excellent gymnasts can be found on each continent. Nadia Comaneci received the first perfect score, at the 1976 Summer Olympics deemed in Montreal, Canada. She was coached by the famous Romanian, Bela Karolyi. As per Sports Illustrated, Comaneci scored four of her perfect tens on the uneven bars, two on the balance beam and one in the floor exercise.

Unfortunately, even with Nadia's perfect scores, the Romanians lost the gold medal to the Soviets. Nadia will always be remembered as "a fourteen year old, ponytailed little girl" who showed the world that perfection could be attained.

In 2006, a new point system was put into play. Rather of being marked 1 to 10, the gymnast's start value depends upon the difficulty rating of the exercise routine. Also, the deductions turned higher: before the new point system developed, the deduction for a fall was 0.5, and now it is 0.8. The need for a new point system was to reducethe chance of gymnasts getting a perfect score. The game can comprise children as young as three years old and sometimes younger doing kindergym and children's gymnastics, recreational gymnasts of all ages, competitive gymnasts at varying levels of skill, as well as world class athletes.

THE GAME

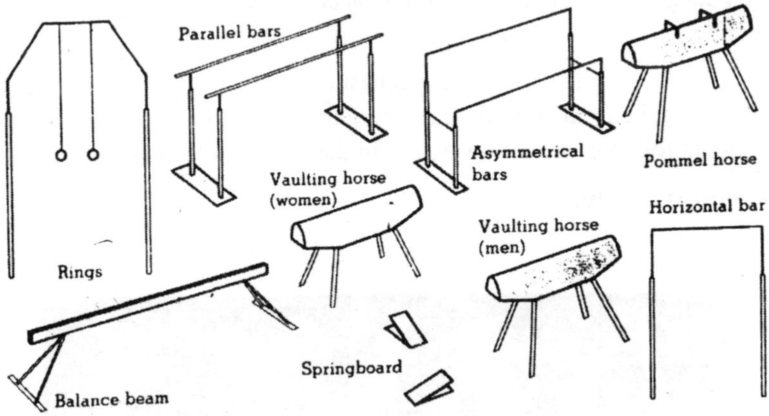

Fig.Instruments used in Gymnastics

Artistic Gymnastics

Artistic gymnastics is normallynormally divided into Men's and Women's Gymnastics. Every group does dissimslar events; Men contend on Floor Exercise, Pommel Horse, Still Rings, Vault, Parallel Bars, and High Bar, while women contend on Vault, Uneven Bars, Beam, and Floor Exercise. In some countries, women at one time contended on the rings, high bar, and parallel bars (for example, in the 1950s in the USSR). Though routines executed on each event may be short, they are physically exhausting and push the gymnast's strength, flexibility, endurance and consciousness to the limit.

Fig.Artistic Gymnastics

Traditionally, at the international level, competitions on the various apparatus consisted of two dissimslar performance categories:

compulsory and optional. For the compulsory event, each gymnast executing on a particular apparatus accomplished the similar required routine.

At the optional level, the gymnast executed routines that he or she choreographed. At present, each country may utilize compulsory and optional routines at their discretion in the training of young gymnasts.

Women's Events

Fig. Decals

Vault: In the vaulting events gymnasts: sprint down a 25 meter (about 82 feet) runway, jump onto a beatboard - a kind of springboard, (run/ take-off segment), land momently, in general inverted on the hands, on the vaulting horse or vaulting table, (pre flight segment), then spring or block off of this platform to a two footed landing (post flight segment). The post flight segment may comprise one or more multiple saltos or somersaults, and or writhing movements.

In 2001, the traditional vaulting horse was substituted with a new apparatus, sometimes known as a tongue or table. The new apparatus is more static, wider, and longer than the older vaulting horse - approx. 1m in length and 1m in width, gives gymnasts a larger blocking surface, and is hence safer than the old vaulting horse. With the increase of this new, safer vaulting table, gymnasts are trying more difficult and dangerous vaults.

Uneven Bars: On the uneven bars (also known as asymmetric bars, UK), the gymnast navigates two horizontal bars set at dissimilar heights. The height is in general fixed, but the width may be adjusted.

Gymnasts execute swinging, circling, transitional, and release moves,that may pass over, under, and among the two bars. Movements may pass through the handstand. Gymnasts often mount the Uneven Bars utilizing a beatboard (springboard).

Fig. Men's Exercise on Balance Beam

Balance Beam: The gymnast performs a choreographed routine from 60 to 80 seconds in length comprising of leaps, acrobatic skills, somersaults, turns and dance components on a padded sprung beam.

Apparatus norms set by the International Gymnastics Federation (used for Olympic and most elite competitions) determine the beam must be 125 cm (4' 1") high, 500 cm (16' 5") long, and 10 cm (4") broad. The event requires particularly, balance, flexibility and strength.

Fig: *Women's Exercise on* Balance Beam

Floor: The floor event occurs on a carpeted 12m × 12m square, normallynormally comprising of hard foam over a layer of ply wood, which is supported by springs or foam blocks in general called a "sprung" floor. This provides a firm surface that will react with force when compressed, permitting gymnasts to achieve extra height and a softer landing than would be possible on a regular floor. Female gymnasts execute a choreographed exercise 70 to 90 seconds long. In levels 7 and up, they can choose an accompanying music piece, which must be instrumental and cannot comprise vocals.

In the USA, the other levels must execute a routine that is choreographed for them by USAG and these routines come with music. The routines of a female gymnast consist of tumbling passes, series of jumps, dance elements, acrobatic skills, and turns. A gymnast normally performs three or four tumbling passes that comprise three or more skills or "tricks". Elite gymnasts can have up to six or seven tumbling passes.

At the required levels (1-6) gymnasts are labeled on a scale of 10, but as they reach the higher levels, particularly levels 9 and 10, the gymnasts' start-values may vary depending upon a number of dissimslar elements such as skill level and skill combinations. Also, each skill has a letter grade describing its difficulty. At level nine, to reach a start value of ten, the gymnast has to acquire bonus points, which she can attain by associating two or more skills of a certain high level of difficulty.

Compulsory levels of gymnastics have choreographed routines, and all women contending at that level do the similar routines. In the United States, compulsory levels go from 1-6; most gymnasts start at levels 1-4 . In optional level competitions, however, all routines are dissimilar and have dissimslar floor music. Optional levels in the U.S. comprise levels 7 - 10 (elite). The Olympics, and college level gymnastics are also nonmandatory. In the Olympics, gymnasts are believed elite level gymnasts, which is higher level than the U.S. level 10.

Men's Events

Floor Exercise : Male gymnasts also execute on a 12m. by 12m. sprung floor A series of tumbling passes are executed to present flexibility, strength, and balance. The gymnast must also show strength skills, as well as circles, scales, and press handstands. Men's floor routines normally have four passes that will total between 60–70 seconds and are executed without music, unlike the women's event. Rules expect that gymnasts touch each corner of the floor at least once during their routine.

Still Rings : Still Rings is arguably the most physically involving event. The rings are suspended on wire cable from a point 5.75 meters off the floor, and adjusted in height so the gymnast has room to hang freely and swing. He must execute a routine demonstrating balance, strength, power, and dynamic motion while preventing the rings themselves from swinging. At least one static strength move is needed, but some gymnasts may comprise two or three. A routine should have a dismount equal in difficulty to the difficulty of the routine as a whole.

Vault : Gymnasts sprint down a runway, which is a maximum of 25 meters in length, before hurdling onto a spring board. The body position is held while "punching" (blocking utilizing only a shoulder movement) the vaulting platform. The gymnast then rotates to a standing position. In advanced gymnastics, multiple twists and somersaults may be contributed before landing. Successful vaults depend on the speed of the run, the length of the hurdle, the power the gymnast yields from the legs and shoulder girdle, the kinesthetic consciousness in the air, and the speed of rotation in the case of more difficult and complex vaults.

Parallel Bars: Men execute on two bars a little further than a shoulder's width apart and normally 1.75m high while performing a series of swings, balances, and releases that require great strength and coordination.

High Bar : A 2.4cm thick steel bar aroused 2.5m above the landing area is all the gymnast has to hold onto as he performs giants (revolutions all over the bar), release skills, twists, and alterations of direction. By utilizing all of the momentum from giants and then releasing at the proper point, enough height can be attained for spectacular dismounts, such as a triple-back salto. Leather grips are normallynormallynormally used to help maintain a grip on the bar.

Fig. High Bar Exercises

As with the women, male gymnasts are also judged on all of their events, for their execution, degree of difficulty, and overall presentation skills.

Rhythmic Gymnastics

The discipline of rhythmic gymnastics is contended only by women (even though there is a new version of this discipline for men being pioneered in Japan, and involves the performance of five different routines with the use of five apparatus — ball, ribbon, hoop, clubs, rope — on a floor area, with a much greater emphasis on the aesthetic rather than the acrobatic. Rhythmic routines are scored out of a possible 20 points, and the music used by the gymnast can contain vocals, but may not contain words.

Trampolining and Tumbling: Trampolining and tumbling consists of four events, individual, synchronized, double mini and power tumbling. Since 2000 individual trampoline has been admitted in the Olympic Games. Individual routines in trampolining involve a build-up phase throughout which the gymnast jumps repeatedly to achieve height, succeeded by a sequence of ten leaps without pauses throughout which the gymnast performs a sequence of aerial skills. Routines are marked out of a maximum score of 10 points. Additional points (with no maximum at the highest levels of competition) can be earned depending upon the difficulty of the moves. In high level competitions, there are two beginningroutines, one which has only two moves scored for difficulty and one where the athlete is free to execute any routine. This is succeeded by a final routine which is optional. Some competitions restart the score from zero for the finals, other add the final score to the preliminary results.

Synchronized trampoline is similar except that both competitors must execute the routine together and marks are granted for synchronicity as well as the form and difficulty of the moves. Double mini trampoline involves a smaller trampoline with a run-up, two moves are performed for preliminaries and two more for finals. Moves cannot be repeated and the scores are marked in a similar manner to individual trampoline. In power tumbling, athletes execute an explosive series of flips and twists down a sprung tumbling track. Scoring is similar to trampolining.

Display Gymnastics: General gymnastics enables people of all ages and abilities to participate in performance groups of 6 to more than 150 athletes. They execute synchronized, choreographed routines. Troupes may be all one gender or mixed. There are no age divisions generally gymnastics. The largest general gymnastics exhibition is the quadrennial World Gymnaestrada which was first deemed in 1939.

Aerobic Gymnastics

Fig. Aerobic Gymnastics

Aerobic gymnastics (formally Sport Aerobics) involves the performance of routines by individuals, pairs, trios or groups up to 6 people, emphasizing strength, flexibility, and aerobic fitness rather than acrobatic or balance skills. Routines are performed on a small floor area and in general last 60-90 seconds.

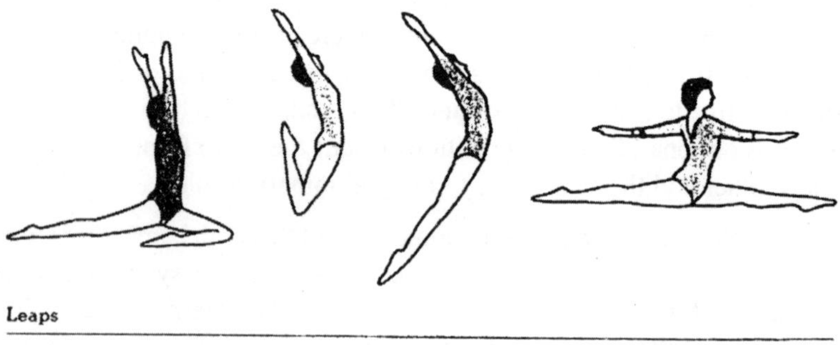

Fig. Aerobic Gymnastics

Acrobatic Gymnastics

Acrobatic gymnastics (formerly Sports Acrobatics), often referred to as acrobatics, "acro" sports or simply sports acro, is a group gymnastic discipline for both men and women. Acrobats in groups of two, three and four execute routines with the heads, hands and feet of their partners. They may pick their own music, but lyrics or Disney music are not permitted.

Performers must contend in preparatory grades A and B, then move on to grades 1, 2, 3, 4 and 5; by 3, 4 and 5 two routines are needed, one for balances and another for tempos.

MAJOR TOURNAMENTS

Olympics

It's one of the most popular Olympic sports for good reason: the gymnastics competition will feature incredible skills, feats of strength, balance and coordination, and near-perfect performances.

ADMINISTRATIVE BODIES

International Federation of Gymnastics

The Fédération Internationale de Gymnastique (FIG) or International Federation of Gymnastics (IFG) is the governing body of competitive gymnastics. Its headquarters is in Moutier, Switzerland. It was established on July 23, 1881 in Liège, Belgium, making it the most former international sport organisation. Primitively called the European Federation of Gymnastics, it had three member countries — Belgium, France and the Netherlands — until 1921, when non-European countries were admitted, and it was renamed to its existing name.

The federation draws up the rules, known as the Code of Points, which regulate how gymnast's performance is evaluated. Six gymnastics disciplines are governed by the FIG: Artistic gymnastics (further classified as Men's Artistic Gymnastics — MAG and Women's Artistic Gymnastics — WAG), Rhythmic gymnastics (RG), Aerobic gymnastics (AER), Acrobatic gymnastics (ACRO) and Trampolining (TRA).

Additionally, the federation has been believed the authority in charge for deciding whether gymnasts are old enough to participate in the Olympics. In spite of there being controversies concerningthe described ages of Chinese athletes He Kexin and Yang Yilin in the 2008 Olympics, the International Olympic Committee has deferred to the FIG age verifications.

The main organizations of the federation are the President and Vice-Presidents, the Congress, deemed all two years, the Executive Committee, the Council and seven Technical Committees — for each of the subjects (WAG and MAG have discrete ones; for GG it's called General Gymnastics Committee).

FAMOUS PLAYERS

Vera Caslavska

Vera Caslasvska (born May 3, 1942) is a Czech gymnast. Blonde, cheerful and possessing impressive stage presence, she was in general famous with the public and won a total of 22 international titles.

Calavska is the most adorned Czech gymnast in history and is one of only two female gymnasts, along with Soviet Larissa Latynina, to win the all-around gold medal at two successive Olympics.She was also the 1966 all-around World Champion and the 1965 and 1967 all-around European Champion.

Caslavska has the peculiarity of holding more Olympic individual event titles than any other gymnast, a record she has now deemed for over 40 years. She is also the only gymnast, male or female, ever who has won Olympic gold on each individual event (all-around, vault, uneven bars, beam, floor exercise). Between 1964 and 1968 Caslavska was unbeatable in the all-around in main international competition; to date, she is the only female gymnast ever to win each Olympic, World Championships and European Championships all-around title from one Olympiad to the following.

In addition to her gymnastics success, Caslavska is known for her tactful support of the Czechoslovak democratization movement and her opposition to the Soviet-led invasion of Czechoslovakia. At the 1968 Olympics in Mexico City, she took this dissent to the world stage by quietly looking down and away while the Soviet national anthem was played throughout the medal ceremonies for the balance beam and floor exercise event finals. While Èáslavská's actions were spatted by her countrymen, they resulted in her turning a persona non grata in the new regime. She was forced into retirement and for many years was denied the right to travel, work and attend sporting events.

Caslavska situation bettered in the 1980s after the intervention of members of the International Olympic Committee, and after the fall of Communism, her status improved dramatically. Throughout the 1990s she deemed various positions of honour, counting a term as President of the Czech Olympic Committee. As of 2008, she still rests in Prague and has opted to remain largely out of the public eye.

Born in Prague and primitively a figure skater, Caslavska debuted internationally at the 1958 World Championships, winning a silver medal in the team event. She first took partin the Olympic Games in 1960, also winning a silver medal with the Czechoslovakian team. By 1962, she fought for the all-around title at the World Championships, deemed off only by Larissa Latynina.

Caslavska was at her peak at the 1964 Summer Olympics in Tokyo, distinctly winning the overall title and taking gold medals in the balance beam and the vault, in addition to another silver medal in the team event. She would eventually win a team gold at the 1966 World Championships, breaking the Soviet monopoly in that event.

She was once again prevailingat the 1968 Summer Olympics, winning medals in all six events: She opposed her all-around title and won extra gold medals on the floor, uneven bars and vault, as well as two silvers, for the team competition and balance beam.Her use of the "Jarabe tapatío" as the music for her floor routine made her immensely famous with the Mexican crowd. Shortly after the end of the competition, Caslavska married runner Josef Odlozil, who had been a silver medalist at the 1964

Olympics in Tokyo. The ceremony, which was held at the Mexico City Cathedral, drew a crowd of thousands.Caslavska was cited as being the most famous female athlete at the Olympics.

Caslavska's countrymen respected her for her brave demonstration on the world's biggest stage. Her federation, however, was none too pleased. For her consistent support of the Czechoslovak democratization movement (the so-called "Prague Spring") in 1968, and during the purges which succeeded the Soviet-led invasion in August 1968, she was deprived of the right to travel abroad and participate in public sport events both in Czechoslovakia and abroad. Caslavska was effectively forced into retirement, and was believed a persona non grata for many years in her home country.

Czech authorities declined to issue her autobiography, and insisted that it be heavily censored when it was released in Japan.She was granted leave to work as a coach in Mexico, but apparently only when the Mexican government threatened to cease oil exports to Czechoslovakia.In the late 1980s, following pressure from Juan Antonio Samaranch, the president of the International Olympic Committee, who presented her with the Olympic Order, Caslavska was at last permitted to work as a gymnastics coach and judge in her home country.

Maxi Gnauck

Maxi Gnauck born on October 10, 1964 in Berlin, East Germany was a German Artistic Gymnast. Her parents were awaiting a boy and they planned to name him Max so, when the baby turned out to be a girl, they simply contributed an i.

With a total of 27 medals at the Olympic Games, World Championships, World Cups, and European Championships she is believed one of the most flourishing woman gymnasts that Germany has ever developed.

Maxi was 5; her mother took her to a gymnastics centre in their area. By age 8, Maxi had gained her first medals at the Kreisspartakiade. When she was 9 she transferred to the Club SC Dynamo Berlin, where she was coached by Jurgen Heritz. Believed one of the greatest Uneven Bars workers of her time, Maxi was also a super tumbler. She was one of the first girls to execute a triple twist on Floor.

In April 1986, Maxi officially declarted her retirement and started studying to become a coach. Throughout 1988, Maxi was badly injured while sliding down a waterslide while she was working as an aid at a children's summer camp by the Baltic Sea. Maxi broke her C5 vertebra and was almost paralyzed. Three vertebrae were later reenforced with a metal plate.

From 1993 Maxi has worked as a full-time coach at the Norderstedt Gymnastics Center in Hamburg. In 2000, she was induced into the International Gymnastics Hall of Fame, She is the first German gymnast to be granted that honour.

Bart Conner

Bart Wayne Conner born on March 28, 1958 in Chicago, Illinois is a former American gymnast who, as a member of the gold medal-winning men's gymnastics team at the 1984 Summer Olympic Games won a single gold on the parallel bars. Conner was also the 1979 World Champion on the parallel bars. Conner is the only American male gymnast to have gained gold medals at each level of competition, as well as international, national and collegiate. Conner presently owns and controls the Bart Conner Gymnastics Academy in Norman, Oklahoma along with his wife, Romanian gold medalist Nadia Comaneci. He is also a commentator for telecasted gymnastics events and an editor of International Gymnast magazine.

Conner was also part of the 1976 and 1980 USA Olympic gymnastics teams. He gained the World Cup in 1979, and the American Cup in 1976, 1980, and 1981. He has been induced into various Halls of Fame, as well as those of the US Olympic Committee, USA Gymnastics, International Gymnastics, and Oklahoma Sports.

Active in sports as a child, Conner began gymnastics at the age of ten, after a school physical education coach noticed his talent. He started training with the Niles West High School team and contending in local meets, where he moved on rapidly but seldom won. After a few years, he also started training and contending at the local YMCA. Conner's first substantial gymnastics victory was the 1972 AAU Junior Olympics, succeeded soon after in 1974 by the USGF Junior National Championships. Immediately following his high school graduation in 1976, he went on to join the United States team as its youngest member at the 1976 Summer Olympics in Montreal.

He went to grade school at Park View School in Morton Grove, Illinois, and went to Niles West High School in Skokie, Illinois. When he went to Park View, his trainer induced him walk to and from class on his hands. He was on the gymnastics team at Niles West, where he set records that haven't been broken to this day.

Conner went to the University of Oklahoma in order to work with coach Paul Ziert on the gymnastics team, which was then rated 19th nationally by the NCAA. Accoding to Ziert, Conner is comparatively unsuited physically for gymnastics due to his relative lack of spinal flexibility, and his weakness in tumbling skills. However, Ziert continues, Conner's motivation and commitment to the game combined with his other physical abilities helped him rapidly advance to the world-class level. In 1979, he won the parallel bars event at the World Championships with an original move called the "Conner Spin." In this move, the gymnast executes a complete 360-degree turn on one bar in a straddled position, and then presses to a handstand.

Much of Conner's early career was seen as a enmity within himself and fellow American Kurt Thomas, another top contender whose style differed from his own. Thomas, a more physically gifted gymnast than Conner, impressed judges with his explosive strength and unusual degree of difficultness in his routines; whereas Conner's strengths were in his solid steadiness and artistic presentation. The media made much of this rivalry, and though the two were good friends, the publicity all over their rivalry and media exaggeration incited ill feeling within them for a time.

Conner was the first qualifier for the 1980 Olympic gymnastics team, and did not support the US protest of the Games. He made various media appearances in which he described the boycott as "futile," and protested the Olympics being used for political purposes. However, due to a torn biceps he received throughout the Olympic Trials, it is unlikely he would have performed well had he contended. Because he extended training after this injury, his recovery lasted well over a year. In December 1983, contending at the Chunichi Cup, Conner tore his left biceps throughout his rings routine. Due to various bone chips floating all over his elbow, his arm mobility was limited, which rated undue stress on the muscles of the upper arm throughout the strenuous activities of competitive gymnastics.

Following surgery and intensive physical therapy, Bart squeaked onto the 1984 Olympic team, after contending in only one of the two qualifying events, the Olympic Trials. He had begun contending in the earlier National Championships, but various serious falters, as well as a headfirst landing on the floor exercise, made it clear that he had not yet made a full recovery. Conner was granted a petition by the USGF to conceive only the Trials scores, with which he was selected for the team.

After vivid training to return to the level of contest he had reached before his injury, Conner's consistently good scores (as well as a perfect 10 on the parallel bars) helped the US men's team earn its first team gold. Conner took sixth place in the individual all-around competition, with his total isolated from gold medalist Koji Gushiken by .35 points.

He got eligble for two individual event finals, on floor exercise and parallel bars. He had a lackluster floor exercise, scoring a 9.75 for fifth place. In the parallel bars final just hours later, he marked a perfect 10 to win the event.

Former rival Kurt Thomas, who had retired from gymnastics, was a commentator for ABC Sports. Coach Paul Ziert saw his judgments of Conner's performance as being more fair and precise than any others'.

Conner and Nadia Comaneci were engaged on November 12, 1994, (Nadia's 33rd birthday), and got married on April 27, 1996 in Bucharest, Romania. The couple for the first time met at the 1976 American Cup, where Conner won the men's, and Comaneci the women's title. They joined in 1991, when Comaneci fled Romania. They presently own the Bart Conner Gymnastics Academy, Perfect 10 Production Company, and various sports equipment shops, and are editors of International Gymnast magazine. They also are heavily involved in charity work. Conner is also a gymnastics commentator, and accepts speaking engagements.

Conner turned a father when Comaneci gave birth to their first child, a boy called Dylan Paul Conner, on the morning of June 3, 2006 in Oklahoma City, Oklahoma. Dylan was born three weeks early, weighing in at just 4lbs. However, Dylan left the hospital after a short stay and instantly thrived.

Conner has seemed in films in 1986 and 2006. In 1986, he played a character named Bart in the cult BMX film Rad! In 2006 he seemed as himself in two movies about gymnastics, Stick It and Peaceful Warrior. In 1997 Conner was induced into the International Gymnastics Hall of Fame.

REFERENCES

Cochrane, Tuovi Sappinen:*International Gymnastics for Girls and Women.* Reading, MA: Addison-Wesley Publishing Co., 1968.

Gerber, Ellen. W.:*Innovators and Institutions in Physical Education.* Philadelphia: Lea and Febiger, 1971.

Goodbody, John.:*The Illustrated History of Gymnastics.* London: Stanley Paul, 1982.

Ryan, Joan.:*Little Girls in Pretty Boxes: The Making and Breaking of Elite Gymnasts and Figure Skaters.* New York: Doubleday, 1995.

9

Handball

Handball alsocalled as team handball, field handball, European handball, or Olympic handball is a team sport in which two teams of seven players each pass and bounce a ball to throw it into the goal of the opponent team.

The game has a goal smaller than the association football, though caring the ball involves the players' hands rather than feet. The game has been played internationally since the 1920s.

Team handball has sources reaching as far as antiquity: urania in ancient Greece, harpaston in ancient Rome, fangballspiel in medieval Germany as examples. There are also records of handball-like games in medieval France, and amongst the Inuit in Greenland, in the middle Ages, and in Ancient Africa, mainly Egypt. By the nineteenth century, there survived similar games of haandbold from Denmark, hazena in the Czech Republic and Slovakia, gandbol in Ukraine, torball in Germany, as well as versions in Ireland and Uruguay.

The team handball game of now was shaped by the end of the nineteenth century in northern Europe, mainly Denmark, Germany, Norway and Sweden. The Dane Holger Nielsen drew up the rules for modern handball (handbold) in 1898 and issued them in 1906, and R.N. Ernst did something alike in 1897.

Another set of team handball rules was issued on 29 October 1917 by Max Heiser, Karl Schelenz and Erich Konigh from Germany. After 1919 these rules were improved by Karl Schelenz. The first international games were commenced under these rules, among Germany and Belgium for men in 1925 and among Germany and Austria for women in 1930.

In 1926, the Congress of the International Amateur Athletics Federation appointed a committee to draw up international rules for field handball. The International Amateur Handball Federation was established in 1928. The International Handball Federation was established in 1946

Men's field handball was played at the 1936 Summer Olympics in Berlin at the petition of Adolf Hitler. It was withdrew, to return as team handball for the 1972 Summer Olympics in Munich. Women's team handball was brought at the 1976 Summer Olympics.

The International Handball Federation formed the men's world championship in 1938 and all 4 (sometimes 3) years from World War II to 1995. Since the 1995 world championship in Iceland, the contest has been every two years. The women's world championship has been played since 1957. The IHF also prepares women's and men's junior world championships.

By February 2007, the IHF listed 159 member federations - approximately 1,130,000 teams and 31 million players, trainers, officials and referees.

HISTORY

In order to settle down the belongings of the handball, the investigators try to look for similarities and meeting points with own games of the Greeks and the Romans. even though to anybody he gets away, however, that the nimbleness of the man with its hands could take to him already in the first known civilizations to utilize them for its games. It is an incongruencia to confirm that there he was where the handball was born. But in a point they are almost all in agreement: the handball, so and as is realized now, been a game in real very young, of the first quarter of our century.

In any case, also it is sure that in old Greece the "game of Uranian" survived in which the ball of measures was used similar to an apple that had to be maintained in the air. In one of central books of classic Literature, the Odyssey, Homero speak of this game and explain how two of their protagonists sent the ball to the air in the direction of clouds and they took it jumping, before their feet came back to step on the ground. Some scenes of this type of recreation were found in the wall of Athens in 1926.

Later, also among the Romans the doctor Soft Claudius had suggested to his patients the practice of the "Harpaston", a modality that was made with a ball and the hands. That was held all over years 150 to of C. Much moderner, already in the Average Age, the trovador Walter Von der Vogelwide also described the "game of the ball", that consisted of capturing the ball in flight of a form alike to as the players go now of handball. He was practiced primarily in the Court and the trovadores baptized it like the "First Game of Summer". Anyway, it was a not planned sport practice, without no type standard nor of norms.

These are the fundamental ascendants that were used later on for the creation as a called game "handball", that is practicing at the moment in more than 100 countries of the entire world, with all over a quarter of million equipment and more than 5 million players.

The modern sources of the handball date from end of century XIX, when it was used as accompaniment to train and to develop the gymnasts. In 1982, a professor of gymnastic, Konrad Koch, produced "raffballspied", with characteristics very similar to the present handball. In this time, in Czechoslovakia a game exercised in the schools in which each equipment was established by seven players. "hazena" was designated and its first regulation looked in 1905.

Many historians ensure that the origin of the existinghandball is in Germany. But seeking concrete data we were with various versions, with important points of discrepancy. In any case, it seems clear that year 1848, in an institute of average education of Denmark, a professor of gymnastics, Holger Nielsen, devised a game to which called "haandbold", giving him to rules and a system of game. Was to put goals in one portería, of a similar way to soccer, but handling the ball with the hands. Few years later this game was brought in in Sweden, Karlskrona concretely, through G. Wallstrom. It was year 1910.

More unbelievable it seems the South American version, as per which the Uruguayan professor of gymnastics Antonio Valera made in 1914 a basketball mixture, rugby and soccer, that exercised in some zones of the Argentine coast and which was made a first authorized encounter in the stage of Montevideo in 1916. This strange game was seen, as per the similar version, by sailors Germans who were interested in him and when concluding the war transferred Germany, where would finish polishing until fetching the present handball.

Anyway everything objectsat a professor Berliner of physical education, Max Heiser, that isacceptedlike the true and legitimate "father" of this game modality. The historians German assure that Heiser was enthused by some sports that already exercised like "raffbold", "volkerball" and "koreball", for the creation of one new one: "torball". One gambled in a room or outdoors (concretely it played with his students in one of the main avenues of Berlin), on a land of 40 ms by 20 and a medicinal ball or one of soccer was used. With the ball in the hand it was not possible to be run more than three seconds; the zone was situated to 4 ms and portería measured 2,50 by 2 ms.

Heiser invented east game to occupy the free short whiles of the workers of the Siemens company. Accordingly, the quarrels and the hand-to-hand combat were not permitted. The rules were not, yet, overly clear and, even though it got to have a good number of medical instructors, finished later dying just a short time. But "torball" left its seed. The invention of Heiden in 1915 was gathered years later by the German professor Carl Schelenz and served as it bases of which it called "handbold". The share of Schelenz, later trainer of Germany, Austria and Switzerland, was critical because it recognised norms, it altered the previous ones and it took the game to the football grounds with matching rules to those of this one with the difference of which it gambled with the hands.

Among most prominent it was the fact that the new game had to gamble with 11 components and that the zone moved to the 11 ms. Porterías was identical to those of soccer. "dribling" was also brought in and the fight by the self-command of the ball, which offered more spectacle and dynamism.

The new game had also been planned so that the men practiced. And perhaps for that reason it found more affirms for his future growth. The similar Secretary General of the Association the International of Soccer in 1912, the Hirschmann German, made an effort in formulating the handball. In his beginnings it was left in the Federation the International of Athletics enrolled. Schelenz confronted the handball in Europe in 1919. A year later, Carl Diem, director of the German School of Physical education and president of Liga de Atletismo de Brandedurg, it gave officiality in his country to this game and it brought in it in the Navy, with which soon it developed a great growth in Germany.

After that whole he was very fast. In 1926 the congress of the Federation the International of Athletics Amateur, reunified, named a committee in charge to establish a clear and brief regulation. The 11 of August of 1927, in Amsterdan, the handball committee admitted of authorized form, the regulation that was being used in Germany for this game that extended practicing with 11 players. In the 25 session of the Olympic Committee the International, Monaco 1927, took another very important step when the inclusion in the Olympic program was asked for for the first time.

THE GAME

Playing Field

Handball is played on a court 40 meters long by 20 meters broad (40m x 20m), with a goal in the center of each end. The goals are bounded by a near-semicircular area, called the zone or the crease, outlined by a line six meters from the goal.

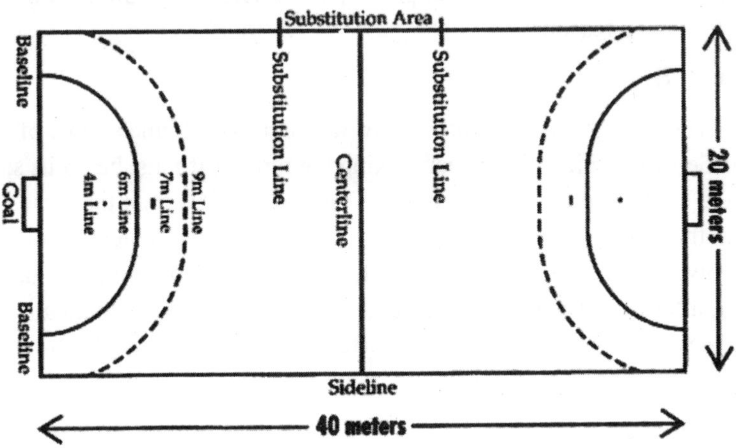

Fig. Handball Court

Only the defending goalkeeper is permitted inside this perimeter, and normally the defense aligns itself along this line and tries to protect this zone. Nevertheless, the court players may catch and touch the ball in the air inside it. As long as the player starts his jump outside the zone and frees the ball before he lands, the play is legal. If a player contacts the ground inside the goal perimeter he must take the most direct path out of it. Should a defender contact an attacker in the goal perimeter, his team is penalized with a direct attempt at the goal, with only one assaulter on the seven-meter line and the opposing goalkeeper involved.

There is also a dashed near-semicircular line nine meters from the goal, which marks the free-throw line. Play is resumed after a fault with all assaulting players outside this line, and the defensive players at least three meters from the ball. Play restarts at the site of the fault if not the fault is inside this region, in which case play restarts at the nearest point on this nine meter line.

After a goal, the team conceding the goal resumes the game with a pass off from center court. Once the player with the ball is under control the referee will blow his whistle to resume play. All players of the team which are resuming the play must be behind the line on their own half, or else the resuming throw will have to be retaken.

Duration

A standard match has two periods of 30 minutes with a 10 minute half-time. Teams may switch sides of the field, as well as benches.Each team may call one time-out per period. The referee may call timeout for the following reasons:

Game Start

The game begins at center court, with a throw-off and a blow of the whistle by the referee. The team taking the throw-off must be on its side of the court, and the defending team must be no less than three meters from the thrower. The thrower tries to throw the ball to a member of his/her own team. Throw-offs occur after every goal. To permit for faster play, after a goal is scored, the game can resume before all antagonists are back on their side of the court (the team taking the throw-off, however, must still be on its own half).

Possession

A player who is in possession of the ball may stand stationary for only three seconds and may only take three steps. They must then either shoot, pass or dribble the ball. Dribbling is similar to dribbling in basketball. As in basketball, the player can not have multiple series of dribbling. Once the player holds the ball with both hands after dribbling they must either shoot or pass.

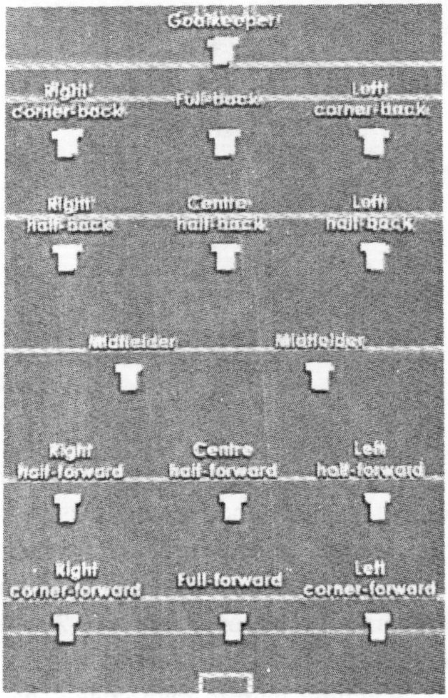

Ball Advancement

The ball is moved down the field toward the goal by passing it among team members. A team member may stop, catch, throw, bounce and strike the ball in any direction, with any part of the body above the knees.

Normal league games are normallynormally permitted to end in a draw, but in knockout tournaments, such as the Olympics, two extension periods of 5 minutes are played, and if they also end in a draw another two times 5 minutes has to be played.

If each of these ends in a tie after the extra time the winner is decided by an individual shootout from the 7-meter line, where each team is given five shots. The rules of the shootout are similar to football shootouts, where, if a winner is not found inside the first ten shots, the players return to the shooting, until one team has missed and the other scored.

In two Olympic Finals of women's handball penalty shootouts had to be used - both of them with Denmark taking part (in opposition to Hungary in 1996 and South Korea in 2004); in both, Denmark was the winner.

Fig. Ball

The usual formations of the defense are 6-0, when all the defense players line up among the 6 meter and 9 meter lines to form a wall; the 5-1, when one of the players cruises outside the 9 meter perimeter, normallynormally targeting the center forwards while the other 5 line up on the six meter line; and the lesser common 4-2 when there are two such defenders out front. Very fast teams will also try a 3-3 formation which is close to a switching man-to-man style. The formations vary greatly from country to country and reflect each country's style of play. The usual attacking formation includes two wingmen, a left backcourt and a right backcourt who normallynormally excel at high jumps and shooting over the defenders, a center backcourt who is the playmaker and the handball equivalent of a basketball point guard and the circle or pivot player, who tends to intermingle with the defense, setting picks and attempting to disrupt the defense formation.

The game is quite fast and includes body contact as the defenders try to stop the attackers from approaching the goal. Contact is only permitted when the defensive player is completely in front of the offensive player, i.e. among the offensive player and the goal. Any contact from the side or especially from behind is believed dangerous and is normally met with penalties. When a defender effectively stops an attacking player, the play is stopped and restarted by the attacking team from the spot of the infraction or on the nine meter line. Unlike in basketball where players are permitted to commit only 5 fouls in a game (6 in the NBA), handball players are permitted an unlimited number of "faults," which are believed good defense and disruptive to the attacking team's rhythm.

Goals are quite common in handball; normally both teams score at least 20 goals each, and it is not uncommon to have a match end 33-31. This was not true in the earliest history of the game, when the scores were more akin to that of ice hockey. But, as offensive play has improved, particularly the use of counterattacks (fast breaks) after a failed attack from the other team, goal scoring has increased.

The authorized adult size ball is essentially a size 3 football ball for men and a size 2 ball for women, with the idea being that players be able to manipulate the ball with a single hand (though contact with both hands is permitted, except while dribbling). The ball is moved all over by passing, running and dribbling, similar to basketball. A player may only hold the ball for three seconds and may only take three steps with the ball in hand (as in basketball, pivoting counts as steps taken) before he is required to pass, shoot or make a dribble. At any time taking more than three steps is believed moving and results in a turnover. A player may dribble as many times as he wants (though since passing is faster it is the preferred method of attack) as long as during each dribble his hand contacts only the top of the ball. Hence basketball-style carrying is completely prohibited, and results in a turnover. After the dribble is picked up, the player has the right to another three seconds or three steps. The ball must then be passed or shot as further holding or dribbling will result in a "double dribble" turnover and a free throw for the other team. Other offensive infractions that result in a turnover comprise, charging, setting an illegal screen, or carrying the ball into the six meter zone.

Goal throw

Free throw—direction

Referee throw

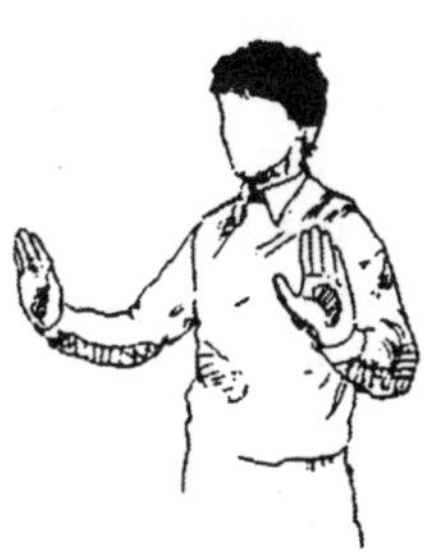
Keep the distance of 3 meters

Warning (yellow) Disqualification (red)

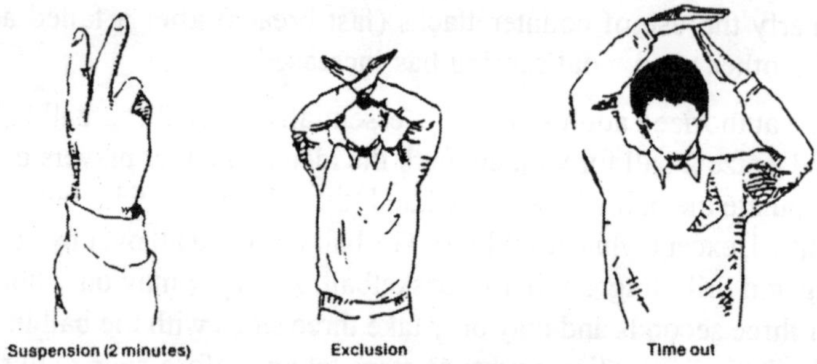

Fig. Referee Signals

Penalties

Penalties are given to players, in progressive layout, for fouls that require more punishment than just a free-throw. "Actions" directed primarilyprimarily at the antagonist and not the ball (such as reaching all over, holding, forcing, hitting, tripping, or jumping into antagonist) as well as contact from the side or from behind a player are all believed illegal and subject to penalty. Any infraction that prevents a clear scoring chance will result in a seven-meter penalty shot.

Normally the referee will give a warning yellow card for an illegal action, but if the contact was in particular dangerous the referee can forego the warning for an immediate two-minute suspension. A player can only get two warnings before obtaining a two minute suspension. One player is only allowed three 2-minute suspensions; after that he/she will be shown the red card.

A red card results in an ejection from the game and a two minute penalty for the team. A player may obtain a red card directly for particularly rough penalties. For instance any contact from behind throughout a fast break is now being treated with a red card. A red carded player has to leave the playing area completely. A player who is disqualified may be substituted with another player after the two minute penalty is served. A Coach/Authorized can also be penalized progressively. Any coach/ authorized who receives a 2-minute suspension will have to pull out one of his players for two minutes - note: the player is not the one punished and can be substituted in once again, because the main penalty is the team playing with a man less than the other.

If a player attacks an umpire, an opponent or any other person, the referee can expel the player forming a cross over his head with his arms, which will tell the player that he/she will have to leave the game wholly and his team will have to play a man down for the remainder of the game. This expulsion is the most severe penalty possible in handball.

After having lost the ball throughout an attack, the ball has to be laid down rapidly or else the player not following this rule will face a 2-minute suspension. Also gesticulating or verbally questioning the referee's order, as well as arguing with the officials decisions, will normally result in a 2-minute suspension. If it is done in a very provocative way, a player can be given a second 2-minute suspension if he/she does not walk straight off the field to the bench after being given a suspension, or if the referee deems the tempo intentionally slow. Illegal substitution, any substitution that does not take place in the specified substitution area or where the entering player enters before the exiting player exits is also punishable with a 2 minute suspension.

MAJOR TOURNAMENTS

Olympics

Team Handball was brought in as an Olympic game for men at the 1936 Summer Olympics, in Berlin, but neglected after that, only to be resumed at the 1972 Summer Olympics, once again on German territory. Women's team handball competition was brought in at the 1976 Summer Olympics.

World Men's Handball Championship

The World Championship in team handball for men has been coordinated by the International Handball Federation since 1938.

In 1938, the first indoor handball world championship was played in the Deutschlandhalle in Berlin,Germany on 5 February and 6 February. This first Tournament was deemed with only four taking part teams and played as a Single-Group-Tournament without a knockout-system. Germany turned the champion by defeating each of its Opponents, one of which was Austria which would become a part of Germany only a month later. The other competitors were Sweden and Denmark, which sent the club team of Ajax Kobenhavn to the championship. Indoor handball was spread only in Scandinavia at this point in time and there had only been one single authorized international match played indoor before the Championship. In Germany, where the Tournament was held, the indoor game was practically unknown to this point. Nevertheless the Deutschlandhalle was attended by 18,000 spectators in the two days, who were reportedly very pleased by the fast and exciting example of handball. The first World Championship can be said to have been an obscure spectaculum for pure entertaining purposes. Matches lasted only 20 minutes (10 per half-time) and the players were recruited from field handball teams which sought an chance to execute their game throughout winter. A first field handball WC was deemed in July of the similar year in Berlin and other german cities, which was also won by Germany who were then olympic champions (in 1936) and dual world champions. Both WC tournaments were administered by the IAHF (International Amateur Handball Federation), the forerunner organisation of 1946 established IHF, which was established in 1928, and meant to be celebrational events for the 10th "birthday" of the Organisation.

In 1946, at the initiative and invitation of Denmark and Sweden, France, the Netherlands, Norway, Poland, Sweden and Switzerland established the International Handball Federation (IHF). The IHF's authorized birthday is 11 July.

Five months after the IHF was established, the first authorized international match was played under its aegis, with Sweden defeating Denmark 9-7 in Gothenburg on 6 November 1946. In those days, the classic eleven-a-side outdoor game of field handball, so dear to the central Europeans, and the still-up-and-coming game of seven-a-side handball, played indoors on a small court the form preferred in Scandinavia, were evenly famous. Both disciplines had their fans: in 1955, 50,000 spectators watched the final of the field handball World Championships among Germany and Switzerland (25-13) in Berlin, but the indoor final among Sweden and Czechoslovakia in East Berlin in 1958, which ended 22-12, was also played in a packed hall in front of 6,500 spectators. The dominating nations at that time were Sweden, Czechoslovakia, Germany, and Denmark.

European Men's Handball Championship

The European men's handball championship is the authorized competition for senior men's national handball teams of Europe, and takes place every two years. In addition to crowning the European champions, the tournament also serves as a qualifying tournament for the World Championship. Sweden have won four of the eight championships that have been deemed since 1994, while Spain have been runners-up three times.

In 1946, the International Handball Federation was established by eight European nations,and though non-European nations contended at the World Championships, the medals had always been taken by European nations until the establishmentof the European Handball Federation in 1991.At the similar time (1995), the World Championship was altered from a quadrennial to a biannual event, and the European Handball Federation now started its own championship – which also acted as a regional qualifier for the World Championship.

The first championship was deemed in Portugal in June 1994.The host nation that had not managed to qualify for any World Championship thus far, and they completed 12th and last after losing all six games, as well as 21–38 to Romania in the 11th-place play-off. Sweden turned the first European champion after defeating Russia by 34–21 in the final, Russia's heaviest loss in their international history.Both teams had gone through the tournament without loss, but Sweden's fast breaks turned the key in the final; they scored 14 of their 34 goals on fast breaks. Russian winger Valeri Gopin scored 50 goals and was top scorer.

Norway was the host country for the 2008 tournament. Matches were played in Bergen, Drammen, Lillehammer, Stavanger and Trondheim. Croatia, Norway, Hungary and France won their beginninggroups, but two of the teams failed to utilise their advantage; Norway drew with Poland and lost to Slovenia, and required to beat Croatia in the final match of the group stage. Instead, Ivano Balic scored the 23–22 goal with twenty seconds to spare, and only a late equaliser gave Norway third position in the group. Hungary, Spain and Germany had all gone through with two points from Group C, and Germany sealed their qualification with a two-goal win over Sweden in a match where a draw would have been enough for the Swedes.In the first semifinal Croatia played France in a game prevailed by strong defense by both teams, with the Croats winning a three-goal lead twice, only to see France come back strong. Croatia goalkeeper Mirko Alilovic saved a shot from Nikola Karabatic with six seconds to go as Croatia won 24–23. Denmark came back from 7–12 down to beat Germany, in spite of the Germans equalising with in the final minute, as Lars Christiansen slotted home a penalty shot with three seconds left over. Croatia began off well in the final, scoring the first four goals, but with eight saves more from Denmark's keeper, Kasper Hvidt, Denmark won 24–20 and took their first main trophy.

ADMINISTRATIVE BODIES

European Handball Federation

The European Handball Federation (EHF) is the umbrella organisation for 49 member federations and one linked member (Kosovo) – stretching to all corners of the European continent – with its headquarters in Vienna, Austria. Since its establishmentin November 1991, the EHF has taken on the role of ambassador to European handball, acting as a common voice for the European member federations and representing the entire European Handball Family on the international sporting stage.

Commencing with the very conception of the European Handball Federation, the body structure of the EHF has altered in line with its dynamic business philosophy and new and changing trends inside the spheres of European handball. This change has brought with it new initiatives and indeed new challenges.

The EHF focuses its intensities and invests its resources on the growth of the game of handball generally with the overall objective to optimize product placement on the competitive sporting market, delivering the delights of handball in the form of high-profile branded events.

The European Handball Federation – is the accelerator behind the growths in handball on the European stage. Handball is a one of the quickest and most technical team sports in the world – with high-powered, dynamic, exciting, intense and passionate play. The athletes are the protagonists of the game and are highly-disciplined, polished and shaped to perfection through complex training programmes which encompass the latest enterprises from the fields of game science, nutrition and medicine and high standard equipment.

Handball has long since recognised a firm position on the European sporting market and is a game enjoyed by many all over Europe, both live in the arena and on television, radio and ever progressively on the web. The sheer nature of this team sport tries for mutual support and tactical, target-driven, strategic planning – an complex partnership of all members of the European Handball Family.

On 17th November 2006, the European Handball Federation (EHF) celebrated it 15 Year Anniversary. Over 15 years ago, the idea of a continental federation, helping the European Handball Family was just a sight, 15 years on and the vision has turn a reality, with the EHF taking on the role of ambassador to the game of handball in Europe, acting as a common voice for the, now, 49 Member Federations and constituting the European Handball Family on an international stage, as well as clubs, players, referees, delegates and many more.

The headquarters of the EHF are in Vienna, Austria and have been since the Foundation Congress, which was held in 1991 in Berlin. The

EHF has formulated substantially since the initial 29 countries turned signatory to the European Handball Charter of Partnership. At all times, the European governing body tries to serve the game, innovate and develop handball. The EHF faces adversity in many areas, the sporting market is endlessly changing, the political map has orginated substantially, challenges are overcome, achievements are celebrated, yet the overall goal never disappears from view.

The EHF has a duty to guarantee the growth of the game in all areas and puts it name to a wide-spectrum of activities inside its compendium, varingfrom its top products at the apex of the scale, namely the Men's and Women's European Handball Championships and the EHF Champions League - which extend to break TV and media records, to growth initiatives such as Beach Handball, Handball at School and Wheelchair Handball.

The Men's and Women's European Championships have been held out a total of 15 times (including 2008 Men's European Handball Championship), in host countries all over Europe. Sixteen of the greatest national teams in the world take part in each of these events and they extend to reach new heights. In recent times published figures show a continuous upwards spiral, with a accumulative audience in the 2008 men's event of over 1 billion views and more than 1000 hours of programming. A significant part of EHF business revolves all over the further growth of the game itself and handball inside the European Handball Family. Events and projects of 2006, which proved to be accelerators for this growth, admitted the EHF Youth Handball Convention, a variety of referee and delegate courses, coaches' course and, for example, the EHF Foster Project, where the "big brothers" of the European handball world guide and give a helping hand to developing handball nations.

Professional handball management has turn a business like any other. From the establishmentof the EHF, the organization has rated huge importance on its open and pro-active communication strategy and the swap of information. The EHF is the voice of Europe on handball matters and is in permanent reference with all its partners. Each year, many meetings, workshops, conferences, congresses and events take place to assure that this communication process falls into position and that the key link among all handball protagonists from all fields of the game is reinforced even further.

The EHF never loses sight of handball's exceptional passion and speed and tries to utilize these characteristics as the underlining statement in the growth of the game.

Pan-American Team Handball Federation

The Pan-American Team Handball Federation, often denoted to by the acronym PATHF, is the administrative and operating body the national handball associations of North, Central and South America and Caribbean.

FAMOUS HANDBALL PLAYER

Nadine Krause

Nadine Krause (born 25 March 1982 in Waiblingen) is a German handball player. She made her debut on the German A-Team in 1999, 17 years old. She was top scorer at the 2005 World Championships, and was voted IHF World Player of the Year 2006.

Ivano Balic

Ivano Balic is a Croatian handballer. He is believed to be the topmost handball player in the world and was voted 6 times in a row most important player in major international competitions. Also he is believed to be one of the topmost handball players of all time.

Before playing handball Balic coached with the basketball club KK Split. He started his handball career with RK Split. Balic was a member of the Croatian national team that won the 2003 World Men's Handball Championship in Portugal. He won a gold medal at the 2004 Summer Olympics and silver at the 2005 World Championship in Tunisia.

Balic was acknowledged the IHF World Player of the Year in 2003 and 2006 as well as the topmost player in Croatia 2003. After playing for RK Metkovic he moved to Portland San Antonio. At the 2006 European Championship in Switzerland he was declared the tournament MVP. Even though Croatia won the 5th position on the European Men's Handball Championship 2007 in Germany, he was declared the tournament's MVP. In the 2008 European Men's Handball Championship he was the equal top scorer with 44 goals as he led Croatia to a silver medal and was also voted to be in the All-Star Team for the tournament.

Arpad Sterbik

Arpad Sterbik (born November 22, 1979 in Senta, SAP Vojvodina) is a Spanish (as of 2008) handball player of Serbian/Hungarian origin, presently playing for the Spanish club BM Ciudad Real. He received bronze medals at the 1999 World Championships with the National team of Serbia-Montenegro, and again at the 2001 World Championships. He is Spanish citizen from 2008. Arpad Sterbik was voted World Player of the Year 2005 by the International Handball Federation.

REFERENCES

Alter, S.: *Science of Flexibility*, 2nd edn, Human Kinetics, Champaign, IL, 1996.

Alter, S.: *Sport Stretch*, Human Kinetics, Champaign, IL, 1998.

Dintiman, G. and Ward, R.:*Sport Speed*, Leisure Press, Champaign, IL, 1988.

Ellison, D.: *Performance Stretching*, Human Kinetics, Champaign, IL, 1999.

Goldberg, B. (ed.): *Sports and Exercise for Children with Chronic Health Conditions*, Human Kinetics, Champaign, IL, 1995

Newsholme, E., Leech, T. and Duester, G.: *Keep on Running*, John Wiley & Sons, Chichester, UK, 1994

Reaburn, P. and Jenkins, D.: *Training for Speed and Endurance*, Allen & Unwin, Sydney, 1996

Rowland, T.W.: *Developmental Exercise Physiology*, Human Kinetics, Champaign, IL, 1996

Sports weekly Magazine

Sports Illustrated Magazine

10

Ice Hockey

Ice hockey, often named simply as hockey, is a team sport played on ice. It is a fast paced and physical game. Ice hockey is most famous in areas that are sufficiently cold for natural, dependable seasonal ice cover, though with the advent of indoor artificial ice rinks it has become a year-round pastime at the amateur level in main metropolitan areas such as cities that host a National Hockey League (NHL) or other professional-league team. It is one of the four main North American professional sports, and is presented by the National Hockey League (NHL) at the highest level, and the National Women's Hockey League (NWHL), the highest level of women's ice hockey in the world. It is the authorized national winter sport of Canada, where the game enjoys immense popularity. Only six of the thirty NHL franchises are established in Canada, but Canadian players outnumber Americans in the league.

Although there are 66 total members of the International Ice Hockey Federation (IIHF), Canada, the Czech Republic, Finland, Russia, Slovakia,

Sweden and the United States have completed in most of the coveted 1st, 2nd and 3rd positions at IIHF World Championships. Of the 63 medals granted in men's contest at the Olympic level from 1920 on, only six did not go to the one of those countries, or a former entity thereof, such as Czechoslovakia or the Soviet Union. Only one of those six medals was above bronze. Those seven nations have also acquired 162 of 177 medals granted at 59 non-Olympic IIHF World Championships, and all medals since 1954.Similarly, all nine Olympic and 27 IIHF World Women Championships medals have gone to one of those seven countries.

HISTORY

Games among teams hitting an object with curved sticks have been played during history; 4000 year-old drawings at the huge tombs in Egypt depict a game resembling field hockey.The 1366 Statutes of Kilkenny in Ireland mentions "the plays which men call horlings, with great sticks and a ball upon the ground, from which great evils and maims have arisen", which was forbidden so that men would be fit and able to oppose the land.The 1527 Galway Statutes, also in Ireland, made reference to "the horlinge of the litill balle with hockie stickes or staves." The history of the word hockey is incertain. It may derive from the Old French word hoquet, shepherd's crook, or from the Middle Dutch word hokkie, meaning shack or doghouse, which in famous use meant goal. Many of these games were formulated for fields, though where conditions permitted they were also played on ice. Seventeenth century Dutch paintings show townsfolk playing a hockey-like game on a frozen canal.

European immigrants brought various interpretations of hockey-like games to North America, such as the Irish game of hurling, the closely-related Scottish game of shinty, and versions of field hockey played in England. Where necessary these seem to have been adjusted for icy circumstances; for example, a colonial Williamsburg newspaper records hockey being played in a snow storm in Virginia. Early paintings show "shinney", an early form of hockey with no standard rules, being played in Nova Scotia. Author Thomas Chandler Haliburton wrote in a book of fiction, about boys from King's College School in Windsor, Nova Scotia, playing "hurley on the ice" when he was a student there all over 1800 (Haliburton was born in 1796).To this day, "Shinny" (derived from Shinty) is a famous Canadian term for an informal type of hockey, either on ice or as street hockey. These former games may have also engaged the physically aggressive aspects of what the Mi'kmaq Aboriginal First Nation in Nova Scotia called dehuntshigwa'es (lacrosse).

In 1825 Sir John Franklin penned that "The game of hockey played on the ice was the morning sport" while on Great Bear Lake throughout one of his Arctic expeditions. In 1843 a British Army officer in Kingston, Ontario, wrote "Began to skate this year, improved rapidly and had great fun at hockey on the ice."A Boston Evening Gazette article from 1859 makes extension to an early game of hockey on ice taking place in Halifax in that year.

The first commemorated hockey games were played by British soldiers stationed in Kingston and Halifax throughout the mid 1850s. In the early 1870s, the first known set of ice hockey rules was drawn up by students at Montreal's McGill University. These rules recognised the number of players per side to 9 and substituted the ball with a square puck.

Established on Haliburton's writings, there have been claims that modern ice hockey developed in Windsor, Nova Scotia, and was named after an individual, as in 'Colonel Hockey's game'. Proponents of this theory claim that the surname Hockey exists in the district surrounding Windsor. In 1943, the Canadian Amateur Hockey Association declared Kingston the place of origin of hockey, established on a commemorated 1886 game played among students of Queen's University and the Royal Military College of Canada.

The Society for International Hockey Research has had an "origins of hockey" committee examining this debate since 2001 and they outlined hockey as: "a game played on an ice rink in which two contradicting teams of skaters, utilizing curved sticks, try to drive a small disc, ball or block into or through the opposite goals."

The committee found manifest of stick and ball games played on ice on skates in Europe in the sixteenth through eighteenth centuries, and viewed these actions as being more declarative of a hockey-like game than Halliburton's reference.

They found no prove in the Windsor position of a association from whatever form of hockey might have been played at Long Pond to the game played elsewhere and to modern hockey. The committee viewed as conjecture the affirmation that King's schoolboys brought in the game to Halifax. They noted that the assertion that hockey was not played outside Nova Scotia until 1865 overlooks diary manifest of shinny and hockey being played at Kingston in the 1840s.

The committee resolved that Dr. Vaughan and the Windsor Hockey Heritage Society had not offered credible prove that Windsor, Nova Scotia, is the place of origin of hockey.

The committee proposed no opinion on the birth date or place of origin of hockey, but took note of a game at Montreal's Victoria Skating Rink on March 3, 1875. This is the earliest eyewitness account known to the committee of a particular game of hockey in a particular position at a particular time, and with a commemorated score, among two identified teams.

As per the Society for International Hockey Research, the word puck is deduced from the Scottish and Gaelic word "puc" or the Irish word "poc", meaning to poke, punch or deliver a blow. This definition is explained in a book published in 1910 entitled "English as we Speak it in Ireland" by P.W. Joyce. It defines the word puck as "The blow given by a hurler to the ball with his caman or hurley is always called a puck".

The establishmentof the modern game centres on Montreal. On March 3, 1875 the first organized indoor game was played at Montreal's Victoria Skating Rink by James George Aylwin Creighton and various McGill University students. In 1877, various McGill students, as well as Creighton, Henry Joseph, Richard F. Smith, W.F. Robertson, and W.L. Murray codified seven ice hockey rules. The first ice hockey club, McGill University Hockey Club, was established in 1877succeeded by the Montreal Victorias, organized in 1881.T

he game turned so famous that the first "world championship" of ice hockey was featured in Montreal's annual Winter Carnival in 1883 and the McGill team captured the "Carnival Cup".In 1886, the teams which contended at the Winter Carnival would organize the Amateur Hockey Association of Canada(AHAC) league.

In Europe, it is conceived that in 1885 the Oxford University Ice Hockey Club was established to play the first Ice Hockey Varsity Match in opposition to traditional rival Cambridge in St. Moritz, Switzerland, even though this is undocumented. This match was won by the Oxford Dark Blues, 6-0.The first photographs and team lists date from 1895. This continues to be the most former hockey rivalry in history.

In 1888, the new Governor General of Canada, Lord Stanley of Preston, whose sons and daughter turned hockey enthusiasts, attended the Montreal Winter Carnival tournament and was impressed with the hockey spectacle. In 1892, recognizing that there was no recognition for the greatest team in all of Canada, (various leagues had championship trophies) he purchased a decorative bowl for use as a trophy. The Dominion Hockey Challenge Cup, which later turned more awesomely known as the Stanley Cup, was first granted in 1893 to the Montreal HC, champions of the AHAC. It continues to be granted at present to the National Hockey League's championship team.

By 1893, there were nearly a hundred teams in Montreal alone, and leagues all around Canada. Winnipeg hockey players had incorporated cricket pads to better protect the goaltender's legs. They also brought in the "scoop" shot, later called as the wrist shot.

1893 also saw the first ice hockey matches in the U.S., at Yale University and Johns Hopkins University. The U.S. Amateur Hockey League was established in New York City in 1896, and the first professional team, the Portage Lake hockey club was established in 1903 in Houghton, Michigan (even though there had been individual professionals in Canada before this).

The five sons of Lord Stanley were implemental in bringing ice hockey to Europe, defeating a court team (which admitted both the future Edward VII and George V) at Buckingham Palace in 1895. By 1903 a five-team league had been established. The Ligue Internationale de Hockey sur Glace was established in 1908 to rule international competitions, and the first European championships were won by Great Britain in 1910. In the mid-twentieth century, the Ligue turned the International Ice Hockey Federation.

THE GAME

While the general features of the game are the similar wherever it is played, the exact rules depend on the peculiar code of play being used. The two most significant codes are those of the International Ice Hockey Federation (IIHF) and of the North American National Hockey League (NHL).

Ice hockey is played on a hockey rink. Throughout normal play, there are six players, as well as one goaltender, per side on the ice at any time, each of whom is on ice skates. The aim of the game is to score goals by shooting a hard vulcanized rubber disc, the puck, into the opponent's goal net, which is rated at the opposite end of the rink. The players may assure the puck utilizing a long stick with a blade that is normally curved at one end.

Players may also redirect the puck with any part of their bodies, subject to specificlimitations. Players can angle their feet so the puck can redirect into the net, but there can be no kicking motion. Players may not deliberately bat the puck into the net with their hands.

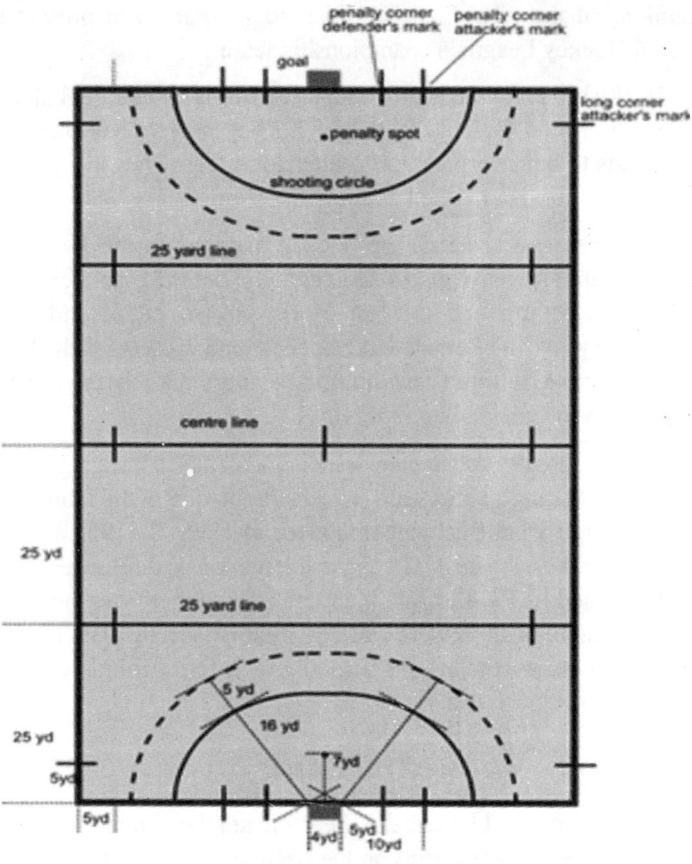

Fig. Field

Hockey is an "offside" game, entailing that forward passes are permitted, unlike in rugby. Before the 1930s hockey was an onside game, meaning that only backward passes were permitted. The period of the onside game was the golden age of stick-handling, which was of prime significance in moving the game forward. With the arrival of offside rules, the forward pass transmuted hockey into a truly team sport, where individual heroics diminished in importance relative to team play, which could now be co-ordinated over the entire surface of the ice as contradicted to merely rearward players.

The five players other than the goaltender are normally divided into three forwards and two defencemen. The forward positions consist of a centre and two wingers: a left wing and a right wing. Forwards often play together as units or lines, with the similar three forwards always playing together. The defencemen normally stick together as a pair, but may change less often than the forwards. A substitution of an entire unit at once is called a line change. Teams normally employ alternate sets of forward lines and defensive couplings when shorthanded or on a power play.

Substitutions are permitted at any time throughout the course of the game, even though during a stoppage of play the home team is permitted the final change. When players are replaced during play, it is called altering on the fly. A new NHL rule added in the 2005-2006 season prevents a team from altering their line after they ice the puck.

The boards surrounding the ice help keep the puck in play and they can also be used as tools to play the puck. The referees, linesmen and the exteriors of the goal are "in play" and do not cause a stoppage of the game when the puck or players are determined (by either bouncing or colliding) into them. Play can be stopped if the goal is knocked out of position. Play often goes for minutes without interruption. When play is stopped, it is restarted with a faceoff. Two players "face" each other and an official drops the puck to the ice, where the two players seek to gain control of the puck.

There are three main rules of play in ice hockey that limit the movement of the puck: offsides, icing, and the puck going out of play. The puck goes "out of play" when it goes past the perimeter of the ice rink (onto the player benches, over the "glass", or onto the protective netting above the glass) and a stoppage of play should be called by the officials. It also does not matter if the puck comes back onto to the ice surface from those areas as the puck is believed dead once it leaves the perimeter of the rink.

Under IIHF rules, each team may persuade a maximum of 20 players and two goaltenders on their roster. NHL rules limit the total number of players per game to 18 plus two goaltenders.

Equipments

Two things that are universal, non-protective equipment are the hockey puck and the hockey sweater. On top of the defensive gear, players wear a jersey or sweater which displays the team's logo or crest and colors, as well as the player's name and number. Players also put on thick wool or polyester socks that match the jersey colors and have no "foot" (as the material would cause the player's foot to move in the skate, decreasing stability). They are used to cover the kneepads and supply some lower-body insulation as many kneepads have little or no backing.

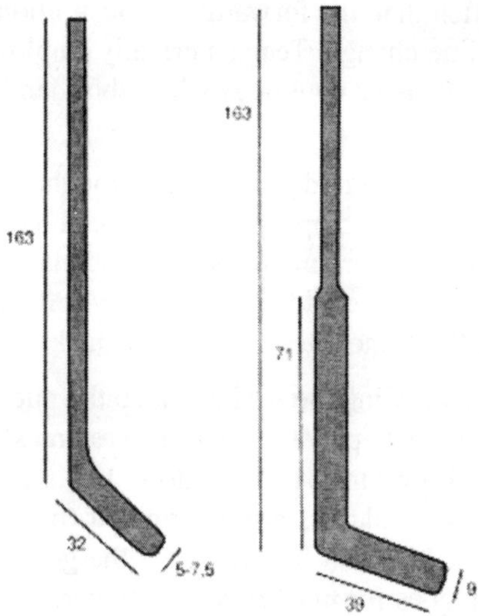

Fig. Stick

- Helmet Combo — compiled of a helmet with strap, and optionally a face cage or visor
- Neck Guard — helps escape injury from skates, sticks and pucks to the neck and throat. It is normally optional as it limits neck movement.
- Shoulder Pads — also admits torso and spine protection from flying pucks and most collisions.
- Elbow Pads — provides forearm and tricep safety in opposition to pucks in addition to a reinforced elbow cup.
- Hockey Gloves — protects the hands; player's gloves are built with a very thin palm and fingers while providing considerably more padding to the outside of the hands; also rewards the thumb to prevent it turning backwards.
- Hockey Pants — incorporates thigh, pelvic, hip and tailbone pads
- Shin Guards — incorporating a kneepad as well, the shin guard has a hard shell in front to protect in opposition to pucks, but normally has little or no safety on the calf.
- Mouthguard — many versions subsists from standard plastic guards to custom-moldable compounds that make speaking easier.
- Ice skates — comprise a rigid shell, often reinforced with metal mesh to precludea skate blade cutting through. Unlike figure

skates, hockey skates have a rounded heel and no toe picks as these can be severe in a "pile-up".

- Hockey Stick — Made of wood or composite materials.

Goalies are permitted special variations on equipment, both to increase their chance of stopping pucks and for extra safety. They offer more safety from frontal impacts, while in general providing little or no safety to the goalie's back. This is because a goalie should always face the action and a hit on a non-padded area is in general a mistake on the part of the goalie.

- Goal stick — comprises a larger blade than player sticks as well as a extended flat shaft. Mostly used to block but the goalie can play the puck with it.
- Goal skates — thicker blade with a larger blade radius and less ankle affirm allows a goalie to slide off his skates to make "pad stops" more easily.
- Goalie mask or helmet and wire facemask — Masks are equipped to the player's face and can withstand multiple high-speed impacts from pucks. Most leagues as well as the NHL now require goalies to hang a throat protector and/or wear a neck pad to protect in opposition to pucks and skate blades.
- Chest and arm protector — more profusely padded in the front than a player's shoulder pads, also incorporating forearm, elbow and bicep safety.
- Blocker — worn on the hand that holds the stick. It is a glove with a square pad on the back, used to forfend shots.
- Catch glove — worn on the opposite hand, used to pick up the puck on the ice or catch a flying shot.
- Goal jock or jill — better pelvic safety and more padding in front of the cup than a player's jock.
- Goal pants — incorporating thicker thigh padding and additional pelvic/hip safety, but reduced groin safety (this is mitigated by the jock and allows for increased flexibility)
- Goal pads — thickly padded leg pads screening the top of the skate, the player's shin and the knees. Pads are 11' or 12" broad (recent NHL rule alterations reduced the width of the pads) and sized to fit the individual player's legs. Most shots are blocked by some method of "pad stop".

- Socks — covering the leg from the foot to just above the knee or above. Normally this is the only safety afforded to a goalie's calves, as the back of the goal pads are simply a series of straps.

Normally the stick has a left-hand curve, is deemed in the right hand with the blocker, and the catch is on the left. Nevertheless, "full right" goalies reverse this, holding a right-hand curve stick in the left hand and catching with the right. This is largely personal predilection, depending largely on which hand the goalie is most comfortable catching with

Penalties

Altercations often occur near the goal after a stoppage of play, since defensive players are exceptionally concerned with protecting their goaltender. All rulebooks call for penalties if an offensive player intervenes with a goaltender's capability to oppose the goal.

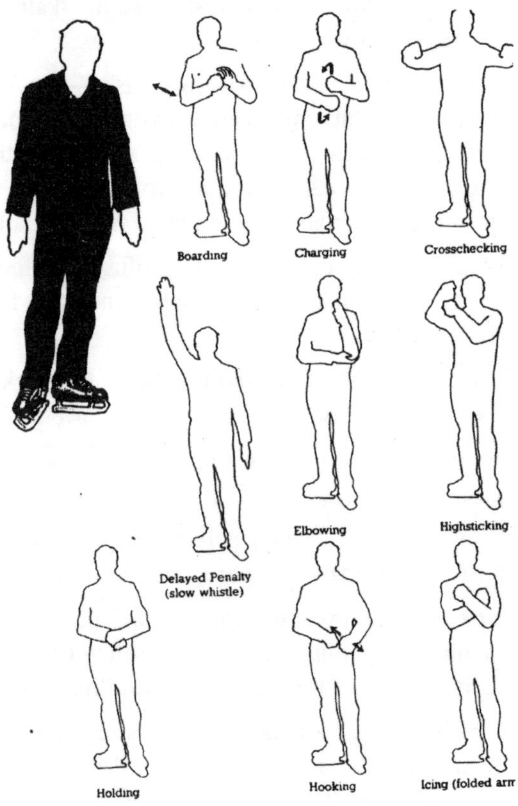

Fig. Referee Signals

With most penalties, the offending player is sent to the penalty box and his team has to play without him and with one less skater for a short amount of time. Most penalties last for two minutes unless a main penalty has been measured. The team that has taken the penalty is said to be playing shorthanded while the other team is on the power play.

A two-minute minor penalty is often demanded lesser violations such as tripping, elbowing, roughing, high-sticking, too many players on the ice, illegal equipment, charging (leaping into an opponent or body-checking him after taking more than two strides), holding, encumbrance, delay of game, hooking, or cross-checking. In the 2005-06 NHL season, a minor is also assessed for diving, where a player embellishes a hook or trip. More egregious fouls of this type may be penalized by a four-minute double-minor penalty, in particular those which (inadvertently) cause injury to the victimized player. These penalties end either when the time runs out or the other team scores on the power play. In the case of a goal scored throughout the first two minutes of a double-minor, the penalty clock is set down to two minutes upon a score (effectively expiring the first minor). Five-minute main penalties are called for especially violent illustrations of most minor infractions that result in intentional injury to an opponent, as well as for fighting. Main penalties are always served in full; they do not terminate on a goal scored by the other team. The foul of 'boarding', defined as "checking an opponent in such a manner that causes the opponent to be thrown violently in the boards" by the NHL Rulebook is penalized either by a minor or main penalty at the discretion of the referee, established on the violence of the hit. A minor or main penalty for "Boarding" is also often assessed when a player checks an opponent from behind and into the boards.

Some varieties of penalties do not always demand the offending team to play a man short. Five-minute main penalties in the NHL normally result from fighting. In the case of two players being assessed five-minute fighting mains, they both serve five minutes without their team incurring a loss of player (both teams still have a full complement of players on the ice). This differs with two players from opposing sides getting minor penalties, at the similar time or at any intersecting moment, leading from more common infractions. In that case, both teams will have only four skating players (not counting the goaltender) until one or both penalties expire (if one expires before the other, the opposing team gets a power play for the remainder); this applies regardless of existing pending penalties, though in the NHL, a team always has at least three skaters on the ice. Ten-minute misconduct penalties are served in full by the penalized player, but his team may immediately substitute another player on the ice unless a minor or main penalty is measured in conjunction with the misconduct (a two-and-ten or five-and-ten). In that case, the team designates another player to serve the minor or main; both players go to the penalty box, but only the designee may not be substituted, and he is released upon the expiration of the two or five minutes, at which point the ten-minute misconduct begins. In addition, game misconducts are assessed for deliberate intent to inflict severe injury on an opponent (at the officials' discretion), or for a main penalty for a stick infraction or repeated main penalties. The offending player is ejected from the game and must immediately leave the playing surface (he does not sit in the penalty box); in the meantime, if a minor or main is assessed in addition, a designated player must serve out that segment of the penalty in the box (similar to the above-mentioned "two-and-ten").

A player who is stumbled, or illegally obstructed in some way, by an opposer on a breakaway – when there are no defenders except the goaltender among him and the opponent's goal – is granted a penalty shot, an attempt to score without opposition from any defenders except the goaltender. A penalty shot is also granted for a defender other than the goaltender covering the puck in the goal crease, a goaltender intentionally displacing his own goal posts throughout a breakaway in order to avoid a goal, a defender intentionally displacing his own goal posts when there is less than two minutes to play in regulation time or at any point throughout overtime, or a player or coach intentionally throwing a stick or other object at the puck or the puck carrier and the throwing action interrupts a shot or pass play.

Officials also stop play for puck movement violations, such as utilizing one's hands to pass the puck in the offensive end, but no players are penalized for these offences. The sole exceptions are intentionally falling on or gathering the puck to the body, holding the puck in the hand, and shooting the puck out of play in one's defensive zone (all penalized two minutes for delay of game).

A new penalty in the NHL enforces to the goalies. The goalies now are not able to play the puck in the "corners" of the rink near their own net. This will result in a two-minute penalty in opposition to the goalie's team. The area instantly behind the net is the only area behind the net in which the goalie can play the puck.An extra rule that is not a penalty in the new NHL is the two line offside passes. There are no more two-line offside pass whistles blown. Now players are capable to pass to teammates who are more than the blue and centre ice red line away.

The NHL has taken on steps to speed the game of hockey up and create a game of finesse, by drawing back from the past where illegal hits, fights, and "clutching and grabbing" amongst players was commonplace. Rules are now much more strictly enforced leadingin more violations being penalized which in turn provides more safety to the players and allows for more goals to be scored.

There are many violations for which a player may be assessed a penalty. The governing body for United States amateur hockey has held outmany new rules to cut down the number stick-on-body occurrences, as well as other detrimental and illegal facets of the game ("Zero Tolerance").

In men's hockey, but not in women's, a player may utilize his hip or shoulder to hit some other player if the player has the puck or is the last to have touched it. This utilize of the hip and shoulder is called body checking. Not all physical contact is legal — particularly, hits from behind and most types of forceful stick-on-body contact are illegal.

Officials

A distinctive game of ice hockey has two to four officials on the ice, accused with imposing the rules of the game. There are normally two linesmen who are responsible only for calling offside and icing intrusions, and one or two referees, who call goals and all other penalties. Linesmen can, however, report to the referee(s) that a penalty more severe than a two-minute minor penalty should be assessed in opposition to an offending player, or when a too many men on the ice violation occur. On-ice officials are assisted by off-ice officials who act as goal judges, time keepers, and official scorers.

The highly wide-spread system in use at present is the 3-man system that chracterise one referee and two linesmen. With the first being the National Hockey League, a number of leagues have began to implement the 4-authorized system, where an extra referee is added to aid in the calling of penalties normally difficult to assess by one single referee. The system has proven quite fortunate in the NHL and the IIHF have adopted it for the World Championships, slightly discussed throughout the 2008 World Championships in Quebec City and Halifax, Canada. Many other leagues are adopting the system for the following season, which only downside at the moment is the increased cost for the leagues.

Officials are choosen by the league for which they work. Amateur hockey leagues utilize guidelines recognised by national organizing bodies as a basis for selecting their officiating staffs. In North America, the national organizing bodies Hockey Canada and USA Hockey approve officials as per their experience level as well as their capability to pass rules knowledge and skating capability tests. Hockey Canada has officiating levels I through VI. USA Hockey has officiating levels 1 through 4.

Tactics

An significant defensive tactic is checking – attempting to take the puck from an opponent or to remove the opponent from play. Fore checking is checking in the other team's zone; back checking is checking while the other team is advancing down the ice toward one's own goal. These terms normally are applied to checking by forwards. Stick checking, sweep checking, and poke checking are legal uses of the stick to recieve possession of the puck. Body checking is utilizing one's shoulder or hip to strike an opponent who has the puck or who is the last to have touched it (inside a short period of time after possession; normally less than three seconds). Often the term checking is used to denote to body checking, with its true definition in general only propagated amongst fans of the game.

Offensive tactics comprise improving a team's position on the ice by progressing the puck out of one's zone towards the opponent's zone, increasingly by gaining lines, first your own blue line, then the red line and finally the opponent's blue line. NHL rules instated for the 2006 season specified icing to make the two-line pass legal; a player may pass the puck from behind his own blue line, past both that blue line and the centre red line, to a player in front of the opponents' blue line. As a matter of fact, an errant pass that would usually result in an icing call is negated if the player for whom the pass was intended gains possession of the puck before it crosses the opponents' goal line; thus a "three-line pass" can be attempted with a fast forward as long as an offside is not committed. Offensive tactics are designed finally to score a goal by taking a shot. When a player deliberately directs the puck towards the opponent's goal, he or she is said to shoot the puck.

A deflection is a shot which redirects a shot or a pass towards the goal from another player, by permitting the puck to strike the stick and carom towards the goal. A one-timer is a shot which is struck straightaway off a pass, without obtaining the pass and shooting in two different actions. A deke (short for decoy) is a feint with the body and/or stick to fool a defender or the goalie. Headmanning the puck, also called as cherry-picking or breaking out, is the tactic of quickly passing to the player farthest down the ice.

A team that is turning a loss by one or two goals in the last few minutes of play will often elect to pull the goalie; that is, getting rid of the goaltender and substituting him or her with an extra attacker on the ice in the hope of earning enough advantage to score a goal. However, it is an act of desperation, as it sometimes leads to the opponents team extending their lead by scoring a goal in the empty net.

A delayed penalty call happens when a penalty offense is invested by the team that does not have possession of the puck. In this circumstance the team with possession of the puck is permitted to complete the play; that is, play continues until a goal is scored, the puck is shot, stopped and assured by the opposing goalie, a player on the opposing team gains control of the puck, or the team in possession perpetrates an infraction or penalty of their own. Because the team on which the penalty was called cannot control the puck without stopping play; it is not possible for them to score a goal; however, it is possible for assuring team to mishandle the puck into their own net. In these cases the team in possession of the puck can pull the goalie for an extra assaulter without fear of being scored on. If a detained penalty is signaled and the team in possession scores, the penalty is still measured to the offending player, but not served.

Even though it is officially disallowed in the rules, at the professional level in North America fights are sometimes used to affect morale of the teams, with aggressors hoping to demoralize the opposing players while exciting their own, as well as settling personal scores. Both players in an altercation obtain five-minute main penalties for fighting. The player held to be the "instigator" of an NHL fight, if one is decided to exist, is penalized an additional two minutes for instigating, plus a ten-minute misconduct penalty. If there is no instigator, both players stay in the penalty box for five minutes, and neither team loses skaters. They point to less extreme on-ice violence throughout the era before the rule was brought in. Toronto Maple Leafs owner Conn Smythe famously observed that "If you can't beat 'em in the alley you can't beat 'em on the ice."

Periods and Overtime

A game comprises of three periods of twenty minutes each, the clock running only when the puck is in play. The teams change ends for the second period, once again for the third period, and once again at the commence of each overtime played. Recreational leagues and children's leagues often play shorter games, in general with three shorter periods of play.

Various processes are used if a game is tied. In tournament play, as well as in the NHL playoffs, North Americans favour sudden death overtime, in which the teams keep on to play twenty minute periods until a goal is scored. Up until the 1999-2000 season regular season NHL games were settled with a single five minute sudden death period with five players (plus a goalie) per side, with the winner granted two points in the standings and the loser no points. In the case of a tie (if the overtime was scoreless), each team was granted one point.

From 1999-2000 until 2003-04 the National Hockey League decided ties by playing a single five minute sudden death overtime period with each team having four players (plus a goalie) per side to "open-up" the game. In the case of a tie, each team would still obtain one point in the standings but in the case of a victory the winning team would be granted two points in the standings and the losing team one point. The only exception to this rule is if a team opts to pull their goalie in exchange for an extra skater throughout overtime and is later scored upon (an 'Empty Net' goal), in which case the losing team receives no points for the overtime loss.

International play and various North American professional leagues, as well as the NHL (in the regular season), now utilize an overtime period succeeded by a penalty shootout. If the score remains tied after an extra overtime period, the later shootout consists of three players from each team taking penalty shots. After these six total shots, the team with the most goals is granted the victory. If the score is still tied, the shootout then proceeds to a sudden death layout. Regardless of the number of goals scored throughout the shootout by either team, the final score commemorated will grant the winning team one more goal than the score at the end of regulation time. In the NHL if a game is settled by a shootout the winning team is granted two points in the standings and the losing team is granted one point. Ties no longer occur in the NHL.

MAJOR TOURNAMENTS

Olympic Games

Ice hockey tournaments have been presented at the Olympic Games since the 1920 Summer Olympics. The game entered the Winter Olympic Games program for the first Winter Games in 1924. A women's ice hockey tournament was added to the Olympic program for the 1998 Winter Olympics.1920 and 1968, the Olympic hockey tournament was also believed the Ice Hockey World Championships for that year.

The ice hockey competition wasprimarily prevailed by teams from Canada, who won 6 of the first 7 tournaments. Canada's medal count tolerated in the decades to follow, which saw more and more top players drawn into professional hockey, excluding them from Olympic eligibility. The team withdrew entirely throughout the 1970s, and did not send a team to the 1972 or 1976 games. The team's fortunes improved by the 1998 Nagano games, when the National Hockey League started shutting down to permit its players to participate. Professionals had been permitted since 1988, but NHLers were otherwise committed. This also led to the improvement of teams such as Sweden and the USA, which also had large numbers of professional players.

The era without master players (ending by 1988) was prevailed by the Soviet Union, who used full-time hockey players who were given military titles to maintain a guise of amateurism. When the Soviet Union first participated in the Winter Olympics in 1956, they were instantly successful, and would win 7 gold medals in the nine appearances of the nation. As well as the successor teams of the Unified Team in 1992 and Russia since 1994, Soviet or ex-Soviet hockey teams have won 12 medals (8 gold) in 14 total appearances.

The women's tournament has been prevailed by teams from Canada and the United States, who normally would only ever lose to each other and hence, win gold and silver at every woman's hockey tournament. Sweden broke this trend with a surprise defeat of the United States in 2006 to claim the silver medal

Ice Hockey World Championships

The Ice Hockey World Championship is a yearly event organized by the International Ice Hockey Federation.They were preceded by the European Championship which was deemed from 1910 to 1932, and determined at the 1920 Summer Olympics for the first time. Subsequently ice hockey sported at the Winter Olympics, where the World Championship was decided when the two eventstook placeconcurrently. The last time the World Championship was decided throughout the Olympic Games was at the 1968 Winter Olympics.

The 73rd championship will be deemed from April 24 and May 10, 2009 Zurich and Berne, Switzerland.In the early days of the Championship, the teams from Canada prevailed. From 1930 and 1939, Canadian teams won the tournament eight times. Thistook placedespite the fact that Canada sent a dissimslar club team each year, as in those days Senior Amateur teams normally represented Canada.

World War II caused the Championship to be cancelled from 1940-46.Canadian teams extended to dominate the tournament in the early post-war era, but from 1954 onwards, the Championship turned progressively competitive, as the USSR joined them this year, and the teams from Czechoslovakia and Sweden bettered their skill level.

While the top European players were officially able to contend in the World Championship while holding back their amateur status, players in the National Hockey League and other North American minor professional leagues were forbidden for many years from entering in the tournament. As the great mainity of these players were Canadian nationals, this rule was seen by many as discriminatory in opposition to Canadian players.

Throughout this period the Soviet ice hockey team prevailed, winning almost all the World Championships. In 1970, the IIHF permitted Canada to send nine professionals from the ranks of the NHL and its affiliated minor leagues (though as the tournaments were deemed throughout the Stanley Cup playoffs, only a handful of them could actually contend). However, these rules were later rescinded after officials developed many reciprocal claims in opposition to them. It upset the Canadians, who felt that they should be permitted to send their greatest players as well. Canada boycotted the World Championship for seven years as a result, throughout which the IIHF moved the championships out of the Olympics in 1972 and 1976 in an attempt to resolve the issue.

In 1976, a new president of the IIHF finally permitted professionals on all teams, and Canada came back to competition the following year. By this time, the quality of play of European hockey had bettered so much that even Canadian rosters filled with NHL players whose teams had missed the playoffs could not prevail. Not until 1994, 33 years after its previous championship, would Canada win the tournament once again.

By the early 1990s the breakup of the Soviet Union, which prevailed the Championship for much of the three decades after Canada's supremacy ended, and of Czechoslovakia, which won in most of the years in which the Soviets did not, brought about extraordinary parity to the international game for two grounds:

Players in the former USSR and Czechoslovakia had the freedom to play in the NHL. Thus many European countries' greatest players were also contending in the NHL, and so unable to send their greatest to the Championship

The breakup of the USSR and Czechoslovakia meant that the left over core states, respectively Russia and the Czech Republic, had fewer talented players to draw from, even amongst those not playing in the NHL throughout the Championship.

The breakup of USSR and Czechoslovakia produced a challenge for the IIHF because new national teams like Belarus, Czech Republic, Kazakhstan, Latvia, Russia, Slovakia, and Ukraine wanted to take part in the Championship at the highest level of play, pool A. The IIHF ruled that Czech Republic and Russia would be allowed immediate entry to pool A, but the other new national teams would have to start at pool C. It turned clear that the new teams were or would soon be, better than many of the existing, but less elite, pool A teams. The Championship ran the risk of grounded countries from Western Europe, such as Austria, France, Germany, Italy, Norway, and Switzerland, being displaced from pool A by the new teams from Eastern Europe as they advanced from pool C. As the IIHF depended on advertising revenue derived from the recognised Western European countries, it decided to expand pool A to accommodate the existing pool A teams plus the new rising teams.

In recent championships, the two nations of the former Czechoslovakia have got along exceptionally well in international play, accounting for four straight championships from 1999-2002 – the first three by the Czech Republic and the latter by Slovakia. (The Czech side also won the 1998 Winter Olympic gold medal in Nagano, Japan). Canada has in recent times came back to prominence with an international trophy binge, fascinating the 2003, 2004, and 2007 World Championships as well as the 2002 Winter Olympic gold medal at Salt Lake City and the 2004 World Cup of Hockey.

The modern layout for the World Championship features a minimum of 40 teams: 16 teams in the main group, 12 teams in Division I and 12 teams in Division II. If there are more than 40 teams, the rest contend in Division III.The main group features 16 teams. In the Beginninground the 16 teams are split into 4 groups (Groups A through D) and the teams play each other in a round robin layout, and the top 3 teams in each division advance into the Qualifying round. The Qualifying round is another round of group play with 2 groups of 6; the top three teams from group A and group D are rated together and the top three teams from group B and group C are rated together. In the Qualifying round teams maintain their results from the Beginninground in opposition to other teams who have also advanced, and only play in opposition to teams which they have not before played in opposition to. The top four teams in each Qualifying round group advance into the knockout playoff stage. In the quarterfinals the first place team from one group plays the fourth position team from the other group, and the second position team from one group plays the third position team from the other group. The winners advance to the semi-finals. The winners of the semi-finals advance to the Gold medal game, and the losers advance to the Bronze medal game.

The bottom teams in the Beginninground play in another group as well; this group will decide relegation. After a round-robin layout, the bottom two teams are normally relegated to Division I. Japan was normally never relegated, as the IIHF deemed a "Far East Qualifier" with an automatic berth from 1998 to 2005 to develop the popularity of the game in the Far East. Japan had always won this tournament, but due to the lack of famous support in the Far East, little improvement in the quality of play, and poor prospects for any related marketing, the IIHF has discontinued the practice in the 2005 Championships, relegating Japan to contend in Division I.

Below the World Championship group are two 6-team Division I round robin groups, the winner of which is encouraged to the World Championship group, while each last position team is demoted to Division II. Division II works likewise to Division I, with two 6-team groups where each last position team is relegated to a Division III group. There is no relegation from Division III.

The IIHF consists of 5 tournaments. Championship tournament is the primary one and everything below that is attempting to get to the championship round. At the end of the tournaments the top 2 teams in each division (Except the Championship division) get promoted to the following highest division. The Bottom 2 Teams in each Division (Except Division III) get relegated to the following lowest division. The Bottom 1 in Division III gets booted out and has to Qualify for Division III.

ADMINISTRATIVE BODIES

English Ice Hockey Association

The English Ice Hockey Association has administered ice hockey in England since 1982. In that time the number of teams has risen from 60 to 298 (plus 19 elite teams). There are presently 33 affiliated clubs and this year there are over 8000 licensed players, officials and coaches.

The EIHA is presently handled by an Executive Committee comprising of Chairman - Ken Taggart, Secretary - Irene Jones, Treasurer Neville Moralee, Bob Wilkinson, Geoff Hemmerman, Rob Laidler and David Hurn. Malcolm Preen is the EIHA webmaster and Mohammed Ashraff is the IT manager.

International Ice Hockey Federation

The International Ice Hockey Federation (IIHF) was established in 1908 as the Ligue Internationale de Hockey sur Glace and is the universal governing body for ice hockey and in-line hockey. It is established in Zurich, Switzerland and has 66 members. It is responsible for the management of international ice hockey tournaments, and maintains the IIHF World Ranking.

In spite of its universal authority, the IIHF has little control of hockey in North America where the NHL is the most eminent hockey organization. Its base of power rests in Europe with the respective national governing bodies and leagues. Canada (Hockey Canada) and the United States (USA Hockey) are the only members who have their own rulebooks.Decisions of the IIHF can be invoked to the Court of Arbitration for Sport in Lausanne, Switzerland.

The IIHF museum was situated inside the International Hockey Hall of Fame Museum situated in Kingston, Ontario, Canada from 1992 to 1997. After terminating the partnership with the International Hockey Hall Of Fame, the IIHF signed an agreement with the NHL to house their museum inside the Hockey Hall of Fame. In 1998 the IIHF museum relocated to Toronto, Ontario, Canada occupying over 3,500 Sq. Ft. inside the Hockey Hall of Fame.

The IIHF maintains the IIHF Hall of Fame. It was established in 1997, with 30 initial members, and has had inductions yearly since then. The Hall of Fame includes players and builders.As part of the centennial celebrations of the IIHF's founding, the 2008 IIHF World Championship were granted to Canada, the place of origin of hockey, the first time the championships were hosted in Canada.

National Hockey League

The National Hockey League (NHL) is a professional ice hockey league composed of 30 teams in North America. It is believed to be the premier professional ice hockey league in the world, and one of the North American main professional sports leagues. The Stanley Cup, the most former professional sports trophy in North America, is granted yearly to the league champion at the end of each season.

The league was established in 1917 in Montreal, Quebec, Canada from a predecessor organization, the National Hockey Association (NHA), established in 1909. It began with four teams, and through a series of expansions, contractions and relocations, the league is now compiled of

30 teams, 24 of which are established in the United States and six in Canada. After a labour dispute that led to the cancellation of the entire 2004–05 season, the league has staged a successful comeback, as well as revenue and profit growth.

The NHL draws many highly skilled players from all over the world. Presently, the league has players from about 20 dissimslar countries. Canadians have in the past constituted a large majority of the players in the NHL because both the sport and the league developed in Canada. In the past 25 years, the percentages of American and European players have increased because of the NHL's extended expansion into the United States, its high standard of play equated to other leagues, and the availability of highly skilled European players.

Each National Hockey League regulation game is an ice hockey game played between two teams and is hour long. The game is framed of three 20-minute periods with an intermission of either 15½ or seventeen minutes (if nationally televised) from periods.Television timeouts are taken at the first stoppage of play after six, ten, and 14 minutes of elapsed time unless there is a power play or the first stoppage is the result of a goal. In these cases, the timeout will occur at the first stoppage after the penalty expires or the following stoppage after the goal, respectively.

A new rule was brought in for the 2007-08 season that if the first stoppage of play is an icing, the TV timeout does not occur. This is to prevent players from getting a break in spite of not being permitted to change. At the end of the sixty-minute regulation time, the team with the most goals wins the game. If a game is tied after regulation time, overtime ensues. Throughout the regular season, overtime is a five-minute, four-player on four-player sudden-death period, in which the first team to score a goal wins the game. Until the 2005–06 season, if no team was able to score in the five-minute overtime, the game ended in a tie.

Commencing in the 2005–06 season, if the game is still tied at the end of overtime, the game enters a shootout. Three players for each team in turn take a penalty shot. The team with the most goals throughout the three-round shootout wins the game. If the game is still tied after the three shootout rounds, the shootout continues but becomes sudden death.

Whichever team finally wins the shootout is granted a goal in the game score and thus granted two points in the standings. The losing team in overtime or shootout is granted only one. Shootout goals and saves are not tracked in hockey statistics; shootout statistics are tracked separately.

Shootouts do not occur throughout the playoffs. In the playoffs, sudden-death 20-minute five-on-five periods are played until one team scores. While a game could theoretically continue forever, only four games have arrived at five extra time, two have reached six, and none have gone beyond six.There are no television timeouts throughout playoff overtime periods; the only break is to clean the loose ice at the first stoppage after the period is halfway completed.

FAMOUS PLAYERS

Alexander Ovechkin

Alexander Mikhaylovich Ovechkin (born September 17, 1985) is a Russian professional ice hockey left winger for the Washington Capitals of the National Hockey League (NHL). In January 2008, he signed a thirteen-year contract extension worth $124 million with the Capitals, the most valuable contract in NHL history. He lives in Arlington, Virginia. He is often referred to as "AO".

He was the first overall choice in the 2004 NHL Entry Draft, but due to the 2004-05 NHL lockout, he started play in the 2005-06 NHL season. Throughout the 2007-08 season, he led the NHL with 65 goals and 112 points to capture the Rocket Richard and Art Ross Trophies. That season he also won the Lester B. Pearson Grant as the top player voted by the NHLPA and the Hart Memorial Trophy as the league's MVP.

Alexander Ovechkin is the son of Mikhail Ovechkin, a former professional football (soccer) player, and Tatyana Ovechkina who won two Olympic gold medals while contending for the Soviet women's basketball team in the 1976 Summer Olympics at Montreal and in 1980 at Moscow.The first signs of the Ovechkin's future came when he was a child. At the age of two, in a Soviet toy store, Alexander caught a toy stick and helmet and declined to let go. His parents treasure the picture to this day. As a small child, whenever he saw a hockey game on TV, he "threw all his toys" and ran to the TV. He "protested strongly" if his parents tried to change the channel. His parents say they knew he would be an athlete when Alexander chose to run up the steps to their apartment rather than take the elevator.

He started playing hockey at the age of 7. Soon after he started, however, he had to postpone his hockey career because his parents were not able to take him to the rink. But one of Ovechkin's coaches saw Ovechkin's talent and communicated to his parents that he should keep to play hockey. Ovechkin's brother, Sergei, who later died in a car accident, saw that Alexander loved hockey and insisted that he be permitted to return.Since he examined at the Military Institute for Border Guards, Ovechkin did not have to go through compulsory military service.

In Russia, hockey teams form players in their systems from childhood. Ovechkin started playing in the Dynamo Moscow system. At 16, he made his debut for Dynamo Moscow in the Russian Superleague in the 2001-2002 season.In the 2003-2004 seasons, he won the Superleague grant for Best Left Wing and turned the youngest Dynamo Moscow player to lead the team in scoring.

In 2004-2005, he missed nearly two months of play because of a shoulder injury confirmed in the Gold Medal Game in opposition to Canada in the World Junior Championships.Ovechkin was the first overall draft selection in the 2004 NHL Entry Draft, going to the Washington Capitals. He had been projected as the first overall pick for nearly two years, and had earned comparison to Mario Lemieux. He was so highly considered, the Florida Panthers attempted to draft him in the 2003 NHL Entry Draft in the 9th round, even though his birthday was two days after the cuttoff (September 15th, 1985). Rick Dudley, the general manager of the Panthers, exacted the pick was legitimate, saying that utilizing leapyears Ovechkin was old enough.

Following the 2004-05 NHL lockout, Alexander Ovechkin played his first game with the Capitals on October 5, 2005, hitting two goals in a 3-2 victory over Columbus. In a shootout in opposition to Anaheim, Ovechkin marked the winning goal to end the game at 5-4.Ovechkin was named the NHL Rookie of the Month for December 2005.On January 13, 2006, in Anaheim, Ovechkin scored his first career hat trick in opposition to Jean-Sébastien Giguère of the Mighty Ducks of Anaheim to help Washington win the game.

On January 16, 2006, Alexander Ovechkin scored a goal that veteran hockey reporter Bill Clement called "one of the greatest goals of all time." Knocked down by Paul Mara, a defenseman for the Phoenix Coyotes, then sliding on his back and confronting away from the net, Ovechkin was able to hook the puck with one hand on his stick and slide it into the net past goalie Brian Boucher for his second goal of the night.

On February 1, 2006, Ovechkin was named NHL Rookie of the Month for January 2006 as well as being named Offensive Player of the Month, fetching only the third player in NHL history to earn both honours in a single month.Ovechkin led 2005-2006 NHL rookies in goals, points, power-play goals, and shots. He completed third overall in the NHL in scoring and tied for third in goals.

His 425 shots led the league, set an NHL rookie record, and was the fourth-highest total in NHL history. Ovechkin's point total was the second-greatest in Washington Capitals history and his goal total tied for third in franchise history. He was also named to the NHL First All-Star Team, the first rookie to obtain the honour in 15 years. After the season ended, Ovechkin received the Calder Memorial Trophy, granted to the NHL's greatest rookie. EA Sports made him one of the cover athletes for NHL 07.

Following the 2006-2007 NHL season, Ovechkin was granted the Kharlamov Trophy, which is named after Valery Kharlamov and presented by Sovetsky Sport. The Kharlamov Trophy honours the greatest Russian NHL player as voted by other Russian NHL players.Ovechkin played beside fellow young phenom Sidney Crosby of the Pittsburgh Penguins in the 2007 NHL All-Star Game, deemed on January 24, 2007, in Dallas, Texas. He scored his first All-Star game goal.

On December 29, 2007, Ovechkin notched his third hat trick in opposition to Ottawa Senators netminder, Martin Gerber. Ovechkin tallied 5 points that night: 4 goals and 1 assist to lead the Capitals to a 8-6 victory. On January 31, 2008, he had another 5-point performance (4 goals, 1 assist) in a 5-4 overtime victory in opposition to the Montreal Canadiens.After much hypothesis, Ovechkin signed a 13-year contract extension worth $124 million with the Capitals on January 10, 2008. The contract, which averages $9.5 million per year, is the richest in NHL history. Working without an agent, Ovechkin negotiated with Capitals owner Ted Leonsis and general manager George McPhee.

On March 3, 2008, Ovechkin notched his fourth hat trick, in opposition to the Boston Bruins. He made his 50th, 51st, and 52nd goals of the season, the second time he has hit the 50-goal mark in three seasons with the Capitals.On March 21, 2008, Ovechkin scored his 59th and 60th goals of the season in opposition to the Atlanta Thrashers. He was the first NHL player to score 60 goals in a season since 1996. He is the 19th player ever to reach the 60 goal plateau. On March 25, Ovechkin scored his 61st goal to hold the Washington Capital's team record for regular season goals before deemed by Dennis Maruk. He would break Luc Robitaille's record for most goals by a left winger in one season on April 3, 2008, by scoring two goals, his 64th and 65th of the season.

Alex Ovechkin completed the 2007-08 NHL season as the leader in points (112) and goals (65), and was granted both the Art Ross Trophy and the Rocket Richard Trophy.In his first NHL playoff game, Ovechkin made the game-winning goal with less than five minutes left.The day after he obtained the Hart Memorial Trophy as league MVP, he was given the key to the city by Washington mayor Adrian M. Fenty for being the first Washington MVP winner in a main game since Joe Theismann of the Washington Redskins in 1983.

On June 11, 2008, Ovechkin also established his own line of designer Streetwear with CCM.At the age of 16, Ovechkin served lead the Junior National Team to the Gold medal with two hat tricks, one in opposition to Switzerland and one in opposition to USA, and an assist.At the age of 17, when he was chossen by Russian coach Victor Tikhonov to play in the Ceska Pojistovna Cup Euro tour tournament, Alexander turned the youngest skater ever to play for the Russian National Team in the history of Russian hockey. In that tournament he also turned the youngest player ever to score for the National Team.

At the age of 18, Alexander Ovechkin was called Captain of the Junior Russian National Team. Russia completed 5th in the tournament.At the age of 19, Ovechkin was called to the Russian National Team for the 2004 World Cup of Hockey. He was the youngest player in the tournament.Also at the age of 19, Alexander Ovechkin was called Captain of the Junior National Team in the 2005 World Junior Ice Hockey Championships. The tournament, lasting from December 25, 2004, to January 4, 2005, was Ovechkin's third and last. At the end of the tournament he had accumulated 7 goals (tied for tournament lead). His team obtained the silver medal after losing the gold medal game to Canada on January 4, and Ovechkin was named the Best Forward of the tournament as well as selected to the tournament All-Star Team.

In 2005 Ovechkin played in his first IIHF men's World Championships. He scored five goals and three assists, putting down eighth in the top scorers list and sharing third place in goal scoring.In 2006, Ovechkin played in his very first Winter Olympic Games.

Even though Russia came away from the games without a medal, Ovechkin scored 5 goals in the tournament, as well as the game-winner in opposition to Canada's Martin Brodeur, eliminating Canada from the tournament. Ovechkin was the only player not on Sweden (Gold) or Finland (Silver) to be called to the all-tournament team.At the 2006 IIHF World Championships, Ovechkin marked six goals and three assists (nine points) in seven games before losing 4-3 to the Czech Republic in the quarterfinals. For his efforts, Ovechkin was one of six players took Media All-Star Team.At the 2008 IIHF World Championships, Ovechkin served led Russia to the gold medal by completing with twelve points (six goals, six assists) in nine games. He was selected to the Media All-Star Team for the second time in five tournament appearances.

Isobel Stanley

One of two daughters to Governor General Lord Stanley of Preston, Isobel Stanley inherited her father's passion for hockey, turning a fixture on the rink outside Government House in Ottawa. After serving her first organized contest at the Montreal Winter Carnival in 1889, Isobel donned the customary long skirt to play in the regular ladies shinny games at Rideau Hall. A photograph taken there in 1890 of Isobel and her Government House teammates is thought to be the first commemorated image of women's participation in hockey.Isobel made an even more outstanding contribution to the game she loved when, with the help of her brothers, she convinced her father to purchase a silver cup to present yearly to the greatest amateur team in the Dominion of Canada.

Dan Bain

One of Canada's first great athletes, Donald H. (Dan) Bain went on to turn hockey's original extra time hero. Born in Belleville, Ont., Bain grew up in Winnipeg, where he shone at a host of sports and joined the Victorias of the Manitoba Hockey League near the end off the nineteenth century .

Believed one of the finest playmakers of the pre-NHL era, the muscular Bain scored the Stanley Cup-winning goal in Winnipeg's stunning upset of the mighty Montreal Victorias in 1896 – the first time a team from beyond Montreal won hockey's most coveted prize.

Bain developed more heroics five years later, turning the first player to net the Cup-winner in overtime as the Winnipeg Victorias traumatized the powerful Montreal Shamrocks. Dubbed the "Masked Man" after he donned a rudimentary wooden shield to protect a broken nose, Bain was called Canada's top sportsman of the last half of the nineteenth century and received induction into the Hockey Hall of Fame upon its opening in 1945.

REFERENCES

Alter, S.: *Science of Flexibility*, 2nd edn, Human Kinetics, Champaign, IL, 1996.

Alter, S.: *Sport Stretch*, Human Kinetics, Champaign, IL, 1998.

Dintiman, G. and Ward, R.:*Sport Speed*, Leisure Press, Champaign, IL, 1988.

Ellison, D.: *Performance Stretching*, Human Kinetics, Champaign, IL, 1999.

Goldberg, B. (ed.): *Sports and Exercise for Children with Chronic Health Conditions*, Human Kinetics, Champaign, IL, 1995

Newsholme, E., Leech, T. and Duester, G.: *Keep on Running*, John Wiley & Sons, Chichester, UK, 1994

Reaburn, P. and Jenkins, D.: *Training for Speed and Endurance*, Allen & Unwin, Sydney, 1996

Rowland, T.W.: *Developmental Exercise Physiology*, Human Kinetics, Champaign, IL, 1996

Sports weekly Magazine

Sports Illustrated Magazine

11

Judo

Judo, meaning "gentle way", is a modern Japanese martial art and combat game, that developed in Japan in the late nineteenth century. Its most outstanding feature is its competitive element, where the object is to throw one's opponent to the ground, immobilize or otherwise subdue one's opponent with a grappling maneuver, or force an opposer to submit by joint locking the elbow or by applying a choke. Strikes and thrusts (by hands and feet) - as well as weapons defences - are a part of judo, but only in pre-arranged forms and are not permitted in judo competition or free practice (randori).

Finally, the philosophy and resultant pedagogy formulated for judo turned the example for almost all modern Japanese martial arts that developed from "traditional" schools .Practitioners of judo are called judoka.

HISTORY

The early history of judo is indivisible from its beginner, Japanese polymath and educator Jigoro Kano (1860–1938). Kano was born into a well-to-do Japanese household. His grandfather was a self-made man: a sake brewer from Shiga prefecture in central Japan. Nevertheless, Kano's father was not the eldest son and hence did not inherit the business. Instead, he turned a Shinto priest and government official, with enough influence for his son to enter the second incoming class of Tokyo Imperial University.

Cian was a small, frail boy, who, even in his twenties, did not weigh more than a hundred pounds (45 kg), and was often picked on by bullies. He first began pursuing jujutsu, at that time a dying art, at the age of 17, but met with little success. This was in part due to troubles finding a teacher who would take him on as a student. When he went to university to study literature at the age of 18, he extended his martial arts studies, finally gaining a referral to Fukuda Hachinosuke (c.1828–c.1880), a master of the Tenjin Shin jo -ryu and grandfather of Keiko Fukuda (born 1913), who is Kano's only surviving student, and the highest-ranking female judokain the world. Fukuda Hachinosuke is said to have emphasized technique over formal exercise, sowing the seeds of Kano's emphasis of free practice in judo.

A little more than a year after Kano joined Fukuda's school, Fukuda turned ill and died. Kano then turned a student in another tenjin shin yo-ryu school that of Iso Masatomo (c.1820–c.1881), who put more emphasis on the practice of pre-arranged forms than Fukuda had. Through dedication, Kano rapidly earned the title of master instructor and turned assistant instructor to Iso at the age of 21. Unfortunately, Iso soon took ill, and Kano, feeling that he still had much to learn, took up another style, turning a student of Iikubo Tsunetoshi (1835–1889) of Kito-ryu. Like Fukuda, Iikubo rated much emphasis on free practice.

By this time, Kano was devising new techniques, such as the "shoulder wheel" (kata-guruma, known as a fireman's carry to Western wrestlers who utilize a slightly dissimslar form of this technique) and the "floating hip" throw. However, he was already thinking about doing far more than just expanding the canons of Kito-ryu and Tenjin Shinyo-ryu. Full of new ideas, Kano had in mind a main reformation of jujutsu, with techniques established on sound scientific principles, and with focus on growth of the body, mind and character of young men in addition to growth of martial prowess. At the age of 22, when he was just about to finish his degree at the University, Kano took nine students from Iikubo's school to study jujutsu under him at the Eisho-ji, a Buddhist temple in Kamakura, and Iikubo came to the temple three days a week to help teach. Even though two years would pass before the temple would be called by the name "Kodokan", or "place for teaching the way", and Kano had not yet been accorded the title of "master" in the Kito-ryu, this is now regarded as the Kodokan's founding.

Judo was in the beginning known as Kano Jiu-Jitsu or Kano Jiu-Do, and later as Kodokan Jiu-Do or simply Jiu-Do or Judo. In the early days, it was also still concerned to generically simply as Jiu-Jitsu.

THE GAME

The traditional rules of judo are meant to avoid injuries to the participants and ensure proper etiquette. Some later additions to the rules were prompted by a desire to make the game more fascinating to observers.

Penalties may be given for being inactive throughout the match, or for utilizing illegal techniques. Fighting must be stopped if a player is outside the designated area on the mat (tatami). If the referee and judges need to discuss something throughout groundwork, the referee will call sonomama (which means "do not move") and both fighters must stop in the position they are in. When they are done, the referee says yoshi and the match continues.

Fig. Different Judo Positions

All scores and penalties are given by the referee. The judges can make a decision that changes the score or penalty given by the referee. There are slight deviations to IJF rules to conciliate blind judo.

Mixed Martial Arts

Utilizing their knowledge of ne-waza/grappling and tachi-waza/standing-grappling, accomplished judo practitioners have also contended in mixed martial arts matches. Former Russian national judo champion Fedor Emelianenko is normally ranked as mixed martial arts' greatest heavyweight. Karo Parisyan fights in UFC's welterweight division, and Rameau Thierry Sokoudjou and Hidehiko Yoshida, an Olympic gold medalist in 1992 and World Judo Champion in 1999, were also fighters in the now defunct PRIDE FC. Other Olympic gold medalist and world champion judokas such as Pawel Nastula, Yoon Dong-Sik and Jung Bu-Kyung also fight in MMA. Undefeated WEC middleweight champion Paulo Filho has accredited judo and jiu-jitsu for his achievemnt. Fighters Sanae Kikuta and Hayato Sakurai also come from judo backgrounds.

Styles

Kano Jigoro's Kodokan Judo is the most famous and well-known style of judo, but is not the only one. The terms judo and jujutsu were quite interchangeable in the early years, so some of these forms of judo are still known as jujutsu or jiu-jitsu either for that reason, or simply to differentiate them from mainstream judo. From Kano's original style of judo, various related forms have orginated—some now broadly believed to be distinct arts:

- Olympic Judo: This is the preprevailingform of Kodokan judo.
- Brazilian Jiu-Jitsu: Mitsuyo Maeda brought in judo to Brazil in 1914. Maeda taught judo to Carlos Gracie (1902–1994) and others in Brazil. Brazilian Jiu-Jitsu did not follow later changes in international judo rules that were added to emphasise the standing phase of the fight, nor those rules that were brought in to ban the more dangerous techniques. Even though all the techniques are virtually the similar, BJJ's quite dissimslar point scoring system and absence of judo's various rules that require the competitors to recommence fighting from a standing position are largely responsible for giving it its dissimslar character. BJJ is closer to the original early 1900s judo than existing Olympic judo is.
- Judo-do: In Austria, Julius Fleck and others formulated a system of throwing intended to lead judo that they called "judo-do".
- Kawaishi-ryu jujutsu: Teaching in France, Mikonosuke Kawaishi developed Kawaishi-ryû jujutsu as an alternative approach to

instruction that extended to teach many techniques banned in modern Olympic/Kodokan judo competition.

- Kosen Judo, Kosen Judo: As a sub-style of Kodokan Judo that turned popularised in early twentieth century Japanese inter-scholastic competition, Kosen style has the similar range of techniques but greater latitude is permitted for ground technique. Like BJJ, this style of judo is closer to the original early 1900s judo than existing Olympic judo is.
- Russian Judo: This distinctive style of judo was determined by Sambo. It is represented by well-known coaches such as Alexander Retuinskih and Igor Yakimov, and mixed martial arts fighters such as Igor Zinoviev, Fedor Emelianenko and Karo Parisyan. In turn, Russian judo has determined mainstream judo, with techniques such as the flying armbar being accepted into Kodokan judo.
- Sambo (especially Sport Sambo): Vasili Oshchepkov was the first European judo black belt under Kano. Oshchepkov went on to create Sambo from judo's influence, incorporating other contentious techniques into his new system. Oshchepkov died throughout the political purges of 1937 for rejecting to deny his education in Japanese judo under Kano. In their History of Sambo, Brett Jacques and Scott Anderson wrote that in Russia "judo and SOMBO were believed to be the similar thing" - albeit with a dissimslar uniform and some differences in the rules.

Safety

Research shows that judo is a in particular safe sport for youths, though adult competitive judo has a comparatively higher incidence of injuries equated to non-collision or non-contact ball-sports for example, but similar to other competitive contact sports.

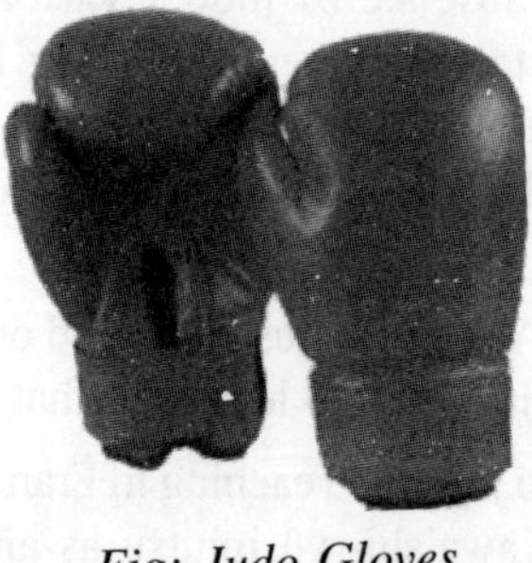

Fig: Judo Gloves

Fig: Knee Protector

Chokes

Even though chokes are potential lethal techniques, a properly-applied chokehold, if released soon enough after submission or unconsciousness, causes no injury.

There is ample data manifesting the safety of applying chokeholds and training includes emergency care and resuscitation (kappo.)

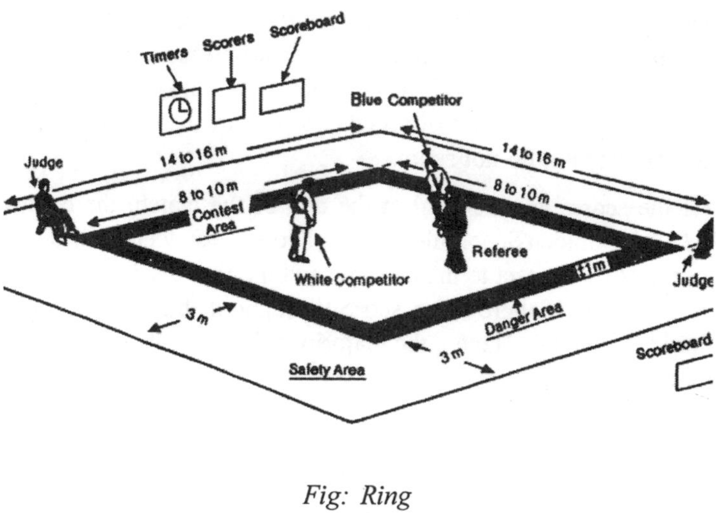

Fig: Ring

Competition Scoring

The object in a judo match is to throw the opposer to the ground on his shoulder; to pin him to the ground primarily on his back; or to force him to submit to a choke, strangle or an armlock. Any of these score ippon, instantly winning the match.

Judo has four grades of score: ippon, waza-ari, yuko, and koka. An ippon literally means "one point" and wins the match.An ippon is granted for

- a throw that lands the opponent largely on their back in a assured manner with speed and force;
- for a mat hold of sufficient duration (twenty five seconds); or
- for opponent submission. A waza-ari is granted for a throw that does not quite have enough power or control to be believed ippon; or for a hold of twenty seconds.

A waza-ari is a half-point, and, if two are scored, they constitute the full point required for a win.

Yuko and koka are lower grades of score, and only count as tie-breakers - they are not accumulative with one another. Scoring is lexicographic; a waza-ari beats any number of yuko, but a waza-ari and a yuko beat a waza-ari with no yuko. It is not not common for a match to be decided established on koka.

A fifteen-second hold down scores yuko and a ten-second hold down scores koka. If the person who secured the hold down already has a waza-ari, they only need to hold the hold down for twenty seconds to score ippon by way of two waza-ari (waza-ari-awasete-ippon). Throws further lacking the necessities of an ippon or a waza-ari might score a yuko or a koka. So-called "skillful takedowns" are also allowed (e.g. the flying arm-bar) but do not score.

If the scores are identical at the end of the match, the contest is settled by the Golden Score rule. Golden Score is a sudden death situation where the clock is reset to match-time, and the first dissident to achieve any score wins. If there is no score throughout this period, then the winner is resolved by Hantei, the majority opinion of the referee and the two corner judges.

Presentation of Scores

Judo scoreboards show the number of waza-ari, yuko and koka scores scored by each player. Often an ippon is not presented on the scoreboard, because upon award of an ippon the match is directly terminated. Some computerised scoreboards will briefly show that an ippon has been scored.

Scoreboards usually also show the number of penalties enforced on each player, and sometimes the number of medical visits for each. (Only two "medical" attentions are permitted for each competitor during a match — most often for minor bleeds.)

Electronic scoreboards also normally comprise timers for measuring both competition time and osekomi time.

A match with the first player hitting one waza-ari, two yuko, and two koka, defeating his opponent who scored one fewer kokas would be exhibited on the scoreboard as: "122" vs. "121"; while in print such a result would often be presented as: "1W2Y2K" vs. "1W2Y1K".

Self-defense

In 1902, Barton-Wright wrote: "Judo and jujitsu were not planned as primary means of attack and defence in opposition to a boxer or a man who kicks you, but were only to be used after coming to close quarters, and in order to get to close quarters it was absolutely necessary to understand boxing and the use of the foot."

While throws performed with proper break falls on soft mats may seem comparatively light and graceful, their more practical application on a hard surface can be very dangerous (especially with greater intent to harm.)

Moreover, ground grappling had been shown to be an effective form of self-defence.

Though the game is in itself an efficient means of self-defence, the amount of training offered that adapts it more specific to self-defence positions changes from dojo to dojo, ranging from very little in some dojos through to a strong stress in others (especially with Russian Judo.)

Techniques & Practice

While judo includes a variety of rolls, falls, throws, hold downs, chokes, joint-locks, and strikes, the chief focus is on throwing, and groundwork . Throws are separated in two groups of techniques, standing techniques (tachi-waza), and sacrifice techniques,. Standing techniques are further separated into hand techniques,, hip techniques and foot and leg techniques, . Sacrifice techniques are divided into those in which the thrower falls directly backwards and those in which he falls onto his side.,

The ground fighting techniques are divided into attacks in opposition to the joints or joint locks (, kansetsu-waza), strangleholds or chokeholds (shime-waza), and holding or pinning techniques.

A kind of sparring is exercised in judo, known as randori, randori, meaning "free practice". In randori, two adversaries may attack each other with any judo throw or grappling technique. Striking techniques such as kicking and punching, along with knife and sword techniques are held in the kata. This form of pedagogy is normally reserved for higher ranking practitioners but are forbidden in contest, and normally not allowed in randori for reasons of safety. Also for reasons of safety, chokeholds, joint locking, and the sacrifice techniques are subject to age or rank restrictions. For example, in the United States one must be 13 or older to utilize chokeholds, and 16 or older to utilize arm locks.

In randori and tournament exercise, when an opposer successfully executes a chokehold or joint lock, one submits, or "taps out", by tapping the mat or one's opponent at least twice in a manner that clearly shows the submission. When this occurs the match is over, the tapping player has lost, and the chokehold or joint lock ceases.

MAJOR TOURNAMENTS

World Judo Championships

The World Judo Championships are the most eminent level of international judo competition, along with the Olympic judo competition. The championships are deemed once every two years by the International Judo Federation, and qualified judoka contend in their respective categories as representatives of their home countries. Team competitions have also been deemed since 1994. The men's championships started in 1956, though the layout and periodicity of the championships have altered overtime. The 26th edition of the championships will take place in Rotterdam, Netherlands in 2009.

The first edition of the world championships happened in Tokyo, Japan in 1956. There were no weight classes at the time and Japanese judoka Shokichi Natsui turned the first world champion in history, defeating fellow countryman Yoshihiko Yoshimatsu in the final. The second world championship was also deemed in Tokyo two years later, with the Japanese winning the top two spots in the competition for the second time. In 1961, the championship was deemed outside of Japan for the first time, and Dutch judoka Anton Geesink overcame the prior world champion, Koji Sone, in Paris, France, to become the first non-Japanese world champion.

The 1965 World Judo Championships were deemed in Rio de Janeiro, Brazil, and weight classes were held outfor the first time with the addition of the -68 kg, -80 kg, and +80 kg categories. Judo had turn an Olympic sport at the 1964 Summer Olympics deemed in Tokyo, and a permanent sport after a brief absence at the 1968 Summer Olympics.

In spite of this progressive enlargement, it took until 1980 for women to participate in the world championships. The first women's world championships were held in New York in 1980, and were held in alternating years as the men's championships until the 1987 World Judo Championships in Essen, where the two competitions were merged into one world championship.

The mixed championships have been held biannually since 1987. In 2005, the world championships made its debut on the African continent in Cairo, Egypt. In the International Judo Federation meeting held in Rio de Janeiro, Brazil in 2007 (throughout the 2007 World Judo Championships), it was decided that France would host the world championships for the fifth time in 2011.

The World Judo Championships team competition started in 1994, and was held once every four years until 2006. The competition will be held every year from 2007. Judoka who take part in the individual world championships often do not take part in the team competition.

Olympics

Judo was first admitted in the Summer Olympic Games at the 1964 Games in Tokyo, Japan. After not being admitted in 1968, judo has been an Olympic sport in each Olympiad since then. Only male judoka participated until the 1988 Summer Olympics, when women participated as a demonstration sport. Women judoka were first granted medals at the 1992 Summer Olympics.

Judoka compete in weight classes. Gold and silver medals are granted established on a single elimination bracket. Two bronze medals are granted in each weight class; two judoka from a repechage for those who are ruled out by one of the eventual semifinalists face the two semifinal losers for the bronze medals.

There have been among 4 and 8 Olympic weight classes over the years (presently 7), and the definition of each class has altered various times, as shown in the following table.

Judoka from forty-five nations have won medals, presenting each continent except Antarctica. Japan leads the medal count with fifty-eight medals, succeeded by France and South Korea, each with thirty-three.

ADMINISTRATIVE BODIES

International Judo Federation

The International Judo Federation was established in July 1951. The IJF was primitively composed of judo federations from Europe plus Argentina. Countries from four continents were affiliated over the following ten years.

There is substantial discontent (ranging to outrage) in Japan that there is no Japanese member in the IJF as the game is primitively Japanese and because some of the rules are either counter to Japanese tradition (like weight classes) or make it more difficult for the smaller Japanese competitors (such as some of the rules concerning Judogi.

FAMOUS PLAYERS

Masahiko Kimura

Masahiko Kimura was a Japanese judoka (Judo practitioner) who is broadly believed one of the most outstanding judoka of all time. Kimura (5ft 7in 170cm; 85 kg, 187lb) was born on September 10, 1917 in Kumamoto, Japan.Kimura at age 24 with the Emperor's tantogift after winning the Ten-Ran Shiai tournament

At age 16, after six years of judo, Kimura was elevated to 4th dan. He had defeated six opponents (who were all 3rd and 4th dan) in a row. In 1935 at age 18 he turned the youngest ever godan (5th degree black belt) when he defeated eight successive opponents at Kodokan (headquarters for the main governing body of Judo). Kimura's remarkable success can in part be attributed to his fanatical training regimen. He reportedly lost only four judo matches in his lifetime, all occurring in 1935.He believed quitting judo after those losses, but through the encouragement of friends he started training once again.

All through the nights, he practiced osoto gari, a basic leg throw, in opposition to a tree. After six months, his technique was such that daily randori or sparring sessions at various dojos ensued in 10 people with concussions. Fellow students frequently asked him not to utilize his unorthodox osoto gari. At the height of his career, Kimura's training involved a thousand push-ups and nine-hours practice each day. He was promoted to 7th dan at age 30, a rank that was frozen after disputes with Kodokan over turning a professional wrestler, refusing to return the All Japan Judo Championship flag, and issuing dan ranks while in Brazil.

In 1955, Kimura, at 38 years old, took part in a match in which he defeated Hélio Gracie of the famous Gracie Jiu Jitsu household in a submission judo match deemed in Brazil. Throughout the fight, Kimura threw Gracie repeatedly with Ippon Seoinage (one arm shoulder throw), Osoto Gari (main outer reap) Kimura's signature throw. He threw Helio 3 times with Osoto Gari., Ouchi Gari (main inner reap), Uchimata (inner thigh throw), and Harai Goshi (sweeping hip throw). Kimura reportedly threw Gracie repeatedly in an effort to knock him unconscious. However, the floor of the fighting area was evidently too soft to permit this to happen.

Kimura also inflicted painful, suffocating grappling techniques on Gracie such as kuzure-kamishiho-gatame (altered upper four corner hold), kesa-gatame (scarf hold), and sankaku-jime (triangle choke). Finally, thirteen minutes into the bout, Kimura positioned himself to apply a reverse ude-garami (arm entanglement, a shoulderlock). Gracie declined to submit, even after his arm broke, forcing Kimura to continue the lock on Gracie's broken arm. At this point, Carlos Gracie, Helio's older brother, threw in the towel to end the match to protect his brother's health. In 1994, Helio admitted in an interview that he had in fact been choked unconscious earlier in the match, but had revived when Kimura issued the choke.

As a tribute to Kimura's victory, the reverse ude-garami technique has since been commonly referred to as the Kimura lock, or simply the Kimura, in Brazilian Jiu-Jitsu and, more in recent times, mixed martial arts circles.

In the early 1950s, Kimura was asked for by Rikidozan to contend as a professional wrestler. They performed both as tag team partners and as opponents, but Kimura was not marketed or advertised as much as Rikidozan, mainly due to Rikidozan's own opposition (Rikidozan was in reality Zainichi Korean, and thus he reportedly felt conflicted or insecure about having a real Japanese in competition with him for publicity. The Rikidozan vs. Kimura match for the Japanese Professional Wrestling Heavyweight title was the first high-profile match among two native professional wrestlers. The match, as per Kimura, was supposed to go to a draw and establish a series of rematches. But Rikidozan, whether it was premeditated or in the heat of the moment, shot (started fighting for real) on Kimura and battered him unconscious with a series of open hand strikes, punches, and kicks (some of which were to the groin), and won the match by knockout. Kimura never obtained a rematch with Rikidozan.

Kimura established International Pro Wrestling Force (IPWF), a promotion established in his hometown of Kumamoto, as a local affiliate of The Japan Wrestling Association (JWA). Even though JWA later took over operations, IPWF is remembered for being the first Japanese promotion to bring in Mexican Lucha Libre wrestlers.

Some biographers mention that his professional wrestling career started shortly after his wife was diagnosed with tuberculosis, and it is pondered by some that he started professional wrestling to pay for her medication. Indeed, the predicament was likely beyond the financial means of a police instructor, which was his paying job prior to professional wrestling.Kimura died of lung cancer at age seventy-five.

Isao Okano

Isao Okano (, Okano Isao, born January 20, 1944) is a retired judoka who contended in the middleweight (-80 kg) division. He was born in Ryûgasaki, Ibaraki, Japan.

He entered the 1964 Summer Olympics while learning at Chuo University's law school, and won the gold medal in the middleweight division. He won another gold medal at the World Judo Championships in 1965, turning the champion of his division at only 21 years of age. He also won the Open weight class division of the All-Japan Judo Championships in 1967 and 1969, and rated second in the competition in 1968. He stays the lightest ever competitor to win the Open weight class of the All-Japan Championships, as he weighed around 80 kg all over his career. He suddenly retired from competitive judo at only 25 years of age, and established the Shoki Juku (presently the Ryutsu Keizai University's judo team) in 1970, where he instructed future Olympic gold medalist Kazuhiro Ninomiya. He also served as a coach for the Japanese Olympic judo team throughout the 1976 Summer Olympics. He later worked as a judo instructor at Keio University from 1989-1998, and the University of Tokyo from 1989-2000. He is presently an instructor and professor at Ryutsu Keizai University

Shiro Saigo

In August 1883, Shiro Saigo (153 cm, 5 ft, 56 kg, 123 lbs) along with Tsune-jiro Tomita were the first judoka to receive black belts. In 1888, at age twenty-one, Saigo was also the first to receive Go-dan.

Saigo was born in 1867 in Nigata Prefecture, Japan. As a child, he liked to become an army general. However, due to his short stature, he was not permitted to enter the military academy. At age 14, he started practicing jiu-jitsu at Inouye Dojo (Jigoro Kano's Sensei). Saigo was born with octopus toes (irregular shaped feet with long and curved toes) which bettered his balance and made him very hard to throw. One year later, Kano recruited Saigo to Kodokan to train. Commencing in October 1882, Saigo, Tomita, and Kano lived a 12 mat dojo and exercised all day. He was promoted to Yon-Dan in 1885 and Go-Dan in 1888.

REFERENCES

Alter, S.: *Science of Flexibility*, 2nd edn, Human Kinetics, Champaign, IL, 1996.

Alter, S.: *Sport Stretch*, Human Kinetics, Champaign, IL, 1998.

Dintiman, G. and Ward, R.:*Sport Speed*, Leisure Press, Champaign, IL, 1988.

Ellison, D.: *Performance Stretching*, Human Kinetics, Champaign, IL, 1999.

Goldberg, B. (ed.): *Sports and Exercise for Children with Chronic Health Conditions*, Human Kinetics, Champaign, IL, 1995

Newsholme, E., Leech, T. and Duester, G.: *Keep on Running*, John Wiley & Sons, Chichester, UK, 1994

Reaburn, P. and Jenkins, D.: *Training for Speed and Endurance*, Allen & Unwin, Sydney, 1996

Rowland, T.W.: *Developmental Exercise Physiology*, Human Kinetics, Champaign, IL, 1996

Sports weekly Magazine

Sports Illustrated Magazine

12

Snooker

Snooker is a cue game that is practised on a large baize-covered table with pockets in each of the four corners and in the middle of each of the long side cushions. A regulation (full-size) table is 12 ft × 6 ft (3.6 m x 1.8 m). It is played utilizing a cue and snooker balls: one white cue ball, 15 red balls worth one point each, and six balls of dissimslar colours yellow (2), green (3), brown (4), blue (5), pink (6) and black (7). A player (or team) wins a frame (individual game) of snooker by scoring more points than the opponent(s), utilizing the cue ball to pot the red and coloured balls. A player wins a match when a certain number of frames have been won.

Snooker is particularly famous in many of the English-speaking and Commonwealth countries,and in China, with the top professional players achieving multi-million pound career gainings from the game.

HISTORY

The game of snooker is a spin-off of billiards which dates back to the 16th century but the game of snooker did not in really come into being until the 1800s. Billiards had turn famous between the British Armed Forces stationed in India. As billiards was only a two player game, however, new games such as Life Pool and Pyramid Pool was developed in order to accommodate more players. Finally these two games were combined to form one which is now called snooker.

Billiards was first played in the 1500s. It was not played by many people, though, as it in general only was held in royal palaces with aristocrats. This gave the game a reputation of being a 'gentleman's game'. The tables used back then did not consist of any side rails, pockets or cushions, however. They only contained holes for the balls to be potted. This meant that each time that a pot was attained the ball would fall on to the ground. The table was not the only thing dissimslar from modern billiards equipment as the balls were then made of ivory.

In the 1800s the game had become quite famous amongst the British Armed Forces that were stationed in India. They played this to pass the time due to the monsoon rain. With only 3 balls used in billiards which admitted a cue ball for each player it was unsuitable for any more than 2 players. This was when multi-player versions were established. These comprise both Life Pool and Pyramid Pool. Life Pool was where various coloured balls were used as both cue balls and object balls. In Pyramid Pool 15 red balls were used and a cue ball. Each player received one point per red ball potted. As well as games being formulated the tables were being improved. Tables had now formulated into something alike as the ones we know now. Cushions, side rails and pockets had all been added as the players were fed up of balls falling on to the floor.

Black Pool was the following version to be created. This was similar to Pyramid Pool except that the black ball from Life Pool was added to the game and could be potted for more points. In 1875, however, at the officers' mess in Jabalpur a colonel Sir Neville Francis Fitzgerald Chamberlain suggested that the other coloured balls should also be added to the new version. The game was now turning more like snooker is at present, even though both the blue and brown balls were added in later years.

The name for the new version came after the Colonel, Sir Neville Chamberlain, called one of the players 'a real snooker', when he had missed a shot, denoting to his lack of experience. 'Snooker' was a slang term for a first year cadet. This term was then linked with the game and so it was snooker. The first authorized set of rules for the new game were drafted up in 1882 in Ootacamund. When the British Billiard Champion, John Roberts, travelled to India in 1885 he met Chamberlain and then he decided to bring in the game to England when he arrived back there.

It took various years for the first authorized competitions to take place, but in 1916 the English Amateur Championships were first played and in 1927 Joe Davis helped to establish the first Professional World Championship. The winner of this was also Joe Davis who took home the winning prize of £6.10s. At the time the standard was not very high as the highest break of that tournament was just 33. Snooker, though, was commencing to become the most famous cue game especially in 1930s.

Joe Davis extended to dominate the era as he won each World Championship up to when he retired in 1946. He also seemed to be ahead of his time as he commemorated a maximum break and also had many of the skills and techniques of future generations. Soon afterwards, however, a dispute developed between the games then governing body, the Control Council, and the Billiards Association. As a result they were only two participants in the authorized World Championship, even though an unofficial one was organised and the winner of this at the time was in general regarded as the greatest player in the world. Horace Lindrum won the authorized one and so his name is engraved on the trophy. This happened from 1952 and 1957. The popularity of snooker declined all over the 50's and 60's and hence no world championship was held from 1958 and 1963.

In 1969, however, a new tournament called Pot Black was founded by the BBC as a result of the introduction of colour T.V. The programme proved to be huge success and helped put snooker back into the public's view. It was productive into the 1980s when it was discontinued but a new version has been run in recent years.

The World Championship was first televised in 1973 as snooker started to grow in popularity once once again. World Rankings were brought in in 1976 and in 1977 the World Championship was staged in the Crucible Theatre in Sheffield where it has been ever since. More money pullulated into the game due to the rise in popularity and a new breed of player began to emerge, like Steve Davis, who were young, serious and dedicated. Snooker reached its peak in popularity in 1985 with a titanic match in the World Championship final among Steve Davis and Dennis Taylor. Davis was favourite for the match and title due to his ascendency of the decade. Everything was going to plan for him when he raced into a 7-1 lead in the first session but Taylor came storming back and it finally went to a final frame decider which was decided on the final black ball at 00.20 in the morning with Taylor being the victor. This match received a huge U.K. T.V. rating of 18.5 million.

Snooker extended to be famous in the 1990s and into the new millennium. Stephen Hendry had been the prevailingforce during the 90's with his aggressive style. He broke many of Steve Davis's records as well as winning seven world championships. Snooker's grow in popularity seems to have stagnated now especially with the number of tournaments cut down than on previous years and also the blow of losing sponsorships for tournaments like the Masters and World Championship after it turned illegal in the U.K. for tobacco companies to sponsor sports tournaments. A big plus point for snooker, though, is its huge popularity in China. With many Chinese players taking up the game as well as the most outstanding, Ding Junhui who has already won a couple of ranking tournaments the future of the game

THE GAME

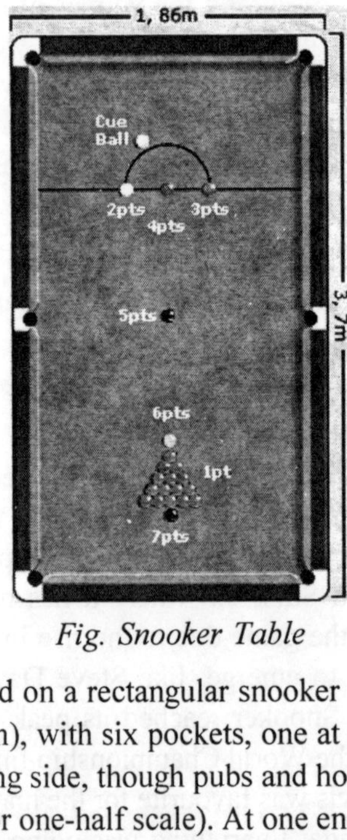

Fig. Snooker Table

Snooker is played on a rectangular snooker table, usually 6 feet by 12 feet (1.8 m x 3.6 m), with six pockets, one at each corner and one in the middle of each long side, though pubs and homes often have smaller versions (two-thirds or one-half scale). At one end of the table (thebaulk end) is the so-called baulk line, which is 29 inches (74 cm) from the baulk cushion (the short cushion at the baulk end). A semicircle of radius 11½ inches (29.5 cm), named the D, is drawn behind this line, centred on the middle of the line. The cushion on the other side of the table is called as the top cushion.

As of the large size of rules snooker tables, smaller tables are common in domestic positions and other situations where space is fixed. These are often around 6 feet (1.8 m)in length, and all the dimensions and markings are scaled down accordingly. The balls used are sometimes also scaled down, and/or reduced in number (in the case of the reds) such that the longest row of balls in the rack is omitted.

The Balls

Snooker balls, like the balls for all cue sports, are normally made of phenolic resin, but are smaller than pool balls. Regulation snooker balls (which are specified in metric units) are nominally 52.5 mm (approximately 2-D_{15} inches) in diameter, though many sets are actually manufactured at 52.4 mm (about 2-D_{16} in.) Some re created sets (which are normally not measured metrically) are 2-D_8 in. (about 54 mm) up to as large as pool balls, at 2-D_4 in. (about 57.2 mm); larger ball size requires wider pocket openings. Miniature sets also exist, for half-size home tables. There are fifteen red balls, six "colour" balls (yellow, green, brown, blue, pink, and black), and one white cue ball. Normally none of the balls are numbered, though the six colour balls often are in the US, where they are easily mistaken at first glance for pool balls (the design is similar, but the numbering does not match pool's scheme).

Fig. Balls

At the commencing of a frame, the balls are set up in the arrangement shown in the illustration. The six colours (a term referring to all balls but the white and the reds) are rated on their own spots. On the baulk line, looking up the table from the baulk end, the green ball is situated where the "D" meets the line on the left, the brown ball in the middle of the line, and the yellow ball where the "D" meets the line on the right. This order is often remembered utilizing the mnemonic God Bless You, the first letter of each word being the first letter of the three colours. At the exact centre of the table sits the blue ball. Further up the table is the pink ball, which sits midway among the blue spot and the top cushion, succeeded by the red balls, arranged in a tightly-packed triangle behind the pink (the apex must be as close as possible to the pink ball without touching it). Finally, the black ball is placed on a spot 32.5 cm (12.75 in.) from the top cushion.

Objective

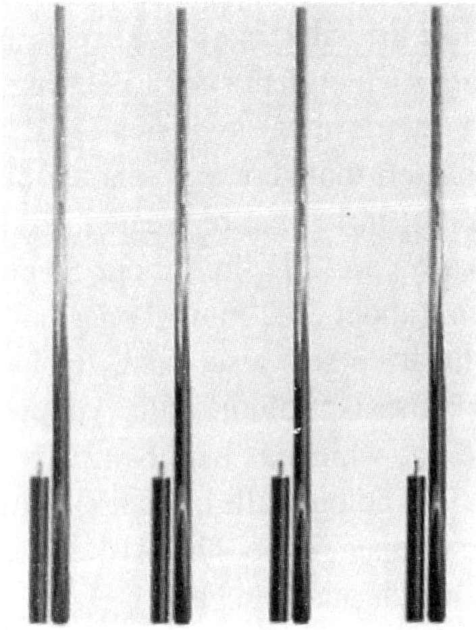

Fig. Cue

The aim of the game of snooker is to strike the white cue ball with a cue in the direction of other object balls and to pot these object balls in one of the six pockets. This must be done as per the rules of the game, which are described below. By potting object balls points can be scored. The player who marks most points wins the frame, and the player who wins most frames wins the match.

Snooker Match

A snooker match normally consists of an odd fixed number of frames. A frame begins with setting up the balls as described above. A frame ends when all balls are potted, or when one of the players confesses defeat because he is too far behind in score to equal or beat the score of the other player. A match ends when one of the players has won the most of the set number of frames and the other player can hence not equal this. For example, when a match consists of 19 frames, the match ends when one of the players has reached 10 frames.

Game Play

At the commencing of each frame the balls are set up by the referee as explained. This will be succeeded by a break-off shot, on which the players take turns. At the break-off, the white cue ball can be placed anywhere inside the D, even though it is common for players to start by placing the ball on the line, among the brown ball and either the green or yellow ball.

Players take turns in visiting the table. When one player is at the table, the other cannot play. A break is the number of points scored by a player in one single visit to the table. A player's turn and break end when he fails to pot a ball, when he does something in opposition to the rules of the game, which is called a foul, or when a frame has ended.

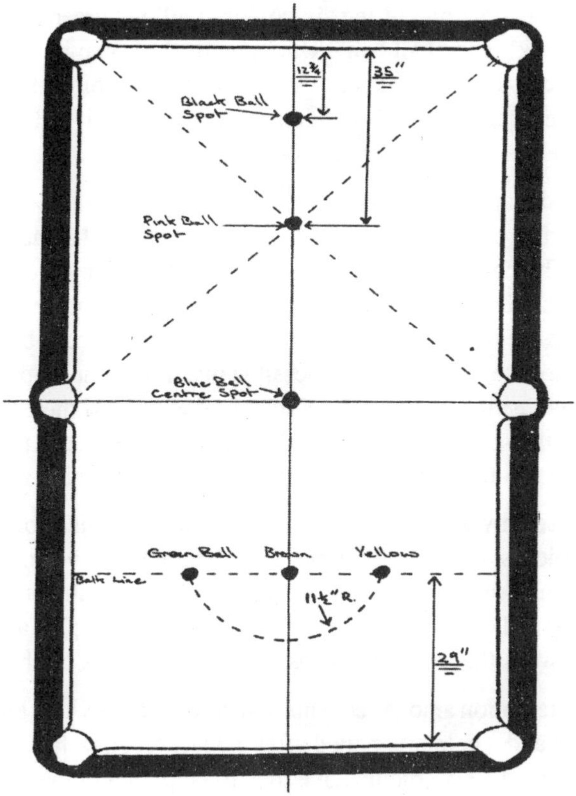

Fig. Snooker Table Measurements

The ball or balls that can be hit first by the white are called the ball(s) "on" for that particular stroke. The ball(s) "on" differ from shot to shot: a red ball, if potted, must be succeeded by a colour, and so on until a break ends; if a red is not potted, any red ball stays the ball "on". Only a ball or balls "on" may be potted legally by a player. If a ball not "on" is potted, this is a foul.

The game of snooker in general consists of two phases. The first phase is the situation in which there are still red balls on the table. In the first phase, at the commencing of a player's turn, the balls "on" are all left over red balls. The player must hence attempt to first hit and pot one or more red balls. For each red ball potted, the player will obtain 1 point. When a red has been potted, it will stay off the table and the player can continue his break. If no red has been potted or a foul has been made, the other player will come into play.

In case one or more red balls have been potted, the player can extend his break. This time one of the six colours (yellow, green, brown, blue, pink and black) is the ball "on". Only one of these can be the ball "on" and the patterns of the game state that a player must nominate his desired colour to the referee, even though it is often clear which ball the striker is playing and it is not necessary to nominate.

When the appointed colour is potted, the player will be granted the correct number of points (yellow, 2; green, 3; brown, 4; blue, 5; pink, 6; black, 7). The colour is then taken out of the pocket by the referee and placed on its original spot. If that spot is covered by another ball, the ball is placed on the highest accesible spot. If there is no accesible spot, it is placed as close to its own spot as possible in a direct line among that spot and the top cushion, without touching another ball. If there is no room this side of the spot, it will be placed as close to the spot as possible in a straight line towards the bottom cushion, without touching another ball.

Because only one of the colours is the ball "on", it is a foul to first hit multiple colours at the similar time, or pot more than one colour (unless a free ball has been granted). If a player fails to pot a ball "on", it being a red or appointed colour, the other player will come into play and the balls "on" are always the reds, as long as there are still reds on the table.

The alternation among red balls and colours ends when all reds have been potted and a colour is potted after the last red, or a failed attempt to do so is made. All six colours have then to be potted in the correct order (yellow, green, brown, blue, pink, black). Each turns the ball "on" in that order. Throughout this phase, when potted, the colours stay down and are not substituted on the table, unless a foul is made when potting the colour, in which case the colour is respotted. When the colours have been potted, the frame is over and the player who has scored most points has won it.

Fouls

A foul is a shot or action by the striker which is in opposition to the rules of the game. When a foul is made throughout a shot, the player's turn is ended and he will obtain no points for the foul shot. The other player will obtain penalty points.

Common fouls are:

- failing to hit any other ball with the cue ball
- first hitting a ball "not-on" with the cue ball
- potting a ball "not-on"
- potting the white (in-off)
- hitting a ball other than the white with the cue
- making a ball land off the table
- touching a ball with something other than the tip of the cue
- playing a "push shot" - a shot where the cue, cue ball and object ball are in simultaneous contact
- playing a "jump shot", which is where the cue ball leaves the bed of the table and jumps over a ball (even if touching it in the process) before first hitting another ball
- playing a shot with both feet off the ground

Should a cue ball be "in-hand", i.e. when breaking-off or playing from the "D" after being potted, be touched with the tip, a foul is not confided as long as the referee is satisfied that the player was only placing the ball, and not playing, or preparing to play, a shot.

When a foul is made, the other player will obtain penalty points. Penalty points are at least 4 points and at most 7 points. The number of penalty points is the value of the ball "on", or any of the "foul" balls, whichever is highest. When more than one foul is made, the penalty is not the added total — only the most highly valued foul is considered.

Not hitting the ball "on" first is the most common foul. Players can make life difficult for an opponent by making sure that they cannot hit a ball "on" directly. This is most commonly called "snookering" your opponent or instead "laying a snooker" or putting the other player "in a snooker".

Since players obtain points for fouls by their opposers, snookering your opponent a number of times in a row is a possible way of winning a frame when potting all the balls on the table would be deficient for you to win.

If a player commits a foul, and his opponent considers that the position left is unattractive, he may request that the offender play once again from that position.

If a foul has been committed by not hitting a ball "on" first, or at all, and the referee judges that the player has not made the greatest possible effort to hit a ball "on", and neither of the players are in need of snookers to win the frame, or would be after the penalty points were applied, then "foul, and a miss" is called. In this instance the other player may request that all balls on the table are came back to their position before the foul, and the opponent play the shot once again. (In top class play, this will normally require only the cue ball and a couple of other balls to be moved.) It should be noted that this rule is often applied less stringently, if at all, in amateur matches.

When a player leaves an opposer unable to hit both sidelong extremities of at least one ball "on" after a foul, the opponent will obtain a free ball. This means any colour can be appointed and played as the ball "on". The number of points for potting the free ball is not the worth of the appointed ball but of the original ball "on". For example, if the ball "on" is a red, and the free ball is a pink, the player will obtain one point for potting the pink. After embedding the free ball as a red, a player can nominate and pot a colour as usual. The only exception to this rule is if the "on" ball is a red that is being impeded by another red. For example, if the player breaking-off hits the white too soft and it does not hit the triangle of reds, a free-ball would not be called, even though no red can be hit on both sides, since the only thing preventing some of the reds being hit on both sides is another red.

Free Ball

Free ball occurs after a foul shot where the outcome layout of the table leaves the opponent snookered (unable to hit any legitimate ball on either side). The opponent of the player who confided the foul can choose any other ball on the table as a replacement for the ball in question, and pot this as if it were the intended ball. If this was a red, then he continues to pot a colour which is, if productive, succeeded by another red etc.

If free ball occurs with all 15 reds still on the table, it gives a chance to an offended player to compile a break higher than 147 (147 is attained by potting 15 reds and 15 blacks with all colours afterwards); in theory a break of 155 could be played but it has never been attained in a professional tournament.However, breaks of 149 and 148 did occur in a professional tournament and Jamie Cope managed a 155 break, but only in a practice session.

It is permitted to play a snooker utilizing the free ball, providing the snooker is not behind the ball which has just been used as the ball 'on'. It is permitted to cannon a ball nominated as a red into another red, so as to pot this (a plant).

A free ball scenario also occurs when the ball bogs down at the edge of a pocket jaw in such a manner that the player is not able to hit any legitimate ball. In this case also the player can play by calling any other ball as the "on" ball.

Miss

A miss wili be cried if a player does not hit the ball "on" first and is held by the referee to not have made a good enough attempt at the shot. This gives his opponent the option to have the balls substituted as they were and have the fouling player take his shot once again. A miss would not normally be called should the offending player require snookers, but there are exceptions to this scenario. Firstly, it may be possible to make full central contact on the ball "on" with a plain straight stroke, in which case a miss would be called each time an unsuccessful attempt at hitting it was developed. Secondly, it is still up to the referee's discretion whether an adequate attempt at hitting the object ball was made. If the referee deems that the snookered player has made no genuine effort to hit the ball, a miss can still be called in spite of snookers being needed.

The rule was brought in to prevent players from playing professional fouls, i.e. intentionally fouling so as to leave the balls in a safe position, reducing the risk of giving a frame-winning chance to the opponent. Multiple misses often occur because players attempt to hit a shot thinly, in situations where such a contact would leave their opponent no potting chance. This can lead to a relatively easy full-ball escape being retaken various times, as players feel that it is better to concede many points but leave a safe position, than concede none and leave a frame-winning chance.

However, the applied rendering of the rule has proved controversial, as players sometimes narrowly miss a shot many times. Sometimes this is due to pure bad luck, or the trouble of the snooker - meaning that a good snooker can pay more dividends than a great pot.

The End of a Frame

If the score is tied after the final black is potted, the black is "respotted" and the cue ball put "in hand". The referee will then toss a coin, with the player winning the toss choosing who will take first strike at the black. Play then continues usually until the black is potted or another frame-ending situation occurs. A frame usually ends in one of three ways:

A concession, when one player gives up due to being too far behind to have a realistic chance of winning the frame (normally when at the snookers-required stage).

When the pink is potted in the final stage of the frame, and the potting player leads by more than seven points as a result. The striker may pot the black, for example to complete a high-scoring break, if he so desires. The final black is potted legally (as well as after a respot), and the seven points scored puts one player ahead.

There are three less common ways to end a frame:

A foul on the black, when the seven-point penalty puts the fighting player ahead by any score. It is sometimes wrongly assumed that play extends after a foul on the black if there are less than seven points among the scores. This is not the case: the player who has made such a foul loses the frame.

Failure to hit a ball "on" three times in a row, if the player has a clear sight of the ball. The referee will warn a player after a second such miss that a third miss will mean forfeiting the frame. This rule does not apply if the player is snookered. As missing due to averting a direct shot on a ball is normally a tactical, rather than skill-related, outcome, this rule is rarely raised, as a player will simply hit the ball directly on the third shot.

If the referee deems a player is taking too long to take his shot, the player may be warned. If the player extends to hesitate, the frame may be granted to the other player at the discernment of the referee. In practice, a delay of over two minutes can result in such forfeiture.

Highest Break

The highest break that can be made under normal conditions is 147. To achieve that, the player must pot all 15 reds, with the black after each red, succeeded by potting the six left over colours. This "maximum break" of 147 rarely occurs in match play.

If an opponent fouls before any balls are potted, and leaves the player a free ball, the player can then nominate a colour and play it as a red ball. Then, black can be nominated as the following colour. This means it is really possible to score the value of 16 reds and blacks (16 * 8), plus the values of all the colours (27), which equal 155 points scored. This has never been done in a professional tournament. The highest break in tournament play is 149, and the highest break in professional matchplay is 148.

MAJOR TOURNAMENTS

World Snooker Championship

The World Snooker Championship, presently deemed at the Crucible Theatre in the English city of Sheffield, is the climax of snooker's annual calendar and the most important snooker event of the year in terms of prestige, prize money and world ranking points. The existing champion is Ronnie O'Sullivan.

The first championship was deemed in 1927, and the legendary Joe Davis helped to organise the event. Matches were deemed at various venues, and the final was held at Camkin's Hall, Birmingham. Joe Davis won the event, defeating Tom Dennis 20-11. His prize money was £6.10s. The highest break of the tournament was 60 by Albert Cope.

In subsequent years, finals were deemed at various venues. Joe Davis won every year until 1940, when he just beat his younger brother Fred 37-36. No tournaments were organised throughout the remaining war years, and it only resumed in 1946 when Joe Davis won once again for the 15th time, a record that still stands. Joe Davis never contested the world championship once again, though he extended to play professional snooker. Some have speculated that he did not want to risk losing his unbeaten record.

Walter Donaldson won in 1947, but it was Fred Davis who prevailed the following few years, winning it three times in 1948, 1949 and 1951.

In 1952, as a result of a disagreement among the governing bodies (the Billiards Association and Control Council), and some of the players, two tournaments were deemed. The World Matchplay, organized by the players and broadly viewed as the "real" world championship, extended until 1957. The BA&CC event only lasted one year. Meanwhile the 'authorized' world championship did attract two entrants in 1952, Horace Lindrum (Australia) defeating New Zealander Clark McConachy – and it is Lindrum's name that is inscribed on the familiar trophy.

Snooker then went into a period of decline, and no tournament was deemed from 1958 and 1963. In 1964 it was revived on a challenge basis, a layout which lasted until 1968. This meant that matches was held on an irregular basis, sometimes more than once a year. John Pulman completely prevailed throughout this period, overcoming all challengers in a total of seven matches.

The championship reverted back to a knockout tournament in 1969. That year it was won by John Spencer, but it was Ray Reardon who was to dominate over the coming years, winning six times from 1970 and 1978.

1976 was the first year the championships were sponsored by the cigarette brand Embassy. The following year, the event moved to the Crucible Theatre in Sheffield, UK, and the BBC began providing main television coverage. The Crucible provides a unique atmosphere to the tournament, both for spectators and live television viewers. The venue seats fewer than a thousand people with the front row of seats only a few feet from the players.

This was about the time snooker began pulling very large television audiences, and for most fans The Crucible is synonymous with snooker. The most productive players at The Crucible are Steve Davis, who won six times in the 1980s, and Stephen Hendry, who won seven times in the 1990s. In recent times, the tournament has been more open, with six dissimslar winners in the last six years (2002-07). The most famous finaltook placein 1985, when Dennis Taylor beat Steve Davis 18-17 in one of the most closely contested matches of all time.

In 2004, the championship offered a total of £1,378,920 ($2,665,589) in prize money, as well as £250,000 ($483,274) for the winner and £125,000 ($241,637) for the runner-up. A further £147,000 ($284,165) was on offer for a 147 break, though no player attained this.

Recent United Kingdom legislation has placed restrictions on tobacco advertising, as well as sponsorship of sporting events. Embassy had a special dispensation to continue snooker sponsorship until 2005. The Championship is presently without a title sponsor after 888.com pulled out of their five year sponsorship deal after three years. Throughout the 2005 Championship it was declarted that the Championship would remain at the Crucible for at least another five years. Plans to build a purpose-built billiardrome in the city are in their early stages. It is anticipated that the World Championships will be switched to the new venue once the existing Crucible contract ends.

A recent contract ensures that the BBC will continue to televise this event (along with three others) until 2011. IMG Media (initially as TWI) have developed the BBC's Snooker coverage since 1998.

Premier League Snooker

Premier League Snooker, is a professional snooker tournament. It has been running since 1987. The tournament is played in a league formatTemplate:Clariflyme over a number of weeks, normally from mid-September to early-December, all over the other main WPBSA events. It is not a ranking event.

The league is an invitation-only event, contended primarilyprimarily by players in the World's Top 10. The combination of players is chosen though to have maximum televisual appeal, so it is usual for a mixture of high-ranked players, upcoming youngsters yet to reach the top 10, famous older players now out of the top 10 and players with an appeal to international (i.e. non-UK) markets such as Asia or Australia to be selected. The players play each other once in a 6-frame match. Unlike other snooker events, a draw is a possible result in the league. 2 points are granted for a victory, and 1 for a draw. At the end of the round-robin stage, the top 4 players in the league table go forward to the greatest of 9 semi-finals stage. The final is then played over the greatest of 13 frames.

The main difference from other tournaments is the presence of a shot clock. Each player has 25 seconds to strike the cue ball from the time the clock starts. This is decided by the timing official, and the clock normally starts when the balls have come to rest from the previous shot. The penalty for exceeding the limit is 5 points. Each player is permitted 5 time outs per match where the clock is stopped and they may have as long as they require to take their shot. A player is permitted no more than 3 time outs per frame.

The event commenced in 1987 with Steve Davis winning for the first 4 years. It has been prevailed by Davis, Stephen Hendry and Ronnie O'Sullivan, who among them have taken 17 of the 22 titles in the competition's history. O'Sullivan has won the most titles, having won 7 in total.

The 2007 event was contended by Ronnie O'Sullivan, Ding Junhui, John Higgins, Neil Robertson, Stephen Hendry, Jimmy White and Steve Davis. It ran from 6 September to 2 December.

In the semi-finals, Higgins defeated Ding 5–3, while O'Sullivan beat Hendry 5–1.The final was a greatest-of-13 match finally won by O'Sullivan 7–4 over Higgins.This was O'Sullivan's 4th succeedingfinal victory in this event, winning this event finals 7 times in total.

ADMINISTRATIVE BODIES

World Professional Billiards and Snooker Association

The World Professional Billiards and Snooker Association (WPBSA, also called as the World Snooker Association) is the governing body of world snooker and English Billiards. It is sometimes mistakenly presumed that the "P" in "WPBSA" stands for "Pool", but in fact, the organisation does not comprise pool in its remit.

It was established in 1968 as the Professional Billiard Players' Association. Its subsidiary, World Snooker, is responsible running and administering snooker's main ranking circuit events. The WPSBA is also responsible for organising invitation events such as the Masters. The head office is established in Bristol, England. The WPBSA is also responsible for the rules and regulations of snooker, as well as disciplinary matters. The existing chairman of the WPBSA board is Sir Rodney Walker.

International Billiards and Snooker Federation

The International Billiards & Snooker Federation (IBSF) is the organisation that rules non-professional snooker and English billiards all over the world.

In 1971 the World Billiards and Snooker Council was established, changing its name in 1973 to the International Billiards and Snooker Federation. The name change came about because of the dissatisfaction of many abroad national associations that the Billiards and Snooker Control Council (then the Billiards Association and Control Council) should be the ruling body of both the English domestic game and the game at international level. Accordingly, the IBSF took control of the organisation of the non-professional championships of both snooker and billiards.

The IBSF is made up of over sixty affiliated countries all of which belong one of the five Olympic regions: Africa, Americas, Asia, Europe and Oceania.

The IBSF Board of Directors has four executive officers, namely the President, Vice-President, Secretary and Treasurer, plus two spokespeople from each Olympic Region. These four executive officers are responsible for the day to day running of the Federation and are responsible to IBSF members at the Annual General Meeting. The IBSF AGM is normally deemed throughout the period of the IBSF World Snooker Championships.

The aims and objectives of the IBSF are to co-ordinate, promote and develop the sports of billiards and snooker on a non-professional level and, as the world governing body, to decide championship conditions, formats, dates and venues.

The IBSF also encourages and fosters snooker and English billiards with all other bodies with similar objectives.

The IBSF is the snooker division of the World Confederation of Billiard Sports (WCBS). The WCBS is an organisation that encourages cue sports in the form of carom, pool and snooker. Its primary aim is to gain the acceptation of these three cue sports disciplines into the Olympic Games.

The IBSF also works towards preserving a healthy relationship with the professional side of the game, the World Professional Billiards and Snooker Association (WPBSA), so as to ensure maximum growth for snooker and English billiards universal.

FAMOUS PLAYERS

Ronnie O'Sullivan

Ronald Antonio "Ronnie" O'Sullivan (born 5 December 1975 in Wordsley, West Midlands), nicknamed "The Rocket" due to his fast playing style, is an English professional snooker player, and the reigning World No. 1. He has been world champion on three occasions (2001, 2004 and 2008) and is second on the all time prize money list with career earnings of all over £5.8 million, behind only Stephen Hendry. He has won a total of 21 ranking titles.

O'Sullivan is believed by many fans, critics and fellow professionals such as Steve Davis and Stephen Hendry as the most naturally talented player in the history of the game. He has also been involved in a number of controversial incidents throughout his career, being a famous figure for many British tabloids.

O'Sullivan grew up and still lives in the exclusive Manor Road area in Chigwell, Essex and attended Wanstead High School. He began his career at an early age. He first attained a century break at the age of 10, making a 117; scored a 147 or maximum break at 15; and turned professional at 16. He won his first 38 matches as a professional – a record that still stands – on his way to the 1993 World Championship, where he stays the youngest-ever player to qualify. He lost in the first round 10-7 to Alan McManus and ended his debut season ranked 57. He was the youngest ever winner of a ranking tournament when he won the 1993 UK Championship aged 17, defeating Stephen Hendry in the final, and commencing one of the most outstanding rivalries in the game. In 1995, he won his first Masters title.

In the 1996 World Championship, snooker's ruling body found him guilty of assaulting Mike Ganley, then a media official, now the tournament director. He was given a two-year suspended sentence and a £20,000 fine, and advised to donate £10,000 to charity.

On 21 April 1997, in the first round of the World Championship in opposition to Mick Price, he made the fastest-recorded maximum break (and also his first), 5 minutes and 20 seconds, an average of one shot every 9 seconds. In November, he won his second UK title, defeating Hendry 10-6 in the final.

After winning the 1998 Benson & Hedges Irish Masters in opposition to Ken Doherty, he was stripped of his title after a drugs test found cannabis in his system.

O'Sullivan made it to the semi-finals of the 1999 Embassy World Championship, losing 17-14 to Stephen Hendry, in a match featuring many century breaks among the two players. O'Sullivan's foreboding campaign in the 1999–2000 season (when he won three ranking titles) ended in disappointment, however — following his solid performance the previous year, he was a favourite for the 2000 world title, especially after Hendry's unexpected 10-7 first-round loss to Stuart Bingham. However, O'Sullivan was also ruled out in the first round by David Gray, who came from 5-1 and 9-7 down to edge out O'Sullivan 10-9 for a place in the second round. In this particular match, O'Sullivan made five centuries (three in consecutive frames, equalling the record deemed by John Higgins), all to no avail, and Gray commemorated four.

In 2001, O'Sullivan arrogated his first World Championship title (dedicated to his father), with an 18-14 victory over John Higgins, and his third UK title, with a 10-1 victory over Doherty. He commenced the 2002/2003 season ranked number 1.

In 2002, before his World Championship semi-final with Hendry, O'Sullivan accused him of bad sportsmanship after the latter's quarter-final victory over Doherty; the similar day O'Sullivan edged his quarter-final in opposition to Stephen Lee 13-10 to set up a meeting with Hendry in the semis. Referring to a previous match in opposition to Hendry in 1999 at a pre-match interview, he pointed out: "I know if I do get beat and he comes up and does a moonie in front of me and goes 'Ne ne ne', I'll just look at him and say 'well done' and say 'go back to your sad little life'.In the match, O'Sullivan had the better of the first day's play, opening up an 8-5 lead; but on the second day Hendry rallied back to 12-12 going into the final session. Hendry afterwards outplayed O'Sullivan and won convincingly 17-13. Hendry didn't comment on his opponent's outburst following the match, even though O'Sullivan did obtain some unfavorable judgment for his remarks from Steve Davis and Clive Everton. O'Sullivan later apologised to Hendry for his comments.

In 2003, following a season that saw him win the Scottish Masters, the European Open and Irish Masters, O'Sullivan's season ended on another dissatisfactory note when he was knocked out of the World Championship in the first round for the third time in his career, losing 10-6 to the unseeded Marco Fu, in spite of making another maximum 147 break in the match. This defeat saw him drop to number three in the rankings.

In 2004, O'Sullivan's father telephoned 1970s six-time World Champion Ray Reardon and asked if he could give O'Sullivan some proposal. With Reardon's backing, O'Sullivan came into top form and claimed the World Championship, defeating Graeme Dott very convincing in the final by 18 frames to 8. He lost the first five frames of the match, however, which he assigned to his opponent's (and O'Sullivan's former) coach's mind games – entering O'Sullivan's dressing room minutes before the match. He also beat Hendry 17-4 in the semi-final – the heaviest defeat ever in a World Championship semi-final. He was ranked number one for the following two seasons.

O'Sullivan plays in a fast and attacking manner. He is a prolific breakbuilder and solid tactical player, even though he has stated his disdain for long, drawn-out games, saying that it harms the game of snooker. He is a good front-runner, even though tends to become demoralised when behind and not playing well, and is liable to lose multiple consecutive frames. When behind and needing snookers, he tends to concede more often than other players, even though after Ray Reardon's coaching he does seem to carry on with the frame a lot more than before.

O'Sullivan is right-handed, but can play to a high standard with his left hand. While not quite possessing the similar power in his left arm, being ambidextrous enables him to attempt shots with his left hand that would otherwise require awkward cueing with a rest or spider. O'Sullivan sometimes plays with a variety of bridge hands.

When he first displayed this left-handed capability in the 1996 World Championship in opposition to Alain Robidoux, the Canadian accused him of disrespect. O'Sullivan responded that he played better with his left hand than Robidoux could with his right. O'Sullivan was cited to a disciplinary hearing in response to Robidoux's formal complaint, where he had to prove that he could play to a high level with his left hand. He played three frames of snooker in opposition to former world championship runner-up Rex Williams, winning all three. The charge of bringing the game into disrepute was subsequently dropped.

He is believed by many to be the most naturally-talented player in the history of the game, with many such as Steve Davis labelling him a 'genius'; some have said that his highest level of play is above any other player's highest level of play; and many have hailed him as the greatest player ever, even though a temperamental streak sometimes lead to a lack of confidence or interest, and he has performed inconsistently during his controversial career thus far, with observers noting the 'two Ronnies' aspect of his character.

As per Stephen Hendry after his defeat at the World Snooker Championship 2008, "O'Sullivan is the greatest player in the world by a country mile".

O'Sullivan is also the most famous player on the circuit – along with Jimmy White, another very famous English player – and is noted for being a 'showman'. He is perhaps the biggest draw in the game at present, and has helped improve the image of snooker to the general public. O'Sullivan himself has stated his desire for entertaining the watching public, and said that slow, gritty games put viewers off.

He has often been equated to Alex Higgins and Jimmy White because of both his natural talent and popularity.O'Sullivan has compiled over 500 competitive centuries throughout his career, second only to Hendry who has played as a pro 7 years longer.

Stephen Maguire

Stephen Maguire (born March 13, 1981) is a Scottish professional snooker player from Glasgow. When he was young, he was so keen to play the game that his grandparents knocked a wall out of their flat to assure that a table would fit.Maguire almost qualified for the 2000 World Championships, heading eventual semi-finalist Joe Swail 9-6 in the final qualifying round before losing 10-9, but first served notice of his true potency by knocking out Stephen Lee in the first round of the UK Championship in 2002.

Maguire was the surprise winner of the 2004 European Open. Ranked 41 in the world at the time, he beat well proved top-16 player Jimmy White 9-3 in the final. It was in that similar season that he qualified for the World Championship for the first time, losing 6-10 in the first round to Ronnie O'Sullivan. After losing 6-9 to John Higgins in the final of the British Open, Maguire then went on to win the UK Championship on 28 November 2004 with an emphatic 10-1 victory over David Gray in the final, after having knocked out world number one Ronnie O'Sullivan before in the tournament. He has played O'Sullivan five times so far in his career, also losing to him in a World Snooker Championship first-round match for a second successive year in 2005, 9-10, having led 9-7. The second half of his 2004/2005 season was less successful, but he still moved up to #3 in the world rankings. In the 2005/2006 season, he only reached one quarter-final, demonastrating evidence of a loss in form, especially when losing 13-4 to qualifier Marco Fu in the second round of the World Championships.

Maguire has a rivalry with Shaun Murphy. In a 2004 Grand Prix match, Murphy was involved in having one of Maguire's frames forfeited. As the match was about to commences, Maguire realized he had forgotten to bring his chalk with him. He asked referee Johan Oomen for permit to leave the arena. While he was away, Murphy spoke to the referee; the tournament director Mike Ganley was summoned and he docked Maguire a frame for not being ready to start at the scheduled time.Maguire later won the match 5-2. Later that year, whilst playing in the final of the UK Championships, David Gray forgot his chalk. However, Maguire let him get it without a frame being docked. After the before mentioned 2006 World Championship match with Marco Fu, Maguire said, 'I don't want to be a fat world champion', a dig at Murphy, which may have simply reflected Maguire's own disappointment at his season, which saw him slide from 3 to 9 in the rankings.

In 2007, he showed his greatest run at the World Championship reaching the semi-final, where he lost 15-17 to ultimate champion John Higgins having led 14-10. In the 2008 World Championships, he was edged out by Joe Perry in the quarter-finals 13-12.

Stephen once again beat Shaun Murphy in the 2007 UK Championship semi-final 9-5 only to lose 10-2 to Ronnie O'Sullivan in the final. In the 2008 China Open, he compiled a 147 in completely defeating his friend Welshman Ryan Day 6-5 in the semi-finals, before edging out Shaun Murphy once again in the final by 10 frames to 9.

In spite of losing at the quarter-final stage of the 2008 World Championship in another final frame decider (12-13) to Joe Perry, he turned the world number 2, his highest ever rating, for the 2008/09 season. Having severed most of his ties the previous summer, Maguire formally left Management Company 110sport in the summer of 2008.

Shaun Murphy

Shaun Murphy (born August 10, 1982 in Harlow, England) is an English professional snooker player and the 2005 World Snooker

Champion. Murphy is noted for his broadly acclaimed cue action and his consistent long potting. He is also part of a small group of players that can play with their left hand as well as their right. For the 2007-2008 season, Murphy was rated at number three, his highest ever, and he retained this for the following season.

Murphy commenced playing snooker at the age of 8 when he was given a snooker cue that his father had bought from a jumble sale. He soon joined a club and exercised heavily, making his first century break by the age of 10. At the age of 13, he gave an interview to the BBC, stating his ambitions of winning the World Championship and turning world number one. Aged 13 he had already secured a £5,000-a-year sponsorship deal. He turned professional at 15.

In 2000, he was granted World Snooker Newcomer of the Year and Young Player of Distinction of the Year, but his advance was gradual until his World Championship victory. In the similar year, he won the Amateur English Open and the Benson & Hedges Championship, and made a maximum break in the following year's Benson & Hedges tournament. He reached the semi-finals of the British Open in 2004, his first run past the last 16 of a rating event. He reached the Crucible in 2002 and 2003, losing 10-9 to Ken Doherty on the final black in the latter, and lost a specifying match to Stuart Pettman in 2004.

Throughout the 2005 tournament, he beat former world champions John Higgins (13-8), Steve Davis (13-4), Peter Ebdon (17-12), and competitor Matthew Stevens (18-16) to win the World Championship. His run echoed the first championship win of his childhood idol Davis, who also beat three world champions (Alex Higgins, Cliff Thorburn and Terry Griffiths) to reach the final.

The tournament doubled his previous career prize money and his run to the final earned him the nickname Magician. He purchased a Mercedes-Benz E-Class and a house with the proceeds of his win.

At the age of 22, Murphy turned the second youngest player ever to win the World Championship, following Stephen Hendry who first lifted the title when he was 21. He also turned only the second-ever qualifier to win the World Championship, the other being Terry Griffiths in 1979.

Murphy commenced the 2005 World Championship rated number 48 in the world rankings and with the odds of 150-1. He had to play two qualifying matches to reach the final stages. No former world champion had played that many matches (seven in total) to lift the title.

He was rated number 21 after his title win, which made him the first world champion to start the new season outside of the top 16. However, he qualified automatically for each tournament in the season as the number two seed (and number one seed for the 2006 World Championship). In the first three events of the season he attained the last 16, missing deciding-frame matches to Stuart Bingham, Neil Robertson and Graeme Dott respectively. He was more successful at the Welsh Open, reaching the final earlier losing to Stephen Lee. In the 2006 World Championship, he fell victim to the "Crucible Curse" (no first-time champion ever successfully defending the title at the Crucible) when he was defeated in the quarter-finals 13-7 by Peter Ebdon, after victories over James Wattana and Steve Davis. His overall performances over the previous two seasons moved him up to number five in the world rankings. He spent some of the coming summer doing work for a Christian charity group in Zimbabwe with his wife.

After 22 months without a title, Murphy won the 2007 Malta Cup in February 2007, defeating Welshman Ryan Day by 9 frames to 4 in the final. In his very following match, in opposition to Jamie Cope in the Welsh Open, he scored centuries in four consecutive frames, turning only the second player ever to do this (after John Higgins in the 2005 Grand Prix final) and the only person to do so in a greatest-of-nine match. Murphy reached the semi-finals of the 2007 World Championship after a 13-12 victory over Matthew Stevens in the quarter-finals. Murphy came from 11-5 and 12-7 down to defeat Stevens, knocking the latter out of the top 16 in doing so. However, he lost to Mark Selby in the semi-finals in another deciding frame. He ended the season ranked number three, his highest ever ranking.

In the 2007 Grand Prix, he won four out of five matches in his group, only losing out to Marco Fu, before defeating Ryan Day and Peter Ebdon to reach the semi-finals, where he lost 6-5 to Ronnie O'Sullivan, in spite of being 2-5 up at one point. He reached the semi-finals of the Northern Ireland Trophy and the UK Championship, making it three consecutive semi-final appearances and four of the last five. Before the UK Championship, he was provisionally ranked number one.

Murphy successfully defended his Malta Cup title in 2008, defeating Irishman Ken Doherty 9-3 in the final (the 2008 event, however, was not a ranking event). He has reached the final of Pot Black twice, losing to Matthew Stevens in 2005 and Ken Doherty in 2007. He was coached by Steve Prest, who helped Murphy perfect his cue action and develop the tactical side of his game. Murphy was coached early on in his career by

Joe Johnson, another surprise winner of the World Championship. He has also received tactical guidance from Ray Reardon.

Murphy has a rivalry with Stephen Maguire, another member of the 2000 Young Players of Distinction. In a 2004 Grand Prix match, Murphy was involved in having one of Maguire's frames forfeited. As the match was about to commences, Maguire realised he had forgotten to bring his chalk with him. He asked referee Johan Oomen for permission to leave the arena.While Maguire was away, Murphy spoke to the referee; the tournament director Mike Ganley was marshalled and he docked Maguire a frame for not being ready to start at the scheduled time.Maguire later won the match 5-2. After defeating Murphy in the 2007 Welsh Open, Maguire said of the incident, "That put the icing on the cake, but we've always had a rivalry. I dislike him and I think he dislikes me. I try hard to beat everyone, but it would have hurt more if I'd lost to him." Before their 2007 Northern Ireland Trophy semi-final clash, Murphy remarked that the media had amplified the rift, commenting that "It might add spice for you (the media), but I said hello to Stephen in the practice room this morning. He's a fantastic player and I've got great respect for him. I'm willing to get on with him and if there's a problem it's not at my end".They played each other once again at the following tournament, the UK Championship, once more at the semi-final stage, which Maguire won as well. And in the final of the 2008 China Open Maguire defeated him once once again, but this time only in a final frame decider: 10-9.

Murphy was born in Harlow, but lives in Rotherham with his wife Clare, whom he met on an online Christian chat room. He is a devout Christian and prays in his dressing room before every match. Murphy is a keen piano player and single-figure handicap golfer.

Throughout the 2007 World Championship it was described in some newspapers that he had developed a rift with his father, Tony, who is a member of the World Snooker board. He revealed that this happened 18 months earlier and that they had not spoken since. He did, however, state on BBC snooker coverage that he would happily speak to his father once again if he was called.

REFERENCES

Garnier, Albert.:*Scientific Billiards. Garnier's Practice Shots, with Hints to Amateurs.* New York: D. Appleton & Company, 1880.

Collender, H.W.:*Modern Billiards*. New York: The Brunswick-Balke-Collendar Co., 1884.

Drayson, Major-General A.W., F.R.A.S. 1897.

Bennett, Joseph.:*Billiards.* London: Thos. De la Rue & Co. Ltd. Edited by Cavendish, 1899.

Stancliffe: Fun On The Billiard Table- Being a collection of amusing tricks & games for amateurs with diagrams. London, 1900 or 1914.

Woerz:*Woerz' Billardbuch.* W. Berlin: Grieben-Verlag, 1904.

Roberts, Charles:Robert's Billiards for Everybody. London: George Routledge, 1906.

Billiards Association & Control Council:*The Rules of Snooker.* London: The Billiards Association & Control Council, 1919.

Horemans, E.J.F.:*Het Biljartspel.* Rotterdam: Nijgh & Van Ditmar's Uitgevers-Mij, 1919.

Daly, Maurice:Daly's Billiard Book. Chicago: A.C. McClurg & Co., 1920.

Roberts, John: *The Game of Billiards and How to Play It.* London: C. Arthur Pearson Ltd, 1922.

13

Squash

Squash is a racquet game that was formerly called squash rackets, a reference to the "squashable" soft ball used in the game (equated with the harder ball used in its parent game Rackets. The game is played by two players (or four players for doubles) with "standard" rackets in a four-walled court with a small, hollow rubber ball. Squash is characterized as a "high-impact" exercise that can place strain on the joints, notably the knees. Squash isacceptedby the IOC and stays in contention for incorporation in a future Olympic program.

HISTORY

The game of squash was developed established on other pre-existing racquet sports, especially rackets and fives, a set of sports played predominantly by boarders at British independent schools. Squash itself was formulated at one of these schools, London's Harrow School, in the early nineteenth century, when the boys noted that puncturing a rackets' ball caused it to squash when attaining the wall, allowing a greater variety of shots. By the end of the century it had spread to Britain's other private schools as well as Oxford and Cambridge universities. In 1908 a squash sub-committee of the Tennis and Rackets Association was established to regulate the game, succeeded in 1928 by the British Squash Rackets Association.

THE GAME

Court

The court size was statute in the 1920s at 975 cm (32 feet) and 640 cm (21 feet) broad. The front wall has a "front wall line" 457 cm (15 feet) above the floor, associated by a raking "front" line meeting the "out" line on the back wall at 213 cm (7 feet) above the floor. The front wall also has a "service line" whose top is 183 cm (6 feet) above the floor with the "board" (the equivalent of a net) 48 cm (18.9 inches) high. The floor is noticed with a transverse "half-court" line and further divided into two rear "quarter courts" and two "service boxes", as shown in the diagram above.

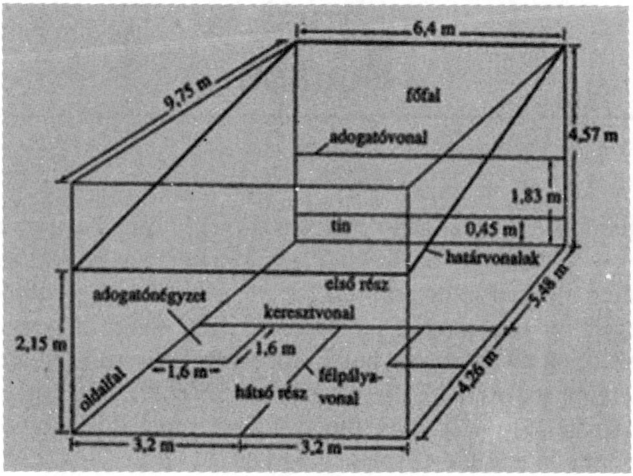

Fig. Court

The historical"American" court for the U.S. game, (now referred to as "hardball squash") is a similar size, but minuter at 18 feet 6 inches (564 cm). The floor and wall markings differ slightly from the "International" court and the tin is lower, at 15 inches (38 cm) high. However, hardball squash was substituted by softball in America as the standard version of squash and has since almost completely died out.

A "Converted Court" is the result of changing racquetball courts to squash. Racquetball courts are 20 feet (610 cm) broad and 40 feet (1220 cm) in length, so it is relatively easy to install a back wall, developing a squash court of 20 feet (610 cm) broad by 32 feet (975 cm) long.

Playing Equipment

Standard rackets are governed by the rules of the game. Traditionally they were made of laminated timber (normally Ash), with a small strung area utilizing natural gut strings. After a rule change in the mid-1980s, they are now almost always made of composite materials or metals (graphite, kevlar, titanium, boron) with synthetic strings. Modern rackets have maximum dimensions of 686 mm (27.0 in.) long and 215 mm (8.5 in.) broad, with a maximum strung area of 500 square centimetres (approx.

90 sq. in.), the permitted maximum weight is 255 grams (approx. 9 oz.), but most weigh from 110 and 200 grams (4-7 oz.).

Squash balls are 39.5 mm and 40.5 mm in diameter, and weigh from 23 and 25 grams. They are made with two pieces of rubber compound, glued together to form a hollow sphere and buffed to a matte finish. Dissimslar balls are provided for varying temperature and atmospheric conditions and standards of play: more experienced players utilize slow balls that are smaller and have less bounce than those used by less experienced players (slower balls tend to die in court corners, rather than standing up to permit easier shots). depending upon its particular rubber composition, a squash ball may have the property that it bounces more at higher temperatures. Players tend to warm up balls by bouncing them on the ground prior to play. As a rally progresses, play is complicated as the ball normally becomes hotter and faster. Interestingly, given the broadly perceived dangers, no-one has ever been blinded playing squash.

Fig. Raquet

Small coloured dots on the ball show its dynamic level (bounciness), and thus the standard of play for which it is suited. The distinguished speed colours showing the degree of dynamism are:

Balls are manufactured to these standards by Prince, Dunlop, Pointfore, Wilson, Black Knight and others. The "double-yellow dot ball", brought in in 2000, is presently the competition standard, replacing the earlier "yellow-dot" that was long believed the competition standard. There is also a high-altitude "orange dot" ball, used in places such as Mexico

City, Calgary, Denver, and Johannesburg. In North America, the Dunlop "green dot" ball is often used at high altitude, as well.

Given the game's vigorousness, players must wear comfortable sports clothing and robust indoor (non-marking) sports shoes. In competition, men normally wear shorts and a t-shirt or a polo shirt. Women normally wear a skirt and a t-shirt or a tank top, or a sports dress. Towelling wrist and head bands may also be needed in humid climates. Polycarbonate lens goggles are advocated, as players might be struck with a fast-swinging racket or the ball, that normally reaches speeds exceeding 200 km/h (125 mph). In the 2004 Canary Wharf Squash Classic, John White was recorded driving balls at speeds over 270 km/h (170 mph). Many squash venues mandate the utilize of eye safety and some association rules require that all juniors and doubles players must wear eye safety.

Play and Scoring

The players normally spin a racket to decide who begins serving at the start of the match, and this player starts the first rally by electing to serve from either the left or right service box. For a legal serve, one of the server's feet must be in that box and, after being struck by the racket, the ball must strike the front wall above the service line and below the out line and land in the opponent quarter court, unless volleyed by the receiver.

The players then take turns hitting the ball in opposition to the front wall (referred to as "rallying"). The ball may be volleyed (hit whilst still in the air) or hit after its first bounce and before the second. To be believed good, the ball must reach the front wall below the "out" line and above the "board" or "tin" before touching the floor. A ball landing on either the out line or the line above the tin, contrary to tennis, is believed to be out. The ball may also be struck in opposition to any of the other three walls before reaching the front wall. Shots that are first played off the side or back walls are referred to as "boasts" or "angles".

The rally continues until a player is unable to return his or her opponent's shot or makes a mistake or a "let" or "stroke" is granted by the referee for interference.

A point is scored only by the server (when the receiver is unable to return the ball to the front wall before it has bounced twice). When the receiver wins the rally, they are granted only the right to serve. They may choose to serve from either service box.

Games are normally played to 9 points (alternatively, the receiver may opt to call "set two" and play to 10 when the score first reaches 8-

8). Competition matches are normally played to "greatest-of-five" (i.e., the player to win the most out of 5 games).

Alternatively, in the point-a-rally scoring system, points are scored by the winner of each rally, whether or not he or she served. Normally, PARS scoring was up to 15 points (or the receiver calls 15 or 17 when the game reaches 14-14). However, in 2004, the PARS scoring was reduced to 11 for the professional game (if the game reaches 10-10, a player must win by two clear points). PARS is now used on the men's Professional Tour, and the tin height has been lowered by two inches for the men's professional tournaments (these alterations have been made in a hope to shorten the length of the rallies and hence the match). The women's Professional Tour uses the original tin height, but began utilizing the PARS to 11 scoring system as of July 2008.

In the International game, club, doubles and recreational matches are normally played utilizing the traditional British scoring system, but the European Squash Federation (ESF), World Squash Federation (WSF) and various national federations are now utilizing PARS to 11 on a trial or permanent basis. Scoring systems and rules can be adapted subtly to accommodate shorter game time or multiple players. The British scoring is in general used for USSRA (United States Squash Rackets Association) matches.

Strategy and Tactics

The scheme of the game is to hit the ball straight up the side walls to the back corners referred to as a "rail," straight drive, wall, or "length", then move to the centre of the court near the "T" to be well placed to recover the opponent's return. Attacking with soft or "short" shots to the front corners (referred to as "drop shots") causes the opponent to cover more of the court and may result in an outright winner. "Angle" shots are used for deception and once again to cause the opponent to cover more of the court.

A key strategy in squash is known as "dominating the T" (the intersection of the red lines near the centre of the court where the player is in the greatest position to retrieve the opponent's following shot). Skilled players will return a shot, and then move back toward the T before playing the following shot. From this position, the player can rapidly access any part of the court to retrieve the opponent's following shot with a minimal of movement.

Rallies among experienced players may involve 30 or more shots and hence a very high premium is placed on fitness, both aerobic and anaerobic. As players become more skilled and, in particular, better able to retrieve shots, points often become a war of attrition. At higher levels of the game, the fitter player has a main advantage.

Almost all players will fall into the following categories of style of play:

- Retriever- Normally a very fit player, plays patiently, can retrieve most shots hit by an opponent, but doesn't have a particularly strong attacking game.
- Shooter or attacking player- May be a patient player as well, but is more comfortable trying to hit winning shots or going for "nicks". In general has very good shot accuracy and deception skills.
- Power Player- Tries to overpower their opponent by hitting the ball with extreme pace. Not known for their fitness, or patience.
- All-Around Player- Is comfortable playing all dissimslar styles and places, comfortable in all areas of the court.
- Attritional Attacking- Most professional players fit into this category,with the likes of David Palmer and James Willstrop; where they are prepared to rally down the wall, however as soon as the player leaves a loose ball inches from the side wall, they are ready to kill the ball into the nicks.

Capability to change the direction of ball at the last instant is also important to off-balance the opponent. Expert players can anticipate the opponent's shot a few tenths of a second before the average player, giving them a chance to react sooner. Such skill is normally acquired by a lot of practice and game experience.

MAJOR TOURNAMENTS

British Open Squash Championships

The British Open Squash Championships is one of the most former and most established tournaments in the game of squash. It is broadly believed to be one of the two most honoured tournaments in the game, alongside the World Open. (Indeed prior to the establishment of the World Open in the 1970s, the British Open was in general believed to be the effective world championship of the sport.) The British Open Squash Championships are now often referred to as being the "Wimbledon of Squash". The men's and women's events were deemed separately until 1983. Since then, the two competitions have been deemed as a joint event.

The most fortunate players in the history of the championships are Heather McKay, who won the women's event 16 consecutive times from 1962-77, and Jahangir Khan, who won the men's title 10 successive times from 1982-91.

World Team Squash Championships

The World Team Squash Championships are an international squash competition played among teams representing dissimslar nations. Countries enter teams of three or four players to represent them in the championships. In each round of the competition, teams face each other in a greatest-of-three singles matches contest. The competition is deemed once every two years, with the venue changing each time. Normally the men's and women's events are deemed separately in dissimslar years in two dissimslar locations.

World Open

The World Open is a squash event which serves as the individual world championship for squash players. The World Open is broadly believed to be one of the two most honoured titles in squash, alongside the British Open (which was believed to be the effective world championship of the game prior to the World Open's establishment). The men's World Open was first deemed in 1976, and the women's World Open was inaugurated in 1979.

Prior to the establishment of the men's World Open, a tournament called the World Amateur Individual Championship was deemed in the late-1960s and 1970s. The winners of this touranment for male players admitted some of the game's heading figures such as Geoff Hunt and Cam Nancarrow. However many players and fans did not consider this event to be a proper world championship because various of the game's top players were ineligible to participate as they had turned professional. The British Open had for many years been gerenerally believed to be the game's effective world championship, and this extended to be the case until the World Open was established.

The women's World Open was deemed once every two years until the early-1990s, when it turned an annual event. The men's event has been deemed every year since 1979, except for a two-year gap in 2000 and 2001 when it was not deemed due mainly to difficulties in securing sponsorship.

In recent years, the men's World Open has been part of the PSA Super Series.The venue for the World Open alterations every year.

Normally the men's and women's events are deemed separately in two dissimslar locations.

World Doubles Squash Championships

The World Doubles Squash Championships is an international squash tournament, as well as Men's Doubles, Women's Doubles, and Mixed Doubles events. Under the rules of the championship, double pairs must be made up of two players from the similar country. The event has been deemed three times – in 1997, 2004, and 2006.

ADMINISTRATIVE BODIES

World Squash Federation

The Squash was first played over 100 years ago and is now delighted in over 150 nations, on 125,000 courts, with its popularity continuing to grow quickly. To harness this development and to encourage and co-ordinate the sport the International Squash Rackets Federation was established in 1967, its name being altered in 1992 to the World Squash Federation. The WSF is recognized by the International Olympic Committee (IOC) as the International Federation for Squash and is also in membership of the General Association of International Sports Federations (GAISF) and the Association of the IOC Recognised International Sports Federations (ARISF).

The WSF has 141 Members, all of which are National Associations of Squash, recognized by their National Olympic Association or Ministry of Sport as the sole and unchallenged rulingbody for the sport in the country. Members obtain a number of votes to be utilized at General Meetings depending upon the number of Squash courts in their country. Member nations are commanded also to be in membership of one of the five Regional Squash Federations, which are an integral part of the world structure.

The WSF is handled by a Management Committee, accountable for day-to-day control of the Federation and an Executive Committee which aids Management Committee in the strategy and policy making action. The Management Committee of the WSF is elected by the Members at General Meeting and comprises of a President and three Vice-Presidents, who each serve two year terms of office. The Executive Committee of the WSF consists the Management Committee plus one Regional Vice-President nominated by each of the five Regional Federations. The WSF employs professional staff who are answerable for implementing the decisions of the committees.

A Rules and Referees Committee repeatedly monitors the Rules of the sport and builds recommendations for alter every four years. The Committee has liability for implementing and running a Referee Programme which trains, accredits and evaluates the top two grades of official, International Referee and World Referee.

The WSF sets criteria for all technical aspects of Squash as well as court construction, rackets, balls, eye safety and clothing and monitors the carrying out on them. Through its Technical Committee it inspects and accredits court components which meet the qualifications and works with its partner companies to promote good practice in court build-up world-wide. The numerous courts in the world now stands at 50,000, increasing at all over 2000 courts per annum.

The Federation works intimately with the two player connections - the Professional Squash Association (PSA) and the Women's International Squash Players Association (WISPA) to control and coordinate the world calendar for Squash. Championships are deemed in all main Squash playing nations and are incorporated with the World Championships and Main Games calendar to assure that there are no clashes of dates and timings.

The WSF is accountable for the functioning and promotion of World Championships for men, women, boys, girls and masters at individual and team levels in both singles and doubles. World Championships for each are deemed every two years and are run by WSF member nations, who tender for the events four years in advance.

The WSF is accountable for co-ordinating the curriculum of Coaching training and awards by member nations and putting up a comparative table of qualifications. Coaching courses are run in new and growing Squash nations to allow for the resource for future development.

One of the most vital of all the functions undertaken by the WSF is the growth of Squash, not only in countries where it is a new sport but also where it is already instituted. Advice on all growth matters is given to members and held outthrough a group of WSF accredited specialists. Regional Committee Directors discover needs for growth projects in their area and suggest activity plans to the WSF for resources and funding.

Women's International Squash Players Association

Women's International Squash Players Association (WISPA) is an organisation for female squash professionals. The goals of the association are to:

- enable more players to consider a career in professional squash viable through the growth of a world tour;
- produce and publish world rankings;
- increase exposure for the sport and its players;
- promote professionalism amongst its members;
- raise the administrative standards at events;
- increase the level of support and advice offered to promoters; and
- improve communication and relationships with other squash organizations and the press.

The association was established in 1983 as the Women's Squash Players Association

FAMOUS PLAYERS

F. D. Amr Bey

Abedel Fattah Amr, also calledas "F.D. Amr Bey", or simply "Amr Bey", was a squash player from Egypt. He gained the British Open men's title six successive times from 1933-1938.

Amr is broadly believed to be the first truly prevailingplayer in the sport of squash. He was not a professional person, but he beat all the top professional players of his time and has been named the first "professional amateur" in squash because his training for the game turned the key center of his life.

The British Open men's title was only in recent times inaugurated at the time Amr emerged on the scene, but it rapidly turned the most substantial title in the game and came to be looked at by many to be the equivalent to a world championship for the sport. The men's final at the time was played under a "challenge" system, with a competitor taking on the defending champion in a greatest-of-three-legs match-up, with matches being played at both the two players' respective squash clubs. In 1933, Amr took on Don Butcher, who had gained the title in 1931 and 1932. The first match of the tie took place at Butcher's club, the Conservative Club, with Amr winning 9-0, 9-7, 9-1. The second leg was played at Amr's club, the Bath Club, which Amr won 9-5, 6-9, 9-2, 9-1, 9-4 to capture the title.

No challenger came out to take on Amr in the British Open final in 1934, so he held the title by default. Butcher challenged Amr once again in the 1935 final, with Amr once again succeeding in two matches – 9-4, 8-10, 10-8, 9-0 and 9-6, 6-9, 9-2, 0-9, 9-5.

In 1936-38, Amr confronted Jim Dear in three successive British Open finals, with Amr succeeding on all three occasions in two straight matches.In summation to his six British Open titles, Amr also gained the British Amateur Championship six times, as well as several other titles.Amr is broadly believed to have aroused the level of the sport of squash to a new heights through both his marvellous shot-making capability, and his exceptional speed and fitness

Hashim Khan

Hashim Khan is a former squash player from Pakistan. He won the British Open seven times from 1951 and 1958. He is broadly believed to be one of the most outstanding squash players of all time, and was the first great player to arose from a Pakistani dynasty of squash players which prevailed the international game for decades.

Hashim Khan was born in Nawakille a small village near Peshawar, in British India. The year of his birth is normally described as 1916, though this has been challenged (some conceive that he may have been born as much as five years before this). Hashim's father, Abdullah Khan, was the Head Steward at club in Peshwar where British army officers stationed in the area played squash. As a youngster, Hashim assisted as an unpaid ballboy at the club, retrieving balls that were hit out of court by the officers. When the officers had completed playing, Hashim and the other ballboys would take over the courts.

In 1942, Hashim turned a squash coach at a British Air Force officers' mess. In 1944, he gained the first All-of-India squash championship in Bombay, and successfully defended this title for the following two years. When Pakistan turned an independent state, Hashim was nominated a squash professional at the Pakistan Air Force, and won the first Pakistani squash championship in 1949.

In 1950, Abdul Bari, a distant relative of Hashim's who had selected to remain in Bombay after the division of India and Pakistan, and who Hashim had beaten in various tournaments in India before division, was sponsored by the Indian Government to play at the British Open where he completed runner-up to the great Egyptian player Mahmoud Karim. (The British Open was believed to be the effective world championship of the sport at the time.) This spurred Hashim to seek backing to contend in the British Open the following year.

In 1951, Hashim locomoted to the United Kingdom to play in the British Open, and won the title defeating Karim in the final 9-5, 9-0, 9-0. He once again beat Karim in the final in 1952 9-5, 9-7, 9-0. He won once again for the following four successive years, defeatingdefeating R.B.R.

Wilson of England in the 1953 final; his younger brother Azam Khan in two tight five-set finals in 1954 and 1955; and Roshan Khan (another Pakistani who was a distant relative of Hashim and Azam's) in the final of 1956. Hashim was runner-up to Roshan in 1957, and gained his seventh and final British Open title in 1958, when he beat Azam in the final.

Hashim also gained five British Professional Championship titles, three US Open titles, and three Canadian Open titles.In his later years, Hashim has nailed down in Denver, Colorado, and has extended to appear in veterans' matches at the British Open.Hashim had a total of 12 children. His eldest son Sharif Khan turned the prevailingplayer on the North American hardball squash circuit in the 1970s, winning a record 12 North American Open titles. Four other sons – Aziz, Gulmast, Liaqat Ali (Charlie), and Salim (Sam) – also turned top-level hardball squash players.

Geoff Hunt

Geoffrey Brian (Geoff) Hunt, MBE born on March 11, 1947, in Melbourne, Australia), is a retired Australian squash player who is broadly believed to be one of the most outstanding squash players of all time.

Hunt won the World Open title four times. He was the event's inaugural champion, winning the competion on the first four occasions it was deemed (1976, 1977, 1979 and 1980). He also won the World Amateur Individual Championship three times (1967, 1969, and 1971), and the British Open (which was believed to be the effective world championship event concerning both amateurs and professionals before the World Open started) eight times from 1969 and 1981.

Hunt won 178 of the 215 tournaments he contended throughout his career. He was ranked the World No.1 squash player from 1975 to 1980.

After retiring as a player, Hunt assisted as the Head Squash Coach at the Australian Institute of Sport from 1985-2003, where he assisted formulate a new generation of Australian squash stars.

Hunt has been induced into the World Squash Federation Hall of Fame and the Australian Sport Hall of Fame.

REFERENCES

Alter, S.: *Science of Flexibility*, 2nd edn, Human Kinetics, Champaign, IL, 1996.

Alter, S.: *Sport Stretch*, Human Kinetics, Champaign, IL, 1998.

Dintiman, G. and Ward, R.:*Sport Speed*, Leisure Press, Champaign, IL, 1988.

Ellison, D.: *Performance Stretching*, Human Kinetics, Champaign, IL, 1999.

Goldberg, B. (ed.): *Sports and Exercise for Children with Chronic Health Conditions*, Human Kinetics, Champaign, IL, 1995

Newsholme, E., Leech, T. and Duester, G.: *Keep on Running*, John Wiley & Sons, Chichester, UK, 1994

Reaburn, P. and Jenkins, D.: *Training for Speed and Endurance*, Allen & Unwin, Sydney, 1996

Rowland, T.W.: *Developmental Exercise Physiology*, Human Kinetics, Champaign, IL, 1996

Sports weekly Magazine

Sports Illustrated Magazine

14

Swimming

The goal of competitive swimming is to be the quickest over a given distance. Competitive swimming turned popular in the nineteenth century, and comprises 36 individual events - 18 male events and 18 female events, nevertheless the IOC only recognizes 34 events - 17 male and 17 female events. Swimming is an event at the Summer Olympic Games, where male and female athletes contend in 13 of the recognized events each. Olympic events are controlled a fifty meter pool. Competitive swimming's international organization is FINA (Federation Internationale de Natation), the International Swimming Federation.

The four competitory strokes are the butterfly, backstroke, breaststroke, and front crawl (freestyle). "Freestyle" and "front crawl" are often used interchangeable, but "freestyle" properly mentions to an unregulated competitive event rather than to any particular stroke. Swimmers generally choose to swim front crawl in a freestyle event since it is the fastest stroke. In events that demand specific strokes, disqualification will occur if the stroke is not swum correctly, for instance if the swimmer does not touch the wall with two hands during breaststroke or butterfly.

There are two types of meets. 'A' meets are official meets that permit qualification for a special or bigger meet if the qualifying time is met. Scores are maintained to see how each team did at the end of the season. 'B' meets are utilized as practice meets, where the normal, or prime stroke is swum if not yet specified. Scores are not maintained.

HISTORY

In 1804 the lifebelt was devised by W. H. Mallison, the device being known at that time as the "Seaman's Friend". Nevertheless, the lifebelts took up valuable space on ships, and the United States Navy was worried about the devices being used by sailors to desert.The first German swimming club was established in 1837 in Berlin. A journal mentions "swimming skates" in France, which may be an early version of a surfboard.

One watershed event was a swimming contest in 1844 in London. Some Native Americans took part in this competition. While the British raced using breaststroke, the Native Americans swam a version of the front crawl, which had been used by people in the Americas, West Africa and some Pacific islands for generations, but was not recognized to the British. As the front crawl is much faster than the breaststroke, the Americans easily beat the British: Flying Gull gained the medal, swimming the 150 feet (46 m) in 30 seconds, and second place went to another American named Tobacco. Their stroke was reported as making a motion with the arms "like a windmill" and kicking the legs up and down. As this produced considerable splashing, it was conceived barbaric and "un-European" to the British gentlemen, who favored to keep their heads above water. Subsequently, the British extended to swim only breaststroke until 1873.

The first indoor swimming pool was constructed in England in 1862. An Amateur Swimming Association of Great Britain was prepared in 1880 with more than three hundred members. The primary swimming styles were the breaststroke and the recently formulated side stroke. In the sidestroke, the swimmer lies on one side. Initially, the arms were brought forward under water, but this was soon altered to bring the arm forward over water to cut down resistance and to improve the speed, leading in an overarm sidestroke. The legs were forced together in a scissor style. In 1895, J. H. Thayers of England swam 100 yards (91 m) in a record-breaking 1:02.50 using a sidestroke.

Sometime within 1870 and 1890 (the date is most often given as 1873), John Arthur Trudgen reintroduced the front crawl to England, having learned the stroke from Native Americans during a trip to South America. His stroke, a variant of the front crawl, came to be called the Trudgen or Trudgeon. The arms were brought forward, alternating, while the body rolled from side to side. The kick was a scissors kick such as that familiarly used in breaststroke, with one kick for two arm strokes, although it is conceived that the Native Americans had so utilized a flutter kick. Front crawl variants used different ratios of scissor kicks to arm strokes, or alternated with a flutter (up-and-down) kick. The speed of the new stroke was presented by F.V.C. Lane in 1901, swimming

100 yards (91 m) in 1:00.0, an improvement of about ten seconds equated to the breaststroke record. This style is the first European version of the front crawl, the quickest swimming style known today. Due to its speed the Trudgen turned very quickly popular around the world, despite all the ungentlemanlike splashing.

Captain Matthew Webb was the 1st man to swim the English channel (between England and France), in 1875. He used breaststroke, swimming 21.26 miles (34.21 km) in twenty-one hours and forty-five minutes. No other man or woman swam the channel for the next thirty-one years. He died in 1882 while undertaking to swim the Niagara Falls. The first European amateur swimming competitions were in 1889 in Vienna.

In 1879 King Ludwig II of Bavaria built a swimming pool in castle Linderhof. This is conceived to be the first artificial wave pool and also sported electrically heated water and light.Synchronized swimming commenced in the late nineteenth century, and the 1st contest was in 1891 in Berlin, a men's-only event.

THE GAME

Butterfly Stroke

Fig. Start Positions

The butterfly, (fly for short) is a swimming stroke swum on the breast, with both arms moving at the same time. The butterfly kick was formulated one by one, and is also known as the "dolphin kick". While other styles like the breaststroke, front crawl, or backstroke can be swum easily even by beginners, the butterfly demands very good technique to be feasible. Many students conceive it the hardest style of swimming. It is the newest swimming style swum in competition, first swum in 1933.

Technique: The butterfly technique with the dolphin kick comprises of synchronous arm movement with a synchronous leg kick. Good technique is essential to swim this style in effect. The wave-like body movement is also very substantial, as this is the key to easy synchronous over-water recovery and breathing.

In the initial position, the swimmer lies on the breast, the arms are extended to the front, and the legs are extended to the back.

Arm Movement: The butterfly stroke has three major parts, the pull, the push, and the recovery. These can also be further split up. From the initial position, the arm movement starts very likewise to the breast stroke. At the commencing the hands sink a little bit down with the palms confronting outwards and slightly down at shoulder width, then the hands move out to create a Y. This is called catching the water. The pull movement follows a semicircle with the elbow higher than the hand and the hand pointing towards the center of the body and downward. Do not constitute the traditional taught "keyhole" when using this stroke, as it disrupts the flow and speed of the stroke. The arms should be pushed directly back after the Y is formed.

The push forces the palm backward through the water underneath the body at the beginning and at the side of the body at the end of the push. The swimmer only forces the arms 1/3 of the way to the hips, making it easier to enter into the recover and making the recovery shorter and making the breathing window shorter. The movement gains speed during the pull/push phase until the hand is the fastest at the end of the push. This step is called the release and is crucial for the recovery. The speed at the end of the push is used to help with the recovery.

The recovery swings the arms sideways over the water surface to the front, with the elbows straight. The arms should be swung out forward from the end of the underwater movement, the prolongation of the tricep in combination with the butterfly kick will allow the armd to be brought forwards relaxed yet quickly. It is important not to enter the water too early, as this would generate extra resistance as the arms moved forward in the water against the swimming direction, however, during longer distances, this cannot be forefended, and it should be noted that it is more substantial to avoid dropping one's hips. A high elbow recovery, as in front crawl, would be negative because of the natural undulations that are partially caused by the recovery and the relaxed movement caused by the momentum of a tricep extension. Restrictions of the shoulder movement in the human body make such a motion unlikely.

The arms enroll the water with the thumbs first at shoulder width. A wider entry loses movement in the next pull phase, and a smaller entry, where the hands touch, wastes energy. The cycle repeats with the pull phase. Nevertheless, some people favor to touch in front, as it helps them catch water, as long as they can do this efficiently, they arent losing anything. The underwater part is really more like a keyhole than it isn't, contrary to what was said in the 1st paragraph.

In general, viewed from below, the arm movement forms a fat "keyhole" figure throughout the stroke cycle in the water. Nevertheless, more recently, a straighter arm pull has been favored in competitive swimming.

Leg Movement: The leg movement is alike to the leg movement in the front crawl, except the legs are synchronized with each other, and it uses a wholly different set of muscles. The shoulders are brought above the surface by a strong up and medium down kick, and back beneath the surface by a strong down and medium up kick. A smooth undulation fuses the motion together.

The feet are agitated together to prevent loss of water-pressure. The feet are naturally pointing downwardly, giving downwards thrust, moving up the feet and pressing down the head.

There is no actual condition in competitive butterfly patterns that a swimmer make a fixed number of pulses in butterfly–the swimmer may kick as little or as much as he or she may wish. While competitive rules allow such a choice, the typical method of swimming butterfly is with two kicks.

As butterfly initiated as a variant on breaststroke, it would be performed with a breaststroke or whip kick by some swimmers. While breaststroke was differentiated from butterfly in 1953, the breaststroke kick in butterfly was not officially outlawed until 2001. Nevertheless a number of Masters swimmers were upset with the alteration since they came from a time when butterfly was usually swum with a breaststroke kick. FINA was then convinced to allow a breaststroke kick in Masters swimming. Given the option, most swimmers choose to utilize a dolphin kicking action, but there still is a small minority of swimmers who prefer the breaststroke kick, for recreational swimming and even for competition.

Rules and Regulations: These are the official FINA regulations. They apply to swimmers during official swimming competitions.

From the beginning of the first arm stroke after the start and every turn, the body shall be kept on the breast. Under water kicking on the side is allowed. It is not permitted to roll onto the back at any time.

Both arms shall be brought forward together over the water and brought backward at the same time through-out the race, except after the start and at turns

All up and down movements of the legs must be simultaneous. The position of the legs or the feet need not be on the similar level, but they shall not alternate in relation to each other. A breaststroke kicking movement is not allowed.

At every turn and at the finish of the race, the touch shall be made with both hands simultaneously, at, above or beneath the water surface.

At the start and at turns, a swimmer is allowed one or more leg kicks and one arm pull under the water, which must bring him to the surface. It shall be permissible for a swimmer to be totally submerged for a distance of not more than 15 meters after the start and after every turn. By that point, the head must have broken the surface. The swimmer must stay on the surface until the next turn or finish. Only the meter distances are admitted in the official Olympics. Must do open wall turn.

Backstroke

The backstroke, also often called the back crawl, is one of the four swimming styles regulated by FINA, and the only regulated style swum on the back. This has the advantage of easy breathing, but the disadvantage of the swimmer not being able to see where they are going. It is also the only competition swimming style that starts in the water. The swimming style is alike to an upside down front crawl. Both backstroke and front crawl are long-axis strokes.

Technique: In the initial position, the swimmer lies flat on their back, arms stretched forward, and legs extended backwards.

Arm movement: In backstroke, the arms contribute most of the forward movement. The arm stroke consists of two main parts: the power phase (consisting of three separate parts) and the recovery. The arms alternate so that always one arm is underwater while the other arm is recovering. One complete arm turn is considered one cycle. From the initial position, one arm sinks slightly under water and turns the palm outward start the Catch phase (first part of the power phase). The hand enters downward about ten inches, catching the water.

During the power phase the hand follows a semi-circular path from the Catch to the side of the hip. The palm is always facing away from the swimming direction, and the elbow always points downward towards the bottom of the pool. This is done so that both the arms and the elbow can push the maximum amount of water back in order to push the body forward. At the height of the shoulders the upper and lower arms should have its maximum angle of about 90 degrees. This is called the Mid-Pull of the power phase.

The Mid-Pull phase consists of forcing the palm of the hand as far down as possible with the fingers pointing upward. Again, the goal is to push the body forward against the water. At the very end of the Mid-Pull, the palm flaps down for a last push forward down to a depth of 45 cm, creating the Finish of the Power phase. Besides forcing the body forward this also helps with the rolling back to the other side as part of the body movement. During the power phase, the fingers of the hand can be slightly apart, as this will increase the resistance of the hand in the water due to turbulence.

To prepare for the recovery phase, the hand is rotated so that the palms point towards the legs and the thumb side points upwards. At the beginning of the recovery phase of the one arm, the other arm begins its power phase. The recovering arm is moved in a semicircle straight over the shoulders to the front. During this recovery, the palm rotates so that the small finger enters the water first and the palms point outward. After a short gliding phase, the cycle repeats with the preparation for the next power phase.

A variant is to move both arms synchronized and not alternating, similar to an upside down butterfly stroke. This is easier to coordinate, and the peak speed during the combined power phase is faster, yet the speed is much slower during the combined recovery. The average speed will usually be less than the average speed of the alternating stroke.

Another variant is the old style way of swimming backstroke, where the arm movement formed a complete circle in a windmill type pattern. However, this style is nowadays no longer used for competitive swimming, as a lot of energy is spent on forcing the body up and down instead of forward. Furthermore, the added strain on the shoulder is considered less than ideal and can lead to injuries.

It is also possible to move only one arm at a time, where one arm moves through the power and recovery phases while the other arm rests. This is slow, but it is used frequently to teach students the movement, as they have to concentrate on only one arm.

Leg Movement: The leg movement in backstroke is similar to the flutter kick in front crawl. They make a small contribution to the forward speed, yet are very significant for stabilizing the body.

The leg stroke is also alternating, with one leg sinking down straight to about 30 degree out of the horizontal. From this position the leg makes a fast kick upward, slightly bending the knee at the beginning and then stretching it again in the horizontal. However, there are also frequent variants with four or only two kicks per cycle. Usually, sprinters tend to utilize 6 kicks per cycle, whereas long distance swimmer may utilize less.

It is also possible to utilize a butterfly (dolphin) kick, although this is rare except the butterfly kick after the start and the turns. This dolphin kick is essential for many top athletes because it is the fastest part of the race. It may also constitute the majority of the race. ie(in the 100 yd backstroke the swimmer may kick underwater dolphin for 15 yds per length which equates to as much as 60 yds kicking in a 100 yd race) A great example of this is Olympic gold medalist Natalie Coughlin. Breaststroke kicks are most comfortable if the arms are used synchronized, as the breaststroke kick has difficulty to compensate for a rolling movement due to alternating arm cycles. The butterfly kick can be done slightly to one side depending on the rolling of the body.

Rules and Regulations: These are the official FINA rules. They apply to swimmers during official swimming competitions.

Prior to the commencing signal, the swimmers shall line up in the water facing the commencing end, with both hands holding the commencing grips. Standing in or on the gutter or bending the toes over the lip of the gutter is prohibited.

At the signal for commencing and after turning the swimmer shall push off and swim upon his back throughout the race except when executing a turn as set forth in SW 6.4. The normal position on the back can include a roll movement of the body up to, but not including 90 degrees from horizontal. The position of the head is not relevant.

Some part of the swimmer must break the surface of the water throughout the race. It shall be permissible for the swimmer to be completely submerged during the turn, at the finish and for a distance of not more than 15 meters after the start and every turn. By that point the head must have broken the surface.

During the turn the shoulders may be turned over the vertical to the breast after which a continuous single arm pull or a continuous simultaneous double arm pull may be used to initiate the turn. Once the body has left the position on the back, any kick or arm pull must be part of the continuous turning action. The swimmer must have returned to the position on the back upon leaving the wall. When executing the turn there must be a touch of the wall with some part of the swimmer's body.

Upon the finish of the race the swimmer must touch the wall while on the back. The body may be submerged at the touch.

Breaststroke

Breaststroke is a swimming style swum on the breast. It is the most popular recreational style due to its stability and the ability to keep the head out of the water at all times. In most swimming classes, beginners learn either the breaststroke or the front crawl first. But in competitive swimming, the breaststroke is regarded as one of the most difficult strokes, requiring comparable endurance to other strokes.

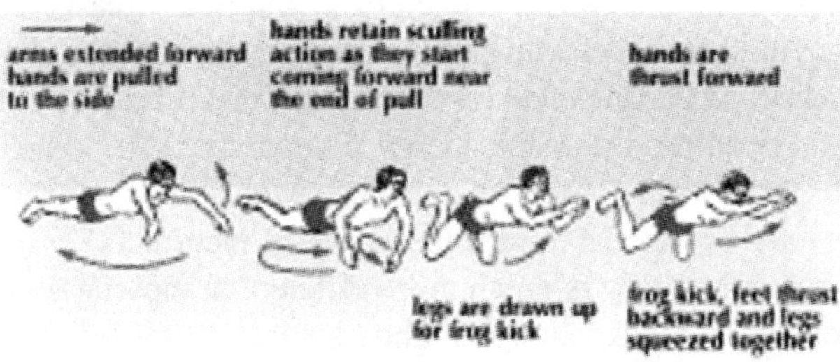

Fig. Breaststroke

Breaststroke is the slowest of the four official styles in competitive swimming. The fastest breaststroke swimmers can swim about 1.57 meters per second. Although it is the slowest of the four competitive strokes, it is commonly agreed that it is the most difficult when done correctly. It is also often the hardest to teach to rising swimmers due to the importance of timing and the coordination required to move the legs properly.

Breaststroke is swum while leaning on the chest, with the arms only breaking the surface of the water slightly and legs always underwater, while the head is underwater for the second half of the stroke. The kick is sometimes referred to as a "frog kick" because of the resemblance to a frog's kick, but when done correctly it is more of a "whip kick" due to the whip-like motion that moves commencing at the core down through the legs.

The body is often at a steep angle to the forward movement. This slows down the swimmer more than any other style. Professional breaststrokers utilize abdominal muscles and hips to add extra power to the kick, although most do not perfect this technique until the collegiate level. This much faster form of breaststroke is referred to as "wave-action" breaststroke and fully incorporates the whip-kick.

A special feature of competitive breaststroke is the underwater pullout. From the streamline position, one uses the arms to pull all the way down past the hips. As the arms are pulling down, one downward dolphin kick is allowed (as of the 2005 season), though still optional (However, any upward motion with the dolphin kick is strictly forbidden, and will result in a disqualification). This is followed by the recovery of the arms to the streamline position once more, and then a kick. The pullout at the start and after the turns contributes significantly to the swimming times. Therefore one way to improve the swimming times is to focus on the start and the turns.

Of the four competitive strokes of swimming, breaststroke is the most efficient in terms of energy consumption, though it is the slowest. Race breaststroke has the most resistance in water compared to the other strokes and requires the most energy compared to the other strokes. Many often assume that, because it can be swum slowly quite easily, this translates to what it's like to race it, but this is incorrect. For example, a properly swum butterfly is much more efficient at moving forward than breaststroke is, and thus requires slightly less power to be fast. However, the roles are reversed when it comes to leisure swimming.

Arm Movement: There are three steps to the arm movement: outsweep, insweep, and recovery. The movement starts with the outsweep. From the initial position, the hands sink a little bit down and the palms face inward, and the hands rotate outward and move apart. During the outsweep the arms stay almost straight and parallel to the surface. The outsweep is followed by the insweep, where the hands point down and push the water backwards. The elbows stay in the horizontal plane through the shoulders.

The hands push back until approximately the vertical plane through the shoulders. At the end of the insweep the hands come together with facing palms in front of the chest and the elbows are at the side at the body. In the recovery phase the hands are moved forward again into the initial position under water. The entire arm stroke starts slowly, increases speed to the peak arm movement speed in the insweep phase, and slows down again during recovery. The goal is to produce maximum thrust during the insweep phase, and minimum drag during the recovery phase.

As a variant, it is possible to recover the arms over water. This reduces drag, but requires more power. Some competitive swimmers utilize this variant in competition.

Another variant is the underwater pull-down, similar to the push phase of a butterfly stroke. This stroke extends the insweep phase and forces the hands all the way to the back to the sides of the hip. This greatly increases the push from one stroke, but also makes recovery more difficult. This style is well suited for underwater swimming. However, FINA allows this stroke only for the first stroke after the start and every turn. In late 2005, FINA has also introduced a new rule which allows you to perform a single downward kick after the push off the wall.

Leg Movement: The leg movement, colloquially known as the "frog kick", consists of two phases: bringing the feet into position for the thrust phase and the insweep phase. From the initial position with the legs stretched out backward, the feet are moved together towards the posterior, while the knees stay together. The knees should not sink too low, as this increases the drag. Then the feet point outward in preparation for the thrust phase. In the thrust phase, the legs are moved elliptically back to the initial position. During this movement, the knees are kept together. The legs move slower while bringing the legs into position for the thrust phase, and move very fast during the thrust phase. Again, the goal is produce maximum thrust during the in sweep phase, and minimum drag during the recovery phase.

As a variant, some swimmers move the knees apart during the preparation phase and keep them apart until almost the end of the thrust phase. Moving both knee and foot outwards like a real frog avoids the extreme rotation in the lower leg.

Another variant of the breaststroke kick is the scissor kick, however, this kick violates the rules of the FINA as it is no longer symmetrical. Swimming teachers put a great effort into steering the students away from the scissor kick. In the scissor kick, one leg moves as described above, but the other leg does not form an elliptical movement but merely an up-down movement similar to the flutter kick of front crawl. Some swimming teachers believe that learning the front crawl first gives a higher risk of an incorrect scissor kick when learning breaststroke afterwards.

Breaststroke can also be swum with the dolphin kick in butterfly, yet this also violates the FINA rules. One kick is allowed, however, at the start and at the turn providing that it is part of the body's natural movement.

The harmonic movements of the dolphin kick and flutter kick are in contrast to the breaststroke whip kick, which really deserves the name kick. Scissor kick and frog kick are intermediate. Humans have strong muscles in the legs and would need swim fins (like a frog) to bring all their power into the water and stand with the sole of the feet on the water. Rather the leg grabs almost as much water as the foot and a small amount of water is accelerated to high kinetic energy, but not much impulse is transferred. The toes are bent, the feet point 45° outwards, the sole points backwards, to mimic a hydrofoil. While closing in a V shape to the rear a small "lifting" force can be felt. Unlike in the other kicks, the joints are moved into extrema. Before the kick the knee is maximally bent and the upper leg is rotating along its axis to its extreme outer position and the lower leg is twisted to extreme, at the end of the kick the ankles are maximally turned to the inside so that the soles clap together to achieve a nozzle effect like in a jelly fish. Therefore training involves getting flexible in addition to fitness and precision. The sudden sideway stress on knee at the kick can lead to uncomfortable noise and feeling for the beginner and to wear for the senior.

On recovery the lower leg stays in the wake of the upper leg. Around 2000 the distance between the knees in the recovery phase was reduced to harmonize it with the optional body undulation.

Rules and Regulations: These are the official FINA rules. They apply to swimmers during official swimming competitions.

From the beginning of the first arm stroke after the start and after every turn, the body shall be kept on the breast. It is not permitted to roll onto the back at any time. Throughout the race the stroke cycle must be one arm stroke and one leg kick in that order.

All movements of the arms shall be simultaneous and in the similar horizontal plane without alternating movement.

The hands shall be pushed forward together from the breast on, under, or over the water. The elbows shall be under water except for the final stroke before the turn, during the turn and for the final stroke at the finish. The hands shall be brought back on or under the surface of the water. The hands shall not be brought back beyond the hip line, except during the first stroke after the start and every turn.

During every complete cycle, some part of the swimmer's head shall break the surface of the water. After the start and after every turn, the swimmer may take one arm stroke completely back to the legs. The head must break the surface of the water before the hands turn inward at the widest part of the second stroke. A single downward dolphin kick followed by a breaststroke kick is permitted while wholly submerged. Following which, all movements of the legs shall be simultaneous and in the similar horizontal plane without alternating movement.

The feet must be turned outwards during the propulsive part of the kick. A scissors, flutter or downward dolphin kick is not permitted except as in. Breaking the surface of the water with the feet is allowed unless followed by a downward dolphin kick.

At every turn and at the finish of the race, the touch shall be made with both hands simultaneously at, above, or beneath the water level. The head may be submerged after the last arm pull prior to the touch, provided it breaks the surface of the water at some point during the last complete or incomplete cycle preceding the touch.

Front Crawl

The front crawl, or forward crawl, is a swimming style usually regarded as the fastest of all the styles developed. It is one of two long axis strokes, the other being the backstroke. Unlike the backstroke, butterfly, and breaststroke, the front crawl is not regulated by FINA, but it is nearly universally swum in freestyle competitions. This style is sometimes referred to as the Australian crawl or the American crawl, although these are, in fact, more specific variants, both of which qualify as front crawl strokes. This style is also sometimes called freestyle although it is technically only one of the freestyle strokes.

Technique: The first position for front crawl or Freestyle is the streamline position, that is to say on the stomach with both arms stretched out to the front and both legs extended to the back.

Arm movement: The arm movement alternates from side to side. In other words, while one arm is pulling/forcing, the other arm is recovering. The arm strokes also provide most of the forward movement. The move can be separated into three parts, the pull, the push, and the recovery.

From the initial position, the arm sinks slightly lower and the palm of the hand turns 45 degrees with the thumb side of the palm towards the bottom. This is called catching the water and prepares for the pull. The pull movement follows a semicircle, with the elbow higher than the hand, and the hand pointing towards the body center and downward. The semicircle ends in front of the chest at the beginning of the ribcage.

The push forces the palm backward through the water underneath the body at the beginning and at the side of the body at the end of the push.

Sometime after the beginning of the recovery of the one arm, the other arm begins its pull. The recovery moves the elbow in a semicircle in a vertical plane in the swimming direction. The lower arm and the hand are completely relaxed and hang down from the elbow close to the water surface and close to the swimmer's body. The beginning of the recovery looks similar to pulling the hand out of the back pocket of a pair of pants, with the small finger upwards. Further into the recovery phase, the hand movement has been compared to pulling up a center zip on a wetsuit. The recovering hand moves forward, with the fingers trailing downward, just above the surface of the water. In the middle of the recovery one shoulder is rotated into the air while the other is jumping backwards to avoid drag due to the large frontal area which at this specific time is not covered by the arm. To rotate the shoulder, some twist their torso while others also rotate everything down to their feet.

Beginners often make the mistake of not relaxing the arm during the recovery and of moving the hand too high and too far away from the body, in some cases even higher than the elbow. In these cases, drag and incidental muscle effort is increased at the expense of speed. Beginners often forget to utilize their shoulders to let the hand enter as far forward as possible. Some say the hand should enter the water thumb first, reducing drag through possible turbulence, others say the middle finger is first with the hand precisely bent down, giving thrust right from the start. At the beginning of the pull, the hand acts like a wing and is moved slower than the velocity of the swimmer while at the end it acts like an oar and is moved faster than the velocity of the swimmer.

A recreational variation of front crawl involves only one arm moving at any one time, while the other arm rests and is stretched out at the front. This style is called a "catch up" stroke and requires less strength for swimming. This is because the immersed length of the body is longer and more streamlined. This style is slower than the regular front crawl and is rarely used competitively: however, it is often used for training purposes even by professional swimmers, as it increases the body's awareness of being streamlined in the water. Total Immersion is a similar technique.

Leg Movement: The leg movement in freestyle is called the flutter kick. The legs move alternately, with one leg kicking downward while the other leg moves upward. While the legs provide only a small part of the overall speed, they are important to stabilize the body position. This lack of balance is apparent when using a pull buoy to neutralize the leg action.

The leg in the initial position bends very slightly at the knees, and then kicks the lower leg and the foot downwards similar to kicking a football. The legs may be bent inward slightly. After the kick the straight leg moves back up. A frequent mistake of beginners is to bend the legs too much or to kick too much out of the water.

Ideally, there are 6 kicks per cycle, although it is also possible to utilize 8 kicks, 4 kicks or even 2 kicks. Franziska van Almsick, for example, swims very successfully with four kicks per cycle. When one arm is pushed down the opposite leg needs to do a downwards kick also, to fix the body orientation, because this happens shortly after the body rotation. Alternatively, front crawl can also be swum with a butterfly kick, although this reduces the stability of the swimming position. A breaststroke kick with front crawl arms (the Trudgen) is awkward, because the breathing pattern for front crawl needs a rotation, yet a breaststroke kick resists this rotation.

MAJOR TOURNAMENTS

Olympics

Swimming has been part of the Games since the beginning of the modern Olympiad in 1896 but the first two Games were rather quirky aquatic affairs, and exclusively male.

The first was a 100 metres (or thereabouts) race between three Greek sailors across the Bay of Zea near Piraeus (not far from a place where cave drawings offer evidence of an ancient game) that began with the rivals jumping from a rowing boat. The winner was Ioannis Malokinis in 2 minutes and 20 seconds.

The second Games, in Paris, involved races up the Seine, one in which obstacles were placed in the way of swimmers and one where the point was to swim the whole distance under water - not much fun for the spectators! Still, at least the races were held with the tide, not against it. That helped John Arthur Jarvis on his way to capturing the 4,000 metres freestyle (an event never seen before or since) in less than an hour - a time many of those who swim for charity these days would be quite proud of.

The first indication of the modern race programme emerged in St Louis, in 1904, with races of 50, 100, 200, 400 and 1,500 metres, all of which will be raced in Sydney. Yet there were still no women, who raced for the first time in the 1912 Games of Stockholm.

The early glamour of the game opened up vast opportunities to the likes of Duke Paoa Kahanamoku, a Haiwaiian who became a Hollywood actor and won the 1912 and 1920 100 metres freestyle titles. The man who beat him for the title in 1924 would become yet more famous on the silver screen; Johnny Weissmuller, the American who became the first to swim faster than a minute for 100 metres freestyle (in 1922), an event he won at both the 1924 and 1928 Games before going on to become the original Tarzan in Hollywood.

In 1932, Buster Crabbe got his passport to Hollywood in the similar way. He won the 400 metres freestyle by what he described as the tenth of a second that "changed my life".

The early programme relied heavily on the freestyle races, with only 200 metres races being held on breaststroke and backstroke until 1964, when the modern Olympic programme began to emerge. It was in Tokyo in 1964 that the first medley race appeared, over 400 metres. The 200 metres was introduced in 1968 but was dropped in 1976 and 1980 before returning in 1984.

Don Schollander, of the United States, was the first man to win four gold medals at the similar Games in swimming.

Eight years later, Mark Spitz became an Olympic immortal with that all-time record of seven gold medals at one Games. In the month in which the US Olympic trials and the Munich Olympic Games were staged in the summer of 1972, Spitz set 14 world records, an achievement unsurpassed. Matt Biondi, the Freestyle and butterfly sprinter of the US, won five gold medals in 1988, the closest any man has come to emulating Spitz, whose success was so magnificent that it overshadowed one of the greatest Olympic efforts by a woman swimmer in history.

Shane Gould held each freestyle world record between 100 and 1,500 metres simultaneously and arrived at the Games in Munich as favourite to win the four freestyle races she had entered. Against fierce opposition from the US, Gould won three gold medals (200 and 400 metres freestyle and 200 metres medley), a silver (800 metres) and a bronze (100 metres).

The most successful swimming nation is the United States, though in men's freestyle races Americans have struggled to keep up with Australians and Europeans in the past 16 years.

Australia defeated the United States for the first time in terms of gold medal tally at the Pan Pacific championships in 1999. Australian strength lies in its male freestylers, Thorpe, Grant Hackett and Michael Klim, and in Susie O'Neill, the reigning Olympic champion, who aims to remove the longest swimming record - over 200 metres butterfly - from the books. If she does it at Homebush, or even retains her title, the wall of sound from the crowd may itself be the stuff of swimming legend.

FINA Swimming World Cup

The FINA Swimming World Cup is an international professional swimming competition in short course meters organised by the International Swimming Federation since 1989. Swimmers from the members of the International Swimming Federation are allowed to compete. 1st, 2nd, and 3rd place finishers are granted prize money.

The events are the similar for all meets, but the competition order may vary. All events are swum in prelims finals except for 800 m and 1500 m Freestyle, which are swum in timed finals. The competition are held over two days, with prelims in the mornings and finals in the evening, with the noted exception of the Brazilian meets where prelims have been in the evening with finals the following morning (hence the 3-day format).

Series events (all in 25 m pools):

Freestyle: 50 m, 100 m, 200 m, 400 m, 800 m for women, 1500 m for men

Backstroke: 50 m, 100 m, 200 m

Breaststroke: 50 m, 100 m, 200 m

Butterfly: 50 m, 100 m, 200 m

Individual medley: 100 m, 200 m, 400 m

ADMINISTRATIVE BODIES

International Swimming Federation

Fédération Internationale de Natation (FINA) is the International Federation (IF) recognized by the International Olympic Committee (IOC) for administering international competition in the aquatic sports (its name translated from French is "International Swimming Federation"). It is one of various IFs which administers a given game/discipline for the IOC and/or international community. It is based in Lausanne, Switzerland.

FINA presently oversees competition in five aquatic sports: swimming, diving, synchronized swimming, water polo and open water swimming. The present President of FINA is Mustapha Larfaoui of Algeria. FINA presently organizes various events in all the disciplines it oversees.

The biggest FINA event is the now biennial World Championships, presently held each odd year. It features events in all five aquatic disciplines, and was most recently held in Melbourne, Australia, in March 2007. Prior to 2000, the event was held each 4 years, in the even year between Olympic (Summer) Games.

FAMOUS PLAYERS

Johnny Weissmuller

Johnny Weissmuller (June 2, 1904 – January 20, 1984) was an American swimmer and actor who was one of the world's topmost swimmers in the 1920s, succeeding five Olympic gold medals and one bronze medal. He won fifty-two US National Championships and set sixty-seven world records. After his swimming career, he was the sixth actor to portray Tarzan in films, a role he played in twelve motion pictures. Dozens of other actors have also played Tarzan, but Weissmuller is by far the best known. His character's distinctive, ululating Tarzan yell is still often used in films.

As a teen, Weissmuller dropped out of school and worked various jobs including a stint as a lifeguard at a Lake Michigan beach. While working as an elevator operator and bellboy at the Illinois Athletic Club, Weissmuller caught the eye of swim coach William Bachrach. Bachrach coached Weissmuller and in August 1921, Weissmuller won the national championships in the 50-yard and 220-yard distances. Though he was foreign-born, Weissmuller gave his place of origin as Tanneryville, Pennsylvania, and his birth date as that of his younger brother, Peter Weissmuller. This was to ensure his eligibility to compete as part of the United States Olympic team, and was a critical issue in being issued an American passport.

On July 9, 1922, Weissmuller broke Duke Kahanamoku's world record on the 100-meters freestyle, swimming it in 58.6 seconds. He won the title in that distance at the 1924 Summer Olympics, beating Kahanamoku on February 24, 1924. He also won the 400-meters freestyle and the 4 x 200 meters relay. As a member of the American water polo team, he also won a bronze medal. Four years later, at the 1928 Summer Olympics in Amsterdam, he won another two Olympic titles.

In all, he won five Olympic gold medals, one bronze medal, won fifty-two U.S. National Championships and set sixty-seven world records.

Johnny Weissmuller never lost a race and retired from his amateur swimming career undefeated.

Johnny Weissmuller (1904 – 1984) was one of the greatest swimmers in history. He turned popular from his film career and water polo. Johnny Weissmuller had never lost a swimming competition in his entire career, turned fifty two times national champion of the USA and broke sixty sevenworld records. He was the first swimmer to swim the 100 meters freestyle in less than 1 minute.

On the 1924 Olympic Games in Paris, he won the gold medal on the 100 meter and 400 meter freestyle and on the 4 x 200 meter freestyle relay. 4 years later he would add another 2 gold medals (100 meter freestyle and 4 x 200 meter freestyle) on the Olympics in Amsterdam.

He contended with the USA national water polo team on 2 Olympic Games and won the bronze medal on the 1924 Olympics, finishing after France (gold) and Belgium (bronze). He once said: "Water polo's a rough game. That's where I learned to duck. It came in handy when Cheetah started throwing coconuts." Johnny Weissmuller died in 1984 from a heart condition, lonely and broke after 4 failed marriages

Dawn Fraser

Dawn Lorraine Fraser AO, MBE (born on 4 September 1937) is an Australian champion swimmer. She is one of only two swimmers to win the similar Olympic event three times, in her case, the 100 meters freestyle.

Inside Australia, she is known for her controversial behaviour and larrikin character as much as for her athletic ability. Fraser won eight Olympic medals, including four gold medals, and six Commonwealth Games gold medals. She also held 39 records. The 100 meters freestyle record was hers for 15 years from 1 December 1956 to 8 January 1972.

She is the first of only two swimmers in Olympic history (Krisztina Egerszegi of Hungary being the other) to win individual gold medals for the similar event at three successive Olympics (100 meters freestyle - 1956, 1960, 1964).

In October 1962, she was the first woman to swim 100 meters freestyle in less than one minute. It was not until 1973, eight years after Fraser retired, that her 100m record of 58.9 secs was broken. During the 1964 Summer Olympics in Tokyo, Fraser angered swimming team sponsors and the Australian Swimming Union (ASU) by marching in the opening ceremony against their wishes, wearing an older swimming costume because it was more comfortable than the one supplied by the sponsors, and allegedly climbing a flagpole at Emperor Hirohito's palace to steal the Olympic flag. In 1965, the ASU placed Fraser under a ten-year ban, to which she responded by announcing her retirement.

At the 1964 summer olympics she was alleged to have swum the moat to the Emperor's palace and stolen a flag. She was arrested but released without charge. The Emperor gave her the flag as a souvenir. However, the Australian Swimming Union suspended her for 10 years. They repented a few months before the 1968 Games but by then it was too late for Fraser, at 31, to prepare.

She would later deny swimming the moat to steal the flag, telling The Times in 1991: "There's no way I would have swum that moat. I was terrified of dirty water and that moat was filthy. There's no way I'd have dipped my toe in it."

She was named the Australian of the Year in 1964, was made a Member of the Order of the British Empire in 1967, and appointed an Officer of the Order of Australia (AO) in 1998. Also in 1998, she was voted Australia's greatest female athlete in history. She was named Australian Female Athlete of the Century by the Sport Australian Hall of Fame. In 1999 the International Olympic Committee named her the World's Greatest Living Female Water Sports Champion.

She was one of the bearers of the Olympic Torch at the opening ceremony of the 2000 Summer Olympics in Sydney. She carried the Olympic Torch at the stadium, as one of the runners for the final segment, before the lighting of the Olympic Flame. The Australian Sport Awards includes an award named in honour of and presented by Fraser.

REFERENCES

Armbruster, David A., Sr., and Lawrence E. Morehouse : *Swimming and Diving*. 3rd ed., St. Louis, Missouri, C. V. Mosby Co., 1958.

Broer, Marion: *Efficiency of Human Movement*. Philadelphia, W. B. Saunders Co., 1966.

Counsilman, James: *The Science of Swimming*. Englewood Cliffs, New Jersey, Prentice-Hall, Inc., 1968.

Clotworthy, Robert: *Diving*. Camden, N. J., Thomas Nelson and Sons, 1962.

Curtis, Katherine Whitney: *Rhythmic Swiming*. Minneapolis, Minnesota, Burgess Publishing Co., 1942.

Council for National Cooperation in Aquatics: *Water Fun for Everyone*. 291 Broadway, New York City 10007, Assoc. Press, 1965.

Downing, W. H.: *Every Boy and Girl a Swimmer*. New York, N. Y., Skiffington & Sons.

Fairbanks, Anne Ross: *Teaching Springboard Diving*. Englewood Cliffs. New Jersey, Prentice-Hall, Inc., 1963.

Goss, Gertrude: *Swimming Analyzed*. 200 West Foster Street, Melrose, Massachusetts 02176,

Goss, Gertrude: *Stunts and Synchronized Swimming*. 200 West Foster Street, Melrose, Massachusetts 02176.

Gundling, Beulah, and Peg Seller: *Aquatic Art*. 403 Iowa Theater Building, Cedar Rapids, Iowa, 1957.

Hobden, F. W.: *Springboard Diving*. 42 Great Russell Street, London, England, William Clowes & Sons, Ltd.

Jarvis, Margaret: *Swimming for Teachers and Youth Leaders*. London, England, Faber and Faber, 1947.

Kiphuth, Robert J.: *Swimming*. New York, N. Y., A. S. Barnes & Co, 1942.

Lukens, Paul W.: *Teaching Swimming*. Minneapolis, Minnesota, Burgess Publishing Co., 1948.

Moriarty, Phillip: *Diving*. New York, N. Y., The Ronald Press, 1959.

Newman, Virginia Hunt: *Teaching an Infant to Swim*. New York, N. Y., Harcourt, Brace, 1967.

Peppe, Mike, and Coles Phinizy: *Sports Illustrated Book of Diving*. Philadelphia, Pa., J. B. Lippincott Co.

Rackham, George: *Synchronized Swimming*. London, England, Faber and Faber.

Spears, Betty: *Beginning Synchronized Swimming*. 2nd ed. Minneapolis, Minnesota, Burgess Publishing Co., 1958.

Torney, John A., and Robert Clayton: *Aquatic Instruction, Coaching and Management*. Minneapolis, Minnesota, Burgess Publishing Co., 1970.

Yates, Fern, and Theresa W. Anderson: *Synchronized Swimming*.

15

Table Tennis

Table tennis, also called as ping pong, is a game in which two or four players hit a lightweight, hollow ball to and fro to each other with rackets (also known as 'bats' or 'paddles'). The game occurs on a hard table separated by a net. Players must permit a ball played towards them only one bounce on their side of the table and must return it so that it bounces on the other side. Points are scored when a player fails to return the ball inside the rules. Play is fast and calls quick reactions. A skilled player can add various varieties of spin to the ball, changing its trajectory and restricting an opponent's options to great advantage.

The game is assured by the International Table Tennis Federation (ITTF), established in 1926. Since 1988, table tennis has been an Olympic sport which admits four events. From 1988 until 2004, the events were men's singles, women's singles, men's doubles and women's doubles. Since 2008 the doubles have been substituted by the team events (Beijing was the first time where table tennis had an Olympic team event).

The game is played with two or four players striking a ball with rackets to and fro to each other on a table, in a manner similar to tennis. The rules are slightly dissimslar, but the concept is very similar. In singles play, the serve is not needed to cross from the server's right-hand court to the receiver's right-hand court (or left to left) as it is in tennis. However, serving over is needed in doubles play. Ball spin, speed, placement, strategy and tactics play an significant part in competitive table tennis matches. The speed of the ball can alter from slow serves with much spin to smashes that travel as fast as 112.5 kilometers per hour (70 mph).

The game is played on a 274 cm × 152.5 cm × 76 cm high (9 ft × 5 ft × 30 inches high) playing surface. The International Table Tennis Federation requires an area not to a lesser extent than 14 m long, 7 m broad and 5 m high for competitions. No restrictions in size or shape are determined. Modern rackets normally have a thin layer of rubber covering the racket's striking surface. The rubber may have pimples pointing outwards or inwards, as well as a thin layer of sponge among the plywood center and the rubber surface. Since spin plays a large role in the modern game of table tennis, the composition of the rubber and the combination of sponge and rubber is planned to maximize the amount of spin and speed a player can impart onto the ball. Other technological betterments comprise the use of carbon or other synthetic layers as part of the blade to increase the size of the sweet spot or the stiffness of the blade.

The ball used in table tennis has a diameter of 40 mm, is made of celluloid, and is hollow. A three star rating on a ball normally involves a top quality ball, in relation to its bounce, roundness and their respective uniformity among balls of the similar make and type.

The winner is the first to score 11 points or more while being ahead by 2 points or more. Players interchange serves every two points. At 10-10 (or deuce) the players alternating with each serve; the winner is then the first person to gain a clear two points advantage over his opponent. The 11 point game is an International Table Tennis Federation (ITTF) change whichtook placein 2001. All games played at national level and at international tournaments (ITTF) are played to 11 points in either a greatest of five (5) games (preliminaries) or greatest of seven (7) games layout (championship matches).

HISTORY

The game has its roots in England as an after-dinner amusement for upper-class Victorians in the 1880s. Mimicking the game of tennis in an indoor environment, daily objects were primitively enlisted to act as the equipment. A line of books would be the net, a rounded top of a champagne cork or knot of string as the ball, and a cigar box lid as the racket.

Table tennis orginated into the modern game in Europe, the United States and Japan. The fame of the game led game manufacturers to trade the equipment commercially. Early rackets were often pieces of parchment stretched upon a frame, and the sound generated in play gave the game its first nicknames of "whiff-whaff" and "Ping-pong." A number of sources show that the game was first brought to the attention of Hamley's of Regent Street under the name "Gossima". The name "ping-pong" was in broad use before English producer J. Jaques & Son Ltd trademarked it in 1901. The name "Ping-Pong" then came to be used for the game played by the rather costly Jaques equipment, with other producers calling theirs table tennis. A similar situation came to exist in the United States where Jaques sold the rights to the "Ping-Pong" name to Parker Brothers.

The following main invention was by James Gibb, an English enthusiast of table tennis, who founded novelty celluloid balls on a trip to the U.S. in 1901 and found them to be ideal for the game. This was succeeded by E.C. Goode who in 1901 devised the modern version of the racket by fixing a sheet of pimpled, or stippled, rubber to the wooden blade. Table tennis was developing in popularity by 1901 when table tennis tournaments were being organized, books on table tennis were being written, and an unofficial world championship was deemed in 1902. Throughout the early twentieth century the game was banned in Russia due to a belief that was deemed by the rulers at the time that playing the game had an adverse effect on players' eyesight. In 1921, the Table Tennis Association was established in England, and the International Table Tennis Federation succeeded in 1926. London hosted the first authorized world championship in 1927. Table tennis was brought in as an Olympic sport at the Olympics in 1988.

In the 1950s rackets that used a rubber sheet merged with an underlaying sponge layer altered the game dramatically, premising greater spin and speed. These were brought in to England by the sports goods manufacturers S.W. Hancock Ltd. The use of speed glue enhansed the spin and speed even further, leading in alterations to the equipment to "slow the game down."

Toward the end of 2000, the ITTF laid various rules alterations aimed at making table tennis more executable as a televised spectator game. First, the older 38 mm (1.5 inch) balls were officially substituted by 40 mm balls. This increased the ball's air resistance and successfully slowed down the game. By that time, players had begun modifying the thickness of the fast sponge layer on their rackets, which made the game excessively fast, and difficult to watch on television. Secondly, the ITTF altered from a 21 to an 11 point scoring system. This was intended to make games more fast-paced and exciting. The ITTF also altered the rules on service to prevent a player from hiding the ball throughout service, in order to gain the average length of rallies and to reduce the server's advantage. Variants of the game have came out. "Large-ball" table tennis uses a 44 mm ball which slows down the game significantly. This has seen some acceptance by players who have a hard time with the extreme spins and speeds of the 40 mm game. The ball's mass is 2.47 grams.

There is a move towards revitalizing the table tennis game that existed prior to the introduction of sponge rubber. Classic table tennis or "Hardbat" table tennis players reject the speed and spin of reversed sponge rubber, favoring the 1940-60s play style, with no-sponge, short pimpled rubber equipments, when defense is less difficult by diminishing the speed and eliminating any meaningful magnus effect of spin. Because hardbat killer shots are almost not possible to hit in opposition to a skilled player, hardbat matches focus on the strategic side of table tennis, requiring skillful maneuvering of the opponent before an attack can be successful.

THE GAME

Ball

The international rules determine that the game is played with a light 2.7 gram, 40 mm diameter ball. In general, it is the most-used ball. The rules state that the ball shall bounce up 23cm when dropped from a height of 30cm thereby having a coefficient of restitution of 0.88. The 40 mm ball was brought in after the 2000 Olympic Games. However, this created some controversy as the Chinese National Team contended that this was merely to give non-Chinese players a better chance of winning. A 40 mm table tennis ball is slower and spins less than a 38 mm one. The ball is made of a high-bouncing gas-filled celluloid, colored white or orange, with a matte finish. The selection of ball color is made as per the table color and its surroundings. For example, a white ball is gentler to see on a green or blue table than it is on a grey table. Stars on the ball show the quality of the ball. 3 stars show that it is of the most eminent quality.

Table

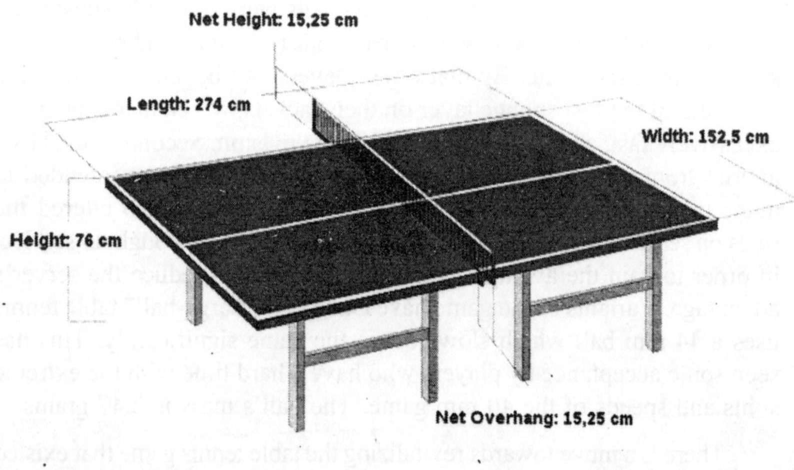

Fig. Table

The table is 2.74 m (9 ft) long, 1.525 m (5 ft) broad, and 76 cm (30 inch) high with a Masonite (a type of hardboard) or likewise produced timber, layered with a smooth, low-friction coating. The table or playing surface is separated into two halves by a 15.25 cm (6 inch) high net. The table surface can either have a green or blue color.

Racket

Players are equipped with a laminated wooden racket covered with rubber on one or two sides depending upon the grip of the player. This is called either a paddle, racket or bat depending upon where in the world the game is being played. In the USA the term "paddle" is common, in Europe the term is "bat," and the authorized ITTF term is "racket." This section will use the ITTF term.

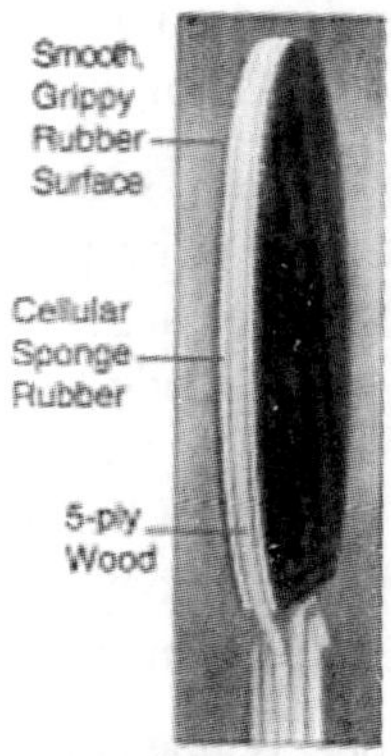

Fig. Racket

Table tennis regulations permit dissimslar surfaces on each side of the racket. The dissimslar types of surfaces provide various levels of spin or speed, or in some cases, nullify spin. For example, a player may have a rubber that provides much spin on one side of his racket, and no spin on the other side of the racket. By flipping the racket in play, dissimslar types of returns are possible. To help a player distinguish among dissimslar types of rubber used by his opposing player, international rules determine that one side must be red while the other side must be black. The player has the right to inspect his opponent's racket before a match to see the type of rubber used and what color it is. In spite of high speed play and rapid exchanges, a player can see clearly what side of the racket was used to hit the ball. Existing rules state that, unless damaged in play, the racket cannot be exchanged for another racket at any time throughout a match.

Recent years have seen progress in technology of table tennis blades. Materials of dissimslar properties may be combined with the wood in the blade to enhance its playing execution. Many blades at present feature one or more carbon layers inside them to enhance their 'sweet spot', and to give the player a greater margin of error when playing powerful shots. Materials incorporated into table tennis blades at present comprise titanium, acrylate, aramids, fiberglass, and aluminium.

The rubber coating may be of pimpled rubber, with the pimples outward, or it may be a rubber that is compiled of two materials, a sponge layer, covered up by a pimpled rubber, with the pimples pointed inwards or outwards. Some rackets are not covered up with rubber at all, because a "naked" racket is more resistant to a spin. However, it is illegal to use these types of racket in competition as they are not sanctioned by the ITTF. Some types of rubbers are also not sanctioned. Sanctioned rubbers have the ITTF emblem on the base of the rubber.

Players have many options and versions in rubber sheets on their racket. Even though a racket may be purchased with rubber by the manufacturer, most serious tournament players will produce a customized racket. A player selects a blank blade (i.e. a racket without rubber), established on his playing style. The type of wood and synthetic layers used to make up the blade will allow for a slower or faster blade. The player can choose from dissimslar types of rubber sheets which will provide a certain level of spin, speed and particular playing characteristics.

Normally, a sheet of rubber is glued to a blade utilizing rubber cement and not taken out until the rubber wears out or becomes damaged. In the 1980s, a new technique was formulated where the player would use special glue called speed glue to apply the rubber each time he played. The glue would help allow for more spin and speed by providing a "catapult" effect. This technique is known as "regluing" and has turn a standard technique for top players.

The surface of a racket will formulate a smooth glossy patina with use. The rubber surface needs to be on a regular basis cleaned to assure it holds a high friction surface to impart spin to the ball. Players use a commercial cleaner, or just water and detergent as cleaning agents.

Racket construction and new rubber technology (skilled elite players normally choose and attach the rubber to their own rackets and glue them before every match) lead significantly to the amount of deflection from the anticipated ball flight path. The fairly recent growth of speed glue speeds up the departure of the ball from the rubber substantially, though at the cost of some ball control on touch shots where little or no spin is put on the ball. Speed glue was permitted for the final time in the 2008 Summer Olympics. From the 2012 Summer Olympics on speed glue will be banned at the Olympic games.

Starting a Game

In top-flight competition, service is determined by a coin toss. At lower levels it is common for one player (or the umpire/scorer) to hide the ball in one or the other hand (normally hidden under the table), permitting the other player to guess which hand the ball is in. The correct or incorrect guess gives the "winner" the option to choose to serve, obtain, or to choose which side of the table to use. Another method is for one player to hit the ball to the other and he or she retorts it or by hitting it to and fro four times and then playing out the point. This is ordinarily referred to as PING. Then, they play one point to see who serves first. Players also decide the first to serve by placing a racket on the table with the handle off the board, taking turns throwing the ball at their opponent's racket. The first to strike the opponent's racket without receiving a return shot gets the serve.

Service

In game play, the player serving the ball begins a point. Standing so that the ball is deemed behind the endline of the table, with the ball in the palm of the free hand - over the table's height - and the racket in the other, the server tosses the ball without spin, upward, at least 16 centimeters (about 6 inches). In casual (non-tournament) games, many players do not toss the ball upward, nevertheless this is technically illegal and can give the serving player an unfair advantage. The ball must stay above the height of the table at all times. The server cannot use his body or clothing to block sight of the ball; the opponent and the umpire must have a clear view of the ball at all times.

He or she then must hit the ball from backside of the baseline such that it bounces once on his or her half of the table, and then bounces at least one time on the opponent's half. If the ball hits the net but does not strike the opponent's half of the table, then a point is granted to the opponent. However, if the ball hits the net, but however goes over and bounces on the other side, it is called a let (or net-in). Play stops, and the ball must be served once again with no penalty. A player may entrust any number of lets without penalty.

If the service is "good", then the opposer must then make a "good" return — by delivering the ball before it bounces on his or her side of the table a second time. Bringing back the serve is one of the hardest parts of the game, as the server's first move is often the least predictable - due to the many spin options at his or her disposal - and thus most advantageous to him or her.

Hitting the Ball

Any hitting of the ball must be done such that the ball passes over or all over the net. If the ball is struck such that it travels all over the net, but still lands on the opponent's side of the table, the hit is legal and play should be extended. If the opponent cannot return it over (or around) the net and make it bounce on your side, then you win the point.

Scoring

Points are granted to the opponent for any of various errors in play:

Allowing the ball to bounce on one's own side twice

Double hitting the ball. Note that the hand above the wrist is believed part of the racket and making a good return off one's hand or fingers on the racket-holding hand is permitted, but hitting one's hand or fingers and subsequently hitting the racket is a double strike and an error.

Permitting the ball to strike anything other than the racket.

Causing the ball not to bounce on the opponent's half (i.e., not making a "good" return)

Placing one's free hand on the playing surface or moving the playing surface

Offering and failing to make a good serve (i.e., making a service toss and failing to strike the ball fairly into play)

Making an illegal serve: (e.g., one preceded by a player's hiding the ball or his failing to toss the ball at least 16 centimetres (six inches) in the air).

Hitting the net with racket or any body part.

By volleying the ball (not allowing the ball to bounce on your side)

Alternation of Service: Service alternates among opponents every two points (regardless of winner of the rally) until a player reaches 11 points with at least a two-point lead, or until both players have 10 points a piece. If both players reach 10 points, then service alternates after each point, until one player gains a two-point advantage.

In doubles, service alternates every two points among sides, but also rotates among players on the similar team. At the end of every two points, the receiving player becomes the server, and the partner of the serving player becomes the receiver.

In the older 21-point game system, service would alternate every 5 points. If both players reached a score of 20, then service would alternate each point until one player gains a two-point advantage.

Series of Games

After each game, players switch sides of the table and in the fifth or seventh, game "for the match", players switch sides when the first player scores 5 points, regardless of whose turn it is to serve. In competition play, matches are normally best of five or seven games.

Doubles Game: In addition to games among individual players, pairs may also play table tennis. In doubles, all the rules of single play apply except for the following. A line painted along the long axis of the table to create doubles courts bisects the table. This line's only aim is to facilitate the doubles service rule, which is that service, must originate from the right hand "box" in such a way that the first bounce of the serve bounces once in said right hand box and then must bounce at least once in the opponent side's right hand box (far left box for server).

Play then continues normally with the exception that players must alternate hitting the ball. For example, after a player serves, the receiving player makes his or her return, the server's partner returns the ball and then the service receiver's partner would play the ball. The point proceeds this way until one side fails to make a legal return and the point is then granted to the other team.

Also, when the game reaches the final set, the teams must switch side and the team that receives the service must switch receiver when one of the teams reach 5 points. Singles and doubles are both played in international competition, as well as the Olympic Games since 1988 and the Commonwealth Games since 2002. In 2005, the ITTF declarted that doubles table tennis will only be featured as a part of teams events in the 2008 Olympics.

Types of Shots

The strokes break down into in general offensive and defensive. The types of strokes comprise backhand and forehand. The shots vary from the forehand loop to the backhand smash.

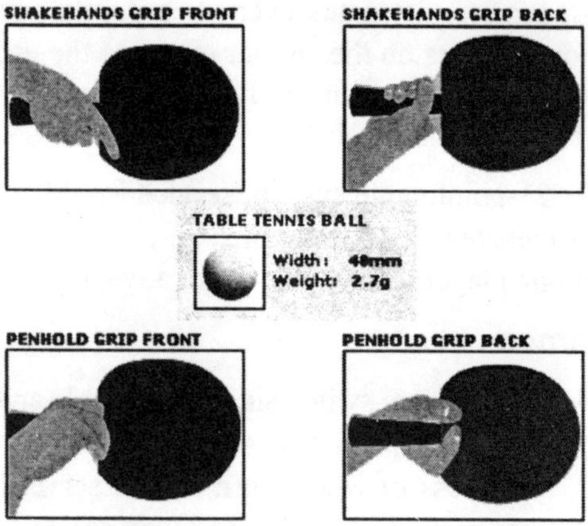

Fig. Grisp

Speed drive: These strokes vary to ones from other racket sports like tennis. The racket is mainly perpendicular to the direction of the stroke, and most of the energy employed to the ball results in speed rather than spin, producing a shot that does not arc much, but is fast enough that it can be difficult to return. A speed drive is used largely for keeping the ball in play, applying pressure on the opponent and potentially opening up an chance for a more powerful attack.

Loop Drive: Essentially the reverse of the speed drive. The racket is much more parallel to the direction of the stroke ("closed") and the racket thus grazes the ball, leadingin a large amount of topspin. A good loop drive will arc quite a bit, and once striking the opponent's side of the table will jump forward, much like a kick serve in tennis. Returning a loop drive may not be as hard to return as a speed drive; however, because of its topspin, it is more likely to rebound off the opponent's racket at a very high angle, setting up an easy smash on the follow up. As the loop drive requires a lot of topspin, players in general use their entire body to produce the movement needed. Fluctuations in spin and speed add to the effectiveness of this shot.

Counter Drive: Normally a counter attack in opposition to drives (normally high loop drives). You have to close the racket and stay close to the ball (try to predict its path). The racket is deemed closed and near to the ball, which is hit with a snippy movement "off the bounce" (before reaching the highest point) so that the ball moves faster to the other side. If executed correctly, a well-timed, precise counter-drive can be as effective as a smash.

Flip: When a player attempts to attack a ball that has not bounced outside the edge of the table, he/she does not have the room to wind up in a backswing. The ball may still be attacked, nevertheless, and the resulting shot is called flip because the backswing is compacted into a quick wrist action. A flip is not a single stroke and can correspond either a drive or a loop in its features flick.

Smash: A player will normally perform a smash when his or her opposer has returned back the ball that bounces too high and/or too close to the net. Smashing is fundamentally self-explanatory — large backswing and rapid acceleration contributing as much speed on the ball as possible. The goal of a smash is to get the ball to move so rapidly that the opposer simply cannot bring back it. Because the ball speed is the main aim of this shot, often the spin on the ball is something other than topspin. Sidespin can be used effectively with a smash to alter the ball's trajectory significantly, even though intermediate players will smash the ball with little or no spin. An offensive table-tennis player will think of a rally as a build-up to a winning smash; only a calculated series of smashes can guarantee a point in opposition to a good opponent. However, most players will be able to return at most one or two smashes consistently. Allowed that the opponent is not too close to the table or too far away from the ball, a smash can be lobbed, chopped, blocked or even counter-looped, albeit with some hardness. A player who smashes in general works out a series of smashes (and possibly drop-shots) to rush the opponent out of position, put him off balance, or both. Smashers who fail to do this find it difficult to win a point in opposition to an excellent defense.

Push: The push is very easy and normally used for holding the point alive and producing offensive opportunities. A push resembles a tennis slice: the racket cuts below the ball, imparting backspin and causing the ball to float slowly to the other side of the table. While not obvious, a push can be hard to attack because the backspin on the ball causes it to drop toward the table upon striking the opponent's racket. In order to attack a push, a player must normally loop the ball back over the net. Often, the greatest option for beginners is to easily push the ball back once again, leadingin forcing rallies. For good players it may be the worst option as the opponent will counter with a loop, putting you in a defensive position from which most likely you will lose, unless you are a good chopper. Another option to forcing is to flip the ball when it is close tc the net. Forcing can have advantages in some conditions. Players should only push when their opponent makes easy mistakes. Offensive players should only push for fluctuation and not for general rallies. A push can easily be counter-looped into the opposite corner if it is not short enough. The goal of most player's pushes is to make the ball land too short to be assaulted, rather than undertaking to over-spin the opponent.

Chop : A chop or cut is the defensive, backspin counterpart to the offensive loop drive. A chop is basically a bigger, heavier slice, assumed well back from the table. The racket face points chiefly horizontally, perhaps a little bit upward, and the direction of the stroke is straight down. The aim of a defensive chop is to match the topspin of the opponent's shot with your own backspin. A good chop will float nearly horizontally back to the table, in some cases having so much backspin that the ball actually rises. A chop such as this can be exceptionally hard to return due to the enormous amount of backspin. Sometimes a defensive player can impart no spin on the ball throughout a chop, or frequently add right- or left-hand spin to the ball. This may further confuse his/her opponent. Chops are hard to execute, but are devastating when completed properly because it takes a significant quantity of topspin on a loop drive to return the ball back over the net.

Block : The block or short is a simple shot, barely worthy of being called a "stroke," but nevertheless can be devastating in opposition to an attacking opponent. A block is performed by simply putting the racket in front of the ball — the ball bounces back toward the opponent with nearly as much energy as it came in with. This is not as easy as it sounds, because the ball's spin, speed, and location all influence the correct angle of a block. It is very credible for an opponent to execute a perfect loop, drive, or smash, only to have the blocked shot come back at him just as fast. Due to the power demanded in offensive strokes, often an opponent simply cannot recover rapidly enough, and will be unable to return his own shot blocked back to him/her. Blocks almost always produce the similar spin as was received, which is nearly always topspin.

Push-Block : High level players may utilize what is called push block or active block, adding speed to the ball (with a small topspin movement). When playing in the Penhold Grip, many players utilize push blocks when being forced on the backhand. Chinese pen-hold players denote to it as a push-block as they literally "push" their backhand forward, rather of simply blocking it.

Side Drive : This spin shot is consequently used as a defensive and offensive maneuver. The basis of this move is to put a spin on the ball either to the right or the left of the racket. The carrying out of this move is alik to a slice, but to the right or left rather of down. This spin will outcome in the ball curving to the side but bouncing in the reverse direction when the opponent returns it. Do not attempt a right-side spin (moving your arm to the right when hitting the ball) when too close to the left side of the table, and visa versa. To bring back, simply execute the similar sided spin as your opponent just gave you.

Lob : The defensive High Ball or Lob is perhaps the most visually-impressive shot in the game of table tennis, and it is deceptive in its ease. To execute a High Ball, a defensive player first backs off the table 8-10 meters; then, the stroke itself consists of simply lifting the ball to an tremendous height before it falls back to the opponent's side of the table. A High Ball is inherently a creative shot, and can have nearly any kind of spin you can think. Top quality players utilize this fact to their benefit in order to control the spin of the ball. For example, though the opponent may smash the ball hard and fast, a good defensive Lob could be more difficult to return due to the unpredictability (and heavy amounts) of the spin on the ball. Thus, though backed off the table by tens of feet and evidently running and leaping just to reach the ball, a good defensive player can still win the point utilizing good High Balls but majority of the time you will lose the point so it is not suggested unless it is in real necessary.

Drop Shot : The drop shot is a high degree stroke, used as another fluctuation for close-to-table strokes (like harai and slice). You have to place the racket close to the ball and just let the ball touch it (without any hand motion) in a way that the ball stays close to the net with almost no speed and spin and touches on the other side of the table more than twice if the opposer doesn't reach it. This stroke should be used when opponents are far from the table and not prepared to get close to the table. This technique is most normally done by pen-holders and players who utilize long or short pimples. A very betraying technique, this could outcome in the opponent failing to reach the ball after misjudging the distance of the ball. A perfectly carried out stroke after a topspin sequence can win a point.

MAJOR TOURNAMENTS

European Champions League

European Champions League (ECL) is the cyclic table tennis contest for the highest ranked European club teams and is regarded as the most important international club competition in Europe. It is coordinated by the European Table Tennis Union (ETTU) and substituted the European Club Cup of Champions (ECCC), the previous outstanding club competition, since the 1998/99 season. Primitively there is only a men competition while a women competition was innovated in the 2005/06 season. The competition starts in September and the champions are normally decided in May in recent years.

Belgian club La Villette Charleroi is the most prosperous club in the history of the men's competition, being the champions from 2001 to 2004 and having won the competition for five times, while Italy's topclub Sterilgarda TT Castelgoffredo has won the women's league twice, being the most fortunate club in the women's competition. The Finals of 07/08 season were deemed in April to early May, with Austrian club SVS Niederösterreich turned the champions of the men's competition, and Dutch club MF Services Heerlen has been announced to be the winner of the women's league after German club FSV Kroppach are calledto be not ableto play on the set date of the second leg.

The Men's Champions League was first directed in the 1998/99 season, with the intention to substitute the European Club Cup of Champions, the previous highest level European club competition since 1960/61 season. In the second season (99/00), the playing system is altered. The maximum number of games had been reduced from 7 to 5, and the double had been cancelled, with the intention of having a better presentation in TV and more excitation for the spectators. The competition came into a new era in 2005/06, when the Women's Champions League commenced with 8 clubs and the men's league was expanded from 8 to 16 clubs, enabling a greater number of nations to take part. These alterations were undertaken in the hopes of making table tennis more famous in a European level as well as motivating the coming generation.

For the Men's competition, the 4 semi-finalists of the last year are automatically admitted in the competition. The left over 12 places are filled by the 12 teams with the highest total number of ranking points for their three greatest ranked players on the existing world ranking, with only one "foreign player" being believed.

For the women's league, last year's two finalists will contend in the competition with the six teams with the largest total number of ranking points for their three greatest ranked players, also with only one "foreign player" being believed.

Moreover, there is a restriction on the number of clubs from the similar nations. Not more than 4 or 3 clubs, Men's and Women's respectively, from the similar association are entitled the right to enter in the competition. In the Men's competition, if the semi-finalists of the former year came from the similar association and a 5th team has the highest ranking points, the ranking of the final national team championships will determine on the qualification.

The league is accomplished in two stages. The first stage is the group round robin matches while the second stage is the straight 2-leg knock-out stage.

For the men's league, the 16 teams are separated into 4 groups inside which they play round robin matches. The 4 teams with the highest ranking points will be seeded and play in the 4 groups respectively. Throughout the group stage, 2 match points are granted for a win, 1 for a loss and 0 for a loss in a not played or uncompleted match, and the ranking order is decided by the numbers of match points earned.

If 2 or more teams have earned the similar number of match points, their relative position are decided by the results only of the matches among them, taking successively the numbers of match points, the ratios of wins to losses in individual matches, games and points, as far as it is essential to resolve the order. Lot is used to decided the position if teams are equal in all of the above criteria.

The top two teams in each group certified for the knock-out stage. Those 8 teams will play in a single knock-out system, with quarter-finals, semi-finals and finals, to decide the winner of the competition. At any stages 2 legs, home and away, are played for each tie, and teams win the tie if they win both legs. If each team wins one leg, the result is decided by totality score first in individual matches, then in games and finally in points.

The women's competition is deemed in similar layout with the men's league, with the exception that the 8 teams are separated into 2 groups and the 2 teams with the largest ranking points will be the seeds.

The contest is played under the new Swaythling Cup system (greatest of 5 singles). A team is comprised of 3 players selected from those appointed for the event. The opposite teams play 5 single matches with the match order A v X, B v Y, C v Z, A v Y, B v X. The team match will end if one of the teams has won 3 matches.

ADMINISTRATIVE BODIES

International Table Tennis Federation

The International Table Tennis Federation (ITTF) is the governing body for all national table tennis associations. Led by representatives of

Germany, Hungary, and England, the International Table Tennis Federation was founded in 1926. The first international tournament was held in January 1926 in Berlin. Austria, Germany, Hungary and Sweden were charter members.

The role of the ITTF includes overseeing rules and regulations and seeking technological improvement for the sport of table tennis. The ITTF runs numerous international competitions, including the Table Tennis World Championships that has continued since 1926.

Toward the end of 2000, the ITTF instituted several rules changes aimed at making table tennis more viable as a televised spectator sport. The older 38 mm balls were officially replaced by 40 mm balls. This increased the ball's air resistance and effectively slowed down the game. By that time, players had begun increasing the thickness of the fast sponge layer on their paddles, which made the game excessively fast, and difficult to watch on television.

On February 29, 2008, the ITTF announced several rules changes after an ITTF Executive Meeting in Guangzhou, China with regards to a player's eligibility to play for a new association. The Olympic eligibility of registered players for the 2008 Summer Olympics will not be affected and will not be applied retroactively. The new ruling is to encourage associations to develop their own players. There are currently 205 member organizations associated with the ITTF. The seat of the ITTF is in Lausanne, Switzerland. The current president of the ITTF is Adham Sharara, a Canadian.

FAMOUS PLAYERS

Richard Bergman(Austria)

Regarded as the best defensive player in history, Bergman won seven World Championships during his professional career.

Andrzej Grubba (Poland)

One of the best Eastern European players in the history of the sport, Grubba won the World Cup in 1988, three bronze medals at the World Championships as well as medals at twelve European Championships.

Jiang Jialiang (China)

World Champion of two consecutive competitions, Jialiang is known for his extremely effective service return.

Kong Linghui (China)

Becoming the third Grand Slam winner in 2000, Linghui won three Olympic medals, two World Cup titles and a gold medal at the World Championships during her career.

Ma Lin (China)

One of the world's most feared players today, Lin won the table tennis World Cup in 2000, 2003, 2004 and 2006 as well as the gold medal for doubles at the 2004 Olympics.

REFERENCES

Barna, Victor:*Table Tennis Today*. London: Arthur Barker, 1962.

Bellak, Laszlo:*Table Tennis: How A New Sport Was Born.* N.p., 1990.

Bergmann, Richard:*Twenty-One Up*. London: Sporting Handbooks Ltd., 1950.

Clark, Coleman:*Modern Ping-Pong: And How To Play It.* New York: John Day, 1933.

Montagu, Ivor:*Table Tennis:* London: Sir Isaac Pitman & Sons, 1936.

Reid, Philip: *Victor Barna*. Lavenham, Suffolk, U.K.: Eastland Press, 1974.

Schaad, Cornelius G.:*Ping-Pong: The Game, Its Tactics and Laws*. Boston: Houghton Mifflin, 1930.

Schiff, Sol.: *Table Tennis Comes Of Age*. New York: Henry Holt, 1939.

Stewart, William R.: *Table Tennis Tactics.* Chicago: Martin, 1933.

Uzorinac, Zdenko: *Od London 1926 Do Sarajeva 1973*. Zagreb: NISP "Vjesnik.", 1973)

16

Taekwondo

Taekwondo is the Korean martial art and the national game of South Korea. It is the world's most famous martial art in terms of number of practicians.Kyeorugi, or sparring, is an official Olympic sporting event. In Korean, tae signifies "foot"; kwon means "fist"; and do signifies "way"; so taekwondo is loosely transformed as "the way of the foot and fist" but can be better translated as, "the art of kicking and punching."

Taekwondo's popularity has led in the altered evolution of the martial art into various domains: as with many other arts, it merges combat techniques, self-defense, game, exercise, meditation and philosophy. Taekwondo is also used by the South Korean armed forces as part of its training.

Traditional taekwondo is specifically not competition-oriented but roots from military roots with great stress on offense. Modern Taekwondo, on the other hand, tends to accent control and self-defense. Officially, there are two main styles of taekwondo.

One comes from the Kukkiwon, the roots of the sparring system shihap kyeorugi which is now an event at the summer Olympic Games and which is ruled by the World Taekwondo Federation (WTF), the other arrives from the International Taekwondo Federation (ITF).

Even though there are doctrinal and technical differences among the two main styles and among the various organizations, the art generally stresseson kicks thrown from a mobile stance, employing the leg's greater reach and power (compared to the arm). Taekwondo training in general admits a system of blocks, kicks, punches, and open-handed strikes and may also comprise various take-downs or sweeps, throws, and joint locks.

HISTORY

The history of taekwondo has been a subject of controversy. Taekwondo organizations formally state that taekwondo was deduced from former Korean martial arts. Others state that taekwondo is derived from native Korean martial arts with influences from neighboring countries or that it was chiefly derived from karate studied by Koreans throughout the Japanese occupation.

The most former Korean martial art was a merger of unarmed combat styles formulated by the three rival Korean kingdoms of Goguryeo, Silla and Baekje. Young men were coached in unarmed combat techniques to develop strength, speed, and survival skills. The most famous of these techniques was subak, with taekkyeon being the most famous of the segments of subak.

Those who presented strong natural aptitude were choosen as trainees in the new especial warrior corps, called the Hwarang. It was conceived that young men with a talent for the liberal arts may have the grace to become competent warriors. These warriors were taught in academics as well as martial arts, learning philosophy, history, a code of ethics, and equestrian sports. Their military training incorporated an extensive weapons program demanding swordsmanship and archery, both on horseback and on foot, as well as lessons in military tactics and unarmed combat utilizing subak. Even though subak was a leg-oriented art in Goguryeo, Silla's influence added hand techniques to the practice of subak.

Throughout this time a few choose Sillan warriors were given training in Taek Kyon by the early masters from Koguryo. The Taek Kyon coached warriors then turned known as the Hwarang. The Hwarang establish a military academy for the sons of royalty in Silla called Hwarang-do, which means "The way of flowering manhood." The Hwarang examined Taek Kyon, history, Confucian Philosophy, ethics, Buddhist Morality, and military tactics. The guiding principles of the Hwarang warriors were loyalty, filial duty, trustiness, valor, and justice. The makeup of the Hwarang-do education was established on the Five Codes of Human Conduct written by a Buddhist scholar, fundamental education, Taek Kyon and social skills. Taek Kyon was spread during Korea because the Hwarang traveled all all over the peninsula to learn about the other regions and people.

In spite of Korea's rich chronicle of ancient and traditional martial arts, Korean martial arts faded into obscurity throughout the Joseon Dynasty. Korean society turned highly centralized under Korean

Confucianism and martial arts were poorly regarded in a society whose ideals were typified by its scholar-kings. Formal exercises of traditional martial arts such as subak and taekkyeon were reserved for sanctioned military uses. However folks practice of taekkyeon as a kicking game still remained into the nineteenth century . There are numerous associations of Taekwon-do, including (not limited to) the ITF, ITA, WTF, WTA, and the ATA.

The Japanese line of work of Korea officially commenced in 1910, under control of all facets of Korean identity admitting folk culture, language and history. Koreans were stormed to take Japanese names and to worship at Shinto shrines; Korean-language newspapers and magazines were prohibited; and throughout the war, hundreds of thousands of Koreans were forced into service to support Japanese war efforts. Martial arts such as taekkyeon (or subak) were also banned throughout this time; however, taekkyeon survived through underground teaching and folk custom. Throughout the line of work the few Koreans who were capable to study in Japan were showing to Japanese martial arts in some cases getting black belts. Others were buncovered to martial arts in China and Manchuria.

When the occupation ended in 1945, Korean martial arts schools (kwans) commenced to open in Korea under various influences.There are differing regards on the origins of the arts taught in these schools. Some conceive that they taught martial arts that were based chiefly upon the traditional Korean martial arts taekkyon and subak or upon a variety of martial arts such as taekkyon, kungfu and karate. Others conceive that these schools taught arts that were almost totally based upon karate.

In 1952, at the peak of the Korean War, there was a martial arts expo in which the kwans exhibited their skills. In one presentation, Nam Tae Hi smashed thirteen roof tiles with a forefist punch. Following the presentation, South Korean President Syngman Rhee instructed Choi Hong Hi to bring in the martial arts to the Korean army.

By the mid-1950s, nine kwans had came forth. Syngman Rhee ordered that the various schools unify under a single system. The name "taekwondo" was either stated by Choi Hong Hi, or Song Duk Son of Chung Do Kwan and was recognized on April 11, 1955. As it stands at present, General Choi is the founder of Taekwondo. The Korean Taekwondo Association (KTA) was established in 1961 to facilitate the unification. Shortly thereafter, taekwondo made its début universal. Standardization efforts in South Korea stalled, as the kwans extended to teach differing styles. Another petition from the Korean government for conjugation resulted in the formation of the Korea Tae Soo Do Association, which altered its name back to the Korean Taekwondo Association in 1965 succeeding a change of leadership.

Presently, Taekwondo is practiced in 188 countries with over 70 million practitioners and 4 million people with black belts during the world. It is now one of only two Asian martial arts that are included in the Olympic Games; it turned a demonstration event commencing with the 1988 games in Seoul, and turned an official medal event commencing with the 2000 games in Sydney.

THE GAME

Taekwondo is acknowledged for its emphasis on kicking techniques, which differentiates it from martial arts such as karate or southern styles of kung fu. The rationale is that the leg is the longest and strongest weapon a martial artist has, and kicks thus have the most cracking potential to perform powerful strikes without successful retaliation. One determining kick of taekwondo is the back kick.

Taekwondo as a game and exercise is famous with people of all sexes and of many ages. Physically, taekwondo formulates strength, speed, balance, flexibility, and stamina. An instance of the union of mental and physical discipline is the breaking of boards, which demands both physical mastery of the technique and the concentration to focus one's strength.

A taekwondo student normally wears uniform often white but sometimes black or other colors, with a belt tied all over the waist. The belt shows the student's rank. The school or place where instruction is given is called the dojang .

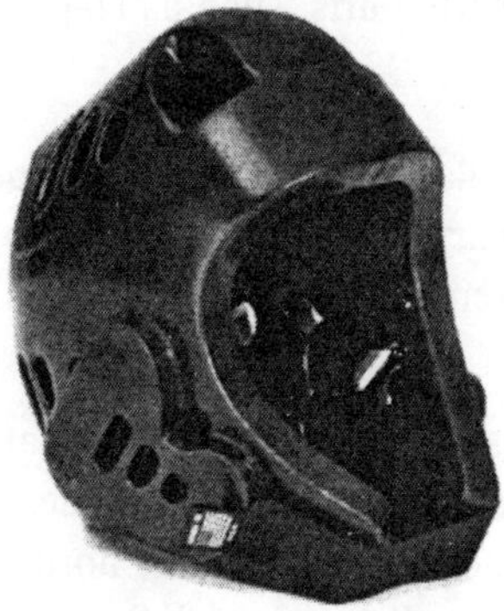

Fig. Protective Helmet

Even though each taekwondo club or school will be dissimslar, a taekwondo student can normally expect to take part in most or all of the following:

- Studying the techniques and curriculum of taekwondo
- Both anaerobic and aerobic workout, including stretching
- Self-defense techniques
- Patterns Sparring which may comprise 3-, 2- and 1-step sparring, free-style sparring, formatted sparring, point sparring, and other types
- Relaxation and meditation exercises
- Throwing and/or falling techniques
- Breaking utilizing techniques to break boards for testing, training and martial arts demonstrations. Demonstrations often also incorporate bricks, tiles, blocks of ice or other materials. Can be isolated into two types:
- Power breaking - utilizing straightforward techniques to break as many boards as possible.
- Special techniques - breaking fewer boards but utilizing jumping or flying techniques to achieve greater heights, distances, or to clear obstacles.
- Exams to progress to the following rank
- A focus on mental and ethical discipline, justice, etiquette, respect, and self-confidence

Some taekwondo instructors also incorporate the utilize of pressure points, known as ji ap sul, as well as catching self-defense techniques borrowed from other martial arts, such as Hapkido and Judo.

Techniques

Because the particular Taekwondo techniques checked to progress to the following rank vary from school to school, this is only a partial listing of techniques generally. Overall, there are 3200 techniques in Taekwon-do.

These techniques are all united into various set self-defense techniques, improvised self-defense techniques, and longer set forms. These change from school to school, but normally at least one person who knows the "traditional" forms or defenses can be found.

Kicks

All kicks can be accomplished as jump kicks, spin kicks, jump spin kicks or multi-rotational spin kicks. Also, all can be executed by the front or rear leg in a given stance.

Some of the best-known Taekwondo kicks comprise:

- Front Kick — This is a very linear kick. The practitioner raises the knee to the waist, pulls the toes back and rapidly extends the foot at the target. It is also known as the snap kick. The front kick is one of the first kicks learned in TKD; if mastered it can turn one of the most powerful.
- Side Kick — A very powerful kick, first the practitioner at the same time raises the knee and rotates the body 90 degrees, and then rapidly stretches the leg, hitting with the heel or the side of the foot.
- Roundhouse Kick (Turning Kick or Round Kick) — The practitioner lifts the knee, turns the hips, pivots on the non-kicking foot, and snaps the kick horizontally into the target at a 90-degree angle, either with the instep or with the ball of the foot (in the latter case, with the toes moved back out of the way as in a front kick).

  Back Kick — Here the practitioner twists the body away from the target and forces the back leg straight toward the target, hitting it with the heel while watching over the shoulder. The turning motion assists to give this kick a lot of power.

- Reverse Side Kick — Similar to the back kick, here the body turns further, permitting the heel to strike the target with the foot indicating to the side as in a regular side kick, instead of more downward as in a true back kick.
- Hook Kick — A less famous kick traditionally, it has found increasing favor in modern competitions. The practitioner raises the knee in a fashion similar to the roundhouse kick, then extends the foot outward then snaps it all over in a dorsal arc, with the heel as the intended striking weapon.
- Axe Kick — Another kick that has enhansed its popularity due to sparring competitions. The leg is produced in front of the body. The leg stays straight or close to straight as it rises, then the leg is pulled down with the heel pointed downward. It is normally targeted toward the head or shoulders and demands substantial flexibility to employ effectively.
- Crescent Kick — There are two versions of this kick: the outer crescent and the inner crescent. In the outer, the practitioner lifts the extended leg as high as possible, and slightly up across the body, (a bit acros the centerline of the body), then sweeping outward to the side, in a circular movement. In the inner, the motions are thesimilar but the instruction of the kick changes, this time arising from the outside of the body, heading towards the inside, or centerline of the body. These kicks are also called "Inside Kick" and "Outside Kick" at some taekwondo schools, and "Inside-Outside" and "Outside-Inside" at others.
- Spin Kicks — There are various spinning kicks that require the rotation of the entire body and head before the kick is expelled. Spinning kicks comprise the back pivot kick (dweel chagi), spinning hook kick (dweel huryeo chagi), spinning axe kick, butterfly kick, reverting kick, 360 turning kick, and a number of other kicks of varying popularity.
- Jump Kicks — There are also many kicks that call for jumping before their performance. These comprise jumping front kick, jumping side kick flying side kick, jumping axe kick, jumping roundhouse, jumping spinning hook kick, jumping spinning roundhouse kick, butterfly kick or "shuffle jump kick," jumping (or counter) back kick, and jump spinning side kick. Normally, jumping kicks involve extracting the back leg to help gain height throughout the jump and then executing the kick itself with the front leg.

- Advanced Kicks — There is a lots of kicks that can be used in combination or stem out from a simple kick to produce harder ones. Some of these comprise 540 Kick (One spins 1 1/2 times in mid-air and does a kick, normally a back spinning hook kick) and Triple Aero Kicks (One does round house kick, back spinning hook kick, and another round house kick in mid-air).
- Fast Kicks — Also, many kicks can be applied utilizing a fast kick style. The practitioner shuffles the back leg forward to the front leg, and the front leg arises and kicks closer to the enemy than the practitioner had been before execution. This can be utilized with side kick, roundhouse kick, front kick, hook kick, and axe kick. They are called Fast "insert kick name".

Ranks, Belts and Promotion

Traditional tae kwon do uses only 10 "geups" or ranks. At present's more present-day schools often have added to this system or have varied it based on age and such. Taekwondo ranks are sometimes isolated into "junior" and "senior" or "student" and "instructor" sections. The junior section normally consists of ten ranks indicated by the Korean word geup (also Romanized as gup or kup).

The junior ranks are normally identified by belts of various colors, depending upon the school, so these ranks are sometimes called "color belts". Geup rank may be indicated by stripes on belts rather than by colored belts. Students commences at tenth geup (normally indicated by a white belt) and advance toward first geup (normally indicated by a red belt with a black stripe).

The senior section is built up of nine full ranks of black belt. These ranks are yelled dan, also referred to as "black belts" and "degrees" (as in "third dan" or "third-degree black belt"). Black belts commences at first degree and encourage to second, third, and so on. The level is often showed on the belt itself with stripes, Roman numerals, or other methods; but sometimes black belts are plain and unadorned regardless of rank.

To progress from one rank to the following, students normally complete promotion tests in which they demonstrate their proficiency in the various aspects of the art before a panel of judges or their teacher. Promotion tests vary from school to school, but may comprise such elements as the execution of patterns, which combine various techniques in particular sequences; the breaking of boards, to demonstrate the capability to utilize techniques with both power and control; sparring and self-defense, to present the practical application and control of techniques;

and answering questions on terminology, concepts, history, and so on, to demonstrate knowledge and understanding of the art. For higher dan tests, students are sometimes needed to take a written test or to submit a research paper in addition to taking the practical test.

Promotion from one geup to the following can proceed fairly quickly in some schools, since schools frequently allow geup promotions every two, three, or four months. Students of geup rank learn the most canonic techniques first, then move on to more advanced techniques as they access first dan. Many of the older and more traditional schools will often take longer to earn rank in than newer, more contemporary schools as they may not have standard testing intervals.

In contrast, advancement from one dan to the following can take years. The universal rule is that a black belt may advance from one rank to the following only after the number of years equivalent to the rank pursued. For example, a newly-promoted third-degree black belt may not be permitted to promote to fourth-degree until four years have passed. Some organizations also have age requirements related to dan promotions, and may grant younger students pum (junior black belt) ranks rather than dan ranks until they reach a certain age. Black belt ranks normally have titles linked with them, such as "master" and "instructor". Taekwondo organizations have their own rules and standards when it comes to ranks and the titles that go with them.

Stripes are placed on the final belt the student gained, until the student tests for his/her following belt. As the student gains higher belts, it takes longer time to test. Once at black belt, students must wait years instead of months to test for their following degree. If a student is not ready to test, the instructor awaits until he or a she is prepared to test in many schools

MAJOR TOURNAMENTS

Olympics

Taekwondo has been component of the Summer Olympic Games from 2000 Games, after being a presentation sport in 1988 and 1992.

Taekwondo has now been a sport in the Olympic games for three editions.

Medals are granted in four dissimslar weight classes for both men and women.

Event	Men	Women
Flyweight	58 kg	49 kg
Lightweight	58-68 kg	49-57 kg
Middleweight	68-80 kg	57-67 kg
Heavyweight	+80 kg	+67 kg

South Korea and China are amongst the top two nations winning a total of 12 and 5 medals in Olympics respectively.The third position is took by USA with 6 medals.

Asian Games

Taekwondo first took place from December 7 to December 10 at the 2006 Asian Games in Doha, Qatar. Men's and women's competitions were held in eight weight categories for for each one. All competition took place at the Qatar Sports Club Indoor Hall. South Korea and China are once again the top two nations with 11 and 6 medals respectively in Asian Games.

ADMINISTRATIVE BODIES

International Taekwondo Federation

The International Taekwon-Do Federation or (ITF) exists to promote and promote the development of the Korean martial art of taekwondo. Its main purposes are to co-ordinate and approve tournaments and seminars, arranging standards for teaching (patterns, sparring, destruction), co-operating with affiliated member organizations, and servicing members in regards to rank and certifications.

The International Taekwon-Do Federation was established in 1955, 11 April by General Choi Hong Hi in Seoul, Korea. In 1972 the headquarters for the ITF was locomoted to Toronto, Canada. In 1985 the headquarters for the ITF was locomoted to Vienna, Austria. After the death of General Choi Hong Hi the administration headquarters has moved to Rome, Italy.

On 2002, 15 June, since the death of General Choi Hong Hi, Russell McClellan turned acting president.

On 2003, 13 June, Tran Trieu Quan was nominated president of the ITF at the 14th Congress of ITF in Warsaw, Poland. Tran Trieu Quan was born in Vietnam, but came over to Canada to attend Laval University in Quebec City. He started many taekwondo schools.

On 2007, 1 June, President Tran Trieu Quan was re-elected to be the president of ITF for another 4 years.

Patterns, or tool in Korean, primitively called hyeong, form an significant aspect of training in taekwondo. They are equal to the kata in karate. The majority of the patterns (excepting Eul-Ji and Tong-Il) begin with a defensive move, which stresses taekwondo's defensive nature. All of the patterns start and end at the similar location. This assures that the practitioners' stances are the correct length, width, and in the proper direction.

There are 24 patterns in the functionary ITF syllabus; this is symbolic of the 24 hours in a day. The names of these patterns specially denote either to events in Korean history or to important people in Korean history. Basics of the patterns may also be historical references, such as the number of moves, the diagram, the way the pattern ends, and so on.

ITF competition sparring rounds are two minutes and in national and international levels of competition they withstand two rounds each two minutes with a one minutes rest in between. Certain rules are no strikes beneath the belt, no hitting to the back of the head, no elbow strikes, no knee strikes, no out of control fighting, no falling down, no going beyond of the ring. The ring is a twenty-four foot by twenty-four foot ring labeled by square mats or tape rather of a traditional style kickboxing rings with ropes. It has no sides permitting the fighter to move out of bounds. Whenever a fighter produces an infraction of the rule's the center referee will issue a warning to the fighter who produced the infraction. Three warnings equals a minus point. If a fighter does not listen to the referee's instruction he or she may be given a foul which is an automatic minus point and if the fighter extends to not listen they can be disqualified. ITF taekwondo is contended in continuous point sparring. Four judges score the fights in each of the corners in the square ring. After the fight a judge votes for which ever fighter has the most points and a winner is announced. In the case of a draw the battlers go to a one minute overtime round. If there is another draw the fighters go to a sudden death round where the fighter who scores first is declared the winner.

World Taekwondo Federation

The World Taekwondo Federation (WTF) is the International Federation (IF) member of the International Olympic Committee (IOC) for the competition events of the martial art of Taekwondo. It was founded in South Korea on May 28, 1973, at its inaugural meeting deemed at the

Kukkiwon with participation of 35 representatives from the world. The present president is Chungwon Choue who was elected for a four-year term in 2005.

The WTF, which only rules the function of Taekwondo competitions and related support services, should not be bewildered with the World Taekwondo Headquarters, also known as Kukkiwon, which is a center of learning and research of Taekwondo situated in Yuksam Dong, a dissimslar part of Seoul. Kim successfully lobbied to comprise Taekwondo sparring competition as a demonstration game in the 1988 and 1992 Summer Olympics, and official Full Medal Olympic sport commencing in 2000, and is a member of the Association of Summer Olympic International Federations.

As per the WTF, "Taekwondo is a Korean unarmed martial art. It is not only kicking and punching, but also a way of thinking and living. The primary goal of Taekwondo is to attain total body and mind control by proper training."

Only national associations may be members of the WTF, there are no private members. Presently, there are 5 regional unions: the African Taekwondo Union, Asian Taekwondo Union, European Taekwondo Union, Oceania Taekwondo Union, and the Pan-American Taekwondo Union, inside each union there are multiple member countries. The member association corresponding the United States is inside the Pan-American Taekwondo Union, and is called USA Taekwondo, Inc. A prospective member (an individual) in the United States would register for membership with USA Taekwondo. This individual membership would be with USA Taekwondo, and would not be a member with the WTF. In the UK, member affiliation is acted by the BTCB (British Taekwondo Control Board).

The organisational structure of the WTF has diverisifed at various times over its more than thirty year history to incorporate the various changes, affiliations and associations over these years of development. As of 2007 the organization islead up by a General Assembly made up from members of the 182 member National Associations from the 5 world regions it represents. This in turn comprises of a WTF Council compiled of an Executive Committee and various sub committees. The Executive Committee consists a president, secretariat, and an Advisory Council. The sub committees are made up of various departments among the organisation, admitting a technical committee and representative committees of games, women's, legislative, financial, medical, athletic and PR areas.

FAMOUS PLAYERS

Lee H. Park

Great Grandmaster Park was a recognized ninth Dan Black Belt by the World Tae Kwon Do Federation in 1985. He was a qualified ninth Dan Black Belt in Hapkido by the Moo Sul Kwan Hapkido Federation and a 5th Dan Black Belt by the Korea Yudo Association. He was one of the two most eminent ranking Moo Sul Kwan instructors all over the world. In 1980, he was recipient of the Outstanding Coach Award at the fifth National Collegiate Tae Kwon Do Championships in St. Louis, Missouri.

Great Grandmaster Park conceived in and taught a traditional approach to the martial arts. Discipline, hard work and commitment got him to a pinnacle that few others have attained. He committed his life to teaching and encouraging the martial arts. His spirit is held on by the Black Belt instructors that survive him and extend the tradition of Moo Sul Kwan.

Great Grandmaster Lee H. Park was born in Korea on Dec. 25, 1939. In 1969 Great Grandmaster Park locomoted to the United States and was employed at Southeast Missouri State University. It was at this time that Great Grandmaster Park commenced Moo Sul Kwan in Cape Girardeau.

Great Grandmaster Park was beginner of the American Martial Arts Sports and Education Association, vice-president of the International Council on Martial Arts Education, and was chairperson of the Teacher Certification Committee for the International Council on Martial Arts Education. Great Grandmaster Park had previously served as a Delegate At Large for the National AAU Tae Kwon Do Committee, and was a preceding president of the American Hapkido Association, preceding chairperson of the Sub-committee Safety and Equipment Growth for the National AAU Tae Kwon Do Committee and a preceding chairperson of the Regional Board of Examiners for the American Tae Kwon Do Association.

Chu Mu-yen

Chu Mu-yen born on March 14, 1982 is a Taekwondo athlete of Taiwan. He is the 2nd Taiwanese athlete and 1st male to gain a gold medal at the Olympics, winning in men's under 58-kilogram class in Taekwondo at the Athens 2004 Games. He was twenty-two years old and 1.73 meters tall when he gained the Gold at Athens, and often contended against larger, stronger players in his Olympic Fly division. In the 2008 Olympics, Chu won the bronze medal in the men's under 58-kilogram class in Taekwondo.

Chen Shih-Hsin

Chen Shih-Hsin born on November 16, 1978 is the 1st Taiwanese athlete to gain a gold medal at the Olympics. She gained the gold medal in the women's 49-kilogram category in taekwondo at the 2004 Summer Olympics on August 26.

Chen was acknowledged as one of the Taiwanese Ten Outstanding Young Persons in 2001. Presently, she is an associate professor in Taipei Physical Education College.

REFERENCES

Alter, S.:*Science of Flexibility*, 2nd edn, Human Kinetics, Champaign, Il, 1996

Alter, S.: *Sport Stretch*, Human Kinetics, Champaign, IL, 1998

Dintiman, G. and Ward, R.:*Sport Speed*, Leisure Press, Champaign, IL, 1988

Ellison, D.: *Performance Stretching*, Human Kinetics, Champaign, IL, 1999

Goldberg, B. (ed.):*Sports and Exercise for Children with Chronic Health Conditions*, Human Kinetics, Champaign, IL, 1995

Micheli, L.J. (ed.): *Clinics in Sports Medicine: The Young Athlete*, W.B. Saunders, Philadelphia, PA., 1995

Newsholme, E., Leech, T. and Duester, G.:*Keep on Running*, John Wiley & Sons, Chichester, UK, 1994

Reaburn, P. and Jenkins, D.: *Training for Speed and Endurance*, Allen & Unwin, Sydney, 1996

Rowland, T.W. *Developmental Exercise Physiology*, Human Kinetics, Champaign, IL, 1996

Sports weekly Magazine

Sports Illustrated Magazine

17

Water Polo

Water polo is a team water sport. A team comprises of 6 field players and 1 goalkeeper. The winner of the game is the team that hits more goals. Gameplay requires swimming, players passing the ball while being opposed by opponents, and scoring by throwing into a net defended by a goalie. As such, water polo has associations to football (soccer) and netball.

HISTORY

The history of water polo as a team game commenced as a presentation of strength and swimming skill in late nineteenth century England and Scotland, where water sports and racing exhibitions were a feature of county fairs and festivals. Men's water polo was the between the first team sports brought in at the modern Olympic games in 1900. Water polo is now famous in many countries all over the world, notably Europe (particularly in Hungary, Greece, Italy, Russia, Croatia, Serbia, Montenegro), the United States, Canada and Australia. The present-day game calls for teams of seven players (plus up to six substitutes), with a water polo ball similar in size to a soccer ball but built of waterproof nylon.

The principles of water polo were primitively formulated in the late 19th century in Great Britain by William Wilson. The modern game developed as a form of rugby football played in rivers and lakes in England and Scotland with a ball made of Indian rubber. This "water rugby" came to be called "water polo" based on the English pronunciation of the Balti word for ball, pulu. Early play permitted brute strength, wrestling and holding fighting players underwater to recover the ball; the goalie stood outside the playing area and defended the goal by jumping in on any opposer attempting to score by placing the ball on the deck.

By the 1880s, the game orginated to comprise fast-paced team play with a soccer-sized ball that stressed swimming, passing, and scoring by shooting into a goal net; players could only be undertook when holding the ball and could not be taken under water. To deal with alterations in regional rules, in 1888, the London Water Polo League was established and sanctioned a set of rules to allow team competition, organizing the basis of the present game. The first English championships were acted in 1888. In 1890, the first international water polo game was played; Scotland defeated England, 4-0.

From 1890 and 1900, the game formulated in Europe, with teams competing in Germany, Austria, France, Belgium, Hungary and Italy, utilizing British rules. A dissimslar game was being played in the United States, recognized by rough play, holding, diving underwater, and soft, semi-inflated ball that could be gripped tightly and held underwater. As a consequence, European teams did not contend in the 1904 Olympic championships in St. Louis. By 1914, most US teams agreed to conform to international rules.An international water polo committee was established in 1929, comprising of representatives from Great Britain and the International Amateur Swimming Federation (FINA). Rules were formulated for international matches and put into effect in 1930; FINA has been the international governing body for the game since that time.

Over the years, both technical and rule alters had affected the nature of the game. In 1928, Hungarian water polo coach Bela Komjadi invented the “air pass,” or “dry pass”, a technique in which a player instantly passes the ball through the air to another player, who obtains it without the ball hitting the water. Previously, players would let the ball drop in the water first and then reach out for it, but the dry pass made the offensive game more dynamic, and contributed to Hungarian dominance of water polo for 60 years.In 1936, James R. (“Jimmy”) Smith, California water polo coach and author of various books on water polo mechanics, developed a water polo ball made with an inflatable bladder and a rubber fabric cover, which bettered performance.

The previous leather ball absorbed water and turned heavier throughout the game. In 1949, rule changes permitted play to continue uninterrupted after an umpire whistled an ordinary foul, speeding up play. In the 1970s, the exclusion foul substituted a point system for major fouls; players guilty of this foul were ejected for a 1 minute penalty and their team pushed to play with fewer players. Possession of the ball was limited to 45 seconds before a scoring attempt. Time of penalties and possession have been reduced since then. The direct shot on goal from the seven (7) meter line after a free throw was permitted in 1994, and altered to a five meter throw in 2005.

THE GAME

Overview

Seven players from each team (six field players and a goalkeeper) are permitted in the playing area of the pool throughout game play. Visiting team field players wear numbered and normally dark blue caps, and home team field players wear normally white caps (though any other contrasting colours are now permitted); both goalies wear quartered red caps, numbered "1". Both teams may substitute players. Throughout game play, players enter and exit in front of their team bench; when play is stopped, they may enter or exit anywhere.

The game clock is stopped when the ball is not 'in play' (from a foul being committed and the free throw being taken, and among a goal being scored and the restart). As a consequence, the average quarter lasts all over 12 minutes 'real time'. A team may not have possession of the ball for longer than 30 secondswithout shooting for the goal unless an opponent commits an ejection foul. After 30 seconds, possession passes to the other team. Nevertheless, if a team shoots the ball inside the allotted time, and recovers control of the ball, the shot clock is readjust to 30 seconds. Each team may call 2 one-minute timeouts in the four periods of regulation play, and one timeout if the game goes into overtime. Throughout game play, only the team in possession of the ball may call a timeout.

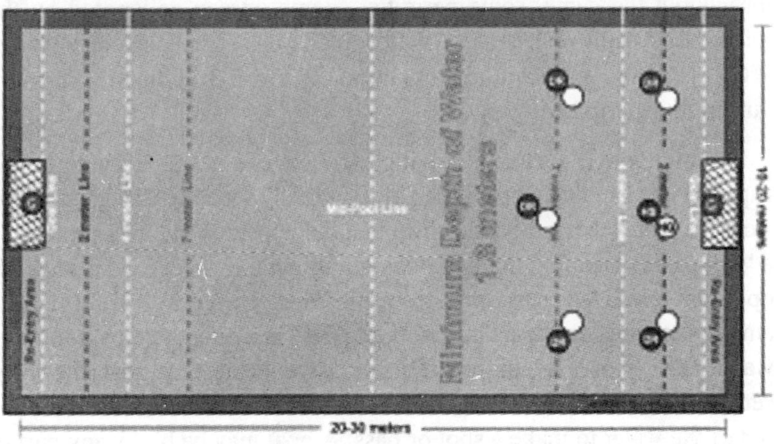

Fig. Dimensions of Pool

Dimensions of the water polo pool are not fixed and can change among 20 x 10 and 30 x 20 meters. Minimal water depth must be least 1.8 meters (6 feet), but this is often waived for age group or high school games if such a facility is unavailable. The goals are 3 meters broad and 90 centimetres high. Water polo balls are in general yellow and of varying size and weight for juniors, women and men. The middle of the pool is assigned by a white line. In the past, the pool was divided by 7 and 4 meter lines (distance out from the goal line). This has been merged into one 5 meter line since the 2005-2006 season. Along the side of the pool, the center area between the 5 meter lines is marked off by a green line. The "five meters" line is where penalties are shot and it is designated by a yellow line. The "two meters" line is indicated with a red line and no player of the attacking team can be inside this line without the ball.

One player on each team is designated the goalkeeper, assigned to deflect or catch any shots at goal. The goalkeeper is the only player who can touch the ball with both hands at any time, and, in a shallow pool, the only player permitted to stand on the bottom. Players can move the ball by throwing it to a teammate or swimming while forcing the ball in front of them. Players are not permitted to push the ball underwater when being tackled, or push or hold an opposing player unless that player is holding the ball. Fouls are very common, and result in a free throw throughout which the player cannot shoot at the goal unless beyond the "5 meter" line. If a foul is called outside the 5 meter line, the player is either able to shoot or pass the ball. Water polo players need remarkable stamina due to the significant amount of holding and forcing that occurs throughout the game, some permitted, some unseen or ignored by the referees (normally underwater). Water polo is a physically involving game; action is continuous, and players normally swim 3 kilometers or more during four periods of play.

Water polo is a game involving excellent eye-hand skillfulness. The capability to handle and pass the ball flawlessly separates the good teams from the great teams. A pass thrown to a field position player is preferably a "dry pass" (meaning the ball does not touch the water) and allows for optimum speed when passing from player to player with fluid motion among catching and throwing. A "wet pass" is a deliberate pass into the water, just out of reach of the offensive player nearest the goal (the "hole set") and his defender. The hole-set can then lunge towards the ball and out of the water to make a shot or pass. A goal may be hit by any part of the body except a clenched fist, or a foot.

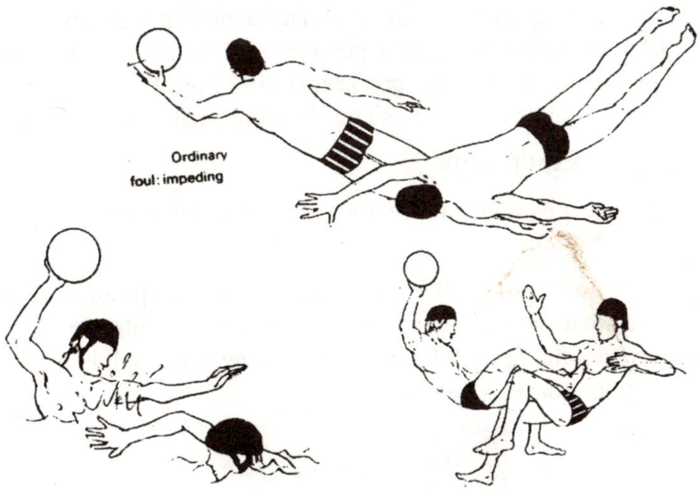

Fig. Different Positions

Scoring in water polo can be quite dissimslar than in other sports. For example, a "skip" or "bounce" shot is fired intentionally at the water with significant force so it will bounce back up. The ball normally hits the water inside a metre of the net, where the goalie cannot anticipate and block the shot. Another shot, called a "lob" is thrown with a large vertical arc. Often these shots are more difficult to stop than a faster shot, as they are normally thrown over a net at such an angle the goalie must not only shift position from one side of the net to the other rapidly, but also at the similar time propel out of the water more than for other shots. Pump faking is effective when utilizing any kind of shot. The player gets in the position to shoot but stops halfway through his motion, causing the defending goalkeeper to invest too early to block the subsequent shot.

The referee's whistle for a foul is listened much more in water polo than in other sports. A defender will often foul the player with the ball as a tactic to disrupt the opponent's ball movement. Play extends uninterrupted in most cases, but the attacker must now pass the ball instead of advancing or taking a shot. (An exception allows players to rapidly pick up the ball and shoot if fouled outside of the five meter mark.) Nevertheless, as in ice hockey, a player caught committing a major foul, is sent out of the playing area with his team a man-down for 20 seconds, but may return sooner if a goal is scored or his team regains possession. If the foul is adjudicated to be brutal, the player is ejected for the remainder of the game, with substitution by another teammate after four minutes have elapsed. A player, coach or spectator can also be ejected for arguing with the referees. Throughout a man up situation leadingfrom exclusion foul, the aggressing team can anticipate to score by passing around to move the goalkeeper out of position. A player that has been ejected three times must sit out the whole match with substitution.

Water Polo Equipment

Little player equipment is required to play water polo. Items needed in water polo comprise:

Ball: A water polo ball is manufactured of waterproof material to permit it to float on the water. The cover has a particular texture so it won't slip from the hands of a player. The size of the ball is dissimslar for men's and women's games.

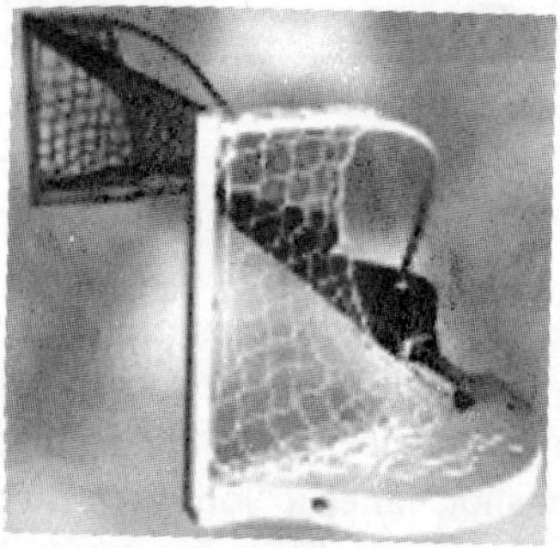

Fig. Goal

Caps: A water polo cap is utilized to protect the players' heads and to identify them. Home team field players wear numbered light or dark caps, and visiting team field players wear contrasting caps. Both commencing goalkeepers wear (quartered) red caps, numbered "1", and substitute goalies caps are numbered either "1-A" in NCAA play or "13" for FINA international play. Caps are fitted with ear protectors.

Goals: Two goals are required in order to play water polo. These can either be put on the side of the pool, or in the pool utilizing floaters.

Swimwear: Male water polo participants often wear swim briefs. Some players prefer to wear two briefs for more security throughout play. Female players must wear a one-piece swimsuit. Most of these suits do not have straps as normal suits, but havezipper-backed.

Basic Skills

Swimming: Water polo is a team water sport involving an capability to swim. Field players must swim end to end of a 30-meter pool non-stop many times throughout a game without touching on the sides or bottom of the pool. The front crawl stroke used in water polo differs from the usual swimming style in that water polo players swim with the head out of water at all times to observe the field. The arm stroke used is also a lot shorter and quicker and is used to protect the ball at all times. Backstroke is used by opposing field players to track progressing attackers and by the goalie to track the ball after passing. Water polo backstroke differs from swimming backstroke; the player sits almost upright in the water, utilizing eggbeater leg motions with short arm strokes to the side instead of long straight arm strokes. This allows the player to see the play and rapidly switch positions. It also allows the player to rapidly catch an oncoming pass with a free hand.

Ball Handling Skills: As all field players are only permitted to touch the ball with one hand at a time, they must develop the capability to catch and throw the ball with either hand and also the capability to catch a ball from any direction, including all around the body utilizing the momentum of the incoming ball. Experienced water polo players can catch and release a pass or shoot with a single motion. The size of the ball can overwhelm a small child's hand making the game more desirable for older children.

Treading Water

The most common form of water treading is in general referred to as "egg-beater", named as the circular movement of the legs corresponds the motion of an egg-beater. Egg beater is used for most of the match as the players cannot touch the bottom of the pool. The advantage of egg-beater is that it permits the player to keep a constant position to the water level, and uses less energy than other forms of treading water such as the scissor kick, which result in the player bobbing up and down. It can be utilized vertically or horizontally. Horizontal egg-beater is used to resist forward motion of an attacking player. Vertical eggbeater is used to keep a position higher than the opponent. By kicking faster for a brief period the player can get high out of the water (as high as their suit—below their waistline) for a block, pass, or shot.

Reflexes and Awareness: At higher levels of the game the pace of play quickly enhances, so that anticipation and mental formulation is vital. "Field sense" (i.e. staying aware of the surroundings) is a main advantage in scoring, even if a player misses the speed of an opponent.

Positions

There are six field player places and a goalkeeper on each team. Unlike most common team sports, there is not any position play; field players often will fill various positions during the game as situations demand. Players who are skilled at various offensive or defensive roles are called utility players. Utility players tend to come away of the bench, though this isn't absolute. Some body types are more suitable for particular positions, and left-handed players are particularly coveted on the right-hand side of the field, permitting teams to launch 2-sided attacks.

Offense

The offensive positions comprise: one center (a.k.a. two-meter offense, hole set, hole man, bucket, pit player or pit-man), two wings, two drivers (also called "flats"), and one "point" man, placed furthest from the goal. The center aims the attack, and the wings, drivers and point are often known as the perimeter players.

The most fundamental positional establish is called as a 3-3, due to the fact that there are two lines in front of the opponent's goal, both comprising three players. Another set up, used more by professional teams, is known as an "arc," umbrella, or mushroom; perimeter players form the shape of an arc all over the goal, with the center forward as the handle or stalk. As yet another option for offensive set is called a 4-2 or double hole; there are 2 center forward offensive players ahead of the goal. Double hole is most frequently used in "man up" situations, or when the defense has only one skilled hole D, or to draw in a defender and then pass out to a perimeter player for a shot ("kick out").

The center forward lays up ahead of the defending team's goalie and normally scores the most individually (especially during lower level play where perimeter players do not have the needed strength to effectively penetrate and then pass to teammates like the point guard in basketball). The center's position closest to the goal grants explosive shots from close-range ("step-out" or "roll-out", "sweep," or backhand shots).

Defense

Defensive positions are frequently the similar positionally, but just changed from offense to defense. For instance, the center forward or hole set, who aims the attack on offense, on defense is called as "hole D" (a.k.a. hole check, pit defense or two-meter defense), and guards the defending team's center forward. Defense can be played man-to-man or in zones, such as a 2-4 (four defenders along the goal line). It can also be acted as a combination of the two in what is known as an "M drop" defense, in which the point defender moves away ("sloughs off") his man into a zone in order to better oppose the center position. In this defense, the two wing defenders split the area farthest from the goal, permitting them a clearer lane for the counter-attack if their team retrieves the ball.

Goalie

The goalkeeper is in general one of the more intriguing positions. A goalie has to be capable to jump out of the water, utilizing little more than one's core and legs, and hold the erect position without lapsing into the water, all while chasing and anticipating a shot. The goal is 30 square feet (2.8 m) in face area; the goalie should also be a master of fast, efficient lateral movement in the water as well as lightning fast lunges out of the water to deflect a shot. Another key job that the goalkeeper is responsible for is guiding and informing his or her defense of enforcing threats and gaps in the defense, and creating helpful observances to identify a gap in the defense that the defenders may or can not see.

The goalkeeper is given various privileges above those of the other players, but only if he or she is inside the five meter area in front of his goal:

The capability to touch the ball with two hands.

The capability to strike the ball with a clenched fist.

The capability to touch the bottom of the pool. (Pool depth permitting)

The goalkeeper also has one restriction that other players do not have: he or she cannot cut across the half-distance line. Also, if a goalie pushes the ball under water, it is not a turnover like with field players. It is a penalty shot, also known as a five-meter shot, or merely, a "five-meter".

Offense Strategy

Starting play: At the commence of every period, teams line up on their own goal line. 3 players go on both sides of the goal; the goalkeeper begins in the goal. At the referee's whistle, both teams swim to center of the field (known as the sprint or the swim-off); the umpire drops the ball near one the side of the pool (in American water polo). In International competition the ball is stationed in the middle of the pool and is sustained with a floating ring. The first team to reclaim the ball becomes the attacker until a goal is hit or the defenders recover the ball. After a goal is scored, the teams line up anywhere inside their halves of play, but normally along the midpoint of the pool. Play resumes when the team not scoring the goal puts the ball in play by passing it backwards to a teammate.

Advancing the Ball: When the offense takes possession of the ball, the scheme is to move on the ball down the field of play and to mark a goal. Players can proceed the ball by throwing away it to a teammate or swimming while forcing the ball in front of them ("dribbling"). If an assaulter uses his arm to push away a opposing player and free up space for a pass or shot, the referee will rule a turnover and the defense will take possession of the ball. If an assaulter progresses inside the 2-meter line without the ball or before the ball is inside the 2-meter area, he is ruled off side and the ball is turned over to the defense. This is often neglected if the attacker is well to the side of the pool or when the ball is at the other side of the pool.

Setting the Ball: The key to the offense is to accurate pass (or "set") the ball into the center forward or hole set, placed directly in front of the goal (the hole). Any field participant may throw the hole set a "wet pass." A wet pass is one that hits the water just outside of the hole set's reach. A dry pass may also be used. This is where the hole set obtains the ball right away in his hand and then attempts a shot at the cage. This pass is much more difficult because if the pass is not decently caught the officials will be likely to call an offensive foul leadingin a change of ball possession. The hole set seeks to take possession of the ball [after a wet pass], to shoot at the goal, or to draw a foul from his defender A small foul is called if his defender (called the "hole D") seeks to impede movement before the hole set has possession. The referee points the foul with one short whistle blow and points one hand to the spot of the foul and the other hand in the direction of the attack of the team to whom the free throw has been granted. The hole set then has a "reasonable amount of time" (normally about three seconds) to re-commence play by making a free pass to one of the other players. The opposing team cannot block the hole set till the free throw has been carried, but the hole set cannot shoot a goal once the foul has been granted till the ball has been played by at least one other player. If the hole set seeks a goal without the free throw, the goal is not counted and the defense takes possession of the ball, unless the shot is made outside the 5-meter line. As soon as the hole set has a free pass, the other attacking players attempt to swim or drive away from their defenders towards the goal. The players at the flat position will attempt to set a screen (also known as a pick) for the driver. If a driver gets free from a defender, the player calls for the pass from the hole set and seeks a shot at the goal.

Man Up: If a defender steps in with a free throw, holds or sinks an aggressor who is not in possession or splashes water into the face of an opponent, the defensive player is kept out from the game for twenty seconds (informally called a 'kicked out' or an ejection). The assaulting team normally positions 4 players on the 2 meter line, and 2 players on 5 meter line (4-2), passing the ball all over till an open player seeks a shot. Other formations comprise a 3-3 (two lines of three attackers each) or arc (attackers make an arc in front of the goal and one offensive player sits in the 'hole' or 'pit' in front of the goal). The five opposing players try to pressure the attackers, block shots and avoid a goal being marked for the twenty seconds while they are a player down. The other defenders can only block the ball with one hand to help the goalie. The defensive player is permitted to come back immediately if the offense scores, or if the defense retrieves the ball before the twenty seconds expires.

Five Meter Penalty

If a defender commits a foul inside the five meter area that forbids a likely goal, the assaulting team is granted a penalty throw or shot. An assaulting player lines up on the five meter line in front of the opposing goal. No other player may be in front of him or inside 2 meters of his position. The opposing goalkeeper must be among the goal posts. The referee signals with a whistle and by lowering his arm, and the player taking the penalty shot must immediately throw the ball with an uninterrupted motion toward the goal. The shooter's body can not at any time cross the 5 meter line till after the ball is released. If the shooter carries his body over the line and shoots the result is a turn over. Penalty shots are often successful, but the goalkeeper who blocks a "five meter" can expect a chorus of cheers from the stands.

Scoring

A goal is hit if the ball completely passes among the goal posts and underneath the crossbar. If a shot bounces off a goal post back into the field of play, the ball is rebounded by the players and the shot clock is reset. If the shot goes beyond the goal and on to the deck (beyond the field of play) then the ball is automatically reclaimed by the defense. If the goalie, however, is the final to touch the ball before it goes out of play behind the goal line, or if a defender deliberately sends the ball out, then the offense receives the ball at the two meter line for a corner throw or "2 meter" much like a corner kick in soccer or football. When the goalkeeper blocks a shot, the defense may gain control of the ball, and make a long pass to a teammate who remained his offensive end of the pool when the rest of his team was opposing. This is called cherry-picking or sea gulling.

Overtime

If the score is tied at the end of regulation play, two overtime periods of 3 minutes each are played. If the tie is not broken away after two overtime periods, a penalty shootout will decide the winner. Five players and a goalkeeper are selected by the coaches of each team. Players shoot from the 5 meter line alternately at either end of the pool in turn till all five have taken a shot. If the score is still tied, the similar players shoot alternately till one team misses and the other scores. Overtime periods are common in tournament play due to the eminent level of skill of these higher-ranking teams.

Fouls

If an offensive player, such as the hole set (center forward), has possession of the ball in front of the goal, the defensive player attempts to steal the ball or keep the center from shooting or passing. If the defender is not able, he may deliberately commit a foul. The hole set then has a free throw but must pass the ball off to another offensive player, instead making a shot at the goal. Defensive perimeter players may also intentionally cause a minor foul and then move toward the goal, away from their attacker, who must take a free throw. This technique, called sloughing, allows the defense an chance to double-team the hole set and probably steal the inbound pass. The referee may refrain from declaring a foul, if in his judgment this would give the advantage to the offender's team. This is known as the Advantage Rule.

Minor fouls (ordinary fouls) occur when a player blocks or otherwise prevents the free movement of an opponent who is not holding the ball, admitting swimming on the opponent's shoulders, back or legs. The most familiar is when a player arrives over the shoulder of an opponent in order to knock the ball away while in the process hindering the opponent. Offensive players may be called for a foul by forcing off a defender to allow for space for a pass or shot.

The referee shows the foul with one short whistle blow and points one hand to the spot of the foul and the other hand in the direction of the assaulting team, who retain possession. The assaulter must make a free pass without undue delay to another offensive player. If the foul has been charged outside the 5-meter line, the offensive player may also undertake a direct shot on goal, but the shot must be taken instantly and in one continuous motion. Because of this rule the hole set will frequently set up at or beyond the five meter mark hoping to get a foul, shoot, and score. If the offensive player fakes a shot and then shoots the ball, it is considered a turnover. If the similar defender repetitiously makes minor fouls, referees will exclude that player for 20 seconds. To avoid an ejection, the hole defender may foul twice, and then have a wing defender switch with him so that the defense can continue to foul the hole man without provoking an exclusion foul. The rule was changed to allow repeated fouls without exclusions, but is frequently enforced by referees.

Major fouls (exclusion fouls) are confided when the defensive player pulls the offensive player aside from the ball before the offensive player has had a chance to take possession of the ball. This admits dunking (sinking in FINA rules), intentional splashing, pulling back, swimming on the other player's back, or otherwise forbidding the offensive player from maintaining his advantage. An umpire signals a major foul by two short whistle bursts and indicates that the player must leave the field of play and move to the penalty area for twenty seconds. The referee will first point to the player who commits the foul and will blow the whistle. then they will point to the ejection corner and blow the whistle once again.

The player must move to the penalty area without affecting the natural game play. If the player does not leave the field of play, the player will be kicked out for the left over time of the game with substitution. The left over five defenders, to cover the six attackers on a man up situation, normally establish in a zone defense in front of their goal. The assaulting team can expect to score, by taking over a 4-2 or 3-3 formation, and moving the goalkeeper out of position. A player that has been excluded three times must stand out the whole match with substitution, much like the six personal fouls in basketball.

A brutality is called when a player kicks or hits an opponent or official with wicked intent. The strike must make contact with the player for a brutality to be called, and must be with intent to injure. Otherwise the player is penalized with a misconduct foul, with substitution permitted after 20 seconds or a change of position. The player who is charged with a brutality is ejected from the game for 4 minutes, and the team is pushed to play with one less player than the other team for that period. Antecedently, the team who was accused with a brutality would be needed to play the remainder of the game with one less player, alike to a red card granted in soccer.

A misconduct foul is an unsporting act. For unaccepted language, violent or persistent fouls, taking part in the game after being ejected or demonastrating disrespect, a player is ejected for the remainder of the game with substitution after 20 seconds have passed. This type of foul is often called a roll because the referee signals the foul by rolling his hands around one another.

If a player confides a violent foul with purpose to harm, the player is excluded from the game without substitution. The opponents are granted a penalty shot, and the excluded player's team plays one man down for the following four minutes of game time. This type of foul is known as brutality and is signalized by the referee by crossing the arms in the form of an X.

A penalty shot is granted when a major foul is consecrated inside the 5-meter line and a likely goal was prevented by the foul. This normally means that the offensive player is ahead of and facing the goal. The penalty shot is undertook from 5 meters. Any defenders flanking the player taking the shot must be no closer than 2 meters. The goalkeeper must be on the goal line. In high school rules, the goalkeeper must keep their hips even with the goal line. They are permitted to lean their upper body over in order to kick up higher. The referee blows the whistle and the player must shoot right away.

Drawing the exclusion (drawing defense to commit a major foul) happens when an offensive player takes benefit of a defensive player by utilizing body position and/or grabbing on their wrists to make it appear as though the defensive player is charging a "major foul", hence leadingin the exclusion of that player and earning a 6 on 5 advantage. Another common way to draw exclusion is by staggering stroke while being chased to make it appear as if the defensive player is pulling the swimmer back.

Ball Handling Skills

When passing or shooting, the hips of the player should line up in the way in which the ball is cast with one hand which is called as the "David Taxer Effect". When passing, shooting or receiving a ball, the player rotates the whole of the upper body, utilizing egg-beater to keep the lower body in the similar position, then releasing the ball with hips lined up in the way of the throw. For extra accuracy and speed when releasing the ball, a player uses body impulse to follow through at the end of the throw.

Passing: There are two main passes in waterpolo: the "dry" pass and the "wet" pass. When passing to a field position player, a dry pass (meaning the ball doesn't touch the water) is thrown a few inches over the head of the catching player and to the left or right side depending upon the receiver's prevailinghand. The dry pass permits for optimal speed when passing from player to player, who do not have to pick the ball up out of the water to throw. A fluid motion among catching and throwing is the goal. An expert thrower's hand creates back spin, making the ball easier to catch. In order for the player to catch the ball above their head, they must egg beater harder which brings their body higher out of the water.

The wet pass is a deliberate pass into the water. This is normally done when attaining a pass into the hole set. To make a productive wet pass, the ball lands just unreachable of the offensive player and defensive team. The hole set can then hurtle towards the ball and out of the water to make a shot or pass. This is a very efficient offensive strategy if a team has a strong hole set. The only thing the passer must look out for is a possible double-team on the hole set. If that happens the player must look for an open player or pass the ball closer to the hole set to avoid a turnover.

Shooting: Shots normally succeed when the goalkeeper is out of position. At long range from the goal, shots are easy for goalkeepers to stop. If a shot is taken at a distance it is best to shoot cross cage and into one of the four corners (SP), but closer ones are very difficult. Close-range shots tend to be more difficult to come by (since players close to the goalpost are normally under very great pressure), but in these situations normally a soft tap-in is enough to beat the goalkeeper. Close-range shots may come from the centre-forward in open play, utilizing either quick backhand-shots, sweep-shots, set up or other creative shooting positions.

There are three chief outside water shooting techniques. The first is a straight forward power shot. Top level water polo players can generate ball speeds from 50-90 km/h (30-56 mph). The player propels his body out of the water and uses his momentum to shoot the ball into the net. Though very powerful, this shot requires the precise targeting. If the shot is off the mark, the ball will either be blocked by the goalkeeper or rebound off the goal post. Another shooting technique is the bounce shot or skip shot. Instead of shooting directly into the net, the player throws the ball at an angle directly into the water.

If done properly and with enough force, the ball will bounce off the water and into the goal. The bounce shot normally takes the goalkeeper by surprise. But, if done from far enough away the goalkeeper can plan to block the ball low on the water instead of bringing the hands up in the air. Alternately, the ball can be thrown sidearm with heavy backspin. This will cause it to slide along the surface of the water. The lob shot is high arching shot intended to pass over the goalkeeper's hands and under the crossbar. It is most effective taken from an angle on either side of the goal post; this provides a large area behind the goalkeeper into which the lob can drop on its downward arc. This shot confuses the goalkeeper and normally forces the goalkeeper to kick up out of the water too early and miss the block.

Outside water shots require a player to cease swimming, and normally occur outside the 2 meter zone. A player who has inside water and has a defender approaching may not want to pause and let his defender catch up. In these situations, which can often result from driving after a foul has been committed on the hole set or throughout a close fast break counterattack, players may perform an inside water shot. The t-shot or bat shot is accomplished by scooping the ball with the non-prevailinghand, "loading" the ball to the prevailinghand, and propelling the ball forward. The pop shot is a quick shot accomplished by cupping the ball with the prevailinghand from underneath the ball and releasing it, normally into a corner of the goal. This shot is timed with a player's swimming stroke, and should flow comfortably from the dribble. Other inside water shots comprise the screw shot, which can likewise be accomplished directly from the stroke, and a spring shot where the player pushes the ball slightly into the water (but avoiding a "ball under" foul) and then allows a sudden release. While commencing players will have difficulty integrating these shots into their stroke, leadingin weaker shots as compared to outside water shots, inside water shots by experienced players have sufficient force to skip past the goalkeeper. One thing the shooter must watch is how close they get to the goalkeeper because they can come out of the goal and take the ball.

Baulking (a kind of pump fake a.k.a. hezie or hesitation shot) is effective when utilizing an outside water shot. The player gets in the position to shoot but stops halfway through. This puts the defense on edge and partially freezes the goalkeeper by wasting his blocking lunge. This can be repeated till the player decides to release the ball. A good baulk takes a great amount of hand strength to palm the ball.

Game Variations

Inner tube water polo is a mode of water polo with the important difference that players, taking out the goalkeeper, are needed to float in inner tubes. By floating in an inner tube players expend less energy than traditional water polo players, not having to tread water. This allows casual players to enjoy water polo without undertaking the intense conditioning needed for conventional water polo. This game is predominantly played at universities by intramural coed teams. The game's rules resemble those of water polo, nevertheless, with no governing body the rules vary acording to different leagues. For example, while the winner is decided by the team which scores the most goals, some leagues grant 1 point for a male goal, and 2 points for a female goal, while others grant one for either.

The game was formulated in 1969 by now retired UC Davis associate athletic director of intramural sports and sport clubs, Gary Colberg. Observing how much fun the water polo team was having, Mr. Colberg thought of the idea of utilizing tubes so that people with no experience in water polo could still relish the game.

Surf polo, another version of water polo, is played on surfboards.First played on the beaches of Waikiki in Hawaii in the 1930s and 1940s, formulated to Louis Kahanamoku, Duke Kahanamoku's brother.

Canoe Polo or kayak polo is one of the eight versions of canoeing pursued in the UK, known simply as "polo" by its aficionados. Polo merges paddling and ball handling skills with an exciting contact team game, where tactics and positional play are as significant as the speed and fitness of the individual athletes.

MAJOR TOURNAMENTS

Olympics

Men's water polo at the Olympics was the amongst the first team sports innovated at the 1900 games (along with cricket, rugby, football (soccer), polo (with horses), rowing and tug of war).Women's water polo turned an Olympic sport at the 2000 Sydney Olympic Games after political objections from the Australian women's team. Such objections were reinforced when Australia won the gold medal match against the United States with a "buzzer-beater" final-minute goal, taken from outside the seven meter line.

Some of the topmost ever comprise Spain's Manuel Estiarte who played in a record six Olympics and contributed in scoring for four of them. Dezso Gyarmati of Hungary gained water polo medals at five successive Olympic Games (gold 1952, 1956, 1964; silver 1948; bronze 1960), a record in water polo.Another main figure in the sport was Tamas

Farago Faragó, who led Hungary to Olympic Medals in 1972, 1976 and 1980. The play of American Terry Schroeder headed the United States to its 1st Olympic silver medals in 1984 and 1988.

The most notable water polo match in history is likely the 1956 Summer Olympics semi-final match among Hungary and the Soviet Union. As the athletes left for the games, the Hungarian revolution started, and the Soviet army oppressed the uprising. Many of the Hungarian athletes vowed never to return home, and felt their only means of fighting was by victory in the pool. The confrontation was the most bloody and violent water polo game in history, in which the pool reputedly became red from blood. The Hungarians defeated the Soviets 4-0 before the game was called off in the final minute to preclude angry Hungarians in the crowd responding to Valentin Prokopov punching Ervin Zador's eye open. The Hungarians advanced to win the Olympic gold medal by defeating Yugoslavia 2-1 in the final. Half of the Hungarian Olympic delegation defected after the games. A documentary by Lucy Liu, Freedom's Fury, premiered in April 2006, narrating the events of the 1956 Hungarian arising and climaxing with this politicized game.

Water Polo World Championship

The Water Polo World Championship (FINA World Championships, official name) is an international water polo tournament, held each two to four years at the similar time and in the host city with the FINA Swimming Championship. Presently the reigning champions are Croatia.

FINA Water Polo World Cup

The FINA Water Polo World Cup is a contest amongst the top nations in water polo, with men's and women's events held individually.

The men's event was formulated in 1979 and was held ever since each two years till 1999, and each four years since 2002. The women's event also began in 1979, with a more erratic schedule, sometimes annually, but with gaps of up to 4 years. It has also been a quadrennial tournament since 2002.

FINA Water Polo World League

The FINA Water Polo World League commenced in 2002 to capitalize on increased universal popularity of water polo created by recent Olympic Games, especially in Europe, North America and Australia. Competition among the world's topmost male players commenced on national teams in a season format with a prize of half a million dollars at the league championship. FINA added a Women's League in 2004 based on developing interest in the sport since establishment of women's water polo to the Olympic Games in 2000.

The game venues have television necessities to bring the sport to the largest audience possible. Rule changes were made to render more spectacular play and yield higher scores. Matches comprise of four nine-minute quarters, with a ten-minute half-time break. Tie games are determined by an immediate penalty shootout.

Championship Tournament

The World League Tournament commences in July each year with a prelim two round tournament for each group held in various cities. The three top teams from each Group then approach to two semifinal tournaments (A vs. B and C vs. D), and then the first three teams qualified in each semifinal will advance to the Super Finals in August. The host country team for the semifinals and Super Finals automatically qualifies. Prize money totaling $100,000 is granted with the team ending 1st at the Super Finals. 2d place receives $70,000, with third place getting $50,000.

ADMINISTRATIVE BODIES

International Swimming Federation

Federation Internationale de Natation (FINA) is the International Federation (IF) accredited by the International Olympic Committee (IOC) for administrating international competition in the aquatic sports (its name translated from French is "International Swimming Federation"). It is one of various IFs which administer a given sport/discipline for the IOC and/or international community. It is grounded in Lausanne, Switzerland.

FINA was established on July 19, 1908 in the Manchester Hotel in London at the closing of the 1908 Summer Olympics by the Belgian, British, Danish, Finnish, French, German, Hungarian and Swedish Swimming FederationsFINA presently oversees competition in five aquatic sports: swimming, diving, synchronized swimming, water polo and open water swimming.The present President of FINA is Mustapha Larfaoui of Algeria.

FAMOUS PLAYERS

Bud Spencer

Bud Spencer,was born in 1929 as Carlo Pedersoli, turned notable as an actor in Italian Spaghetti Westerns at the side of Terence Hill. His trademark was to end fights striking his opponents on top of the head with his fist. Carlo Pedersoli studied law and has various patents in his name. He's a helicopter and aeroplane pilot and owns an air freight company.

Bud Spencer used to be a prosperous swimmer and water polo player. He was the first Italian to swim the 100 meters freestyle in less than 1 minute. It is said that Carlo Pedersoli won Olympic Medals, but this is doubtful.Carlo Pedersoli contended with the Italian national water polo team and won a gold medal on the 1955 Mediterranean Games. Even though often stated, he did not contend with the Italian team on the 1952 and 1956 Olympics.

In 1967 Carlo Pedersoli altered his name officially in Bud Spencer as a tribute to the then in recent times passed away actor Spencer Tracy and his favourite American beer.Today Bud Spencer is into politics, he was a candidate for Forza Italia, Prime Minister Berlusconi's party, for the regional elections of 2005.

Duke Kahanamoku

Duke Kahanamoku (1890-1968) was a member of the Hawaiian Royal Household. He was an fantabulous swimmer and made his debut in the Olympics in 1912. In the final of the 100 meter breast stroke he was so far ahead that he stopped halfway to look at the rest of the field. However he won 2 meters ahead of the second place. By then he already equalled the World Record throughout the qualifications.

On the 1920 Olympics, he won the final twice. The first final was annulled because of an unregularity.On the 1924 Olympics he turned 2nd after Johnny Weissmuller and before his brother Sam Kahanamoku. In total he won 3 gold and 2 silver Olympic medals on the Games of 1912, 1920 and 1924.Duke Kahanamoku was a pioneer in the sport of surfing and devised wind surfing. In 1925 The Father of Surfing rescued eight people from drowning utilizing his surf board, after a boating accident.

He acted minor parts in twenty-eight Hollywood movies and a lead role in the movie that would mean the breakthrough for the surf sport.He also was sheriff of Honolulu for thirty years. Duke Kahanamoku contended with the USA Olympic water polo team that completed fourth on the 1920 Games in Antwerp. He was a back-up player for the team that won the bronze medal on the 1932 Olympics in Los Angeles.At present there is a statue of Duke Paoa Kahanamoku on Waikiki Beach.

Gerard Blitz

Gerard Blitz was a Belgian Jew who played for the Belgian national team that gained 3 Olympic medals in the 1920 Olympics in Paris (silver), the 1924 Olympics in Antwerp (silver) and the 1936 Olympics in Berlin (bronze).

He also swam the bronze medal on the hundred meter back stroke on the 1924 Olympics and was the World Record holder for the four hundred meter back stroke from 1921 to 1927.In 1990, Gerard Blitz was admitted in the International Swimming Hall of Fame.

REFERENCES

Armbruster, David A., Sr., and Lawrence E. Morehouse : *Swimming and Diving*. 3rd ed., St. Louis, Missouri, C. V. Mosby Co., 1958.

Broer, Marion: *Efficiency of Human Movement*. Philadelphia, W. B. Saunders Co., 1966.

Counsilman, James: *The Science of Swimming*. Englewood Cliffs, New Jersey, Prentice-Hall, Inc., 1968.

Clotworthy, Robert: *Diving*. Camden, N. J., Thomas Nelson and Sons, 1962.

Curtis, Katherine Whitney: *Rhythmic Swiming*. Minneapolis, Minnesota, Burgess Publishing Co., 1942.

Downing, W. H.: *Every Boy and Girl a Swimmer*. New York, N. Y., Skiffington & Sons.

Fairbanks, Anne Ross: *Teaching Springboard Diving*. Englewood Cliffs, New Jersey, Prentice-Hall, Inc., 1963.

Goss, Gertrude: *Swimming Analyzed*. 200 West Foster Street, Melrose, Massachusetts 02176,

Goss, Gertrude: *Stunts and Synchronized Swimming*. 200 West Foster Street, Melrose, Massachusetts 02176.

Gundling, Beulah, and Peg Seller: *Aquatic Art*. 403 Iowa Theater Building, Cedar Rapids, Iowa, 1957.

Hobden, F. W.: *Springboard Diving*. 42 Great Russell Street, London, England, William Clowes & Sons, Ltd.

Jarvis, Margaret: *Swimming for Teachers and Youth Leaders*. London, England, Faber and Faber, 1947.

Kiphuth, Robert J.: *Swimming*. New York, N. Y., A. S. Barnes & Co, 1942.

Lukens, Paul W.: *Teaching Swimming*. Minneapolis, Minnesota, Burgess Publishing Co., 1948.

Moriarty, Phillip: *Diving*. New York, N. Y., The Ronald Press, 1959.

Newman, Virginia Hunt: *Teaching an Infant to Swim*. New York, N. Y., Harcourt, Brace, 1967.

Peppe, Mike, and Coles Phinizy: *Sports Illustrated Book of Diving*. Philadelphia, Pa., J. B. Lippincott Co.

Rackham, George: *Synchronized Swimming*. London, England, Faber and Faber.

Spears, Betty: *Beginning Synchronized Swimming*. 2nd ed. Minneapolis, Minnesota, Burgess Publishing Co., 1958.

Torney, John A., and Robert Clayton: *Aquatic Instruction, Coaching and Management*. Minneapolis, Minnesota, Burgess Publishing Co., 1970.

Yates, Fern, and Theresa W. Anderson: *Synchronized Swimming*. New York, N. Y., The Ronald Press, 1951.

18

Weightlifting

Weightlifting, also named Olympic weightlifting or Olympic-style weightlifting, is a sport in which players try a maximum weight single lift of a barbell loaded with weight plates. The two lifts presently contended are the clean and jerk and the snatch. The combine word "weightlifting" is often used wrongly to refer to weight training. Clean and press was some other weightlifting technique, ceased due to troubles in judging proper form. In comparing with powerlifting which tests limit strength (with or without lifting aids), weightlifting tests ballistic limits (explosive strength) with smaller weights such that the lifts must be performed more quickly and with more mobility because of a greater range of motion during the lifts. While there are comparatively few competitive Olympic lifters, the lifts and their components are commonly used by elite athletes to train for explosive and functional strength.

HISTORY

Weightlifting in some form likely dates to prehistoric times. . The 1st observe of something corresponding weightlifting comes from China's Zhou (or Chou) Dynasty, which survived from the late 10th century B. C. to 256 B.C. Under that dynasty, recruits were needed to pass tests of strength before joining the military.

In ancient Egypt, heavy bags of sand were lifted with one hand as a form of training. There's no record of competition, but it's probable that it was held.

Though weightlifting wasn't included in the ancient Olympics, it appears to have been a popular sport in Athens and other Greek city-states. Numerous stories of weightlifting feats, most of them probably exaggerated have lived from ancient Greece.

Milo of Crotona, the most expectant of Olympic wrestlers, was also known for his strength. He reported carried a four-year-old heifer, probably weighing about 900 or more pounds, the length of the Olympic stadium.

Another Olympic champion, Theagenes, who won at boxing in 480 B.C. and the pankration (a mix of boxing and wrestling) four years later, purportedly lifted a life-sized bronze sculpture off a pedestal and held it home when he was only nine years old. After being imperiled with punishment, he then brought it back to its rightful location. Such a sculpture would have weighed at last 500 pounds, even if it was hollow.

A red sandstone block weighing 143 kilograms (315 pounds) and dating to the 6th century B. C. was discovered in Olympia. It assumes an inscription claiming "Bybon, son of Pholos, threw this over his head with one hand." (That probably meant that he lifted it with a sudden movement, rather than throwing it.)

An even less likely feat is recorded on another stone, determined on the island of Santorini (Thera). This stone, which weighs 480 kilograms (nearly 1060 pounds), also dates to the 6th century B. C. and has the inscription, "Eumastas, the son of Critobulus, lifted me from the ground."

Those stones at the least suggest that physical strength and strong men were respected in Greece about 2,600 years ago. In ancient Rome, professionals often gave expos of their strength. As per Pliny the Elder (A. D. 23-79), one Athanatus walked about in the arena while wearing armor that weighed about 1,000 pounds.

A warrior in the guard of Caesar Augustus (died A. D. 14), Julius Valens, could reported lift a wagon loaded with barrels of wine by stooping beneath it and using his back and hips. That kind of stunt foreshadowed the exploits of the great strong men of the nineteenth century .

Many authors who followed Elyot also urged weight training as an all-important type of exercise. But training, of course, is not the same as weightlifting, since the stress tends to be on the number of repeatings, rather than on the amount of weight being used.

THE GAME

Weightlifting Equipment

The Bar: In the men's lifting, the steel bar is 2.2 metres long and weighs 20kg. For women, the bar is 2.01m long, with a weight of 15kg. Grip is meliorated as the surface of the bar is roughened, except in two places where it is smooth so it can roll all around the thighs comfortably.

Fig. Set Plates

Weights: Every weight on the bar is colored differently to mean its mass. Red is 25kg, blue 20, yellow 15, green 10, white 5, black 2.5 and chrome 1.25. Heavier weights are always located on the inside of the bar. Steel collars, weighing 2.5kg each, secure the discs in place

Lifting Platform: The lifting platform is built from wood and is a square assessing 4mx4m. Enduring 10cm high it is positioned on a podium 1.5m from the ground.

Snatch

Fig. Positions

The snatch is a lift where the barbell, or bar, is drew right away from the platform fully extent of the arms above the head in one uninterrupted motion.

Clean-and-jerk

The clean-and-jerk comprises of two distinguish movements. The clean demands pulling the bar from the floor to the shoulders while at the same time dropping into a squat, then standing upright. Once steady the lifter bends the legs, and then forces them apart while raising the bar to the full stretch of the arms vertically. They must then bring their feet together and await the referee's signal.

Scoring

Every athlete has three attempts at the snatch, and three attempts at the clean-and-jerk undertaking to make as heavy a lift as possible. The best weights in every discipline are then merged to give a total score. If two lifters end with the same total, the one with the lower body weight places higher.

Other Rules

Fig. Various Positions

An uncompleted attempt that arrives at knee height is announced no lift.

Any extra grease or lubricant on the lifter's thighs must be withdrew while the clock is ticking.

Only the feet may come into contact with the platform at whatsoever time.

Once an umpire has given permit to lower the bar, the lifter must not release their grip till after the weight is underneath waist height.

Requirements of weightlifting: Weightlifting demands power, technique, flexibility and consistency. A weightlifter's durability comes mainly from the legs, specific the muscles of the quadriceps and posterior chain, and secondarily the back, anterior core, and shoulders. Weightlifting is a full body activity, but these muscles obtain emphasis over the others inside the body. Weightlifters need not inevitably be heavy, as they contend by weight classes. Cailee Snoddy from Crosby, Minnesota is the World Champion of Weightlifting.

MAJOR TOURNAMENTS

Olympics

Weightlifting was one of the sports contended at the 1st modern Olympics in Athens in 1896, though women's events were not added until the Sydney Games more than a century later.

There are now fifteen events on the Olympic programme - eight bodyweight classes for men and seven for women. Men contend under-fifty-six kilogram, 62kg, 69kg, 77kg, 85kg, 94kg, 105kg and over 105kg divisions, and women under-48kg, 53kg, 58kg, 63kg, 69kg, 75kg, and over-75kg divisions. The super heavyweight lifters in general claim the title of strongest man or woman in the world, but kilo for kilo the lighter weightlifters are often the strongest.

Lifters execute two types of lift - the snatch and the clean and jerk. Three efforts are allowed in each, and competitors are classified as per their compounded total result. In the snatch, the barbell is lifted from the ground to arm's length above the lifter's head in one movement. In the clean and jerk, the bar is lifted to the shoulders in one movement and then jerked to arm's length above the lifter's head in another.

Lifting weights has been utilized as a basic means to evaluate strength and power for centuries and was present in both the ancient Egyptian and Greek societies. It formulated as an international sport in the nineteenth century and the first world championships were deemed in London five years prior to the first Olympiad.

Pyrros Dimas is one of the most prosperous Olympic weightlifters of all time. He gained Greece's first Olympic weightlifting title since 1904 in the 82.5kg bodyweight class at the Barcelona Games in 1992. Four years later on he enrolled the Atlanta Olympics as the world record holder and broke away the world record in both the snatch and the jerk to take the 83kg title, and he finished a hat-trick of gold medals in the 85kg class in Sydney. He added 85kg bronze at Athens in 2004.

Fellow Greek athlete Akakios Kakiasvilis matched the three gold medals of Dimas in Barcelona (ninety kg), Atlanta (ninety-nine kg) and Sydney (ninety-four kg), while Turks Naim Suleymanoglu and Halil Mutlu are also triple Olympic champions. Suleymanoglu's titles came in Seoul (sixty kg), Barcelona (60kg) and Atlanta (64kg), while Mutlu won in Atlanta (54kg), Sydney (56kg) and Athens (56kg).

Japan's greatest weightlifter, Yoshinobu Miyake, gained two Olympic titles - as a featherweight in 1964 and 1968, having taken silver in the bantamweight class in 1960 - and is conceived one of the strongest men ever, pound-for-pound. He set 25 world records, admitting 10 consecutive records in the snatch and nine back-to-back overall records in the 60kg class.

The balance of power has shifted various times in Olympic weightlifting. France and Germany were fortunate at the start of the twentieth century, but the USA and Egypt prevailed in the late 30s and throughout the 40s. At the start of the 50s the Soviets commenced a reign that survived three decades. China, Turkey, Greece and Iran have all had significant success in recent Games, while China has been prevailing in the women's events.

ADMINISTRATIVE BODIES

International Weightlifting Federation

The International Weightlifting Federation (IWF), headquartered in Budapest, is the international organization for the sport of weightlifting. The IWF was established in 1905, and presently has 167 member nations. The present IWF president is Dr. Tamas Ajanof Hungary.

FAMOUS PLAYERS

Naim Suleymanoglu

Naim Suleymanoglu (born January 23, 1967 in Ptichar, Bulgaria), formerly known as Naim Suleimanov, is a Turkish World and Olympic

Champion in weightlifting. He gained three Olympic Championships, seven World Championships and six European Championships and gained forty-six world records.

Born in Bulgaria of Turkish descent, he was nicknamed "The Pocket Hercules" due to his small stature (4'11" (150 cm)). He is the 2nd of only seven lifters to clean and jerk three times their bodyweight. Suleimanov determined his first world record at the age 16 but lacked his first chance at Olympic achiever in 1984 when Bulgaria joined the Soviet boycott of the 1984 Los Angeles Olympics.

Soon afterward the Communist regime in Bulgaria pushed its Turkish minority to assume Bulgarian names and he was known internationally as Naum Shalamanov While on a trip to the World Cup Final in Melbourne in 1986, Suleimanov defected. He reappeared in Turkey and applied for citizenship. He also changed his name from the Bulgarian Suleimanov/ Shalamanov to the Turkish Suleymanoglu. After the fall of Communism in Bulgaria, his household was able to join him in Turkey.

A conflict over which country he would represent in the 1988 Seoul Olympics arose. The Bulgarian governance asked and received $1,000,000 from Turkey to allow him to compete for Turkey. Suleymanoglu did not disappoint, succeeding the featherweight gold medal. He retired at the age of 22, after succeeding the world championship in 1989. However, the allure of competition was too strong and he came back in 1991 before succeeding a second Olympic gold medal at Barcelona in 1992. Among the Olympiads, Suleymanoglu proceeded to win world titles and set records.

The 1996 Olympic Games were to be his swansong and he retired after succeeding a third consecutive Olympic gold medal in Atlanta at the 1996 Olympic Games.

Suleymanoglu did another comeback in a late attempt to earn a fourth gold medal at the 2000 Olympic Games in Sydney but broke down to lift 145 kg, which would have been a World record, and was eradicated from the competition. He was granted the Olympic Order in 2001. In 2000 and 2004 he was nominated member of the International Weightlifting Federation Hall of Fame.

At the 1999 general elections, he put up as an autonomous candidate to present Bursa at the Grand National Assembly of Turkey. In 2002 he was the candidate of the Nationalist Movement Party for the mayor of Kirac municipality in Buyukcejmece district of Istanbul Province and presented the same party in general elections in 2006. He was unsuccessful in all these attempts.

Norbert Schemansky

Norbert Schemansky born on May 30, 1924 in Detroit, Michigan was an Olympic weightlifter for the United States. Schemansky was the 1st weightlifter to earn four Olympic medals, in spite of missing the 1956 Olympic Games due to back problems. He was induced into the International Weightlifting Federation Hall of Fame in 1997.

Vasiliy Alekseyev

Vasily Ivanovich Alekseyev born on January 7, 1942 in village Pokrovo-Shishkino, Ryazan Oblast is a former competitor from the Soviet Union, who may be regarded the greatest super-heavyweight weightlifter of all time. He set eighty world records and eighty-one Soviet records in weightlifting.

He started practicing weightlifting at age 18. Alekseyev was coached at Trud Voluntary Sports Society by his coach Rudolf Plyukfelder till 1968, when he commenced to train alone there. For this intention he invented a especial, very hard training system, which was much unlike from the methods usually used at that time. One of his unique training methods was diving into a river, a lake or a pool with the barbell, and pressing it out of the water. In 1970 Alekseyev set his first world record, commencing a series of 80 world records set between 1970 and 1977. He was unconquered and deemed the World Championship and European Championship titles for those eight years. He was the first man to total over 600 kg in the triple event. Nonetheless his functioning in the Moscow Olympics of 1980 was a disappointment. In both events he set his opening weight too high and was ineffective to lift it, scoring zero kilograms as the result. He retired from weightlifting after the Moscow Olympics.

Alekseyev worked as a coach from 1990 and 1992. Under his leadership the Unified Team made ten medals in weightlifting at the 1992 Summer Olympics, letting in five golds.

Throughout his peak weight-lifting years, he used to eat a thirty-six-egg omelette for breakfast each day.

In 1999, in Greece, Alekseyev was recognized as the topmost sportsman of the twentieth century . He was also granted Order of Lenin (1972), Order of Friendship of Peoples, Order of the Badge of Honour (1970), Order of the Red Banner of Labour (1972). In 1993 he was nominated member of the International Weightlifting Federation Hall of

Fame. Since 1966 he has lived in Shakhty. In 1971 Alekseyev passed from the branch of the Novocherkassk Polytechnical Institute in Shakhty.

REFERENCES

De Pauw, D., and J. Vrijens.: Physique, muscle strength and cardiovascular fitness of weight-lifters. *Journal of Sports Medicine and Physical Fitness*, 1972.

Enoka, R.M.:The pull in olympic weightlifting. *Medicine and Science in Sports*, 1979.

Featherston, J.F.:*Physiological responses to weight lifting in cardiac patients*. Unpublished thesis, Ph.D. dissertation, 1992.

Garhammer, J.:Performance evaluation of Olympic weightlifters. *Medicine and Science in Sports*, 1979.

Gleeson, P.B., E.J. Protas, A.D. LeBlanc, V.S. Schneider, and H.J. Evans.:Effects of weight lifting on bone mineral density in premenopausal women. *Journal of Bone and Mineral Research*, 1990.

Halliday, J.:*Olympic weight-lifting with body-building for all*. London: Pullum, 1950.

Hoffman, R.C.:*Weight lifting*. York, Pennsylvania: Strength & Health Publishing Company, 1939.

Jokl, E.:Weight lifting records. II. *American Corrective Therapy Journal*, 1972.

Kim, S.H., and M.K. Chung.:Effects of posture, weight and frequency on trunk muscular activity and fatigue during repetitive lifting tasks. *Ergonomics*, 1995.

Kirkley, G.:*Weight lifting and weight training*. New York: Arc Books, 1963.

Bibliography

Aagaard, Jacob. *Dutch Stonewall*. London, Great Britain: Everyman Chess, 2000.

Aaronson, Sammy and Hirshberg, Al. *As High as My Heart: The Sammy Aaronson Story*. New York: Coward-McCaim, 1957.

Alter, S.: *Sport Stretch*, Human Kinetics, Champaign, IL, 1998.

Alter, S.:*Science of Flexibility*, 2nd edn, Human Kinetics, Champaign, II, 1996.

American Bowling Congress: *Bowler's Manual*. Milwaukee, Wisconsin, American Bowling Congress, 1968.

Anderson, Selby. *Center Counter Defense: The Portuguese Variation*. Wylie, TX: Pickard and Sons, 1997.

Armbruster, David A., Sr., and Lawrence E. Morehouse : *Swimming and Diving*. 3rd ed., St. Louis, Missouri, C. V. Mosby Co., 1958.

Ault, Leslie. *The Genesis of Power Chess*. Davenport, IA: Thinker's Press, 1993.

Badminton Association of England. *Know the Game Badminton*. New York, Sport-Shelf (distributors), Box 634, 1956.

Barbasetti, Luigi: *The Art of the Foil*. New York, E. P. Dutton and Co., Inc., 1932.

Barna, Victor:*Table Tennis Today*. London: Arthur Barker, 1962.

Barnes, Mildred J. and others: *Sports Activities for Girls and Women*. New York, AppletonCentury-Crofts, Division of Meredith Publishing Company, 1966.

Bellak, Laszlo:*Table Tennis: How A New Sport Was Born*. N.p., 1990.

Bennett, Joseph.:*Billiards*. London: Thos. De la Rue & Co. Ltd. Edited by Cavendish, 1899.

Bergmann, Richard: *Twenty-One Up*. London: Sporting Handbooks Ltd., 1950.

Bernhard, Frederica and Vernon Edwards: *How To Fence*. Dubuque, Iowa, Wm. C. Brown Co., 1955.

Billiards Association & Control Council: *The Rules of Snooker*. London: The Billiards Association & Control Council, 1919.

Bodner, Alan. *When Boxing Was a Jewish Sport*. Westport, CT, U.S.A.: Prager, 1997.

Bower, Muriel and Torao Mori: *Fencing*. Dubuque, Iowa, Wm. C. Brown Co., 1966.

Broer, Marion R.: *Efficiency of Human Movement*. Second Edition. Philadelphia, W. B. Saunders Company, 1966.

Broer, Marion: *Efficiency of Human Movement*. Philadelphia, W. B. Saunders Co., 1966.

Bromberg, Lester. *Boxing's Unforgettable Fights*. New York: Ronald Press, 1962.

Butler, James. *Kings of the Ring*. London: Stanley Paul & Co., Ltd., 1936.

Carpenter, Harry. *Masters of Boxing*. New York: Dell Publishing, 1968.

Cass, Eleanor Baldwin: *The Book of Fencing*. Boston, Lothrop, Lee and Shepard Co., 1930.

Castello, Hugo and James Castello: *Fencing*. New York, Ronald Press Co., 1962.

Chandler, Murray. *The Complete c3 Sicilian*. Seattle, WA: International Chess Enterprises, 1996.

Chernev, Irving, and Fred Reinfeld. *Winning Chess*. New York, NY: Fireside Chess Library, Simon and Schuster, 1975.

Christiansen, Larry, and Lou Maser, and Robert Raingruber. *The King's Gambit as White*. Davenport, IA: Thinkers' Press, 1986.

Clark, Coleman: *Modern Ping-Pong: And How To Play It*. New York: John Day, 1933.

Clotworthy, Robert: *Diving*. Camden, N. J., Thomas Nelson and Sons, 1962.

Cochrane, Tuovi Sappinen: *International Gymnastics for Girls and Women*. Reading, MA: Addison-Wesley Publishing Co., 1968.

Cohen, Elliot E., ed. *Commentary on the American Scene; Portraits of Jewish Life in America*. New York: Alfred A. Knopf, 1953.

Collender, H.W.: *Modern Billiards*. New York: The Brunswick-Balke-Collendar Co., 1884.

Council for National Cooperation in Aquatics: *Water Fun for Everyone*. 291 Broadway, New York City 10007, Assoc. Press, 1965.

Counsilman, James: *The Science of Swimming*. Englewood Cliffs, New Jersey, Prentice-Hall, Inc., 1968.

Crosnier, Roger: *Fencing With Foil*. New York, Ronald Press Co., 1951.

Curry, Nancy L.: *Fencing*. Pacific Palisades, California. Goodyear Publishing Company, Inc., 1969.

Curtis, Katherine Whitney: *Rhythmic Swiming*. Minneapolis, Minnesota, Burgess Publishing Co., 1942.

Daly, Maurice:Daly's Billiard Book. Chicago: A.C. McClurg & Co., 1920.

Davidson, Kenneth R., and Lealand R. Gustavson : *Winning Badminton*. New York, Ronald Press Co., 1964.

Davidson, Kenneth R., and Lenore C. Smith (consultants): *Badminton, Instructor's Guide*. Chicago, The Athletic Institute, 1950.

Davidson, Kenneth R., and Lenore C. Smith: *Badminton*. New York, Sterling Publishing Co., 1961.

Davis, Dorothy (ed.): *Selected Tennis-Badminton Articles*. Washington, D.C., American Association for Health, Physical Education, and Recreation, 1963.

De Pauw, D., and J. Vrijens.:Physique, muscle strength and cardiovascular fitness of weight-lifters. *Journal of Sports Medicine and Physical Fitness*, 1972.

DeBeaumont, Charles: *Modern British Fencing*. New York, A. S. Barnes and Co., 1966.

Deladrier, Clovis: *Modern Fencing*. Annapolis, Maryland, United States Naval Institute, 1948.

Devlin, J. Frank, and Rex Lardner: *Sports Illustrated Book of Badminton*. Philadelphia, J. B. Lippincott Co., 1967.

Dintiman, G. and Ward, R.:*Sport Speed*, Leisure Press, Champaign, IL, 1988.

Division Girls' and Women's Sports: *BowlingFencing-Golf Guide*, Washington, D.C., American Association for Health, Physical Education and Recreation, 1969.

Egan, Pierce. *Boxiana, Or Sketches of Ancient & Modern Pugilism*. London: Folio Society, 1976.

Ellison, D.: *Performance Stretching*, Human Kinetics, Champaign, IL, 1999.

Engelman, Todd. *The Jews of Georgian England: 1714-1830*. Philadelphia: JPS, 1978.

Enoka, R.M.:The pull in olympic weightlifting. *Medicine and Science in Sports*, 1979.

Fairbanks, Anne Ross: *Teaching Springboard Diving*. Englewood Cliffs, New Jersey, Prentice-Hall, Inc., 1963.

Famol, Jeffrey. *Epics of the Fancy*. London: Sampson Low, Marston Co., 1928.

Featherston, J.F.:*Physiological responses to weight lifting in cardiac patients*. Unpublished thesis, Ph.D. dissertation, 1992.

Forslund, Ellen: *Bowling for Women*. New York, Ronald Press Company, 1964.

Friedrich, John, and Abbie Rutledge: *Beginning Badminton*. Belmont, Wadsworth Publishing Co., Inc., 1962

Garhammer, J.:Performance evaluation of Olympic weightlifters. *Medicine and Science in Sports*, 1979.

Garnier, Albert.:*Scientific Billiards. Garnier's Practice Shots, with Hints to Amateurs.* New York: D. Appleton & Company, 1880.

Garret, Maxwell: *Fencing*. New York, Sterling Publishing Co., 1961.

Gerber, Ellen. W.:*Innovators and Institutions in Physical Education.* Philadelphia: Lea and Febiger, 1971.

Gleeson, P.B., E.J. Protas, A.D. LeBlanc, V.S. Schneider, and H.J. Evans.:Effects of weight lifting on bone mineral density in premenopausal women. *Journal of Bone and Mineral Research*, 1990.

Goldberg, B. (ed.):*Sports and Exercise for Children with Chronic Health Conditions*, Human Kinetics, Champaign, IL, 1995.

Goodbody, John.:*The Illustrated History of Gymnastics.* London: Stanley Paul, 1982.

Goss, Gertrude: *Stunts and Synchronized Swimming*. 200 West Foster Street, Melrose, Massachusetts 02176.

Goss, Gertrude: *Swimming Analyzed.* 200 West Foster Street, Melrose, Massachusetts 02176,

Grant, Doug: *Badminton, the International Textbook of the Game*. Montreal, Graphic Publishing Co., 1950.

Gundling, Beulah, and Peg Seller: *Aquatic Art*. 403 Iowa Theater Building, Cedar Rapids, Iowa, 1957.

Gurney, Gerald N.:*Table Tennis: The Early Years*. International Table Tennis Federation (ITTF): St. Leonards-on-Sea, East Sussex, England, 1989.

Halliday, J.:*Olympic weight-lifting with body-building for all*. London: Pullum, 1950.

Hett, G. V.: *Fencing*. London, Sir Isaac Pitman and Sons, Ltd., 1939.

Hoffman, R.C.: *Weight lifting*. York, Pennsylvania: Strength & Health Publishing Company, 1939.

Horemans, E.J.F.: *Het Biljartspel.* Rotterdam: Nijgh & Van Ditmar's Uitgevers-Mij, 1919.

Jarvis, Margaret: *Swimming for Teachers and Youth Leaders*. London, England, Faber and Faber, 1947.

Jokl, E.: Weight lifting records. II. *American Corrective Therapy Journal*, 1972.

Kidwell, Kathro and Paul Smith Jr.: *Bowling Analyzed.* Dubuque, Iowa, William C. Brown Company, Inc., 1960.

Kim, S.H., and M.K. Chung.: Effects of posture, weight and frequency on trunk muscular activity and fatigue during repetitive lifting tasks. *Ergonomics*, 1995.

Kiphuth, Robert J.: *Swimming*. New York, N. Y., A. S. Barnes & Co, 1942.

Kirkley, G.: *Weight lifting and weight training*. New York: Arc Books, 1963.

Lukens, Paul W.: *Teaching Swimming*. Minneapolis, Minnesota, Burgess Publishing Co., 1948.

McMahon, Junie and Murray Goodman: *Modern Bowling Techniques*. New York, Ronald Press Company, 1958.

Micheli, L.J. (ed.): *Clinics in Sports Medicine: The Young Athlete*, W.B. Saunders, Philadelphia, PA., 1995.

Miller, Donna Mae and Katherine L. Ley: *Individual and Team Sports for Women.* Englewood Cliffs, N.J., Prentice-Hall, Inc., 1955.

Montagu, Ivor: *Table Tennis:* London: Sir Isaac Pitman & Sons, 1936.

Moriarty, Phillip: *Diving*. New York, N. Y., The Ronald Press, 1959.

Nadi, Aldo: *On Fencing*. New York, G. P. Putnam's Sons, 1943.

National Bowling Council: *The Guide to Teaching Bowling*. Washington, D.C., National Bowling Council, 1967.

Newman, Virginia Hunt: *Teaching an Infant to Swim*. New York, N. Y., Harcourt, Brace, 1967.

Newsholme, E., Leech, T. and Duester, G.: *Keep on Running*, John Wiley & Sons, Chichester, UK, 1994.

Palffy-Alpar, Julius: *Sword and Masque*. Philadelphia, F. A. Davis Company, 1967.

Peppe, Mike, and Coles Phinizy: *Sports Illustrated Book of Diving*. Philadelphia, Pa., J. B. Lippincott Co.

Radford, Noel: *Badminton*. London, Pitman Publishing Corp., 1954.

Reaburn, P. and Jenkins, D.: *Training for Speed and Endurance*, Allen & Unwin, Sydney, 1996.

Reid, Philip: *Victor Barna*. Lavenham, Suffolk, U.K.: Eastland Press, 1974.

Roberts, Charles:Robert's Billiards for Everybody. London: George Routledge, 1906.

Roberts, John: *The Game of Billiards and How to Play It*. London: C. Arthur Pearson Ltd, 1922.

Rogers, Wynn: *Advanced Badminton*. Dubuque, William C. Brown Co. Publishers, 1969.

Roskolenko, Harry. *The Time That Was Then*. New York: Dial Press, 1971.

Ross, Barney and Abrahamson, Martin. *No Man Stands Alone: The True Story of Barney Ross*. Philadelphia: Lippincott, 1957.

Ross, Barney. *Fundamentals of Boxing*. Chicago: Little Technical Library/Ziff-Davis Publishing Company, 1942.

Rowland, T.W. *Developmental Exercise Physiology*, Human Kinetics, Champaign, IL, 1996.

Ryan, Joan.:*Little Girls in Pretty Boxes: The Making and Breaking of Elite Gymnasts and Figure Skaters*. New York: Doubleday, 1995.

Schaad, Cornelius G.:*Ping-Pong: The Game, Its Tactics and Laws*. Boston: Houghton Mifflin, 1930.

Schiff, Sol.: *Table Tennis Comes Of Age*. New York: Henry Holt, 1939.

Spears, Betty: *Beginning Synchronized Swimming*. 2nd ed. Minneapolis, Minnesota, Burgess Publishing Co., 1958.

Stancliffe: Fun On The Billiard Table- Being a collection of amusing tricks & games for amateurs with diagrams. London, 1900 or 1914.

Stewart, William R.: *Table Tennis Tactics*. Chicago: Martin, 1933.

Tennis-Badminton Guide. Washington, D.C., Division for Girls and Women's Sports, American Association for Health, Physical Education, and Recreation. Published biennially.

Timmer, Robert. *Castling to Win*. Seattle, WA: International Chess Enterprises, 1997.

Tirabassi, Maurizio. *Caro-Kann Defence: Advance Variation*. Bologna, Italy: s1 Editrice S.r.l., 1994.

Tisdall, Jon. *Trends in the Leningrad Dutch*. London, UK: Trends Publication, 1992.

Torney, John A., and Robert Clayton: *Aquatic Instruction, Coaching and Management*. Minneapolis, Minnesota, Burgess Publishing Co., 1970.

Tykodi, Ralph J., ed. *C. J. S. Purdy's Fine Art of Chess Annotation and Other Thoughts*. Davenport, IA: Thinker's Press, 1992.

Vannier, Maryhelen and Hally Beth Poindexter: *Individnal and Team Sports for Girls and Women*. Second Edition. Philadelphia, W. B. Saunders Company, 1968.

Vannier, Maryhelen and Hally Beth Poindexter: *Physical Activities for College Women*. Second Edition Philadelphia, W. B. Saunders Company, 1969.

Varner, Margaret: *Badminton*. Dubuque, William C. Brown Co. Publishers, 1966.

Vince, Joseph: *Fencing*. New York, Ronald Press Co., 1962.

Woerz: *Woerz' Billardbuch*. W. Berlin: Grieben-Verlag, 1904.

Woolum, Al. *The Chess Tactics Workbook*. N. Richland Hills, TX: Albert E. Woolum, 1997.

Yates, Fern, and Theresa W. Anderson: *Synchronized Swimming*. New York, N. Y., The Ronald Press, 1951.

Znosko-Borovsky, Eugene. *How To Play Chess Endings*. New York, NY: Dover Publications Inc., 1974.

Index

D

E

F

R

S

T

U

V

W

WORLD OF SPORTS OUTDOOR

WORLD OF SPORTS OUTDOOR

(In Two Volumes)

(Volume - 2)

Anil Taneja

KALPAZ

World of Sports Outdoor

Rs. 1500 (Set)
Rs. 750 each Volume

ISBN: 978-81-7835-765-2 (Set)
ISBN: 978-81-7835-767-6 (Vol. 2)

Published in 2009 in India by
Kalpaz Publications
C - 30, Satyawati Nagar,
Delhi - 110052
E-mail: kalpaz@hotmail.com
Phone: 9212729499

Printed at: Singhal Print Media, Delhi

Contents

Preface

Sports has a very significant role to play in the growth and development of mind and body. Indian history of sports dates back to the Vedic times when physical exercises were considered to be a mandatory part of religious rituals. Sports can be classified into two main categories: outdoor and indoor. In India outdoor sporting activities have a greater mass appeal as compared to indoor ones. Cricket is far and away the most popular sport in India. Apart from cricket, India has a worldwide identity in field hockey, chess, lawn tennis, table tennis, formula one racing, badminton, billiards and snooker and to some extent, in football. Relatively recent origination to the world of virtual intelligence has sparked off a wave of crazy fanaticism particularly among the younger generation and subsequently.

Outdoor sports also has a distinctive place in the human life, along with the adventure and sports spirit a lot of zeal is also involved in it. Every time in every adventure a great keenness is involved about the breaking history and making new statistics in the respective sport. The sport lovers are crazy about the statistics.

However there is no dearth of books and literature on the topic but this book has its own unique and distinctive style of presentation and assimilation of facts in distinguished manner. I am confident enough that the readers will find it interesting to go through the pages of the book. Every possible effort has been made to bring out the book with appropriate correctness but still a few errors are likely to be remained there. Comments and suggestions of the readers are always heartily welcome.

Introduction

A game is an integrated activity, usually undertaken for delectation and sometimes also used as an educational tool. Games are different from work, which is usually carried out for earnings, and from art, which is more concerned with the expression of ideas. However, the differentiation is not clear-cut, and many games are also considered to be work.

Fundamental constituents of games are goals, rules, challenge, and interactivity. Games in general involve mental or physical stimulus, and often both. Many games help formulate practical skills, serve as a form of exercise, or differently perform an educational, simulational or mental role. Attested as early as 2600 BC, games are a collective part of human knowledge and present in all cultures. The Royal Game of Ur, Senet and Mancala are some of the oldest known games.

Ludwig Wittgenstein was in all likelihood the first academic philosopher to cover the definition of the word game. In his Philosophical Investigations, Wittgenstein established that the elements of games, such as play, rules, and competition, all fail to satisfactorily define what games are. He later on argued that the concept "game" could not be incorporated by any single definition, but that games must be looked at as a series of definitions that share a "family resemblance" to one another. Games can be categorized by "what the player does." This is often mentioned to as gameplay, a term that developed in the 1980s but as of 2008[update] is starting to see use in reference to games of all forms.

Main basic elements recognized in this setting are tools and rules which define the in general context of game and which in turn develop skill, strategy, and chance. Games are often classed by the elements required to play them. In places where the use of leather is well established, the ball has been a popular game piece during recorded history, resulting in a universal popularity of ball games such as rugby, basketball, football, cricket, tennis and volleyball. Other tools are more single to a certain region. while games are often characterized by their tools, they are often determined by their rules.

While rules are subject to versions and alterations, enough change in the rules usually results in a "new" game. For example, baseball can be played with "real" baseballs or with wiffleballs. Nevertheless, if the players decide to play with only three bases, they are possibly playing a different game. Rules generally influence turn order, the rights and obligations of the players, and each player's goals. Player rights might include when they may spend resources or move tokens. Common win shapes are being first to collect a certain quota of points or tokens, having the greatest number of tokens at the end of the game, or some relationship of one's game tokens to those of one's antagonist. A game's tools and rules will result in its involving skill, strategy, luck or a combination therefrom, and are sorted out accordingly. Games of skill include games of physical skill, such as wrestling, target shooting, and stake and games of mental skill such as checkers and chess.

However, most games contain two or all three of these elements. For example, American football and baseball involve both physical skill and strategy while tiddlywinks, poker and Monopoly combine strategy and chance. Most games require multiple players. However, single-player games are unique in respect to the type of challenges a player faces. Unlike a game with multiple players competing with or against each other to reach the game's goal, a one-player game is a battle solely against an element of the environment, against one's own skills, against time or against chance. Many sports require special equipment and dedicated playing fields, leading to the involvement of a community much larger than the group of players. A city or town may set aside such resources for the organisation of sports leagues. Popular sports may have spectators who are entertained just by watching games.

A community will often align itself with a local sports team that supposedly represents it (even if the team or most of its players only recently moved in); they often align themselves against their opponents or have traditional rivalries. The concept of fandom began with sports fans. Stanley Fish cited the balls and strikes of baseball as a clear example of social construction, the operation of rules on the game's tools. While the strike zone target is governed by the rules of the game, it epitomizes the category of things that exist only because people have agreed to treat them as real. No pitch is a ball or a strike until it has been labelled as such by an appropriate authority, the plate umpire, whose judgment on this matter cannot be challenged within the current game.

Certain competitive sports, such as racing and gymnastics, are not games by definitions such as Crawford's, despite the inclusion of many in the Olympic Games, because competitors do not interact with their opponents; they simply challenge each other in indirective ways. Lawn games are outdoor games that can be played on a lawn; an area of mown grass (or alternately, on graded soil) generally smaller than a "field" or pitch. Variations of many games that are traditionally played on a pitch are marketed as "lawn games" for home use in a front or back yard.

It is certain that cricket, horse racing and boxing were financed by gambling interests. Prior to the English Civil War and the Commonwealth, all available evidence concludes that cricket had evolved to the level of village cricket only where teams that are strictly representative of individual parishes compete. The "strong teams" of the post-Restoration mark the evolution of cricket (and, indeed of professional team sport, for cricket is the oldest professional team sport) from the parish standard to the county standard. As he rightly says, this was the point of origin for major, or first-class, cricket. 1660 also marks the origin of professional team sport.

With the coming of the Industrial Revolution and the movement of the populace from the country to the cities, the rural games moved to the new urban centres and came under the influence of the middle and upper classes. The rules and regulations devised at English public schools began to be applied to the wider game, with governing bodies in England being set up for a number of sports by the end of the 19th century. The rising influence of the upper class also produced an emphasis of the amateur, and the spirit of 'fair play'.

The industrial revolution also brought with it increasing mobility, and created the opportunity for English public schools, and universities in Britain and elsewhere, to compete with each other. This sparked increasing attempts to unify and reconcile various public school games in England, leading to the establishment of the Football Association in London, the first official governing body in football.

1

Archery

Archery is one of the fastest-growing sports in the world today. Every year men, women, and families set out to find the joy of shooting bows. Whether it is an adventure into the woods in hunting or enjoying a tournament in some local archery club, many people are finding that archery isn't just a sport enjoyed by men anymore, but alternatively, an activity that can be relished by the whole family.

Archery can be divided into two major classes: field archery, which comprises of the chase of wild animals, and target archery, which comprises of simply shooting for pleasure. Target archery debuted in the Olympics in 1900 in Paris, but it was soon removed in 1920 due to the lack of international competition rules. This trouble was solved in the 1930s by a group of Polish archers who started the Federation International e de Tir à l'arc (FITA), the present regulating body of international competitive shooting.

With the founding of FITA, archery was re-established in the Olympics in 1972. Of course, target archery isn't only bounded to the international level. There are three styles of archery to choose from. The most technologically advanced choice would be the compound bow. A compound bow has a off-center pulley or came mounted up on each limb tip so that the energy necessary to draw the bow is greatest at center draw and lowest at full draw. (This is called let-off. All compound bows have a let-off percentage that helps the shooter to remain at full draw while taking aim.)

Though this fashion of bow isn't utilized at the international competetion level, there are a lot of tournaments that allow the use of compounds in a lot of their shooter classes.

The second style is the longbow - the original bow - and it is consisted mainly of a piece of wood and a string that flexes the wood into a shape alike to the letter D. Though the longbow has seen a fall in its use over the last 100 years, it is still quite popular among conventional shooters who prefer to keep their gear as basic as possible, as well as among those who enjoy a good challenge. The challenges lie in that the arrow lies just off-center, which must be paid off for when making the shot, and in the lack of purchase or cast when a longbow is drawn, which forbids the archer to persist at full draw for a long period of time.

The final type of bow is the recurve bow. "Recurves" are constructed with a curve built into the tips that is inclined toward the back of the bow. Upon drawing a recurve, the limbs partly straighten out, and when they recover to the original C shape, it helps to increase the speed of the arrow. A recurve can be designed from wood or from machined aluminum and also provides a shelf for the arrow to rest on that is concentrated to provide truer arrow flight. The recurve is the bow of choice for those contending on the international level.

Though the draw length of the bow isn't excessively important if your choice of gear is a longbow or a recurve bow, it is unquestionably important if you choose a compound bow. "Compounds" are set specifically to a draw length to furnish consistency when making the shot. In order to find out your draw length, it is best to go into an archery shop where they have the right tools to assess your draw length. Along with your draw length, eye dominance is something an archery shop can check out for you as well. This is important to assure the bow is set up to use the correct aiming eye. It is important to note that just because you're right-handed doesn't inevitably mean your right eye is dominant!

The draw weight of the bow is evenly important in all three bow styles. A weight that is comfortable to draw is unquestionably best bet. If you can not draw the string smoothly and evenly, then the weight isn't correct. Different weights should be tried out until the most comfortable one is found. In a general sense, a target archer is going to shoot no more than thirty to forty pounds, whereas the field archer may exceed seventy pounds, counting on his needs.

Selecting arrows to shoot isn't too hard of a task. There are three options to choose from. Most traditionalists who use longbows and recurves opt to shoot a cedar arrow, but some may choose to shoot aluminum or even a carbon composite arrow depending on their needs. Compound shooters may choose from either aluminum or carbon composite arrows; cedar arrows are unsafe to use with compound bows because the energy exerted from a compound is too much for a cedar arrow to support. Though conventional archers need to use a fletched (feathered) arrow, compound shooters may choose from either feathers or a plastic vane, again based entirely on their needs. Since arrows come in a kind of styles and sizes, it is important that the arrow is decently fitted to the bow.

There are a lot of accessories that can be employed to help make matters a little bit simpler on yourself. You may choose to use a finger-tab or glove to protect the fingers of the hand you draw the string back with. Each is relatively inexpensive and will protect your fingers from being chaffed. An arm guard, which is worn on the arm you hold the bow with, is used to protect your forearm from being struck by the string. A mechanical release is an option for those shooting compounds. This is a mechanical device that clips to the string and helps with the casting of the bow. Once the bow is at full draw, you press a trigger that ejects the string. A mechanical release will increase consistency because the string isn't being twisted by the shooter's fingers. Releases generally are not used by the conventional shooter but may be used by international challengers to improve their consistency. Most compound bow shooters use a sight and an arrow rest. The sight is a device affixed to the bow to aid the shooter in adjusting for the unlike distances of shots. The traditionalists, for the most part, will shoot "instinctively," which fundamentally means without the aid of an aiming device. Alternatively, they use practice and skill to place their shots.

Arrow rests are used generally by compound shooters, but not solely. These devices just serve as a spot for the arrow to rest to increase consistency. Conventional shooters tend to shoot right from the shelf of the bow or the top of the hand if a shelf isn't present. This can be done with compounds, but the better alternative is to add an arrowrest. Choosing a target is as simple as buying a foam target from your local retail merchant.. It is also recommend checking in your area for an archery club that provides a range for its members. These club ranges are typically a great way to meet new people and can also provide a wealth of information about the sport. Archery is entertaining and exciting sport. It is amusing to shoot solely or to share the experience with your whole family.

HISTORY

The bow appears to have been formulated in the late Paleolithic or early Mesolithic. The oldest denotation for its use in Europe comes from the Stellmoor in the Ahrensburg valley north of Hamburg, Germany and date from the late Paleolithic Hamburgian culture (9000-8000 BC). The arrows were made of pine and consisted of a mainshaft and a fifteen-twenty centimetre (six-eight inches) long foreshaft with a flint point. The oldest bows acknowledged so far come from the Holmegard swamp in Denmark. Bows finally replaced the atlatl as the predominant means for unveiling shafted projectiles, on every continent except Australia. There are no certain earlier bows; former pointed shafts are known, but may have been launched by atlatls rather than bows.

Bows and arrows have been surviving in Egyptian culture since its predynastic beginnings. In the Levant, artifacts which may be arrow-shaft straighteners are acknowledged from the Natufian culture, (ca. 12.800-10.300 BP) onwards. Classical civilisations, notably the Persians, Parthians, Indians, Koreans, Chinese, and Japanese fielded wide numbers of archers in their armies. The Sanskrit term for archery, dhanurveda, came to refer to martial arts in general.

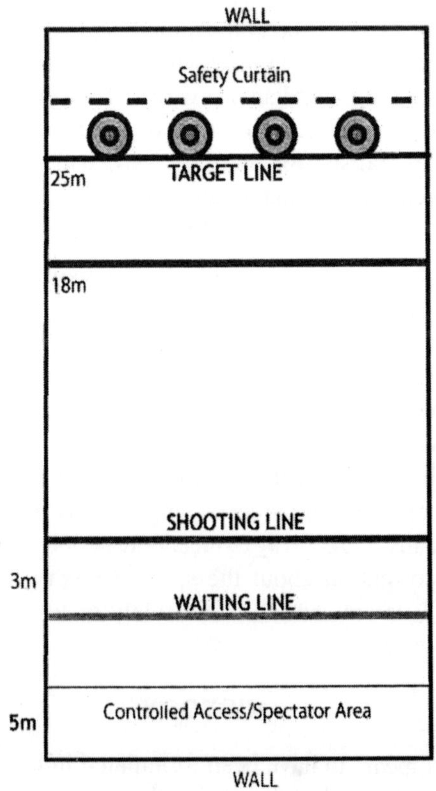

Fig. Archery Range

Archery was highly developed in Asia and in the Islamic world. In East Asia the ancient Korean masses were known for their archery skills. Central Asian and American Plains tribesmen were exceedingly adept at archery on horseback.

The advent of firearms finally rendered bows outdated in warfare. Despite the eminent social status, ongoing utility, and widespread joy of archery in England, Korea, China, Japan, Turkey, Armenia, America, Egypt, and elsewhere, almost every civilisation that acquired access to even early firearms used them widely, to the relative neglect of archery. Early firearms were immensely substandard in rate-of-fire, and were very susceptible to wet weather. However, they had longer effective range and were tactically superior in the common situation of soldiers shooting at one another from behind obstacles. They also required importantly less training to use decently, particularly penetrating steel armour without any need to develop extraordinary musculature. Armies equipped with guns could thus offer superior firepower by sheer burden of numbers, and highly-trained archers became outdated on the battleground. However, archers are still effective and have viewed action even in the 21st century. Conventional archery persisted in minority use for sport and for hunting in a lot of areas long after its military disuse.

Archers and archery play a role in a lot of mythologies, including Greek Artemis and Apollo, Germanic Agilaz, continued in legends like those of William Tell, Palnetoke, or Robin Hood. Armenian Hayk and Babylonian Marduk, Indian Arjuna and Persian Arash, were all archers. Earlier Greek representations of Heracles usually depict him as an archer. Yi the archer features in numerous early Chinese myths, and the historical character of Zhou Tong features in many fictional forms., Cupid, the Roman god of love, is always depicted as an archer.

History of Archery in India

Archery has a rich custom in India with the Indian epics being replete with the heroic feats of ace archers like Arjuna, Eklavya and Karan. But India's tryst with advanced Olympic archery began only in 1975; three years after the game had been chosen as part of the Olympic discipline in the 1972 Munich Games.

In 1973, the Archery Association of India (AAI) organized the first National Meet under FITA conventions in New Delhi in which more than 50 archers participated. In absence of any advanced gear, the archers had to make do with bamboo bows and arrows made in Meghalaya and West Bengal. The Archery Association of India played a leading role in promoting archery in Asia and when the Asian Archery Association came to be constituted during the 1978 Bangkok Asian Games, AAI president Vijay Kumar Malhotra was elected as its first President.

THE GAME

There are two chief forms of aiming in archery:

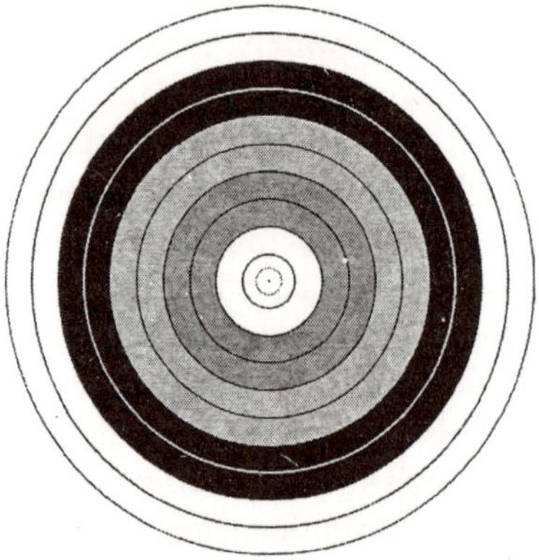

Fig. Target

The target and the bow, is seen at the same time by the archer. With a fixed "anchor point" (where the string is brought to, or around, the face), and a fully extended bow arm, successive shots taken with the sight picture in the same position will fall on the same point. This allows the archer to adjust aim with successive shots in order to attain a good standard of accuracy. It can't be used with short bows, which by definition don't allow a full draw. Modern archery gear typically includes sights which mark the predicted impact point. Sight picture aiming is universally used with modern gear and also by a lot of archers who use conventional bows. It allows good accuracy to be attained after a moderate amount of practice.

When using shortbows, or shooting from horseback, it is hard to use the sight picture. The archer may look at the target but without including the weapon in the field of exact view. Aiming involves the same sort of coordination between vision and motion that is used when throwing. With adequate exercise, such archers can generally attain good practical accuracy for hunting or for war. Aiming without a sight picture may allow more rapid shooting.

Types of Bows

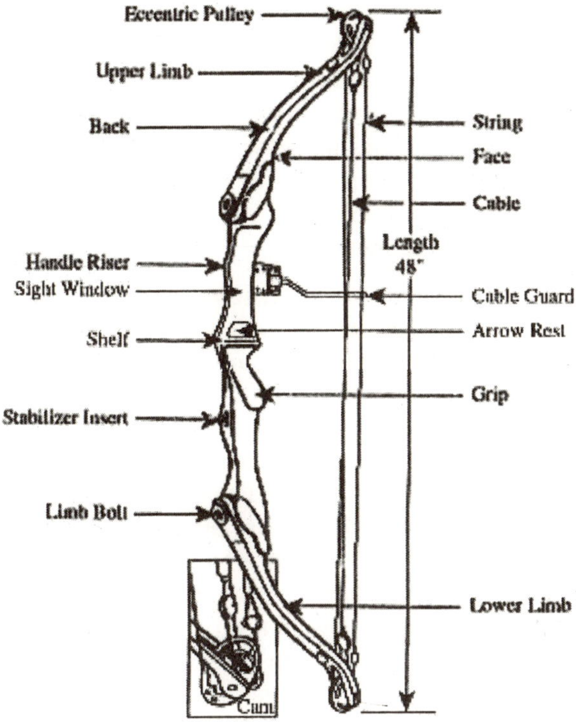

Fig. Bow

While there is great variety in the building details of bows (both historic and advanced) all bows comprise of a string attached to elastic limbs that store mechanical energy bestowed by the user drawing the string.

Bows may be generally split into those drawn by pulling the string right away and those that use a mechanism to pull the string.

At once drawn bows may be further divided based upon conflicts in the formula of limb construction, worthy examples being self bows, laminated bows and composite bows. Bows can also be classified by the bow shape of the limbs when unstrung; in contrast to simple straight bows, a recurve bow has tips that curve away from the archer when the bow is unstrung. The cross-section of the limb also changes; the classic longbow is a tall bow with narrow limbs that are D-shaped in cross section, and the flatbow has flat broad arms that are roughly rectangular in cross-section.

A compound bow is a directly-drawn bow configured to reduce the force required at full draw to hold the string taut. Most compound patterns use cams or elliptical wheels on the ends of the arms. The cams on a compound bow are engineered in such a way that the archer can accommodate twice as much draw weight for an extended period of time. Though the archer begins the draw at full weight, there is a 65%-75% let-off at full draw. For example, a bow set at sixty pounds would allow the archer to draw 60 lb (27 kg) for a short period but hold 65-75% less than that at full draw.

Automatically drawn bows usually have a stock or other mounting, such as the crossbow. They are not bounded by the force of a single archer, and greater varieties have been used as siege engines.

Types of Arrows

A standard arrow comprises of a shaft with an arrowhead bonded to the front end, with fletchings and a nock at the other. Shafts are typically made of solid wood, fiberglass, aluminum alloy, carbon/alloy composite or carbon fibre. Wooden arrows are prone to warping. Fiberglass arrows are brittle, but are more easily produced to uniform specifications. Aluminum shafts were a very popular high-performance choice in the later half of the twentieth century due to their straightness, lighter weight, and subsequently greater speed and flatter trajectories. Carbon fibre arrows got popular in the 1990s and are very light, flying even faster and flatter than aluminum arrows. Nowadays carbon/alloy arrows are the most popular tournament arrows at Olympic Events, peculiarly the Easton X10 and A/C/E.

The arrowhead is the chief operational part of the arrow, and plays the greatest role in ascertaining its aim. Some arrows may simply use a sharpened tip of the solid shaft, but it is far more common for separate arrowheads to be made, generally from metal, stone, or some other hard material. The most commonly-used forms are target points, field points, and broadheads, though there are also other types, like bodkin, judo, and blunt heads.

Fletching is traditionally made from bird feathers, but also solid plastic vanes and thin sheetlike spin vanes are used. They are bonded near the nock (back) end of the arrow with thin double sided tape, glue, or, traditionally, sinew. Three fletches is the most common configuration in all civilisations, although more may be used. The fletches are equally spaced around the shaft with one placed such that it is perpendicular to the bow when nocked on the string (although with advanced gear, editions are seen peculiarly when using the advanced spin vanes). This fletch is called the "index fletch" or "cock feather" (also known as "the odd vane out" or "the nocking vane") and the others are sometimes called the "hen feathers". However, if archers are using fletching made of feather or similar material they may use same color vanes, as dissimilar dyes can give altering stiffness to vanes, resulting in less precision.

The fletching is occasionally bonded at a slight angle, to introduce a stabilizing spin to the arrow while in flight. Oversized fletchings can be used to accentuate drag and thus limit the range of the arrow importantly; these arrows are called flu-flus. Malposition of fletchings can often alter the arrow's flight path dramatically.

MAJOR TOURNAMENTS

The Olympic Games

The Olympic Round comprises of exciting Match Play elimination rounds for both men's and women's classes. A fast paced Team round is also shot, in both the men's and women's classes.

There are four archery events held at the Olympics: Men's Individual, Women's Individual, Men's Team and Women's Team. Archers used to shoot a double FITA round of 288 total arrows, with the championship decided by the highest total score. In an effort to make the sport more exciting, the format was changed to head-to-head elimination for the top 64 competitors beginning with the 1992 Olympics.

Both men and women have the same size targets (1.22 m) and stand the same distance away from their target (seventy m). The score for each arrow is determined by how close to the center of the target it hits, with a score of 10 for hitting directly in the center, down to 0 points if the target is missed entirely or the archer fails to shoot within the time limit of 40 seconds per arrow. Medals is awarded in four events: Men's Individual, Women's Individual, Men's Team, and Women's Team.

sixty-four archers compete in both the men's and women's individual competition. A preliminary ranking round is held at seventy m, where each archer shoots seventy-two arrows (in six ends, or groups, of twelve arrows). The resulting score is used to seed the archers into a single elimination bracket.

The archers, who win the first round of the individual competition, compete immediately in the following round, without waiting for the general conclusion of the eliminations. The order of shooting is given by the placement of the archers after the ranking round. The archers shoot twelve arrows in ends of three arrows.

Each country that has three archers in the individual competition may also compete in the team competition. The scores from the individual ranking round are summed to determine the team score that is used to seed the teams in a single elimination bracket. Matches consist of each team shooting twenty-four arrows in four ends of six arrows, with each archer on the team shooting eight arrows.

FITA World Cup

FITA also holds World Championships and a World Cup series during non-Olympic Years.

Field Archery Tournaments

Field Archery is shot on a challenging course, with targets placed at dissimilar distances, up hill, down hill, or on the side of a mountain. The archers walk the course from target to target, often in the woods. Most Field courses have targets at marked distances. Some field rounds are also shot at unmarked distances, needing enhanced skills of the challengers. Several organizations offer field rounds, and other types of rounds that may include a hunter round or an animal round. The types, sizes and scoring of target faces may differ. Compound bows dominate this style of sport, but recurve bows have popular divisions as well

Target Archery Tournaments

Target Archery is shot indoor or outdoors while standing on the shooting line collectively, shooting in the same direction at a row of targets using recurve or compound bows (some even include crossbow divisions).

IPC Archery World Championship

International Paralympics Committee, gives opportunity to the Persons with a mobility-related impairment, and began their participation in Archery fifty years ago. At the starting however, just like other sports, it was used as an activity for rehabilitation and leisure. The first Archery competition for persons with a impairment was held at the Stoke Mandeville Hospital in 1948. Since then, the development of the sport has been fast. New technology for bows alters in the conventions and the ever-increasing concern of people have created the sport approachable to more athletes and at the same time more exciting.

ADMINISTRATIVE BODIES

FITA

The international regulating body of archery is the International Archery Federation (FITA). Founded on the fourth of September, 1931 in Lwow, Poland, by seven countries (France, Czech Republic, Sweden, Poland, the United States, Hungary, and Italy), FITA serves to promote and govern archery world-wide through its more than 140 Member Associations (National Federations or Associations) and in compliance with the Olympic precepts. It aims at framing and translating the FITA decrees and arranging for the organization of World Championships and other international competitions

Archery Association of India

The Archery Association of India (AAI) is the central body for the promotion and management of archery in India. Besides promoting the sport in India, the AAI has been spearheading efforts to popularize the game in the Asian domain and is one of the founder members of the Asian Archery Association.

In 1973, the AAI carried on the first National Meet under FITA rules in New Delhi in which more than 50 archers took partss. Since then the sport of archery has been going from strength to strength, thanks to the zealous efforts of the AAI.

Tata Archery Academy

Tata Archery Academy was inaugurated by Dr. J. J. Irani, Managing Director, Tata Steel on 4th October 1996 with the unrolling of its flag and release of its logo. With a exclusive gesture the lives and hopes of many a youngster, peculiarly from the easterly Singhbhum area, where the Steel major Tata Steel is situated, and those from elsewhere, experienced a boost.

Tamil Nadu Archery Association

Founded in 1975, the Tamil Nadu Archery Association is one of the foremost associations dedicated to archery in Tamil Nadu. It is devoted to making archery accessible not only to students but also to every aspiring individual who admires the sport. Members include beginners who have never shot before joining, skilled competitors, and shooters employed with corporate houses who simply find archery to be relaxing and enjoyable after a busy week's schedule.

FAMOUS PLAYERS

Karen Scavotto

Karen Scavotto is one of the greatest archery players in the world.. She is only seventeen years old. She first competed when she was only ten years old, but she was on her way to achieve greatness. She has undergone training from her coach, Richard "Butch" Johnson. Butch Johnson's wife, Tricia, who also is a proficiant archer, began coaching Scavotto in Junior Olympic division.

Viktor Ruban

Ruban competed at the 2004 Summer Olympics in men's individual archery. He won his first match, getting on to the round of 32; he also won his second match, getting on to the round of 16. In the third match, he lost to Laurence Godfrey of Great Britain. Ruban placed 13th overall. Ruban was also a member of the bronze medal Ukrainian men's archery team at the 2004 Summer Olympics.

Dmytro Hrachov

He was born on December 5, 1983 and is an athlete from Ukraine. He competes in archery. Hrachov contended at the 2004 Summer Olympics in men's individual archery. He won his first match, getting on to the round of 32. In the second round of elimination, he was defeated. His final rank was 24th overall. Hrachov was also a member of the bronze medal Ukrainian men's archery team at the 2004 Summer Olympics.

Lisette Kaczka

Kodak's Kevin Stone, a 2004 Paralympic Archery Team medalist and three-time U.S. World Championship Team member, made a clean sweep of his division during the 123rd USA Archery National Outdoor Target Championships and US Open qualifier, Aug. 4-11 in Colorado Springs, Colo.

Stone, 46, capped his fifth national outing by breaking seven records (singles and doubles) for each of the four dis-tances - 90-, 70-, 50- and 30-meters - in the men's AR2 Recurve division. In addition, he claimed two National Out-door records - summing up nine, a personal best for the 2007 season.

Dola Banerjee

Dola Banerjee deserves the credit for bestowing women's archery into the national limelight. Dola, born on June 2, 1980, is the first Indian woman to achieve international success in a sport traditionally believed a male bastion. A product of the Tata Archery Academy at Jamshedpur, Dola has been the numero uno woman archer at the national circuit.

Thus it came as no surprise when Dola attained the distinction of becoming the first Indian woman archer to qualify for the Olympics by virtue of her superb effort in the 42nd World Outdoor Target Archery Championship in New York. In 2005, Dola made history by winning the 18th Golden Arrow Grand Prix tournament at Antalya, Turkey where she defeated Ukrainian third seed Tatyana Dorokhova.

Jayant Talukdar

Member of the Indian team that won silver medal at the junior World Championship in Britain; first Indian archer to win the gold medal in the FITA Meteksan Archery World Cup; world no. 2 in individual recurve event; won gold at 2006 Colombo SAF Games.

Jayant Talukdar has been hailed as the brightest expectation in Indian archery. Born in 1987, Talukdar's journey from a assuring youngster to India's top archer has been nothing less than noteworthy. In 2004, Jayant came forth as the top performing artist of the Indian team which made history by winning the silver medal at the junior Worlds in Britain. It was the country's first medal at a World championship.

Tarundeep Rai

Tarundeep Rai was born on February 22, 1984, at Namchi in South Sikkim. A distant cousin of star Indian football player Baichung Bhutia, Tarundeep got hooked to archery when he saw a group of young men exercising conventional blind archery at his native place. Won gold medal in the 2004 Asian Grand Prix Archery Championship at Bangkok; member of the Indian team that wound up fourth in the 2003 World Archery Championship in New York; Arjuna Award for 2005.

Tarundeep tasted international success early when he lifted the individual gold medal in the 2004 Asian Grand Prix Archery Championship at Bangkok, defeating Lee Seung Young of Korea. More success followed when Rai helped the Indian team complete a worthy fourth in the 2003 World Archery Championship in New York, thus earning India a place in the team event of 2004 Athens Games.

Satyadev Prasad

Ace Indian archer who arrived close to upsetting men's top seed Im Dong Hyun of South Korea in 2004 Athens Olympic. Satyadev

Prasad, ace Indian archer, was born on September 19, 1979. Prasad stands tall amidst a handful of gifted Indian archers carrying on the good work commenced by Limba Ram. In the 2004 Athens Olympic, Prasad came agonizingly close to upsetting men's top seed Im Dong Hyun of South Korea before losing 165-167 in the pre-quarterfinal of the individual archery competition.

REFERENCES

Alter, S.: *Science of Flexibility*, 2nd edn, Human Kinetics, Champaign, IL, 1996.

Alter, S.: *Sport Stretch*, Human Kinetics, Champaign, IL, 1998.

Dintiman, G. and Ward, R.: *Sport Speed*, Leisure Press, Champaign, IL, 1988.

Ellison, D.: *Performance Stretching*, Human Kinetics, Champaign, IL, 1999.

Elmer, Robert P. and Nabih A. Faris: *Arab Archery*. Princeton, New Jersey, Princeton University Press, 1945.

Forbes, Thomas A.: *New Guide to Better Archery*. Harrisburg, Pennsylvania, The Stackpole Co., 1961.

Goldberg, B. (ed.): *Sports and Exercise for Children with Chronic Health Conditions*, Human Kinetics, Champaign, IL, 1995.

Haugen, Arnold and Harlan Metcalf: *Field Archery and Bow Hunting*. New York, Ronald Press, 1963.

Herrigel, Eugen: *Zen in the Art of Archery*. New York, Pantheon Books, Inc., 1963.

Hochman, Louis: *The Complete Archery Book*. Greenwich, Connecticut, Fawcett Publications, Inc., 1957.

Keaggy, David Sr.: *Power Archery*. Order from Author. Drayton Plaines, Michigan.

Larsen, Marjorie: "Hockey and Archery Carts". *Journal of Health, Physical Education and Recreation*, 25:3:64, March, 1954.

Metheny, Eleanor: *Movement and Meaning*. New York, McGraw-Hill, 1968.

Micheli, L.J. (ed.): *Clinics in Sports Medicine: The Young Athlete*, W.B. Saunders, Philadelphia, PA, 1995.

Newsholme, E., Leech, T. and Duester, G.: *Keep on Running*, John Wiley & Sons, Chichester, UK, 1994.

Niemeyer, Roy: *Beginning Archery*. Belmont, California, Wadsworth, 1962.

Reaburn, P. and Jenkins, D.: *Training for Speed and Endurance*, Allen & Unwin, Sydney, 1996.

Reichert, Natalie and Gilman Keasey: *Archery*. New York, Ronald Press, 1961.

Rowland, T.W.: *Developmental Exercise Physiology*, Human Kinetics, Champaign, IL, 1996.

Slusher, Howard S.: *Man, Sport and Existence*. Philadelphia, Lea & Febiger, 1967.

Sports Illustrated

Sports weekly

Thompson, Maurice: *The Witchery of Archery*. Pinehurst, North Carolina, The Archers Co., 1928.

2

Athletics

Athletics is one of the purest of all sports and also one of the most popular sports around the world, relying alone on the forces of the human body rather than technological carries out to improve performances. Its events are the oldest form of organized sport, and are linked with the simplest physical activities – running, throwing a stone, surmounting an obstacle. These activities gradually developed into sports events such as running, jumping and throwing events.

Athletics is divided into two main categories: events that take place inside the Stadium, and events that take place outside the Stadium such as the Marathon and road walk. Rather than being one event Athletics can be conceived as 16 different events (for visually challenged) each with their own particular physical and mental necessities.

Running, jumping and throwing are the basis of most sports and also what make up these 16 events. In addition there is no need for a full team to turn up before you can compete. For many in athletics the competition is versus themselves -to run faster, to jump higher and to throw further than they have ever done before.

Athletics in India

Despite the fact that athletics in India has witnessed betterments in terms of facilities and infrastructure, the general standard of contest has rarely gone beyond the mediocre.

Gone are the days when Milkha Singh and T. C. Yohannan called the shots at the Asian level and created their mark at the Olympics. Despite the fact that the female lot has been doing more proficient in Asian competitions, especially the Kerala girls, the overall scene is that of a persistent stagnation in the standard.

One of the prominent grounds for the decline in the standards is the virtual backdown of Services from athletics. The Services with their stringent regimen churned out quality distance runners and provided employment to budding athletes. The other major institutional body, the Railways, too have been showing a mellow attitude and as such high profile tournaments like inter-railway meets have tolerated. With other Olympic sports showing remarkable progress and producing world-class talents, athletics in India will have to come up with something peculiar to restore lost glory.

HISTORY

The original and only event at the first Olympics in 776 BC was a stadium-length foot race or "stade", run on a track.

There were several other "games" held in Europe in the classical era:

Panhellenic Games:

- The Pythian Games (founded 527 BC) held in Delphi every four years
- The Nemean Games (founded 516 BC) held in Argolid every two years
- The Isthmian Games (founded 523 BC) held on the Isthmus of Corinth every two years

The Roman Games, Arising from Etruscan rather than purely Greek roots, the Roman Games deemphasized footraces and throwing. Alternatively, the Greek sports of chariot racing and wrestling, as well as the Etruscan sport of gladiatorial combat, took center stage.

The Tailteann Games (claimed foundation 1829 BC), held near modern Telltown in Ireland, this thirty-day meeting included foot races and stone-throwing events

Other peoples, such as the Celts, Teutons and Goths who succeeded the Romans, loved athletic contests. However, these were often related to combat training. In the Middle Ages the sons of noblemen would be trained in running, leaping and wrestling, in summation to riding, jousting and arms-training. Competitions between rivals and friends may have been common on both official and unofficial grounds.

Annually, from 1796-1798, L'Olympiade de la Républíque was held in revolutionary France, and is an early forerunner to the modern summer Olympic Games. The premier event of this competition was a footrace, but several ancient Greek disciplines were also on display. The 1796 Olympiade also marks the debut of the metric system into sport.

In the 19th century the conventional organization of the modern events quickened - in France, Germany, and Great Britain in particular. This included the incorporation of regular sports and practice into school regimes. The Royal Military College, Sandhurst has claimed to be the first to adopt this in 1812 and 1825, but without any supporting evidence. The earliest recorded meeting was coordinated at Shrewsbury, Shropshire in 1840 by the Royal Shrewsbury School Hunt. There are details of the meeting in a series of letters written 60 years later by C.T. Robinson, who was a student there from 1838 to 1841. The Royal Military Academy at Woolwich held an organised competition in 1849, but the first regular series of meetings was held by Exeter College, Oxford from 1850.

Modern athletic events are commonly organized around a 400 metre running track on which most of the running events take place. Field events (vaulting, jumping, and throwing) often take place on the infield, inside the track.

Athletics was included in the first modern Olympic Games in 1896 and has made their backbone ever since. Women were first allowed to take part in track and field events in the 1928 Olympics.

An international organization, the International Amateur Athletics Federation (IAAF), was established in 1912; it adopted its current name, the International Association of Athletics Federations, in 2001. The IAAF founded separate outdoor World Championships in 1983. There are a number of regional games as well, such as the European Championships, the Pan-American Games, and the Commonwealth Games. In addition there is a professional Golden League circuit, gathering in the IAAF World

Athletics Final, and indoor championships such as the World Indoor Championships. The sport has a very high profile during major championships, particularly the Olympics, but otherwise is less popular.

The AAU (Amateur Athletic Union) was the governing body in the United States until it collapsed under pressure from advancing professionalism in the late 1970s. A new governing body called The Athletics Congress (TAC) was constituted. It was later renamed USA Track & Field (USATF or USA T&F). An additional, less structured organization, the Road Runners Club of America (RRCA), also exists in the United States to encourage road racing.

In modern times, athletes can receive money for racing, putting an end to the so-called "amateurism" that existed before.

Events

There are other versions besides the ones listed below, but races of strange length (e.g. 300 m) are run much less often. The unusual races are typically held during indoor season because of the shorter 200 m indoor track.

With the exception of the mile run, races based on majestic distances are rarely run on the track any longer since most tracks have been changed from a quarter mile (402.3 m) to 400 m; almost all record keeping for imperial distances has been ceased. However, the IAAF record book still includes the mile world record (currently held by Hicham El Guerrouj of Morocco for men and Svetlana Masterkova of Russia for women) because of its worldwide historic significance.

Men and women do not contend against each other, though they may sometimes run in the same races due to time constraints at high school meets. Women generally run the same distances as men though hurdles and steeplechase barriers are lower and the weights of the shot, discus, javelin and hammer are less.

Track and Field is the most approachable sport for anybody to take part in. It only takes two people to have a race, or one can simply race a stopwatch. In events called All Comers Track Meets, anybody who wishes to participate is welcome; there is no exclusion because you do not have a team or even equipment. Most such meets are low cost or even free. While races are usually seeded based on the entrant's anticipated level of ability, the most elite of athletes can and do use these meets as training grounds.

Running and Racewalking Events: Running events carried on a track (generally 400 metres, except indoors):

Fig. Sprint

Sprints are events up to and including the 400 metres. Events ordinarily contested are:

- 60 metres (indoors only)
- 100 metres
- 200 metres
- 400 metres

Middle Distance Events are events longer than sprints and up to 3000 metres. Events ordinarily contested are:

- 800 metres
- 1000 metres
- 1500 metres
- One mile
- 3000 metres
- 3000 metres steeplechase

Long Distance Events are events over 3000 metres. Events ordinarily contested are:

- 5000 metres
- 10,000 metres

Hurdles events require the runner to run over evenly spaced barriers during the race. Events commonly contested are:

- 60 metres hurdles (indoors only)
- 100 metres hurdles (women)

- 110 metres hurdles (men)
- 400 metres hurdles

Relay races are events in which four athletes take part as a team, passing a metal baton in between. Events commonly contended are:

- 4 × 100 metres relay
- 4 × 400 metres relay

Some events, such as medley relays, are rarely run except at large relay carnivals. Typical medley relays include:

Sprint Medley Relay (SMR): the four legs are 400 metres, two 200 metre legs, 800 metres; or alternately 200 metres, two 100 metre legs, 400 metres.

Distance Medley Relay (DMR): the four legs are 1200 metres, 400 metres, 800 metres, 1600 metres.

Road Races are events organized on open roads, sometimes finishing on a track. Events ordinarily contested are:

- 10 km
- 20 km
- Half marathon (21.0975 km)
- Marathon (42.195 km). The marathon is the only usual road-racing distance run in major international athletics championships, such as the Olympics.

Racewalking may be contested on either the track or on open roads. Events commonly contested are:

- 10 km
- 20 km
- 50 km

Field Events:

Throwing Events

- Discus Throw
- Hammer Throw
- Javelin Throw
- Shot Put

Fig. High Jump

Jumping Events

- High Jump
- Pole Vault
- Long Jump
- Triple Jump

Fig: Triple Jump

Multiple Event Competitions

Multiple event competitions include events from both the track (running) and field events.

Pentathlon: the Pentathlon includes the following five events:

- High Hurdles (110 metres for men, 100 metres for women)
- Shot Put
- Long Jump
- High Jump
- Middle distance (1500 metres for men, 800 metres for women)

Heptathlon: the Heptathlon includes the following seven events:

Outdoors (usually only women):

- 100 metre high hurdles
- High Jump
- Shot Put
- 200 metres
- Long Jump
- Javelin Throw
- 800 metres

Indoors (commonly only men):

- 60 metres
- Long Jump
- Shot Put
- High Jump
- 60 metres hurdles
- Pole Vault
- 1000 metres

Decathlon: the Decathlon includes the following ten events:

- 100 metres
- Long Jump
- Shot Put
- High Jump
- 400 metres
- 110 metre high hurdles

- Discus
- Pole Vault
- Javelin
- 1500 metres

Fig. High Jump

Fig. Discus Throw

Fig. Relay race

Fig. Hurdle Race

Fig. Hammer Throw

Fig. Javelin Throw

Fig. Shot put

Organization and Tournaments

Top-level competition in athletics is still restricted to the amateur athlete, though the definition of "amateur" continues to evolve. The IAAF over time has cut down its definition of an amateur athlete to the simplest possible terms: "An amateur is one who abides by the eligibility rules of the IAAF" is the complete rule, allowing for alteration whenever the federation alters any of its other rules.

Until the 1980s the IAAF undertook to keep its athletes from profiting financially from the sport. This was always a conflict, however, as star athletes and eager meet promoters managed to circumvent the rules. So did entire nations: eastern European countries provided government aid to athletes, other countries boosted military personnel to concentrate on track-and-field training, and U.S. athletes got college scholarships in return for their skills. Financial aid was made acceptable in the 1980s through the use of trust funds. Athletes were allowed to accept payment for appearing in competition, for doing well, for appearing in television commercials, or for other sport-related activities. The money was placed in trust; training expenses could be charged to the fund, with the remaining funds, if any, going to the athlete on retirement from competition. Some athletes were reported to have made several hundred thousand dollars a year under the new system.

The chief functions of the IAAF are to assert a set of conventions that are consistent throughout the world, to approve world records for outdoor and indoor competition, and to promote international athletics. While continuing to administer athletics competition in the Olympic

Games, the IAAF began its own quadrennial World Championships in 1983, constituted World Cup competitions, and established walking, cross-country, marathon and other road races, indoor track and field, and junior competitions.

Each IAAF member nation has its own set of rules and maintains its own set of records in line with international guidelines. The amateur athletic federations of individual countries conduct their own national championships.

In the United States, for instance, The Athletic Congress (TAC) alone has the power to select international teams (except for the Olympic team, which is under the legal power of the United States Olympic Committee), to establish rules, and to accept or reject records. It also conducts the national championships and other competitions. Meets in which involvement is restricted to college or university athletes usually are regulated by the decrees of the National Collegiate Athletic Association (NCAA), National Association of Intercollegiate Athletics (NAIA), or one of two junior (two-year) college groups. Most secondary schools in the United States come under the aegis of the National Federation of State High School Athletic Associations.

The particulars of the conduct of athletics competitions vary with the location and the level and type of meet. To a great level the basic sport has been standardized by the rules of the IAAF. Outdoor track events take place on the 400-metre (about 440-yard) oval running track. Track compositions differ greatly. Once almost all tracks were of natural materials (dirt, clay, cinders, and broken brick being the most common), but all major competition tracks now are made of synthetic materials. The synthetic track provides more consistent and faster footing in all weather conditions. Field event performers also benefit from improved footing; jumpers and javelin throwers perform on the same materials used for synthetic tracks, while the throwers of the shot, discus, and hammer work in circles made of concrete.

Indoor track meets adapt themselves to widely varying and often limiting conditions. Tracks range in size generally from 150 to 200 metres or 160 to 220 yards and have synthetic surfaces over wood. Some tracks have banked curves, others are unbanked. Cross-country running utilizes any terrain that is available—parks, golf courses, and farmland. The prescribed IAAF distance in international races for men is approximately 12,000 meters (7.5 miles) and for women 4,000 meters (2.5 miles). Road events include walking, marathon, and other road runs of widely varying distances

THE GAME

Track Events

Fig: Marathon

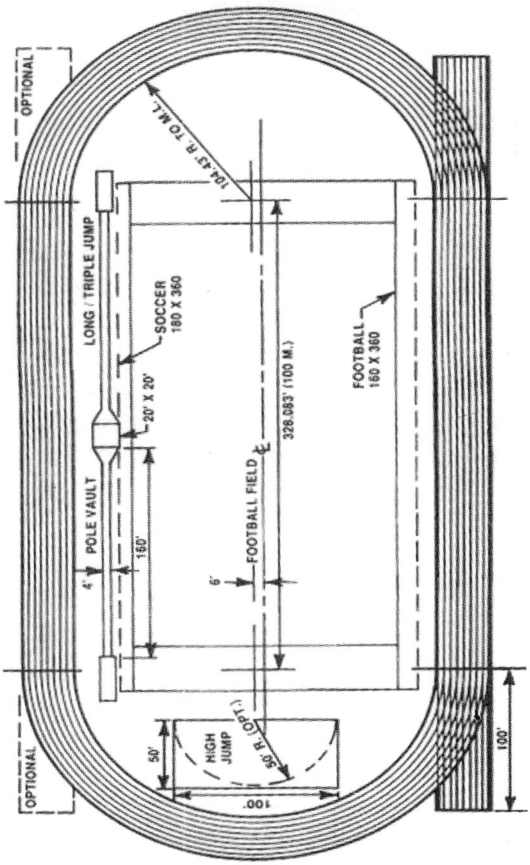

Fig. Track and Measurements

The rules of track athletics or of track events in athletics as observed in most international athletics competitions are set by the Competition Rules of the International Association of Athletics Federations (IAAF). The most recent complete set of rules is the 2008 rules.

Fig. Track Event

Key rules of track events are those regarding starting, running and finishing.

Starting

The start of a race is marked by a white line 5cm wide. In all races that are not run in lanes the start line must be curved, so that all the athletes start the same distance from the finish. Starting blocks must be used for all races up to and including 400 m (including the first leg of the 4 x 200 m and 4 x 400 m) and may not be used for any other race. No part of the starting block may overlap the start line or extend into another lane. All races must be started by the report of the starter's gun or approved starting apparatus fired upwards after he or she has ascertained that athletes are steady and in the correct starting position. An athlete may not touch either the start line or the ground in front of it with his hands or his feet when on his marks. At most international competitions the commands of the starter in his own language, in English or in French, shall, in races up to and including 400 m, be "On your marks" and "Set". When all athletes are "set", the gun must be fired, or an approved starting apparatus must be activated. However, if the starter is not satisfied that all is ready to proceed, the athletes may be called out of the blocks and the process started over.

False start: An athlete, after assuming a final set position, may not commence his starting motion until after receiving the report of the gun, or approved starting apparatus. If, in the judgment of the starter or recallers, he does so any earlier, it is considered a false start. It is deemed a false start if, in the judgment of the starter an athlete fails to comply with the commands "on your marks" or "set" as appropriate after a reasonable time; or an athlete after the command "on your marks" disturbs other athletes in the race through sound or otherwise. Any athlete making a false start must be warned.

Running the Race

In all races run in lanes, each athlete must keep within his allocated lane from start to finish. This also applies to any portion of a race run in lanes. If an athlete leaves the track or steps on the line demarking the track, he should be disqualified. Also, any athlete who jostles or obstructs another athlete, in a way that impedes his progress, should be disqualified from that event. However, if an athlete is pushed or forced by another person to run outside his lane, and if no material advantage is gained, the athlete should not be disqualified.

The Finish

The finish of a race is marked by a white line 5cm wide. The athletes must be placed in the order in which any part of their bodies (i.e. torso, as distinguished from the head, neck, arms, legs, hands or feet) reaches the vertical plane of the nearer edge of the finish line.

Ties between different athletes are resolved as follows: In determining whether there has been a tie in any round for a qualifying position for the next round based on time, a judge (called the chief photo finish judge) must consider the actual time recorded by the athletes to 1/1000th of a second. If the judge decides that there has been a tie, the tying athletes must be placed in the next round or, if that is not practicable, lots must be drawn to determine who must be placed in the next round. In the case of a tie for first place in any final, the referee decides whether it is practicable to arrange for the athletes so tying to compete again. If he decides it is not, the result will stand. Ties in other placings remain.

MAJOR TOURNAMENT

Olympics

The Olympic Games is an international multi-sport event established for both summer and winter games. There have been two generations of the Olympic Games; the first were the Ancient Olympic Games held at Olympia, Greece. The second, known as the Modern Olympic Movement, were first held in 1896, in Athens, Greece. The modern Olympics feature the Summer Games and Winter Games. The

Paralympic and Youth Olympic Games are variations on the Modern Olympic Movement.

ADMINISTRATIVE BODIES

International Amateur Athletic Federation (IAAF)

The International Amateur Athletic Federation was founded in 1912 by 17 national athletic federations who saw the need for a governing authority, for an athletic programme, for standardised technical equipment and world records.

But what was the sport the IAAF was meant to govern? For participants, athletics was about enhancing the quality of life; it was something done for love and other noble principles. This permitted a limited group of athletes to achieve high-level performances by virtue of a privileged social and financial situation.

Yet with the continual evolution of modern society came tremendous enthusiasm for sport. This growing interest and the improvement of individual performances boosted the stature of athletics. Beginning in the 1960s, TV coverage of athletics greatly increased and many companies began to see commercial value in the sport. It became harder to follow the amateur principle in the traditional sense, especially considering the time and resources needed to train and maintain elite athletes. Faced with this commercially demanding world, the IAAF made changes to benefit the athlete, spectators and all other members of the "Athletics Family".

In 1982, the IAAF abandoned the traditional concept of amateurism and in 1985 created trust funds for athletes. The way to high performance was opened to larger groups of extremely talented athletes. Steadily, there has been a change from the so-called amateurs to financially motivated and secure athletes at the highest levels and this development has continued with the introduction of the IAAF Competition Awards in 1997, which offered prize money to successful athletes for the first time in the history of IAAF competitions. The development of applied sports sciences, improved equipment and new training and competition techniques, brought even more changes to the sport. Sadly, performance enhancing drugs became more prominent at this time as well, jeopardising the moral fabric of sport as well as the health and lives of young people. The IAAF has subsequently led the sports movement worldwide in the development and application of an extensive anti-doping programme involving testing both in and out of competition.

FAMOUS PLAYERS

Michael Jordan

Jordan was born on Feb. 17, 1963 in Brooklyn, N.Y., the fourth of five children. That spring, the family moved to Wilmington. After playing junior varsity basketball as a high school sophomore, Jordan made the varsity his final two years, starring as a senior and earning a scholarship to North Carolina.

Jordan is recognized as an icon. Tall, dark and bald, he is the first man of the planet. The former Chicago Bulls guard had the rarest of gifts, the ability to transcend his sport. His fame and skill were intertwined, much as they were in earlier generations for a select few, such as the Babe and Ali.

He won the regular-season MVP five times and the Finals MVP six times. In 1991 and 1992, he became the only player to win back-to-back regular season and Finals MVP awards, and in 1993 he became the first to win the Finals MVP three consecutive years, a feat he repeated from 1996-98.

On Jan. 13, 1999, Jordan, at 35, retired - again. This time, his Airness said he was at peace with his decision and that it appeared to be for good. "I know from a career standpoint I have accomplished everything that I could as an individual," he said.

Michael Johnson

Johnson was born Sept. 13, 1967 in Dallas, the youngest of five children. His parents, Paul Johnson Sr., a truck driver, and Ruby Johnson, an elementary school teacher, emphasized education, and Michael was regularly placed in classes for gifted children.

He started with the 200, and unlike most runners, he went up in distance, not down. With Georgia 1996 on his mind, he announced his intention of becoming the first man to win both the 200 and 400 at the same Olympics. Call it a double dare of the highest order. Especially coming from a man who had failed in his two previous Olympics; once because of injury, once because of illness.

But Johnson came with the proper credentials, the No. 1 ranking in the world five times in the 400 and four times in the 200 in the 1990s. He was the first man to break both 44 seconds in the 400 and 20 seconds in the 200.

He warmed up for the 1996 Atlanta Olympics with two dress rehearsals. He won both titles at the U.S. national championships in June 1995 in Sacramento, Calif., becoming the first man to take both races at a major meet since Maxie Long at the U.S. championships in 1899.

In June 1997, Johnson's 58-final, eight-year winning streak in the 400 ended in Paris as he finished fifth, with Antonio Pettigrew winning the race. But Johnson came back that summer to win his fifth individual World Championships gold, taking the 400.

Anju Bobby George

Anju Bobby George's emergence as a champion long-jumper has given a fillip to the otherwise dreary world of Indian athletics. Anju was born on April 19, 1977, in Changanassery in Kerala.

Though Anju started with Heptathlon, she later began to concentrate on her jump events, triple and long jump. In 1999 Anju set the national record for triple jump in the Bangalore Federation Cup and two years later she bettered her own record in long jump to 6.74 m in the National Circuit Meet at Thiruvananthapuram.

Anju made history when she won the bronze medal in Long Jump at the 2003 World Championships in Athletics in Paris, thus becoming the first Indian athlete ever to win a medal in a World Championships. After such a commendable show, expectations were high about an Olympic medal, but even a personal best of 6.83 m at the 2004 Olympic Games at Athens could bring her the sixth position.

P. T. Usha

P. T. Usha, arguably the greatest ever Indian women athlete, inspired generations of young Indian girls to seek glory in track and field and for a long time, was synonymous with Indian athletics. Usha, born on June 27, 1964, was nicknamed Payyoli Express for her dazzling runs. In 1978, at the age of 14, P. T. Usha shot into limelight as a junior athlete in National Inter State meet at Kollam. Her budding talent was noticed by Coach O. M. Nambiar and under his tutelage Usha went to achieve greater success.

After winning silver medals in the 100 m and the 200 m events in the 1982 New Delhi Asiad, a year later at the Asian Track and Field Championship in Kuwait Usha clinched gold in the 400 m with a new Asian record.

Milkha Singh

He won the 200 and 400 meters events in the 1956 Tokyo Asian Games; won the 400 meters at the 1958 Cardiff Commonwealth Games; broke the Olympic record for the 400 meters event while finishing fourth in the 1960 Rome Olympic Games

Milkha Singh is undoubtedly the greatest athlete India has ever produced. Despite losing to his parents to the Partition mayhem of 1947, Milkha went on to earn the sobriquet of "The Flying Sikh" by dint of hard work and sheer determination. Milkha Singh shot into limelight during the National Games at Patiala in 1956 and two years later he broke the 200 and 400 meters record in the National games at Cuttack. The same year, at the Tokyo Asiad, Milkha continued with his record-breaking spree while winning the 200 and 400 meters title.

In the 1958 Cardiff Commonwealth Games (then known as the Empire Games), Milkha won the 400 meters, his favourite event, in 46.6 seconds beating celebrated South African sprinter Malcolm Spence. Thus Milkha was on a roll, beating some of the top athletes in the European circuit and peaking nicely for the 1960 Rome Olympic Games.

When the big occasion finally arrived, the 400 meter event saw some of the greatest athletes producing dazzling runs even at the qualifying stage. In the final, Milkha took off the blocks with great speed and led the pack for 200 meters but then decided to slow down to preserve energy for the final burst. But gradually he was overtaken by other runners and despite giving his best shot Milkha couldn't erase the deficit in the last 100 meters. The sheer quality of that fateful race can be gauged from the fact that the winner Ottis Davis and Kaufman broke existing world record while Malcolm Spence and Milkha Singh broke the Olympic record in finishing third and fourth.

REFERENCES

Alter, S.: *Science of Flexibility*, 2nd edn, Human Kinetics, Champaign, IL, 1996.

Alter, S.: *Sport Stretch*, Human Kinetics, Champaign, IL, 1998.

Dintiman, G. and Ward, R.: *Sport Speed*, Leisure Press, Champaign, IL, 1988.

Ellison, D.: *Performance Stretching*, Human Kinetics, Champaign, IL, 1999.

Goldberg, B. (ed.): *Sports and Exercise for Children with Chronic Health Conditions*, Human Kinetics, Champaign, IL, 1995.

Micheli, L.J. (ed.): *Clinics in Sports Medicine: The Young Athlete*, W.B. Saunders, Philadelphia, PA, 1995.

Newsholme, E., Leech, T. and Duester, G.: *Keep on Running*, John Wiley & Sons, Chichester, UK, 1994.

Reaburn, P. and Jenkins, D.: *Training for Speed and Endurance*, Allen & Unwin, Sydney, 1996.

Rowland, T.W.: *Developmental Exercise Physiology*, Human Kinetics, Champaign, IL, 1996.

3

Baseball

Baseball is a game played between two teams of nine players each. The game is divided up into nine innings, each separated into two halves. In the top half of the inning, the players of one team successively come to bat and attempt to score runs, while the other team plays in the field and attempt to stop the revolting team from scoring. In the bottom half, the teams switch places. The team with more runs at the end of nine innings is the winner of the game.

The game is played on a diamond-shaped playing field, the four corners of the diamond being conceived by home plate, first base, second base and third base. In the middle of the infield is the pitcher's mound, where the pitcher stands to pitch the ball to the batter. The area on the far side of the infield, bordered by the first and third baselines, is called the outfield.

During an inning, the pitcher of the protective team throws the ball toward member of the offensive team presently in batting position at home plate. The batter attempts to hit the ball with the bat to a location out of the range of the defensive players in the field and run around the bases. If he is able to round the bases and come back to home plate, he scores a run. But if the ball is captured, or can be thrown to first base before he arrives at the base, then the batter is out. A batter is also put out if he strikes out, or fails to hit the baseball three times after three good pitches. The revolting team's time at bat is over when it gets three outs.

Each cycle that is played this way (where each team has played on discourtesy for three outs and on defense for three outs) is denoted to as an inning. The game is generally concluded at the end of a specified number of innings, at which point the winner is the team with the most runs scored. In most baseball leagues, a winning team must be announced (no ties can exist). This extra time scenario is adverted to as "extra innings", which involves the two teams playing more innings than normal, with the game being accomplished when one team scores more runs in one of the innings than the other team.

Contrary to most other sports, baseball exists outside of time, there is no clock to control game play or judge a player's performance. Nevertheless, a dizzying array of statistics record almost every aspect of the game in astonishing particulars, and permits fans (and team managers) to equate the performance of one player against another.

HISTORY

The question of the origins of baseball has been the subject of debate and disputation for more than a century. Baseball (and softball), as well as the other advanced bat, ball and running games, cricket and rounders, improved from earlier folk games.

Throughout the early part of the 19th century, small towns constituted teams, and baseball clubs were constituted in larger cities. In 1845, Alexander Cartwright desired to formalize a list of decrees by which all teams could play. Much of that original code is still in place today. Though popular legend says that the game was contrived by Abner Doubleday, baseball's true father was Cartwright.

The first recorded baseball competition took place a year later, in 1846. Cartwright and his Knickerbocker Base Ball Club of New York City lost to the New York Baseball Club in a game at the Elysian Fields, in Hoboken, New Jersey. These amateur games turned more frequent and more popular. In 1857, a rule of amateur teams was called to discuss decrees and other matters. Twenty five teams from the northeast sent delegates. The following year, they constituted the National Association of Base Ball Players, the first organized baseball league. In its first year of operation, the league supported itself by once in a while charging fans for admission. The future looked very bright.

Though the roots of baseball are English, alike games have also been played in other parts of the world. Oina is a Romanian ball sport, alike in some ways to baseball. Russia had a bat and ball game called Lapta since the 1300s. Germans played a game called Schlagball, which was alike to rounders. A "bowler" threw a ball to a "striker," who hit it with a club and then tried to run around a circuit of bases without getting hit with the ball by a defender.

Americans played a version of the English game rounders in the early 1800s which they called "Town Ball". In fact, early forms of baseball had a number of names, including "Base Ball", "Goal Ball", "Round Ball", "Fletch-catch", and merely "Base". In at lowest one version of the game, teams pitched to themselves, runners went around the bases in the opposite direction of today's game, and players could be put out by being hit with the ball like in Schlagball. Like today, however, it was three strikes and you're out.Few particulars of how the advanced games evolved from earlier folk games are acknowledged. Some think that varied folk games resulted in a game called town ball, from which baseball was finally born. Others conceive that town ball was independent from baseball.

The History of baseball in the United States can be traced to the 18th century, when amateurs played a baseball-like game by their own informal conventions using temporary gear. The popularity of the sport inspired the semi and amply professional baseball clubs in the 1860s. By the following decade, American newspapers were adverting to baseball as the "National Pastime" or the "National Game." The first attempt at constituting a "major league" raised the National Association, which endured from 1871 to 1875. In response to the shortcomings of the National Association, the current National League was constituted in 1876. After a series of rival leagues were organised but failed, the current American league, developing from the minor Western League of 1893, was constituted in 1901.

In the former part of the 20th century, known as the "dead-ball era," baseball rules and gear favored the "inside game" and the game was played more violently and aggressively than it is today. This period finished in the 1920s with several alterations that gave advantages to hitters. In the largest parks, the outfield fences were brought closer to the infield. In addition, the strict enforcement of new rules regulating the size, shape and building of the ball caused it to travel farther when hit.

The first professional black baseball club, the Cuban Giants, was organized in 1885. Consequent professional black baseball clubs played each other independently, without an official league to organize the sport. Rube Foster, a past ballplayer, founded the Negro National League in 1920. A second league, the Eastern Colored League, was constituted in 1923. These were known as the Negro Leagues. The Negro National League did well until 1930, but folded during the great depression.

From 1942 to 1948 the Negro League World Series was recreated. This was the golden era of Negro League baseball, a time when it produced some of its greatest stars. In 1947, Jackie Robinson signed a contract with the Brooklyn Dodgers, breaking the colour barrier that had prevented talented African American players from getting in the white-only major leagues. Though the transformation wasn't instantaneous, baseball has since become fully amalgamated. In 1948, the Negro Leagues faced fiscal difficulties that effectively stopped their existence.

Pitchers dominated the game in the 1960s and early 1970s. In 1973 the assigned hitter (DH) decree was adopted by the American League, while in the National League pitchers still bat for themselves to this day. The DH rule now comprises the elementary conflict between the two leagues. During the late 1960s, the Baseball Players Union became much stronger and differences between owners and the players' union led to major work stoppages in 1972, 1981, and 1994. The 1994 baseball strike led to the cancellation of the World Series, and wasn't settled until the spring of 1995. In the wake of the 1994 players' strike, functions that had been administered individually by the two major leagues' administrations were combined under the rubric of Major League Baseball.

THE GAME

Players

Baseball is a bat-and-ball sport played between two teams of nine players each. Team all of the time includes a pitcher, who throws the ball with his full durability and accuracy. Each team is directed by a captain, who's responsible for making decisions.

Umpires

In baseball, the umpire is the person charged with officiating the game, including commencement and closing the game, implementing the decrees of the game and the grounds, making judgment calls on plays, and meting out discipline.

There are total of four umpires on the ground.

In a game officiated by two or more umpires, the umpire-in-chief (generally referred to as the "plate umpire") is the umpire who's placed behind home plate. This umpire calls balls and strikes, calls fair balls and foul balls short of first/third base and makes most calls regarding the batter or pertaining baserunners near home plate.

Other umpires are called base umpires and are generally posted near the bases. When two umpires are used, the second umpire is merely the base umpire. This umpire will make most calls regarding runners on the bases and nearby plays, as well as in the middle of the outfield. When three umpires are used, the second umpire is called the first-base umpire and the third umpire is called the third-base umpire, even though they may move to dissimilar places on the field as the play necessitates.

When four umpires are used, each umpire is named for the base at which he is stationed. Occasionally a league will allow six umpires; the extra two are placed along the outfield foul lines are called the left-field and right-field umpires. In Major League Baseball, outfield umpires are only used during the post-season playoffs and World Series and the All-Star Game. Rulings on catches of batted balls are usually made by the umpire closest to the play.

Playing Field

The baseball is played in a diamond shaped ground. The Infield is a 90-foot square and the Outfield is the space between the two foul poles/lines.

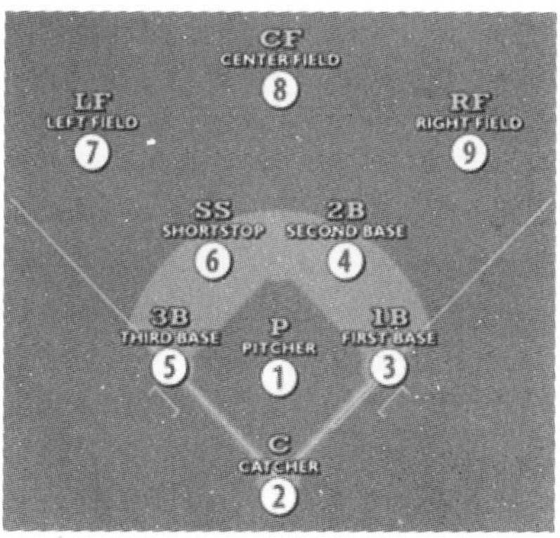

Fig. Baseball Ground

The beginning point for much of the action on the field is home plate, which is an uneven white rubber pentagon 17 inches by 8 1/2 by 12 by 12 by 8 1/2 inches. Next to each of the two parallel 8 1/2-inch sides is a batter's box. The point of home plate where the two 12-inch sides meet at right angles, is at one corner of a ninety-foot square. The other three corners of the square, in counterclockwise order from home plate, are addressed first base, second base, and third base. Three canva.. bags fifteen inches (38 cm) square mark the three bases. These three bags along with home plate form the four bases at the corners of the infield.

A subtlety about the bases is that first and third base, along with home plate, lie completely within the ninety-foot square made by the four bases. They are placed this way to help the umpires, as any ball hitting those bases must inevitably be in fair territory. Home plate has its special shape in order to help the plate umpire adjudicate whether a pitch is over the plate or not, that is, whether it might be in the strike zone. The second base bag, which is fully within fair territory, is based so that its center coincides exactly with the corner or "point" of the ninety-foot infield square. Thus, though the "points" of the bases are 90 feet aside, the physical distance between each successive pair of base markers is closer to 88 feet.

The lines from home plate to first and third bases extend to the closest fence, stand or other obstruction and are addressed the foul lines. The part of the playing field between (and including) the foul lines is fair territory; the rest is foul territory. Thc area in the vicinity of the square constituted by the bases is called the infield; fair territory outside the infield is known as the outfield. Most baseball fields are confined with a fence that marks the outer border of the outfield. The fence is generally set at a distance ranging from 300 to 410 feet (90 to 125 m) from home plate. Most professional and college baseball fields have a right and left foul pole. These poles are at the crossing of the foul lines and the respective ends of the outfield fence. Another common feature of baseball fields is a cautionary track, a narrow dirt path that follows the outer edge of the outfield at the fence that serves to warn outfielders chasing a long fly ball of their proximity to the wall.

Home Plate: Homeplate is the place from where the batting is done. And the pitching is done from the pitching rubber which is 60 feet and 6 inches away from the homeplate.The dimensions and the ordinances are given for distances between home and the bases, and the foul lines in the outfield.

- A 17 × 17 inch plate that sets at the center of a 26-foot diameter, making up the home plate area. From here, players must cover a 90-foot sprint to reach each sequential base.
- Beginning from home plate, foul lines must extend at least 325 feet to where a pole marker stands. These poles can be set farther, but the minimum must be met. At the pole's halfway point, the wall or fence must be 400 feet from home plate.

Bases: There are total of three bases on the field. Each one of it is a 15 inch square, and 90 feet aside from each other with 13 foot surrounding arcs.

Pitching: The pitcher faces the catcher and throws the ball to its utmost speed. The ball is pitched towards the plate using the throwing arm. All of pitchers momentum went right away towards the plate.

Fielding: There are 9 fielding positions on the field. Each position conventionally has an connected number (from 1 to 9) which is used to score putouts.

For instance: If the third baseman fields a ball and throws it to first, it is registered as a 5-3 out. A double play where the second baseman fields, throws to the shortstop at second base, who throws to the first baseman is registered as a 4-6-3 double play.

Scoring the Runs: In baseball, a run is scored when a player approaches safely around first, second and third base and comebacks safely to home plate, touching the bases in that order, before three outs are recorded. A player may score by hitting a home run or by any combination of plays that puts him safely "aboard" (that is, on first, second, or third) as a runner and afterward brings him home. The object of the game is for a team to score more runs than its opposition.

In baseball statistics, a player who approaches around all the bases to score is credited with a run (R), occasionally adverted to as a "run scored." While runs scored is regarded a important individual batting statistic, it is considered as less significant than runs batted in (RBIs)-superiority in the latter, for example, is one of the elements of the extraordinary batting accomplishment known as the Triple Crown. Both individual runs scored and runs batted in are heavily context-dependent; for a more sophisticated judgement of a player's share towards acquiring runs for his team, see runs made.

Fig. Helmet

Fig. Baseball & Bat

Batting: In baseball, batting is the act of facing the opposing pitcher and attempting to make offense for one's team. A batter or hitter is a person whose turn it is to face the pitcher. The goals of batters are to make runs, but the methods and schemes they use to do so vary. The three main goals of batters are to become a baserunner, drive runners home, or advance runners along the bases for others to drive home.

In general, batters try to get hits. They may also draw a walk if they do not obtain a pitch they can hit decently. In cases when there is a runner on third and fewer than two outs, they can effort to hit a sacrifice fly to drive the runner in. When there are fewer than two outs and runners on base, they can try to sacrifice bunt. They might even be hit by a pitch, reach on an error or-if first is vacate or there are two outs-on a dropped third strike.

The defense tries to get the batter out. The pitcher's chief role in this is to throw the ball in such a way that he or she either strikes out or can't hit it flawlessly so that the defense can get him or her out.

Uniform: A baseball uniform is a type of uniform worn by baseball players, and occasionally by non-playing personnel, such as managers and coaches. It is worn to indicate the person's role in the game and, through use of logos and colours, to distinguish the two teams and officials. Most baseball uniforms include the player's name and uniform number, generally on the back (and sometimes the front) of the shirt, which helps the viewers distinguish the different players within a team. Uniform items usually include shirts, pants, shoes, socks, caps, and gloves.

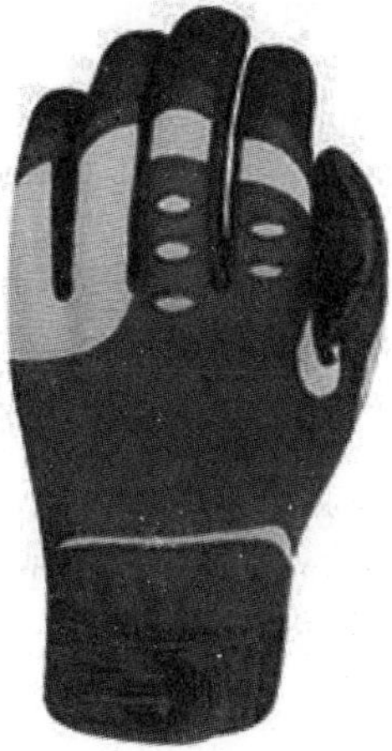

Fig. Baseball Glove

MAJOR TOURNAMENTS

Major League Baseball

Major League Baseball (MLB) is the highest level of play in North American professional baseball compiled of 30 teams. More specifically, Major League Baseball refers to the organization that operates the National League and the American League, by means of a joint organizational structure that has existed between them since 1903. Each season comprises of 162 games, which usually commences on the first Sunday in April and ends on the first Sunday in October, with the playoffs played in October and occasionally in early November. The same rules and ordinances are played between the two leagues with one exception: the American League operates under the assigned Hitter convention, while the National League doesn't. Utilization of the DH Rule in Interleague play, the All-Star and World Series games are ascertained by the home team's league rules. In 2000, two leagues were formally disbanded as separate legal entities with all rights and functions consolidated in the commissioner's office. MLB effectively operates as a single league and as such it comprises one of the major professional sports leagues of North America.

MLB is operated by the Major League Baseball Constitution that has gone through several incarnations since 1876 with the most recent alterations being made in 2005.

Under the direction of Commissioner of Baseball, Major League Baseball hires and asserts the sport's umpiring crews, and negotiates marketing, labor, and television contracts. As is the case for most North American sports leagues, the "closed shop" aspect of MLB effectively forbids the yearly promotion and relegation of teams into and out of the Major League by virtue of their performance. Private enterprises is largely funded by Major league Baseball, but also partly funded straightaway by public taxes. Major League Baseball preserves a unique, controlling relationship over the sport, including most aspects of minor league baseball. This is due in large part to a 1922 U.S. Supreme Court ruling in Federal Baseball Club v. National League, which held that baseball is not interstate commerce and therefore not subject to federal antitrust law. This ruling has been weakened only slightly in consequent years.

Minor League Baseball

Minor league baseball is a hierarchy of professional baseball leagues in North America that contend at levels below that of Major League Baseball. All of the minor leagues are controlled as autonomous businesses, and many are members of Minor League Baseball, an umbrella organisation for leagues that have agreements to operate as affiliates of Major League Baseball. Various leagues, known as autonomous leagues, don't have any links to Major League Baseball, and thus are not members of "organized baseball." Many alumni of independent baseball, however, have worked their way to the Major Leagues and many former MLBers play in independent baseball.

Each league affiliated with Minor League Baseball comprises of teams that commonly are independently owned and controlled, but always, with the exception of the Mexican League, right away "affiliated" with (and at times named after) one Major League team through a standardised Player Development Contract (PDC). Major and Minor League teams may enter into a PDC for a two- or four-year term and may reaffiliate at the expiration of a PDC term, although many relationships are revived and endure for extended time periods. For instance, the Omaha Royals (concisely renamed the Omaha Golden Spikes from 1999-2001, but altered back to Royals in 2002) have been the Class AAA affiliate of the Kansas City Royals since the Royals united the American League in 1969, but the Columbus Clippers altered affiliations for the 2007 season from the New York Yankees to the Washington Nationals. A small number of minor league teams are directly owned by their Major League parent club, such as the Springfield Cardinals, possessed by the St. Louis Cardinals, and all of the Atlanta Braves' affiliates except for the Myrtle Beach Pelicans. Minor League teams that are possessed right away by the Major League Club don't have PDCs with each other and are not component of the reaffiliation shuffles that happen every other year. The aim of the system is to prepare players available to play in the Major Leagues on demand.

World Baseball Classic

The WBC is the first international baseball tournament for national teams to feature professional players from the major leagues of North America and Japan (thus the first real "World" Series); the Summer Olympics have on a regular basis featured college and minor-league players because the Games battle with the major league seasons in both domains, and the Baseball World Cup historically hasn't had major leaguers participate. In addition to furnishing a format for the best baseball players in the world to compete against one another while representing their home countries, the World Baseball Classic was made in order to further promote the game around the globe.

The tournament was declared in May 2005. Major League Baseball (MLB) had been trying to create such a tournament for at least two years; negotiations with the Major League Baseball Players Association (MLBPA)-the players' union-and with the team owners had held the plan back. Owners, notably New York Yankees owner George Steinbrenner, had been interested about their star players being wounded in international play before the commencement of spring training, and the professional season.

Tara Sawyer Memorial Tournament

Those who have played in TSM tournament before understand how special this tournament isn'tt only to the Sawyer Family, but to each team that takes part and each player that gets the prestigious Barnabas Award.

Yearly more than 120 youth baseball teams from surrounding states convene in North Texas for the Tara Sawyer Classic. With an average of twelve players per team, coaches, admirers and fans, thousands of people are involved in this weekend-long event. More than just your average baseball tourney, the Tara Sawyer Classic incorporates family-friendly amusement through a Saturday night "chief Event", raffles, auctions, children's entertainment and more.

ACC Baseball Tournament

The ACC Baseball Tournament is the conference championship tournament in baseball for the Atlantic Coast Conference (ACC). It is a two-group round robin tournament with the winners of each group facing each other in a one-game match for the championship. The championship tournament is traditionally held in Jacksonville, Florida at the Baseball Grounds of Jacksonville.

Southland Conference Baseball Tournament

The Southland Conference Baseball Tournament is an eight team double-elimination tournament held every year at different locations in the Southland Conference region. The eight teams with the best conference record at the end of the regular season earn berths in the tournament. The winner gets an automatic bid to the NCAA Division I Baseball Tournament.

The Southland Conference tournament commenced in 1964. From 1964 through 1966 the tournament comprised of three teams. In 1967 and 1968 the tournament expanded to a four team double-elimination tournament. From 1969 until 1992 the Southland Conference did not have a baseball tournament.

In 1993 the conference began holding a baseball tournament again. From 1993 through 1995, the tournament was a four team double-elimination tournament. In 1996 it expanded to become a six team double-elimination tournament and stayed that way until 2007. In 2008, the tournament once again expanded and became an eight team double-elimination tournament.

The Mountain West Conference Baseball Tournament

The Mountain West Conference Baseball Tournament is a six team double-elimination tournament held yearly at varied locations in the Mountain West Conference region. The six teams with the best conference record at the end of the regular season earn berths in the tournament. The winner incurs an automatic bid to the NCAA Division I Baseball Tournament.

ADMINISTRATIVE BODIES

The International Baseball Federation

The International Baseball Federation (IBAF) is the worldwide regulating body for the sport of baseball. It approves play between teams sponsored by the national baseball federations of member countries through competition tournaments including the Baseball World Cup, the World Baseball Classic (in conjunction with Major League Baseball), the Intercontinental Cup, and the Olympic baseball tournament (in conjunction with the International Olympic Committee). Its headquarters are in Lausanne, Switzerland.

IBAF was established in 1938. It changed its name several times in its history - in 1944 it took on the official name Federación Internacional de Béisbol Amateur (FIBA), in 1973 it spawned the rival Federación Mundial de Béisbol Amateur (FEMBA), which united back with FIBA in 1976 under the name International Baseball Association (AINBA), altering the official acronym to IBA in 1984, before coming back to its original name and abbreviation in 2000.

Colleyville Baseball Association

Colleyville Baseball Association is a non-profit organization dedicated to offering the administrative body for youth baseball between the ages of 3 to 14 in which players are grouped into leagues for the Colleyville and Grapevine-Colleyville autonomous School District. The individual age appropriate leagues are designed to provide organized baseball activities focusing on individual instruction and teamwork in a positive, constructive and fun environment. CBA considers that if you teach young people to play by the rules, they'll learn to live by the decrees.

The leagues are designed to help young people develop into better adults through engagement in organized, managed competitive athletics. Sportsmanship, teamwork, self reliance, and self-discipline are some of the positive characteristics that are learned, along with how to win and how to accept defeat, by involvement in organized league play. The Association (known as CBA) offers a variety of programs for inexperienced players to seasoned veterans looking for a competitive environment.

George Khoury Association of Baseball League

The Khoury Association is a non-profit, non- denominational organization of affiliated circuits and leagues, using a hub system of control and administration. The Association Is configured to administer anything from one (1) four-team league to a network of leagues within a 125-mile radius of a large town or city serving as the network hub, however, the Association is adaptable enough to operate larger circuits, such as State or territorial.

FAMOUS PLAYERS

Honus Wagner

Johannes Peter "Honus" Wagner was born on February 24, 1874 and dies on December 6, 1955, nicknamed "The Flying Dutchman" due to his superb speed and German heritage, was an American Major League Baseball shortstop who played in the NL from 1897 to 1917, almost exclusively for the Pittsburgh Pirates.

In 1936, the Baseball Hall of Fame inducted Wagner as one of the first five members, getting the second-highest vote total behind Ty Cobb and tied with Babe Ruth. Though Cobb is often cited as the grooviest player of the dead-ball era, some contemporaries considered Wagner as the better all-around player, and most baseball historians regard Wagner to be the greatest shortstop ever. Cobb himself called Wagner "maybe the greatest star ever to take the diamond".

Barry Bond

Barry Lamar Bonds was born on July 24, 1964 in Riverside, Californiaand is a Major League Baseball outfielder who is presently a free agent. He is the son of previous major league All-Star Bobby Bonds, the godson of Hall of Famer Willie Mays, the nephew of 1964 Olympian Rosie Bonds, and a remote cousin of Hall of Famer Reggie Jackson. He debuted in the Major Leagues with the Pittsburgh Pirates in 1986 and joined the San Francisco Giants in 1993, where he stayed through 2007. Bonds filed for free agency following the 2007 World Series.

Bonds' achievements place him among the greatest baseball players of all-time. He has a record-setting seven Most Valuable Player awards, including a record-setting four sequential MVPs. He is a fourteen times All-star, eight time gold glove-winner and he holds several Major League Baseball records. He presently holds the all-time Major League Baseball home run record with 762, and is also the all-time career leader in both walks (2,558) and intentional walks (688). He holds several other records, including the single-season Major League record for home runs (73), set in 2001.

Since 2003, Bonds has been a key figure in the Bay Area Laboratory Co-operative (BALCO) scandal. He was under investigation by a federal grand jury regarding his testimony in the BALCO case, and was indicted on perjury and obstacle of justice accuses on November 15, 2007. The indictment alleges that Bonds lied while under oath about his alleged use of steroids.

Charles Bernard Lear

Charles Bernard Lear (born January 23, 1891, in Greencastle, Pennsylvania, died October 31, 1976) was a professional baseball player who played 2 seasons for the Cincinnati Reds of Major League Baseball.

William David Holland

William David Holland (born June 4, 1915 in Varina, North Carolina) is a previous relief pitcher in Major League Baseball who played for the Washington Senators during the 1939 season. Listed at 6'1", 190 lb., he batted and threw left handed.

Daniel Edward Barone

Daniel Edward Barone was born on April 4, 1983, in San Jose, Californiaand is a Major League Baseball pitcher for the Florida Marlins. He was called up on August 10, to become the fifth starting pitcher in the Florida Marlins rotation, filling the vacate spot after Florida sent Byung-Hyun Kim to the Arizona Diamondbacks on waivers. He went to the bullpen when the Diamondbacks released Kim and the Marlins picked him back up. Barone attended Sonoma State University, an NCAA Division II school in Rohnert Park, California. He was an 11th round selection of the Marlins in the 2004 Major League Baseball Draft.

Robert Burns Conley

Robert Burns Conley (born February 1, 1934 in Mousie, Kentucky) is a previous beginning pitcher in Major League Baseball who played shortly for the Philadelphia Phillies during the season. Listed at 6' 1", 188 lb., he batted and threw right-handed.

REFERENCES

Filthy, ed. *Patrick Brown*, no. 1 Spring 2003.

Jolie Solomon, "*Baseball Is a Game of Hits, Runs, Errors and Lyric Poetry*," Wall Street Journal, 4 February 1987.

Ken LaZebnick, "*Opinion," Minneapolis Review of Baseball* 1, no. 4 Fall 1981: 20-21.

Mark Schraf, *Cooperstown Verses* Jefferson NC: MacFarland, 2001.

Mudville Diaries: *A Book of Baseball Memories, collected by Mike Schacht* New York: Avon Books, 1996.

Pig Iron: *Baseball*, ed. Jim Villani and Rose Sayre, no. 9 1982.

Steve Lehman, "*Introduction: The Minneapolis Review of Baseball," Base Paths: The Best of the Minneapolis Review of Basebal*l, ed. Ken LaZebnick and Steve Lehman Dubuque IA: William C. Brown, 1991.

The Best of Spitball: *The Literary Baseball Magazine*, ed. Mike Shannon New York: Pocket Books, 1988.

4

Canoeing

Canoeing is the activity of paddling a canoe for the aim of recreation (also called a float trip), sport, or conveyance. It generally refers solely to using a paddle to propel a canoe with exclusively human muscle power. A kayak is moved using a paddle with two blades where the paddler sits with their legs generally broadened in front of them, whereas canoes are propelled using single- or double-bladed paddles where the paddler - a "canoeist" or "canoer"- is kneeling or sitting on seat or thwart, with their knees bent and their legs more or less beneath them. Kayaks are generally closed-decked boats with a spraydeck, while canoes are generally open boats. There are also open kayaks and closed canoes. Technically, a kayak can be seen as a particular kind of canoe. When exactly a canoe can be called a kayak is hard to determine although, and often arbitrary. Internationally, the term canoeing is used as a generic term for both forms although the terms "paddle sports" or "canoe/kayak" are also used. In North America, however, 'canoeing' generally refers only to canoes, as opposed to both canoes and kayaks. Paddling a kayak is also denoted to as kayaking.

Open canoes may be 'poled' (punted), sailed, 'lined and tracked' (using ropes) or even 'gunnel-bobbed'.

In advanced canoe sport, both canoes and kayaks may be closed-decked. Other than by the minimum competition specifications and seating arrangement it is difficult to distinguish most competition canoes from the equivalent competition kayaks. The most common divergence is that competition kayaks are always seated and paddled with a double-bladed paddle, and competition canoes are usually kneeled and paddled with a single-bladed paddle. Exceptions include Canoe Marathon (in both European and American competitive forms) and sprint (high kneeling position). The most conventional and former canoes didn't have seats;

the paddlers merely kneeled on the bottom of the boat. Recreational canoes and kayaks employ seats and whitewater rodeo and surf variants increasingly employ the use of 'saddles' to give greater boat control under extreme circumstances.

Most canoeing takes place on the rivers and estuaries of the south-west corner, from Perth around to Albany. Sea kayaking is growing in fame along interesting sections of our long coastline.

Further north the climate becomes very hot with the rivers paddleable only after summer cyclones. The distances are vast and many areas are inaccessible. Then there are man-eating crocodiles to watch out for! Only the nearly intrepid and adventurous paddler will want to search the Kimberley, its coast and islands by canoe or kayak.

HISTORY

Since Remote times human beings have been using distinct types of crafts for voyaging through the rivers, lakes and seas.

Searching in the history, the oldest testimony that we find represents a canoe and a paddle, of silver, with more than six thousand years of antiquity, discovered by the English archaeologist Sir Leonard Wooley, in the tomb of the Sumerian King, "en Ur", at the banks of the Eufrates river. With this craft the king could carry out his last trip on the after life river. This motive will repeat along the humankind history, in other civilisations.

On ancient Egyptian drawings appears crafts propelled with paddles. Egyptians, in the pyramids age, piloted the Nile waters aboard narrow boats built with lots of rush, tied with ropes and leather straps. At the peninsula of Yucatan (Central America), in Chichen Itzá, another representation of canoes appears in a thousand hundred fifty year-old BC mural, and at the ruins of Tikal, in the heart of Guatemala, there are bones of 700 BC with engravings that represent canoes.

In the Caribbean coasts, when Christopher Columbus arrived to the American Continent, the Indigenous approached to the three Colon's ships, with boats constructed from a single piece. A big trunk of tree was hollowed with fire, and the tips were sharpened for a better water cutting. These canoes were carried on building and using until the present time.

In the literary field Christopher Columbus is the one who, through his writings, brings in the word "canoe"(Indian canoe) in Europe, and

Garcilaso de La Vega was the one that defined the concept like a craft without cover. On the other hand the English adopted the word canoe for defining this type of crafts in general.

The natives of the costs and rivers of Africa used from remote times the same method of canoes constructing applied by the American Indigenous. The actual origin of the canoe was in the eastern coast of Canada, for this reason is now usually called as "Canadian Canoe". Used by the primitive people of Canada to travel large distances with their goods, or to carry the mail, taking advantage in some cases for the kindness of the waters and on the other hand, overcoming the aggression of rapids and currents. The 'Red Indians' of North America used the canoes as their medium of life, for the transport, hunting, fishing and the war.

In their origins this type of crafts were constructed with hollow trunks of trees or skins of animals, antecedent treated. Afterwards were constructed with wood and bones framework, covered with birch-bark skins and animal's leathers. The colonists, leather's hunters and gold searchers, soon adopted this transport medium for the rivers and lakes of Canada.

In Britain, primitive crafts were evolved in slightly a different way, and called "Coracles". These were made almost round, with a skin covering over a wattle framework.

In Ireland, the "Curraghs" were the forerunners of much advanced canoe constructing techniques, though the shape is practically the same of some of the primitive canoes.

The British also took the idea of canoes in America, and commenced to construct some canoes with varnished wood ribbons, covered up with waterproof canvas, for recreational and touring use.

The current kayak, descend from the "boat of men" (Ka-i-ak) from the Eskimos. Built with bones and skins of animals, practically covered up in its totality and whose uttermost sophistication is achieved in Greenland. Fundamentally used to hunt and to fish. The firsts to know of the Esquimo kayak were the British, who acquainted it to Europe at the end of the IXX century (1890). In the 1840's decade, the kayaking began to function as a sport.

The birth of kayaking as we know nowadays is generally assumed to date from the kayak originated in 1865 by the Scottish John MacGregor, a barrister resident in London. He is the most well known universal traveler in the world of the canoeing. During 1865, MacGregor was dedicated to travel over the British rivers.

For the adjacent years he contracted several trips by lakes and rivers of the Nordic countries and of Central Europe (France, Germany and Switzerland); with his Rob Roy's kayak also arrived to the Red Sea, piloted in the Jordan, in the Suez channel and in the Nile River. He named it "Rob-Roy", in honor to the renowned "Rob-Roy" of the Scottish tribe MacGregor. He conceptualised the idea of light boat, just big enough to carry himself, decked over except for a small hole at the middle of the boat, in which he sat, and moved, by a double-bladed paddle or a small sail.

The kayak "Rob-Roy" has a length of 4 m, a width of 75 cm and its weight is of about 30 Kg. It was built in the conventional method, from a wood framework, covered up with waterproof canvas. John MacGregor, attained such a prestige that he was solicited to visit Paris in 1867 by Napoleon III, so that he organized a regatta in the Sena river with reason of the Universal Exhibition. His book, A Thousand of Miles in the canoe Rob Roy, associates this singular navigator's adventures. At the European continent, the first kayaks appeared in 1890, diffusing in Switzerland and Germany. Used at the commencement for excursionist purposes, and afterwards for competition too.

The first kayaks built in Europe were made in the same way and with the same materials used by the Eskimos. During long time, the "Rob-Roy" was the standard kayak model.

Due to the main purposes were touring and comfort, the kayaks were built with detachable frameworks, which allowed them to be comfortable transported inside a knapsack, and rapidly assembled at the desired place.

Later on, the kayaks were constructed with more width in the stern than in the remainder craft, until one day when a German called Heyman, had the happening to say: "Nature is our model", and then, he initiated to build kayaks with a fish shape: wide in the bow, and narrow in the stern. Inclusive they were the fastest of the moment.A typical detachable kayak was initiated in Germany during the IXX century, and named "Faltboote" (Foldboat). It was constructed with a wood framework, and covered with a waterproof canvas.

The I.C.F (International Canoe Federation) was established on January 19th, 1924, in the face of the necessity for regrouping the several Canoeing Associations that survived at world level, most dedicated to the Nautical Touring, though some competitions were executed at local level.

In that moment the International Canoe Federation is recognized with the name of Internacionale Repräsentantschaft fur Kanusport, and was constituted by Austria, Denmark, Germany and Sweden. But previously, toward 1880, a high number of Canadian canoes had begun the popularity of this sport. In Europe the Association that was founded in Wroclaw, in 1876, is the one known as the most veteran.

For the first time, at the Olympic games of Paris in 1924, took place some Kayak exhibitions with 11 canoeists, but it is not until 1936, at the Olympic games of Berlin, when for the first time this sport acquires the Olympic category. At the exhibitions of 1924, the Germans with their "fish-kayaks" contended and were get over by the new tetrahedral kayaks designed and paddled by the Swedes. On 1936, for the Olympiad of Berlin, was made the ordinances that established the official kayak dimensions that presently conventions.

Another great creations were made by the Austrians, who acquainted in these Olympic Games the kayaks constructed from "bark", with smooth surfaces and unvarying finish of appreciable advantages, because the smooth surface reduces to a minimum the water resistance, and makes easy the advance of the kayak. Someday near the end of the 1930's decade, William Fronde, a British naval designer, detected that the kayaks were faster if they were longer. Then, everyone got down to build kayaks more and more long, because at that time, the competition kayaks were of free measures and shapes.

Little by little, these crafts were altering up to the present-sophisticated competition kayaks and canoes.presently, according to the competition rules of the I.C.F, it can be used any kind of material for the kayak building, but the total weight, shape and water contact-surface of the kayak must be the designated by the conventions.

The possibility to use any building material has been exploited to a highest by the kayak constructors, using treated woods, metals, plastics and fibers, that makes the kayaks more light with developed resistance and long-standing. Presently, the noblest wood, worked meetly, has taken to the building of canoes and kayaks exceedingly slight and, more latterly, the carbon and kevlar fibers, have added a superior resistivity and less weight to these crafts. After the Second World War, kayaking has turn highly popular; at first possible because it offered a cheap method of getting afloat and navigate, when supplies were short. The general boating boom of the 1950's profited it. The fame of "Slalom" as a spectacle did much to show kayaking to the public, and to educate them on this method, for the most part through the television media at the first instance.

THE GAME

The International Canoe Federation is the world wide canoeing organisation and makes the standard decrees for the dissimilar disciplines of canoe/kayak competition. The ICF recognises a lot of competitive and non-competitive disciplines of canoeing; of which Sprint and Slalom are the only two competing in the Olympic Games. The United States Canoe Association is widely regarded the American authority in sport and recreational canoeing, and recognizes many ICF classes. Other national competition conventions are generally based on the decrees of the ICF.

Fig. Canoeing

Sprint

The oldest discipline of ICF canoeing, occasionally referred to as "Flatwater Racing". It implies:

Kayak:

K1 — single seat kayak

K2 — double seated kayak

K4 — 4 seated kayak

Canoe:

C1 — single kneeling canoe

C2 — double kneeling canoe

C4 — 4 person kneeling canoe

Flatwater races are over 200m, 500m, 1000m, and "long distance racing" such as 2 km or 6 km.

Slalom

Competitors are timed in completing a descent down the rapids of a whitewater course, in the process steering their canoes or kayaks through "gates" (a pair of suspended poles about 1 m apart), including going up versus the flow, across the flow, and surfing the standing waves of the rapids. Again, there are both kayak and canoe classes:

Kayak:

K1 — single kayak

Canoe:

C1 — solo canoe

C2 — tandem canoe

Marathon

Longer distance races over largely flatwater courses, possibly including one or more portages. Course lengths commonly deviate from about 2 miles to the epic 125 mile Devizes to Westminster International Canoe Marathon on the Thames, and the 260 mile "World's Toughest Boat Race", the Texas Water Safari. USCA conventions specify that a Marathon course may not have rapids over class II on the International Scale of River trouble whereas, in the United Kingdom and Ireland, courses may be of any trouble and with any hazards including weirs, like those found in the Liffey Descent. The most extreme courses can be found in South Africa, and grade V sections are not unusual in for instance, the Fish River Marathon. Australia's most renowned marathon race is the Hawkesbury Canoe Classic.

Canoe Polo: A fast-action competitive goal-scoring ball game on water, between two teams of 5 players.

Whitewater Racing: (Also acknowledged as Wild Water Racing) - Competitors race specialized canoes or kayaks down a whitewater river (usually class II to IV whitewater is used).

Canoe Sailing: Racing a canoe using sail power. There a number of disciplines.

Unclassified Styles

- Dragon boat - Since the 1970s racing of the traditional Chinese Dragon Boats has been arranged. In general there are about 18-20 paddlers per boat, plus a drummer and a helmsman. In a few types of dragon boat races, an additional flag catcher is part of the crew; the flag catcher must grab a flag at the finish line for the boat to be considered as finished. The International Dragon Boat Federation (IDBF) is the international governing body for Dragon Boats, discussions with the ICF about co-operation are taking place.
- Playboating (or Rodeo) - a form of canoeing or kayaking where the challenger executes tricks and stunts in standing waves such as front and back surfing, flatspins, cartwheels, and blunts, and gets points for the variety of moves executed inside a fixed time. Points are also granted for style.
- Extreme racing - a form of canoeing competition involving racing down grievous whitewater rivers (often with many grade V rapids and generally requiring excellent river running skills).
- Outrigger canoeing - racing of conventional Pacific Ocean outrigger canoes. Very popular in Hawaii (it is the state sport), Tahiti, and other Pacific nations including Australia and New Zealand; well established in western North America and the eastern US, also catching on in Asia and Europe. International governing body is the International Va?a Federation (IVF). Outrigger canoes are traditionally referred to as wa?a, va?a, or waka ama (wa?a, va?a, and waka are words meaning canoe in different Polynesian languages; ama refers to the outrigger float). Standard racing canoes carry six paddlers; one and two person canoes are also widely raced. Races include both short distance sprint races and long distance races.
- Surf skiing - The canoeing equal of surfing, but in a specialised surf kayak. Points are scored for the diversity and caliber of moves executed on a wave. Also whitewater kayakers and playboaters often surf non-competitively. Races for the fastest time in open water with waves are also done.

In some countries, these forms of paddling may come under the national canoeing organisations, but they are not universally accepted as canoeing, despite the fact that they involve propelling a small craft with a paddle.

- Wave skiing - paddling a small, maneuverable craft (surf ski) a little like a bigger surfboard, amongst the breaking waves of the sea or ocean, variously sliding down the face of the wave or executing tricks on the face of a breaking wave. Close affinity to surfing. The paddler sits on top of the ski and can be strapped in. Competition is based on points for tricks and style.
- Surf ski - paddling a long (about 22'), slim racing craft on the sea. Able to handle going in and out of breaking waves, but not for maneuvering on breaking waves. The paddler sits in a bucket manner seat and uses a kayak like paddle. Most common races are long distance in the open ocean where they can catch swells and get the feeling of skiing the ocean.
- Rafting - one or a group of people paddle a small or large inflatable raft down a wild water river. Has much in common with White Water Touring.

MAJOR TOURNAMENTS

Flatwater

Yearly, five regattas are held at the National Water Sports Centre, which incorporate an interclub championship and age group National Championships. Local regattas are also held at other UK locations throughout the year. Women compete in K1, K2 and K4. Men contend in K1, K2 and K4, as well as C1, C2 and C4.

Slalom

British National Championships are held yearly. Slalom canoeists are ranked according to their performance in events held throughout the season, with points accumulated for the fastest time in each individual race. There are four chief divisions (with Division 4 being the lowest, for casual canoeists with basic skills, and Division 1 being for advanced paddlers). A Premier Division, above Division 1, is restrained for the highest performing sportsmen and women. Promotion and relegation between the divisions occurs every season. There are K1 events women and men, with C1 and C2 events for men only. There are also team events.

Wild Water

National Championship events are held throughout the season in the Sprint and Classic categories. There are K1 events for men and women, C1 and C2 events for men only. There are also team events. Points are accrued throughout the season, the winner being the competitor with the highest points total. The Perception Wavehopper Challenge Series is more of a fun competition, targeted at newcomers to the sport.

Marathon

The primary focus of the UK Marathon scene is the Hasler Series. This is a divisional arrangement, with rankings determined by performance in a series of events (over 60 races in all) held between September and August. Races are accommodated over distances of 4, 8 and 12 miles depending on the division. Promotion and relegation goes on each season. An equivalent series for junior competitors (age 8-12) is also held, and is known as 'The Lightning Series'.

Canoe Sailing

The National Championships (incorporating the one-day Sailing Challenge Cup Race) are contested over the course of five days. They consist nine races, six of which count towards the final standings. The Travellers' Series consists of five Premier Events, four nominated Open Meetings and the National Championships. Points are awarded for the position earned in each of these races and ascertain the overall winner of the series.

Dragon Boat

The BDA National League is a series of dragon boat racing events which take place over the summer season. The format is a series of regattas, with points granted for the overall placing achieved at each event. Races are held over a distance of 200m and 500m.

Freestyle

The Peak UK WW Challenge is a major event in UK Freestyle, with canoeists completing two 45 second sessions, or rides, in a play hole or wave on the water. The two scores are added and challengers progress through the rounds to knock-out finals.

Canoe Polo

Canoe Polo teams compete in a National League, and local Polo Leagues also operate in various UK regions. The season runs from

October to April. National Club Canoe Polo Championships are held yearly at the end of May, and the once-yearly National Championships are run over a weekend during the summer.

A number of outdoor tournaments are arranged by clubs during the summer months, notably the Merseyside International, Hull International Challenge and the Welsh Open.

ADMINISTRATIVE BODIES

International Canoe Federation

The International Canoe Federation (ICF) is the world regulating body for paddlesports. The ICF is responsible for ensuring that international competitions are regularised by Competition conventions adapted to the development of the sport. The British Canoeing Union (BCU) is the National Federation for Britain, overseeing regulation of the sport in the home nations.

With the great diversity of paddlesports, decrees are very much particular to the particular canoeing discipline. Rules govern the size and shape of the craft that may be used, the format and duration of the course and/or competition, the number of challengers, penalties, rights of way, grievous play/positioning and many other areas.

American Canoe Association

The American Canoe Association (ACA) is the nation's largest paddle sports organization, upgrading canoeing, kayaking, and rafting. The ACA sponsors more than seven hundred events each year, along with safety education, instructor certification, waterway preservation and public information campaigns. There are more than four thousand ACA certified canoe and kayak instructors. More than two hundred local paddling clubs and fifty thousand individuals are members.

The ACA was founded in 1880 by Scottish lawyer, John MacGregor, who had established the British imperial Canoe Club (RCC) in 1866. In 1883, ACA Secretary Charles Neide and adjourned sea captain "Barnacle" Kendall paddled and sailed over three thousand miles from Lake George, New York to Pensacola, Florida. The Lake George shore where Neide and Kendall launched not only their own boat, but formation of the American Canoe Association is presently part of Wiawaka. In 1886 the ACA and the RCC held the first international canoe sailing regatta. Mostly through the efforts of Waldemar Van B. Claussen of the ACA, representatives of nineteen national clubs met in Copenhagen in 1924 to establish the Internationale Repräsentantenschaft des Kanusport (IRK).

Canadian Canoe Association

The Canadian Canoe Association was established in 1900 in Brockville, Ontario. There were nine initial charter clubs: Carleton Place Canoe Club (Carleton Place), Brockville Rowing Club (Brockville), Brockville Y.M.C.A. (Brockville), Bohemian Amateur Athletic Association (Brockville), Lachine Boat & Canoe Club (Montreal), Grand Trunk Boating Club (Montreal), Britannia Boat House Club (Ottawa), Ottawa Canoe Club (Ottawa), Kingston Yacht Club (Kingston). Carleton Place Canoe Club is the only surviving charter member within the organization though the Lachine club has endured through revival. Brockville Rowing, Ottawa, Britannia and Kingston still operate but outside of the organization.

The Association was founded in an effort to coordinate Canadian canoe clubs into a national competition separate from that of the American Canoe Association (to which these clubs belonged until 1900). The national championship was started in 1900 though no club champion was designated until 1904, the Ottawa Canoe Club becoming the first official Canadian Champion at that time.

Championships were invalidated during the years 1916-1918 and 1942-1945 due to the two world wars. While the national championship continues to this day and is regarded the premier national regatta, provincial divisions and regions have organized a variety of events to fill out the seasonal schedule of events for competitors. CanoeKayak Canada also runs annual selection trials to determine their national team squad - athletes chosen to contend in international events including Pan American Games, Junior and Senior World Championships, and the Olympic Games.

British Canoe Union

The British Canoe Union (BCU) is the National regulating Body for the sport of canoeing and kayaking in the UK, helping and inspiring people to go canoeing. It formulates standards for coaching programmes with certification degrees and accredits instructors to teach canoeing.

1887 saw the formation of the British Canoe Association, which survived about thirty years. Revived in 1933, it blended with the Canoe Section of the Camping Club of Great Britain. In March 1936, representatives of the Canoe Section of the Camping Club, Clyde Canoe

Club, Manchester Canoe Club and the Royal Canoe Club constituted the British Canoe Union.

The BCU is an umbrella organisation which brings conjointly Britain's separate paddlesport organisations: Canoe England, The Scottish Canoe Association, The Welsh Canoeing Association and The Canoe Association of Northern Ireland. It is concerned with all paddlesports in the UK, recreational as well as competitive, in open and closed craft, paddled with single and double-bladed paddles, on inland and coastal waters as well as Open Ocean.

FAMOUS PLAYERS

Jon Lugbill

Jon Lugbill is widely believed to be the greatest whitewater canoe slalom racer ever. During the 1980s, he mastered international racing in Men's Individual C1 (a decked canoe, similar to a kayak). He is the only slalom racer to ever come out on the Wheaties box. He revolutionised the sport while making innovations in paddling method and boat design.

Jon began canoeing in the 1970s in the Washington, D.C. area. He often trained daily in his C1 using slalom gates set up on a feeder canal next to the Potomac River near Great Falls. During the winter, Jon and his fellow paddlers also trained in the David Taylor Model Basin. He and some other fellow racers (notably David Hearn) formulated new designs of low volume decked canoes, applying nylon, kevlar and fiberglass cloths mixed with epoxy resin.

In 1979, Jon won the C1 Men's Individual World Championship in Canoe Slalom at the first World Championships to be held on the North American continent at Jonquière (Canada). This was the first time an American had acquired a gold medal in the world whitewater canoe slalom championships. Jon went on to win gold in his category many more times; 1981 at Bala (Wales), 1983 at Merano (Italy), 1987 at Bourg St. Maurice (France), and 1989 at the Savage River (USA). In 1985 at Augsburg (Germany), Lugbill had to settle for the silver medal after David Hearn bested him for the gold.

Cliff Meidl

Cliff Meidl is a two-time U.S. Olympic athlete who took part in the 1996 Summer Olympics and the 2000 Summer Olympics, where he was chosen to be the U.S. Flag Bearer. After a building accident that caused him to suffer critical electrical burns and the near loss of his legs at age 20, he battled to recover, and rose to become a two-time Olympian in the sport of kayaking. His fellow athletes elected him to bear the flag and lead Team USA into the Olympic Stadium during the Opening Ceremonies of Sydney 2000. Meidl's inspiring story received major television and press coverage during the Sydney 2000 Summer Olympics.

Nathan Baggaley

Nathan Baggaley was born on December 6, 1975 in Byron Bay, New South Wales and is an Australian flatwater canoer and surfski champion. He is a three-time world champion in the single kayak (K1) 500m event and has also won two Olympic silver medals.

He made his international debut for Australia in 1997, initially competing in the K2. In 1999 he switched to the K1 and attained the 500m semi-finals at the Sydney Olympics in 2000.

Since then he has become one of the top stars in the sport, winning three back-to-back K1 500m world championships. At the Athens Olympics however he had to settle for the silver medal in the K1 500m final where he was edged out by Canadian Adam van Koeverden. In the K2 race he partnered Clint Robinson to additional silver medal. He was voted the Australian Institute of Sport's Athlete of the Year in 2004. He came back to win in K1 500m in 2005 in Zagreb just before being banished for 24 months for doping.

Robin Bell

Robin Bell was born on 16 November 1977 in Kaapstad, South Africa and is an Australian slalom canoer and Olympic bronze medallist, who was born in South Africa.

Contending in the C-1 event, he ended up ninth at the 2000 Summer Olympics and fourth in the 2004 Summer Olympics. He was named Western Australian Sports Star of the Year in 2005, and became world number one in 2006. At the 2008 Summer Olympics, he won bronze on the 12th August in the C-1 event at the Shunyi Olympic Rowing-Canoeing Park.

Caroline Brunet

Caroline Brunet was born on March 20, 1969 in Quebec City, Quebec and is a Canadian kayaker, who contended in five Summer Olympics for her native country, beginning in 1988. She commenced kayaking at age eleven. She has won two silver medals at the Olympics in the women's K1 500 m event (in 1996 and 2000) and a bronze in the same event at the 2004 Summer Olympics.

On top of that, she has won ten world championship golds, seven silvers and four bronze medals:

- 1993 in Copenhagen, Denmark: bronze in K1 500 m.
- 1994 in Mexico City, Mexico: bronze in K4 200 m, and K1 200 m.
- 1995 in Duisburg, Germany: silver in K1 500 m, and K1 200 m; gold in K4200 m.
- 1997 in Dartmouth, Canada: gold in K1 1000 m, K1 500 m, and K1 200 m.
- 1998 in Szeged, Hungary: silver in K1 1000 m; gold in K1 500 m, and K1 200 m
- 1999 in Milan, Italy: silver in K2 500 m; gold in K1 1000 m, K1 500 m, and K1 200 m.
- 2002 in Seville, Spain: silver in K1 500 m and K1 200 m
- 2003 in Gainesville, Georgia: bronze in K2 1000 m; silver in K1 500 m; gold in K1 200 m.

REFERENCES

Cameron, A. "Some Mechanical Aspects of Rowing". Rowing- A Scientific Approach, J.P.G. Williams, ed. A.S. Barnes, New York, 1967.

Churbuck, D. C. "The Book of Rowing". Overlook Press, Woodstock, NY, 1988.

Davenport, M. "The Nuts and Bolts Guide to Rigging", Mouse House Ink, Church Hill, MD, USA, 1993.

Herberger, Dr. Ernst, et al. "Rowing (Rudern)". Sport Books Publisher, Toronto, 1993.

McMahon, Thomas A. "Rowing: A Similarity Analysis". Science. Vol. 173, (1971) pp. 349-351.

Ramsey, Wm. D. "Lift and Drag Characteristics of Rotating Oar Blades". Thesis, BS, MIT Dept. Mechanical Engineering, 1993.

Young, Ken. "Rowing Physics". Paper, USRA Convention, Seattle, WA, 1991

5

Cricket

Cricket has been an established team sport for many centuries. It originated in its advance font in England, and is famous chiefly in the Commonwealth countries. In few countries in South Asia, including India, Pakistan, Bangladesh, and Sri Lanka, cricket is the most famous sport. Cricket is also a major sport in England, Australia, New Zealand, South Africa, Zimbabwe and the English-speaking countries of the Caribbean, which are known in cricketing world as the West Indies.

Cricket is played in three very different forms. The first is test match format, in which a particular number of hours of playing time are allocated and each team plays two innings. The second is restricted overs, in which every team play one innings of a pre-determined number of overs. In T20 cricket, both teams bat for 20-20 overs.

The length of the game is varied. A T20 match can last up to six or more hours and a test match can be long lasting up to five days. The several intervals and the terminology are many aspects which can often befuddle those not familiar with the sport.

Cricket is a team sport played between two teams having eleven players each. It is a bat-and-ball game played on a roughly elliptical grass field, in the centre of which is a hard, flat strip of ground 20.12 m (22 yards) long is known as the pitch.

At each end of the pitch stand a set of three wooden poles known as stumps which is conventionally built from the wood of the ash tree, it along with two smaller wooden rods known as bails, form the wickets. A player from one team (the bowler) throws a hard ball of fist-sized (which has a cork core wrapped in worsted yarn, and a leather cover) from one wicket towards the other. A player from the conflicting team (the batsman) attempts to defend the wicket from the ball with a wooden cricket bat, conventionally built of willow. Another (the non-striker) stands in an motionless role near the bowler's wicket.

If the batsman hits the ball with his bat, he may run to the other wicket, switching places with the non-striker. This scores a run. The batting team seeks to score as many runs as it can, members of the bowling team collect the ball and return it to either wicket. If the ball hits a wicket while the nearest batsman is still running, the batsman is considered as out. Batsmen can also be considered out by other means, such as failing to defend the bowled ball from hitting the wicket, or hitting a catch to a fielder.

Once out, a batsman is switched by another batsman in the team. As there must invariably be two batsmen on the field, if and when the tenth batsman is out, the team's turn to bat or innings is over, and the other team may bat while the first team takes the field. Depending upon the particular conventions of the match, one or two innings may be played, possibly with a fixed number of legally-bowled balls determining the end of an innings instead of ten batsmen having been dismissed. At the end of the match, the winner is the team that has scored the most runs. However, the game may run out of time before it is finished up, in which case it is a draw, even if one team is irresistibly winning at that point. This is occasionally prodigious to those not familiar with the game, but it does add concern to one-sided games by providing the substandard team the incentive to try and attain a draw even if they cannot win.

HISTORY

Cricket's most likely birth place is the Weald, an area in south-east England that lies across Kent and Sussex. The game was probably designed by children of the Weald's farming communities. There are grounds to suggest that it subsisted as a children's game for many centuries before it was taken up by adults around the starting of the 17th Century.

According to few other theories, cricket initiated outside England and was brought there by the Normans after 1066. As early as the 8th century, bat and ball games were played in the Punjab region of southern Asia (the ancestors of games such as gilli-danda and may be polo). Like the other great recreational import of the time, chess, these sports are considered to have transmigrated via Persia and through Constantinople into Europe. There are 8th and 9th century accounts of bat and ball games being played in the Mediterranean region, occasionally as church-sponsored events to raise community spirit. But all of this is contemplation and there is usual agreement among cricket historians that the sport did start in south-east England.

Until the 17th Century, cricket may have evolved chiefly as a boy's game. The first reference to it being played as an adult sport was in 1611, when two men in Sussex were prosecuted for playing cricket rather than going to church.

Throughout the 18th Century, cricket thrived because of the money it attracted through patronage and gambling to become a big sport. By this time, cricket had drew the attention of aristocrats like the Duke of Richmond who were prepared to stage matches at great expense in the hope of significant returns.

Cricket must have had agreed conventions, subject to local variations, for a long time but the most former known Laws were ratified in 1744. The game continued to disperse and, in 1751, Yorkshire is first mentioned as a venue. The primitive kind of bowling (rolling the ball along the ground as in bowls) was superseded sometime after 1760 when bowlers startedstarted to pitch the ball and study variations in line, length and pace. Scorecards startedstarted to be kept on a steady basis from 1772 and since then we have an increasingly clear picture of the sport's growth. The Laws of Cricket were updated in 1774 and it was at this time that present characteristics like the third stump and lbw came into being.

The popular Hambledon Club first attainedattained prominence in 1756 and was the focal point of the game for the next thirty years until the establishment of MCC and the opening of Lord's in 1787. MCC quickly turned the game's premier club and the custodian of the Laws.

THE GAME

The game is played in accordance with 42 dissimilar laws, evolved by the Marylebone Cricket Club in agreement with chief cricketing countries. There are a number of adjustments to conventions in various types of matches.

Players

A team comprises of eleven players. A player may be classed as a specialist batsman or bowler. Teams invariably include a specialist wicket-keeper. Each team is leaded by a captain, who is responsible for making decisions.

Umpires

Two on-field umpires control over a match. One umpire stands behind the bowler's wicket, and settles most decisions. The other one, square leg umpire, stands with a side view of the batsman and helps in decision making for which he has a better view. Also the facility subsists for them to refer few decisions to a third umpire, who has the aid of television replays.

Fig. Umpire Signals

Playing Field

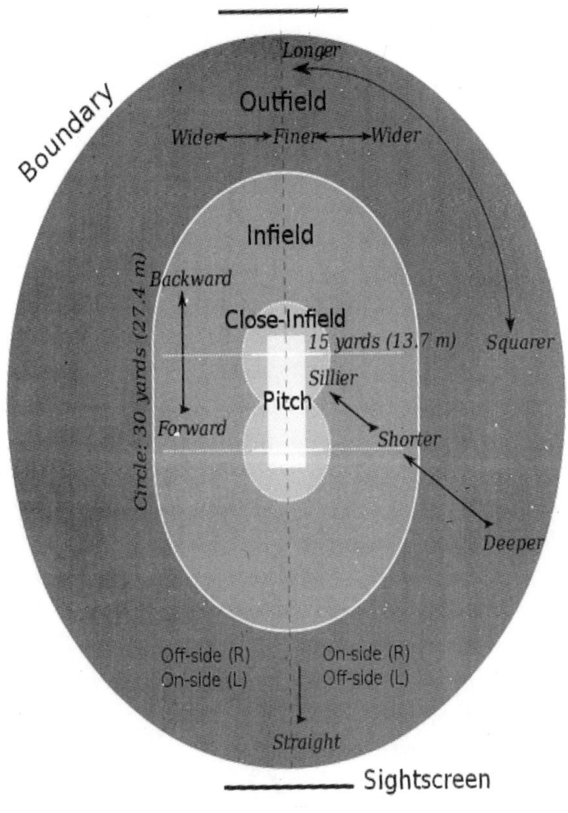

Fig. Cricket Field

The cricket field is a large, circular or oval-shaped, grassy ground. There are no fixed dimensions for the field but its diameter normally varies between 450 feet and 500 feet. The perimeter of the field, called the boundary, is marked, often with a rope or a painted line.

Pitch

A wicket comprises of three stumps that are anchored into the ground with two bails on top of them. Most of the game is played in the centre of the ground, on a rectangular clay strip normally with short grass known as the pitch. The pitch measures 10 × 66 feet. At each end of the pitch three upright wooden stakes, known as the stumps, are hammered into the ground.

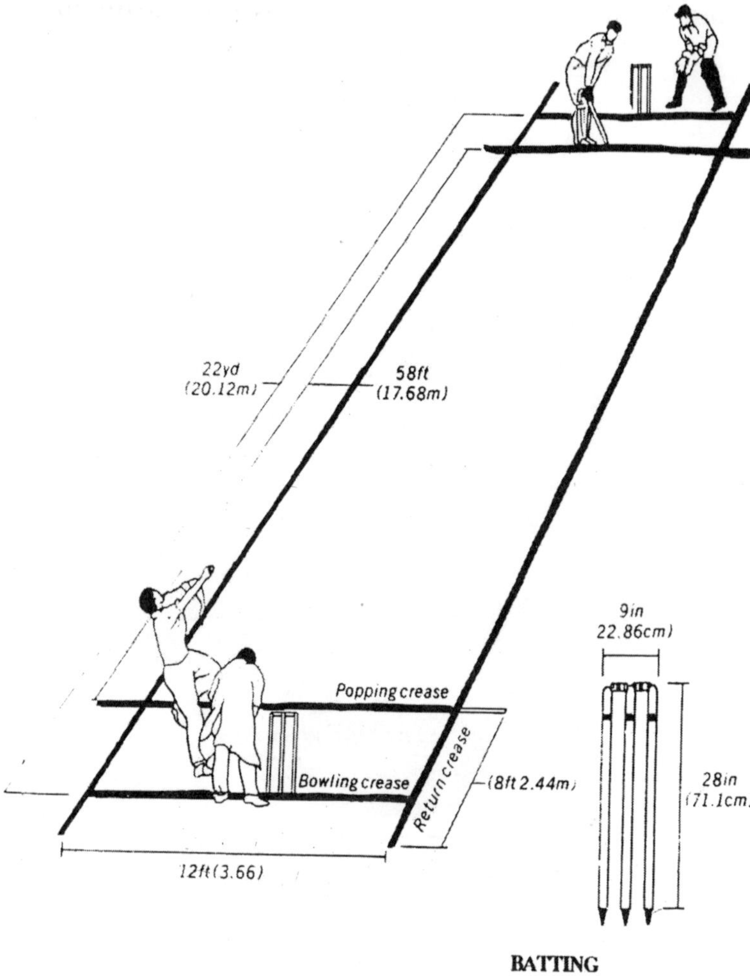

Fig: Pitch

Two wooden crosspieces, known as the bails, sit in grooves atop the stumps, linking each to its neighbour. Each set of three stumps and two bails is jointly known as a wicket.

One end of the pitch is assigned the batting end where the batsman stands and the other is assigned the bowling end where the bowler runs in to bowl. The area of the field on the side of the line connecting to the wickets where the batsman holds his bat is called the off side, the other as the leg side or on side.

Parts of the Field

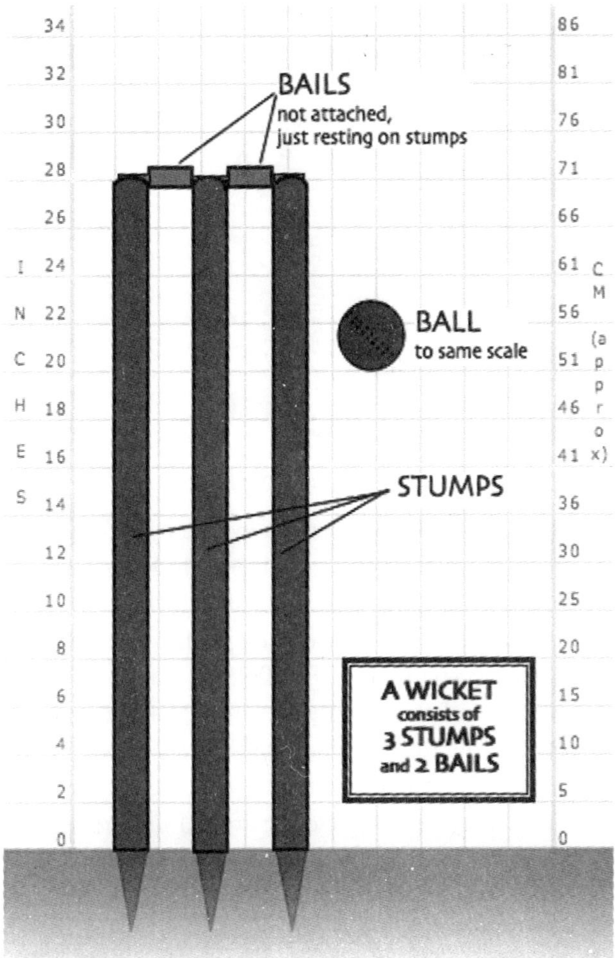

Fig. Stamps

For few restricted-over matches, there are two additional field markings. A painted oval is built by drawing a semicircle of 30 yards radius from the centre of each wicket with respect to the breadth of the pitch and uniting them with lines parallel, 30 yards to the length of the pitch. This line, ordinarily known as the circle, divides the field into an infield and outfield. Two circles of radius 15 yards, centered on each wicket and often marked off by dots, define the close-infield. The infield, outfield, and the close-infield are employed to enforce fielding restrictions.

Players' Positions

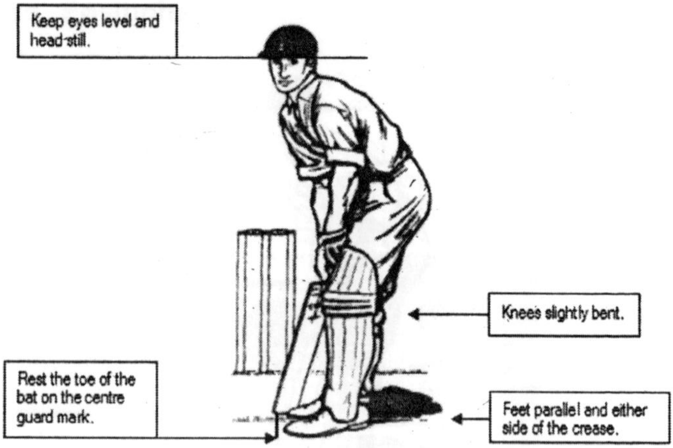

Fig. Batting Stance

The bowler and wicket-keeper are invariably in roughly the same position, and there are only nine other fielders. The batting team invariably has two batsmen on the field. One batsman called the striker faces and plays the balls bowled by the bowler. His partner stands at the bowling end and is called the non-striker. The fielding team has eleven players on the ground. One of them is the bowler. The wicket-keeper, who usually acts in that role for the whole innings, stands behind the wicket at the batting end. The captain of the fielding team spreads out his or her left over nine players, the fielders, around the ground, positioned according to the team's strategy.

Toss

The two captains toss a coin before the match, and the captain who wins chooses either to bat or bowl first.

Overs

Each innings is split up up into overs, comprising of six consecutive legal deliveries bowled by the same bowler. No bowler may bowl two consecutive overs, so at the end of the over the bowler takes up a fielding position and another bowler bowls. Overs are bowled from the end of the pitch; at the end of each over the umpires switch their places, the umpire at the bowler's end moving to square leg, and the umpire at square leg moving to the new bowler's end.

End of an Innings

An innings is finished if:

- A captain declares his team's innings closed (in test match).
- Ten out of eleven batsmen are out.
- The predetermined number of overs has been bowled.
- The team batting last reaches the score needed to win the match.

Playing Time

In test match, two-innings matches are played. One-innings matches are normally played in one day, and can last for six hours or more. There are normally intervals on each day for lunch and tea, and brief informal breaks for drinks. There is also a smallinterval between innings. A one-day match is played on a single day. Each team gets only one innings, and that innings is limited to a maximum number of overs (50, 55 or 60 overs). Each innings is over at the end of the stipulated number of overs.

A T20 game is finished in approximately two and half hours, with each innings lasting around 75 minutes.

Batting

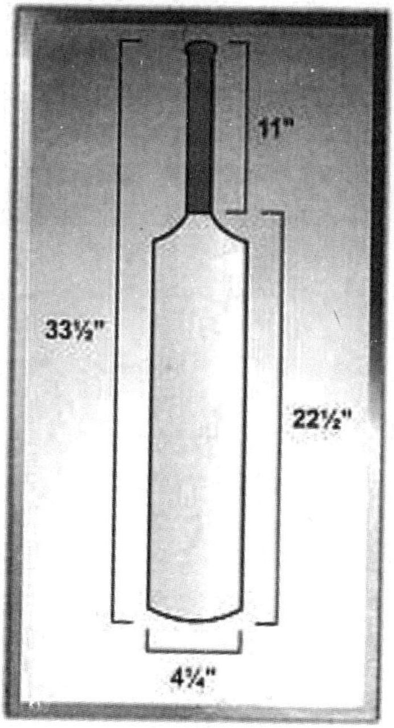

Fig. Bat Dimensions

Batsmen come out to bat in a batting order, decided by the team captain. The batting order is not agreed beforehand, and if a wicket falls any player who has not batted yet may bat next. The batsman plays a shot, trying to hit the bowled ball with the flat surface of the bat. Shots are named according to the style of swing and the direction aimed.

Fig. Various Batting Stances

Run Scoring

To score a run, a striker must run to the opposite end of the pitch, while his non-striking partner runs to his end. To make a successful run, both runners must touch the ground behind the crease with either their bats or their bodies. If the striker hits the ball well enough, the batsmen may double back to score two or more runs and is known as over throw.

If a fielder knocks the bails off the stumps with the ball while no part of the batsman is grounded behind the popping crease, the batsman nearer the broken wicket is run out. The batsman may ground the bat, provided he or she is holding it.

If the ball reaches the boundary, then runs are automatically scored: six if the ball goes over the boundary without touching the ground inside the boundry, four if it touched the ground inside the boundry. These are scored rather than any runs the batsmen may have already run (unless they have run more, which is unlikely), and they return to the ends at which they began. Every run made by the batsmen contributes to the team's total. A team's total also includes a number of runs which are unaccredited to any batsmen.

Bowling

Fig. Cricket Ball

A bowler delivers the ball toward the batsmen. The bowler's goal is to get the batsman out; the most common modes of dismissal (except run out) are credited to the bowler, who is said to have taken a wicket.

Fig. Googly

Fig. In Swing

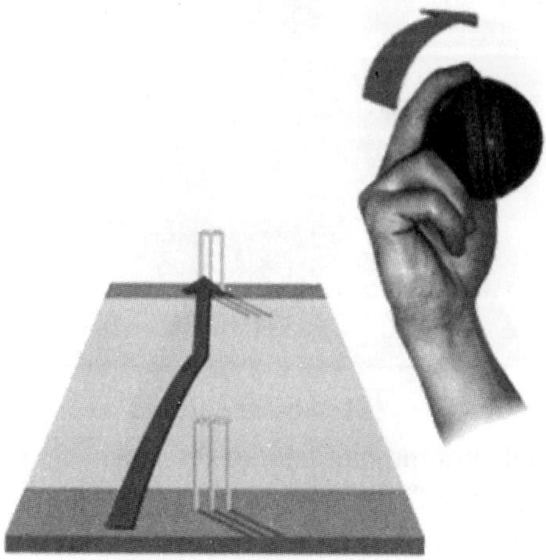

Fig. Leg Break

Fig. Off Break

Fig. Out Swing

Dismissal

There are ten ways in which a batsman may be dismissed. Once a batsman is dismissed, he leaves the field to be replaced by another batsman. The ten ways are:

- Caught out: When a fielder catches the ball before it bounces and after the batsman has struck it with the bat or it has come into contact with the batsman's glove while it is in contact with the bat handle.
- Bowled: When a delivered ball hits the stumps at the batsman's end, and dislodges one or both of the bails.
- Leg before wicket (LBW): When a delivered ball hits the batsman's leg, pad or body, and the umpire judges that the ball would otherwise have struck the stumps.
- Run out: When a fielder, bowler or wicket-keeper removes one or both of the bails with the ball by hitting the stumps whilst a batsman is still running between the two ends.
- Stumped: When the batsman leaves his crease in playing a delivery, voluntarily or involuntarily, but the ball goes to the wicket-keeper who uses it to remove one or both of the bails before the batsman has remade his ground.
- Hit wicket: When the batsman knocks the stumps with either the body or the bat, causing one or both of the bails to be dislodged.
- Handlling the ball: When the batsman deliberately handles the ball without the permission of the fielding team.
- Hitting the ball twice: When the batsman deliberately hits the ball a second time, except for the sole purpose of guarding his wicket.

- Obstructing field: When a batsman deliberately obstructs a fielder trying to field the ball.
- Timed out: When a new batsman takes more than three minutes to take his position in the field to replace a dismissed batsman.

Fielding

Fielders assist the bowlers either by taking catches to dismiss a batsman, or by saving runs by intercepting the ball and returning it, possibly running out the batsman. The wicket-keeper is the only fielder allowed to wear gloves. A fielder may stop the ball with any part of his body.

MAJOR TOURNAMENTS

There are various international competitions such as ICC Test Championship, World Cup, Champions Trophy, Asia Cup, Twenty20 World Cup and national tournaments such as Ranji Trophy, Irani Trophy, Duleep Trophy, Deodhar Trophy, Indian Cricket League and Indian Premier League.

ICC Test Championship

The ICC Test Championship is a competition run by the International Cricket Council in the sport of cricket for the ten nations that play Test cricket. In essence, after every Test series, the two teams involved incur points grounded on a mathematical formula. The total of each team's points total is split up by the total number of matches to give a 'rating', and the Test-playing teams are ranked by order of rating.

The points for winning a Test match or series are greater than the team's rating, increasing the rating, and the points for losing the match or series are invariably less than the rating, reducing the rating. A drawn match between higher and lower rated teams will benefit the lower-rated team at the expense of the higher-rated team. An 'average' team that wins as often as it loses while playing a mix of stronger and weaker teams should have a rating of 100.

Cricket World Cup

Cricket World Cup is the most popular international tournament in One Day International cricket. The event is organized by the International Cricket Council (ICC), with preliminary qualification rounds leading up to a finals tournament which is held every four years. The first Cricket World Cup competetion was organized in England in 1975. The finals of the Cricket World Cup are contended by all ten Test-playing and ODI-playing nations, jointly other nations that qualify through the World Cup Qualifier. Australia has been the most successful of the five teams to have won the tournament, taking four titles. The West Indies have won twice, while India, Pakistan, and Sri Lanka have each won one time.

The Test-playing nations and ODI-playing nations qualify automatically for the World Cup finals, while the other teams have to qualify through a series of preliminary qualifying tournaments. Qualifying tournaments were brought in for the second World Cup, where two of the eight places in the finals were granted to the leading teams in the ICC Trophy. The number of teams selected through the ICC Trophy has changed during the years; presently, six teams are selected for the Cricket World Cup. Under the present qualifying process, all 91 Associate and Associate members of the ICC are able to qualify for the World Cup. Associate and Associate members must play between two and five stages in the ICC World Cricket League to qualify for the World Cup finals, depending upon the Division in which they start the qualifying process.

Champions Trophy

The ICC Champions Trophy is second in significance only to the Cricket World Cup. It was inaugurated as the ICC Knock Out tournament in 1998 and has been played every two years subsequently, changing its name to the Champions Trophy in 2002. Primitively, all ten full members of the International Cricket Council took part; together with (for the first four competitions) two associate members. From 2008, this was altered to the 8 highest-ranked ODI teams as placed 6 months out from the tournament.

The Champions Trophy varies from the World Cup in a various methods. The Champions Trophy takes place every two years, while the World Cup is held every four years. The matches in the Champions Trophy are held over a period of around two weeks, while the World Cup may last for over a month. Unlike the World Cup, no team plays another more than once in the Champions Trophy. For 2002 and 2004, twelve teams played a round robin tournament in four pools of three, with the top team in each pool moving forward to the semi-final.

A team would play only four matches (two in the pool, semi-final and final) to win the tournament. In 2006, eight teams played in two pools of four, with the top two teams in each pool playing in the semi-finals. Losing even a single match would potentially mean elimination from the tournament. The format employed in the Knock Out tournaments differed from the formats employed in the Champions Trophy. The competition was a straight knock out, with no pools and the loser in each game being eliminated.

Asia Cup

The Asia Cup is an international cricket tournament. It was commenced in 1983 when the Asian Cricket Council was made as a measure to raise goodwill between Asian countries. It was primitively scheduled to be held every two years. The first tournament was held in 1984 in Sharjah, UAE where the council's offices were based until 1995. The International Cricket Council has ruled that all games played for the Asia Cup have official One Day International status. India along with Sri Lanka has lifted the Asia cup the most times (four times). India appeared in every final apart from the 1986, 1993 and 2000 cups. Sri Lanka, however, have appeared in every final since the cup's commencement.

Twenty20 World Cup

The ICC World Twenty20 is the international championship of Twenty20 cricket. The event is organized by the sport's regulating body, the International Cricket Council. The tournament comprises of 12 teams and is contended by all Test-playing nations plus qualifiers. The championship is expected to be held around every two years. The inaugural event, the 2007 ICC World Twenty20 was staged in South Africa from September 11, 2007 to September 24. 2007. The inaugural champion of the ICC World Twenty20 is India who defeated Pakistan in the final at Johannesburg by five runs.

Ranji Trophy

Ranji Trophy, "The Cricket Championship of India," is undoubtedly the most important tournament in India's domestic cricket season. The first Ranji Trophy fixtures took place in the 1934-35 season.

The trophy was donated by the then Maharaja of Patiala, H.H.Bhupender Singh to the BCCI in fond memory of Sir Ranjitsinghji Vibhaji of Nawanagar, who has the honour of playing test cricket for England and is widely considered as one of the finest batsmen the game has ever seen.

Bombay won the first Ranji Trophy Championship by defeating North India. Ranji Trophy is composed of teams representing the states that make up India. Few states have more than one cricket team, e.g.

Maharashtra and Gujarat. There are also teams like Railways, and Services representing the armed forces. The various teams employed to be grouped into zones - North, West, East, Central and South. Commencing with the 2002-03 season, the zonal system has been abandoned and a two-division structure has been adopted with two teams being raised from the plate league and two relegated from the elite league.

Irani Trophy

The Irani Trophy tournament was conceptualised throughout 1959-60 to mark the completion of 25 years of the Ranji Trophy championship and was named after the late Z.R. Irani, who was a keen patron of the game. The first match, played between the Ranji Trophy champions and the Rest of India was played in 1959-60. Since 1965-66, it has conventionally heralded the start of the new domestic season. The Irani Trophy game ranks very high in fame and significance. Leading players take part in the game which has often been a sort of selection trial to pick the Indian team for foreign tours.

Duleep Trophy

The Duleep Trophy was commenced by the Board of Control for Cricket in India in 1961-62 with the aim of providing a greater competitive edge in domestic cricket. The Duleep Trophy was also meant to help the selectors in assessing form. The primitive format was that five teams, drawn from the five zones, play each other on a knock-out basis. From the 1993-94 season, the competition has been converted to a league format.

Deodhar Trophy

Deodhar Trophy was commenced in 1973-74 by Board of Control for Cricket in India, it is the present one-day cricket competition in Indian domestic cricket. Five zonal teams - North zone, South zone, East zone, West zone and Central zone feature in the competition. North zone have won this competition eleven times.

Indian Cricket League

Indian Cricket League (ICL) is a private cricket league that runs parallel to the subsisting cricket league managed by BCCI. At the moment, matches in the ICL pursue the Twenty20 format. In the third edition the league was expanded to eight teams, almost doubling the number of group stage games from 15 to 28. Players taking part in this league have been banished by various cricket boards of their respective countries as this is a private league.

The first edition of the league began on 30 November 2007. The league comprised of six teams with the matches played at Panchkula, near Chandigarh. It concluded on 16 December 2007 with the Chennai Superstars winning the first title. The second edition was a 50 over tournament played from 7 January 2008 to 28 January 2008 at Mayajaal Cricket Ground, near Chennai, with Chennai Superstars winning again. A third edition which started on 9 March 2008 saw the league expanded to eight teams and matches being played at two further venues, Hyderabad and Gurgaon. Hyderabad Heroes won the 3rd edition.

There are eight teams of private clubs. These are:

- Ahmedabad Rockets
- Chandigarh Lions
- Chennai Superstars
- Delhi Giants
- Hyderabad Heroes
- Kolkata Tigers
- Lahore Badshahs
- Mumbai Champs

Indian Premier League

The Indian Premier League (IPL) is a Twenty20 cricket competition made by the Board of Control for Cricket in India (BCCI). The first season of the Indian Premier League started on 18 April 2008, and finished on 1 June 2008. Teams play with each other two times in a round robin arrangement, with equal number of home and away matches. The top four ranking sides progress to the semi-finals. The eight teams which that took part were Kolkata Knight Riders, Chennai Super Kings, Mumbai Indians, Hyderabad Deccan Chargers, Rajasthan Royals, Royal Challengers Bangalore, Delhi Daredevils, and Kings XI Punjab.

The inaugural 2008 tournament began on 18 April 2008 in Bangalore and held out for 45 days, with 59 matches scheduled, out of which 58 took place and 1 was washed out due to rain. The IPL 2008 tournament was won by the Rajasthan Royals on 1 June 2008.

ADMINISTRATIVE BODIES

There are many cricket administrative bodies on international and national basis such as International Cricket Council, Asian Cricket Council, Cricket Australia, England and Wales Cricket Board, Board of Control for Cricket in India, Pakistan Cricket Board and Sri Lanka Cricket.

International Cricket Council

The International Cricket Council (ICC) is the international regulating body of cricket. It was established as the Imperial Cricket Conference in 1909 by representatives from England, Australia and South Africa, renamed the International Cricket Conference in 1965, and took up its present name in 1989. The ICC has 104 members: Ten Full Members that play standard Test matches, 34 Associate Members, and 60 Associate Members. The ICC is responsible for the organization and governance of cricket's major international tournaments, most notably the Cricket World Cup.

It also appoints the umpires and referees that officiate at all approved Test matches, One Day International and Twenty20 Internationals. It promulgates the ICC Code of Conduct, which sets professional standards of discipline for international crickets, and also co-ordinates action versus corruption and match-fixing. The working ICC President is David Morgan the chairman of the England and Wales Cricket Board. He will be at this post until 2010, when he will be replaced by Sharad Pawar, the present president of the Board of Control for Cricket in India.

Asian Cricket Council

The Asian Cricket Council was established as the Asian Cricket Conference in 1983 to push and grow the game of cricket within Asia. It is the regional administrative body and is sub-ordinate to the International Cricket Council. It turned Asian Cricket Council in 1995, and it is presently headquartered in Kuala Lumpur, Malaysia. There are 22 members of the ACC.

Membership in the ACC is split up between four full Test Status members, seven associate members, and eleven associate members. The full members are Bangladesh, India, Pakistan, and Sri Lanka. The associate members are Hong Kong, Kuwait, Malaysia, Nepal, Singapore, Thailand, and United Arab Emirates. The associate members are Afghanistan, Bahrain, Bhutan, Brunei, China, Iran, Maldives, Myanmar, Oman, Qatar, and Saudi Arabia.

The ACC runs evolving programs that includes coaching, umpiring, and sports medicine programs in member countries. The ACC funds this program from television revenues accumulated throughout the officially approved ACC tournaments including the Asia Cup, Asian Test Championship and Asian Cricket Junior Tournaments.

Board of Control for Cricket in India

Board of Control for Cricket in India (BCCI), is the peak administration body for cricket in India. The board was established in 1929. It is a society, registered under the Tamil Nadu Societies Registration Act. The state-level clubs choose their representatives who in turn choose the BCCI officials. As a member of the International Cricket Council (ICC), it has the authorization to choose players, umpires and officials to take part in international events.

BCCI hold yearly elections at its Annual General Meeting for all posts, with a bar on re-election of an officeholder president outside two successive years, "rendered that the General Body may in its discretion re-elect the same person as president for the third consecutive year". The current President of BCCI is Sharad Pawar.

State Cricket Associations

In India there are state cricket associations, and states have more than one association. Maharashtra state, for example, has Maharashtra Cricket Association, Mumbai Cricket Association and Vidarbha cricket association and Gujarat state has Gujarat Cricket Association, Baroda cricket association and Saurashtra cricket association. Railways and Armed Services are also members. All these organizations are members of BCCI.

FAMOUS PLAYERS

Donald Bradman

Sir Donald George Bradman (1908—2001), often known as Don Bradman or The Don, was an Australian cricketer who is universally considered as the greatest batsman of all time. Among those who have a meaningful Test match batting average through batting in more than 20 innings, his figure of 99.94 is over 63% higher than that attained by any other cricketer.

Born in Cootamundra, New South Wales, raised in Bowral, Bradman exercised obsessively throughout his youth. He devoted himself to cricket, playing for local sides before attracting enough attention to be drafted into grade cricket in Sydney at the age of 18. Within a year he was selected for New South Wales, and within three years he made his Test first appearance.

In the English summer of 1930 he scored 974 runs over the course of the five Ashes tests, the highest individual total in any test series.

Braɑman himself rated his 254 in the second Test at Lord's as his best ever innings. His 334 in the third Test at Headingley, of which he scored a test record 309 runs on one day, was then the highest individual score in Test cricket.

Over an international career spanning 20 years from 1928 to 1948, Bradman's batting accomplishments are unique. His career statistics are far superior to those of any other batsman, and a testament to his strange powers of concentration. He broke scoring records for both first-class and Test cricket.

Bradman scored centuries at a rate of better than one every three innings. He converted very nearly a third of his centuries into double hundreds, and his total of 37 first-class double hundreds is the most attained by any batsman. In a biographical essay in Wisden, he is hailed as the greatest phenomenon in the history of cricket, indeed in the history of all ball games.

Sachin Tendulkar

Sachin Ramesh Tendulkar was born on 24 April 1973, he is n famous Indian cricketer. He holds many batting records, including the most Test centuries and the most one-day international centuries, and was rated in 2002 by Wisden as the second greatest Test batsman ever, after Sir Don Bradman. He obtained the Rajiv Gandhi Khel Ratna, India's highest sporting honour, for 1997-1998, and the civilian award Padma Shri in 1999. Tendulkar was a Wisden Cricketer of the Year in 1997

He is the first batsman to score 10,000 runs in one-day cricket, making the record in the third game of a five-match series versus Australia on 31st of March 2001. He arrived at the landmark when he scored 34 runs in his 266th match and 259th innings. Tendulkar, 27, in his amazing 12-year career, has scored a world record 28 hundreds and 50 half-centuries in his 10,000 runs.

Born in Mumbai (Bombay) into a middle-class family, he went to Sharadashram Vidyamandir School where he began his cricketing career under Coach Ramakant Achrekar. While at school, he was involved in a mammoth 664 run partnership in a Harris Shield game with friend and team mate Vinod Kambli.

Sachin played his first international match versus Pakistan in Karachi in 1989. He made just 15 runs, being bowled by Waqar Younis, who also made his first appearance in that match. Tendulkar persued it up with his maiden Test fifty a few days afterwards at Faisalabad. His One-day International (ODI) first appearance on December 18 was equally disappointing, where he was dismissed without making a run, again by Waqar Younis. Tendulkar truly came into his own in the 1991-1992 tour of Australia that included a brilliant century on the fast and bouncy track at Perth. He has been Man of the Match 11 times in Test matches and Man of the Series twice, both times in the Border-Gavaskar Trophy versus Australia.

His first ODI century came on September 9, 1994 versus Australia in Sri Lanka at Colombo. It had taken Tendulkar 79 ODIs to score a century. Sachin Tendulkar is the only player to score a century while making his Ranji Trophy, Duleep Trophy and Irani Trophy first appearance. Wisden named Tendulkar one of the Cricketers of the Year in 1997, the first calendar year in which he scored 1,000 Test runs. He repeated the feat in 1999, 2001, and 2002.

Tendulkar also holds the record for scoring 1,000 ODI runs in a calendar year. He has done it six times - 1994, 1996, 1997, 1998, 2000 and 2003. In 1998 he made 1,894 ODI runs, still the record for ODI runs by any batsman in any given calendar year. While not a regular bowler, Tendulkar has 37 wickets in 132 tests.

Vivian Richards

Sir Isaac Vivian Alexander Richards was born on 7th March 1952, better known by his second name, Vivian or, more famously, simply as Viv is a former West Indian cricketer. Richards was a highly assaulting right-hand batsman, a good fielder, an occasional spin bowler, and a successful captain. His impressive style of play, and relaxed but determined demeanour made him a great crowd favourite. He often entirely reigned conflicting bowlers both physically and mentally.

Richards made his Test match first appearance for the West Indian cricket team in 1974 versus India in Bangalore. He made an unbeaten 192 in the second Test of the same series in New Delhi. In his Test career, he scored 8,540 runs in 121 Test matches at an average of 50.23 (including 24 centuries). He won 27 of 50 matches as a Test captain, and lost only 8. He is also the scorer of the fastest ever Test century. His highest innings of 291 is sixth on the list West Indies' highest individual scores.

He was chosen as a Wisden Cricketer of the Year for 1977. In 2000, Richards was named by a 100-member panel of experts one of the five Wisden Cricketers of the Century. Richards obtained 25 votes, behind Sir Donald Bradman (100 votes), Sir Garfield Sobers (90 votes), Sir Jack Hobbs (30 votes) and Shane Warne (27 votes).

Garfield Sobers

Sir Garfield St Auburn sobers was born on July 28, 1936, often acknowledged as Garry Sobers is a erstwhile West Indies cricketer, widely considered as the greatest all-rounder (batsman and bowler) the game has ever seen. Sobers was a cricket all-rounder, excelling at both batting and bowling.

He was also an outstanding fielder, normally fielding close to the wicket. Sobers was a gifted left-handed batsman, with a brilliant career Test batting average of 57.78, one of the highest attained by any player. He scored 8,032 runs in his career, which was a record at the time. Sobers was also a versatile bowler, taking 235 Test wickets at an average of 34.03. He bowled left-arm spin and also left-arm fast-medium.

Sobers played his first Test Match in 1953 aged 17. Just with in five years afterwards, in 1958 he set a Test cricket record by scoring 365 runs in 614 minutes in a single innings that included 38 fours and, interestingly, not one six versus Pakistan. It was his first Test century, and a record which stood for over 36 years, until it was surpassed by Brian Lara. However, Sobers' innings still persists the highest maiden Test century ever.

He played his last Test in 1974 versus England in Trinidad. In 1968 Sobers turned the first ever batsman to hit six sixes off one over of six consecutive balls in first-class cricket. In 2000 Sobers was named by a 100-member panel of experts as one of the five Wisden Cricketers of the Century.

Sunil Gavaskar

Sunil Manohar Gavaskar was born on July 10, 1949, nicknamed Sunny, was a cricket player throughout the 1970s and 1980s for India. Widely considered as one of the greatest opening batsman in Test history, Gavaskar set world records throughout his career for the most runs and most centuries scored by any batsman. He held the record of 34 Test centuries for almost two decades before it was broken by Sachin Tendulkar in December 2005. He was widely admired for his technique versus fast bowling, with a specially high average of 65.45 versus the West Indies, who possessed a four-pronged fast bowling attack considered as the most vicious in Test history.

Jack Hobbs

Sir John Berry Hobbs (1882-1963), usually known as Jack Hobbs, played cricket for Surrey and England. Renowned as a very modest and self-effacing man, he was popularly referred to as "The Master". He was the only English cricketer and the only opening batsman to be selected as one of the five Wisden Cricketers of the (20th) Century.

REFERENCES

Allen Guttmann, *Games and Empires: modern sports and cultural imperialism* New York: Columbia University Press, 1994.

David Underwood, *Start of Play: Cricket and Culture in Eighteenth Century England* London: Allen Lane, 2000.

Eric Midwinter, *Quill on Willow: Cricket in Literature* Chichester: Aenaes, 2001.

Gillian Beer, *Darwin's Plots* London: Routledge & Kegan Paul, 1983.

J.A. Mangan (ed.), *The Cultural Bond: Sport, Empire, Society* London: Cass, 1982.

J.A. Mangan, *The Games Ethic and Imperialism* London and Portland, OR: Frank Cass, 2002.

Quoted in Bernice Martin *A Sociology of Contemporary Cultural Change* Oxford: Blackwell, 1981.

Simon Baraes, 'Truth is the latest casualty as ICC bends to Mugabe'. *The Times* London, 20 Dec. 2002.

Wisden Asia Cricket November 2002.

6

Cycling

Cycling is the use of bicycles, or less typically unicycles, tricycles, quadricycles and other alike wheeled human powered vehicles (HPVs) as a means of transport, a form of recreation or a sport. It is done on roads and paths, across open country or even over snow and ice (icebiking).

As a sport, cycling is regulated internationally by the Union Cycliste Internationale in Switzerland (for upright bicycles) and by the International Human Powered Vehicle Association (for other HPVs, or human-powered vehicles). Cycling for transport and touring is raised on a European level by the European Cyclists' Federation, with associated members from Great Britain, Japan and elsewhere. Scheduled conferences on cycling for transport are held under the auspices of Velo City; global conferences are organised by Velo Mondial.

In many countries, the most typically used vehicle for road transport is a utility bicycle. These have frames with relaxed geometry, protecting the rider from shocks from the road, and facilitating steering at low speeds.

Road bikes tend to have a more upright shape and a shorter wheelbase, which make the bike more mobile but harder to ride tardily. The design, coupled with low or dropped handlebars, needs the rider to bend forward more, which reduces air resistance at high speed.

The price of a new bicycle can range from US$50 to more than US$20,000, depending on caliber, type and weight (the most exotic road bicycles can weigh as little as 3.2kg (7 lb). Being measured for a bike and taking it for a test ride are advisable before buying.

The drivetrain parts of the bike should also be reckoned. A middle grade dérailleur is enough for a beginner, though many utility bikes come furnished with hub gears. If the rider plans an important measure of hillclimbing, a triple-crank (three chainrings) front gear arrangement may be preferable. Otherwise, the comparatively lighter and less costly two chainrings may be better.

Many road bikes include clipless pedals to which special shoes attach via a cleat, allowing the rider to pull on the pedals as well as push. Other conceivable accessories for the bicycle include locks, fenders, baggage carriers and pannier bags, water bottles and bottle cages.

For basic maintenance and repairs, cyclists can choose to carry a pump (or a CO2 cartridge), a puncture fixing kit, an extra inner tube, and tyre levers. Cycling can be more efficient and comfortable with special shoes, gloves, and shorts. In wet weather, riding can be more bearable with waterproof clothes, such as cape, jacket, pants and overshoes.

Items lawfully expected in some jurisdictions, or voluntarily adopted for safety reasons, include bicycle helmets, generator or battery operated and hearable signaling devices such as a bell or horn. Extras include studded tires and a bicycle computer.

Learning to ride with efficiency and safely in traffic is important. In the United Kingdom, many elementary school children take the Cycling Proficiency Test, to help them travel extra safely. However, the Cycling Proficiency Test has now been replaced, for children, by 'Bikeability' and the National Standards for Cycle Training. In countries such as the Netherlands, where cycling is popular, cyclists occasionally ride in bike lanes at the side of or separate from, the main highway. Many primary schools take part in the national road test in which children individually complete a circuit on roads near the school while being observed by testers.

Types of Bicycle Racing

Fig. Olympic Symbol for Cycling

Road Bicycle Racing: Road bicycle racing is a popular bicycle racing sport held on roads (following the geography of the area), using racing bicycles. The term 'road racing' is generally applied to events where competing riders begin at the same time (unless riding a handicap event) with the winner being the first at the end of the course (individual and team time trials are different form of cycle racing on roads).

Road racing is popular all over the world, but particularly in Europe. The most competitive and dedicated countries are Belgium, France, Germany, Italy, Luxembourg, the Netherlands, Spain and Switzerland, though the sport is popular also in Australia, Russia, and the United States. Road bicycle racing began as an organized sport in 1868. The first world championship was in 1893 and cycling has been part of the Olympic Games since the advanced sequence began in Athens in 1896.

Cyclo-Cross: Cyclo-cross (occasionally cyclocross, CX, cyclo-X or 'cross) is a form of bicycle racing. Races take place generally in the autumn and winter (the international or "World Cup" season is September-January), and comprises of many laps of a short (2.5-3.5 km or 1.5-2 mile) course featuring pavement, wooded trails, grass, steep hills and obstacles needing the rider to speedily dismount, carry the bike whilst navigating the blockage and remount in one motion. Races for senior classes are usually between 30 minutes and an hour long, with the distance varied depending on the ground conditions. The sport is strongest in the conventional road cycling countries such as Belgium (and Flanders in particular), The Netherlands and the Czech Republic.

Mountain Bike Racing: The Union Cycliste Internationale (UCI) recognised the sport of mountain bike racing comparatively late in 1990, when it authorised the world championships in Purgatory, Colorado. The first mountain biking world cup series took place in 1991. Its nine-race circuit embraced two continents - Europe and North America - and was sponsored by Grundig. In 1992, the Grundig-UCI world cup circuit expanded to ten races, and continued a trans-Atlantic series. Cross-country racing was the only world cup sport at this time, then in 1993 a six-event downhill world cup was brought in.

In 1996, cross country mountain biking events were added to the Olympic Games. NORBA refers to the Board of Trustees that represent the sport of mountain bike racing for USA Cycling. There are three USA Cycling Mountain Bike National Calendars- survival, Gravity and Ultra-Endurance. USA Cycling runs the USA Cycling Mountain Bike National Championships. In 2006 cross Country Mountain biking events will become section of the World Deaf Cycling Championships for the first time in San Francisco, USA.

Track Cycling: Track cycling is a bicycle racing sport generally held on specially-built banked tracks or velodromes (but many events are held at older velodromes where the track banking is comparatively shallow) using track bicycles. Track racing is also done on grass tracks marked out on flat sportsfields. Such events are specially common during the summer in Scotland at Highland Games assemblages, but there are also steady summer events in England.

BMX Racing: BMX racing is a type of off-road bicycle racing. The format of BMX was derived from motocross racing. BMX bicycle races are sprint races on purpose-built off-road single-lap race tracks. The track generally comprises of a starting gate for up to eight racers, a groomed, serpentine, dirt race course made of varied jumps, and a finish line. The course is banked and has flat corners. The sport of BMX racing is facilitated by a number of territorial and international sanctioning bodies.

They provide decrees for regulating the conduct of the races, specify age-group and skill-level classifications among the racers, and maintain some kind of points-accumulation arrangement over the racing season. The sport is mostly participant-driven, with the average age of close to 9 or 10 years. Professional ranks exist for both men and women, where the average age is 18 to 21.

A BMX "Class" bike is a strong, quick-handling, lightweight derivative of the standard 20-inch (510 mm)-wheel, single-speed youth bicycle. Variants include a larger 24-inch (610 mm)-wheel "cruiser" class. Cruisers are made for adults who can not fit the 20-inch (510 mm)-wheel bikes, but some kids have mastered the cruiser.

HISTORY

The first authentic claim for a practically-used bicycle belongs to German Baron Karl von Drais, a civil servant to the Grand Duke of Baden in Germany. Drais invented his Laufmaschine (German for "running machine") of 1817 that was addressed Draisine (English) or draisienne (French) by the press. Karl von Drais patented this design in 1818 which was the first commercially successful two-wheeled, steerable, human-propelled machine generally called a velocipede, nick-named hobby-horse or dandy horse. It was at the start made up in Germany and France. It was manufactured almost completely of wood.

Hans-Erhard Lessing found from circumstantial evidence that Drais' interest in finding an alternative to the horse was the starvation and death of horses caused by crop failure in 1816 ("eighteen hundred and froze to death," following the volcanic eruption of Tambora). On his first reported ride from Mannheim on June 12, 1817, he covered 13 km (eight miles) in less than an hour.

The wooden draisine weighed 22 kg (48 pounds), had brass bushings within the wheel bearings, a rear-wheel brake and 152 mm (6 inches) of trail of the front-wheel for a self-centering castor effect. This designing was welcomed by mechanically minded men daring to balance and several thousand copies were built and used, mainly in Western Europe and in North America. Its fame speedily faded when; partially due to increasing numbers of accidents some city authorities began to prohibit its use. However in 1866 Paris a Chinese visitor named Bin Chun could still observe foot-pushed velocipedes.

Briefly after, the concept was picked up by a number of British cartwrights; the most notable being Denis Johnson of London. We can assume a name alteration occurred when Johnson patented his vehicle and named it "pedestrian curricle" or "velocipede," but the public preferred nick-names like "hobbyhorse," after the children's toy or, worse still, "dandyhorse," after the foppish men who often rode them. Johnson's machine was betterment on Drais's, being notably more elegant: his wooden frame had a serpentine shape rather of Drais's straight one, which permitted the use of larger wheels without raising the seat higher. During the summer of 1819 the "hobby-horse", thanks in part to Johnson's marketing skills and better patent protection, became the craze and fashion in London society. The dandies, the Corinthians of the Regency, adopted it, therefore the poet John Keats referred to it as "the nothing" of the day. Riders wore out their boots astonishingly quickly, and the fashions ended inside the year, after riders on sideways were penalised two pounds.

Nevertheless, Drais' velocipede provided the basis for further growths: in fact, it was a draisine which inspired a French metalworker around 1863 to add rotary cranks and pedals to the front-wheel hub, to make the first pedal-operated "bicycle" as we now understand the word.

Scottish Innovations

The first mechanically-propelled 2-wheel vehicle was considered to have been built up by Kirkpatrick MacMillan, a Scottish blacksmith, in 1839. A nephew later claimed that his uncle formulated a rear-wheel drive design applying mid mounted treadles joined by rods to a rear crank, similar to the transmission of a steam locomotive. Proponents associate him with the first recorded instance of a bicycling traffic offence, when a Glasgow newspaper reported in 1842 an accident in which an unknown “gentleman from Dumfries-shire... bestride a velocipede... of ingenious design” knocked over a pedestrian in the Gorbals and was fined five British shillings.

However, the evidence connecting this with MacMillan Is not even circumstantial, since the artisan MacMillan would not have been termed a gentleman. A similar machine was said to have been created by Gavin Dalzell of Lesmahagow. The first documented manufacturer of rod-driven 2-wheelers was Thomas McCall, of Kilmarnock in 1869. The design could not compete with the front-crank velocipede of the Lallement/Michaux type, however, despite McCall’s all steel version of 1869.

Boneshaker

The first genuinely popular and commercially flourishing design was a French one (an example of the style is held in the Museum of Science and Technology (Ottawa)). At the start developed around 1863, it sparked a fashionable craze concisely during 1868-70. Its design was simpler than the Macmillan bicycle; it used rotary cranks and pedals mounted to the front wheel hub. Pedaling made it more comfortable for riders to propel the machine at speed, but the rotational speed restriction arising from stability and comfort pertains would lead to the large front wheel of the “penny farthing”. It was hard to pedal the wheel that was used for steering. The use of metal frames decreased the weight and allowed sleeker, more elegant designs, and also permitted mass-production. Different braking mechanisms were used depending on the manufacturer. In England, the velocipede earned the name of “bone-shaker” because of its rigid frame and iron banded wheels that resulted in a “bone-shaking experience for riders.”

The velocipede’s renaissance commenced in Paris during the late 1860s. Its early history is complex and has been shrouded in some mystery, not least because of conflicting patent claims: all that has been stated for sure is that a French metalworker bonded pedals to the front wheel; now, the earliest year bicycle historians agree on is 1864. The identity of the person who bonded cranks is still an open question at International Cycling History Conferences (ICHC). The claims of Ernest Michaux and of Pierre Lallement, and the lesser claims of rear-pedaling Alexandre Lefebvre, have their supporters within the ICHC community.

Bicycle historian David V. Herlihy documents that Lallement claimed to have made the pedal bicycle in Paris in 1863. He had seen somebody riding a draisine in 1862 then primitively came up with the idea to add pedals to it. It is a reality that he filed the earliest and only patent for a pedal-driven bicycle, in the USA in 1866. Lallement's patent drawing shows a machine which looks exactly like Johnson's draisine, but with the pedals and rotary cranks impounded to the front wheel hub, and a thin piece of iron over the top of the frame to act as a spring supporting the seat, for a slightly more comfortable ride.

By the early 1860's, the blacksmith Pierre Michaux, besides creating components for the carriage trade, was producing "vélocipède à pédales" on a small scale. The rich Olivier brothers Aimé and René were students in Paris at this time, and these shrewd young entrepreneurs adopted the new machine. In 1865 they travelled from Paris to Avignon on a velocipede in only eight days. They recognized the potential profitability of creating and selling the new machine. Together with their friend Georges de la Bouglise, they formed a partnership with Pierre Michaux, Michaux et Cie ("Michaux and company"), in 1868, debarring use of the Olivier family name and staying behind the scenes, lest the venture prove to be a failure. This was the first company which mass-produced bicycles, replacing the early wooden frame with one made of two pieces of cast iron bolted conjointly otherwise, the early Michaux machines look exactly like Lallement's patent drawing.

Conjointly with a mechanic named Gabert in his hometown of Lyon, Aimé Olivier made a diagonal single-piece frame built of wrought iron which was much stronger, and as the first bicycle craze took hold, many other blacksmiths started forming companies to make bicycles using the new design. Velocipedes were costly, and when customers soon set out to complain about the Michaux serpentine cast-iron frames breaking, the Oliviers realised by 1868 that they needed to replace that design with the diagonal one which their challengers were already using, and the Michaux Company continued to dominate the industry in its first years.

On the new macadam paved boulevards of Paris it was gentle riding, though at the start still using what was essentially horse coach technology. It was still addressed "velocipede" in France, but in the United States, the machine was generally called the "bone-shaker," because its ride was so rough. Later advances included solid rubber tires and ball bearings. Lallement had left Paris in July 1865, crossed the

Atlantic, settled in Connecticut and patented the velocipede, and the number of associated innovations and patents soared in the US.

The fame of the machine arose on both sides of the Atlantic and by 1868-69 the velocipede craze was strong in rural areas as well. Even in a realtively small city such as Halifax, Canada, there were five velocipede rinks, and riding schools started to opening throughout many major urban centres. Fundamentally, the velocipede was a stepping stone that made a market for bicycles that led to the development of more boosted and efficient machines.

However, the Franco-Prussian war of 1870 destructed the velocipede market in France, and the "bone-shaker" enjoyed only a short period of fame in the United States, which ended by 1870. There is debate among bicycle historians about why it failed in the United States, but one explanation is that American road surfaces were much worse than European ones, and riding the machine on these roads was merely too hard. Certainly another factor was that Calvin Witty had bought Lallement's patent, and his royalty demands soon lamed the industry. The UK was the only place where the bicycle never fell entirely out of favor.

High-Wheel Bicycle

The high-bicycle was the logical extension of the boneshaker, the front wheel enlarging to enable higher speeds (bounded by the inside leg measurement of the rider), the rear wheel contracting and the frame being made lighter. Frenchman Eugene Meyer is now esteemed the father of the eminent Bicycle by the ICHC in place of James Starley. Meyer invented the wire-spoke tension wheel in 1869 and created a classic high bicycle design until the 1880s.

James Starley in Coventry added the tangent rundles and the mounting step to his celebrated bicycle named "Ariel." He is regarded as the father of the British cycling industry. Ball bearings, solid rubber tires and hollow-section steel frames became standard, reducing burden and making the ride much smoother. Depending upon the rider's leg length, the front wheel could now have a diameter up to 60 in (1.5 m). This type of bicycle was retronymed the "ordinary" (since there were then no other kind) and was later nicknamed "penny-farthing" in England (a penny acting the front wheel, and a coin smaller in size and value, the farthing, representing the rear).

They were fast, but unsafe. The rider was dignitary in the air and journeying at a great speed. If he hit a bad spot in the route he dismissed front wheel and be seriously bruised (two broken wrists were common, in attempts to break a declivity) or even killed. "Taking a header" (also known as "coming a cropper"), which was not at all uncommon, was no laughing matter. The rider's legs were often caught underneath the handlebars, so falling free of the machine was often not possible. The dangerous nature of these bicycles meant cycling was the preserve of adventurous young men. Elderly gentlemen preferred, and women had to ride, the more stable tricycles or quadricycles. Queen Victoria owned Starley's "Royal Salvo" tricycle; although there is no evidence she actually rode it.

To cure some of the hazards, "moustache" handlebars, allowing the rider's knees to clear them, were developed, and ultimately (although too late, afterward the Starley safety bike), with the 1889 American eagle and ace, the position of big and small wheel was overturned. This forbade headers, but left the danger of being befuddled backwards when riding uphill. Other attempts included moving the seat and rearward and beating back the wheel by levers, as in the Extraordinary or eloquent, or gears, by chain as in the Kangaroo or at the hub in the Crypto; a different option was to move the seat well back, as in the intellectual.

Though French and English inventors altered the velocipede into the high-wheel bicycle, the French were still recovering from the Franco-Prussian war, so English entrepreneurs arrange the high-wheeler on the English market, and the machine became very popular there, Coventry, Oxford, Birmingham and Manchester constituting the centers of the English bicycle industry (and of the arms or sewing machine industries, which accepted the necessary metalworking and engineering accomplishments for bicycle manufacturing, as in Paris and St. Etienne, and in New England). Soon bicycles ascertained their way across the English Channel. By 1875, high-wheel bicycles were becoming popular in France, although ridership expanded slowly.

In the United States, Bostonians such as Frank Weston and commenced importing bicycles in 1877 and 1878, and Pope started production of his "Columbia" high-wheelers in 1878, and acquired control of nearly all applicable patents, starting with Lallement's 1866 manifest. Pope lowered the royalty (licensing fee) previous patent proprietors charged, and took his competitors to court over the patents. The courts backed him, and competitors either paid royalties ($10 per bicycle), or he forced them come out of business. There seems to have been no patent issue in France, where English bicycles still dominated the market. By 1884 high-wheelers and tricycles were relatively popular among a small group of upper-middle-class citizenry in all three countries, the largest group being in England. Their use also spread to the rest of the world, chiefly because of the extent of the British Empire.

The 1880s and 1890s.

The development of the safety bicycle was arguably the most crucial change in the history of the bicycle. It shifted their use and public perception from representing a dangerous toy for sporting young men to being an everyday transport tool for men and, crucially, women of all ages.

Apart from the obvious safety troubles, the high-wheeler's direct front wheel drive bounded its top speed. Accordingly, inventors adjudicated a rear wheel chain drive. Though a Henry Lawson invented a rear-chain-drive bicycle in 1879 with his "bicyclette", it still carried a huge front wheel and a small rear wheel. Detractors called it "The Crocodile", and it failed in the market.

John Kemp Starley, James's nephew, produced the first successful "safety bicycle", the "Rover," in 1885, which he never patented. It sported a steerable front wheel that had important castor, equally sized wheels and a chain drive to the rear wheel.

Widely imitated, the safety bicycle completely substituted the high-wheeler in North America and Western Europe by 1890. Meanwhile John Dunlop's reinvention of the pneumatic tire in 1888 had made for a much smoother ride on paved streets; the previous type were quite smooth-riding, when applied on the dirt roads common at the time. As with the original velocipede, safety bicycles had been much less comfortable than high-wheelers precisely because of the smaller wheel size, and frames were often braced with perplexed bicycle suspension bounce assemblies. The pneumatic tire made all of these obsolete, and frame designers found a diamond pattern to be the strongest and most efficient design.

The chain drive improved comfort and speed, as the drive was transferred to the non-steering rear wheels and provided a much more smooth and decompressed and injury free cycling (earlier designs that required pedaling the steering front wheel were difficult to pedal while turning, due to the misalignment between leg and the plane the pedal rotates in). Because stableness was improved, the gyroscopic forces were reduced, and pedaling was easier, the rider did not accept the pneumatic tire, and the diamond frame bettered rider comfort but do not form a significant design or safety feature. A hard rubber tyre on a bicycle is just as rideable but is bone jolting. The frame design allows for a lighter weight, and more simple structure and maintenance, and hence lower price. ve so much difficulty to turn a corner.

The 20th Century

Cycling steadily became more crucial in Europe all over the first half of the twentieth century, but it dropped off dramatically in the United States between 1900 and 1910. Automobiles became the chose means of conveyance. Over the 1920s, bicycles gradually became conceived children's toys, and by 1940 most bicycles in the United States were brought children. In Europe cycling stayed an adult activity, and bicycle racing, commuting, and "cyclotouring" were all popular activities. In addition, specialist bicycles for children appeared before 1916.

Bicycles continued to develop to suit the different needs of riders. The derailleur formulated in France between 1900 and 1910 among cyclotourists, and was improved over time. Interestingly, only in the 1930s did European racing organizations allow racers to use derailleurs; until then they were impelled to use a two-speed bicycle. The rear wheel had a cog on either side of the hub. To shift gears, the rider had to stop, take out the wheel, flip it around, and remount the wheel. When racers were permitted to use derailleurs, racing times instantly dropped.

Racing Bikes, Mountain Bikes and Hybrid Bikes

In the late 1960s, spurred by Americans' increasing awareness of the value of practice and later the advantage of energy efficient conveyance led to the American bike boom. Sales doubled between 1960 and 1970, and doubled again between 1970 and 1972. Most of the new sales were of racing bikes. These lighter bicycles, long used by sincere cyclists and by racers, featured dropped handlebars, narrow tires, derailleurs gears, five to fifteen speeds, and a narrower seat, but generally tendered none of the extra features, including chain guards and fenders, found on their predecessors. By the 1980s, racing bikes dominated the market in North America.

Mountain bikes appeared on retailers' shelves in the later 1980s, their fame spurred by the development of mountain biking and other extreme sports. These cycles featured heavier sturdier frames, large wide tyres, suspensions, and flat handlebars (allowing upright seating). By 2000, their sales had far distanced that of racing bicycles, which were by then used only by long-distance road cyclists.

Fig. Racing Cycle

The 2005 Giant Innova is an example of a typical 700C hybrid bicycle. It has 27 accelerates, front fork and seat suspension, an adjustable stem and disc brakes for wet-weather riding.

Recent years have seen a consumer backfire in North America, as casual cyclists demonstrated dissatisfaction with both the arduous mountain bikes and the more fragile, sometimes uncomfortable racing bikes. Manufacturers responded with the hybrid bicycle, in effect combining the two styles into a lighter weight utility cycle, but with a larger selection of gears and without the accessories found on earlier models. The term is applied flexibly, with bikes ranging from fast and light (often road belting along bikes, with the bars changed to flat bars) to models configured for comfort.

ADMINISTRATIVE BODIES

Union Cycliste International

Union Cycliste Internationale (UCI) is a cycling association that superintends competitive cycling events internationally. It is the world governing body for jurisdiction in the sport of cycling. The UCI is based in Aigle, Switzerland. The English translation is the International Cycling Union.

The UCI brings out racing licenses to riders and enforces disciplinary conventions, such as in matters of doping. The UCI also manages the classification of races and the points ranking system in versatile cycling disciplines including mountain biking, road and track cycling, for both men and women, amateur and professional. It also oversees the World Championships - in which different countries compete instead of trade teams - in various disciplines and in different categories. The winners of these races have the right to wear a special rainbow jersey for the coming year, and have the right to outwear the same rainbow pattern on their jersey collar and cuffs for the balance of their careers.

International Cycling Association

The International Cycling Association (ICA) was the first international body for cycle racing. It began in 1892 to establish a common definition of amateurism and to organise world championships. Its purpose was taken over by the Union Cycliste Internationale (UCI) in 1900.

League of American Bicyclists

The League of American Bicyclists (LAB) is a non-profit membership organization which promotes cycling for fun, fitness and conveyance through advocacy and education. A nonprofit, the League is one of the largest membership organizations of cyclists in the United States.

Founded in Newport, Rhode Island on May 30, 1880 as the League of American Wheelmen, it soon became the chairing national membership organization for cyclists in the United States. The League was also governance for bicycle racing in the U.S. during the late 1800s. Membership peaked at 103,000 in 1898. The League comprised a prominent advocacy group for the improvement of roads and highways in the United States long before the invention of the automobile. The Good Roads apparent motion in the late 19th century was founded and led by the League, which began publishing Good Roads magazine in 1892 (10 years before the founding of the American Automobile affiliation).

European Cyclists' Federation

European Cyclists' Federation is an umbrella governing body for national cycling organisations throughout Europe.

The ECF works to inform policy makers and the public about the potential and several positive effects of cycling for conveyance and pleasure. In doing so they run into many misconceptions about cycling which are far-flung

National Cyclists' Union

The National Cyclists' Union was an association founded in 1878 as the Bicycle Union to organise and govern bicycle racing in Great Britain. It was renamed the National Cyclists' Union in 1883. It banned all cycle racing on public roads in 1890, and - with the exception of the organisation of time trials (run by the Road Time Trials Council, formed in 1922 as the Road Racing Council) and of distance and place-to-place record attempts (overseen by the Road Records Association) - the NCU ran British cycle racing undisputed until 1942.

While several summer Olympic and world championship road races had been run as single time trials, the UCI decided in 1933 that all championships would be massed-start events. As a consequence, the NCU organised its 1933 world championship trial as a circuit race at Brooklands near Weybridge in Surrey. This and Donington Park in the north Midlands rested the sole venues for massed begin racing, including British National Road Race Championships, on mainland Britain until 1942, along with the Snaefell Mountain Course on the Isle of Man.

MAJOR TOURNAMENTS

UCI Continental Circuits

The UCI Continental Circuits are road bicycle racing competitions contended under the auspices of the Union Cycliste Internationale (UCI). The five circuits (one each representing Europe, Africa, Oceania, Asia, and the Americas) are inferior to the UCI ProTour. Both the ProTour and the circuits consist of a series of races in which varied cycling teams compete on a regular basis. The circuits were designed by UCI to export cycle racing beyond the European continent, where it is most popular and where the three Grand Tour stage races are held.

UCI Road World Championships

The UCI Road World Championships for women made its first appearance in Reims, France in 1959. For the first several years (until about 1990), the race changed in length from a low of 46.6 km in 1966 to around 72 km (30 to 50 miles). Beginning in 1991, the race length started to step by step increase, first to 79 km (Stuttgart, Germany), and then to over 100 km in 1996 (Lugano, Switzerland).

Due to the Summer Olympics, the Road World Championships weren't held in 1984, 1988 and 1992. The 2007 version, held in Stuttgart in Germany, is to date the lengthiest ever at 133.7 km.

British Cycling Junior Track Championships

Held at the Welsh National Cycling Centre in Newport (Wales), the best Junior and Under 16 cyclists in Britain came to contend for British Cycling medals and jerseys in the National Championships over five days. The riders contending included those who had just been to the World Track and Road Championships in Austria where the Great Britain team had its most successful competition ever. British Cycling was there for three of the five days bringing you the results and photographs of the racing.

FAMOUS PLAYERS

Beryl Burton

Beryl Burton, order of British Empire was born on 12 May 1937 and died on 8 May 1996, she was an English racing cyclist and one of Britain's grooviest ever athletes.

She mastered women's cycle racing in the UK, fetching more than 90 domestic championships and seven world titles, and setting several national records. She set a women's record for the 12-hour time-trial which surpassed the men's record for two years.

Burton was born Beryl Charnock and lived in the Morley area near Leeds, West Yorkshire area throughout her life, racing chiefly for Morley Cycling Club and later Knaresborough CC. She was brought in to cycling through her husband, Charlie, whom she got married in 1955. Two years later, she took her first national medal, silver in the national 100-mile individual time trial championship, and before the decade was out was contending internationally.

Yvonne Reynders

Yvonne Reynders (born August 4, 1937 in Schaarbeek near Brussels) is a early track and road cyclist from Belgium. With Beryl Burton of Great Britain, Reynders was among the extraordinary female road riders of the 1960s. She won a total number of twelve international medals during her career at the woman's world championships: road race - four gold medals (1959, 1961, 1963, and 1966) and two silver medals, chase - three gold medals (1961, 1964, and 1965) and three silver medals.

Jeannie Longo

Jeannie Longo was born on October 31, 1958, and is a female French racing cyclist, multiple (55 times) French and world champion. Longo is still active in cycling as of 2008 and is widely believed among the greatest female cyclists of all time. She is renowned for her competitive nature and her longevity in a sport where some of her contenders weren't yet born during her first Olympic contest in 1984. She was selected to compete for France in the 2008 Olympics, her seventh Olympic Games. She has stated that this will be her final involvement in the Olympics. In the Women's road race, she finished 24th, 33 seconds behind winner Nicole Cooke, who was one year old when Longo first rode in the Olympics. At the same Olympics, she wound up 4th in the road time trial, just two seconds shy of securing bronze medal.

Rebecca Twigg

Rebecca Twigg was born on March 26, 1963, and is an American early racing cyclist, who won six World Track Cycling Championship titles in the Individual chase event. During her cycling career, she also won 16 U.S. national championships (the first of which the individual time trial took place when she was 18 years old) and two Olympic medals (Silver medal in the 1984 Road Race in Los Angeles, and Bronze medal in the 1992 Track Pursuit in Barcelona).

Twigg also made her mark in road stage races. In 1984-86, she won the first three editions of the Women's Challenge. Twigg was a three-time Olympian (1984, 1992, and 1996). However, her final Olympic appearance, in Atlanta in 1996, ended in disputation when she quit the team in a disagreement with the coach Chris Carmichael and the U.S. Cycling Federation. The national federation had invested in the evolution of the so-called "SuperBike". Twigg, after using the bike in an earlier part of the Games, refused to ride it, citing poor individual fit and claiming that pressure from the staff on her to use the SuperBike and their refusal to grant conventional accreditation to her longtime personal coach, Eddie Borysewicz, left her defocused.

Oenone Wood

Oenone Wood, born on September 24, 1980 in Newcastle, New South Wales, Australia, is a professional cyclist, who started her cycling career in 2001 at the age of 21. She is a member of professional cycling Team Columbia Women (USA) and the Canberra Cycling Club, and erstwhile of the T-Mobile Professional Womens Cycling Team (GER). She lives in Aranda, a suburb of Canberra.

Her biggest success as a road cyclist has arguably been in Australian tours, including the Australian Criterium, Bay Series Criterium and the Geelong Tour, with some success overseas, especially winning Stages of the Giro d'Italia Femminile (ITA) and the Points Classification for the Giro d'Italia Femminile in 2004 and 2005. In the 2004 Summer Olympics Women's Road race she was in the leading group with fellow Australian Sara Carrigan, and when Carrigan and Judith Arndt broke away in the final lap to win the gold and silver medals, Wood had to sprint for the bronze medal with Olga Slyusareva of Russia and Nicole Cooke of Great Britain, coming 4th overall in the race. She is the present-day Australian Open Road champion (in the Elite Women's Road Race event).

REFERENCES

Barnett, John, *Barnett's Manual: Analysis and Procedures for Bicycle Mechanics.* VeloPress, 2003.

Brandt, Jobst, *The Bicycle Wheel* Mountain Air Books, 1993.

Cuthbertson, Tom and Rick Morrall, *Bike Bag Book,* Ten Speed Press, 1981.

DeLong, Fred, *DeLong's Guide to Bicycles and Bicycling: The Art and Science.* Krause Pub, 1978.

Downs, Todd, *Bicycling Magazine's Complete Guide to Bicycle Maintenance and Repair: For Road and Mountain Bikes.* Rodale Press, 2005.

7

Equestrian Events

Equestrianism refers to the skill of riding or driving horses. This broad description includes both use of horses for practical, working purposes as well as recreational activities and competitive sports.

Horses are trained and ridden for practical working purposes such as in police work or for controlling herd animals on a ranch. They are also used in competitive sports including, but not limited to dressage, endurance riding, eventing, reining, show jumping, tent pegging, vaulting, polo, horse racing, driving, and rodeo. Some popular forms of competition are classified together at horse shows, where horses perform in a broad variety of disciplines.

Horses (and other equids such as mules and donkeys) are used for non-competitive recreational riding such as fox hunting, trail riding or hacking. There is public access to horse trails in almost every part of the world; numerous parks, ranches, and public stables offer both guided and autonomous riding. Horses are also used for therapeutic purposes, both in specialized paraequestrian competition as well as non-competitive riding to improve human health and sentimental development.

Horses are also driven in harness racing, at horse shows and in different types of exhibition, historical re-enactment or ceremony, often pulling carriages. In few regions of the world, they are still used for practical purposes such as farming.

Horses continue to be used in public service: in traditional ceremonies (parades, funerals), police and volunteer mounted patrols, and for mounted search and rescue.

Equestrian Activities

Dressage (a French term, most commonly translated to mean "training") is a path and destination of competitive horse training, with competitions held at all levels from amateur to the Olympics. Its fundamental purpose is to grow, through standardised progressive training techniques, a horse's natural athletic power and willingness to perform, thereby maximizing its potential as a riding horse. At the peak of a dressage horse's gymnastic development, it can smoothly respond to a skilled rider's minimal aids by performing the requested movement while remaining relaxed and appearing effortless. Dressage is sometimes referred to as "Horse Ballet". Though the discipline has past roots, dressage was first recognized as an important equestrian pursuit in the West during the Renaissance. The great European riding masters of that period originated a sequential training system that has altered little since then and classical dressage is still believed the basis of trained advanced dressage.

Endurance Riding: Endurance riding is an equestrian sport based on controlled long distance races. It is one of the international competitions recognized by the FEI. There are endurance rides worldwide.

There are two primary types of long distance riding, Competitive trail riding and endurance rides. In an Endurance ride, the winning horse is the first one to cross the finishing line while stopping sporadically to pass a veterinary check that deems the animal in good health and "fit to continue." In the United States, most endurance rides are either 50 or 100 miles (160 km) long, although shorter rides are organized for beginners and a few longer, usually multi-day, rides exist. In the USA, the American Endurance Ride Conference (AERC) sanctions endurance rides. Winning riders finish 100-mile (160 km) rides in 10-12 hours. Any breed can contend, but the Arabian usually dominates the top levels because of the breed's stamina and natural endurance powers.

Eventing: Eventing is an equestrian event which consists of dressage, cross-country and show-jumping. This event has its roots as a comprehensive cavalry test needing mastery of various types of riding. It has three significant formats, the one day event (ODE), two day event and the three day event (3DE). It can also be called Militaire, Horse Trials, and united Training.

Reining: Reining is a western riding competition for horses where the riders guide the horses through a specific pattern of circles, spins, and stops. All work is done at the lope (a slow, at ease version of the horse gait a lot of generally known worldwide as the canter) and gallop; the fastest of the horse gaits. Reining is often described as a Western form of dressage riding, as it requires the horse to be responsive and in tune with its rider, whose aids should not be easily seen, and adjudicates the horse on its power to perform a set pattern of movements.

Show Jumping: Show jumping is also known as "stadium jumping" or "jumpers," is a member of a family of English riding equestrian events that also includes dressage, eventing, hunters and equitation. Jumping classes are generally seen at horse shows throughout the world, including the Olympics. Occasionally shows are limited entirely to jumpers, occasionally jumper classes are offered in conjunction with other English-style events, and occasionally show jumping is but one division of very large, all-breed competitions that include a very wide variety of disciplines. Jumping classes may be governed by various national horse show sanctioning organizations, such as the United States Equestrian Federation in the USA. However, international competitions are regulated by the decrees of the Fédération Équestre Internationale (FEI).

Tent Pegging: Tent pegging is a cavalry sport of old origin, and is one of only ten equestrian disciplines formally recognised by the International Federation for Equestrian Sports. Used narrowly, the term refers to a particular mounted game with ground targets. More broadly, it refers to the whole class of mounted cavalry games involving sharp weapons on horseback, for which the term "equestrian skill-at-arms" is also used.

Equestrian Vaulting: Equestrian vaulting is most often described as gymnastics and dance on horseback, and like these disciplines, it is an art and not a competitive sport. It is one of ten competitive equestrian events acknowledged by the International Federation for Equestrian Sports, along with: dressage, merged driving, endurance riding, eventing, horseball, paraequestrian, reining, show jumping, and tent pegging. Therapeutic or Interactive Vaulting is also used as form of treatment for children and adults who may have balance, attention, gross motor skill, or social deficits.

Polo: Polo is a team sport played outdoors on horseback in which the target is to score goals against an defending team. Riders score by driving a white wooden or plastic ball (size 3-3.5 inches, weight 4.25-4.75 ounces) into the opposing team's goal using a long-handled mallet. Goals are only valid if the scoring rider is mounted. The conventional sport of polo is played outdoors, and each polo team comprises of four riders and their mounts.

The advanced indoor variant is called arena polo. In arena polo, there are 3 instead of four players on each team and chukkers (periods) are 7 1/2 minutes in length. The playing area is 300' x 150'.

Rodeo: Rodeo is a sport which came up out of the working exercises of cattle herding in Spain, Mexico, and later the United States, Canada, South America and Australia. It was based on the skills needed of the working vaqueros and later, a cowboy, of what nowadays is the western United States, western Canada, and northern Mexico. Today it is a sporting event that comprises of numerous dissimilar timed and judged events that involve cattle and horses, designed to test the skill and speed of the human cowboy and cowgirl athletes who take part.

Rodeo, specially popular today within the Canadian province of Alberta and throughout the western United States, is the official state sport of Wyoming and Texas, and the iconic silhouette image of a Bucking Horse and Rider is a federal and state registered trademark of the State of Wyoming.

Rodeo events include the following forms of competition:

1. Barrel racing and pole bending

The timed speed and agility events seen in rodeo as well as gymkhana or O-Mok. Both men and women contend in speed events at gymkhanas or O-Mok-Sees; however, at most professional, approved rodeos, barrel racing is an entirely women's sport. In a barrel race, horse and rider gallop around a cloverleaf pattern of barrels, making agile turns without knocking the barrels over. In pole bending, horse and rider run the length of a line of six upright poles, turn sharply and weave through the poles, turn once again and weave back, then return to the begin.

2. Steer wrestling

Also known as "Bulldogging," this is a rodeo event where the rider jumps off his horse onto a steer and 'wrestles' it to the ground by grabbing it by the horns. This is likely the single most physically dangerous event in rodeo for the cowboy, who runs a high risk of jumping off a running horse head first and missing the steer, or of having the thrown steer land on top of him, occasionally horns first.

HISTORY

Although there is disputation over the accurate date horses were domesticated and when they were first ridden, the best approximation is that horses first were ridden about 4,500 BC. Indirect evidence suggests that horses were ridden long before they were driven. There is some evidence that about 6,000 years ago, near the Dneiper River and the Don River, people were utilising bits on horses, as a stallion that was buried there shows teeth wear consistent with using a bit. However, the most unequivocal early archaeological evidence of equines put to working use was of horses being driven.

Chariot burials about 2,500 BC exhibit the most direct hard evidence of horses used as working animals. In old times chariot warfare was accompanied by the use of war horses as light and heavy cavalry. The horse played an important role throughout human history all over the world, both in warfare and in peaceful pursuits such as conveyance, trade and agriculture.

The word dressage (rhymes with "massage") is derived from a French term meaning "training." It is not only a technique of schooling, but also a competitive equestrian sport. Dressage is believed "classical training," because it uses gymnastic exercises-a series of movements and figures-which have been studied and developed for centuries. The Spanish Riding School in Vienna, Austria, with its white Lipizzan stallions, is perhaps the most familiar institution dedicated entirely to the classical art of riding. Once an activity of royalty, today dressage has developed into a discipline and competitive sport accessible to all horses and riders."

The history of dressage dates back to the Greeks and the Romans. Dressage began as a form of battle campaigns that were very helpful to the soldiers. During the Medieval times, the art of Dressage was lost when the soldiers resorted to very heavy armor and also covered their horses with anywhere from 50 to more than 150 pounds of heavy armor. Dressage became the popular style of riding once again when pistols and rifles turned a usual part of battle. The armor was reduced, seeing as you could take aim from further away, and it was much lighter to take aims with much less armor.

History of Endurance Riding

Although the need to ride long distances has existed since domestication of the horse, Endurance riding as an organized activity was 1st arose in the United States based on European cavalry (peculiarly Polish and Russian WWI) and breeding program tests necessitating the power to carry 300 lb (140 kg) over 100 miles (160 km) in one day. Its beginnings as a sport commenced in the 1950s, at the time when Wendell Robie rode from Nevada to California, following the route of the Pony Express, to finish in under 24 hours. Endurance riding first was brought to Europe in the 1960s.

History of Eventing

Since prehistoric times, people have been riding horses. Two Equestrian events, chariot races and horse races, were first included in the 25th ancient Olympic Games competition schedule, in 680 BC. Eventing obtains its roots from the military. During its first years the sport was so aptly named "The Militaire". Eventing was the military mission of a cavalry officer that had to deliver a message through enemy lines and back again. Eventing was first presented at the Olympic Games in, Stockholm, Sweden in 1912.

It was however earlier in the 19th century, that the three Olympic disciplines had already developed to their ongoing form.

History of Reining

Throughout American history, dating back to the earliest Spanish settlers in what nowadays is Mexico and the Southwestern United States, including Texas and California, ranchers wanted to manage cattle from horseback. Cattle were moved, branded, doctored, sorted, and herded, often on open range without the welfare of fences, barns or other means of holding back the animals. A good cowboy wanted a quick and nimble horse, one that could alter directions rapidly, stop "on a dime," and sprint after an errant cow. The horse needed to be controlled generally by legs and weight, ridden with only one hand and a light touch on the reins, so that the cowboy's attention could also be on tasks that could include managing a lariat (to rope cattle), opening a gate, or simply waving a hand, hat or rope to move along a reluctant herd animal. Informal demonstrations of these ideal characteristics amongst ranch cowboys and vaqueros developed into the sport of reining, as well as the associated events of cutting and working cow horse as well as a lot of other horse show classes.

History of Show Jumping

Show jumping is a comparatively new equestrian sport. Until the envelopment Acts which came into force in England in the eighteenth century there had been little need for horses to habitually jump fences. But with this act of parliament came new challenges for those who accompanied fox hounds. The enclosures act brought fencing and limits to many regions of the country as common ground was distributed amongst the rich landowners. This meant that those wishing to pursue their sport now needed horses which were capable of jumping these obstacles.

In the early on shows held in France, there was a parade of challengers who then took off across country for the jumping. This sport was, however, not popular with viewers as they could not watch the jumping. Thus, it was not long before fences started to appear in the arena. This became known as Lepping. 1869 was the year 'horse leaping' came to prominence at Dublin horse show. Fifteen years later, Lepping competitions were brought to Britain and by 1900 most of the more important shows had Lepping classes. Women, riding side-saddle, had their own classes.

History of Tent Pegging

The term "tent pegging" is, however, for sure associated to the idea that cavaliers mounting a surprise pre-dawn raid on an enemy camp could use the game's skills to sever or uproot tent pegs, thus breaking down the tents on their sleeping occupants and sowing havoc and terror in the camp. However, there are few honest accounts of a cavalry squadron ever employing such tactics.

Because the particular game of tent pegging is the most popular equestrian skill-at-arms game, the whole class of sports became known as tent pegging during the twilight of cavalry in the twentieth century.

History of Equestrian Vaulting

Some trace the origins of vaulting to Roman games, including acrobatic shows on cantering horses. Others see roots in the bull dancers of old Crete. In either case, people have been doing acrobatic and dance-like movements on the backs of running horses for more than 2,000 years. The first known depiction of vaulting was from stone painting, dated at around 1500 BC, of Scandinavian riders standing on horses.

Renaissance and middle Ages history include a lot of references to vaulting or similar activities, and it appears apparent that current gymnastics executed on the "vaulting horse" was evolved from vaulting - letting concentration on the gymnastics without the horse. The present name of the sport comes from the French "La Voltige," which it gained during the Renaissance, when it was a form of riding drill and agility exercise for knights and noblemen, and also used as a symbol of position.

Vaulting was afterwards used to help cavalry troops increase their abilities on the horse, and the troops would start by working on a wooden horse before advancing to a live, moving mount. Advanced vaulting was formulated in post-war Germany as component of set of exercises for improving general riding. Cavalry officers presented the sport at the 1920 Olympic Games in Antwerp as "Artistic Riding," though the sport wasn't continued in the Games. Vaulting is still much more popular in Europe, where it is still included in dressage training, than it is in other portions of the world, although vaulting is a developing sport in Brazil, Australia, Canada, and the United States.

THE GAME

Equipments and Attires

Reining: Riders must use a western saddle. Spurs are permitted, but whips are not. Bridles are western-styled, without a noseband or caveson. The bosal style hackamore is also permitted. There are very rigid conventions about what types of bits and bosals are legal.

For protection, horses generally wear splint boots or polo wraps on the cannons of their lower front legs as well as skid boots on their hind fetlocks. Bell boots, which wrap around the pastern and protect the hoof and coronary band, are also generally seen, occasionally only on the front feet, other times on all four feet.

Riders must wear a long-sleeved shirt, jeans, a cowboy hat, and cowboy boots. In most competitions, they also wear chaps. Gloves are elective. There has historically been less conflict between men's and women's attire in reining than in most western events, although women's clothing is more tempted by fashion trends from Western delight competition, and thus women occasionally wear brighter colors, and are more apt to add a beautified jacket or vest, although generally not as flashy as in other horse show events.

Equestrian Helmet: An Equestrian helmet is worn when riding horses. This type of helmet is particularly designed to protect the rider's head if a person falls off a horse, particularly if they should strike their head on a hard object while falling or unexpectedly be struck in the head by a horse's hoof.

Certified helmets are needed headgear for a lot of competitive riding events, peculiarly where horse and rider must jump or work at high speed. Helmets are worn more often by English-style riders and are gaining acceptance as required headgear for children. They are most widely accepted in fields such as horse racing, eventing or show jumping. They are needed in eventing, in endurance riding and other types of competitions. People who take their horses hacking or trail riding occasionally wear helmets, although there are enormous variations in helmet use in dissimilar parts and cultures.

Dressage

Track: Dressage horses are shown in minimal tack. They are not allowed to wear boots (including hoof or bell boots) or wraps (including tail bandages) during the test, nor are they permitted to wear martingales or training devices such as draw or running reins or the gogue anywhere on the showgrounds during the competition. Due to the formality of dressage, tack is generally black leather, though dark brown is seen from time to time.

An English-style saddle is required for riding dressage, specifically a "dressage saddle" which is modeled entirely for the discipline. It is planned with a long and straight saddle flap, mirroring the leg of the dressage rider, which is long with a slight bend in the knee, a deep seat and generally a pronounced knee block. The saddle is generally placed over a square, white saddle pad. A dressage saddle is needed in FEI classes, though any simple English-type saddle may be used at the lower levels.

Show Jumping

Show jumping challengers use a very forward style of English saddle, most often the "close contact" design, which has a forward flap and a seat and cantle that is flatter than saddles designed for general all-purpose English riding or dressage.

This construction grants greater freedom of movement for the rider when in jumping position, and permits a shorter stirrup, needed in order for a rider to letting the rider to lighten his or her seat. Other saddles, such as those designed for dressage, are intended for riders with a deep seat, can hinder a rider over large fences, forcing them into a location that limits the horse's apparent motion and may put the rider hazardously behind the movement of the horse.

At international levels, saddle pads are generally white and square in shape, permitting the pair to reveal a sponsorship, national flag, or breeding affiliation. (In contrast, riders in show hunters and equitation often use "fitted" fleece pads that are the same shape as the saddle.) Girths vary in type, but generally have a contour to give room for the horse's elbows, and many have belly guards to protect the underside of the horse from its shoe studs when the front legs are tightly folded below.

Bridles may be used with any style of cavesson noseband, and there are few decrees regarding the severity of this gear. The figure-8 cavesson is the most popular type. Bits may also vary in severity, and challengers may use any bit, or even a "bitless bridle" or a hackamore. However, the ground jury at the show has the right, based on veterinary advice, to refuse a bit or bridling scheme if it could cause harm to the horse.

MAJOR TOURNAMENTS

FEI World Equestrian Games

The FEI World Equestrian Games are the major international championships for equestrianism, believed by many horsemen to be more important than the Olympics, and administered by the Fédération Equestre Internationale (FEI). The games have been held every four years, half way between each pair of back-to-back Summer Olympic Games, since 1990. Prior to that year, all ten of the FEI's individual disciplines held apart championships, generally in distinct countries.

The WEG have step by step expanded to include eight of the FEI's disciplines: merged driving, dressage, endurance riding, eventing, paraequestrianism, reining, show jumping, and vaulting. The FEI's two remaining disciplines, horseball and tent pegging, still conduct unintegrated championships. The WEG represent many of the world's top riders and most skilled horses, who contend over 15 days. Riders contending at WEG go through a strict selection process during the 4 years preceding each competition. Each participating country sends teams compiled of the very best equestrians in their discipline. Some 57 countries are represented by 800 athletes.

The Tevis Cup

The Western States Trail Ride, popularly called The Tevis Cup is a 100-mile endurance ride. The amateur event has been held every year since 1955.

The ride is held in Placer County, California, commencing at 5:15 a.m. at Robie Equestrian Park near the town of Truckee, across the crest of the Sierra Nevada near the Squaw Valley Ski Resort, and finishing at 5:15 a.m. near the fairgrounds in Auburn. There are compulsory 60-minute rest stops and veterinarian checks at Robinson Flat (30 milepost) and Foresthill (70 milepost).

Each rider who finishes the 100-mile course within the 24-hour limit and whose mount is judged "fit to continue" is awarded a silver Completion Award Buckle. The ride is sanctioned by AERC, the American Endurance Ride Conference.

The 52nd annual ride was held Saturday, August 5, 2006; the date was chosen to take advantage of the full moonlight. 194 riders departed Robie Park, and 87 riders accomplished the 100-ride to Auburn, so the completion rate was about 45%. The 2006 Tevis Cup winner (first-place finisher at 10:23 PM) was John Crandell of Virginia, who rode an 8-year old Arabian gelding named "Heraldic." The next morning, a team of veterinarians adjudicated the top ten horses for status, and Heraldic also won the coveted Haggin Cup for "best status," thus accomplishing a rare double-trophy status.

ADMINISTRATIVE BODIES

International Federation for Equestrian Sports

The Fédération Équestre Internationale (ordinarily titled as the FEI) or in English, the International Federation for Equestrian Sports, is the international regulating body of equestrian (horse) sports. Recognized competition disciplines include; dressage, merged driving, endurance riding, eventing, para-equestrianism, reining, show jumping, and vaulting. It also recognizes tent pegging and horseball as regional equestrian disciplines. It doesn't regulate or provide rules for horse racing or polo.

It has organized the FEI World Equestrian Games quadrenially (every four years) since 1990.

The FEI headquarters are in Lausanne, Switzerland. An FEI code of conduct [1] protects the welfare of the horses from physical abuse or doping.

The FEI was constituted in 1921 with the joining of the national organizations of Belgium (BEL), Denmark (DEN), France (FRA), Italy (ITA), Japan (JAP), Norway (NOR), Sweden (SWE) and the United States of America (USA). Today, there are 314 National Organizations who are affiliated with the FEI, the newest members being Cameroon and Madagascar, who joined in 2005.

National Reining Horse Association

The National Reining Horse Association (or NRHA) is a nonprofit organisation whose purpose is to promote the reining horse. The NRHA was established in 1966 and the headquarters are situated in Oklahoma City, Oklahoma. The NRHA approves shows for all breeds of horses, and for all levels of riders from starting amateurs to professional trainers. They also sponsor the NRHA Futurity for three year old horses.

The NRHA's objective is to "promote and encourage development of and public concern in agriculture and ranching through the promotion of public Reining Horse Shows; the development of suitable and proper standards of performance and judging intended to regulate all Reining Horse Contests sponsored and approved by the National Reining Horse Association; to encourage the development and breeding of better Reining Horses; and to develop and disseminate informational material deemed desirable to provide contestants and spectators a better understanding of a proper performance of the Reining Horse in the show arena.

American Quarter Horse Association

The American Quarter Horse Association (AQHA), based in Amarillo, Texas, is an international organization devoted to the conservation, improvement and record-keeping of the American Quarter Horse. The association sanctions many competitive events and preserves the official registry. The organization also houses the American Quarter Horse Hall of Fame and Museum and sponsors informative programs. The organization was established in 1940 in Fort Worth, Texas and now has almost 350,000 members.

The American Quarter Horse Association was born at a meeting in March in Fort Worth. The innovational idea had come out of the articles published by Robert M. Denhardt during the 1930s about the history and characteristics of the quarter horse. In an article entitled "The Quarter Horse, Then and Now" in a 1939 Western Horseman magazine, Denhardt also suggested that those curious in forming a breed registry meet in Fort Worth to discuss the idea and hopefully act on the idea. About seventy-five people met on March 15, 1940 to talk over the proposals, with the ultimate conclusion being to form a non-profit stock holding association in Texas to be the registry. Thirty-six people bought stock at the initial meeting. A board of directors and officers were selected.

United States Equestrian Federation

The United States Equestrian Federation (USEF) is the national regulating body for most equestrian sports in the United States. It began on January 20, 1917 as the Association of American Horse Shows, later altered in 1933 to the American Horse Shows Association (AHSA). In 2001, the organization altered its name to USA Equestrian (USAE) and, in 2003 it combined with the United States Equestrian Team (USET) to form the present organization.

Competitions regulated by the USEF include dressage, driving, endurance riding, eventing, hunt seat equitation, hunter, jumper, paralympic, reining, roadster, saddle seat equitation, vaulting, and western riding competition including equitation, western pleasure, reining, trail, and concerned events.

The organization also regulates breed shows held in the United States for the Andalusian, Lusitano, Arabian, ha!f-Arabian, Anglo-Arabian, Connemara, Friesian, Hackney, Morgan, American Saddlebred, National Show Horse, Paso Fino, Shetland, and Welsh breeds.

FAMOUS PLAYERS

Zara Anne Elizabeth Phillips

Zara Anne Elizabeth Phillips, MBE was born on 15 May 1981she is the second child and only daughter of HRH The Princess Anne, Princess Royal and her first husband, Captain Mark Phillips. As the eldest granddaughter of HM Queen Elizabeth II and HRH The Duke of Edinburgh, she is twelfth in the British Order of Succession.

An equestrienne, Zara is the reigning Eventing World Champion who won the World Championship in Aachen and was voted 2006 BBC Sports Personality of the Year that year by the British watching public (an award her mother, Princess Anne, won in 1971). Zara was created a Member of the Order of the British Empire (MBE) in the 2007 New Years Honours List for her services to equestrianism.

Phillip Peter Dutton

Phillip Peter Dutton was born on September 13, 1963.He was an Olympic-level equestrian rider, who contended for Australia. Dutton was born in Nyngan and was educated at Newington College (1976-1979). He pursued his passion for riding in Australia until 1991 when he moved to the United States to train in a more internationally competitive environment. In the 1996 Atlanta and 2000 Sydney Olympic Games he was a member of Australia's Gold Medal Three-day Eventing Team and he has now represented Australia in three Olympics and four World Equestrian Games. He is very active on the U.S. eventing circuit, winning the USEA greatest Rider of the Year title in 1998, and 2000, 2001, 2002, 2003, 2004, 2005, and 2006. In 2005 he was also the number one FEI World Event Rider. Phillip and his wife, Evie, live in Avondale, Pennsylvania with Evie's daughter LeeLee and their twins Mary and Olivia. Phillip's farm. True Prospect Farm, is situated in West Grove, PA. Dutton was presented the Medal of the Order of Australia in 1997.

Yvonne Losos de Muniz

Yvonne Losos de Muñiz is an international dressage rider that represents the Dominican Republic. She latterly won the individual bronze medal at the 2007 Pan American Games in Rio de Janeiro, Brazil, riding her sanctioned Hannoverian stallion Bernstein. With that medal she repeats her performance from the 2003 Pan Am Games held in her home country, where she also obtained the bronze medal riding a dissimilar mount, a Dutch mare named Inatana.

Prior to her Pan Am medals, she also won double individual gold medals at the 2002 Central American Games in El Salvador. In addition to her championship medals, Yvonne has also incurred several wins at honored international events held in West Palm Beach, FL, the Sunshine Tour (Spain), France and Germany. She presently trains in Germany with riding Master Jean Bemelmans, who also coaches the Spanish Olympic team and other top-level riders from Europe.

David McPherson Broome CBE

David McPherson Broome CBE was born on March 1, 1940. He is a adjourned Welsh show jumping champion. Broome was born in Cardiff, South Wales, attended Monmouth School and still upholds his stables at Mount Ballan Manor, Crick, near Chepstow in Monmouthshire. He won the European championships in 1961, 1967, and 1969, individual Olympic bronze medals in 1960 and 1968, the latter on his best-known horse Mr Softee, on which he was only two fences (8 faults) behind the Gold medal position.

In 1960 he was also voted BBC Sports Personality of the Year. He won the World individual championship in 1970, and in the very year was Western Mail Welsh Sports Personality of the year. In 1978 he was part of the world championship winning British team. He turned professional in 1973. David Broome has won the King George V Gold Cup a record six times on six distinct horses between 1960 - 1991, a record yet to be matched. He has enjoyed most of his success on Irish Sport Horses and he has said his favorite horse of all was Sportsman.

REFERENCES

Andreson, C. W.:.*Head Up, Heels Down.* New York, the Macmillan Company, 1944.

Ansell, M. P. (Lt. Col.): *Jumping.* London, The Naldrett Press, Ltd. 1954.

Baucher, F.: *Horsemanship, Including the Breaking and Trainirig of Horses.* 3rd American ed., Philadelphia, Parry and McMillan, 1856.

Benoist-Gironiere, Yves: *The Conquest of the Horse.* Warford, England, Mayflower Press, 1952.

Beudant, E.: *Horse Training, Out-door and High School.* New York, Charles Scribner's Sons, 1950.

British Horse Society and the Pony Club: *Manual of Horsemanship.* London, 6th ed. reprint 1968.

British Show Jumping Association *Know the Game, Show Jumping,* London, Educational Productions, Ltd., 1954.

Chamberlain, Harry D.: *Riding and Schooling Horses.* Washington, D.C., Armoured Cavalry Journal, 1947.

Training Hunters, Jumpers, and Hacks. New York-D. Van Nostrand Co., Inc., 1952.

8

Football

Succinctly described by the great Brazilian Pelé as 'the beautiful game', football is the only sport in the world which can be precisely defined as a global phenomenon. In 175 countries, football is regarded the national sport, representing approximately 90% of the world's nations. This nominal commitment to football is matched by the world population's dedication, with statistics indicating a cumulative audience of 30 billion plus for the 2006 FIFA World Cup in Germany, and well over a billion tuning in for the Final between Italy and France.

Moreover, football's fame is by no means an advanced development. Writing in 1928, J.B. Priestley eloquently defined its appeal to former generations by expressing 'to say that these men paid their shillings to watch twenty-two hirelings kick a ball is simply to say that a violin is wood and catgut, that Hamlet is so much paper and ink'.

That said, the evolution of globalisation and advanced means of communication, united with the natural advancement beyond its roots in Britain, means football nowadays possesses a position beyond that of a mere pastime. It reflects the contemporary world, with no national limitations on players at club level. Indeed, even in international football, foreign coaches are common and have had much success, most notably Otto Rehhagel, the German-born coach who led Greece to glory in the 2004 European Championships.

Football also frequently plays a role in the arts, with films like 'Escape to Victory' (1981), 'Bend It Like Beckham' (2003) and 'The Arsenal Stadium Mystery' (1939) and books such as Nick Hornby's 'Fever Pitch'. The sport's arising centrality in film was instanced in 2007's 'Zidane: A 21st Century Portrait', which demoed actual Madrid's match against Villarreal, but with 17 cameras trained on the great French midfielder Zinedine Zidane.

Advancing the ball with kicks, running with it, passing to other team mates, trying to forward it to the opponent's end of the field, shooting in between the goal posts and scoring a point, this is football. The winning team is the one that has scored several number of points (goals) when a specific length of time has elapsed.

Even faith and politics are not free from football's sphere of influence. The former is distinctly evidenced in the creation of the Iglesia Maradoniana in Argentina; a Church devoted to the legendary Diego Maradona (who led Argentina to the World Cup in 1986) and now counts 15,000 people as members. Likewise in governmental affairs, the Football War between El Salvador and Honduras in June 1969 was so-called because it followed rioting which broke out after El Salvador eliminated Honduras to reach out the 1970 World Cup finals.

The Major Teams of Football are:

- Argentina.
- Australia.
- Brazil.
- Czech Republic.
- England.
- France.
- Germany.
- India.
- Mexico.
- Poland.
- South Korea.
- Spain.
- Ukraine.
- USA.

HISTORY

The origination of football as we understand it nowadays is geographically bounded to British shores, but there is extensive evidence of old games with the same basic precepts as the contemporary incarnation. The first of these was identified as portion of Shang Dynasty China in the 5th century BC, the game's objective being to kick a leather ball through a hole in a piece of cloth which between two 30 foot poles. The Tsu'Chu military practice in 3rd century China was also a concerning elaboration on this theme; the premise once again being to kick a leather ball through a 30-40 centimetre opening.

As the Tsu'Chu exercise lacked the central team element of today's football, attention has also been given to the Greek and Roman games of episkyros and Harpastum respectively. The latter is especially interesting as a game played on a rectangular grass surface with a ball approximately equivalent to a softball nowadays.

Despite some signs of the game we love today in the old World, the true evolution of football came in Medieval Britain by and large, though there are signs of equivalents across Europe (the majority of which were exported). Known as Shrovetide football or Medieval football, the inception point has been claimed as the 3rd century after the defeat of the Romans, but the exercise itself was first recorded in the 9th century as component of the Historia Britonum.

The extent of its fame and rambunctiousness is mirrored in the truth there were more than 30 imperial and local laws which attempted to ban football between 1314 and 1667. However, by the end of the 14th century, the term 'football' was well constituted in England, with Chaucer even referencing it in his Canterbury Tales.

It was by no means alone bounded to the lower orders either, as the Great Wardrobe of Henry VIII in 1526 recorded 'one leather pair (of shoes) for football', and decrees around 1555 were needed to ban football at the colleges of Cambridge and Oxford University. Football was also prevalent beyond English borders, with the game first mentioned in Ireland in the 1527 Statute of Galway and a ball found out in Scotland which dates back to 1540 and was supposedly used for football. Across the continent too, other forms of the game were visible like the 16th century Calcio Fiorentino in Florence and La Soule in Normandy.

The first signs of football developing from its mob roots came with the publication of the naturalist Francis Willoughby's 'Book of Sports' around 1660. In this work, Willughby described the game of 'football', identifying the pitch, two ends with gates known as 'goals', basic positioning (notably that few of each team's best players were left to 'guard the goal') and the aim as scoring the first goal. Even some details were included, such as avoiding high tackles (referred to as 'striking').

That said, it would be almost incisively two centuries until the constitution of the advanced game took place. The decisive moment was

October 26th 1863 when, following a meeting by all the clubs in existence in England at the Freemason's Tavern in London's Great Queen Street, the Football Association was established.

Five subsequent meetings over the adjacent two months saw the drawing up of the code, predominantly informed by the newly published Cambridge decrees but excluding regulations on running with the ball 'decently' and the acceptance of 'hacking'.

The latter caused respectable uproar, with the representative from Blackheath Rugby Club claiming 'hacking is the true football' and thus voicing an opinion echoed nowadays by a lot of ex-footballers became television pundits. The meetings also saw the institution of 'soccer' as a potential abbreviation for 'Association Football' comparable to 'rugger' in rugby, again firing up a debate presently raging as a result of football's increased fame in America (also home to American Football, also known as, Gridiron).

On a practical level, the meetings led to the inauguration of the first coded match between Sheffield and Nottingham (now Notts County), and the consequent foundation of Nottingham Forest FC in 1865 and many other clubs across England.

The FA Challenge Cup accompanied in 1871 with great success and Aston Villa director William McGregor finally mooted the concept of a league competition in 1888 in collaboration with 11 other clubs. At first set up as the Football League, with a 50-50 split between the North and the Midlands on one side and the South on the other, the true First Division only came as a result of the uniting with the rivalling Football Alliance (set up in 1889) in 1892.

The uprise of club football made international football an obvious idea and, the first international match was played between England and Scotland in Partick in November 1872, ending in a unsatisfying 0-0. However, Scotland's influence on England even at this early stage was palpable. After a number of English teams began hiring Scottish players, the debate over football's amateur status was inflamed and resulted in a move to professionalism in 1885.

At first established with a wage limit, this was a massive boon for the northern, predominantly working-class clubs, as contradicted to the 'gentleman' dominated south. The affect on results for the former was irresistibly positive, with the last amateur team to win the FA Cup being the Old Etonians in 1882. Though the wage cap was only abolished in

1959, the foundations of modern-day professional club and international football in Britain had been established.

The fame of football on the continent was well constituted by the 19th century, with the first club being Switzerland's Lausanne Football and Cricket Club, founded in 1860. However, the actual development of the sport came much later. The Italian Football Federation (FIGC) was conceived in 1898 but the league only came about in 1929, while the first Spanish competition was the Copa del Rey in 1902, pursued by La Liga in 1928.

Furthermore, European and worldwide developments were heavily charmed by the aforementioned innovations in England. For example, the first recorded game outside of Europe took place in Argentina in 1867 and involved English workers in the country. Indeed, many clubs across the world today survive due to the efforts of British natives, Corinthians FC being a prime example. Primitively an amateur side based in London, they joined the Amateur Football Association rather than aligning themselves with the Football League and the FA Cup.

Rather than disband although, Corinthians toured the world, inspiring the small Brazilian side in São Paulo, who renamed themselves Sports Club Corinthians Paulista in 1910 and are now one of the most important clubs in South American football, and even encouraging Spain's fledgling Real Madrid CF to copy their trademark white shirts. Likewise, arguably the most successful Italian side in the world, AC Milan, were the brainchild of Alfred Edwards who, in 1899, founded the Milan Cricket and Football Club. Such was Britain's worldwide influence that the Argentina Football Association was established in 1893 by Scotland-born Alexander Watson Hutton.

It is for reasons like these that football can arguably be regarded the greatest export in Britain's long history. What is surely not in question is the unbelievable influence Britain had on the development of modernistic football; laying down the original ordinances, establishing the basic competitions and dispersing the game quite literally worldwide.

Women's Football

Remarkably, women's football has been around since the inception of the sport in the late 19th century, and there is evidence of female engagement in all the forerunners of the game as well as medieval football. Though not as popular with viewers today, it was really exceedingly popular during World War I, with women's industry teams like Dick, Kerr's Ladies from Preston, who also played the first international game with a team from Paris.

The sport was practically ended with the Football Association's decision to ban women's football in 1921 due to supposed bad taste. However, it was finally revived following the formation of the English Women's FA in 1969 and the lifting of the ban in 1971.

On a global level too, the game expanded and, by 1992, Japan was home to the first semi-professional women's league (the L. League). Today, there are major international competitions, most notably the Women's World Cup and the European Championships.

Furthermore, in the UK, statistics showed well over 100,000 registered women's footballers at the end of 2005. This was almost a ten-fold increase from the 11,2000 registered in 1993, attesting both to the fame of women's football in itself and the cross-gender appeal of the sport commonly.

THE GAME

Players

Each team comprises of a utmost of eleven players (excluding substitutes), one of whom must be the goalkeeper. Competition decrees may state a minimal number of players needed to comprise a team; this is generally seven. Goalkeepers are the only players permitted to play the ball with their hands or arms, provided they do so within the penalty area in front of their own goal. Although there are a variety of positions in which the outfield (non-goalkeeper) players are strategically placed by a coach, these positions are not defined or needed by the Laws.

Equipments

The basic equipment or kit players are needed to wear includes a shirt, shorts, socks, footwear and sufficient shin guards. Headgear is not a needed piece of basic gear, but players today may choose to wear it to protect themselves from head injury.

Players are disallowed to wear or use anything that is grievous to themselves or another player, such as jewellery or watches. The goalkeeper must wear clothing that is easily differentiable from that worn by the other players and the match officials.

A number of players may be replaced by substitutes during the course of the game. The maximum number of substitutions permitted in most competitive international and domestic league games is three, although the permitted number may vary in other contests or in friendly matches.

Fig. Ball

Common reasons for a substitution include injury, fatigue, ineffectiveness, a tactical switch, or timewasting at the end of an exquisitely poised game. In standard adult matches, a player who has been substituted may not take further part in a match.

Officials

A game is officiated by a referee, who has "full authority to enforce the Laws of the Game in association with the match to which he has been appointed" (Law 5), and whose decisions are final. The referee is helped by two assistant referees. In many high-level games there is also a fourth official who helps the referee and may replace another official should the need uprise.

Playing Ground

The length of the pitch for international adult matches is in the range 100-110 m (110-120 yd) and the width is in the range 64-75 m (70-80 yd). Fields for non-international matches may be 91-120 m (100-130 yd) length and 45-91 m (50-101 yd) in width, rendered that the pitch doesn't become square. The longer boundary lines are touchlines or sidelines, while the shorter boundaries (on which the goals are placed) are goal lines.

A rectangular goal is placed at the middle of each goal line. The inner edges of the vertical goal posts must be 7.3 m (8 yd) separated, and the lower edge of the horizontal crossbar supported by the goal posts must be 2.44 m (8 ft) above the ground. Nets are generally placed behind the goal, but are not needed by the Laws.

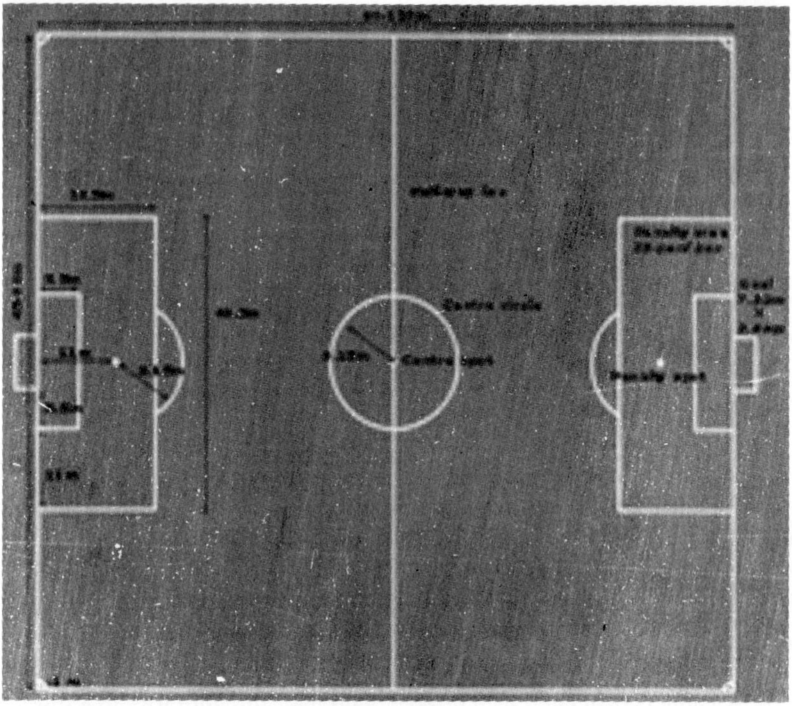

Fig. Field

In front of each goal is an area known as the penalty area. This area is marked by the goal line, two lines beginning on the goal line 16.5 m (18 yd) from the goalposts and extending 16.5 m (18 yd) into the pitch perpendicular to the goal line, and a line linking them. This area has a number of functions, the most prominent being to mark where the goalkeeper may handle the ball and where a penalty foul by a member of the defending team becomes punishable by a penalty kick. Other markings define the location of the ball or players at kick-offs, goal kicks, penalty kicks and corner kicks.

Durations

A standard adult football match comprises of two periods of 45 minutes each, known as halves. Each half runs ceaselessly, meaning that the clock is not stopped when the ball is out of play. There is generally a 15-minute half-time break between halves. The end of the match is known as full-time.

The referee is the official timekeeper for the match, and may make an allowance for time lost through substitutions, injured players requiring attention, or other stoppages. This added time is usually referred to as stoppage time or injury time, and is at the sole discretion of the referee. The referee alone signals the end of the match. In matches where a fourth official is appointed, toward the end of the half the referee signals how many minutes of stoppage time he intends to add. The fourth official then informs the players and spectators by holding up a board showing this number.

The signalled stoppage time may be further extended by the referee. Added time was prefaced because of an incident which happened in 1891 during a match between Stoke and Aston Villa. Trailing 1-0 and with just two minutes remaining, Stoke were granted a penalty. Villa's goalkeeper kicked the ball out of the ground, and by the time the ball had been retrieved, the 90 minutes had elapsed and the game was over.

MAJOR TOURNAMENTS

FIFA World Cup

The FIFA World Cup, at times called the Football World Cup, but generally referred to simply as the World Cup, is an international association football competition contended by the men's national teams of the members of Fédération Internationale de Football Association (FIFA), the sport's global regulating body. The championship has been granted every four years since the first tournament in 1930, except in 1942 and 1946, due to World War II.

The tournament comprises of two sections, the qualification phase and the final phase (formally called the World Cup Finals). The qualification phase, which presently take place over the three years preceding the Finals, is used to determine which teams qualify for the Finals. The current format of the Finals involves 32 teams competing for the title, at venues within the host nation (or nations) over a period of about a month. The World Cup Finals is the most widely-viewed sporting event in the world, with an approximated 715.1 million people watching the 2006 tournament final.

FIFA Confederation Cup

The FIFA Confederations Cup is an official FIFA tournament, held every four years. In modern times, it has been seen as a warm-up event to the FIFA World Cup™, but is by no means a minor competition. In reality, due to the nature of its players, it is often referred to as the 'Champions of Champions' tournament.

The Confederations Cup began life as the King Fahd Cup invitational tournament which pitted hosts and organisers Saudi Arabia against three opted opponents in 1992 and 1995. It was in 1997 that it became an official FIFA tournament and was renamed the FIFA Confederations Cup. From 2005, the scheduling of this antecedently biannual competition was altered to see it played once every four years and staged the year before the FIFA World Cup in the Host Country.

Blue Stars\ FIFA Youth Cup

Established in 1898, FC Blue Stars are one of Zurich's oldest football clubs. In 1921, Blue Stars were among the first Swiss clubs to establish a separate youth section, before expanding their programme to incorporate an yearly tournament in 1939, where Grasshoppers became the first winners entered into the Golden Book. The 1941 event was the first to be staged at the Letzigrund stadium in Zurich. The municipality stepped in as patron as 16 teams combated for the trophy. With penalty shoot-outs yet to be invented, Young Fellows were declared winners by the drawing of lots, following a draw with FC Lugano after extra time.

FIFA Women's World Cup

The FIFA Women's World Cup is recognized as the mo . ımportant International competition in women's football and is played amongst women's national football teams of the member states of FIFA, the sport's global governing body. Contended every four years, the first Women's World Cup tournament, named the Women's World Championship, was held in 1991, sixty-one years after the men's first FIFA World Cup tournament in 1930. The current format has sixteen teams contending every four years for the winner's trophy.

The tournament was primitively the brainchild of the then FIFA president João Havelange. The inaugural tournament was hosted in China in 1991, with twelve teams sent to represent their countries. The 1995 FIFA Women's World Cup was held in Sweden with twelve teams. Over 660,000 viewers attended the 1999 FIFA Women's World Cup in the United States, and almost one billion viewers from seventy countries tuned in to watch sixteen countries fight for the title.

IFA Shield

The Indian Football Association, the association regulating football in the state of West Bengal, came into being in 1893 and in the same year the IFA Shield tournament was commenced.

During the initial years, the IFA Shield, Kolkata's oldest football tournament, was ruled by British army teams. However their stranglehold over the Shield was broken in 1911, when Mohun Bagan turned the first Indian team to win the IFA Shield by defeating East Yorkshire Regiment 2-1. That was a historic moment for Indian football as the natives beat the Englishmen at their own game.

East Bengal Club has won the IFA Shield 27 times while their arch rivals Mohun Bagan has pocketed the honours 21 times. In the 2005 edition, the second team of German giants Bayern Munich made its debut in the tournament and walked away with the honours by thrashing EverReady SA 5-1 in the final.

Federation Cup

Federation Cup is the second most esteemed club football tournament in India after the National Football League (NFL). The tournament was commenced by the All India Football Federation in 1977 and involves all the major NFL teams.

The 27th version of the Federation Cup held in Goa in 2005 got a shot in the arm with Zee Sports rendering live telecast. In an effort to woo the Indian viewers, Zee employed state-of-the-start broadcasting gear and a star commentary team.

Durand Cup

Durand Cup, the oldest football tournament in India, is also 3rd oldest football tournament in the world, after the English FA-Cup and the Scottish FA-Cup.

The Durand Cup football tournament was began in Shimla in 1898 by the then India's Foreign Secretary, Sir Mortimer Durand. Royal Scots Fusiliers bagged the honours in the inaugural Durand cup by defeating Highland Light Infantry with score 2-1.

Since Independence, Mohun Bagan (16) and East Bengal (15) have split 31 cup triumphs between them. The tournament is hosted by the army and is held at the Ambedkar Stadium in Delhi.

Despite the fact that the Durand Cup used to attract huge crowds, the tournament has lost its sheen due to the lack of coordination between the Army and the All India Football Federation (AIFF). With the AIFF investing on the National Football League, like many other domestic competitions, the Durand Cup is also sliding into obscurity.

Santosh Trophy

Before the arrival of the National Football League, Santosh Trophy was India's premier football tournament. The tournament, which was kicked-off in 1941, was named after the late Maharaja Sir Manmatha Nath Roy Chowdhary of Santosh, who had been the President of the Indian Football Association.

In Santosh Trophy, instead of clubs, various Indian provinces vie for the top honour. In the present format, eight teams that are chosen through a qualifying round join the four seeded teams in the quarterfinal league stage. These twelve teams are then divided up into four groups of three each and the subsequent group winners finish the semifinal line-up. The state of Bengal has achieved astounding success in the Santosh Trophy, annexing the title a whopping 29 times.

ADMINISTRATIVE BODIES

FIFA

The Fédération Internationale de Football Association (French for International Federation of Association Football), commonly known by its acronym, FIFA is the international regulating body of association football. Its headquarters are in Zurich, Switzerland, and its present-day president is Sepp Blatter. FIFA is responsible for the organization and administration of football's major international tournaments, most notably the FIFA World Cup, held since 1930.

FIFA has 208 member associations, which is 16 more than the United Nations and 3 more than the International Olympic Committee, although 5 fewer than the International Association of Athletics Federations.

International Football Association Board.

The International Football Association Board (IFAB) is the body that determines the Laws of the Game of association football. IFAB is made up of representatives from each of the United Kingdom's pioneering football associations - England's Football Association (The FA), the Scottish Football Association (SFA), the Football Association of Wales (FAW) and Northern Ireland's Irish Football Association (IFA) - and Fédération Internationale de Football Association (FIFA), the international regulating body for football. Each UK association has one vote and FIFA has four. IFAB deliberations must be sanctioned by at least six votes. Thus, FIFA's approval is essential for any IFAB decision, but FIFA alone cannot alter the Laws of the Game; they need to be agreed by at least two of the UK members.

Union of Europe Football Association

UEFA represents the national football associations of Europe, runs Europewide national and club competitions, and controls the prize money, ordinances and media rights to those competitions. Numerous national football associations which are geographically in Asia or largely in Asia belong to UEFA rather than the Asian Football Confederation (AFC). These nations are Armenia, Georgia, Kazakhstan, Turkey, Israel, Cyprus, Russia and Azerbaijan (Israel and Kazakhstan are former AFC members). Cyprus chose to be classed as a European football nation - it had the choice of Europe, Asia or Africa.

UEFA is one of the biggest of six transcontinental confederations of FIFA. Of all the confederations, it is by far the strongest in terms of riches and influence over the global game. Virtually all of the world's top players play in European leagues in part due to the wages available from the world's richest football clubs, specially in England, Germany, Italy and Spain. Many of the world's strongest national sides are in UEFA. Of the 32 available spots in the 2006 FIFA World Cup, 14 were allocated to UEFA national teams, and presently 14 of the top 20 teams in the FIFA World Rankings are UEFA members.

The Football Association

The Football Association, also known as simply The FA, is the regulating body of football in England and the Crown Dependencies of Jersey, Guernsey and the Isle of Man. The FA has a unique place in the history of football.

The FA is a member of UEFA and FIFA, and bears a permanent seat on the International Football Association Board (IFAB). Contrary to other national football associations, it does not take the national name (ie. English) in its title.

All of England's professional football clubs are members of the Football Association. The FA is responsible for the appointment of the management of the England men's and women's national teams and the organization of the FA Cup (the nation's most honored cup competition). Though it doesn't run the regular operations of the country's top league, the Premier League, it has veto ability over the appointment of the league Chairman and main Executive and over any alterations to league decrees. The Football League, England's second tier league, comprising of The Championship, League One and League Two, is self-governing.

All India Football Federation

The All India Football Federation (AIFF) is the apex administrative body regulating the game of football in India. The AIFF is in charge of the national football team and hosts a number of tournaments including the National Football League.

During the initial years of Indian football, in the absence of a central regulating body, a bevy of provincial associations called the shots at the territorial level. However, the Indian Football Association (IFA), the association regulating football in the state of West Bengal, was recognised as the sport's de-facto regulating body. By virtue of its affiliation to the Football Association of England, the IFA donned the role of the national body and was at the forefront of several promotional activities.

In 1935, the IFA solicited the representatives of the football associations of Assam, Bihar, UP, Delhi, Mysore and Bombay at a conference in Darbhanga, with the aim of constituting a national body. But sharp conflicts among the discussing parties threatened to ruin the conference with the IFA delegates, SN Banerjee and Pankaj Gupta walking out in protest. However, the remaining delegates went ahead and conceived the All India Football Association.

In 1937, the warring factions decided to call peace and arrived at a decision to form the All India Football Federation with one representative from each affiliated association and two each from the IFA and the Army Sports Control Board.

FAMOUS PLAYERS

Ronaldo

His full name is Luís Nazário de Lima Ronaldo, he was born on September 22, 1976, at Bento Ribeiro,Rio de Janeiro, Brazil. His position in the game is forward.

Ronaldo won the FIFA World Player of the Year title in 1996 and 1997, but performed disappointingly in the 1998 World Cup. He scored merely four goals.

He however made a come back becoming the top scorer in the FIFA World Cup 2002 and winning the Golden Boot. He also equated Pelé's Brazilian record of 12 World Cup goals thus helping Brazil lift their fifth world cup title.

On the 2 nd of June 2004, in a qualifier for the 2006 World Cup, Ronaldo scored a hat trick against archrivals Argentina, all of his 3 goals coming from the penalty shots.

Ronaldinho

He was born on 21st march, 1980, at Porto Alegre, Brazil. His position is of midfielder in the game.

Ronaldinho has won the FIFA World Player of the Year Award 2004, 2005, the FIFPro World Player of the Year Title 2005, and the European Footballer of the Year award 2005. This naturally talented player is known for his stunning ball control. He is often spoken of in the same ranks as Pele and Zico. Ronaldinho was acclaimed as the best player of the last World Cup at the age of 22.

David Bekham

His full name is David Robert Joseph Beckham, he was born in England, and is midfielder in the game. David Beckham is the captain of the English football team. As the team goes into the 2006 FIFA World Cup, he would become the sixth player to represent England in three World Cups (along with Sol Campbell and Michael Owen)

His achievements are as follows:

Intercontinental Cup 1999 (Manchester United), Champions League 1999 (Manchester United), Premiership Champions1996, 1997, 1999, 2000, 2001, 2003 (Manchester United), FA Cup 1996, 1999 (Manchester United), League Cup Finals 2003 (Manchester United), League Cup Finals 2004 (Real Madrid).

Zinedine Zidane

His full name is Zinedine Yazid Zidane, he was born on June 23, 1972, at Marseille, France. In 2004, Pelé listed Zidane among the top 125 living footballers. In the same year, in the UEFA Golden Jubilee Poll, he was also voted as the best European player in the past 50 years. Zidane was also among the Athens 2004 Torchbearers.

His achievements are as follows:

FIFA World Cup 1998, European Championship 2000, FIFA World Player of the Year: 1998, 2000, 2003, European Footballer of the Year (Ballon d'Or): 1998.

Diego Maradona

His full name is Diego Armando Maradona, he was born on October 30, 1960, at Villa Fiorito, Argentina.

In his 91 appearings for Argentina, Maradona has scored 34 goals(second highest for Argentina). He has played in four World Cup Tournaments -1982, 1986, 1990, 1994 making 21 appearances in all.

His accomplishments are as follows:

FIFA World Youth Championship 1979, FIFA World Cup winner 1986, Copa Artemio Franchi 1993, Argentine Football Writers' football player of the Year 1979-1981, 1986, South American Footballer of the Year 1979, 1986, 1989, 1990, 1992, Argentine Sports Writers' Sportsman of the Year 1986, Golden Ball for Best Player of the FIFA World Cup 1986, European Footballer of the Year 1986(France Football), finest Footballer in the World 1986-1987 (Onze), World Player of the Year 1986 (World Soccer Magazine), 1996 Golden Ball for services to cccfootball (France Football), Argentine Sports Writers' Sportsman of the Century 1999, FIFA Goal of the Century" 2002 (1986 vs. England; second goal), "FIFA best football player of the century"2000, people's choice.

Baichung Bhutia

He was born in December 15, 1976, Tinkitam, Sikkim. The major teams he played with are: East Bengal Club, JCT Mills, Mohun Bagan AC, Bury FC, India. His playing position is striker.

His accomplishments: First Indian to play professional football in England; led the national football team to title triumph at the LG Cup in Vietnam in 2002; led East Bengal club to LG Asean Club Cup football championship victory in Jakarta in 2003.

Chuni Goswami

His full name was Subimal Chuni Goswami, born on January 15, 1938, Kishoregunj, Bengal. Major Teams he played with: Mohun Bagan AC, India. His playing position was Striker.

He led the Indian team to gold at the 1962 Asian Games in Jakarta. He was awarded Arjuna Award in 1963 and Padma Shri in 1983.

During the golden era of Indian football, Chuni Goswami was one of the mainstays of the national team. Goswami started his professional career with the Mohun Bagan Club in 1954 having graduated through the junior outfit of the club.

Mani Vijayan

His full name is Invalappil Mani Vijayan. He was born on April 25, 1969, Thrissur, Kerala. Major teams he played with: Kerala Police, Mohun

Bagan AC, JCT Mills, FC Kochin, India. His playing Position was Striker. He scored the fastest ever international goal in 1999 SAF Games, was top scorer in 2003 Afro-Asian Games and was awrded Arjuna Award in 2002

The life of I. M. Vijayan, one of most versatile Indian strikers, is the archetypal rags to riches story. From selling soda bottles in the streets of Thrissur to becoming one of the most identifiable faces of Indian football, it is been hard work all the way for IM Vijayan.

REFERENCES

Bower, T.: *Broken Dreams: Vanity, Greed and the Souring of British Football.* London: Simon and Conn, D.: *The Football Business: Fair Game in the 90s.* Edinburgh, 1997.

Corry, D., Williamson, P. and Moore, S,: *A game without vision: The crisis in English football,* 1993.

Freeman, S.: *Own goal! How egotism and greed are destroying football.* London: Orion, 2000.

Fynn, A. and Guest, L.: *Out of time: Why football isn't working.* London: Simon and Schuster, 1994)

Fynn, A.: *Dream On: A year in the life of a Premier League club.* London: Simon and Schuster, 1996.

Garland, G., Malcolm, D. and Rowe, M.: *The future of football: challenges for the twenty-first century.* London: Frank Cass, 2000.

Hamil, S., Michie, J, and Oughton, C. (eds): *The changing face of the football business.* London: Frank Cass, 2001.

Horton, E.: *Moving the goalposts: Football's Exploitation.* Edinburgh: Mainstream, 1997.

Institute for Public Policy Research: *Trust in Football.* London: IPPR, 2004.

Kelly, G.: *Sweet FA.* London: CollinsWillow, 1999.

King, A.: *The End of the Terraces. The transformation of English football in the 1990s.* Leicester, Leicester University Press, 1998.

9

Golf

Fig. Hole Dimension

Golf is a game in which a player, using numerous types of clubs including a driver, a putter, and irons, hits a ball into each hole on a golf course in the lowest possible number of strokes. Golf is one of the few ball games that does not use a standardised playing field; rather, the game is played on golf "courses", each one of which has a unique design and usually comprises of either 9 or 18 holes. Golf is specified in the conventions of Golf as "playing a ball with a club from the teeing ground into the hole by a stroke or successive strokes in accordance with the conventions."

The first game of golf for which records survive was played at Bruntsfield Links, in Edinburgh, Scotland, in A.D. 1456, recorded in the archives of the Edinburgh Burgess Golfing Society, now The Royal Burgess Golfing Society. The advanced game of golf spread from Scotland to England and has now become a worldwide game, with golf courses in the majority of countries.

Golf competition may be played as stroke play, in which the individual with the lowest number of strokes is announced the winner, stableford points play (as devised in 1931 by Dr. Frank Stableford of the Wallasey & Royal Liverpool Golf Clubs), in which the individual with the highest points score is declared the winner, or as match play with the winner determined by whichever single or team posts the lower score on the most individual holes during a whole round. In summation, team events such as fourball have been brought in, and these can be played using either the stroke, stableford or matchplay format. Alternative methods to play golf have also been introduced, such as miniature golf, sholf and disc golf.

Golf has progressively turned into a spectator game, with several varied levels of professional and amateur tours in many parts of the world. People such as Tiger Woods, Jack Nicklaus, Lorena Ochoa, Pádraig Harrington and Annika Sörenstam have become well-recognized sports figures across the world. Sponsorship has also become a huge portion of the game and players often earn more from their sponsorship contracts than they do from the game itself.

Miniature Golf: Minigolf, or miniature golf, is a miniature version of the sport of golf. While the international sports organization World Minigolf Sport Federation (WMF) prefers to use the name "minigolf", the general public in various countries has also many other names for the game: miniature golf, mini-golf, midget golf, goofy golf, shorties, extreme golf, crazy golf, adventure golf, mini-putt and so on. The name Putt-Putt is the trademark of an American company that constructs and franchises miniature golf courses and Family Entertainment Centers.

Sholf: Sholf, a game, is a cross between table shuffleboard and golf. Players take turns putting golf bal Players take turns putting golf balls, attempting to score points, bump opposing golf balls off the green, and/or protect their own golf ball from bump-offs. Each player or team of two players is allotted a golf ball color. ls into scoring zones printed on a putting green. After all eight golf balls have been played, each player re-putts their furthest ball from the scoring end. This is called the mulligan ball. The player who's not in scoring position putts their mulligan ball first. Only the team with the closest ball(s) to the scoring end receive points. Balls must entirely cross the line to get the higher point value. Play then continues in the different direction. The winner of a match is the first to score thirteen points.

Disc Golf: Disc golf is a disc game in which individual players throw a flying disc into a basket or at a target. According to the Professional Disc Golf Association, "The object of the game is to traverse a course from starting to end in the fewest number of throws of the disc."

The golf disc used nowadays is much smaller than conventional flying discs. Also, general-purpose flying discs, such as those used for playing guts or ultimate, have a simple edge to them, whereas disc golf discs have extended lips. They also have a much smaller diameter and profile.There are a wide variety of discs, divided into three basic classes: putters, mid-range discs, and drivers.

HISTORY

Golf is a game the exact roots of which are unclear. The origin of golf is open to debate as to being Dutch or Scottish. However, the most accepted golf history theory is that golf as exercised nowadays sprang up from Scotland in the 1100s. Scholars have claimed references to a form of golf from hieroglyphs found on stone tablets dating to old Egyptian Pharoahs. A game somewhat alike to golf was first mentioned in Dongxuan Records, a Chinese book of 11th century. It was also mentioned on February 26, 1297 in the Netherlands in a city called Loenen aan de Vecht. Here the Dutch played a game with a stick and leather ball. Whoever hit the ball into a target several hundreds of meters away the least number of times, won.

Advanced golf is regarded to be a Scottish invention, as the game was mentioned in two 15th century laws prohibiting the playing of the game of golf. Some scholars have suggested that this refers to another game which is more akin to advanced shinty, hurling or field hockey than golf. A game of putting a small ball into a hole in the ground using clubs was played in 17th century Netherlands. Growing trade over the North Sea during the Middle Ages and early modernistic Period led to much language interaction between Scots, Dutch) and other languages. There are also reports of even earlier accounts of golf like game from continental Europe.

However, these earlier games are more accurately viewed as ancestors of the game we call golf, as the fact remains that the advanced game of golf we understand today originated and evolved in Scotland: The first golf club memberships were conceived in Scotland. The most former permanent golf course started there too, as did the very first written decrees, as did the establishment of the 18-hole course. The first formalized tournament structures also came forth there and competitions were set up between various Scottish cities. Over time, the advanced game dispersed to England and from there to the rest of the world. The oldest playing golf course in the world is The

Musselburgh Old Links Golf Course. Evidence has shown that golf was played here in 1672 though Mary, Queen of Scots reputedly played there in 1567.

As stated, golf courses have not always had eighteen holes. The St Andrews Links occupy a narrow strip of land along the sea. As early as the 15th century, golfers at St Andrews, in Fife, set up a customary route through the undulating terrain, playing to holes whose locations were dictated by topography. The course that came forth featured eleven holes, laid out end to end from the clubhouse to the far end of the property. One played the holes out, turned around, and played the holes in, for a total of 22 holes. In 1764, numerous of the holes were deemed too short, and were therefore joint. The number was thereby brought down from 11 to nine, so that a complete round of the links consisted of 18 holes. Due to the status of St Andrews as the golfing capital, all other courses chose to play along suit and the 18-hole course stays on the standard today.

The major changes in gear since the 19th century have been better mowers, particularly for the greens, better golf ball designs, using rubber and man-made materials since about 1900, and the debut of the metal shaft begins in the 1930s. Also in the 1930s the wooden golf tee was formulated. In the 1970s the use of steel and then titanium to replace wood heads started, and shafts created of "graphite" (also known as carbon fibre) were acquainted in the 1980s. Although wooden tees are still most popular, several designs of plastic tees have been evolved in recent years, and the synthetic materials composing the modern ball continue to be developed.

Golf balls are renowned for "dimples". These small dips in the surface of the golf ball diminish aerodynamic drag which permits the ball to fly more. Golf is also renowned for the use of flags. These show the location of the hole to players when they make their first drive and are too far away from the hole to target accurately. When all players in a group are within putting distance, the flag is removed by a "caddy" or a fellow contender to permit for easier access to the hole.

In 2005 Golf Digest calculated that there were nearly 32,000 golf courses in the world, around half of them in the United States. The countries with most golf courses in regard to population, beginning with the best endowed were: Scotland, New Zealand, Australia, Ireland, Canada, Wales, United States, Sweden, and England (countries with fewer than 500,000 people were barred). Apart from Sweden, all of these countries have English as the majority language, but the number of courses in new territories is increasing rapidly. For instance the first golf course in the People's Republic of China opened in the mid-1980s, but by 2005 there were 200 courses in that country.

The professional sport was at the start dominated by Scottish then English golfers, but since World War I, America has raised the greatest quantity of leading professionals. Other Commonwealth countries such as Australia and South Africa are also conventional powers in the sport. Since around the 1970s, Japan, Scandinavian and other Western European countries have created leading players on a regular basis. The number of countries with high-class professionals continues to increase steadily, particularly in East Asia. South Korea is notably strong in women's golf.

The last decade or so has seen a marked increase in specialised golf vacations or holidays worldwide. This demand for travel which is centered around golf has led to the evolution of luxury resorts which cater to golfers and feature integrated golf courses.

In the United States, the number of people who play golf 25 times or more per year fell from 6.9 million in 2000 to 4.6 million in 2005, according to the National Golf Foundation. The Foundation accounted a smaller decline in the number who played golf at all; it fell from 30 million to 26 million over the same period.

History of Golf in India

Moving on the success of Indian golfers, the game of Golf has caused rapid strides across the length and breadth of India. Over the years, Indian professionals have consistently elevated the bar in international events and the domestic tour is being organized in a professional manner.

The coming of age of Indian golf that began with Ali Sher's memorable Indian Open victory is going on unabated with the golfers breaking fresh grounds in distant lands. Jyoti Randhawa and Arjun Atwal topping the Asian Tour Order of Merit, Gaurav Ghei's qualification to the British Open and Atwal becoming the first millionaire out of the Asian PGA are but a few of the magnificent accomplishments by Indian golfers.

In summation to the good showing by the players, the Indian Golf Union (IGU) is making earnest efforts to improve the standard of the game in the country. In 1995, in a turning point decision, the IGU agreed to form a distinct body called the Professional Golfers' Association of India (PGAI). The game got another shot in the arm when the PGAI chose to hand over the managing and marketing rights of the Tour to a professional company in 1997, with Delhi-based Tiger Sports Marketing winning the rights in an open bid.

THE GAME

Golf Course

Golf is played in an area of land assigned a golf course. A course comprises of a series of holes, each comprising of a teeing area, fairway, rough and other hazards, and the green with the pin and cup. A typical golf course comprises of eighteen holes, but many smaller courses have only nine. Early Scottish golf courses were generally layed out on linksland, soil covered sand dunes straightaway inland from beaches. This gave rise to the common description of a seaside course as a links.

Play

Every round of golf is based on playing a number of holes in a given order. A round generally comprises of 18 holes that are played in the order decided by the course layout. On a nine-hole course, a standard round comprises of two successive nine-hole rounds. Playing a hole on the golf course comprises of hitting a ball from a tee on the teeing box (a marked area specified for the first shot of a hole, a tee shot), and once the ball comes to rest, striking it again. This process is repeated until the ball is in the cup. Once the ball is on the green (an area of finely cut grass) the ball is generally putted (hit along the ground) into the hole. The goal of resting the ball in the hole in as few strokes as conceivable may be impeded by hazards, such as bunkers and water hazards. In most typical forms of gameplay, each player plays his or her ball from the tee until it is holed.

Fig.Start

Par

A hole is assorted by its par, the number of strokes an experienced golfer should need to complete play of the hole. For instance, a skilled golfer anticipates to reach the green on a par-four hole in two strokes (This would be regarded a Green in Regulation), one from the tee (the "drive") and another, second, stroke to the green (the "approach"); and then roll the ball into the hole in two putts for par. Traditionally, a golf hole is either a par-three, -four or -five; some par-six holes exist, but are not generally found on conventional golf courses.

Fig. Grip

Penalties

Penalty strokes are incurred in certain situations. Most often a penalty stroke is assessed because a player has hit into a situation from which they can't or choose not to play the ball as it lies (e.g. in a water hazard), or because they have lost their ball (out of bounds (OB)) and must play a substitute. Penalty strokes are considered towards a player's score as if they were an extra swing at the ball. Penalty strokes can be added on for a lot of dissimilar reasons. It could be a wrongful move that results in a penalty (displacing an object that affects the ball to move.) Or a penalty could be because of a lost ball. Most decree infractions lead to a stroke penalty but also can lead to disqualification. Disqualification could be from cheating, signing for a lower score, or from decree infractions that lead to wrong play.

Hitting of a Golf ball

To hit the ball, the club is swung at the unmoving ball wherever it has come to rest from a side stance. Many golf shots make the ball travel through the air (carry) and roll out for some more distance (roll).

Fig. Golf Ball

Every shot is a compromise between length and precision, and long shots are often less accurate than short ones. A longer shot may result in a better score if it helps in reducing the total number of strokes for a given hole, but the profit may be more than outweighed by additional strokes or penalties if a ball is lost, out of bounds, or comes to rest on hard ground. Therefore, a skilled golfer must assess the calibre of his or her shots in a specific situation in order to judge whether the possible profits of aggressive play are worth the risks.

The golfer uses gear such as golf clubs, golf balls, golf shoes, golf books, and golf bags.

MAJOR TOURNAMENTS

The Open Championship

The Open Championship was first played on 17 October 1860 at Prestwick Golf Club. The opening tournament was confined to professionals, and attracted a field of eight, who played three rounds of Prestwick's twelve-hole course in a single day. Willie Park Senior won with a score of 174, beating the favourite, Old Tom Morris, by two strokes. The following year the tournament was opened to amateurs; eight of them joined ten professionals in the field.

The Open Championship or simply The Open (often referred to as the British Open outside the UK), is the oldest of the four major championships in men's golf. It is the only major held outside the USA and is administered by the R&A, which is the regulating body of golf outside the USA and Mexico. The Open is played on the weekend of the third Friday in July, and is the third major to take place each year following The Masters and the U.S. Open and before the PGA Championship. The event takes place annually on one of nine historic links courses in the United Kingdom. In 2007, The Open had a prize fund of £4.2 million (at the time, about €6.197 million or $8.638 million). Historically, The Open's prize money was consistently the least of the four majors; since 2002 it is been the highest. Unambiguously among the four Major championships, the Open features a four hole playoff for all golfers tied at the end of standard, with the playoff continuing into sudden death holes if players stay on tied after four holes.

Walker Cup

The Walker Cup is a golf trophy contended biennially in odd numbered years between teams consisting the leading amateur golfers of the United States and Great Britain and Ireland (in political terms the United Kingdom and the Republic of Ireland). The event, officially called the Walker Cup Match, is co-organised by the R&A and the United States Golf Association, and is named in honor of George Herbert Walker (grandfather and namesake of the previous President of the United States George H. W. Bush and great-grandfather of present-day President George W. Bush), who was president of the USGA in 1920 when the series was started.

There was an unofficial event in 1921 and yearly events to 1924. From that time on it became a biennial event, and after World War Two it changed to odd numbered years. It is played alternately on either side of the Atlantic. Half points for matches finishing even were presented for the first time in 1971.

St Andrews Trophy

The St Andrews Trophy is a biennial men's team golf tournament contended between teams of amateur golfers representing Great Britain & Ireland and Continental Europe. It takes its name from St Andrews in Scotland, which is colloquially known as the "Home of Golf". The competition was established in 1955 and first played in 1956. It takes place in even numbered years (Great Britain & Ireland plays in the United States in the Walker Cup in odd numbered years). It is arranged alternately in Great Britain & Ireland and on the Continent, and is organised by the royal and Ancient Golf Club of St Andrews and the European Golf Association. The St Andrews Trophy itself was awarded by the Royal and old Golf Club of St Andrews in 1963.

The event consists of four morning foursomes pursued by eight afternoon singles on two consecutive days. The players are predominantly young men in their late teens and early twenties who are working towards a career as professional golfers. Many leading European golfers have played in the St Andrews Trophy, for instance Colin Montgomerie and José María Olazábal.

Seve Trophy

The Seve Trophy is a biennial golf tournament between teams of professional male golfers representing Great Britain & Ireland and Continental Europe. It is named after five times major winner Seve Ballesteros, the most flourishing golfer ever from Continental Europe who was one of the key instigators of the tournament. He made an extraordinary contribution to the European Ryder Cup successes of the 1980s and 1990s, and came to be considered as an exceptionally keen team man in a generally individualistic sport.

Like the much older Ryder Cup, which is now played between teams representing the whole of Europe and the United States, the Seve Trophy is a team event played over three days, with two days of pairs matches (the accurate formats employed have deviated) and a concluding set of singles matches on the final day. Major differences include the smaller size of the teams, which are ten strong, whereas in the Ryder Cup they are twelve strong, and the fact that there is prizemoney engaged. Players are glad to play in the Ryder Cup for nothing because of its prestige, though they incur large indirect financial compensation from the boost that participation gives to their prestige and profile, but as a new event, established only in 2000.

Hero Honda Indian Open

The Hero Honda Indian Open is the oldest international golf tournament in India and is one of the major events in the Asian PGA Tour.

Born as Indian Open in 1964 and played at the Delhi Golf Club, the tournament was the brainchild of five-time British Open winner Peter Thomson who took up the issue of an international golf tournament with the Indian Golf Union. Thomson, who won the event thrice (1964, 1966 and 1976), was a regular feature and also got top participants like Guy Wolstenholme, Angel Miguel and Graham Marsh to take part in the event.

In 1970, the Indian Open became a part of the Asian Golf Circuit and the field became stronger and tougher thereafter. In 1991, Ali Sher broke the stranglehold of foreign participants when he became the first Indian professional to win this esteemed tournament. Since then a number of top Indian pros like Feroze Ali (1998), Arjun Atwal (1999), Jyoti Randhawa (2000) and Vijay Kumar (2002) have walked away with the top honours. From 1998, the tournament was christened Wills Indian Open after the title sponsor.

In 2005 Hero Honda Motors signed a three-year agreement with the event's promoter, the World Sport Group, to title sponsor the honored tournament and it has came to be known as Hero Honda Indian Open.

Indian Masters

The Indian Masters is a professional golf tournament that was played for the first time from 7-10 February 2008, in a slot used by the Malaysian Open in 2007. It was at the start approved by the European Tour and the Indian Golf Union, making India the 37th territory to stage a European Tour event. The promoters are Golf in Dubai, who also runs the Dubai Desert Classic on the European Tour and the Dubai Ladies Masters on the Ladies European Tour. The tournament is division of the continuing globalisation of the European Tour, which had 12 tournaments in Asia in 2007.

However the declaration of the event drew sharp criticism from both the Asian Tour chairman Kyi Hla Han and the Professional Golf Tour of India (PGTI), as both organisations claimed the European Tour had offended International Federation of PGA Tours protocols by not making advance arrangements with them for co-sanctioning of this event arranged in their area. The Indian Golf Union issued a statement a few days after the tournament was declared expressing that the European Tour had approached it and was willing to offer through the PGTI 20 invitations to Indian domestic players. The Asian Tour agreed terms to co-sanction the tournament in advance of its 2008 first appearance.

ADMINISTRATIVE BODIES

International Golf Federation

The International Golf Federation is an organisation which, despite its grand title, occupies only a small place in the structure of golf. The Federation altered its name from the "World Amateur Golf Council" in 2003. It was established in 1958 for the aim of arranging international amateur competitions and it organises two amateur World Team Championships, the Eisenhower Trophy for men and the Espirito Santo Trophy for women.

United States Golf Association

The United States Golf Association (USGA) is the United States' national association of golf courses, clubs and facilities and the regulating body of golf for the U.S. and Mexico. Unitedly with The R&A, the USGA produces and translates the decrees of Golf. The USGA also provides a national handicap arrangement for golfers, conducts 13 national championships, including the U.S. Open, U.S. Women's Open and U.S. Senior Open, and tests golf gear for conformity with rules. In addition, the USGA is a leader in turfgrass research through its Green Section and it renders hundreds of grants to grass-roots programs through its Foundation in Colorado Springs, Colorado.

The USGA Foundation has offered more than $59 million in grants to programs for underprivileged youth and individuals with impairments. It is the largest contributor to The First Tee program. The USGA is presently led by Executive Director David B. Fay, and President Jim Vernon, and is headquartered at Golf House in Far Hills, New Jersey.

The Bob Jones Award is the highest honor granted by the United States Golf Association in recognition of eminent sportsmanship in golf. The opening award was given in 1955.

The USGA was originally conceived in 1894 to resolve the question of a national amateur championship. Earlier that year, the Newport Country Club and Saint Andrew's Golf Club, Yonkers, New York, both stated the winners of their tournaments the "national amateur champion." That autumn, delegates from Newport, St. Andrew's, The Country Club, Chicago Golf Club, and Shinnecock Hills Golf Club met in New York City to form a national governing body, which would administer the championship and also the conventions of Golf for the country.

On December 22, 1894, the Amateur Golf Association of the United States was officially conceived, and was briefly thereafter renamed the "United States Golf Association." Theodore Havemeyer was the first president, and the U.S. Amateur trophy is named in his honor.

Ladies' Golf Union

The Ladies' Golf Union (LGU) is the regulating body for women's and girls' amateur golf in Great Britain and Ireland. It was established in 1893 and is based in St Andrews, Fife, Scotland, which is often known as the "Home of Golf". Issette Pearson was the founder and first Secretary of LGU.

The LGU is regularised by an elected council with equal representation from England, Scotland, Ireland and Wales (despite the disparities in their populations). It is funded by a levy on women golfers' club membership fees, and indirectly represents over two hundred thousand golfers. It deals with major policy issues, all-Britain and Ireland tournaments, and international competitions. It has affiliates in England, Scotland, Ireland and Wales which organise local tournaments, run the handicapping arrangement, liaise with clubs, and promote the sport at a local level.

Indian Golf Union

The Indian Golf Union (IGU) is the central administrative body for promotion and management of golf in India. Before IGU came into being in 1955, the Royal Calcutta Golf Club was looked upon as the unofficial regulating body of golf in India.

The IGU constitution mentioned six prominent clubs at that time—The Royal Calcutta Golf Club, The Tollygunge Club, The Bombay Presidency Golf Club, The Delhi Golf Club, The Willingdon Sports Club and the Madras Gymkhana-as the founder members of the Union.

As the apex body for golf in India, the IGU is at the forefront of several promotional activities including playing host to a number of international tournaments. The esteemed Indian Open has become a division of the Asian PGA Tour from 1998. The IGU is affiliated to the World Amateur Golf Council, the world body for golf.

FAMOUS PLAYERS

Tiger Woods

Eldrick Tont "Tiger" Woods was born on December 30, 1975; He is an American professional golfer whose accomplishments to date rank him amidst the most successful golfers of all time. Presently the World No. 1, he was the highest-paid professional athlete in 2007, having earned an approximated $122 million from winnings and endorsements. According to Golf Digest, Woods earned $769,440,709 from 1996 to 2007, and the magazine anticipates that by 2010, Woods will become the world's first athlete to pass one billion dollars in earnings.

Woods has won fourteen professional major golf championships, the second highest of any male player, and 65 PGA Tour events, third all time. He has more career major wins and career PGA Tour wins than any other active golfer. He is the youngest player to accomplish the career Grand Slam, and the youngest and fastest to win 50 tournaments on tour.

Woods has held the number one position in the world rankings for the most sequential weeks and for the greatest total number of weeks. He has been presented PGA Player of the Year a record nine times, the Byron Nelson Award for lowest adjusted scoring average a record eight times, and has tied Jack Nicklaus' record of leading the money list in eight dissimilar seasons. He has been named related Press Male Athlete of the Year a record-tying four times, and is the only person to be named Sports Illustrated's Sportsman of the Year more than once.

Nicklaus Jack

Jack William Nicklaus was born on January 21, 1940, also known as "The Golden Bear", is widely considered as the grooviest professional golfer of all time, in important part because of his records in major championships. Nicklaus accrued a record 18 professional majors in a PGA Tour career lasting 25 years, from 1962 to 1986. Later, on the Champions Tour, the senior edition of the PGA Tour, he won 8 of that tour's majors between 1990 and 1996. Both records still stand today.

Nicklaus has also taken part in a lot of off-course activities, including golf course design, golf instruction book writing, and running his own tournament on the PGA Tour, the Memorial Tournament. Unitedly with Arnold Palmer and Gary Player (conjointly known as the "Big Three"), he is credited with turning golf into the major spectator sport it has become. While Palmer brought golf into the television era, it was the evolving Nicklaus-Palmer-Player rivalry that drove subsequent interest.

Lorena Ochoa

Lorena Ochoa was born in Guadalajara, Jalisco on 15 November 1981. She is a Mexican golfer who plays on the U.S.-based LPGA Tour and is presently the number one ranked female golfer in the world. As the first Mexican golfer of either gender to be graded number one in the world, she is regarded the best Mexican golfer of all time.

Ochoa grew up next door to the Guadalajara Country Club and took up golf at the age of five. She won her first state event at the age of six and her first national event at seven. All told as a junior she captured 22 state events in Guadalajara and 44 national events in Mexico. She won five sequential titles at the Junior World Golf Championships and in 2000 she enrolled at the University of Arizona in the United States on a golf scholarship. While a student, with steady tutoring she greatly improved her English by watching movies and reading magazines between practice and tournaments.

Thomas Bjorn

Thomas Bjorn wasborn on 18 February 1971. He is a Danish golfer who plays on the European Tour.

Bjorn played on the Challenge Tour from 1993 to 1995. He then created an immediate impact on the European Tour in his first season, finishing tenth on the 1996 Order of Merit. He has won nine tournaments on the European Tour and has finished in the top ten on the Order of Merit five times with a best finish of fifth in 2000. He has come close to winning a major championship at the 2003 Open Championship when he was in the lead with 4 holes to play before a slump handed victory to Ben Curtis and at the US PGA Championship in 2005, when he tied for the lead before finishing as runner-up to Phil Mickelson in a second-place tie with Steve Elkington.

Bjorn was a member of the winning European Ryder Cup teams in 1997 and 2002. He made the top 10 of the Official World Golf Rankings for one week in 2001 after a second place finish at The Scottish Open at Loch Lomond.

Jeev Milkha Singh

First Indian golfer to become a member of the European Tour; won the Volvo China Open Jeev Milkha Singh, son of legendary Indian athlete Milkha Singh, is the highest graded Indian golfer in the world. Born on December 15, 1971, Jeev was the first Indian golfer to become a member of the European Tour.

After winning his first amateur tournament—American Express Championship in Delhi-at the age of 13, Jeev honed his golfing skills playing in some amateur tournaments in the U.S. Jeev has been a even in the Asian PGA Tour since the mid 1990s and has bagged a number of major competitions. In 1997 he completed seventh at the European Tour qualifying school, and he joined the tour the following year.

In April 2006, Jeev won the Volvo China Open, becoming the second Indian to win on the European Tour after Arjun Atwal.

Arjun Atwal

First Indian to play in the US PGA Tour; first player on Asian PGA to surpass US $1 million in career earnings; first Indian golfer to win a European Tour Order of Merit event; crowned the Asian order of merit in 2003. Arjun Atwal, born on March 20, 1973, is a top Indian professional golfer. Atwal has the distinction of being the first Indian to play in the high profile US PGA Tour.

Atwal learnt the tricks of the trade while playing in the hallowed greens of the Royal Calcutta Golf Club during his teens. After turning professional in 1995 Atwal established himself as one of the leading players on the Asian Tour and topped the order of merit in 2003. In 2003, Atwal became the first player on Asian PGA to exceed US $1 million in career earnings when he claimed a one-stroke victory in the Hero Honda Masters on home soil in the same year.

Gaurav Ghei

First Indian to qualify for the prestigious British Open; won the Gadgil Western Masters in November 1995. Indian golfer Gaurav Ghei was born on September 25, 1968. Ghei's historic win at the $500,000 Gadgil Western Masters in November 1995 catapulted him to national fame.

In 1996, Ghei made international headlines when he defeated Ryder Cup veteran Colin Montgomerie in the 16-nation Alfred Dunhill Cup at St Andrews as India stunned hosts and strong favourites Scotland. In June 1997, Ghei became the first Indian to qualify for the esteemed British Open through the tough Sectional Qualifying event and played at the Royal Troon.

REFERENCES

Alway, Leonore K.: "Indoor Group Golf Instruction". *Journal of Health and Physical Education*, 99: 1, January, 1938.

Armour, Tommy: *A Round of Golf with Tommy Armour*. New York, Simon and Schuster, 1959.

Armour, Tommy: *How to Play Your Best Golf All the Time*. New York, Simon and Schuster, 1953.

Berg, Pattie, and Otis Dypwich: *Golf.* New York, A. S. Barnes & Co., 1941.

Broer, Marion R.: *Efficiency of human Movement*. Philadelphia, W. B. Saunders Company, 1966.

Bruce, Ben and Evelyn Davies: *Beginning Golf.* Belmont, California, Wadsworth Publishing Co., Inc., 1962.

10

Hockey

Hockey is any of a family of sports in which two teams contend by trying out to maneuver a ball, or a hard, round, rubber or heavy plastic disc addressed a puck, into the opponent's net or goal, using a hockey stick.

Field Hockey

Field hockey is played on gravel, natural grass, sand-based or water-based unreal turf, with a small, hard ball. The game is popular among both males and females in many regions of the world, especially in Europe, Asia, Australia, and South Africa. In most countries, the game is played between single-sex sides, though they can be mixed-sex.

The regulating body is the 116-member International Hockey Federation (FIH). Men's Field hockey has been played at each summer

Olympic Games since 1908 (except 1912 and 1924), while Women's Field Hockey has been played each summer Olympic Games since 1980.

Advanced field hockey sticks are J-shaped and manufactured of a combination of wood, glass fibre or carbon fibre (occasionally both) and have a curved hook at the playing end, a flat surface on the playing side and curved surface on the rear side.

There are 4000-year-old drawings in Egypt of a game resembling field hockey being played. While current field hockey appeared in the mid-18th century in England, primarily in schools, it wasn't until the first half of the 19th century that it became firmly constituted. The first club was made in 1849 at Blackheath in south-east London. Field hockey is the national sport of India and Pakistan.

Women's Field Hockey

The All England's Women's Hockey Association was founded in 1895 and readily adopted the male conventions of play. An attempt to join with the male Hockey Association was firmly revolted.Women evolved territorial and international matches and played earnestly. By 1939 England had 2,100 women's clubs, with a smattering throughout the empire.

Fig: Women's Hockey

Constance Applebee introduced the game in the United States, and persisted the most influential figure in the sport for decades. In 1922 she helped found the U.S. Field Hockey Association, which became the regulating body for the 14,000 U.S. women who now play. It was 1980 before women were permitted to play at the Olympics.

Most of the 4.5 million people who play worldwide are probably committed to comparatively nonserious, friendly recreational play, which they can carry on as long as they stay fit.At competitive levels, questions of sponsorship, star players, and their ethics have emerged, products of the high costs engaged in training and international play. But the game persists proudly "amateur," fewer purists than it was but closer to its origins than many other games.

HISTORY

The game of Hockey has been around from the time of early civilisation. Some of the reports find the earliest beginning of the game 4000 years back. Field hockey was reportedly played even before the birth of Christ. Fundamentally known as the "ball and stick" game, it was played since old times in places diverse as Rome, Scotland, Egypt and South America. The game was referred to in varied names but the primary idea of playing the game was the same.

The most apt used term was "Hockie" by the Irish. Although the term was coined centuries ago, the word found out its way through to the present generation.

In the 17th and the early 18th century England, the game acquired a ferociously competitive and chaotic form. Villages would contend against their neighboring hamlets and there were about 100 players in one team. The game was a matter of pride and manhood; so the game acquired a grievous form. The game would last for half a month and many players would end up injured and grievously hurt.

The umpires were there but they were more of mute viewers, who would make a call only if a team asked them to. After some years, common sense and a logical and organised approach to the game came into play with the introduction of revision of conventions. The game was bounded to 30 players for each team. The Eton College of England drafted some conventions to bring sanity to the game. The Hockey Association was formed in the year 1875 and some of the decrees chalked out were applied. The results were quite positive and more decrees like giving the umpire enough authority were soon drawn to improve the calibre of the game.

The game of ice hockey probably developed from the game of field hockey that was played in Northern Europe for hundreds of years. The advanced version of ice-hockey finds its origins in the conventions laid down by a Canadian named J G Creighton. His rules were applied in the first game of ice hockey played in Montreal, Canada in the year 1875.

In fact, the "rink" or the playing area for ice hockey was actually utilised in the game called "curling" in Scotland during the 18th century.

Initially there were as many as thirty players for each side and the goals were two stones frozen on one end of the ice. The conventions for the game of ice hockey were drafted at McGill University in Montreal, Canada in the year 1879. Ice hockey found its way to the US in the year 1893. By the early 1900s, the sport had become prevalent in regions of Europe including the UK.

The hockey stick was introduced in the early 1800s. The first stick was made of wood with a flat blade. In the 1920s, hockey players started to tape their sticks to increase the hold and strengthen the blade. The banana curve or the bend in the blade which we see today was evolved during the phase between the years 1957-1980. A certain player named Bobby Hull broke a stick at a exercise match and started to play around with the "bent" stick and found to his amazement that there was far more accuracy in his shots. In the early 1980s, the sticks were conceived of metals. By the turn of the 21st century, there have been three types of hockey sticks-wood, composite (reinforced wood sticks) and aluminum. The aluminum hockey sticks are most often used today because of its light weight, durable nature and replaceable blades.

The first year that Hockey was played in the Olympics was in the year 1908. Only men were allowed to play the game. It was only in the year 1980, that women got the chance to play Hockey in the Olympics. Ice hockey was played in early April of 1920 as a part of the Olympic Summer Games in Antwerp, Belgium. The tournament was also renowned for being the first World Hockey Championship. Canada was the clear cut winner in the championship. The first Olympic Winter Games are held in Chamonix, France, in the year 1924 with Canada winning all five games.

We have seen how Hockey has come forth as a clear winner through the ages. Just like the way our civilisation has evolved, so has our attitude towards the game. Today also, the game has the same amount of fierceness and raw passion similar with its conventional approach. However the passion is also matched with a drive to play the game in the true spirit of sportsmanship and healthy competition.

History of Hockey in India

Despite the fact that many old civilisations played hockey in dissimilar variants, the advanced game of hockey—the field hockey-evolved in the British Isles in the 19th century.

Hockey was introduced in India by British Army regiments and the game soon found favour among the native Indians. The first hockey club in India came up in Calcutta in 1885-86 and soon Bombay and Punjab pursued suit. Making its Olympic entry at the 1928 Amsterdam Games, Indian hockey team cruised home to its first Olympic gold without conceding a single goal. The hallmark of this ruthless domination was the wizardry of Indian hockey legend Dhyan Chand who mesmerized the Amsterdam crowd with his dazzling skills.

From 1928 to 1956, the Indian hockey juggernaut won six straight Olympic gold medals while winning 24 back-to-back matches. This was the golden era of Indian hockey when India loomed large in world hockey and raised some of the finest players the game has ever seen. The Indian stranglehold over the Olympic hockey gold came to an end when Pakistan defeated India in the final of the 1960 Rome Olympics.

THE GAME

Players and Positions

In hockey, each side has 11 players (one goalkeeper and ten outfield players) from a squad of 16 players. The outfield players can be put into three common classes - defenders, midfielders and attackers, with the side's tactics defining the arrangement that they will play around those positions. Here is a prompt run-down of what each position means:

Fig. Hockey Player

The hockey goalkeeper - The hockey goalkeeper is the only player who is able to touch the ball with any portion of his or her body, but contrary to their counterparts in football, hockey keepers are not permitted to pick the ball up. Goalkeepers wear extraordinary clothing, including protective headgear, pads and gloves. Since they are quite literally in the firing line, goalkeepers need to possess bravery amongst other key attributes including agility and quick reaction speeds.

Fig. Goalkeeper

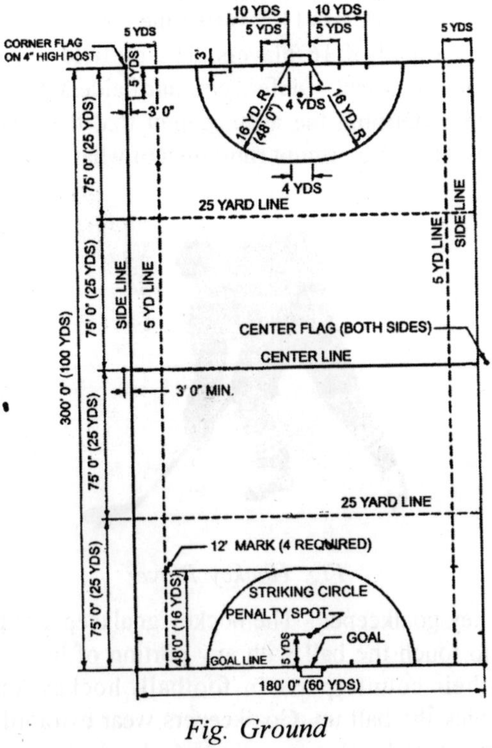

Fig. Ground

Hockey defenders - The hockey defender's main target should be to prevent the opposition from scoring. A defender's strength lies in good anticipation and strong tackles to rob the opposition of possession. They should also be cool in possession of the ball, specially when in their own half as a misplaced pass is often punished by a goal. Defensive hockey positions include full backs, centre-backs and sweepers.

Field hockey midfielders and attackers -Hockey midfielders are the real heartbeat of the side as their purpose is to both to attack and defend. They require to have lots of stamina to get up and down the pitch in both a destructive and productive manner - either putting in the important tackle or interception or playing the important pass to set up a goalscoring chance for an attacker to pounce upon. Positions include holding and attacking midfielders and centres. Hockey has a number of basic ground conventions which are necessary to know before you get involved in a game. These laws include the following:

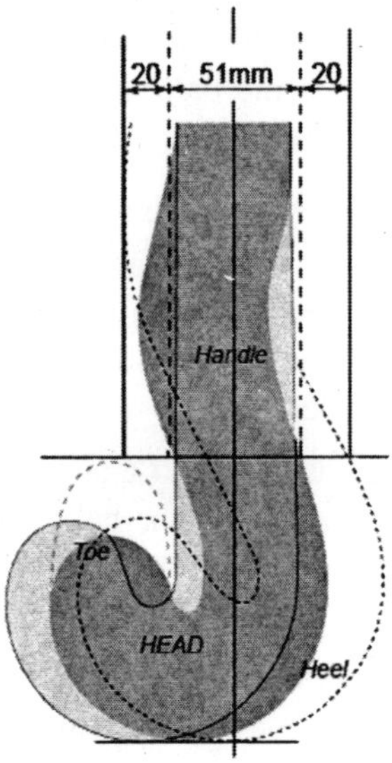

Fig. Head Dimensions

Hockey players can only hit the ball with the flat side of their stick and must not raise the stick above shoulder height when playing the ball.

Field hockey players (other than the goalkeeper) are not permitted to use their feet, or any other portions of the body, to control the ball at any time.

A goal can only be scored either from a field goal, a penalty corner, or from a penalty stroke. A field goal is a goal scored from open play, and can only be scored from inside the 'striking circle', in front of the opponent's goal. If the hockey ball is hit from outside the circle and goes into the goal, it doesn't count as a goal.

Hockey players may not trip, push, charge, interfere with, or physically handle an opponent in any way. Hockey is a non-contact sport and all fouls result in a free hit or a 'penalty corner' for the non-offending team depending on where the infringement took place and the severity of the foul.

Types of Foul in a Hockey Match

A number of dissimilar types of foul may be punished in a game of hockey. Some of the basic ones to watch out for include:

Obstruction - This is presented against a hockey player who uses their body or stick to prevent an opponent from reaching the ball.

Third-party obstruction - This is awarded when a hockey player positions themselves between the ball and an opponent, permitting a team-mate an unobstructed play on the ball.

Undercutting - This is awarded against a hockey player who lifts the ball in a grievous manner.

- Hockey stick interference - This is presented against a hockey player who applies their stick to hit an opponent's stick, either deliberately or accidentally.
- Advancing - This is awarded against a hockey player who shoves, pushes, or advances the ball in any way, utilising any portion of their body.
- Sticks - This is presented against a player who raises their stick hazardously near another hockey player, or plays the ball while carrying the stick above their shoulder level.
- Backsticks - This is presented against a player who strikes the ball with the rounded back of the hockey stick.

Types of Punishment in a Hockey Match

Fouls in a hockey match can be punished in three main ways. These are as follows:

- Free hit - This is a free play presented on any offence that occurs outside of the scoring circle. It generally takes place at the location of the violation. All opposing players must stand at least five yards from where the hit is to be taken.

- Penalty corner - This is presented to the attacking team when the defence either commits a foul inside the striking circle or deliberately hits the ball out-of-bounds over the end line. A penalty corner is taken by an attacking player at a spot on the end-line ten yards away from the nearest goal post. All other attackers must stand outside the striking circle, while five defenders, including the goalkeeper, stand behind the end line until contact is made with the ball. Once the ball has been put in play, all players can rush into the circle to either defend or shoot the ball at the goal.
- Penalty stroke - This is presented to the attacking side when an offence is committed by the defending side which is deemed to have prevented an about certain goal. A penalty is taken seven yards from goal, with the player having only the goalkeeper to beat.

Hockey Umpires

There are two umpires on the hockey field, who are generally accountable for each half of the pitch. A player, who violates the decrees, either by rough or grievous play, misbehaves, or an intentional offence, can be shown a card - green, yellow or red.

Green - This is an official warning given to the hockey player to not breach the decrees.

Yellow - This results in a hockey player being sent off the pitch for five minutes, following an offence.

Red - A red card results in an early bath and is given for more serious offences.

Ground

Traditionally, hockey has been played on grass but advanced technology has meant that artificial or astroturf pitches have become commonplace, specially in Olympic competitions. These types of surface permits play in all types of weather and gives a more even run of the ball along the surface. The hockey pitch surface is generally watered before top competition games. As a result of all this, it is best to get a feel for playing hockey both on and off grass, as an astroturf pitch can see the ball move much faster than on a normal grass pitch.

MAJOR TOURNAMENTS

Hockey World Cup

The Hockey world cup is held once in four year. The first world cup was held in the year 1971. The world cup comes in between the Olympics years. This is the most coveted tournament and every team wants to lift this trophy and be addressed as the world champions.

World Class Hockey Tournament

World Class Hockey was established in 1991 when a Chicago based Bantam team first journeyed to Nybro, Sweden for a hockey tournament. Nowadays, World Class Hockey is the largest American Hockey Tour operator and is a dynamic force in the molding of teams to travel outside America. World-Class Hockey now comprises of nearly 25 trips per year. There are boys' and girls' teams, all-star youth travel teams, high school teams, and senior men's teams who have journeyed overseas to contend in International Events. Since its inception in 1991, World Class Hockey has made great strides in the hockey and extra-curricular development for all players in amateur hockey.

It has offered leadership in proper competition, excellent sites, and the most impressive tours; it has fielded several championship teams; it has rendered the chance for players and parents to take part in the most esteemed hockey events and locations. World Class Hockey has sent over 1500 young players to Sweden, Finland, France, Denmark, Holland, Norway, Germany, Switzerland, Austria, Canada, Italy and Russia. World Class Hockey is the largest provider of American ice hockey trips. It has become constituted as one of the outstanding hockey trip organizing programs in America. It renders programs and leadership chances for players, coaches, families, managers, teams and hockey associations throughout the United States. It has established in the amateur hockey scene as one of the finest hockey programs in America. World Class Hockey is devoted to the evolution of today's youth through Education and Athletic excellence. As another hockey season begins, World Class Hockey will continue this tradition.

Sultan Azlan Shah Cup

Another tournament which is important is the Sultan Azlan Shah cup. This is a tournament which is held in Malaysia. It is considered that the sultan was an ardent fan of hockey and so he commenced this tournament in the year 1983. It started as a tournament to be held once every two years but then was advanced and made a yearly event.

World Champion's Challenge

The world champion's challenge is a great tournament to improve the game of the newly hockey playing countries. In the world cup and Olympics many countries play and get rankings. This is a tournament held to help the teams which rank between 7 and 12. They get a chance to contend and improve their game and rankings.

Premier Hockey League

The Premier Hockey League (PHL) is a new domestic field hockey competition prefaced in 2005, in Hyderabad. The Hyderabad Sultans while in 2006 won this contest, whereas the Bangalore Lions defeated Chandigarh Dynamos to come forth triumphant. The tournament is initiated to revive the concern in the sport.The league is constructed up of two groups, each comprising of five teams. The format is revolutionary and encompasses many innovations such as shorter games, a theme song, and a television friendly format. The Premier Hockey League (PHL) is a joint project of ESPN-Star Sports, Indian Hockey Federation (IHF) and Leisure Sports Management and is modeled on the U.S. NBA league.

All India Aagha Khan Hockey Tournament

In the 1830s the honorific title of Aga Khan was imparted upon Aga Hasan Ali Shah, the 46th Imam of the Ismailis, by Fat'h Ali Shah Qajar, the Shah of Persia. Etymologically the title combines the Turkish military title Agha, meaning a "noble" or "lord", with the Altaic polyvalent title Khan for a local ruler, so the combination means roughly "dominating Chief". In Persia's Qajar court protocol, Khan (and Amir) was ordinarily division of commanders of armed forces and provincial tribal leaders which ranked fourth in precedence amongst the eight title classes for non-members of the dynasty. In 1877, the colonial rulers of India, the British Raj, gave the Aga Khan rank and nobility in recognition of the help in suppressing a regional rebellion against the British, thus the Aga Khan became the only religious or community leader in British India granted a personal gun salute; all other salute dynasties were either rulers of Princely States, or Political Pensioners holding ancestral princely titles in states abolished by the Raj.

Beighton Cup

Beighton Cup is a field hockey tournament. Established in 1895, it is arranged by Bengal Hockey Association and is generally held on the Mohun Bagan ground on the Maidan in Kolkata (earlier called Calcutta) in India. The Beighton Cup was awarded by T.D. Beighton, Legal Remembrancer of the Government of Bengal, and was run at first by the Indian Football Association. The Calcutta Hockey League took off in 1905.

British officers popularised the game amongst soldiers in India; hockey, as an organised sport, arose in Kolkata.

The Anglo-Indian clubs of the time, most importantly, the Calcutta Naval Volunteers Club, now the Calcutta Rangers Club deserve a big share of the credit. Not only did Rangers Club win the Beighton Cup nine times, including in its inaugural year, it was right away responsible for two of the country's Olympic gold medals. When the Indian Olympic Committee didn't have the funds to send the Indian team in 1932 and 1936, it was the generosity of the Rangers Club, rich with funds from its four-times-a-year sweepstakes, which ensured that the team set sail for Los Angeles and Berlin.

ADMINISTRATIVE BODIES

International Street & Ball Hockey Federation

The International Street & Ball Hockey Federation is a registered non-profit organization. It is officially recognised as the regulating body of the sport in Canada by the International Ice Hockey Federation, with many of its member nations officially recognised by their federal sports agencies.

Established in 1993, the International Street & Ball Hockey Federation has catered international competitions since 1995, when the first European Championship was held in Bratislava, Slovakia, with Czechia defeating Slovakia. Canada would claim the first World Championship in 1996, defeating Czechia in Bratislava, in 1996, with seven nations taking part, which also featured Austria, Germany, Russia, Slovakia (bronze medallists), and Switzerland.

Indian Hockey Federation

The Indian Hockey Federation was the Indian branch of the International Hockey Federation. In April, 2008, Kandaswamy Jothikumaran, the IHF's Secretary General, resigned after a television show accused him of corruption. K. P. S. Gill, IHF chief for 14 years, lost his position when the Indian Hockey Federation was suspended by the Indian Olympic Association (IOA) on April 28.

The Indian Olympic Association appointed a new five-member national selection committee. This panel will work in conjunction with the International Field Hockey Federation in managing hockey in India. The panel was guided by Aslam Sher Khan, a previous MP and previous hockey captain and includes Ashok Kumar, Ajit Pal Singh, Zafar Iqbal and Dhanraj Pillay. Aslam Sher Khan has now been substituted by Ajit Pal Singh as the chairman of the national selection committee. Aslam Sher Khan was extremely displeased by this decision, although he stayed as a selector.

In a 30 April 2008 interview with India Today, Khan indicated the impact of the 2007 film about the National Women's Hockey Team, Chak De India, on his future strategy by expressing that he wants "to create a 'Chak De' effect" within Indian hockey.

FAMOUS PLAYERS

Batchelor Stephen

Stephen ("Steve") James Batchelor was born on 22 June 1961 in Beare Green, Surre.He is a past field hockey player, who was a member of the golden winning British squad at the 1988 Summer Olympics in Seoul. Four years earlier, at the 1984 Summer Olympics in Los Angeles, he captured the bronze medal with his team.

In 1980, briefly after leaving Millfield School, Batchelor made his international entry for England as a 19-year-old. He went on to play 48 times for England winning silver medals in the 1986 World cup and the 1987 European Cup. Batchelor, who played for Southgate, represented Great Britain 66 times. At the Seoul Olympics, he either began or came on as a substitute in all seven matches but despite his reputation as a striker he failed to score in the tournament.

Aldo Disorbo

Aldo diSorbo was born in May 23, 1972 and is a very famed international field hockey player. He has participated, throughout his career, at numerous Olympics and was appointed two times as the "World's Best Player of the Year". At the starting of his career, he was one of the youngest players to receive so many Olympic titles.

Aldo diSorbo was supposed to take part in the 2004 Athens Olympics but was prevented due to some arm injuries. That did not stop him from going to the Olympics and being there for his team. He helped them prepare, while assisting the coach and the trainers. Over the years, he has played in over 280 games, having scored around 86 goals.

Robert Hammond

Robert ("Rob") Hammond OAM was born on May 6, 1981 in Townsville, Queensland. He is a field hockey midfielder from Australia, who was a member of the team that won the golden medal at the 2004 Summer Olympics in Athens by beating title holders The Netherlands in the final.

Hammond made his debut for The Kookaburras during the so called Manning Cup against New Zealand in 2001. In the same year he represented Australia at the Junior World Cup in Hobart, before making his senior major tournament entry at the 2002 Champions Trophy in Cologne, Germany. Since the summer of 2006 he is playing club hockey in the Netherlands, at Oranje Zwart from Eindhoven. Hammond was a member of the Australian team that won the bronze medal at the 2008 Beijing Olympics.

Dhyan Chand

Arguably the greatest player the game of hockey has ever raised, Dhyan Chand's genius transcended national boundaries and made myths abound of his phenomenal abilities.

Once a lowly sepoy in the British Indian Army, Dhyan Chand's wizardry with the hockey stick caught the attention of his seniors and soon earned him a place in the Indian national team. Representing India in three Olympics, Dhyan Chand mesmerized the world audience with his audacious jugglery and leadership qualities.

At the 1932 Los Angeles Olympics, when India thrashed the U. S. by 24 goals to one, Dhyan Chand and his brother Roop Singh wreaked havoc in the opposition defence, each scoring eight goals. Four years later, at the Berlin Games, Dhyan Chand was once again in the thick of action when India drubbed the hosts by a huge margin in the final. He won three gold medals in Olympic Games; presented the Padma Bhushan in 1956.

Dhanraj Pillay

Dhanraj Pillay is an ace Indian striker, was born on July 16, 1968 at Kirkee in Maharashtra. The hero of many epic Indian victories, the mercurial Dhanraj has been to Indian hockey what Leander Paes has been to Indian tennis.

Dhanraj polished his raw talent under the tutelage of elder brother Ramesh, who himself was a past India international. After a fine stint with his employers Mahindra & Mahindra and Mumbai in national championships, Dhanraj was called for India duty in the Asia Cup of 1989.

In a magnificent career spanning 15 years, Dhanraj has represented India in four Summer Olympics ('92, '96, 2000, and 2004), four World Hockey Cups, four Champions Trophies, four Asian Games, and four Asia Cups. For a long time, Dhanraj has been synonymous with Indian hockey and his spirited efforts have kept the Indian tricolour flying high in more junctures than one. He is the highest goal scorer in the Bangkok Asian Games; member of World Eleven side during the 1994 World Cup; Padma Shri in 2000; Rajiv Gandhi Khel Ratna Award (1999).

Udham Singh

Udham Singh is without doubt one of the finest hockey players to have donned the India colours. Udham Singh was born on August 4, 1928, in the hockey bastion of Sansarpur in Punjab.

After being picked up to play for a strong Punjab Police team boasting a number of Olympians, Udham Singh missed the 1948 Olympics due to a nagging finger injury. He was a mainstay of the formidable Indian team that won back-to-back gold medals in the 1952 Helsinki and 1956 Melbourne.

After Leslie Claudius only hockey player to win 3 gold and one silver in Olympic Games; Arjuna Award in 1965. Udham Singh made his farewell Olympic appearance in the 1964 Tokyo Games when India avenged their former Olympic final loss to Pakistan to emerge the winners.

Leslie Claudius

Leslie Claudius stands tall among a bevy of Indian hockey legends. Born on March 25, 1927, Claudius was hailed as one of the best right-halves of his time.

For somebody who began with football and even played in the IFA Shield, Leslie's rise in the Indian hockey turf was meteoric. An ace right-half with great distribution and tackling skills, Leslie virtually possessed that position in the world-beating Indian team that won three back-to-back Olympic gold medals from 1948 to 1956.

Despite figuring in the Guinness Book of World Records for having won the highest number of Olympic medals in hockey—three gold and a silver-Lesli Claudius would also be remembered as the captain of the Indian team that lost the Olympic gold in 1960 Tokyo Games after reigning supreme for 28 years.

REFERENCES

Allen, Kevin: *USA Hockey: A Celebration of A Great Tradition.* Chicago: Triumph Books, 1997.

Allen, Kevin: *Why is the Stanley Cup in Mario Lemieux's Swimming Pool?.* Chicago: Triumph Books, 2000.

Baun, Bobby, with Anna Logan: *Lowering the Boom: The Bobby Baun Story.* Toronto: Stoddart Publishing Co. Limited, 2000.

Beardsley, Doug: *Country On Ice*. Canada: Polestar Press., 1987.

Frayne, Trent: *Famous Hockey Players.* New York: Dodd, Mead & Co., 1973.

Frayne, Trent: *The Mad Men of Hockey.* Toronto: McClelland & Stewart. 1974.

McFarlane, Brian: *One Hundred Years Of Hockey.* Toronto: Deneau, 1989.

McFarlane, Brian: *The Youngest Goalie*. Toronto: Summerhill, 1989.

Plante, Jacques: *Goaltending*. New York: Collier, 1972.

Plimpton, George: *Open Net.* New York: W.W. Norton & Co., 1968.

11

Lawn Tennis

Tennis is a sport played between two players (singles) or between two teams of two players each (doubles). Each player employs a strung racquet to smash a hollow rubber ball covered up with felt (most of the time Optic Yellow, but can be any color or even two-tone) over a net into the opponent's court.

The advanced game of lawn tennis initiated in the United Kingdom in the late 19th century as "lawn tennis" and had heavy connections to the old game of real tennis. After its creation, tennis dispersed throughout the upper-class English-speaking population before dispersing around the world.

Tennis is an Olympic sport and is played at all levels of society at all ages. The sport can be played by anybody who can hold a racquet, including people in wheelchairs. In the United States, there is a collegiate circuit organised by the National Collegiate Athletics Association.

Except for the adoption of the tiebreaker in the 1970s, the decrees of tennis have altered very little since the 1890s. A new addition to professional tennis has been the acceptance of "instant action replay" technology coupled with a point challenge system, which permits a player to challenge the official call of a point.

Along with its millions of players, millions of people worldwide follow lawn tennis as a spectator sport, particularly the four Grand Slam tournaments (occasionally referred to as the "majors"): the Australian Open, the French Open, Wimbledon, and the US Open. Traditionally, tennis is played between two people in a Singles match, or four players in a Doubles match. However, popular editions permitting play between three players (of which two or three are on the court at any one time) have emerged.

Singles

In tennis is the body of competition that features individual players contending one-on-one. There are separate singles competitions for men and women. The singles competition exists in counterdistinction to doubles.

Doubles

One team of two players on each side (four players in total). In this version, gender does not matter. Doubles utilizes a wider court than singles matches.

Mixed Doubles

Alike to the doubles game, but this version needs one man and one woman to be a team.

American Doubles

(From the UK) is typically employed in training, and plays one player (playing with a singles court layout) versus two players (playing with a doubles court layout). Often the court rotates game by game taking it in turns to play on your own.

Australian Doubles

Another informal and unsanctioned form of lawn tennis, is played with standardised conventions to the "Kiwi" style, only in this version, players rotate court position after each game. As such, each player plays doubles and singles over the course of a match, with the singles player always serving. Scoring styles diverge, but one popular technique is to assign a value of 2 points to each game, with the server taking both points if he or she holds serve, and the doubles team each taking one if they break.

Canadian Doubles

Is alike to Australian Doubles; however the single player doesn't have to be importantly better than the double team. The single player hits into a doubles court while the side with two players hits into a singles court.

HISTORY

Tennis as the advanced sport can be dated to two unshared roots. Between 1859 and 1865, Major Harry Gem and his friend Augurio Perera evolved a game that united elements of racquets alike to the game of

Poona or Badminton a lot of British soldiers brought from being based in India and the Basque ball game pelota, which they played on Perera's croquet lawn in Birmingham, United Kingdom. In 1872, along with two local doctors, they established the world's first tennis club in Leamington Spa. The Courier of 23 July 1884 recorded one of the first tennis tournaments, held in the grounds of Shrubland Hall.

In December 1873, Major Walter Clopton Wingfield configured a similar game - which he addressed sphairistike (skill at playing at ball), and was shortly acknowledged simply as "sticky" - for the entertainment of his guests at a garden party on his estate of Nantclwyd, in Llanelidan, Wales. He based the game on the newer sport of outdoor tennis or real tennis. According to most tennis historians, advanced tennis terminology also derives from this period, as Wingfield adopted both the name and much of the French vocabulary of genuine tennis and applied them to his new game.

The first championships at Wimbledon in London were played in 1877. On 21 May 1881, the United States National Lawn Tennis Association (now the United States Tennis Association) was conceived to standardise the decrees and organize competitions. The U.S. National Men's Singles Championship, now the US Open, was first held in 1881 at Newport, Rhode Island. The U.S. National Women's Singles Championships were first held in 1887. Tennis was also popular in France, where the French Open dates to 1891. Thus, Wimbledon, the US Open, the French Open, and the Australian Open (dating to 1905) became and have persisted the most esteemed events in tennis. Collectively these four events are called the Grand Slam (a term adopted from bridge).

The comprehensive International Lawn Tennis Federation, now titled the International Tennis Federation, conventions proclaimed in 1924 have persisted outstandingly static in the ensuing eighty years, the one major alteration being the summation of the tiebreaker system designed by James Van Alen.The Davis Cup, an annual competition between national teams, dates to 1900.

In 1926, promoter C.C. Pyle founded the first professional tennis tour with a group of American and French tennis players playing exhibition matches to paying audiences. The most notable of these early professionals were the American Vinnie Richards and the Frenchwoman Suzanne Lenglen. Once a player turned pro he or she could not contend in the major (amateur) tournaments.

In 1968, commercial pressures and rumours of a few amateurs taking money under the table led to the abandonment of this distinction, inaugurating the open era, in which all players could contend in all tournaments, and top players were able to make their living from lawn tennis. With the commencement of the open era, the formation of an international professional tennis circuit, and incomes from the sale of television rights, tennis's fame has spread worldwide, and the sport has shed its upper/middle-class English-speaking image (though it is acknowledged that this stereotype still exists).

In 1954, Van Alen established the International Tennis Hall of popularity, a non-profit museum in Newport, Rhode Island. The building bears a large accumulation of tennis memorabilia as well as a hall of popularity honouring prominent members and tennis players from all over the world. Each year, a grass-court tournament and an induction ceremony honouring new Hall of popularity members are hosted on its grounds.

History of Lawn Tennis in India

The game of lawn tennis was formed by the British and they took the game to their colonies. India was no exception and the game soon caught the fancy of the natives. Mohd. Saleem was one of the former stalwarts of the game and won the Punjab Lawn Tennis Championship consecutively from 1916-20.

The All India Lawn Tennis Association came into beingness in 1920 and soon a number of state associations pursued suit. The AILTA decide to host an annual national championship and work for Indian involvement in the Davis Cup. India made an impressive Davis Cup entry by defeating the formidable French to reach the semi finals.

In the 1930s, Indians like Mohd. Saleem, A. A. Fayzee and Jagat Mohan Lal did well in Davis Cup and the Olympics to fetch laurels for the country. India's growing height was raised by the visits of great tennis players like Bill Tilden and Henry Cochet.

THE GAME

Court

Tennis is played on a rectangular, flat surface, generally grass, clay, or a hardcourt of concrete and/or asphalt. The court is 78 feet (23.77 m) long, and its width is 27 feet (8.23 m) for singles matches and 36 ft (10.97 m) for doubles matches. Additional clear space around the court is needed in order for players to reach overrun balls. A net is stretched across the full width of the court, parallel with the baselines, dividing it into two equal ends. The net is 3 feet 6 inches (1.07 m) high at the posts and 3 feet (91.4 cm) high in the center.

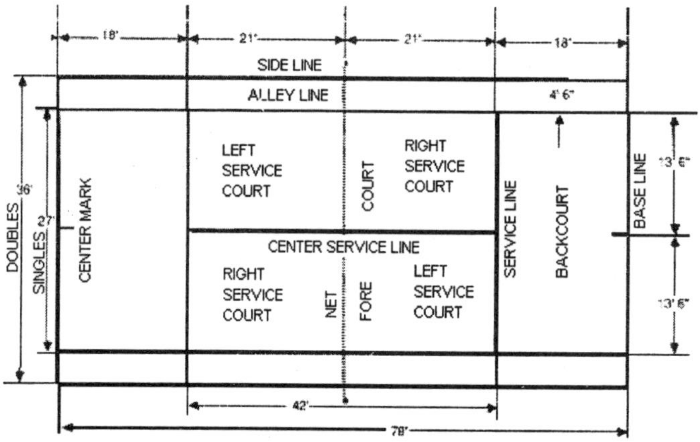

Fig. Court

The design of the lawn tennis court has experienced much evolution. It was Major Walter Clopton Wingfield who, in 1873, designed a court estimate to the current one for his stické lawn tennis (sphairistike). This template was altered in 1875 to the court shape that exists nowadays; the markings homogeneous with Wingfield's design, with the hourglass shape of his court altered to a more linear framework.

Lines

The lines that delineate the width of the court are called the baseline (farthest back) and the service line (middle of the court). The short mark in the center of each baseline is referred to as either the hash mark or the center mark. The outer lines that make up the length are called the doubles sidelines. These are the boundaries used when doubles is being played. The lines to the inside of the doubles sidelines are the singles sidelines and are utilised as boundaries in singles play. The area between a doubles sideline and the closest singles sideline is called the doubles alley, which is regarded playable in doubles play.

The line that runs across the center of a player's side of the court is called the service line because the serve must be rendered into the area between the service line and the net on the receiving side. Despite its name, this isn't where a player lawfully stands when making a serve. The line parting the service line in two is called the center line or center service line. The boxes this center line makes are called the service boxes; depending on a player's position, he will have to hit the ball into one of these when serving.

A ball is out only if none of it has hit the line upon its first bounce. All the lines are needed to be between 1 and 2 inches (51 mm) in width. The baseline can be up to 4 inches (100 mm) wide if so desired.

Racquet

A racquet is a sport implement comprising of a handled frame with an open hoop across which a network of cord is stretched out tightly. It is used for striking a ball in such games as squash, lawn tennis, racquetball, and badminton. Conjointly, these games are known as racquet sports.

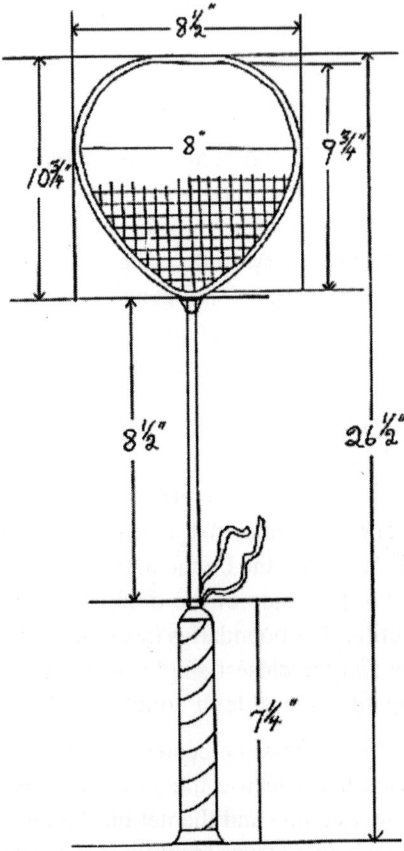

Fig. Racquet

The frame of racquets for all sports was traditionally constructed of laminated wood and the strings of animal intestine known as gut. The conventional racquet size was confined by the strength and weight of the wooden frame which had to be strong enough to hold the strings and stiff enough to hit the ball or shuttle. Manufacturers began adding non-wood laminates to wood racquets to improve stiffness.

Non-wood racquets were made first of steel, then of aluminium, and then carbon fibre composites. Wood is still employed for real tennis, racquets, and xare. Most racquets are now built of composite materials including carbon fibre, glassfibre, metals such as titanium alloys or ceramics. Gut has partially been substituted by synthetic materials including nylon, polyamide, and other polymers. Racquets are restrung when necessary, which may be after every match for a professional or never for a social player.

Officials

In most professional play and some amateur competition, there is an officiating head judge or chair umpire (typically referred to as the umpire), who sits in a raised chair to one side of the court. The umpire has absolute authority to make factual determinations. The umpire may be assisted by line judges, who ascertain whether the ball has landed within the needed part of the court and who also call foot faults. There also may be a net judge who ascertains whether the ball has touched the net during service.

In some tournaments, certain line judges, typically those who would be calling the serve, are substituted by electronic detectors that beep when an out call would have been made. In some open-tournament matches, players are permitted to challenge a confined number of close calls by means of instant replay.

The US Open, the Sony Ericsson Open in Key Biscayne, Florida, the US Open Series, and World Team Tennis began using a "challenge" arrangement in 2006 and the Australian Open and Wimbledon brought in the system in 2007. This used the Hawk-Eye system and the conventions were alike to those used in the NFL, where a player gets a bounded number of instant-replay challenges per match/set. In clay-court matches, such as at the French Open, a call may be questioned by reference to the mark left by the ball's impact on the court surface.

The referee, who is generally located off the court, is the ultimate authority about tennis decrees. When called to the court by a player or team captain, the referee may override the umpire's decision if the tennis decrees were assaulted (question of law) but may not alter the umpire's decision on a question of fact. If, however, the referee is on the court during play, the referee may overrule the umpire's decision.

Match Play

A tennis match is meant to be uninterrupted. Because stamina is a relevant factor, arbitrary delays are not allowed. In most cases, service is needed to occur no more than 20 seconds after the end of the previous point. This is increased to 90 seconds when the players change ends (after every odd-numbered games), and a 120 second break is allowed between sets. Other than this, breaks are allowed only when forced by events beyond the players' control, such as rain, damaged footwear, damaged racquet, or the need to regain an errant ball. Should a player be determined to be stalling repeatedly, the chair umpire may at first give a warning followed by consequent penalties of "point", "game", and default of the match for the player who is consistently taking longer than the permitted time limit.

In the event of a rain delay or other such proponent, the match is resumed at a later time, with the same score as at the time of the delay. Balls wear out rapidly in serious play and, therefore, in ATP and WTA tournaments, they are changed after every nine games with the first change happening after only seven games, because the first set of balls is also applied for the pre-match warm-up. However, in ITF tournaments like Fed Cup, the balls are changed in a 9-11 style. Persistence of the balls' condition is regarded part of the game, so if a re-warm-up is needed after an extended break in play (typically due to rain), then the re-warm-up is done using a separate set of balls, and use of the match balls is resumed only when play resumes. It has latterly been proposed to permit coaching on court during a match on a confined basis.

MAJOR TOURNAMENTS

Grand Slam Tournaments

The four Grand Slam tournaments are regarded to be the most esteemed tennis tournaments in the world. They are held yearly and include, in chronological order, the Australian Open, the French Open, Wimbledon, and the US Open. Aside from the Olympic Games, Davis Cup, Fed Cup, and Hopman Cup, they are the only tournaments governed by the International Tennis Federation (ITF). The ITF's national associations, Tennis Australia (Australian Open), the French Tennis

Federation (French Open), the United States Tennis Association (US Open), and the All England Lawn Tennis and Croquet Club and Lawn Tennis Association (Wimbledon), are designated the obligation to organize these events.

Australian Open: The Australian Open is one of the four Grand Slam lawn tennis tournaments held each year. It is held each January at Melbourne Park. The tournament was held for the first time in 1905 and was contended on grass through 1987. Since 1988, the tournament has been held on hard courts.

Mats Wilander is the only male player to have won the tournament on both grass and hard courts.Like all other Grand Slam tournaments, there are men's and women's singles competitions; men's, women's, and mixed doubles; and junior's and master's competitions. Held in the midway of the Australian summer, the Australian Open is renowned for its notoriously hot days. An extreme-heat policy is put into play when temperatures (and humidity) reach dangerous levels.

French Open: The French Open (French: Les Internationaux de France de Roland Garros or Tournoi de Roland-Garros) is a major tennis tournament carried over two weeks between mid-May and early June in Paris, France, at the Stade Roland Garros. It is the second of the Grand Slam tournaments on the yearly tennis calendar and the premier clay court tennis tournament in the world. It is one of the most esteemed events in tennis, and it has the widest worldwide broadcasting and audience of all events in this sport. Because of the slow playing surface and the five-set men's singles matches without a tiebreak in the final set, some say that the event is regarded to be the most physically demanding tennis tournament in the world.

The event started as a national tournament in 1891 as the Championat de France International de Tennis. The first women's tournament was held in 1897. In 1912, the French tournament was held with a varied surface (at the time all tennis played was lawn tennis), a red clay ("terre battue"), made up from the smashed wastes of red brick. The tournament was open only to tennis players who were certified in France through 1924.

Wimbledon: The Championships, Wimbledon, or simply, Wimbledon, is the oldest tennis tournament in the world and is widely regarded as the most esteemed. It has been held at the All England Club in the London suburb of Wimbledon since 1877. It is the earliest of the four Grand Slam lawn tennis tournaments, and the only one still played on grass courts.The tournament runs yearly for 14 days from late June to early July, with the climax being the men's singles final, scheduled for a Sunday. As of the 2008 tournament, five major events are contended, as well as four junior events and four invitational events. Wimbledon is third in the yearly Grand Slam season.

The hard court Australian Open and clay court French Open precede Wimbledon. The hard court U.S. Open pursues. The grass court Queen's Club Championships also in London is a popular warm up tournament for Wimbledon. Wimbledon customs include the eating of strawberries and cream, royal patronage, strict dress code for challengers, and ball boys and girls. A much unloved custom, "rainfall stops play" calls leading to schedule over-runs, is set to be reduced with the fitting of a retractable roof to Centre Court from 2009. The 2008 men's final, already the longest at about 5 hours of play, was extended to over 7 hours due to rain, stopping in darkness.

US Open: The US Open tennis tournament is one of the oldest tennis championships in the world, first contended in 1881. It was the ultimate event of the Grand Slam Tournament. The tournament is chronologically the fourth and final event of the Grand Slam tennis tournaments. It is held yearly in August and September over a two-week period (the weeks before and after Labor Day weekend).

The main tournament comprises of five championships: men's and women's singles, men's and women's doubles, and mixed doubles, with supplementary tournaments for senior, junior, and wheelchair players. Since 1978, the tournament has been played on acrylic hard court at the USTA Billie Jean King National Tennis Center at Flushing Meadows-Corona Park in Queens, New York City. The US Open varies from the other three Grand Slam tournaments in that there are final-set tie breaks. In the other three majors, the fifth set for the men and the third set for the women continue until somebody wins by two games.

Davis Cup

The Davis Cup is the premier international team event in men's tennis. The greatest yearly international team competition in sports, the Davis Cup is run by the International Tennis Federation (ITF) and is contended between teams of players from contending countries in a knock-out format. The competition commenced in 1900 as a challenge between the United States and Great Britain. In 2005, 134 nations entered teams into the competition.

The most successful countries over the history of the tournament are the United States (winning 32 tournaments and ending up as runners-up 29 times) and Australia (winning 23 times and finishing up second 18 times and also winning on four junctures with New Zealand under the name 'Australasia').

Tennis Masters Series

The Tennis Masters Series is a group of nine tournaments that form the second-highest echelon in men's tennis. Each event is held yearly, and a win at one of these events is worth 500 ranking points. When the Association of Tennis Professionals, led by Hamilton Jordan, started running the men's tour in 1990, the directors designated the top nine tournaments, external of the Grand Slam events, as "Super Nine" events. These finally became the Tennis Masters Series. In November at the end of the tennis year, the world's top eight players contend in the Tennis Masters Cup, a tournament with a rotating locale. It is presently held in Shanghai, China, and will move to London in 2009.

Challenger Series

The Challenger Series for men is the lowest level of tournament administered by the ATP. It is compiled of about 160 events and, as a result, features a more diverse range of countries hosting events. The majority of players use the Challenger Series to work their way up the rankings, including World No. 1s Pete Sampras, Marcelo Ríos, Patrick Rafter, and Gustavo Kuerten. Andre Agassi, between winning Grand Slam titles, plummeted to World No. 141 and used Challenger Series events for match experience and to progress back up the rankings. The Challenger Series offers prize funds of between US$25,000 and US$150,000.

Chennai Open

Chennai Open, South Asia's only Association of Tennis Professionals (ATP) tournament, has been held in Chennai on the first week of January every year since 1997.

Antecedently the tournament was called Gold Flake Open and TATA Open after the main sponsors. In 2004, when the three-year association with Tata finished, the possibility of Chennai losing out on hosting the tournament loomed large, as there was not a title sponsor. But with the Tamil Nadu government deciding to co-sponsor the event along with a consortium of corporate houses, the tournament stayed in Chennai.

Kingfisher Airlines Tennis Open

The inaugural edition of the ATP Mumbai Open will be held from September 25 to October 1, 2006, at the renowned Mumbai Cricket Club. The Cricket Club will be extensively restored to include a new 3,500-seat Center Court plus two match courts and two practice courts.

Mumbai became the second city in India after Chennai to host an ATP tournament when the ATP Board of Directors sanctioned a request to move the $380,000 Vietnam Open tournament from Ho Chi Minh City to Mumbai. World No.7 Tommy Robredo of Spain, No.8 Mario Ancic (Croatia) and No. 9 Radek Stepanek (Czech Republic) are the top-10 players who have assured their participation in the Open. Globosport India, promoted by doubles ace Mahesh Bhupathi, will be responsible for the marketing, management and promotion of the Mumbai Open.

Sunfeast Open

The Sunfeast Open made its introduction in the Women's Tennis Association (WTA) Tour calendar in 2005 with Kolkata playing host to the first version. The tournament, India's first ever Tier III WTA event, was held from September 19-25, 2005 and contained a total prize money of US $170,000.

The tournament, played at the Netaji Subhash Indoor Stadium, saw Russian top seed Anastasia Myskina completing a double by winning both the singles and doubles titles. While the Russian made merry, Indian teen sensation Sania Mirza rammed out of the second round much to the disappointment of the home crowd.

This Sunfeast Open 2005 was brought to Kolkata with the help of the Government of West Bengal and ITC, one of India's corporate giants. Globosport, the sports and entertainment company promoted by tennis star Mahesh Bhupathi were the owners and managers of the Sunfeast Open 2005. The 2006 edition will be played from September 18-24 with ITC Foods being the lead sponsor.

ADMINISTRATIVE BODIES

International Lawn Tennis Federation

The International Tennis Federation is the international regularising and administrative body for the sport of tennis. The International Tennis Federation consists 202 member nations divided amongst 6 territorial regulating bodies. The announced mission of the International Tennis

Federation is to promote tennis globally and regularise the decrees of the game.

The International Lawn Tennis Federation was founded on the 1st of March 1913, when the national federations of 14 lawn tennis playing nations met in Paris to make an overarching regulatory body. The main purpose of the Federation was to ensure uniformity in the conventions of the game, and cooperation between the different national federations.

Since the turn of the century the International Tennis Federation's membership list has grown quickly, and its role in ascertaining the course of international tennis has become more prominent and important.

Lawn Tennis Association

The Lawn Tennis Association (LTA) is the regulating body of tennis in Great Britain, the Channel Islands and the Isle of Man. Its objects are to promote and develop tennis and to advance and safeguard the interests of the sport and the regulating body. It was established on January 26, 1888, and since February 2007 is headquartered at the new National Tennis Centre in Roehampton (South West London) having displaced from its former location at the Queen's Club.

The Women Tennis Association (WTA)

The women tennis association came to life on 23rd September 1970.WTA is like ATP for the main tennis. Bille Jean King is the main man behind formation of this organization. It arranges WTA tours all over the world. It is split up into three parts.

1. The four Grandslams 2. Season ending championship 3. Tier tournaments.

All India Tennis Association

Like many other games, tennis was prefaced in India by the Britishers. The game step by step took root among the locales and a number of tournaments like 'Punjab Lawn tennis Championship' at Lahore (Pakistan) (1885), 'Bengal Lawn Tennis Championship' at Calcutta (1887) and the All India Tennis Championships at Allahabad in (1910) were organised.

In 1920, the All India Lawn Tennis Association (AILTA) came to life at Lahore and the constitution of the Association was framed up. Samuel Perry O'Donnell, an Indian Civil Service officer, was elected the first president at the first AGM of AILTA was held at the Town Hall at Delhi. The AILTA attained force as a number of state associations were associated and India began taking part in the Davis Cup. The Association was renamed All India Tennis Association (AITA) in the early 1980s. The AITA is headquartered at the R. K. Khanna Tennis Stadium in New Delhi and is the central regulating body for tennis in India.

FAMOUS PLAYERS

Roger Federer

Roger Federer is a renowned Swiss tennis player. He was born on August 8, 1981 in Basel, Switzerland. Federer found out his love for tennis when he was 8 years old, when he also had a strong interest in football. Federer devoted himself to tennis and when he was 14 Roger became the the Swiss Junior champion. In 1998 he won the Wimbledon Juniors title and Orange Bowl. Federer has defeated such great tennis stars as Andre Agassi (Tennis Masters Cup 2003 Final), Pete Sampras (Wimbledon 2001 4th Round), and Andy Roddick (Wimbledon 2005 Final).

His few accomplishments:

- 2003- ATP European Player of the Year; Swiss Sportsman of the Year; Swiss of the Year; Michael-Westphal Award.
- 2004- ATP European Player of the Year; ITF World Champion; Sports Illustrated Tennis Player of the Year; Swiss Sportsman of the Year.
- Stefan Edberg Sportmanship Award

Pete Sampras

Pete Sampras was born August 12, 1971, in Washington, DC and has been a World No.1 tennis player. His parents Georgia and Sam are Greek immigrant to the USA. Sampras began his tennis career when he was a child and was discovered in the basement of his home. That was a turning point for his life and within a time and intense training Pete has become one of the best male tennis players on a global scale.

In the year 1988 when Pete Sampras was just 17 years old he won his first first top-level singles title in February 1990 at Philadelphia and by beating Andre Agassi he turned the US Open's youngest-ever male singles champion. Andre Agassi is regarded to be Sampras' greatest rival. During 90's Pete accomplished a great fame and acknowledgement in tennis. But in early 2000's he confronted already the new tennis stars, such as Lleyton Hewitt and Marat Safin. Pete Sampras declared to the world the tennis retirement in the year 2003 (August).

His few accomplishments are:

1990- US Open (Andre Agassi)

1993- Wimbledon (Jim Courier)

1993- US Open (Cedric Pioline)

1994- Australian Open (Todd Martin)

1995- Wimbledon (Boris Becker)

1995- US Open (Andre Agassi)

1996- US Open (Michael Chang)

1997- Australian Open (Carlos Moya)

1998- Wimbledon (Goran Ivanesevic)

1999- Wimbledon (Andre Agassi)

2000- Wimbledon (Patrick Rafter)

2002- US Open (Andre Agassi)

Serena Williams

Serena Williams was born in Saginaw, Michigan, USA on the 26th of September, 1981 to parents Richard and Oracene. Her sister is the renowned tennis star Venus Williams. Her father was very disciplined and had big dreams for his daughters, assisting them both to become champion tennis players.

Serena exhibited her gifted abilities in playing tennis during her childhood by winning her first tournament when she was just four years old. Serena's sister Venus was also into tennis and both sisters rose through the ranks conjointly, to become celebrity tennis players at the top of their game.

Serena's few accomplishments:

1999 Grand Slam Cup (singles) - Champion

2000 Wimbledon (doubles) - Champion

2001 Australian Open (doubles tennis) - Champion

2002 French Open (singles) - Champion

2003 Australian Open (singles and doubles) - Champion

2003 Wimbledon (singles tennis) - Champion

2005 Australian Open (singles tennis) - Champion

Venus Williams

Venus Williams is regarded to be one of the best tennis players in the world. She was born on June 17, 1980 in Lynwood, California, USA.

Her sister, Serena Williams, is also a world famous tennis players, against whom Venus has played many world tennis tournaments between 1998-2003. Venus is the first woman who won an Olympic gold medal in singles and doubles (with Serena) since 1924. Venus had older sister, Yetunde Price, who was shot in the year 2003.

Venus Williams began her career as a tennis player as a child with her father playing a large role in her tennis career. Venus has already attained many achievements and has become one of the leading womens tennis players alongside her sister Serena.

Venus's few accomplishments:

Australian Open F (2003),

French Open F (2002),

Wimbledon W (2000, 2001, 2005),

U.S. Open W (2000, 2001).

Maria Sharapova

Maria Yuryevna Sharapova was born in Nyagan, Russia on the 19th of April, 1987. Born to parents Yuri and Yelena Sharapova, Maria first started playing tennis when she was hardly 4 years old. When Maria Sharapova was just six years of age the renowned tennis player Martina Navratilova discovered her talent and suggested to her parents that she move to the United States to receive professional lawn tennis training.

After her first professional year in 2002 of playing tennis Sharapova was ranked 186th in the world. In 2003 her rankings improved greatly, with her highest ranking being 32nd in the world. In 2004 she carried on to improve, being the 2nd youngest ever to win the Grand Slam Wimbledon Championship and ended the year with $2,506,263 prize money earnings.

Her accomplishments as a single player:

- Year 2004 - Singles Results - Wins 55 / Loss 15
- Year 2003 - Singles Results - Wins 34 / Loss 12
- Year 2002 - Singles Results - Wins 1 / Loss 2

Her accomplishments as doubles player:

- Year 2004 - Doubles Results - Wins 13 / Loss 8
- Year 2003 - Doubles Results - Wins 11 / Loss 6
- Year 2002 - Doubles Results - Wins 1 / Loss 2

Leander Paes

Leander Paes is a rarity in Indian sports arena for his astonishing accomplishments and the never-say-die attitude that he brings to his game. Born on June 17, 1973, Paes has written many a memorable triumphs both at the Davis Cup and in Grand Slam tournaments.

Leander shot into limelight when he won the 1990 Wimbledon Junior title and ascended to No.1 in the junior world-rankings. Despite the fact that he could not make much of an impact as a singles player, Leander teamed up with compatriot Mahesh Bhupathi to form a formidable doubles pair. The year 1999 proved to be a watershed for the duo as they entered the finals of all the four Grand Slam events, finally winning the Wimbledon and the French Open.

He won the 1990 Wimbledon Junior title; No.1 in the junior world-rankings; won the Wimbledon and the French Open doubles title in 1999; bronze medal in the 1996 Atlanta Olympics.

Mahesh Bhupathi

Mahesh Bhupathi may not possess the aura of his more illustrious compatriot Leander Paes, but over the years he has proved to be the more victorious one of the duo.

Bhupathi gained the distinction of becoming the first Indian to win a Grand Slam when he partnered Japan's Rika Hiraki to win the 1997 French Open mixed doubles title. This path breaking victory paved the way for more glory as Bhupathi teamed with Leander to annex a host of esteemed Grand Slam titles.

He became the first Indian to win a Grand Slam by winning the French Open mixed doubles title in 1997; won the Wimbledon and French Open doubles title in 1999; US Open mixed doubles in 1999; Australian Open mixed doubles in 2006.

Vijay Amritraj

Vijay Amritraj, born on December 14, 1953, kept on the Indian flag flying high with his notable performances at the international tennis circuit. Amritraj, along with the father-son duo of Ramanathan and

Ramesh Krishnan, is among the handful of Indians to have fared reasonably well in Grand Slam tournaments.

In 1973, he reached the quarterfinal of Wimbledon but lost to ultimate champion Jan Kodes in a thrilling five-setter. The same year, in the U.S. Open, he lost the quarterfinal clash to tennis great Ken Rosewall after getting the better of Rod Laver in an earlier round. He reached the quarterfinal of Wimbledon in 1973 and 1981; reached the quarterfinal of US Open in 1973 and 1974; division of the Indian team that reached the final of Davis Cup in 1974.

Sania Mirza

First Indian woman to reach the fourth round of a Grand Slam tournament; first Indian woman to win a WTA singles title (Hyderabad Open in 2005); WTA's Most Impressive Newcomer for the year 2005

In a cricket obsessed country like India, tennis player Sania Mirza's hysterical fan following speaks volumes about her accomplishments. Sania's glamorous looks and meteoric ascend to stardom has only added to her aura. Sania became the first Indian woman to reach the third round of a Grand Slam tournament at the 2005 Australian Open. She improved her Grand Slam performance by reaching the fourth round of the US Open in the same year.

On February 12, 2005, Sania became the first Indian woman to win a WTA singles title defeating Alyona Bondarenko of Ukraine in the Hyderabad Open Finals. Her consistency ensured that Sania attained a career high ranking of 31 in singles by mid-October 2005. She was named the WTA's Most Impressive Newcomer for the year 2005.

REFERENCES

Aahper. *Ideas for Tennis Instruction, Lifetime* Sports Education Project. Washington, D.C.: American Association for Health, Physical Education, and Recreation, 1966.

Barnaby, John M.: *Racket Work: the Key to Tennis*. Boston, Allyn and Bacon, Inc., 1969.

Bradlee, Dick.: *Instant Tennis*. New York, Devin-Adair Company, 1962.

Broer, Marion R.: *Efficiency of Human Movement*. Second edition. Philadelphia, W. B. Saunders Company, 1966.

Talbert, William F. and Bruce S. Old: *The Game of Doubles in Tennis*. Philadelphia, J. B. Lippincott Company, 1956.

12

Pentathlon

The Ancient Pentathlon or the "fivefold contest" was one of the most esteemed events played at the ancient Greek Olympics. Players contended in the footrace, long jump, throwing the discus and throwing the javelin. The two men scoring the highest in these events were selected for the final competetion, a wrestling match. The winner of this was announced to be the pentathlete. Three other sports were added in as well, in latter years. The boxing, Pankration and Equestrian events.

In the foot race, the contenders must run around the Olympic stadium which was approximately 200 metres. The long jump was nothing like it is today. They did not have a run up, as they stood and jumped from a standing start. They even employed heavy rocks to help them in getting more distance.

They held onto the weights until just before impact and they then let them go backwards, providing them an extra push. The discus throw was pretty much similar then as it is today. They built their discuses from stone, or afterwards on in the Hellenistic age, they employed iron, lead or bronze. The way they threw the discus was very alike to how athletes do it today.

Javelin was quite dissimilar. The greeks use to use a strap attached to the javelin to move it further. They would wrap the strap around their hand and launch it from a run.

Wrestling to the ancient Greeks was much more then just a sport, but a lifestyle. All soldiers must know how to wrestle. In a wrestling match, a man can only win when the other challenger gives up. In Greek myth, the Pentathlon was invented by Jason. Jason was the ancient Greek hero who was sent to get the Golden Fleece. The Pentathlon was more then likely the climax of the ancient games, with the winner being crowned 'Victor Ludorum'.

There are five events under pentathlon, they are:

Discus Throw

The discus throw is an event in track and field competition, in which an athlete throws a heavy disc itself known as a discus in an effort to mark a farther distance than his or her contenders. It is an ancient sport, as proved by the 5th century BC Myron statue, Discobolus. Though not part of the advance pentathlon, it was one of the events of the ancient pentathlon, which can be dated at least back to 708 BC.

Fig: Discus Throw

A routine part of most advance track and field meets at all levels; it is a sport which is specially iconic of the Olympic Games. The men's competition has been a part of the modern Summer Olympic Games subsequently the first Olympiad in 1896. Images of discus throwers figured prominently in advertising for ancient advance Games, such as fundraising stamps for the 1896 games and the prime posters for the 1920 and 1948 Summer Olympics.

Javelin Throw

The javelin throw is a track and field athletics throwing event where the object to be thrown is the javelin, a spear-like object built of metal, fiberglass and, in few cases, carbon fibre. On April 1, 1986, the men's javelin (800g, 1.76lb) was restyled by the regulating body (the IAAF Technical Committee). They decided to alter the conventions for javelin construction because of the increasingly frequent flat landings and the resulting discussions and protests when these attempts were announced valid or invalid by competition judges.

The javelin throw has been part of the Summer Olympics since 1906. Though the javelin is presently employed only for sport in most areas, it has a long history of use for hunting and warfare. There are, for example, several references to the javelin in ancient Hellenic civilization, who practised a kind of javelin throwing at the ancient Olympics. Few consider the objective was to throw at a aim instead of for distance, but this can not be determined.

Fig: javelin Throw

The javelin throw has a specially strong custom in the Nordic nations of Europe. Of the sixty-six Olympic medals that have been awarded in the event, 30 have gone to contenders from Norway, Sweden, or Finland. Finland is the only nation to have ever swept the medals, and has done so twice, in 1920 and 1932.

Long Jump

The long jump is an athletics (track and field) event in which athletes combine speed, strength, and agility in an attempt to leap as far from the take-off point as possible.

Fig: Jump

Contenders sprint down a runway (normally coated with the same rubberised surface as running tracks, crumb rubber or vulcanized rubber) and jump as far as they can from before a foul line (ordinarily referred to as the "board", and normally defined by the trailing edge of a takeoff board engrafted flush with the runway surface, or a painted mark on the runway) into a pit filled with finely ground gravel or sand.

The distance traveled by a jumper is often referred to as the "mark" because it is the distance to the nearest mark built in the sand from the foul line. If the contender begins the leap with any part of the foot past the foul line, the jump is announced illegal and no distance is registered. At the elite level, a layer of plasticine is placed immediately after the board to notice this occurrence. Otherwise, an official (alike to a referee) will observe the jump and make the determination. The contender can start the jump from any point behind the foul line; however, the distance assessed will invariably be from the foul line. Therefore, it is in the best concern of the contender to get as close to the foul line as possible.

Running

Running is a means for an animal to move on foot. It is defined in sporting terms as a gait in which at few points all feet are off the ground simultaneously. Running is a complex and coordinated process that engage the entire body. Every human being runs in different way, but certain usual characteristics of running movement are common.

Running is accomplished as a sequence of strides, which alternate between the two legs. Each leg's stride can be roughly split up into three phases: support, drive, and retrieval. Support and drive occur when the foot is in contact with the ground. Retrieval occurs when the foot is off the ground. Subsequently only one foot is on the ground at a time in running, one leg is invariably in retrieval, while the other goes through support and drive. Then, briefly, as the runner leaps through the air, both legs are in retrieval. These phases are described in detail below.

Wrestling

Wrestling is the act of physical participation between two people in which each wrestler strives to get an advantage over, or control of, the adversary contender. Physical methods which embody the style of wrestling are clinching, holding, locking, and leverage. Avoiding methods likely to lead to serious injury, the fundamental principle of wrestling are closely related to those of armed forces hand-to-hand combat or self-defence systems. Many styles of wrestling are known all over the world and have long histories. Amateur wrestling has been an Olympic sport for over one hundred years and professional wrestling is a famous kind of amusement as well as an art form.

HISTORY

The ancient Greek pentathlon comprised of five events: discus, javelin, long jump, a foot-race which was most likely a stade long, and wrestling. Of these five events, the first three belonged entirely to the pentathlon while running and wrestling were also different events in and of themselves. Aristotle said of those who contended in the pentathlon, "The pentathletes have the most beautiful bodies, because they are built for strength and speed together"

While the advance discus weighs four pounds, 6.4 ounces and is built out of metal or wood and metal, the ancient discus weighed a great deal more and was built first out of stone and afterwards out of bronze. One ancient discus in the Museum of Fine Arts in Boston weighs 14 pound, 10 ounces; it has an inscription that reads "from the games". While an advance thrower must stand within the boundries of eight foot circle, Philostratos tells us that the ancient throwing area, the balbis, is quite small. He writes, "The balbis is small, large enough for one man standing erect and marked off in all directions except the rear" (Philostratos, On Statues, 1.24). There is only one record of a throw that was registered in ancient times. In the epigram of Phayllus it said "he jumped five over fifty feet, but threw the discus five short of a hundred,"

While the advance javelin is built of metal and must be at least 8.5 feet long and 1.765 pounds, the body of the ancient Greek javelin seems to be 6 feet long and thick as a finger, according to the pictures. It was built of wood, with a metal point on the end. The javelins they threw in war were most likely a great deal heavier, but this athletic event gave soldiers ample of practice for war.

The ancient throwers employed a throwing strap approximately a foot long, wrapped around the center of the body of the javelin. Though there is no definite idea of how far an ancient contender could throw a javelin, a good guess could be approximately 300 feet.

The Greeks exercised only one jump and that is the long jump. The big difference between the ancient and the modern long jump is that the ancient jumpers carried weights, which were known as halteres. These weights were built out of stone or metal, weighed four to eight pounds, and were shaped like telephone hand-pieces, dumbbells or flat-irons. The necessary gear for both the advanced and early long jump is the runway, the takeoff board and the landing pit. Sextus Julius Africanus tells us "In the twenty-ninth Olympics, Chionis of Sparta won the stade; in the jump he did 52 feet." Once again, from Phayllos's epigram, we learn that he jumped fifty-five feet.

History of Discus Throw

Discus throwing was part of the first Olympics held in 776 B.C. The ancient discs were built of unwrought bronze and iron and the Discs were awarded to the winner. In the 8th century BC, Greek poet Homer built references to discus throwing. In the 5th century BC, sculptor Myron produced a statue of a discus thrower (Discobolus). In the 15th century, Indian soldiers employed a lethal throwing Disc weapon known as a Chacarani. In the 1896 Summer Olympics, the mens discus throw was one of two throwing events. Countries such as Finland, Russia and Germany have proven themselves very strong in Discus Throwing.

History of Javelin Throw

The javelin throw has been part of the Summer Olympics since 1906. Though the javelin is presently employed only for sport in most areas, it has a long history of use for hunting and warfare. There are, for example, several references to the javelin in ancient Hellenic civilization, who practised a kind of javelin throwing at the ancient Olympics. Some consider the objective was to throw at an aim instead of for distance, but this can not be determined.

The javelin throw has a especially strong custom in the Nordic nations of Europe. Of the 66 Olympic medals that have been awarded in the event, 30 have gone to contenders from Norway, Sweden, or Finland. Finland is the only nation to have ever swept the medals, and has done so as many as two times, in 1920 and 1932.

History of Long Jump

The long jump was one of the events of the primitive Olympics in Ancient Greece. The athletes carried a weight in each hand, which were known as halteres. These weights were swung forward as the athlete jumped in order to increase momentum. It is usually considered that the jumper would throw the weights behind him in mid-air to increase his forward momentum; however, halteres were held during the duration of the jump. Swinging them down and back at the end of the jump would alter the athlete's center of gravity and permit the athlete to stretch his legs outward, increasing his distance. Most noteworthy in the ancient sport was a man known as Chionis, who in the 656BC Olympics staged a jump of 7 meters and 5 centimeters (23 feet and 1.5 inches).

The long jump has been part of advance Olympic competition subsequently the commencement of the Games in 1896. In 1914, Dr. Harry Eaton Stewart urged the "running broad jump" as a standardised track and field event for women. However, it was not until 1928 that women were permited to contend in the event at the Olympic level

History of Running

The sport of running is undeniably the most ancient kind of athletic competition. The mythological invention of the sport is discovered in such legends as that of Herakles. The sport is so ancient that it is impossible to clarify its accurate time and place of its origin. Because of the strong link between ancient Greek mythology and the sport of running, it is no great surprise that this sport was regarded to be of major importance. Children were civilised at an ancient age in the methods and philosophies of the sport of running, a sport which was formed as a permanent feature in children's education.

History of Wrestling

The first documented proof of wrestling in Egypt came out in circa 2300 BC, on the tomb of the Old Kingdom philosopher Ptahhotep. Throughout the period of the New Kingdom (2000-1085 BC), additional Egyptian artwork (often on friezes), portrayed Egyptian and Nubian wrestlers contending. Carroll notes striking similarities between these ancient portrayals and those of the advance Nuba wrestlers. On the 406 wrestling pairs discovered in the Middle Kingdom tombs at Beni Hasan in the Nile valley, nearly all of the methods seen in advance freestyle wrestling could be discovered. Throughout the period of Ancient Greece (approximately 1100 to 146 BC), Greek wrestling was a famous kind of martial art in which points were awarded for pinning a contender by stretching the adversary prone to the ground or touching his back to the ground, forcing a contender to submit or by forcing a contender out of bounds (arena). Three falls determined the winner. It was at least featured as a sport subsequently the eighteenth Olympiad in 704 BC.

Wrestling is described in the most former celebrated works of Greek literature, the Iliad and the Odyssey. Wrestlers were also portrayed in action on many vases, sculptures, and coins, as well as in other literature. Other cultures featured wrestling at royal or spiritual celebrations, but the ancient Greeks structured their style of wrestling as part of a tournament where a single winner came forth from a pool of contenders. Greek mythology celebrates the rise of Zeus as ruler of the earth after a wrestling match with his father, Cronus. Both Heracles and Theseus were popular for their wrestling versus man and beast. Late Greek custom also said that Plato was known for wrestling in the Isthmian games.

Because of the rise of gymnasiums and athletic clubs, Greco-Roman wrestling and advance freestyle wrestling were soon governed in conventional competitions. On continental Europe, prize money was tendered in large sums to the winners of Greco-Roman tournaments, and freestyle wrestling disperse quickly in the British Isles and in the United States after the American Civil War. Professional wrestling soon raised the fame of Greco-Roman and freestyle wrestling around the world with such contenders as Georg Hackenschmidt, Kara Ahmed, Paul Pons, Stanislaus Zbyszko, William Muldoon, and Frank Gotch.

When the Olympic Games reappeared at Athens in 1896, Greco-Roman wrestling was brought in for the first time. After not being featured in the 1900 Olympics, sport wrestling was encountered again in 1904 in St. Louis; this time in freestyle competition. Since then, Greco-Roman and freestyle wrestling have both been featured, with women's freestyle contributed in the Summer Olympics of 2004. Since 1921, the International Federation of Associated Wrestling Styles (FILA) has governed amateur wrestling as an athletic discipline, while professional wrestling has largely become infused with theatrics but still needs athletic power. The Merriam-Webster dictionary defines wrestling as "a sport or competetion in which two unarmed individuals struggle hand-to-hand with each trying to subdue or unbalance the other".

THE GAME

Discuss Throw

To cast the discus well, an athlete would hold the discus high with only one hand and support it with the other. He would then swing it forcefully down and forward or from the side and forward. This movement uses the shoulder muscles, chest and ribs. The casting of the discus was as follows: A right handed discus thrower stood with his left leg in front and the weight of his body on his right foot. Applying his right hand, he swung the discus up and down a few times. When the discus was above his hand, more support came from his left hand.

Every time the discus swung down and behind, he more or less grew his body to the right. He then shifted his weight from his right foot to his left foot and cast the discus forward with an energetic speeding swing.

Javelin Throw

Conventions are alike to other throwing events: Contenders take three throws after which the top eight take another three, their best legal throw is registered and the winner is the individual with the longest legal throw assessed to the nearest centimetre or foot and inch depending upon country of competition. If the javelin's front point touches the ground first, the throw is marked (measured) from this point. If the throw lands flat then the distance is calculated from the back of the whipcord (grip). If the tail of the javelin lands first, then the throw is not counted and canceled.

The most noticeable difference with the other events is that instead of a throwing circle as employed in discus, shot put and hammer throw, the contenders have a run-up area coated with the same surface employed for running tracks, and a painted line on the surface for little spikes on each shoe. Many athletic tracks have javelin run-ups at each end to take advantage of any potential wind benefit.

Long Jump

Contenders sprint down a runway (normally coated with the same rubberized surface as running tracks, crumb rubber or vulcanized rubber) and jump as far as they can from behind a foul line (ordinarily referred to as the "board", and normally defined by the trailing edge of a takeoff board engrafted flush with the runway surface, or a painted mark on the runway) into a pit filled with finely ground gravel or sand. The distance passed by a jumper is often referred to as the "mark" because it is the distance to the nearest mark built in the sand from the foul line. If the contender begins the leap with any part of the foot past the foul line, the jump is announced illegal and no distance is registered. At the elite level, a layer of plasticine is placed immediately after the board to notice this occurrence. Otherwise, an official will observe the jump and make the determination. The contender can start the jump from any point behind the foul line; however, the distance assessed will invariably be from the foul line. Therefore, it is in the best concern of the contender to get as close to the foul line as possible.

Normally, each contender has a set number of attempts to make his or her longest jump, and only the longest legal jump counts towards the results. Typically, contenders have three try out jumps with which to make their best effort. Higher level competitions are split into two rounds: trials and finals. In competitions bearing a final round, only a choose number of contenders are invited to return for further competition. The number of contenders chosen to return to the final round is decided before the start of the meet by a committee composed of coaches and officials.

It is standard practice to permit one more contender than the number of scoring positions to return to the final round. For example, if a given meet permits the top eight contenders to score points, then the top nine contenders will be selected to contend in the final round. Taking an extra contender to the final round helps to permit that athlete to move into a scoring position if the contender can improve on his or her best mark of the competition. Final rounds are viewed as an additional three jumps, as they do not have any priority to those scored in the trial round. The contender with the longest legal jump (from either the trial or final rounds) at the end of competition is announced the winner.

Running

Leaning forward places a runner's center of mass on the front portion of the foot, which avoids landing on the heel and eases the use of the spring mechanism of the foot. It also makes it more comfortable for the runner to avoid landing the foot in front of the center of mass and the resultant braking effect.

Exercise physiologists have discovered that the stride rates are extremely invariable across professional runners, between 185 and 200 steps per minute. The prime difference between long- and short-distance runners is the length of stride instead of the rate of stride.

Throughout running, the speed at which the runner moves may be computed by multiplying the cadence (steps per second) by the stride length. Running is often assessed in terms of pace in minutes per mile or kilometer.

In walking, one foot is invariably in contact with the ground, the legs are kept generally straight and the center of gravity rides along fairly smoothly on top of the legs; in comparison, humans in reality leap from one leg to the other while running. Each leap raises the center of gravity throughout take-off, and lowers it on landing as the knee bends to absorb the shock. At mid arc, both feet are momentarily off of the ground. This continual rise and fall of bodyweight expends a tremendous amount of energy conflicting gravity and absorbing shock throughout take-off and landing. The act of running involves applying more energy to accomplish travel over the same distance and running is a less efficient means of locomotion in terms of calories expended, although it is faster.

Wrestling

The objective of the sport of wrestling is to put your adversary on his back to pin your adversary. A pin (or fall) is when you put your adversary on his/her back with any part of both shoulders or both shoulder blades of your adversary in contact with the mat for two seconds. When you pin your adversary, the match is considered as over and you are the winner. If nobody gets pinned, the winner is the wrestler who has scored the most points throughout the match. There are five ways to score points in a wrestling match:

1. Takedown - (2 points) you score two points for taking your adversary down to the mat and controlling him/her.
2. Escape - (1 point) you score one point for getting away or getting to a neutral position when your adversary has you down on the mat.
3. Reversal - (2 points) you score two points when your adversary has you down on the mat and you come from underneath and gain control of your adversary.
4. Near Fall (Back Points) - (2 or 3 points) you get near fall points when you almost but not quite get your adversary pinned.

MAJOR TOURNAMENTS

Olympic Games

The Olympic Games is an international multi-sport event established for both summer and winter games. There have been two generations of the Olympic Games; the first were theAncient Olympic Games, held at Olympia, Greece.

The second, known as the Modern Olympic Movement, were first held in1896, in Athens, Greece. The modern Olympics feature the Summer Games and Winter Games. The Paralympic and Youth Olympic Games are variations on the Modern Olympic Movement.

Pentathlon is played in Olympics and is considered as a main sport. Now a days there is modern pentathlon that has emerged, which is being played in modern Olympics.

ADMINISTRATIVE BODIES

International Olympic Committee

The International Olympic Committee (IOC) was founded in 1894 on the initiative of a French nobleman, Pierre Frédy, Baron de Coubertin. His vision was to bring together amateur athletes from around the world to compete in a variety of events. The IOC has become the governing body of the "Olympic Movement," a conglomeration of sporting federations that are responsible for the organization of the Games. The evolution of the Olympic Movement has forced the IOC to change Coubertin's time–honored ideals. The original vision of the pure amateur athlete had to change under the pressure of corporate sponsorships and political regimes intent on the creation of sports "dynasties".

International Amateur Athletic Federation (IAAF)

By the late 1800s, famous enthusiasm for all types of physical workout had caused an expand in participation sports. Athletics was particularly famous, and soon turned central to the practice elements of national educational systems. Organised athletics thrived in well evolved industrial societies and an ever flourishing competition programme evolved in the schools and universities, in military organisations and private clubs.

The International Amateur Athletic Federation was established in 1912 by 17 national athletic federations who saw the need for a regulating authority, for an athletic programme, for standardised technical gear and world records. But what was the sport the IAAF was meant to regulate? For participants, athletics was about raising the quality of life; it was something done for love and other noble principles. This allowed a restricted group of athletes to attain high-level performances by virtue of a privileged social and fiscal situation.

Yet with the continual development of advance society came tremendous enthusiasm for sport. This growing concern and the improvement of individual performances boosted the stature of athletics. Starting in the 1960s, TV coverage of athletics greatly increased and many companies started to see commercial value in the sport. It turned harder to pursue the amateur principle in the conventional sense, particularly regarding the time and resources needed to train and maintain elite athletes. Faced with this commercially demanding world, the IAAF made alterations to benefit the athlete, spectators and all other members of the "Athletics Family".

Jurgen Schult

Jurgen Schult was born on May 11, 1960 in Amt Neuhaus, Lower Saxony, he is a German track and field athlete and the present world record holder in the discus throw since 1986. Schult represented East Germany in the year 1988 Olympic competition in the discus throw held on October 1, 1988, where he won the gold medal

Afterwards in his long sport career he joined the reunified German team. He contended in a second Olympic Games in 1992, getting a silver medal, and the 1999 World Championships, again getting second place. He contended in his final Olympics in 2000 at the age of 40, ending up in 8th place. After he was incapable to contend in the 1984 Summer Olympics in Los Angeles due to his country's boycott of the games, he set a world record in the discus in 1986. With a throw of 74.08 meters he trumped the previous record of Soviet athlete, Yuriy Dumchev, by 2.22 meters.

His accomplishments:

- 1992, Olympic Games: 2nd place (64.94)
- 1993, World championship: 3rd place (66.12)
- 1994, European championship: 3rd place
- 1995, World championship: 5th place (64.44)
- 1996, Olympic Games: 6th place
- 1997, World championship: 3rd place (66.14)
- 1998, European championship: 2nd place
- 1999, World championship: 2nd place (68.18)
- 2000, Olympic Games: 8th place (64.41)

John Gates Powell

John Gates Powell was born on June 25, 1947 in San Francisco.He was an early American athlete. John Powell set the 1975 world record (69.08) in the discus throw, his personal best, set afterwards, is 72.08 m in 1984. It puts him eighth in the all-time performers list. His wife Wally Powell, also known as Mrs. Powell by her students and Ms. Dullea is a 6th Grade Core teacher at La Entrada, home of the Leopards. She is very nice to her students and provides them popcorn, and lets them watch PG-13 movies in class. She's an awesome teacher and the 2002-2003 Blue Core class was her best class ever.

Nicknamed "Roadrunner" in his elite days for his rapid movement across the ring, he took fourth at the 1972 Summer Olympics, bronze at 1976 Montreal and created the doomed U.S. team to Moscow in 1980 before again taking bronze at Los Angeles in 1984. The 1987 meets appear to have been his swan songs on the international level and he was banished from competition after participating in a renegade tour to South Africa.

His accomplishments:

- Fourth with 62.82 in the 1972 Summer Olympics in Munich
- First with 62.37 in the 1975 Pan American Games
- Third with 65.70 in the 1976 Summer Olympics in Montreal
- Third with 65.46 in the 1984 Summer Olympics in Los Angeles
- Second with 66.22 in the 1987 World Championships in Athletics in Rome

Bob Roggy

Bob Roggy was born on 6th august, 1956in Holmdel Township, New Jersey died August 1986) was a javelin thrower from the United States. He set the world best year performance in 1982, throwing 95.80 metres in Stuttgart, West Germany on 29th august, 1982.

A meet was named after him after Roggy's tragic death at age 30 in August 1986. The meet name turned the New Jersey International Meet in 1988, with the Bob Roggy Memorial Javelin Throw a feature event within it. Roggy was killed in an accident in 1986 in Houston, Texas at the first Olympic Sports Festival.

Stephen James Backley

Stephen "Steve" James Backley OBE was born on February 12, 1969 in Sidcup,he is a former athlete from Britain specialist in the javelin throw. Though he is ranked among the great javelin throwers of the modern era, Backley never won a gold medal in a major World athletics event.

He was a firm fixture in the national athletics team for over fifteen years and is the only British track and field contender to win medals at three dissimilar Olympic Games.

He was civilised at Warren Road Primary School, Orpington, and afterwards Beths Grammar School in his teens and afterwards enrolled at Loughborough University in October 1988 to study for a BSc Honours degree in Physical Education, Sports Science and Recreation Management. Though he finished his first year there and persisted a student until 2002, the time he devoted to the javelin prevented him from finishing his studies. However, on December 16, 2002 Loughborough University honoured him with the degree of Doctor of Technology honoris causa. His first significant title was won in 1987 when he threw 75.14 metres to pick up the European junior title, ahead of Vladimir Zossimovich (73.24) of Russia and East German Raymond Hecht (72.78).

Robert Lucien LeGendre

Robert "Bob" Lucien LeGendre was born on January 7, 1898 and died on January 21, 1931. He is an American athlete who contended primarily in the Pentathlon. He contended for a United States in the 1924 Summer Olympics held in Paris, France in the Pentathlon where he won the Bronze medal. In doing so he set a new world record for the long jump of 7.76 metres.

Igor Aramovich Ter-Ovanesyan)

Igor Aramovich Ter-Ovanesyan (born May 19, 1938 in Kiev) is a Russian athlete of Armenian and Ukranian ethnicity, and Olympic medalist in the long jump for the USSR.

Ter-Ovanesyan trained at Burevestnik, first in Kiev, afterwards in Lviv and then in Moscow. He took part in the Olympic Games five times (1956, 1960, 1964, 1968, and 1972) and twice won a bronze medal (in 1960 and 1964). He also repeatedly took medals at the European Championships: golden in 1958, 1962 and 1969, silver in 1966 and 1971.

Armen Nazarian

Armen Nazarian was born on March 9, 1974 in Masis, Armenian SSR, Soviet Union. He is an Armenian/Bulgarian Greco Roman wrestler and a member of the Fila Hall of Fame.

He began wrestling at the age of eight and wrestled for the USSR in international tournaments until the break up of that country in 1991. After which Nazarian wrestled for Armenia, before migrating to Bulgaria in 1995. He obtained Bulgarian citizenship in May 1997. When he was in his prime, Nazarian was one of the most dreaded Greco wrestlers in the world. He is the most decorated of all the active Greco Roman style wrestlers and in his career he has amounted 2 Olympic gold medals, 1 Olympic bronze, as well as 6 world medals to his name.

REFERENCES

Alter, S.: *Science of Flexibility*, 2nd edn, Human Kinetics, Champaign, IL, 1996.

Alter, S.: *Sport Stretch*, Human Kinetics, Champaign, IL, 1998.

Dintiman, G. and Ward, R.: *Sport Speed*, Leisure Press, Champaign, IL, 1988.

Ellison, D.: *Performance Stretching*, Human Kinetics, Champaign, IL, 1999.

Goldberg, B. (ed.): *Sports and Exercise for Children with Chronic Health Conditions*, Human Kinetics, Champaign, IL, 1995.

Micheli, L.J. (ed.): *Clinics in Sports Medicine: The Young Athlete*, W.B. Saunders, Philadelphia, PA, 1995.

Newsholme, E., Leech, T. and Duester, G.: *Keep on Running*, John Wiley & Sons, Chichester, UK, 1994.

Reaburn, P. and Jenkins, D.: *Training for Speed and Endurance*, Allen & Unwin, Sydney, 1996.

Rowland, T.W.: *Developmental Exercise Physiology*, Human Kinetics, Champaign, IL, 1996.

13

Polo

Polo is a team sport played outdoors on horseback in which the objective is to score goals versus a conflicting team. Riders score by driving a white wooden or plastic ball into the conflicting team's goal applying a long-handled mallet. Goals are only valid if the scoring rider is mounted. The conventional sport of polo is played outdoors, and each polo team comprises of four riders and their mounts.

The advance indoor variant is known as arena polo. In arena polo, there are 3 rather than four players on each team and chukkers (periods) are 7 1/2 minutes in length. The playing area is 3002 × 1502.

Another advance variant is snow polo, which is played either outdoor or indoor on snow on a frozen ground or ice. Each team usually comprises of three players and also the gear varies from the sport of polo. Other variants include elephant polo, bike polo and Segway polo. These sports are regarded as different sports because of the differences in the composition of teams, gear, conventions, game facilities etc.

It is a version of polo played whilst riding elephants. It is played in Nepal, Sri Lanka, Rajasthan (India), and Thailand. Equipment comprises of a standard polo ball and six to nine foot cane (alike to bamboo) sticks with polo mallet head on the end. The pitch is three-quarters of the length of a standard polo pitch, due to the slower speed of the elephants. Two people ride each elephant; the elephants are steered by mahouts, while the player tells the mahout which way to go and hits the ball.

Though elephant polo was first played in India at the starting of the twentieth century, the advance game initiated in Meghauly, Nepal, reportedly after a drinking bout. Tiger Tops in Nepal persists the headquarters of elephant polo and the site of the World Elephant Polo Championships. As of December 2007, the world elephant polo champions were Chopard Hong Kong. Elephant Polo in Nepal and Thailand is played under the protection of the World Elephant Polo Association. WEPA enforces strict conventions concerning elephant welfare and game play. As of December 2007, Chopard, Hong Kong is the dominating champion of the World Elephant Polo Association. Other tournaments, such as those played in India and Sri Lanka, are managed solely of each other and the World Elephant Polo Association.

It is a team sport which began to gain few measure of fame after being played by members of the Bay Area Segway Enthusiasts Group (Bay Area SEG) in 2004. The Bay Area SEG was not the first to play polo on a Segway HT; a team sponsored by Mobile Entertainment played in the Metrodome at a Minnesota Vikings halftime show in 2003.

It is alike to horse polo, except that rather than playing on horseback; each player rides a Segway HT or PT on the field. The conventions have been adapted from bicycle polo and horse polo. The conflicting teams' players hit a ball with their mallets, trying to get the ball into the other team's goal.

Though not a major sport, Segway polo is gaining fame and teams have begun forming in the United States, Germany, Spain, and New Zealand among others. Few of these teams have begun to contend versus each other. The International Segway Polo Association (ISPA) has been formed as the official regulating body for Segway Polo.

The Segway Polo world championship is the Woz Challenge Cup which was formed in 2006 when the Silicon Valley Aftershocks played the New Zealand Pole Blacks in Auckland, New Zealand. The result was a 2-2 tie. In 2007, it was played in California, with the Aftershocks defeating the Pole Blacks 5-0. The 2008 Woz Cup was played in Indianapolis, coinciding with Segwayfest 2008. The California Gold Rush defeated the Silicon Valley Aftershocks for the championship by a score of 3-2. The Funky-Move Turtles (Gennany) placed third and the Polo Bears (California) placed fourth.

Water Polo

Water polo is a team water sport. A team comprises of six field players and one goalkeeper. The winner of the game is the team that scores more goals. Gameplay involves swimming, players passing the ball while being guarded by adversaries, and scoring by throwing into a net guarded by a goalie. As such, water polo has similarities to association football (soccer) and netball.

HISTORY

A game of Central Asian source, polo was first played in Persia (Iran) at dates given from the 6th century BC till the 1st century AD. Polo was at first a training game for cavalry units, normally the king's guard or other elite troops. To the warlike tribesmen, who played it with as many as 100 to a side, it was a miniature battle. In time polo turned a Persian national sport played extensively by the nobility. Women as well as men played the game, as pointed by references to the queen and her ladies engaging King Khosrow II Parviz and his courtiers in the 6th century AD. Certainly Persian literature and art give us the richest accounts of polo in antiquity.

Ferdowsi, the popular Iranian poet-historian, gives a number of accounts of royal polo tournaments in his 9th century epic, Shahnameh (the Epic of Kings). In the most former account, Ferdowsi romanticizes an international match between Turanian force and the followers of Siyâvash, a fabled Persian prince from the most former centuries of the Empire; the poet is eloquent in his praise of Siyâvash's skills on the polo field. Ferdowsi also tells of Emperor Shapur II of the Sassanid dynasty of the 4th century who learned to play polo when he was only seven years old.

Worthful for training cavalry, the game was played from Constantinople to Japan by the middle Ages, and is known in the East as the Game of Kings. The name polo is said to have been derived from the Tibetan word "pulu", meaning ball. The advance game of polo, although formalised and popularised by the British, is derived from the princes of the Rajputana (now a state in India) who played the game subsequently time immemorial. The first polo club was formed in the town of Silchar in Assam, India, in 1834.

The origins of the game in Manipur are traced to ancient precursors of Sagol Kangjei. This was one of three forms of hockey in Manipur, the other ones being field hockey (known as Khong Kangjei) and wrestling-hockey (known as Mukna Kangjei). Local rituals such as those connected to the Marjing, the Winged-Pony God of Polo and the creation-ritual episodes of the Lai Haraoba festival acting out the life of his son, Khori-Phaba, the polo-playing god of sports. These may indicate an origin prior to the historical records of Manipur, which go back to the 1st Century A.D.

In Manipur, polo is conventionally played with seven players on each side. The players are mounted on the indigenous Manipuri pony, which stands less than 13 hands high. There are no goal posts and a player scored simply by hitting the ball out of either end of the field. Players were also allowed to carry the ball, although that permited opponents to physically tackle players when they do so. The sticks were built of cane and the balls were built from the roots of bamboo. Colorful cloth pom-poms dangle at sensitive and vulnerable spots around the anatomy of the ponies in order to protect them. Players protected their legs by attaching leather shields to their saddles and girths.

In Manipur, the game was not merely a "rich" game but was played even by commoners who possessed a pony. The kings of Manipur had a royal polo ground within the ramparts of their Kangla Fort. Here they played Manung Kangjei Bung (literally, "Inner Polo Ground"). Public games were held, as they are even today, at the Mapan Kangjei Bung (literally "Outer Polo Ground"), a polo ground just outside the Kangla. Weekly games known as Hapta Kangjei (Weekly Polo) were also played in a polo ground outside the present Palace.

The British are credited with spreading polo worldwide in the late 19th century and the early 20th century. Military officers imported the game to Britain in the 1860s. The formation of polo clubs throughout England and Western Europe persued after the conventional codification of conventions. The 10th Hussars at Aldershot, Hants, brought in polo to England in 1869. The game's regulating body in the United Kingdom is the Hurlingham Polo Association, which drew up the first set of conventional British conventions in 1874, many of which are still in subsistence.

This version of polo played in the 19th century was dissimilar from the faster kind that was played in Manipur. The game was slow and methodical, with little passing between players and few set plays that needed particular motions by players without the ball. Neither players nor horses were trained to play a fast, nonstop game.

This kind of polo lacked the aggressive methods and equestrian skills to play. From the 1800s to the 1910s, a host of teams representing Indian principalities reined the international polo scene. Polo discovered fame in Argentina, Brazil, Chile, Mexico,Pakistan and the United States of America.

James Gordon Bennett, Jr. organized the first polo match in the United States at Dickel's Riding Academy at 39th Street and Fifth Avenue in New York City. Throughout the ancient part of the 20th century, under the leadership of Harry Payne Whitney, polo changed to become a high-speed sport in the United States, dissenting from the game in England, where it needed short passes to move the ball toward the opposition's goal. Whitney and his teammates employed the fast break, sending long passes downfield to riders who had broken away from the pack at a full gallop.

The oldest polo ground in the world is the Imphal Polo Ground in Manipur State formed by the British in India. The history of this pologround is contained in the royal chronicle "Cheitharol Kumbaba" commencing from AD 33. Lieutenant Sherer, the father of modernistic polo visited the state and played on this polo ground in the 1850s. Lord Curzon, the Viceroy of India visited the state in 1901 and assessed the pologround as 225 yards long and 110 yards wide. The oldest royal polo square is the 16th century Gilgit Polo Field, Pakistan, while the highest polo ground in the world is on the deosai Plateau Baltistan, Pakistan at 4307 meters (14,000 ft). The earliest polo club in the world still in subsistence is the Calcutta Polo Club (1862).

Polo is an equestrian sport with its origin engrafted in Central Asia dating back to 6th century BC. At first it was a training game for cavalry units for the King's Guards or other Elite troops. To the warlike tribesmen who played polo with as many as 100 players to a side, it was a miniature battle. It turned a Persian national game in the 6th century AD. From Persia, the game disperse to Arabia, then to Tibet, China and Japan. In China, in the year 910, death of a favourite relative in a game reminded Emperor Apaochi to order beheading of all players.

History of Cycle Polo

The game was invented by an Irishman, Richard J. Mecredy in 1891. That same year the first cycle polo match was played between The Scalp and the Ohne Hast C.C.. Towards the end of the 19th century the game arrived at Great Britain, USA and France. The first international match was played between Ireland and England in 1901. Cycle polo was a demonstration event in the 1908 London Olympics with Ireland winning the gold beating Germany. The sport arrived at its peak of fame in Great Britain throughout the 1930s with the introduction of the regional leagues. Cycle polo also flourished in France throughout this period with the formation of the French league. Internationals between France and Great Britain were held steadily. However the second world war marked the beginning of the demise of cycle polo in Britain.

The sport managed to hang on in France although, with league championships held steadilytill today. The 1980s saw the rise of two new powers in cycle polo, India and USA. The Cycle Polo Association of India was officially made in 1966 and the Bicycle Polo Association of America was made in 1994. International cycle polo matches presented a comeback in the 90s with the first world championship organised in 1996 in USA. Teams from India, USA and Canada took part with India winning the title. The next championship was held in 1999 in Vancouver, Canada which was also won by India. From then on, the championship turned a steady event held every year.

THE GAME

Players and Field

Each team comprises of four mounted players, which can be mixed teams of both men and women. The Number 1 is expected to score the goals and carry out an offensive position. He is generally the least experienced. The Number 2 is also an offensive player but has to be more aggressive subsequently his objective is also to break up the defensive plays of the opposition. The Number 3 is the pivot man, alike to a quarterback in American football, and he is normally the long ball hitter and play maker for the team.

He normally hits the penalty shots and knock-ins. The Number 4, or back, is the defensive player. He is normally the most conservative player and his job is to defend the goal and keep the opposition from scoring. Polo must be played right-handed. Left-handed play was ruled out in 1975 for safety reasons. To date, only 3 players on the world circuit are left-handed.

The field is 300 yards long, and either 200 yards or 160 yards wide if there are side boards—these are usually 6" high. There are lightweight goalposts on each side of the field disperse 8 yards apart. The objective of the game is to score the most goals by hitting the ball through the goal.

In arena polo, played primarily in the United States in large arenas such as armories and riding academies, the size of the field differs due to the size of the floor space, but 100 yards long by 50 yards wide is ideal. Arena polo needs teams of three riders, and goals are made by passing the ball into a 10' goal recessed into the sideboards. Arena polo uses a ball between 12.5" and 15" inches in circumference and looks like a miniature soccer ball but is not the same pattern.

The Beginning of Game

The game starts with the two teams of four lined up each team in line forming two rows with the players in order 1, 2, 3, and 4 facing the umpire in the center of the playing field. There are two mounted umpires on the field and a referee standing on the sidelines. At the starting of a game, one of the umpires bowls the ball in hard between the two teams. Teams alter goals on ends of the field/arena after each score or chukker for indoor to minimize any wind advantage which may subsist. Switching sides also permits each team equal chance to start off with the ball on their right side, as all players must hit right-handed.

Positions of the Players

Each position assigned to a player has certain responsibilities:

1. Number One is the most offensive position on the field. The number one position usually covers the conflicting team's number four.
2. Number Two is the most difficult position on the field to play. The number two has an important offensive role of either running through and scoring himself, or passing to the number one and getting in behind him. Defensively he will cover the conflicting team's number three—usually the other team's best player. Given the difficulty of this position, it is not uncommon for the best player on the team to play number two so long as another strong player is available to play three.
3. Number Three is the tactical leader and must be a long powerful hitter to feed balls to Number Two and Number One as well as maintaining a solid defense. The best player on the team is

normally the Number Three player (Normally wielding the highest handicap).

4. Number Four is the primary defense player and although he can move anywhere on the field, he often tries to prevent scoring. The excessive defense of the number four permits the number three to commit to more offensive plays knowing he will be covered if he loses the ball.

Equipments

The basic dress of a player is a protective helmet (normally of a distinctive color, to be distinguished at the considerable distance from which onlookers are watching the game), riding boots to just under the knees, white trousers (often ordinary denim jeans), and a colored shirt having the number of the player's position. Optional gear includes one or two gloves, wristbands, kneepads, spurs, face mask, and a whip.

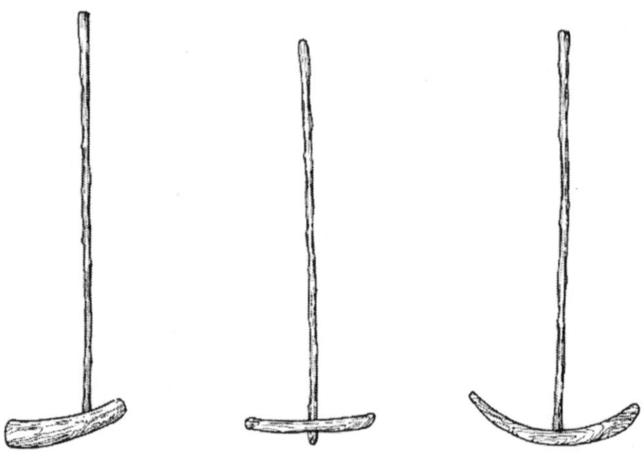

Fig. Polo Sticks

Outdoor Polo

The game comprises of six 7 minute chukkas, between or throughout which players alter mounts. At the end of each 7 minute chukka, play continues for an additional 30 seconds or until a stoppage in play, whichever comes first. There is a four minute interval between chukkas and a ten minute halftime. Play is uninterrupted and is only stopped for penalties, broken tack (equipment) or injury to horse or player. The objective is to score goals by hitting the ball between the goal posts, no matter how high in the air. If the ball goes wide of the goal, the defending team is permited a free 'knock-in' from the place where the ball crossed the goal line, thus getting the ball back into play.

Indoor Polo

The game comprises of four 7 and a half minute periods also known as chukkas, throughout which players may alter mounts. Play is uninterrupted and is only stopped for penalties, broken tack (equipment) or injury to horse or player.

The objective is to score goals by hitting the ball between the goal posts (which is normally a door with motion sensors). Balls cannot go out of bounds unless the arena played in does not have nets or anything to stop the ball going over the 4.5' wall. If the ball goes over it is regarded a dead ball and is then bowled in. The arena is smaller than the field that polo is played on outside. Because of the small size of the arena, indoor polo play is slower than outdoor.

Cycle Polo

Field and Players: Field polo, the older kind of the sport, is played in a rectangular grass field, 150 meters by 100 meters officially, unofficially whatever field is big sufficient. Moreover, standard dimensions can vary between 120 and 150 meters in length on 80 to 100 meters in width. The French conventions however permit for smaller grounds normally 100 by 80 meters. The ball employed is of circumference 12-15 inches and the mallet is of length 1 meter.

There are 6 members (7 in France) in a team of which 4 (5 in France) are on field at a time. The other two are employed as substitutes. International matches are played for a duration of 30 minutes split up into periods of 7.5 minutes each known as as a chukkar. Extra time can be employed to determine the winner in case the scores are tied at normal time. The goal posts are normally widened for extra time.

If a deliberate foul is done at the vicinity of the goal, the team that is fouled is automatically given a goal. There are no penalty strokes. Less severe fouls are awarded 15 metre and 25 metre free hits. In the event of deliberate fouls or grievous fouls, the umpire can issue the Yellow card (warning) and in case of repeated or severe fouls the Red card (ejection). The ejected player can be replaced by a substitute after the end of the current chukkar if the umpire permits it.

Water Polo

One player on each team is assigned the goalkeeper, assigned to deflect or catch any shots at goal. The goalkeeper is the only player who can touch the ball with both hands at any time, and, in a shallow pool, the only player permited to stand on the bottom. Players can move the ball by throwing it to a team member or swimming while forcing the ball in front of them.

Players are not allowed to push the ball underwater when being tackled, or push or hold an conflicting player unless that player is holding the ball. Fouls are very common, and result in a free throw throughout which the player cannot shoot at the goal unless beyond the "5 meter" line. If a foul is known as outside the 5 meter line, the player is either able to shoot or pass the ball. Water polo players need remarkable stamina due to the considerable amount of holding and pushing that occurs throughout the game, few permited, few unseen or ignored by the referees (normally underwater). Water polo is a physically demanding sport; action is uninterrupted, and players ordinarily swim 3 kilometers or more throughout four periods of play.

Water polo is a game needing excellent eye-hand coordination. The power to handle and pass the ball cleanly divides the good teams from the great teams. A pass thrown to a field position player is preferably a "dry pass" (meaning the ball does not touch the water) and permits for optimal speed when passing from player to player with fluid movement between catching and throwing. A "wet pass" is a deliberate pass into the water, just out of reach of the offensive player nearest the goal (the "hole set") and his defender. The hole-set can then lunge for the ball and out of the water to make a shot or pass. A goal may be scored by any portion of the body excluding a clenched fist, or a foot.

MAJOR TOURNAMENTS

Joe Barry Memorial Cup

Named in memory of Joe Barry, a Hall of Fame professional described as "a galloping oak with the soul of a poet". He carried his 9 goal rating to six titles in the U.S. Open, three each in the Gold Cup and Silver Cup, two Butler Handicaps, as well as the Coronation and Camacho Cup.

USPA Gold Cup

The USPA Gold Cup, which started in 1974, is one of the premier tournaments in the United States. Peter Brant's White Birch has won this event a record 12 times. Mariano Aguerre has won the Gold Cup eight times, more than any other professional player.

U.S. Open Polo Championship

The U.S. Open Polo Championship, was first played in 1904 at Van Courtland Park, is one of the three great polo tournaments, along with the British and Argentine tournaments. The U.S. Open Polo Championship attracts the finest polo players in the world for a month long competition.

Courage Cup

The Courage Cup is an IRS assigned 501(c) (3) non-profit corporation which was formed to help at-risk urban youth. We support programs in the mid-Atlantic region which give disadvantaged children individualised attention and a positive alternative activity to keep them in school and off the streets. In addition to supporting these programs fiscally, we also enroll volunteers for their activities.

The long-term goals are to make a scholarship fund for youth who take part in Work to Ride and Inner City Outings. They also hope to add to the list of programs they support with volunteer hours and fiscal donations.

ADMINISTRATIVE BODIES

Federation of International Polo

Federation of International Polo was established in 1983 with headquarters in Beverly Hills, and presntly represents the national polo associations of more than 80 countries.

The Federation of International Polo gives rise to the International Conventions of Polo through a cooperative agreement with the Asociación Argentina de Polo, the Hurlingham Polo Association in the United Kingdom, plus the United States Polo Association.

In addition to organising international tournaments, FIP also evolves international tournaments for children, conducts umpiring and coaching seminars and promotes involvement in the sport of polo at all levels and ages.

Hurlingham Polo Association (HPA)

The Hurlingham Polo Association is the regulating body for polo in the United Kingdom and Republic of Ireland. The Federation of International Polo produces the International Conventions of Polo through a cooperative agreement with the Hurlingham Polo Association, the Asociación Argentina de Polo, plus the United States Polo Association.

Within its jurisdiction, the Hurlingham Polo Association is responsible for applying the conventions of polo and for disciplining player who commit infractions versus these conventions. It also designates handicaps for each of the 2,000 or so players in the UK. It drew up the first set of conventional British conventions in 1874, many of which are still in subsistence.

The association initiated as the Hurlingham Polo Committee in 1875 (which drew up the first English conventions). The Hurlingham Polo Committee was re-titled as the Hurlingham Club Polo committee and elaborated to include representatives on the Council from the Services, the County Polo Association (constituted in 1898 to look after the interests of the country clubs and to run the County Cup Tournaments), the three London polo clubs - Hurlingham, Ranelagh and Roehampton - and from all associations within the Empire where polo was being played in 1903. Afterwards, in 1925, the Hurlingham Club Polo Committee was re-assigned as the Hurlingham Polo Association.

United States Women's Polo Federation

The United States Women's Polo Federation ("USWPF") was established in 2000 at the turn of the century by society horsewoman Kimberly Carr-Cavallo to constitute, organize, coordinate and raise the sport of professional women's polo. The USWPF coordinates the activities of its U.S. member teams, arranging and monitoring national women 's pro polo matches and tournaments. The pro league now advances into its 2006/2007 Season with the formation of the USMPF (U.S. Men 's Polo Federation) National Division, getting the U.S. pro league to what is now being hailed as an unexampled new height in luxury sports. Our undying dedication to keeping alive this historically important sport and insuring its position as a sports stronghold and sporting legacy has begun with the formation of the Atlanta Polo Museum which will be situated in GA in conjunction with the United States Women 's Sports Museum.

Indian Polo Association

Indian Polo Association is a central body which has an executive Committee elected by the member Clubs which looks after the affairs of Polo in the Country and outside. There are approximately twenty six polo Clubs in the Country. The IPA offices are situated at the Rashtrapati Bhavan. The Commandant of the President's Bodyguard by custom acts as Hon Secretary of the IPA. Col Bhawani Singh ex-61 Cav., very good polo player himself is the present Hon. Secretary of the IPA.

Cycle Polo Federation of India

The CPFI is recognised by the Government of India Ministry of Sports and Youth Affairs. It relishes association with the Indian Olympic Association and is a member of the Asian Cycle Polo Federation as well as of the International Bicycle Polo Association.

The affairs of the CPFI are supervised by a duly elected Executive Committee for a term of 4 years. A Technical Committee overlooks all aspects of championships and is creditworthy to conduct National championships every year of boys and girls individually under certain classes.

FAMOUS PLAYERS

Pete Bostwick

George Herbert "Pete" Bostwick was born onAugust 14, 1909and died on January 13, 1982, he was an American court tennis player, a steeplechase jockey and horse trainer, and an eight-goal polo player.

Born in Bisby Lake, New York, Pete Bostwick was the son of Mary Stokes and Albert Carlton Bostwick. His grandfather, Jabez Abel Bostwick, was a founder and treasurer of the Standard Oil Company of New York and a partner of John D. Rockefeller. His grandmother, Helen C. Bostwick, left upon her death in April 1920 a sum of $1,156,818 to him and alike amounts to his siblings.

Pete Bostwick's inherited wealth afforded him the chance to follow a number of sporting interests. His father was a horseman and polo player and Pete Bostwick become one of a leading steeplechase owners, trainers, and riders. Pete Bostwick was a member of The Jockey Club and a patron of the National Tennis Club.

He rode Thoroughbred steeplechase horses from 1927 to 1949 both in the US and Grand National in the UK and also rode in flat racing. At Belmont Park in 1932 he turned the second jockey ever to ride a flat and steeplechase winner on very same day a feat which he repeated again within two weeks. Initially he rode to victory at Belmont Park aboard Thomas Hitchcock's Silverskin in a steeplechase and Latin Stables' Ha Ha in a flat race on the same day. Then repeated the feat two weeks afterwards in the Metropolitan Driving Club, a 1-1/16-mi. flat race on J. F. Byers' Glaneur then won the Chamblet Memorial steeplechase on Mrs. Ambrose Clark's Madrigal II the same day.

Carlos Gracida

Carlos was born in Mexico City, Mexico on September 5, 1960. As a product of the Gracida polo dynasty, Carlos started playing when he was only five years old and started contending at the age of ten. His father Guillermo was a 9-goaler who played in Meadowbrook and Palermo in Argentina and still relished the distinction of 5-goals at the age of 65. Carlos first achieved 10 goals in 1985, and has subsequently spent over fifteen years at this handicap. He was a member of Ellerstina, the legendary team possessed by Australian magnate Kerry Packer, and also of La Espadana, regarded by many as the best polo team of the last twenty years.

1994 was a golden year for Carlos, when he won nearly every potential tournament in the game, letting in the Argentinian Triple Crown of Hurlingham, Tortuguitas and Palermo. That same year, he also won the US Open and the British Open Gold Cup, becoming the only player in history to win the Grand Slam of Polo, in 1987, a feat he afterwards replicated two times, in 1988 and 1994.

Kuldeep Singh Garcha

Kuldeep Singh Garcha is a noteworthy early polo player of India. He had handicap of five gols and captained and coached the Indian polo team for various years. He was presented an Arjuna Award for attaining excellence in sports. He began playing polo when he joined the Indian Military Academy in Dehradun and turned a captain for both the National Defence Academy and the Indian Military Academy. He joined the Indian army and in 1966 was commissioned as a 2nd Lieutenant into the 61st Cavalry. Colonel Garcha with his son Satinder has set up the Jaipur Riding and Polo Club on the outskirts of Jaipur.

REFERENCES

Archetti, E. P.: 'Hibridacion, diversidad y generalizacion en el mundo ideologico del futbol y el polo', *Prismas. Revista de historia intelectual,* 1997.

Archetti, E. P.: '[Nationalisms, football et polo: tradition et creolisation dans la construction de 1 'Argentine moderne', *Terrain,* 1995.

Arlt, R.: *Aguafuertesportenas: cultura ypolitica,* Buenos Aires: losada, 1994.

Armus, D.: Tja idea del verde en la ciudad moderna. Buenos Aires 1870–1940', *Entrepasados. Pevista de Historia,* 1996.

14

Rowing

Alike running, rowing was a means of survival long time ago before it was a sport. The Greeks rowed, the Phoenicians rowed, and the Vikings rowed, as a means of conveyance and as the chief technique of maneuvering during war on the seas. Viking ships from one thousand years ago have been excavated (they were employed in burials) and reconstructed. The typical Viking ship was outfitted for 30 oarsmen. A single square sail was utilised, but only when a tailwind persisted. So, the legacy of piracy and plundering of the Vikings was made possible, in part, by the speed of attack they could attain in their rowing ships.

Fig. Olympic Symbol

Rowing as a sport was originated on the River Thames. Professional watermen contended in the Doggett Coat and Badge Race. "Gentlemen" began contending in 1829 with the Oxford-Cambridge race. The Henly Regatta was started up in 1839. Competitive rowing passed over the Atlantic and the Yale-Harvard race was prefaced on the Charles River (Boston) in 1852. Rowing was the first organised collegiate sport in the United States, accomplished with its own regulating body. Today, collegiate rowing in the U.S. stays on autonomous of the NCAA.

International championships were first set up in 1893, and stay under the direction of the Federation International des Societes d' Aviron (FISA).

International rowing (and collegiate rowing) competitions are standardised at 2000 meters. United States and international Masters rowing chmpionships are contended over a distance of 1000 meters.

At the elite level, 2000 meter races need between 5'20" and 7.5 minutes depending upon boat type. Masters age-group championship races are contended over 1000 meters and last between 2'50" and 5 minutes depending upon boat type and age of the contestents (age 27 to 80+). Other forms of competitive rowing include "head racing" in time trial fashion over a course of about 5 kilometers, as well as ocean rowing. Ocean rowing competitions range from "around the island" races that are very famous in Scandinavia to the "Race across the Atlantic," a 5000 kilometer race for two person teams started in 1997. Rowing among islands and scurries has even conceived the foundation for row-orienteering competitions.

Rowing is split up into distinct disciplines: "sweep" rowing, where each oarsman handles one oar, and "sculling", where he uses two smaller oars. Sweep-oared races are contended in 2, 4, and 8 person boats.

Sculling races are contended in single, double and four man shells. Steering in sweep oared boats is achieved with the use of a mobile rudder handled by either a coxwain (coxed events), or the rower in bow or stroke seat using a foot-controlled rudder. One and two man sculling shells are steered by shifting pressure on the right or left oar. The four person sculling shell is generally controlled with a foot rudder maneuvered by the person rowing in bow (with a contribution from oar pressure shifts by the crew only when the bowman screws up!). International rowing is contended in two weight categories for men and women, lightweight and open. Lightweight oarsmen are confined to a body weight of 72.5 kg (men) and 59kg (women). The average weight of the open class (heavyweight) in international competition is about 92 kg (200 lbs) and 79 kg (173 lbs) respectively.

While rowing, the athlete sits in the boat facing backwards (towards the stern), and uses the oars which are held in place by the oarlocks to propel the boat forward (towards the bow). This may be done on a river, lake, sea, or other prominent body of water. It is a demanding sport needing strong center balance as well as physical durability and cardiovascular endurance.

Whilst the action of rowing and gear used persists moderately consistent throughout the world, there are several different types of competition. These include endurance races, time trials, stake racing, bumps racing, and the side-by-side format used in the Olympic Games. The numerous different formats are a result of the long history of the sport, its development in various regions of the world, and particular local requirements and limitations.

Various Formats of Rowing

Head Race: A head race is a time trial rowing race usually held in the fall or early spring. In this form of racing, competitor's race against the clock and the crew with the fastest time is deemed to be the winner. Racing generally takes place in dissimilar categories of boat class and powers. The length of these races is generally between 3 km and 6 km. Boats begun at 10 to 15 second intervals. To minimize collisions, Boats are generally seeded so that the fastest start first.

The two most reknown head races are the 4¼ mile (6,840 m) Head of the River Race that takes place in month of March every year, on the river Thames in London, United Kingdom and the Head of the Charles race held each October on the 3 mile (4,828 m) Charles River in Boston, Massachusetts, USA.

Other head races include the head of the Trent in Peterborough, Ontario along the Trent-Severn Waterway, the head of the Rideau in Ottawa, Ontario, London in March, the 3¼ mile (5,000m) Head of the Lake through the Montlake Cut in Seattle, Washington, the Fremont 4-Miler also in Seattle, Washington, the 3 mile Head of the Ohio in Pittsburgh, Pennsylvania yearly since 1987 along the Forks of the Ohio River, the 3 mile Head of the Schuylkill in Philadelphia, Pennsylvania, the Head of the Fish, in Saratoga Springs New York, and the Atlanta Race Head of the Hooch in November on the Chattahoochie River in North Georgia.

Bumps Race: A bumps race is a kind of rowing race in which a number of boats trail each other in single file; each boat undertakes to catch ("bump") the boat in front without being caught by the boat trailing. The form is chiefly used intramurally at the University of Cambridge and the University of Oxford. It is specially suited where the stretch of water accessible is long but narrow, precluding side-by-side racing. Bumps racing gives a sharper feel of immediate competition than a head race, where boats are plainly timed over a fixed course.

Bumps races are usually raced over numerous days. Each day the boats line up bow-to-stern, generally along the bank of the river, with a set distance between each boat and the next (ordinarily about one and a half boat lengths of clear water). The commencing positions are generally marked off by a rope attached to the bank, the other end of which is held by each boat's cox. At the start signal the cox let's go of the rope and the crew starts to row, attempting to catch the boat in front while at the same time being pursued by the one behind. A crew that catches the boat ahead of it is said to "bump" it.

Stake Races: The stake format was often employed in betimes American races. Competitors line up at the starting line, race to a stake, moored boat, or buoy some distance away, and return. The 180° turn needs mastery of steering. These races are popular with spectators because one may watch both the start and finish. Generally only two boats would race at a time to avoid collision. The Green Mountain Head Regatta continues to use the stake format but it is run as a head race with an interval start. A same type of racing is found out in UK coastal rowing, where a number of boats race out to a granted point from the coast and then return fighting rough water all the way.

Side by Side: Most races that are held in the spring and summer feature side by side racing also called a regatta - all the boats begin at the same time from a nonmoving position and the winner is the boat that crosses the finish line at first place. The number of boats in a race generally deviates between two to six, but any number of boats can begin collectively if the course is wide enough.

The standard length races for the Olympics and the World Rowing Championships is 2,000 m long, 1,500 m for U.S. High School races on the east coast and 1,000 m for Masters rowers (rowers older than 27). However the race distance can and does vary from 'dashes' or 'sprints', which may be 500 m long, to races of marathon or ultra-marathon length races such as the 'Tour du Léman' in Switzerland which is 160 km, and the 2 day, 185 km Corvallis to Portland Regatta held in Oregon, USA. In the UK, regattas are in general between 500 m and 2,000 m long.

HISTORY

Even since the earliest registered references to rowing, the sporting factor has been present. An Egyptian funerary inscription of 1430 BC records that the warrior Amenhotep (Amenophis) II was also famous for his feats of oarsmanship. In the Aeneid, Virgil mentions rowing constituting part of the funeral games arranged by Aeneas in honour of his father. In the 13th century, Venetian festivals called regata included boat races among others.

The first acknowledged 'advanced' rowing races commenced from competition among the professional watermen that rendered ferry and taxi service on the River Thames in London. Prizes for wager races were often offered by the London Guilds and Livery Companies or wealthy owners of riverside houses. During the Nineteenth Century these races were to become several and famous, attracting large crowds. Prize matches amongst professionals likewise became famous on other rivers throughout Great Britain in the Nineteenth Century, notably on the Tyne. The oldest surviving such race, Doggett's Coat and Badge was first contended in 1715 and is still held yearly from London Bridge to Chelsea. In America, the earliest acknowledged race dates back to 1756 in New York, when a pettiauger defeated a Cape Cod whaleboat in a race.

Amateur competition in England commenced towards the end of the Eighteenth Century. Documentary evidence from this period is sparse, but it is known that the Monarch Boat Club of Eton College and the Isis Club of Westminster School were both in existence in the 1790s. The Star Club and Arrow Club in London for gentlemen amateurs were also in beingness prior to 1800. At the University of Oxford bumping races were first organised in 1815 when Brasenose College and Jesus College boat clubs had the first yearly race while at Cambridge the first registered races were in 1827. Brasenose won Oxford University's first Head of the River and claim to be the oldest constituted boat club in the world. The Boat Race between Oxford University and Cambridge University first ever took place in 1829, and was the second intercollegiate sporting event (following the first Varsity Cricket Match by 2 years). The interest in the first Boat Race and succeeding matches led the town of Henley to start hosting an yearly regatta in 1839.

Established in 1818, Leander Club is the world's oldest public rowing club. The second oldest club which still survives is the Der Hamburger und Germania Ruder Club which was established 1836 and marked the commencement of rowing as an organised sport in Germany. During the Nineteenth Century, as in England, wager matches in North America between professionals went very famous attracting vast crowds. The Detroit Boat Club was constituted as the first rowing exclusive cl[illegible] 839 in the US. In 1843, the first American co[illegible] rowing club was conceived at Yale University. The Harvard-Yale Regatta is the oldest intercollegiate sporting event in the United States, having been contended every year since 1852 (excepting interruptions due to wars).

Women in Rowing

For most of its history, rowing has been a male reigned sport. Though rowing's roots as a sport in the advanced Olympics can be copied back to the original 1896 games in Athens, it wasn't until the 1976 Summer Olympics in Montreal that women were permitted to take part well after their fellow athletes in alike sports such as swimming, athletics, bicycling, and canoeing.

Despite its male domination, women's rowing can be derived back from the early 1800s, and an image of a women's double scull race created the cover of Harper's Weekly in 1870. In 1927, the first rowing event for women between Oxford and Cambridge was held. For the first few years it was an exhibition, and it later turned a race. In 1954, the first women's events were added to the European Rowing Championships.

In 1988, the first Henley Women's Regatta was held. On April 27 1997, one of the last bastions of rowing was violated when, at an exceptional General Meeting, Leander Club voted to admit women as members. This convention met a condition enforced by UK Sport and qualified Leander to receive a £1.5 million grant for renovation from the Lottery Sports Fund.

At international level, women's rowing traditionally has been ruled by Eastern European countries, such as Romania, Russia, and Bulgaria, though other countries such as Germany, Netherlands, Canada, and New Zealand often field competitive teams.

The United States also has often had very competitive crews, and in recent years these crews have become even more competitive given the surge in women's collegiate rowing due to title IX. Because Title IX mandatories equal money spent on men's and women's sports, rowing is specially useful due to the extremely high costs of gear per athlete.

Therefore, many schools open a rowing program only to women to financially counteract the prevalence of men's sports. In the United States, it is important to note that Women's Rowing is a NCAA sport, while Men's Rowing isn't.

THE GAME

Equipments

Racing boats (often addressed "shells") are long, narrow, and broadly curved in cross-section in order to bring down drag to a lower limit. They generally have a fin towards the back, to help prevent roll and yaw and to increase the effectiveness of the rudder.

Primitively made from wood, shells are now almost always made from a composite material (generally carbon-fibre reinforced plastic) for durability and weight advantages. FISA conventions specify minimum weights for each class of boat so that no individual will gain a great advantage from the use of costly materials or technology. There are various different types of boats. They are classified using:

Number of Rowers: In all forms of advanced competition the number is 1, 2, 4, or 8.

Position of Coxswain: Boats are either coxless ("straight"), bow-coxed (also called bowloaders), or stern-coxed.

Steering: Single and double sculls are steered by the scullers pulling harder on one side or the other. In other boats there is a rudder, commanded by the cox, if present, or by among the crew. In the latter case the rudder cable is connected to the toe of one of their shoes which can pivot about the ball of the foot, moving the cable left or right. The steersman may row at bow, who has the best vision when looking over their shoulder, or on straighter courses stroke may steer, since they can point the stern of the boat at some landmark at the beginning of the course. On international courses landmarks for steersmen, comprising of two aligned poles, are provided.

Oars: Oars are used to propel the boat. They are long (250-300 cm) poles with one flat end about 50 cm long and 25 cm wide, called the blade. Classic oars were constructed out of wood, but advanced oars are made from synthetic stuff, the most common being carbon fibre. An oar is often referred to as a "blade" in the case of sweep oar rowing and as a "scull" in the case of sculling.

A sculling oar is shorter and has a smaller blade area than the equivalent sweep oar. The merged blade area of a pair of sculls is however greater than that of a single sweep oar, so the oarsman when sculling is working against a lot of water than when rowing sweep-oared. He is able to do this because the body action in sculling is more anatomically efficient.

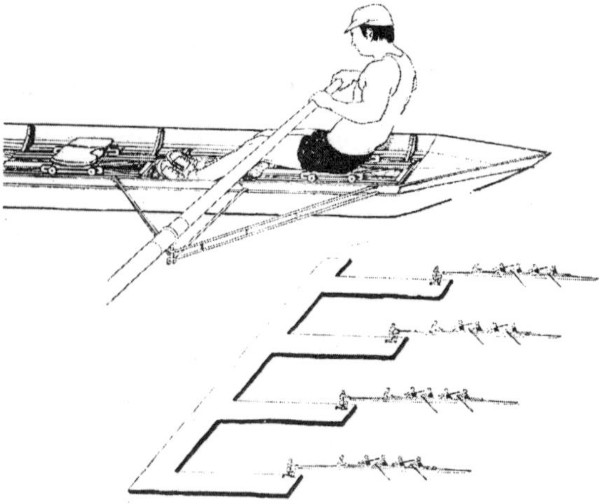

Fig: Crew of Racing Boat

Crew: In all boats, with the exception of single sculls, each rower is numbered in successive order, low numbers at the bow, up to the highest at the stern. The person seated on the first seat is called the bowman, or just 'bow', whilst the rower closest to the stern is called the 'strokeman' or just 'stroke'. There are a few exceptions to this - UK coastal rowers, and in France, Spain, and Italy rowers number from stern to bow.

In addition to this, certain crew members have other titles and roles. In an 8+ the stern pair is responsible for setting the stroke rate and rhythm for the rest of the boat to follow. The middle four (occasionally addressed the "engine room" or "power house") are generally the less technical, but more powerful rowers in the crew, whilst the bow pair are the more technical and usually considered as the pair to set up the balance of the boat. They also have most influence on the line the boat steers.

In most levels of rowing there are different weight categories - usually "open" or "heavyweight" and lightweight. Competitive rowing favours tall, strong athletes due to the additional leverage height renders in pulling the oar through the water as well as the bursting power required to propel the boat at high speed.

Rowing Propulsion: Rowing is a cyclic (or intermittent) sort of propulsion and in the quasi-steady state the motion of the system (rower, oars and boat) is repeated on a regular basis. In order for this perfectly cyclic motion to be maintained the sum all the external forces on the system, averaged over the cycle, must be zero, so that the system as a whole doesn't accelerate.

In that case the average drag (retarding) force on the system must equal the average propulsion force on the system. The drag forces comprises of aerodynamic drag on the superstructure of the system (everything above the waterline) and the hydrodynamic drag on the submerged part of the system.

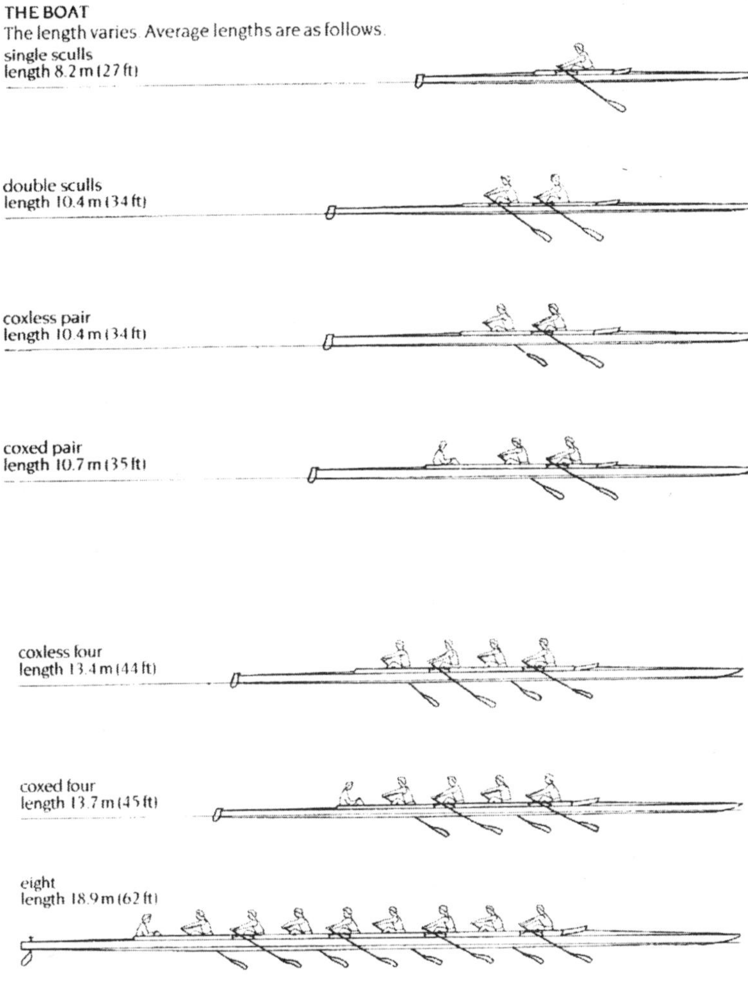

Fig: Various Types of Sculls

The propulsion forces are the forward reaction of the water on the oars while in the water. Of course the oar can be used to provide a drag force (a force working against the forward motion) when the system is brought to rest.

Though the oar can be conveniently thought of as a lever with a "fixed" pivot point in the water, the blade moves sideways and sternwards through the water, so that the magnitude of the propulsion force evolved is the result of a complex interaction between irregular fluid mechanics (the water flow around the blade) and solid mechanics and dynamics.

MAJOR TOURNAMENTS

World Rowing Championships

The World Rowing Championships is an international rowing regatta organised by FISA (the International Rowing Federation). It is a week long event held at the end of the northern hemisphere summer and in non-Olympic years is the highlight of the international rowing calendar.

The first event was held in Lucerne, Switzerland in 1962. The event then was held every 4 years until 1974 - when it became an yearly competition. Also in 1974, Men's lightweight and Women's open weight events were appended to the championships. In 1985, Women's lightweight events were also appended to the schedule.

World Rowing Junior Championships

The World Rowing Junior Championships is an international rowing regatta organised by FISA (the International Rowing Federation). It is open to rowers who are 18 years of age or younger by the end of the prevailing calendar year. During Olympic years it is held at the same location as the Senior World Rowing Championships.

The first FISA Youth Regatta was held in 1967 and has been held annually since then, being aroused to the position of FISA Junior Champs in 1970 and Junior World Champs in 1985.

European Rowing Championships

The European Rowing Championships is an international Rowing regatta organised by FISA (the International Rowing Federation). The first event was held in 1893 and as of 1962 was substituted (one year in four) by the World Rowing Championships, which then became an yearly event from 1974. Women's events were prefaced in 1954, but even then men's and women's events were held on unlike days.

On 27 May 2006 the FISA members voted to reintroduce European Rowing Championships. In the first event there were only 3 events (men's single, coxed four and eight) and only ten entries. Races were 3,000 m long, except for singles - which were only 2,000 m. In 2007, when the European Rowing Championship was re-introduced, there were 14 Olympic boat categories racing over 2,000m.

Rowing at the Summer Olympics

Rowing at the Summer Olympics has been division of the competition since the 1900 Summer Olympics. Rowing was on the program at the 1896 Summer Olympics but was set off due to bad weather. Only men were permitted to contend until the women's events were brought in at the 1976 Summer Olympics in Montreal. Lightweight rowing events were brought in to the games in 1996.

Boston Rowing Marathon

The Boston Rowing Marathon is an event happening on the third Sunday of September yearly in Lincolnshire, England. It is a Head race of exceptionally long distance. The course is along the River Witham from Lincoln to Boston, finishing at the Boston clubhouse; a total of 49 kilometers or 31 miles. The present-day record for this is 2hrs 59mins 45secs, held by a University of London men's eight, set in 1991. It is organised by Boston Rowing Club. The long distance of the event makes it unique in British rowing and thus attracts a lot of entries; some contends for a time, others only desiring to finish the distance. The event is also ususual in accepting entries from all crews and categories. The 2006 marathon had 283 entries.

The current beginning is a set of landing stages at Stamp End Lock, Waterside South, Lincoln, opposite the home of Lincs FM. As of yet there is no rowing club in Lincoln, however a Lincoln RC has been established and its facilities are likely to be used in future when a boathouse is constructed. The race is also a favourite for its witty T-Shirts: "It is long and hard" being a classic reused for the 2006 marathon.

Henley Women's Regatta

Henley Women's Regatta is a kind of rowing regatta held at Henley-on-Thames, England. It was conceived as a result of the lack of women's events at Henley Royal Regatta and first held in 1988. Women's Henley is held on the same stretch of the Thames as Henley Royal but the course is shorter 1,500 m (Henley is 2,112 m) and stops at the Remenham Club. It is held over Friday, Saturday and Sunday, 2 weeks before Henley Royal.

Since 2004 the regatta has used Intermediate, Senior and Elite classes rather than College, Club and Open. This is still up for further review and may change again in the near future.

ADMINISTRATIVE BODIES

Fédération Internationale des Societes d'Aviron (FISA)

The Fédération Internationale des Sociétés d'Aviron, or FISA for short, is the International Rowing Federation which is the regulating body for international Rowing. Its current president is Denis Oswald. The Rowing World Cup, World Rowing Championships, and other such contests are overseen by this organisation.

It was established by rowing representatives from France, Switzerland, Belgium, Adriatica, and Italy on June 25, 1892 in Turin in response to the growing fame of the sport of rowing, and the subsequent need for uniformness of ordinances over such matters as race lengths, boat composition, and weight classes. Also, at the time, betting on rowing was very famous, and the rowers or coaches were themselves often taking bets. Amateur condition was unknown in the sport, a state of affairs which can lead to corruption, such as thrown races.

The first regatta organised by the freshly conceived FISA was the European Rowing Championships and was held in 1893 in Orta, Italy. It only had 10 entries in 3 events and no professional players. By 1925, the 27th European Championships, held in Prague, included 24 entries in 10 varied events.

Amateur Rowing Association

The Amateur Rowing Association (ARA) is the regulating body in the United Kingdom for the sport of rowing. It is also liable for the growth and organisation of rowing in England. The Scottish Amateur Rowing Association (SARA) and Welsh Amateur Rowing Association (WARA) oversee this in their respective countries.

The ARA is a member of the British Olympic Association and the International Federation of Rowing Associations, also acknowledged as FISA.

The ARA had it roots in the want to constitute crews drawn from the leading British clubs 'for the aim of defeating the foreign or colonial invader' though in fact this aim wasn't accomplished until much later.

A series of meetings were held in Putney from 1877 culminating in the constitution of the Metropolitan Rowing Association in 1879 by

Cambridge University Boat Club, Dublin University Boat Club, Kingston Rowing Club, Leander Club, London Rowing Club, Oxford University Boat Club, Royal Chester Rowing Club, Thames Rowing Club and Twickenham Rowing Club. Molesey Boat Club linked up soon afterward. In 1882 the Metropolitan Rowing Association altered its name to the Amateur Rowing Association, having attained additional member clubs from outside London, and started its development into the regulating body of rowing.

National Amateur Rowing Association

The National Amateur Rowing Association (NARA) was established in 1890 to cater for the large number of working class men who were prevented from joining the Amateur Rowing Association (ARA) by virtue of their manual occupations. (According to the interpretation of the specialise definition of Amateur status then imposed by the ARA conventions, these men were to be regarded professionals).

This definition of "amateur" was ultimately resolved in the 1920s and in 1930 NARA was reconstituted, its objectives being "to foster and encourage amateur rowing and to watch over and usually protect its interests.". In 1939 NARA was incorporated as a non-profit making company. The new body earned significant support although practically, the only difference between the two organisations was their outlook on the bar on manual labour; in all other respects the NARA was as strict about amateurism as the ARA. Its first president was the Duke of Fife and its last Lord Iveagh.

FAMOUS PLAYERS

Ernest James Barry

Ernest James Barry born in the year 1882 and died in 1968, was a British rower and Thames Waterman, five times Sculling World Champion during the early part of the 20th century and winner of the Doggett's Coat and Badge Race in 1903. Ernest Barry was brought almost straight from novice to race at the British Championship in 1908 against George Towns who had already won the world championship four times and the British Championship twice. That day, Barry, as well as beating Towns, set up a record which survived for a lot of years.

In August 1910 he contended for the World Professional sculling championship for the first time.

The race was held on the Zambezi River and Barry was defeated by the New Zealander, Richard Arnst, in a 3.25-mile race above the

Victoria Falls, for stakes of $2500 a side, in what may have been the first serious high altitude competition. The Zambezi was selected as a compromise for the race as Arnst, who had held the Championship for three years, objected to the expense of the trip to Europe, while Barry opposed the long journey to New Zealand. Barry lost the World title to Alfred Felton on the same course in October 1919, but retrieved it in 1920 racing against Felton at on the Paramatta River in Sydney, Australia.finally his nephew Bert did go on to turn Champion of the World, but not for another seven years. After Felton's loss to Barry, Richard Arnst promptly challenged and the title finally defaulted to him because three months passed without Barry accepting a challenge.

Alan Campbell

Alan Campbell was born on 9th May 1983, Coleraine, Northern Ireland, is a British sculler. Campbell began rowing for his school, Coleraine Academical Institution for Boys, in Northern Ireland before moving to London and linking up the Tideway Scullers School.

In 2003, Campbell left his degree and won the Diamond Sculls at Henley Royal Regatta. He then made his international debut at the World U23 Championships in 2003, where he was impelled to shift from the double to the single sculls five days before the regatta when his sculling partner became ill. Despite this he finished up 8th.

He contended in the quadruple sculls at the 2004 Summer Olympics, landing up in 12th place. In 2005, Campbell won the men's single at the GB Selection Trials, and raced in the men's quad for the World Cup series, winning the bronze at Lucerne regatta. At the 2005 World Championships in Gifu, Japan, the men's quad narrowly failed to reach the final. In 2006, Campbell shifted to contending in the men's heavyweight single, and won the Munich world cup regatta ahead of Olaf Tufte. He also finished up second in Lucerne, behind Mahe Drysdale, and fourth in Poznan, to win the overall world cup standings. Alan contended in the 2008 Olympics in Beijing where he took part in the Mens 2000m Individual Scull; managing to remain in first for the first 1000m, where he was then over taken by Olaf Tufte and came in fifth position.

Harry Clasper

Harry Clasper was born on 5th July 1812 and died on 13th July 1870. He was a popular Tyneside professional rower and boat-builder. He was an innovational boat designer who pioneered the evolution of the racing shell and the use of outriggers. He is said to have invented spoon-shaped oars. He was the first of three great Tyneside rowers; the other two were Robert Chambers and James Renforth.

Harry Clasper was born in Dunston, now division of the Metropolitan Borough of Gateshead, but then an autonomous village on the south bank of the River Tyne, a mile upriver from Gateshead. Clasper constituted a racing crew with his brother William and two other men. Harry rowed as stroke (the oarsman who sits nearest the stern, opposite to the cox and who sets the stroke rate) and another brother, Robert, acted as cox. The boat was titled "Swalwell". The crew commenced well, winning a lot of races and became known as the Derwenthaugh crew.

Clasper took over the tenancy of the Skiff Inn, Derwenthaugh, and in addition to being a pub landlord; he started to build boats on the same site. He built two skiffs for himself, the Hawk in 1840 and the Young Hawk in 1841. With the latter he won the Durham Regatta single sculls race in 1842. The Derwenthaugh crew was ruling the rowing scene on the Tyne and the logical advancement was to challenge a crew from the River Thames. This was done and the race was held on the Tyne on 16th July 1842. The race was rowed over a five mile course from the Tyne Bridge to Lemington for a stake of £150 a side. The Thames crew attained an easy victory. The Derwenthaugh crew's boat, St Agnes, though much narrower than the Thames boat (29 inches as against 40 inches), was 60% heavier than the Thames boat. Clasper realised that he wanted to design and build a much lighter boat for future races.

John B. Kelly, Sr

He was born on 1889 and died in 1960, American athlete and businessman. He won two gold medals in rowing at the 1920 Olympic Games in Antwerp, Belgium. John Brendan Kelly, Sr., was born in Philadelphia, Pennsylvania. He dropped out of school at an early age to work in his brother's building company. He later worked on as a bricklayer. In 1909 he started to row, contending in four-oared competition, as well as double and single sculls.

Kelly soon turned one of the best American rowers, winning the United States national championship in the single sculls in 1919 and 1920. In 1920 at the Henley Regatta, an esteemed rowing event held near Oxford, England, he was prohibited from contending. The Henley was open only to amateurs, and it was dominated that Kelly's construction work made him a professional. At the Olympics later that year, he won the single sculls race, defeating British rower Jack Beresford, who had won the singles competition at the Henley. With Paul Costello as his teammate, Kelly also won the double sculls race at the Olympics.

REFERENCES

Jolie Solomon, "*Baseball Is a Game of Hits, Runs, Errors and Lyric Poetry*," Wall Street Journal, 4 February 1987.

Ken LaZebnick, "*Opinion,*" *Minneapolis Review of Baseball* 1, no. 4 Fall 1981: 20-21.

Mark Schraf, *Cooperstown Verses* Jefferson NC: MacFarland, 2001.

Mudville Diaries: *A Book of Baseball Memories, collected by Mike Schacht* New York: Avon Books, 1996.

Pig Iron: *Baseball*, ed. Jim Villani and Rose Sayre, no. 9 1982.

The Best of Spitball: *The Literary Baseball Magazine*, ed. Mike Shannon New York: Pocket Books, 1988.

15

Rugby

Rugby is a famous game played by men and women of every race and creed, from five year old child to fifty year old man, in over 100 countries of the world. In a few of those countries it is the national sport, some say religion.

A rugby union match holds out for 80 minutes, (plus stoppage time), with a short-term interval (no more than 10-15 minutes) after the first 40 minutes; at under-19 level and below, games are confined to a maximum of 70 minutes, with an interval after 35 minutes. A match is commanded by a referee, who is helped by two touch judges or assistant referees. For professional matches, a television match official (TMO), generally called the video referee is often employed, generally to advise the referee on matters relating to the scoring of tries and dropped goals.

The object of the game is to score a lot of points as possible. The team that scores the greater number of points is the winner. Points are granted for scoring a try or kicking a goal. A try, which is worth 5 points, is scored when the ball is grounded by a player on the attacking team inside the opponent's in-goal area. A goal is scored by kicking the ball over the crossbar of the opponent's goal while staying on between the posts.

There are three methods to score a goal:

A dropped goal (scored in open play where the ball must hit the ground instantly before it is kicked);

A penalty goal (granted after the defending side infringes against the laws of rugby and may be kicked from a fixed ground position or by drop kick); and

A conversion (granted after a try is scored) by either a drop kick or a place kick. A penalty or the dropped goal has a worth of 3 points; a conversion is worth 2 points.

The pitch must be not more than 100 meters in length, not including the in-goal area. The depth of the in-goal area can deviate but must be at least 10 meters (where practicable) and not more than 22 meters. The width of the pitch may also vary but must be not more than 70 meters wide. The goal posts are located on the centre of the goal line with the upright posts placed 5.6 meters apart and the crossbar is placed 3 meters above the ground in an "H" shape. The overall height of the goal posts must be over 3.4 meters.

A typical game of rugby takes the following form: the team in possession of the ball moves the ball up the field in an attempt to ground the ball over the opponents' goal-line in order to score a try until such time as the ball carrier is tackled. They then form a ruck in order to win the ball back. This process recurs until one team drops off possession, makes a mistake that breaches the laws of the game, moves off the field of play or a try or goal is scored.

The team in possession may choose to proceed by kicking the ball ahead. The ball may be passed from one player to another as long as the ball isn't thrown forward. Rugby union is one of the few ball games where the ball can't be passed ahead. Any team mate closer to the opponent's goal than the ball-carrier is off-side and must not intervene the play, meaning that American football-style blocking is disallowed.

The team not in possession attempts to stop the ball carrier by tackling him, which comprises of grabbing hold of him and bringing him to ground. A tackled player must pass or release the ball, permitting the opponent to contend possession of the loose ball. Play doesn't stop unless there is an infringement of the laws, or the ball/ball-carrier leaves the field of play.

If the ball goes into touch the game resumes with a line-out. If the game stops because of an infringement, play resumes with either a scrum, free kick or penalty kick (depending on the severity of the infringement) granted to the non-infringing team. Tries are the primary form of scoring, and the main aim of most teams is to score tries.

Drop goals and penalty kicks are generally augmenters, a safer choice against a steadfast defense or to punish bad-disciplined opposition. On some (generally rare) junctures, a team may be granted a penalty try, if their oppositions commit a foul which is deemed by the referee to have prevented a probable try, for instance collapsing a scrum or maul close to the try line.

Variants of Rugby

Rugby Sevens: Rugby sevens is a version of rugby union in which only seven players per side feature, rather than the full 15. The variant of rugby union is very famous, with notable competitions including the IRB Sevens World Series and the Rugby World Cup Sevens. Rugby sevens is also played at events such as the Commonwealth Games. Though it was formed as an event for rugby union, rugby league has also followed the sevens format.

Rugby sevens is approved by the (IRB), and is played under considerably the same conventions and on a field of the same dimensions as the 15-player game. While a normal rugby union match lasts upwards of 80 minutes, a normal rugby sevens matches endures about 15 minutes (permitting for the one-minute half-time break, injury time and so forth). Competition finals last somewhat more than 20 minutes; each half in a competition final is ten minutes rather than the normal seven minutes, and the half-time break can be two minutes. (In the IRB Sevens World Series, only the Cup final, which ascertains the overall winner of an event, is played with 10-minute halves; all finals for lower-level trophies are played with regular 7-minute halves.) This permits rugby tournaments to be accomplished in a day or a weekend. However, sevens scores are usually comparable to union scores; scoring happens with much greater regularity in sevens, since the defenders are more spaced out than in rugby union. Scrums still survive within sevens, compiled of just three players from each team. Given the rapid nature of the game, players are typically either from the backline or the trio of loose forwards in fifteens rugby.

Rugby sevens was at the start formed by Ned Haig, a butcher from Melrose, Scotland as a fund-raising event for his local club in 1883. The first ever sevens match was played at the Greenyards, where it was well encountered. The largest sevens tournament in the world is the Rosslyn Park Schools tournament, with an attendance of over 3,000 schoolchildren from around the world. Rugby Sevens specialists Wellington College have reigned the rugby sevens festival winning 6 times out of the last 9 years with a five year undefeated spell between 1998-2003. Results from the tournament can be seen on The Schools' Rugby Website. The first ever formally approved international tournament occurred at Murrayfield as portion of the "Scottish Rugby Union's celebration of rugby" centenary celebrations in 1973. Due to the success of the format, the ongoing Hong Kong Sevens was established three years later. In 1993, the Rugby World Cup Sevens, in which the Melrose

Cup is contended, was established. Two of the best legendary sevens competitions are the Hong Kong Sevens and Wellington Sevens, which now constitute the parts of the IRB Sevens World Series.

Tag Rugby: Tag Rugby is a non-contact team game in which each player wears a belt that has two velcro tags attached to it, or shorts with velcro patches. The mode of play is alike to rugby league with attacking players undertaking to dodge, evade and pass a rugby ball while defenders attempt to prevent them scoring by "tagging" - pulling a velcro connected tag from the ball carrier. Tag Rugby comes in several forms with OzTag and Mini Tag being some of the better acknowledged variations. Tag Rugby has the highest engagement levels in Ireland and Australia.

Rugby League: It is a full-contact team sport played with a prolate spheroid-shaped ball by two teams of thirteen on a rectangular grass field. Rugby league is among the two major codes of rugby football, the other being rugby union. The league code is most spectacular in Great Britain, Australia, New Zealand, and France, where the sport is played professionally. Rugby league is also famous in Papua New Guinea where it is regarded the national sport. The game is played very less in several other countries, such as Russia, the United States and Lebanon.

Rugby league takes its name from what was at the start is a breakaway faction of the English Rugby Football Union (RFU) titled the Northern Rugby Football Union when founded in 1895. Both organisations played the game under similar conventions at first, until alike breakaway factions occurred from RFU-affiliated rugby football unions in Australia and New Zealand in 1907 and 1908, and conceived associations titled rugby football leagues, introducing modified Northern Union decrees to make a new form of rugby football. The Northern Union later altered its name to the Northern Rugby Football League in 1922 (later dropping the 'Northern') and thus, over time the sport itself became known as "rugby league". Over the following decades, the conventions of both variants of rugby were step by step altered, and now rugby league and rugby union are clearly different sports.

Rugby Union: It is an outdoor contact sport, played with an oval ball, by two teams each comprises of 15 players. It is one of the two primary codes of rugby football, the other being rugby league. There is also a seven-a-side version named rugby sevens, which is played under modified laws and with only seven players per team. Rugby union is often referred to as simply rugby, or as football, and in parts where rugby league is played, as union.

A rugby union match endures for 80 minutes, (plus stoppage time), with a short interval (no more than 10-15 minutes) after the first 40 minutes; at under-19 level and below, games are bounded to a maximum of 70 minutes, with an interval after 35 minutes. A match is commanded by a referee, who is helped by two touch judges or assistant referees. For professional matches, a television match official (TMO), generally called the video referee is often employed, generally to advise the referee on matters relating to the scoring of tries and dropped goals.

The objective of the game is to score as many points as possible. The team that scores the greater number of points is the winner. Points are granted for scoring a try or kicking a goal. A try, which is worth 5 points, is scored when the ball is grounded by a player on the attacking team within the opponent's in-goal region. A goal is scored by kicking the ball over the crossbar of the opponent's goal while persisting between the posts.

HISTORY

While playing soccer at Rugby School of England in 1823, William Webb Ellis picked up the ball in his hands and ran with it. This activated an interest, conducting to the foundation of rugby. Cambridge University right away adopted the game, popularised it and made local conventions. The game grew popular at area schools and in 1871, ten years after the common rules of soccer were set, the first Rugby Union was founded in London and firm rules of the game were constituted. In 1895 rugby clubs in northern England called for compensation of lost wages for players. The Rugby League was established as a result and a 13-player game with altered decrees were made for professionals.

Rugby spread across the globe and competition went forth between countries. In the United States, the game went forth chiefly on the West Coast. The lack of accurate conventions, ambiguities in the game and complexity of the sport drew a lot of United States players away from the game and major changes were invoked. In 1880 the scrum was replaced by a line of scrimmage, drawing emphasis from the free-running characteristic of the game.

The game continued to play with rugby conventions until 1905 where the publication of photographs of a harsh game between Sarthmore and Pennsylvania made a stir. President Theodore Roosevelt insisted on reform of the game to lower the viciousness with terror of abolishing the game by edict. In 1906 the forward pass was brought in to the United States game. The conventions of rugby died and the game of American football was born.

Rugby carried on expanding elsewhere, with particular regard to Britain, New Zealand, Australia and South Africa. Though a fistful of clubs persisted in the United States, rugby did not reappear until the 1960's. College campuses turned to the sport because it was one where many could play and escape the rigid discipline and professionalism inherent in college football.

Minimal costs, constant action and the opportunity for frequent play with a primary emphasis on fun also drew in many. The number of clubs grew from about 80 to over 1,000 between 1964 and 1980.

The United States of America Rugby Football Union (USARFU) was constituted in 1975, making added recognition and a measure of organization. The sport carries on growing and now played in over 80 countries worldwide. The conventions of rugby continue to develop and amateurism remains as dominant characteristic.

Medieval football is an advanced term occasionally used for a wide variety of localised football games which were invented and played during the middle Ages in Europe. Alternative names include folk football, mob football and Shrovetide football. Some of these games are played in prevailing times. These games may also be considered as the "ancestors" of modern codes of football. By comparison with later kinds of football, the medieval matches were chaotic and had some conventions.

The middle Ages saw a immense boost in fame of games played yearly at Shrovetide throughout Europe, specially in England. The games played in England at this time may have arrived with the Roman occupation but there is little evidence to indicate this. Certainly the Romans played ball games, in special Harpastum.

There is also one reference to ball games being played in southern Britain prior to the Norman Conquest. In the ninth century Nennian Historia Britonum tells that a group of boys were playing at ball (pilae ludus) the beginning of this account is either Southern England or Wales. Reports of a game played in France specially Brittany, Normandy and Picardy - titled La Soule or La Choule, suggest that football games could have arrived in England as a result of the Norman Conquest.

These archaic variants of football, usually classified as mob football, would be played between neighboring towns and villages, involving an limitless number of players on opponent teams, who would clash in a heaving mass of people struggling to drag an blown up pig's bladder by any means achievable to markers at each end of a town (occasionally rather than markers, the teams would attempt to kick the bladder into thc balcony of the opponents' church).

A legend that these games in England developed from a more ancient and bloody ritual of kicking the "Dane's head" is unlikely to be true. Shrovetide games exist in a number of English towns.

There are astonishingly some images of medieval football. One engraving from the early fourteenth century at Gloucester Cathedral, England, distinctly shows two young men running vigorously towards each other with a ball in mid-air between them. There is a hint that the players may be using their hands to strike the ball.

A second medieval image in the British Museum, London distinctly shows a group of men with a large ball on the ground. The ball distinctly has a seam where leather has been sewed conjointly. It is ill-defined incisively what is happening in this set of three images, though the last image seems to show a man with an injured arm. It is likely that this image highlights the dangers of some medieval football games.

THE GAME

The Field

The field used is made up of grass with the usual exception of mud. The length of the field cannot surpass 100 meters (110 yards) and the width cannot overstep 69 meters (75 yards). Each try zone can't exceed 22 meters (25 yards) in length.

Goal posts alike to those used in American football and shaped in the form of an "H" stand on the goal line at opposite ends of the field, at the commencement of each try zone.

The lines generally drawn inside the field are 22 meters (25 yards) off goal, 10 meters (10 yards) off halfway and the halfway line. Also, a 5 meter (5 yard) alley is drawn along the lengths of the field measured off the touch line (out of bounds).

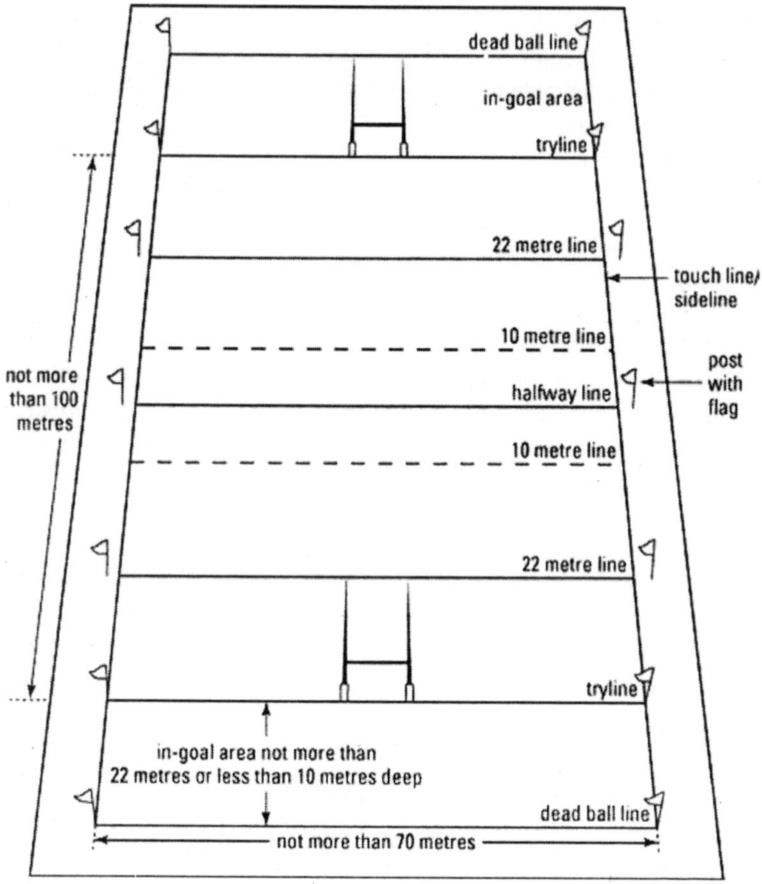

Fig. Rugby Field

Time

The length of play is very elastic and ascertained by the level of play but is generally around an hour to an hour and a half of playing time. The time is divided into two halves, with usually only a 5 minute half time. Substitutions or time-outs are not permitted. Play pauses for penalties, scores, when the ball goes out of touch. The game isn't stopped for injuries until the ball is out of play. Contrary to American football, play doesn't stop with a tackle.

Equipment

Players don't wear any padding or protection except for a mouth guard. The conventional uniform comprises of a long sleeve cotton shirt with a collar. Shorts are generally cotton and rise to about mid-thigh.

Knee-length socks with turnover tops are worn along with boots alike to soccer cleats.

There are strict rules governing the kinds of cleats used. An optional piece of equipment is the scrum cap worn by some forwards which is made from leather or cloth and worn as security for the ears. Any other item than what is named is generally not permitted in play with the inclusion of jewelry. The ball comes in many sizes. It is shaped like an American football, but is bigger. The standard length is about 285 mm (11 inches) and the standard center circumference is about 630 mm (24 inches).

Fig. Rugby Ball

Officials

The referee commands the game and sees that the players maintain good behaviour and obey the laws of rugby. There is only one referee and he is the only judge, timekeeper and score keeper. There are two touch judges, one nominated by each team. They stand outside the touch line and follow the play.

If the ball is kicked out of touch, the touch judge on that side lifts the flag and stands at the point to where the ball went out and marks it. The touch judges also determine if a goal kick is successful. The referee still has absolute authority and makes the end decision even if both touch judges disagree.

The team coaches are not permitted to influence the team once they are on the field. Thus a captain is nominated for each team. The captain makes plays, encourages the players and leads the team. This person is the only means of communication between the team and the referee. Players are not permitted to address the referee unless they are called upon.

Players

15 people play at a time per side, each of which has particular obligations as a player. Players are generally talked about in respect to two classes. Members of the first group are called the forwards, or the pack, and comprise of the first eight players. Members of the second group are called the backs, and comprise of the remaining players. Occasionally the scrum half, number 9, is regarded part of either group.

Position of the players:

1. Prop
2. Hooker
3. Prop
4. Lock (2nd Row)
5. Lock (2nd Row)
6. Flanker (Wing Forward)
7. Flanker (Wing Forward)
8. 8th Man
9. Scrum-Half
10. Fly-Half
11. Weak Side Wing
12. Inside Center
13. Outside Center
14. Strong Side Wing
15. Fullback

The Objective

The objective of the game is to acquire more points than the opponent team within the assigned time of play. A tie is called if the scores are equivalent at the end of play. A try is scored when a player places the ball in the opposition's goal area.

It is counted as 5 points and can be converted to extra 2 points with an eminent place kick made from a line perpendicular to the point at which the ball was scored. A goal can also be scored through a penalty with a free kick or a drop kick from the field of play. A goal counts as 3 points.

MAJOR TOURNAMENTS

Rugby World Cup

The Rugby World Cup is the premier international rugby union competition. The event is organised by the sport's governing body, the International Rugby Board (IRB), and is contested by the men's national teams. The inaugural tournament was held in 1987, hosted by both Australia and New Zealand, and is now contested every four years.

The winners are awarded the William Webb Ellis Cup, named after the Rugby School pupil credited with the game's invention. The tournament is one of the largest international sporting competitions in the world.

The 2007 Rugby World Cup was the sixth Rugby World Cup, a quadrennial international rugby union world championship introduced in 1987. Twenty nations contended for the Webb Ellis Cup in the tournament, which was hosted by France from 7 September to 20 October, and won by South Africa, who defeated England at the Stade de France in St. Denis, Paris. France won the hosting rights in 2003, beating a bid from England. The competition comprised of 48 matches over 44 days; 42 matches were played in ten cities throughout France, as well as four in Cardiff, Wales, and two in Edinburgh, Scotland.

The eight quarter-finalists from 2003 were allotted automatic qualification, while 12 other nations made entry through the regional qualifying competitions that commenced in 2004 - of them, Portugal was the only World Cup debutant. The top three nations from each pool at the end of the pool stage will qualify automatically for the 2011 World Cup.

The competition opened up with a match between hosts France and Argentina on 7 September at the Stade de France in St-Denis. The stadium was also the venue of the ultimate match between England and South Africa on 20 October, which South Africa won by 15 points to 6, awarding them their second World Cup title.

European Nations Cup

The European Nations Cup, ENC or occasionally noted as the Six Nations B is the European Championship for tier 2 and tier 3 rugby union nations. The Championship is fragmented into 7 divisions with 5 or 6 teams in each. The sections play on a two-year cycle with the teams playing each other both home and away.

At present, there is no promotion or relegation between the ENC and the Six Nations. The prevalent champions are Georgia, who won the 2006/2008 First Division title.

Women's European Championship

FIRA's Women's European Championship (it is also known as the European nations Cup) is an international rugby union competition contended between women's national teams who are members of FIRA - Association of European Rugby. The competition has its beginnings in a four nation "European Cup" held in 1988 but didn't become an official FIRA competition until 1995. The competition has grown importantly and is now fractioned into two "Pools" - A and B - with the leading nations in Pool A.

In modern years England and France haven't tended to send their full national teams to the competition, but have rather sent their "A" sides. The English and French unions would not regard games played by these teams as full internationals - however their opponents usually would.

IRB Junior World Championship

The IRB Junior World Championship is an international rugby union competition. The event is organised by the sport's regulating body, the International Rugby Board (IRB), and is contested by 16 men's junior national teams, with an under-20 age necessity. The opening tournament was held in June 2008, hosted by Wales. This event replaced the IRB's previous age-grade world championships, the Under 19 and Under 21 World Championships.

The Junior World Championship is the upper level of a new IRB tournament structure for U-20 national sides. At the same time that the Junior World Championship was set up, the IRB also launched a second-level championship, the IRB Junior World Rugby Trophy, having eight teams. In August 2007, Chile was declared as the host of the inaugural Junior World Trophy to be held in Santiago in April 2008. This was followed in November 2007 by declaring Wales as the host for the inaugural Junior World Championship in June 2008.

ADMINISTRATIVE BODIES

International Rugby Board

The International Rugby Board (IRB) is the world regulating and law-making body for the sport of rugby union, and antecedently for rugby football. It was established in 1886 as the International Rugby Football Board (IRFB) by the unions of Scotland, Wales and Ireland. England originally declined to participate, but in 1890, it became the first non-founding union to become a member. The International Rugby Football Board altered its name to the International Rugby Board in 1997. The IRB's headquarters are situated in Dublin, Ireland.

The IRB has 96 full member Unions, 19 Associate members and six territorial Associations, with the 96 full member unions meeting bi-annually and Regional Associations organising systematic meetings. The IRB organises some of the sport's international competitions, with the Rugby World Cup (taking place every four years) being the most famous and highest profitable competition for the IRB, as seen by the £81.8 million (approximately US$150 million, €118 million, ¥17300 million) gross commercial income of the 2003 tournament. The IRB also provides money to smaller nations, such as the Pacific Islands teams, who are not able to generate their own income.

The IRB has several main functions including:

- Governance of the Laws and ordinances and their enforcement
- Tournament owners and managers
- Global game development through Member Unions funding via grants and Strategic Investment programmes, and delivery of Education & Development programmes
- Game promotion

Confederation of African Rugby

The Confederation of African Rugby (CAR) is regulating body for rugby union within Africa. The Confederation currently has 36 member nations and is responsible for running several rugby tournaments within Africa, particularly the Africa Cup, and CAR Super 16.

The Confederation was formally set in motion in January 1986 in Tunis. The opening members at the meeting were Tunisia, Morocco, Senegal, Ivory Coast, Tanzania, Kenya, the Seychelles and Madagascar. A meeting was held in Casablanca in July 1992, with the view of integrating the SARFU into the confederation. The Confederation now has 36 member nations. The African Rugby Charter was contracted by the President of CAR, Abdelaziz Bougja, the then President of the South African Rugby Union (SARFU) Brian van Rooyen, in the presence of former South African president Nelson Mandela, and the South African Minister of Sport, Makhenkesi Stofile.

Asian Rugby Football Union

The Asian Rugby Football Union (ARFU) is the regulating body of rugby union in Asia under the authority of the International Rugby Board. Established in 1968 by eight charter nations, the Union today has 25 member nations in countries across Asia, stretching out from Kazakhstan to Guam.

The aim of ARFU is: "to bring up physical and moral standards in Asia by education in the healthy chase of Rugby Football and to promote friendship amongst Asian countries."

The ARFU supports regional and pan-Asian tournaments including the freshly established Asian Five Nations competition, women's, men's, and under 19's tournaments in sevens and fifteen-a-side rugby.

FIRA

FIRA was conceived in 1934 to promote, develop, organise and administer the game of rugby union in Europe outside the authority of the International Rugby Board (the world regulating body of rugby union). It became integrated into the IRB in the 90s.

In 1990s the FIRA recognised the IRB as the regulating body of rugby union world wide and after negotiations with the IRB, it agreed to integrate itself within the IRB.

In 1999 it altered its name to "FIRA - Association of European Rugby" (FIRA-A.E.R.), to promote and dominate over rugby union in the European area and to run the junior world championship. FIRA-A.E.R. organised both the under-19 and under-21 world championships until IRB rolled-up them into the under-20 Junior World Championship and Junior World Trophy in 2008.

Touch Rugby Federation of India

The Touch Rugby Federation of India was conceived in December, 2001 and was got registered under the Societies Registration Act XXI of 1860 in February, 2002. It was affiliated with the Federation of International Touch, situated in Australia in January, 2003.

Mr. Tarsem Sharma, a retired Director from Sports Authority of India convoked a meeting of sportspersons on 1st December, 2001 and declared that he has brought a new and attractive game of Touch Rugby to India and gave details of the game being played in about 36 countries including Australia and New Zealand under the Federation of International

Touch stationed in Australia. He moved a resolution to adopt and introduce this game in India.

The Resolution of First December, 2001 was therefore, an historic event when the sportspersons met and decided to adopt, introduce, promote and develop the game of Touch Rugby - a fast and forthcoming game- in India. All were beguiled, that it can be played by people of all ages and needed not much gear except an oval shaped ball and a field of the size of 70 mt X 50 mts.

It can be played by men and women individually and mixed. It needs speed and stamina. The opportunities of injury in this game and decided to constitute a body to promote this game. The thought and concept was interpreted into action and the Touch Rugby Federation of India came into being.

Bangalore Rugby Football Club

Bangalore Rugby Football Club was established in 1996, predominantly by ex-pats. It comprised of only a 1st XV adult team. Today, BRFC still has a truly international flavour but is predominantly Indian with 4 thriving teams feeding into it - the future of rugby in Bangalore is very bright indeed.

The IRFU organises three major tournaments annualy. The Callaghan Cup (Qualificaton for All India) held in Delhi in 2005 we won the Cup by beating the Army in the final, The Hutch All India and South East Asia tournament and the Hutch All India 7s Tournament. The best teams in India qualify and compete. Often foreign teams are solicited to compete.

In 2005 Bangalore ended runners-up in the tournament, British Asian Bulls defeated them in the final; but confirmed our place as India's No.1 rugby team. In 2006 Bangalore shared the Plate with CCFC after torrential rain washed out the final. Bangalore was also delighted to get two teams, Bangalore 1st VII and the Bangalore Refugees to the semi-finals of the 2006 Hutch All India 7s help in Chennai.

FAMOUS PLAYERS

Gonzalo Quesada

Gonzalo Quesada of Argentina is one of the most renowned Rugby Players. He was born in 2nd May in the year 1974 in Buenos Aires.

Gonzalo Quesada-Argentina played for the Argentinian rugby union side and won to his credit 36 caps or the headgear of honour while playing at the position of Fly-half from 1996 to 2003. It was on 14th of September, 1996 that Gonzalo Quesada-Argentina made his first test entry against United States when he was twenty two years old. He scored the highest points in the 1999 Rugby World Cup. The final cap was won by Gonzalo Quesada-Argentina, versus Ireland during the 2003 Rugby World Cup on 26th of October 2003.

His talent and skill is quite apparent from the fact that he scored 12 points out of the Argentina's 15 points although Argentina had to suffer the defeat. Gonzalo Quesada-Argentina, was also the one to score the highest number of points in the Rugby World Cup 1999 in Wales which were 102 points.

Junior Malili Muliaina

Junior Malili Muliaina of New Zealand. He is endlessly playing for 34 matches after his first match. He is the full back player of the team. He is the winner of the Gold medal in the Commonwealth Games in 2002. He was born in 31st July 1980 at Salelesi. Jason Phillip Randall White is the renowned Rugby Player of Scotland. He plays in the forward and he can play in any place. He is the captain of Scottish team of Rugby.

George Chuter

George Chuter was born on 9th of July in Greenwich in the year 1976. He represents the English rugby union. Before he joined the "Leicester Tigers", George Chuter-England, began his career with the "Saracens". It was at the age of 12 that George Chuter-England commenced playing rugby when he went to the Trinity School of John Whitgift in London. He played at the position of the hooker. Afterwards he decided to change his position and began playing in the front row.

George Chuter-England perpetually kept performing at a constant pace and collected the honours for the London Division U18 side while playing for the "Old Mid-Whitgiftians". It was in the year 1994-1995 that George Chuter-England won his first cap for an international match against Scotland. He made a debut for England A playing against France A at Tours.

George Chuter-England, in the same year made a tour for the senior England called as "tour to hell" to the countries like Australia, New Zealand and South Africa. He played against the uncrowned match against the New Zealand Academy at Invercargill.

Joe Roff

Joe Roff, Australia dragged Australia to the victory by scoring the intercept try in the second British Lions Test in 2001 and was the leading try scorer for Australia. This Australian rugby master player declared his retirement in the middle of the super 12 seasons of 2004 and adjourned finally retired at the end of the wallabies test series for the year 2004. His adieu from the super 12 rugby was a great one as the Brumbies came forth triumphant in the super 12 competition. Joe Roff-Australia made a decision to join the University in England after he retired.

He attended the O'Connor Catholic School in Armidale as well as "The Armidale School". Joe Roff is presently following a degree in Politics, Philosophy and Economics at Harris Manchester College. He played for the Oxford University Rugby Football Club by making his amateur return. This club is also acknowledged as "Dark Blues". The match was played on 12th December 2006 at Twickenham Stadium against Cambridge University Rugby Union Football Club. Although Oxford lost this match 15-6, Joe Roff-Australia, was granted the "United Kingdom-based Young Australian of the Year for 2007" which was for his contribution and the valuable services that he rendered to the Australian rugby.

Jaque Fourie

Jaque Fourie was born on 4 March 1983 in Carleton Ville, South Africa. He is a South African rugby union player. His usual position is in the centers, and he has played for the Springboks.He plays for the Lions, erstwhile the Cats, in the international Super 14 competition as well as the Golden Lions in the Currie Cup.

Jaque Fourie in fact made his entry during the World Cup. On October 11, at the 2003 Rugby World Cup, he made his international first appearance at outside centre for the Springboks against Uruguay at Subiaco Oval in Perth, and scored a try on debut. Jaque Fourie also played against Georgia during the pool stages, scoring another try. He was a reserve for consequent World Cup games against Samoa and the All Blacks.

Jaque Fourie next played for the Springboks in June of 2004, playing on the left wing against Ireland, which South Africa won 26 to 17. He played a further three times for the Springboks that year; against England at Twickenham, Scotland at Murray field in November as well as a match against Argentina at Velez Sársfield Stadium in Buenos Aires.

Nasser Hussain

Nasser Hussain was born on March 9, 1980. He is the present captain of the Indian national rugby union team.

He plays for the Bombay Gymkhana Club in Mumbai, India, and has also played abroad for Tynedale RFC & Northumbria University in Newcastle upon Tyne, England. His international first appearance was on October 26, 1998 in Singapore against the host country. As of 2005 he has 18 test caps and has scored 6 tries for his country.

Rahul Bose

Rahul Bose was born on July 27, 1967, he is an Indian actor, screenwriter, film director, social activist, and rugby union player. He is notable for his engagement in the relief efforts that pursued the 2004 Boxing Day Tsunami and is also the founder of the anti-discrimination NGO, The Foundation.

Rahul Bose was born to Rupen and Kumud Bose. He spent his childhood in Kolkata, West Bengal then moved to Mumbai with his family. He is an alumnus of the Cathedral and John Connon School in Mumbai and graduated from Sydenham College. Rahul spent time doing theatre, boxing, and playing rugby, during his college days. His mother introduced him to boxing and rugby union. He plays international rugby in the National Orange Indian Rugby Team. Bose left his job at Rediffusion as a creative director to become a serious actor, writer, and director.

REFERENCES

Arthurson: *Arko: My Game*, Ken Arthurson with Ian Heads,, Ironbark, Sydney, 1997.

Christensen: *Rugby League Year Book 1974 Official Yearbook of the NSWRL*, E E Christensen, NSWRL, Sydney, 1974.

Christensen: *Rugby League Year Book 1973 Official Yearbook of the NSWRL*, E E Christensen, NSWRL, Sydney, 1973.

Coleman: *Fatty The strife and times of Paul Vautin*, Mike Coleman, Ironbark Press, Randwick, 1992.

French: *100 Great Rugby League Players* , Ray French, Macmillan, Melbourne, 1989.

Harris: *The Best of Both Worlds The Michael O'Connor Story*, Bret Harris, Pan Macmillan, Sydney, 1991.

Heads: *The Kangaroos The saga of Rugby Leagues's great tours*, Ian Heads, Lester-Townsend, Sydney, 1990.

Heads: *True Blue The story of the NSW Rugby League*, Ian Heads, Ironbark Press, Randwick, 1992.

Keneally: *The Uitility Player The Des Hasler Story*, Tom Keneally, Pan Macmillan, Sydney, 1993.

Masters: *Inside Out Rugby League Under Scrutiny*, Roy Masters, Ironbark, Sydney , 1997.

McDonald & Henderson: *The Manly Warringah Story* , Charles E McDonald & Captain C W T Henderson, Paul Hamlyn, Dee Why, 1975.

McGregor: *Simply the Best The 1990 Kangaroos*, Adrian McGregor, Queensland of University Press, St Lucia, 1991.

Middleton: *Rugby League 1987-88 Official Yearbook of the NSWRL*, David Middleton (Ed.), Lester-Townsend, Sydney, 1988.

Moorhouse: *At the George And Other essays on Rugby League*, Geoffrey Moorhouse, Hodder & Stoughton, London, 1989.

Mossop: *The Moose That Roared*, Rex Mossop with Larry Writer, Ironbark Press, Randwick, 1991.

O'Connell: *In Defence: The Wally O'Connell Story*, Wally O'Connell, Walter Patrick O'Connell OAM, Sydney, 2005.

Reilly: *Reilly a life in rugby league*, Malcolm Reilly with Ian Heads, Ironbark, Sydney, 1998.

Smith: *The Sea Eagle has Landed The Story of Manly Warringah Rugby League Club* , Robert Smith, Sea Eagle Marketing, Brookvale, 1991.

Video: *Manly the first 50 years*, Video, Sea Eagle Marketing, Brookvale, 1996.

Whiticker: *Captaining the Kangaroos: Rugby League Test and World Cup Captains*, Alan Whiticker, New Holland, Sydney, 2004.

Whiticker: *From the Bush to Brookvale The Cliff Lyons Story*, Alan Whiticker, Gary Allen Pty Ltd, Smithfield, 2000.

Whiticker: *Grand Finals of the NSW Rugby League*, Alan Whiticker, Gary Allen Pty Ltd, Smithfield, 1994.

16

Sailing

Sailing is the art of controlling a sailing vessel. By altering the rigging, rudder and dagger or centre board, a sailor supervises the force of the wind on the sails in order to alter the direction and speed of a boat. Mastery of the skill needs experience in changing wind and sea conditions, as well as knowledge regarding sailboats.

A sailboat sailing ship moves forward because of the reaction to the inertia of moving air on its sails. Subsequently the dawn of history this important technology has afforded mankind greater mobility and capacity for fishing, trade and warfare.

From moving the stones of the great pyramids from Aswan to Giza to permitting man to migrate throughout Polynesia to Nelson's defeat of the French and Spanish navies at the Battle of Trafalgar, mankind's history has been intertwined with this seemingly simple engineering.

There are few sports like sailing; it can be a gentle relaxing activity where the only noise is the wind in the sails and the water lapping versus the hull; or it can be a fast active sport where a gust of wind will catch in the sail driving you forward with an acceleration which you wouldn't have thought possible.

Sailing is easy to get into as the basics can be mastered within a few hours, however, it will invariably offer a challenge which you will never tire of. Controlling the wind demands perpetual attention as it continuously alterations direction and force; this makes sailing not just a thrilling activity but a skilful one as well.

Dingy sailing is an activity with a wide appeal; dissimilar designs of dingy permit sailors who are interested in all action thrills and spills to take part in the same sport as those wanting take a more leisurely sail. In recent years this stimulating sport has continued to develop with a range of new dinghies to sail, when combined with the range of formed dinghies available often at very reasonable cost, dingy sailing really has become a sport for everyone.

Today most people enjoy sailing as a recreational activity. Recreational sailing can be further split up into racing, cruising and "daysailing" or dinghy sailing. There are many production sailboats available, and several of these manufactured models have ownership associations, such as the Islander 36 association.

The energy that moves a sailboat is harnessed by manipulating the relative motion of wind and water speed: if there is no conflict in motion, such as on a calm day or when the wind and water current are moving in the same direction, there is no energy to be drew out and the sailboat will not be able to do anything but drift. Where there is a difference in movement, then there is energy to be drawn out at the interface, and the sailboat does this by placing the sail(s) in the air and the hull(s) in the water.

Sails are airfoils that work by applying an airflow set up by the wind and the movement of the boat. The combination of the two is the apparent wind, which is the relative velocity of the wind relative to the boat's movement. The sails generate lift applying the air that flows around them. The air flowing at the sail surface is not the true wind. The sail alone is not enough to drive the boat in any desired direction, as a sail by itself would only push a boat in the same direction as the wind. Sailboats overcome this by having another physical object below the water line. These include a keel, centerboard, or few other kind of underwater foil or even the hull itself (as in catamarans without centreboard or in a conventional proa). Thus, the physical portion of the boat which is below water can be considered as functioning as a "second sail". Having two surfaces versus the wind and water enables the sailor to travel in almost any direction and to generate an additional source of lift from the water. The flow of water over the underwater hull portions produces a hydrodynamic force.

The combination of the aerodynamic force from the sails and the hydrodynamic force from the underwater hull section permits movement in almost any direction, except straight into the wind. This can be likened, in simple terms, to squeezing a wet bar of soap with two hands which causes it to shoot out in a direction perpendicular to both conflicting forces.

Depending upon the efficiency of the rig, the angle of travel relative to the true wind can be as little as 35 degrees to over 80 degrees. This angle is known as the tacking angle. With a 35 degree tacking angle on either side of the wind, it is possible for a sailboat to sail right away over 290 degrees of the compass (360 - 2x35 = 290 degrees).

When sailing upwind, the sails, when correctly adjusted, will generate aerodynamic lift. When sailing downwind, the sails no longer generate aerodynamic lift and airflow is stalled, with the wind push on the sails providing drag only. As the boat is going downwind, the apparent wind is less than the true wind and this allied to the fact that the sails are not making aerodynamic lift serves to limit the downwind speed.

When moving, the movement of the boat produces its own apparent wind. Apparent wind is what is experienced onboard and is the wind that the boat is in reality sailing by. Sailing into the wind causes the apparent wind to be greater than the true wind and the direction of the apparent wind will be forward of the true wind. Few extreme design boats are capable of traveling faster than the true windspeed.

Few non-conventional rigs purportedly capture energy from the wind in a much dissimilar fashion are capable of feats that conventional rigs are not, such as sailing right away into the wind. One such example is the wind turbine boat, also known as the windmill boat, which uses a large windmill to extract energy from the wind, and a propeller to convert this energy to forward movement of the hull. An alike design, known as the autogiro boat, uses a wind turbine without the propellor, and functions in a manner alike to a normal sail.

HISTORY

Throughout history sailing has been instrumental in the growth of civilization. The most former representation of a ship under sail appears on an Egyptian vase from approximately 3500 BC. Advances in sailing technology from the middle Ages onward enabled Arab, Chinese, Indian and European explorers to make longer voyages into regions with extreme weather and climatic conditions. Improvements were built in the design of sails, masts and rigging, and navigational gear turned more sophisticated. From the 15th century onwards, European ships went further north, stayed longer on the Grand Banks and in the Gulf of St. Lawrence, and finally started to explore the Pacific Northwest and the Western Arctic.

Two thirds of the World's surface is covered by water. The majority of all people on this planet lives by or near to the coast and has done so for millennia. The straining of man to explore and extend his horizon has invariably been constrained by the sea and the restrictions of those vessels that would carry people further and further offshore.

For thousands of years, wind was the only source of energy that would permit man to pass long distances over seas, such as the Mediterranean or the Atlantic Ocean. Distances that proved to be too long to be overcome by the use of muscle power and paddles only. This limitation naturally led dissimilar civilizations to develop dissimilar ways to exploit this only enough source of energy. Commencing from the most primitive vessels – little more than trees with a piece of cloth on top, a construction still employed by many fishermen in developing countries – people quickly improved their skills in navigation and the construction of more sophisticated boats. Phoenician began early to master the Mediterranean, only challenged and finally defeated by the uprising power of Rome.

As most highly evolved civilizations concentrated around the Mediterranean, this naturally favored a strong concern in navigation and all disciplines concerned with it – astronomy, meteorology, shipbuilding and even basic forms of oceanography. Antiquity boosted mankind's skills in passing long distances over the seas. Ample of the knowledge of the Phoenicians, Egyptians, Romans and Greek disappeared and was forgotten throughout the middle Ages. Viking longboats employed generally the power of men at oars and primitive square-sails. The shape of square-sail rigs quickly turned the most common rig type in European nations. The Arabs, however, evolved their own characteristic, triangular sail as a more efficient solution. Arabic dhows could sail upwind very well and proved to be more flexible and navigable than European ships equipped with square-sails.

Completely dissimilar concepts were even further away, in China. The Chinese lugsail is more often referred to as a junk rig, was rigged to a short mast and based on long bamboo battens. The construction of junks was likely to be the most efficient and sophisticated of its days, being cheap and flexible and simultaneously easy to navigate. This permited junks to sail with a relatively small crew on board.

A much simpler construction was made on the Polynesian islands of the Pacific Ocean: the proa comprises of a hollowed-out tree trunk that would hold people and goods, and another piece of wood was attached as a stabilizing outrigger; a simple, but robust construction that was cheap and easily built. It is probably for the same reasons that proas are still widely employed all over the Pacific Ocean. As the leading seafaring nations changed over the course of centuries – Venetian, Spaniards, Portuguese, Arabs, Chinese, and Dutch, the materials persisted essentially the same. Wood was cut into shape or tied together and only very rarely other materials were employed for the construction of the prime body of ships. This should alter with the up rise of Britain after the defeat of the Spanish Armada.

With the industrial revolution, new materials for the construction of sailing vessels turned available. Also, distances turned longer as the British reached out over the oceans built an Empire spanning the globe. The new needs and chances led to a boost in innovative designs and growths. However, it was still wind that would carry most goods and now over thousands of miles of canals that cut Britain into navigable slices. The Thames flatboats are prime instances for innovative designs, easy to navigate even by as few as two men, these little sailing boats were changed from a ground plan into manifold shapes and kinds. This way, they could meet local requirements.

Offshore, the large sailing ships reigned the oceans. Among the most fabled cargo-carrying ships of that period were windjammers and clipper ships. The latter ones were most likely known as that way as they permited trade companies to clip short the time for individual passages, as they were designed to speed up the traffic between the British mother island and its outstations in India, Australia or the Americas.

One of the pioneers of cruising in the advance sense was the British sailor Richard Tyrrell McMullen, who sailed thousands of miles around the area of the British Isles in the second half of the 19th century. He died on his yacht in 1891, at a time when he had already inspired thousands of people to pursue the calling from offshore. Other ancient cruisers included the London barrister John Macgregor and the American Joshua Slocum, who succeeded as the first person to do a single-handed circumnavigation of the globe.

In more recent times, the British couple Eric and Susan Hiscock made cruising tremendously famous and well-known; they themselves did three circumnavigations between 1952 and 1976 in a number of dissimilar yachts which were all known as "Wanderer". A combination of race sailing and cruising arose around the same time.

Cruiser racing proved to be exceptionally famous. Subsequently these days, more and more professionals contend for the most esteemed trophies, and only "private" cruiser races are suitable for spare-time sailors from the club-level. This led to a forking between sailing as a competitive sport and the conventional pleasure yachting. Both areas remain to gain fame from year to year. There are more professional, competitive sailors than ever before and the sport pulls a lot of attention with major events being persued by hundreds of thousands sailing enthusiasts all over the World. On the other hand, sailing yourself for joy has never been easier or more affordable.

Despite of common stereotypes of sailing as being exclusive or a non-affordable luxury, today more and more people discover their passion for this sport. Sailing communities in all countries offer chances to get involved with the sport on any level of concern – from a completely passive one by doing a cruise with a professional crew, to active sailing as a boat owner. Sailing has never been more famous than it is today and seems to go into a bright future!

THE GAME

Running

Sailing the boat within roughly 30 degrees either side of dead downwind is known as a run. This is the easiest point of sail in terms of comfort, but it can also be the most grievous. When sailing upwind, it is easy to stop the boat by heading into the wind; a sailor has no such easy out when running. Severe rolling is more likely as there is less rolling resistivity rendered by the sails, which are eased out. And loss of attention by the helmsman could lead the boat to gybe accidentally, causing injury to the boat or crew. Alternately, if there is a sudden increase in wind strength, the boat can round up very suddenly and heel excessively, often leading to a capsize in smaller boats. This is known as broaching.

Reaching

When the boat is traveling more or less vertical to the wind, this is known as reaching. A 'beam' reach is with the wind exactly at right angles to the boat, while a 'close' reach is halfway between beating and a beam reach, and a 'broad' reach is a little bit away from the wind. For most advance sailboats, that are boats with triangular sails, reaching is the quickest way to travel. The direction of the wind is ideal for reaching because it will maximize the lift generated on the sails in the forward direction of the boat, providing the best boat speed. Also when reaching, the boat can be steered precisely in the direction that is most desirable, and the sails can be trimmed for that direction. Reaching however may put the boat on a parallel course with the waves. When the waves are steep, it may be necessary to sail closer to the wind to avoid waves right away on the beam.

Sailing Upwind

A basic decree of sailing is that it is not possible to sail right away into the wind—at least not for long. Usually speaking, a boat can sail 45 degrees off the wind. When a boat is sailing this close to the wind, it is close-hauled or beating (beating to weather).

Subsequently a boat cannot sail right away into the wind, but the destination is often upwind, one can only get there by sailing close-hauled with the wind coming from the port side (the boat is on port tack), then tacking (turning the boat through the eye of the wind) and sailing with the wind coming from the starboard side (the boat is on starboard tack). By this way, it is possible to reach that destination right away upwind. For a yacht beating upwind to a mark at a distance upwind of one mile, it will cover a distance through the water of over 1.42 miles, if it can tack through an angle of 90 degrees. An old adage describes beating as sailing for double the distance at half the speed and thrice the discomfort.

How closely a boat can sail into the wind depends on the boat's design, sail trim, the sea state, and the wind speed, subsequently what the boat "sees" is the apparent wind, the vector sum of the real wind and the negation of the boat's own velocity. The evident wind speed is what the anemometer on top of the mast shows. The apparent wind angle while sailing close hauled will be less than the true wind angle. A good, advance sloop can sail within 25 degrees of the evident wind. An America's Cup racing sloop can sail within 16 degrees—under ideal conditions. Those figures might translate into 45 degrees and 36 degrees relative to the actual wind, depending upon boat speed.

Types of Sail and Layouts

A conventional modern yacht is technically known as a "Bermuda sloop" (occasionally a "Bermudan sloop"). A sloop is any boat that has a single mast and a headsail (usually a jib) in addition to the mainsail. The Bermuda designation refers to the fact that the sail, which has its forward edge (the "luff") versus the mast (the prime sail), is a sail roughly triangular in shape. Additionally, Bermuda sloops only have a single sail behind the mast.

Other types of sloops are gaff-rigged sloops and lateen sloops. Gaff-rigged sloops have quadrilateral mainsails with a gaff (a small expand) at their upper edge (the "head" of the sail). Gaff-rigged vessels may also have another sail, known as a topsail, above the gaff. Lateen sloops have triangular sails with the upper edge attached to a gaff, and the lower edge attached to the expand, and the expand and gaff are bind to each other via few type of hinge. It is also possible for a sloop to be square rigged (having large square sails like a Napoleonic Wars-era ship of the line). Note that a "sloop of war," in the naval sense, may well have more than one mast, and is not decently a sloop by the advance meaning.

If a boat has two masts, it may be a schooner, a ketch, or a yawl, if it is rigged fore-and-aft on all masts. A schooner may have any number of masts rendered the second from the front is the tallest (known as the "main mast"). In both a ketch and a yawl, the foremost mast is tallest, and thus the main mast, while the back mast is shorter, and known as the mizzen mast.

The difference between a ketch and a yawl is that in a ketch, the mizzen mast is forward of the rudderpost (the axis of rotation for the rudder), while a yawl has its mizzen mast behind the rudderpost. In advance parlance, a brigantine is a vessel whose forward mast is rigged with square sails, while her after mast is rigged fore-and-aft. A brig is a vessel with two masts both rigged square. As one gets into three or more masts the number of combinations rises and one gets barques, barquentines, and full rigged ships.A spinnaker is a large, full sail that is only employed when sailing off wind either reaching or downwind, to catch the maximum amount of wind.

MAJOR TOURNAMENTS

America's Cup

The America's Cup is the most esteemed regatta and match race in the sport of sailing, and the oldest active trophy in international sport, anteceding the Modern Olympics by 45 years. The sport attracts top sailors and yacht architects because of its long history and prestige. Though the most salient aspect of the regatta is its yacht races, it is also a test of boat design, sail design, fundraising, and management skills. The cup, primitively tendered as the Royal Yacht Squadron cup, is now named after the first yacht to win the trophy, the schooner America. The trophy persisted in the hands of the New York Yacht Club of the United States from 1852 or 1857 (when the syndicate that won the Cup donated the trophy to the club) until 1983 when the Cup was won by the competitor, Australia II of Australia, ending the longest winning streak in the history of sport. The skipper of Australia II, John Bertrand, was quoted in saying,

The America's Cup regatta is a challenge-driven yacht series that presently involves a best-of-nine series of match racing (a duel between two boats). Since the 1992 match, the regatta has been sailed with the International America's Cup Class (IACC) sloop, a monohull class.

Boats that conform to the IACC conventions commonly have a length of approximately 75 feet (23 m). Any challenger who meets the requirements specified in the Deed of Gift, which governs the regatta, has the right to challenge the yacht club that holds the Cup. Since 1983, Louis Vuitton has sponsored the Louis Vuitton Cup as a prize for the winner of the challenger selection series (which was inaugurated for the 1970 match). The America's Cup is a race between the winner of the Louis Vuitton Cup and the present holder. If the challenging team wins the cup, the cup's ownership is shifted from the defender's yacht club to the winning team's yacht club.

Sydney Hobart Yacht Race

The Sydney Hobart Yacht Race (occasionally referred to as the 'Bluewater Classic' in the Australian media) is hosted by the Cruising Yacht Club of Australia, commencing in Sydney, Australia on Boxing Day and ending up in Hobart. The race distance is approximately 630 nautical miles (1,170 km). The race is run in co-operation with the Royal Yacht Club of Tasmania.

The race was initially planned to be a cruise by Peter Luke and few friends who had constituted a club for those who enjoyed cruising as opposed to racing, however when a visiting British Royal Navy Officer, Captain John Illingworth, proposed it be made a race, the event was born.

The Sydney to Hobart Yacht Race has grown over the decades; subsequently the first race in 1945, to become one of the top three offshore yacht races in the world and it now draws in maxi yachts from all around the globe. The 2004 race marked the 60th running of the event. The present race record was set in 2005 by Wild Oats XI, which crossed the line in a time of 1 day, 18 hours, 40 minutes and 10 seconds.

Volvo Ocean Race

The Volvo Ocean Race (formerly the Whitbread Round the World Race) is a yacht race around the world, held in every three years. It is named after its present sponsor, Volvo.

Although the route is altered to accommodate several ports of call, the race typically departs Europe in September or October, and in recent years have had either 9 or 10 legs, with in-port races at many of the stopover cities. The next race begins in Alicante, Spain, on October 11, 2008. The route for the 2008-2009 races has been changed from former years to include stopovers in the Middle East and Asia for the first time. This latest route covers almost 39,000 nautical miles, will take over nine months to finish, and is expected to reach a cumulative TV audience of 2 billion worldwide.

Velux 5 Oceans Race

The Velux 5 Oceans Race is a round-the-world single-handed yacht race, sailed in stages. Its name comes from its prime sponsor, Velux, a Danish company. This 2006 race began in Bilbao, Spain, on October 22, 2006. Primitively known as the BOC Challenge, for the title sponsor BOC Gases, the first edition was in 1982. The race was afterwards re-named the Around Alone; the present race is known as the Velux 5 Oceans Race. This event is the longest race for individuals in any sport; though the course has changed over the years, the 2006 edition covered a route of 30,140 nautical miles (55,820 km).

ADMINISTRATIVE BODIES

International Sailing Federation

The International Sailing Federation (ISAF) is the world regulating body for the sport of sailing, specially yacht, dinghy, windsurfing and radio sailing racing. It is composed of "Member National Authorities" (MNA's) from almost every country in the world. The organisation dates from 1996, when the International Yacht Racing Union (IYRU) changed its name to the International Sailing Federation (ISAF).

ISAF is in charge of the Olympic Regatta, the sailing events held as part of the Summer Olympics. ISAF also is in charge of publishing the Racing Conventions of Sailing (RRS, formerly the Racing Conventions of Yachting) and editing the document after every Olympic Regatta based on the input of its MNA's.

The RRS, with few modifications by the MNA's (known as "prescriptions") are persued for the racing of any kind of vessel powered by the wind from remote-controlled sailboats and sailboards to multi-masted vessels, even ice-yachts are included in the scope of the RRS. Another obligation of the ISAF is to approve new classes of sailboats such as the Flying Junior dinghy or the 12-metre class. It also sanctioned subsisting classes, notably the International One Design, the first class it awarded International Classic Yacht status.

Cruising Yacht Club of Australia

The Cruising Yacht Club of Australia (CYCA), formed in 1944 is known as Australia's premier yacht club, and is acknowledged as the leader of ocean racing in the country. However, the club is best known as the host of the popular Sydney to Hobart Yacht Race. Situated in Rushcutters Bay, inner-east Sydney, CYCA facilities include a marina capable of berthing yachts up to 30 meters in length and five-star function rooms and restaurants. It presently has a membership of 2,500.

Inter-Scholastic Sailing Association

The Inter-Scholastic Sailing Association (ISSA) is the organization that serves as the regulating authority for all sailing competition between both public and private secondary schools throughout the United States. Though there are over 350 high schools throughout the United States that field varsity sailing teams, relatively few of these schools own their own boats. Rather, most schools have formed partnerships with community sailing organizations, colleges, or yacht clubs in order to gain access to a fleet of boats. Additionally, most high school sailing teams are involved with fundraising. Many high school sailors go on to take part in college sailing (regulated by the Intercollegiate Sailing Association). Both college varsity teams (such as Yale University) and club teams (such as the Vanderbilt Sailing Club) recruit high school sailors.

Inter-Collegiate Sailing Association

The Inter-Collegiate Sailing Association (ICSA) is a volunteer organization that serves as the regulating authority for all sailing competition at colleges and universities throughout the United States and in few parts of Canada.College sailing has been in uninterrupted subsistence for over a century and the first college sailing club was established in 1881 when the Yale Corinthian Yacht Club was formed in Branford, Connecticut. Organized intercollegiate racing started in 1928 between just a few schools and has subsequently grown to include 218 member programs (150 regular, 19 provisional, 49 associate), although not all continue to contend actively and consistently. While many colleges field fully-funded varsity teams, the majority of programs contend as club teams (although various club teams, such as the University of Vermont and the University of Rhode Island maintain top-level programs despite their sub-varsity status).

FAMOUS PLAYERS

Mike Golding

Mike Golding was born on 27 August 1960, he is an English yachtsman. He is one of the few yachtsmen to have raced round the world non-stop in both ways. He held the individual record for sailing round the world westabout (the most challenging direction for circumnavigation) between 1994 and 2000. Golding, who is a member of Royal Southampton Yacht Club, is the eponymous co-founder of the commercial company Mike Golding Yacht Racing Ltd, a professional and competitive company whose goals are to contend and win on the water and to deliver. His partner in this venture is Jorgen Philip-Sorensen.

Golding led the team Group 4 to second place in the British Steel Challenge in 1992-1993. He did one better in the next edition the BT Global Challenge 1996-1997, taking first place with a new team of amateur sailors, once again onboard Group 4. Golding came seventh in the 2000–2001 Vendée Globe solo non-stop round the world race having lost seven days to the dismasting of his Open 60, again known as Group 4. His present Open 60 campaign is sponsored by Ecover, a Belgian ecological cleaning products company which has sponsored his team since 2001. In 2004 he won the IMOCA World Championship and successfully defended his title the following year, in which he also won the 2005 FICO World Championship. In the 2004 Vendée Globe, Golding finished up third despite losing his keel, an extremely serious accident which has caused boats in former Vendée Globe races to overturn almost immediately on the last day of the race. He sailed the last 50 miles with a tiny sailplan to keep the boat upright.

Philippe Jeantot

Philippe Jeantot began his career as a deep sea diver, working on oil rigs; at one time he jointly held the record for deep diving, at 501 metres (1,644 ft). He turned interested in sailing after reading Bernard Moitessier's book The Long Way; having learned to sail, he made himself a 13.5 metre (44 ft) steel ketch, planning to sail single-handed around the world. After cruising for two years, he entered the first edition of the BOC Challenge (now known as the VELUX 5 Oceans Race) in the year 1982; he won the race, and broke the previous record for a single-handed circumnavigation with a time of 159 days, 2 hours.

In 1984, Jeantot entered the OSTAR, sailing in a new catamaran, Credit Agricole II. He was impelled to retire after a capsize, but saved the boat and entered the 1984 Quebec—St. Malo race, in which he set a new 24-hour speed record. In 1985, he had success in the Grand Prix de Brest, La Baule and Round Europe races. In 1986 he once again entered the BOC Challenge, sailing Credit Agricole III, and was again victorious.

In 1989, Jeantot established a new, single-handed, non-stop, round-the-world race, the Vendée Globe. He entered the race in Crédit Agricole IV, and finished up in fourth place.

Alex Thomson

Alex Thomson was born on april 18, 1974 in Bangor, Wales, he is a British yachter. Alex Thomson was helped early in his sailing career by Sir Keith Mills, the British businessman who ran London's triumphant bid to host the 2012 Olympic Games and Paralympic Games and is presently working with British America's Cup campaign TEAMORIGIN. With Mills backing, Thomson broke into the professional solo sailing circuit at a young age.

He is the youngest captain ever to won a round-the-world yacht race in the year 1998-1999 Clipper Race. He is an around the world solo sailor, and holds the 24-hour world speed sailing record for solo mono-hulls (468 nm at an average speed of 19.5 kts).

Sponsored by Hugo Boss he participated in the Vendee Globe 2004/05 but was pressured to retire after damage to the carbon fitting that is attached to the deck.

REFERENCES

Affeld, K., K. Schichl, and A. Ziemann. "Assessment of Rowing, New York, 1967.

Blades". Thesis, BS, MIT Dept. Mechanical Engineering, 1993.

Cameron, A. "Some Mechanical Aspects of Rowing". Rowing- A, 14, Suppl. 1, pp S39-S41, 1993.

Churbuck, D. C. "The Book of Rowing". Overlook Press, Woodstock, NY, 1988.

Efficiency". International Journal of Sports Medicine. Vol.

Herberger, Dr. Ernst, et al. "Rowing (Rudern)". Sport Books

Ink, Church Hill, MD, USA, 1993.

McMahon, Thomas A. "Rowing: A Similarity Analysis". Science.

Scientific Approach, J.P.G. Williams, ed. A.S. Barnes, Vol. 173, 1971.

Young, Ken. "Rowing Physics". Paper, USRA Convention, Seattle, WA, 1991.

17

Shooting

Shooting is an arousing and absorbing activity and National Shooting Week gives you the chance to try both clay pigeon shooting (with a shotgun) and air rifle shooting. Certain clubs and ranges will take arranged groups to shoot targets with fullbore rifles but this is subject to Home Office legislation. Whether you are a 'first timer' or whether you have already had a certain measure of experience, National Shooting Week will put you in touch with a shooting club or venue near you.

Great Britain has a fantabulous track record of international shooting success, whether at an Olympic, Commonwealth or European level. But the best thing about shooting is that it is not an exclusive sport and it is a great leveller! Across the country, persons from all walks of life enjoy a safe and agitating hobby that can be exceedingly honouring. Shooting is also one of the few sports that offer an actual chance for disabled sportsmen and women to contend on an equal footing to their colleague able-bodied competitors.

Clay pigeon shooting is an outdoor sport, while air rifle shooting may take place either outdoors or within an indoor range, as a general decree avoid bulky or loose fitting jackets, as these make it harder for anyone to fit the stock of the gun comfortably into your shoulder.

Whenever a gun is fired there is recoil which is transferred to the shoulder through the stock of the gun. However, with the gun and cartridge combinations utilised in training, the recoil is very slight, and your coach will make sure that the stock of the gun is tucked tightly into shoulder. That way, one is unlikely to notice the recoil when you fire a shot.

Shooting for the Disabled

Shooting for the handicapped has been a Paralympics sport since the first Paralympics games in 1964. Paralympics competition shooting is separated into rifle and pistol events. Air pistols and air rifles are shot over 10 meters and.22 caliber rifles over fifty meters.

The sport is open to all athletes with a physical impairment, with two classifications of competition depending on the degree of disablement - SH1 (do not use a shooting stand) and SH2 (uses a shooting stand). Most disabilities are eligible, for instance; amputee, spina bifida, spinal cord injured, mild cerebral palsy and muscle or bone degenerative diseases with at least 20% loss of force. Shooting utilises a functional classification system which enables athletes from various disability classes with the same powers to contend jointly. There are men's, women's and mixed events at the Paralympics Games.

Rifle Shooting

- The four Rifle ISSF shooting events (including two Olympic events) comprise of long-time target shooting from distances of 10, 50 and 300 m.
- The two Running Target ISSF shooting events comprise of rapid shooting at a target that moves sideways from distances of 10 and 50 m.

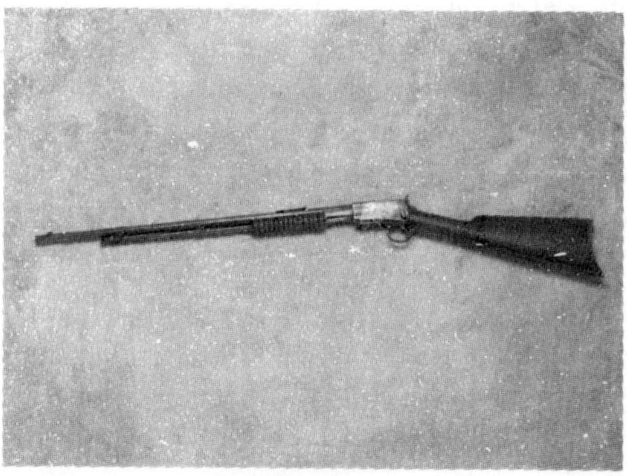

Fig. Rifle

Handgun Shooting

- Advanced pentathlon includes timed shooting with an air pistol as the first of its five parts.
- The six Pistol ISSF shooting events (including four Olympic events) comprise of both precision and rapid-fire target shooting from distances of 10, 25, and 50 meters. In the UK it is not possible to exercise for some of the Olympic events following the Firearms (Amendment) (No. 2) Act 1997.

- The CISM Rapid Fire match is alike to the ISSF 25 m Rapid Fire Pistol event.

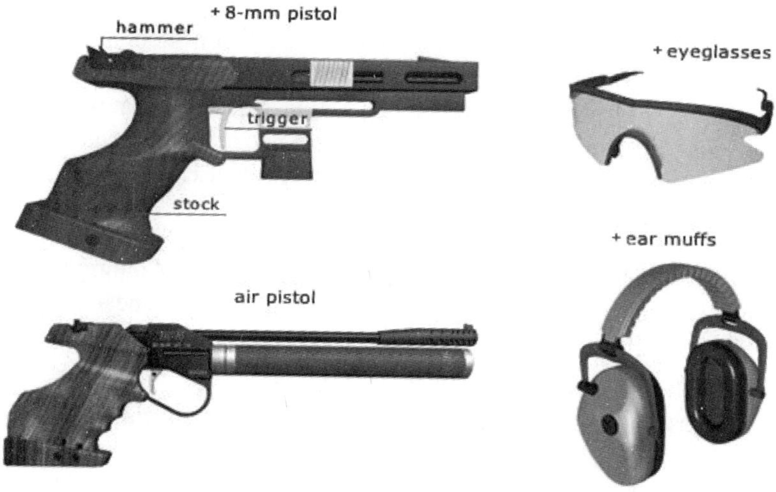

Shotgun Shooting

- Cowboy Action shooting also may involve shotguns.
- The three Shotgun ISSF shooting events (currently all Olympic) are based on quick reaction to clay targets thrown by a machine.
- Other shotgun sports with (at least partial) international recognition include Sporting Clays, providing more fluctuation than the standard ISSF events, and Down-The-Line. Five Stand is also a shotgun shooting sport alike to skeet, but with a lot of target variety. There are five stations, or stands. At each station there is usually a card that lets the shooter know the sequence of birds he or she will be shooting at.

Action Shooting

Action Shooting is a generic term applicable to untraditional shooting sports, usually characterised by fast movement within each shooting stage, where most or all commences with holster draw in the case of handguns. Examples include 'practical pistol' as in the International Practical Shooting Confederation (IPSC), the United States Practical Shooting Association (USPSA) and the International Defensive Pistol Association (IDPA), as well as cowboy action shooting, Action Air gun

(AAG), and 'three-gun' events noted below. The last mentioned two involve use of rifles, handguns, and shotguns within the same event.

However, fast AND accurate shooting as contradicted to just fast shooting - requiring less physical movement than IPSC, IDPA, and Cowboy Action Shooting, also belongs to the action shooting category owing to the rapidity of firing and compulsory holster draw. Discipline such as National Rifle Association's Action Pistol, also known as the Bianchi Cup, is one example where extreme accuracy fired within tight, predetermined time bounds is more dominant than raw speed.

Target Shooting for the Blind

Target shooting for the blind was first seen in this Country in 1948 when some fairly basic gear was installed at St Dunstan's near Brighton. This gear disappeared several years ago and apart from some old photographs very little is known about it.

In 1994 the National Small-bore Rifle Association obtained a sighting arrangement made by an Austrian Company addressed Swarovski Optik which enables blind shooters to accomplish a level of accuracy very close to that of sighted shooters.

To the casual observer the sight, which is designed for use on an air rifle at a range of 10m looks like a traditional telescope sight and is mounted on the rifle in the same way. However, that is where the similarity ends. The sight is designed to accumulate and measure the level of light reflected from the target using a photo-electric cell which is then converted into sound. The midpoint of the target is magnificent white and then moving outwards from the centre progressively darker levels of grey are encountered until off the target is matt black. The closer to the centre of the target you are aiming the greater the level of light mirrored and hence the higher the frequency of sound which is heard by the shooter via a pair of headphones. The sights are adjustable in the regular way to modify the mean point of impact.

For the system to work effectively it has been found that the target requires exceedingly bright illumination. A 50w 12v halogen lamp with a very narrow beam angle of 10° is ideal. This is sufficiently bright to work in all surrounding light levels and there is no need to have the area surrounding the target painted matt black as was originally the case.

Apart from the special sight all that the shooter requires is a helper to ensure safety and to help them "find the target". The rest is up to them! A sighted shooter doesn't seem to benefit using this arrangement,

In fact the opposite may be the case since the blind shooter will not be confused by visual images and may quite possibly have a better evolved sense of hearing. Recent years have seen a enormous increase in the number of centres where these facilities exist with 20 such centres presently offering shooting for the blind and visually impaired all over the country. Few of them are:

- 8th Warwicks (Stratford) Home Guard Rifle Club - Nr Stratford Upon Avon
- Beccles Rifle Club - Beccles, Suffolk
- Bedfordshire Small-Bore Shooting Association - Thorn, Dunstable
- Bon Accord Rifle Club - Aberdeen
- Carmarthenshire Disabled Air Targeters - St Clears, Carmarthenshire
- Chippenham Rifle Club - Chippenham, Wiltshire
- Felixstowe Rifle Club - Felixstowe, Suffolk

HISTORY

Shooting has been played as a sport since very long time. Now it is played on the international level and also become an Olympic sport.

Concerned over poor marksmanship during the American Civil War, veteran Union officers Col. William C. Church and Gen. George Wingate constituted the National Rifle Association in 1871 for the aim of promoting and encouraging rifle shooting on a "scientific" basis. In 1872, with fiscal help from New York State, a site on Long Island, the Creed Farm, was bought for the aim of building up a rifle range. Named Creedmoor, the range opened in 1872, and became the site of the first National Matches until New York politics pressured the NRA to move the matches to Sea Girt, New Jersey. The fame of the National Matches shortly forced the event to be moved to its present, much larger location: Camp Perry. In 1903, the U.S. Congress made the National Board for the Promotion of Rifle exercise (NBPRP), an advisory board to the Secretary of the Army, with a almost identical charter to the NRA. The NBPRP (now titled the Civilian Marksmanship Program) also participates in the National Matches at Camp Perry.

In 1903, the NRA started to constitute rifle clubs at all major colleges, universities and military academies. By 1906, youth programs were in full swing with more than 200 boys contending in the National Matches. Today, more than one million youth take part in shooting sports events and associated programs through groups such as 4-H, the Boy Scouts of America, the American Legion, U.S. Jaycees, NCAA, the Scholastic Clay Target Program, National Guard Bureau, ROTC and JROTC. These programs have all continued to thrive despite political pressures to disband. The success of these programs is often attributed to a stress on safety and education that has resulted in an unprecedented scholastic and collegiate athletic safety record.

French pistol champion and founder of the advanced Olympics, Pierre de Coubertin, took part in a lot of these betimes competitions. This reality for sure contributed to the inclusion of five shooting events in the 1896 Olympics. Over the years, the events have been varied a number of times in order to keep up with technology and social standards. For example, targets that erstwhile resembled humans or animals in their shape and size have are now a circular shape in order to avoid affiliating the sport with any form of violence. At the same time, some events have been dropped and new ones have been summed. The 2004 Olympics featured three shooting disciplines (rifle, pistol and shotgun) where athletes contended for 51 medals in 10 men's and 7 women's events slightly fewer than the early Olympic schedule.

The Olympic Games continue to provide the shooting sports with its greatest public relations chance. The sport has always relished the distinction of presenting the first medals of the Games. Internationally, the International Shooting Sport Federation (ISSF) has oversight of all Olympic shooting events worldwide, while National regulating Body's (NGB) administer the sport within each country.

Having primitively constituted shooting as an organised sport, the NRA was the obvious choice to administer the United States involvement in the Olympic Games. The NRA dutifully managed and financially supported international and conventional shooting sports (ie, National Matches) for over 100 years until the formation of USA Shooting.

Because of its long heritage and broad appeal, the shooting sports are delighted by a large number of players around the world. In recent years, however, the shooting sports have become progressively threatened by social and governmental reforms. In some countries, voters have announced their disapproval toward the private ownership and possession of handguns. This is usually motivated by the perception that handguns are connected with violent crime besides sportsmanship. Some governments, such as the British, have enacted confining gun control legislation that right away affects the shooting sports.

More latterly, a rise in the number of concealed carry permit-holders in the US has led to a surge in interest in several handgun competitions that foster defensive skills, accuracy drills, and personal protection tactics.

The first World Shooting Championships were fired in 1897, when Lyon, France's shooting club organized an international 300-meter rifle match to celebrate its 25th anniversary. Women's events were first instituted at the 1958 Championships, and today World Championships for men and women in all disciplines are fired every four years. At the 1994 Championships in Milan 102 individual and team pistol, rifle, running target, and shotgun events will be contested.

The Emergence of National Federations and the UIT As shooting traditions devel0ped in the V.S. and overseas, many national federations were established in the mid to late 19th century. The National Rifle Association of America (NRA) was founded in 1871 by Colonel William Church and Captain George Wingate of the New York National Guard. The U.S. Revolver Association, founded in 1900, actually selected, trained, and financed Olympic pistol teams through the 1936 Games. The NRA then assumed leadership and developmental responsibilities for pistol, rifle and, beginning in 1960, shotgun shooting in the U.S.

In 1978, the U.S. Olympic Committee selected the NRA as the sole national governing body for Olympic-style shooting in the United States. The NRA's International Shooting Sports division has been designated to fulfill this responsibility from its headquarters office at the Colorado Springs Olympic Training Center. However, organizations such as the Amateur Trapshooting Association(ATA), the Pacific International Trapshooting Association (PITA), and the National Skeetshooting Association (NSSA) actively govern and develop American-style trap and skeet shooting in this country.

History of Shooting in India

In India shooting sport was once the preserve of Maharajas of erstwhile princely states. Expertise with the gun was regarded an necessary part of the royal grooming process and as such some of the leading lights of Indian shooting sport were scions of royal families. Shooting sport in India took a unionised form with the establishment of the National Rifle Association of India in 1951.

THE GAME

Technique and Safety

Shooting method differs depending on factors like the type of weapon utilised, the distance to and nature of the target, the needed precision and the available time. The prone position, the kneeling position and the standing position offer dissimilar amounts of support for the shooter.

The utmost consideration, and one which takes precedence over everything else, is safety. Like many activities such as mountain climbing, skiing, or sky-diving, there is an factor of danger involved. And particularly here, this danger demands a sober understanding and respect for firearms and the particular conventions for the safe handling of them. This is combined by the fact that the danger can easily extend beyond the players.

Safety Guidelines

Many of the shooting conventions and ordinances in the UK have come forth as a result of safety considerations. Because of this, the UK has fewer shooting accidents than a lot of other countries (as long as all shooters are aware of them and make a conscious effort to stick to them whenever they're involved in shooting).

Fig. Target

One of the most important safety conventions centers on loaded guns. It is important that you never point a loaded gun in the direction of another person, even if you do not intend to shoot. The same is true of an unloaded gun as it can still be extremely dangerous. Guns should be offloaded for the majority of the time, except for just before you're ready to shoot.

Types of shooting traps

Double Barrel: Double Barrel shall be shot with two barrels allowed and a score on either barrel to be of equal value.

Single Barrel: The challenger is allowed to load one cartridge only in the gun.

Points Scoring: During an event a hit with the first barrel shall be called and marked "1", a hit with the second barrel shall be called and marked '2". A miss with both barrels shall be marked "zero". At the closing of the event the "1s" shall be valued as 3 points and be added to the 2s and 0s to give a total for the event.

Double Rise: Double rise shall be shot squad system and addressed by the referee "one - one" or "lost - one" or "one - lost" or "lost - lost" whichever the case may be, each target to consider one point. A challenger must shoot at a complete pair pf targets on every juncture. Each target broken by the competitor's shot shall score one point. Two shots must not be fired at either target.

Mixed Targets: A mixed target event shall be a combination of a series of double barrel, single barrel, points score and double rise targets, shot in any order. Shot squad arrangement under conventions applicable to the appropriate section with target numbers and shooting marks in accordance with the suitable championship.

Jury

The Management shall appoint a jury of three. The jury shall be nominated from (in order) members of the Executive conventions Sub-Committee, Executive Committee, decrees Supervisors, Referee Examiners, Qualified Referees on the grounds, to examine the matter.

Should the competitor's appeal be upheld, his deposit shall be returned and the correct ruling shall be applied to the target appealed against. Should the appeal be forbade the deposit shall be confiscate and paid to the club related. There shall be no appeal against a referee's decision in regard to whether a target is legal or whether it has been missed.

For major ISU competition the jury shall be nominated from (in order) UIT Judges, Referee Examiners, Executive Committee Members, conventions Supervisors, and Qualified Referees on the grounds. All members of the appointed jury are eligible to contend.

MAJOR TOURNAMENTS

Olympic Games

The Olympic Games is an international multi-sport event established for both summer and winter games. There have been two generations of the Olympic Games; the first were theAncient Olympic Games held at Olympia, Greece. The second, known as the Modern Olympic Movement, were first held in1896, in Athens, Greece. The modern Olympics feature the Summer Games and Winter Games. The Paralympic and Youth Olympic Games are variations on the Modern Olympic Movement. Shooting is a well known sport played in the Olympics. Several players from around the world takes part in Olympic.

ISSF World Shooting Championships

The World Championships were accommodated annually from 1897 to 1931, with the exclusion of the years 1915-1920 (interruption by World War I) and 1926. From 1933 to 1949, they were held biennially, though the 1941-1945 competitions were called off (again, because of world war). The current schedule, with large World Championships only every four years, was adapted in 1950.

Originally, 300 m Rifle (in several positions) was the only discipline on the programme, despite numerous other events having been included in the Olympics. In 1900, 50 m Pistol was added. This programme was in use until 1929, the only alteration being the addition of 300 m Army Rifle, with mandatory use of the host nation's army weapon, in 1911. The 1929 championships in Stockholm saw the addition of most of the persisting events from the Olympic programme: 100 m Running Deer, 50 m Rifle and Trap. 25 m Rapid Fire Pistol had to wait until 1933. Instantly after World War II, 300 m Standard Rifle (with more strict conventions than 300 m Rifle but less than 300 m Army Rifle) was added along with 25 m Center-Fire Pistol and Skeet.

ISSF World Cup

The ISSF World Cup was brought in by the International Shooting Sport Federation in 1986 to render a consistent system for qualification to the Olympic shooting competitions. It still is carried out in the Olympic shooting events, with four competitions per year in each event. For the best shooters there is since 1988 a World Cup Final.

All-India Police Shooting Championship

It was Border Security Force (BSF) all the way on the penultimate day of the 2nd All-India Police Shooting Championship underway at the BSF's Reoti Range here.

The Force's Vishnu Saste pocketed gold by scoring 1148/1200 in the 50 m Free Rifle event. In the team event, the BSF won with 3,395 points.

Once again, the BSF's Govindaram struck gold in the 300 m Big Bore Free Rifle event by scoring 945/1200. The team event also went to the BSF with 2746/3600.

ADMINISTRATIVE BODIES

International Shooting Sport Federation (ISSF)

International shooting competitions had commenced already with Shooting at the 1896 Summer Olympics, and the first World Championships were held in 1897. However, there was no regulating body until 1907, when eight national federations established the union, soon to be called Union International de Tir (UIT) (French for the International Shooting Union and occasionally referred to in English as the ISU). This was the name until the current name was adapted in 1998.

Over the years, the ISSF has distanced itself from connotations of non-sportive uses of guns. This has included shifting from human-shaped targets to circular ones. The only official ISSF target still portraying a live creature is the wild boar image used in 50 m Running Target.

It is an organization that regulates international shooting sports. While far from the only such organisation, it is the one that is a member of the International Olympic Committee and so it is in charge of the Olympic shooting events. Not all ISSF shooting events are Olympic, however. The organization, with 154 national member federations, has its headquarters in Munich, Germany. Its present-day President is Olegario Vázquez Raña and its Secretary General is Wolfgang Schreiber.

National Rifle Association

The National Rifle Association, or NRA, is a non-profit group dedicated to the protection of the Second Amendment of the United States Bill of Rights and the promotion of firearm ownership rights, marksmanship, firearm safety, and the protection of hunting and self-defense in the United States. It was constituted in New York in 1871 by William Conant Church and George Wood Wingate as the American Rifle Association; its first President was previous Senator and renowned Civil War Union Army General Ambrose Burnside.

The NRA sponsors firearm safety training courses, as well as marksmanship events featuring shooting skills and sports. The NRA is occasionally said to be the single most powerful lobbying organization in the United States.

International Practical Shooting Confederation

IPSC was established at a conference held in Columbia, Missouri, in May 1976. Practical shooting enthusiasts from around the world took part, making a constitution and establishing the decrees regulating the sport. Jeff Cooper served as the first IPSC President.

While IPSC is an international organization, countries have their own organizations under the IPSC umbrella. In the United States, this is the United States Practical Shooting Association (USPSA). In the United Kingdom, this is the United Kingdom Practical Shooting Association (UKPSA).

National Rifle Association of India

The National Rifle Association of India (NRAI) is the central administrative body for the promotion of shooting sport in India. The NRAI was established in 1951 with G. V. Maviankar, the first Speaker of Lok Sabha, as its founder president.

The NRAI is related to the International Shooting Sports Federation (ISSF), the apex body in shooting sport. Digvijay Singh, Minister of State for External affairs is the current president of NRAI.

The NRAI, which has a network of 46 State Rifle Associations/ Units from all over India, holds national level competitions in Rifle, Pistol and Shotgun events. India has as well played host to a slew of international shooting events like the ISSF World Cup and the first Commonwealth Shooting Championship at Delhi in 1995.

The Indian shooting association deserves kudos for the remarkable betterment in the standard of the game in India. It played an active role in the building of the Dr. Karni Singh Shooting Ranges, New Delhi, which was the first range in the country built as per International standards.

FAMOUS PLAYERS

Cai Yalin

Cai Yalin was born on September 3, 1977 in Chengde, Hebei, is a male Chinese sports shooter. He won the 2000 Summer Olympics in the 10m air rifle (beating the Olympic Record of 695.7pts with 696.4pts).

- 1997 National Games - 3rd
- 1998 World Championships - 7th
- 1998 Bangkok Asian Games - 1st 10m air rifle individual, 2nd 10m air rifle team
- 1998 National Shooting Series - 1st (NR)
- 1998 World Championships - 7th
- 2000 Sydney Olympic Games - 1st 10m air rifle (696.4pts, OR)
- 2002 Pusan Asian Games - 1st 10m air rifle team (1788pts, WR) & 50m free rifle team (3472pts, AR)

Zhu Qinan

He was born on November 15, 1984 in Wenzhou and is a male Chinese sport shooter who won the gold medal at the 2004 Athens Olympics in the Men's 10 m Air Rifle event and a silver medal at the 2008 Beijing Olympics in the Men's 10 m Air Rifle event. Zhu presently is learning at Zhejiang University.

Zhu commenced shooting training at Wenzhou Sports School in 1999. From there, in February 2002, he joined the Zhejiang state shooting team. Zhu linked up with the national shooting team on December 14, 2003. At the time of his Olympic triumph, he was still a junior, and his qualification round score of 599 was an equaled junior world record. He repeated this accomplishment at the 2004 ISSF World Cup Final in Bangkok, which he also won. He has since then won several ISSF World Cup competitions in 10 m Air Rifle. His best result in 50 m Rifle is a bronze medal from the 2004 Asian Championships. Zhu is 5'11" tall and weighs 148 pounds.

David Kostelecký

He was Born on May 12, 1975 in Brno, Czechoslovakia and is a male Czech sports shooter. He won the gold medal in the Men's Trap event at the 2008 Summer Olympics. He also ended up second in the 2006 ISSF World Cup final.

Pang Wei

Born on 1986-07-19 in Baoding, Hebei, a male Chinese sports shooter, won both the 2006 ISSF World Shooting Championships and the 2008 Olympic Games in 10 m Air Pistol.

Pang Wei won the gold medal for Men's 10 m air pistol which was China's first gold medal in shooting during the Games. He was presented 2,000,000 RMB (USD$292,600) from Chinese sponsors.

His achievements:

- 2006 World Championships - 1st 10m air pistol;
- 2007 World Cup Final - 3rd 10m air pistol;
- 2007 National Intercity Games - 1st 50m free pistol
- 2008 Summer Olympics - 10 m air pistol

Abhinav Bindra

Abhinav Bindra made a junior world record score of 597/600 in 2001 Munich World Cup and won bronze; gold in 2002 Manchester Commonwealth Games; became the first Indian shooter to win a World Championship gold; Rajiv Gandhi Khel Ratna in 2001. Abhinav Bindra is the most brilliant champion among a Modern breed of talented Indian shooters. Born on September 28, 1983, Bindra is quite often criticised for not delivering on the promise he showed as a child prodigy.

Coming from an affluent family and with the luxury of an indoor range in his backyard, Bindra proved to an early bird and, at 15, was the youngest player at the 1998 Commonwealth Games. Bindra shot into limelight by winning a bronze in the 2001 Munich World Cup with a new junior world record score of 597/600.

In the 2002 Manchester Commonwealth Games, contending in his pet Air rifle event, Bindra won Gold in the Pairs event and Silver in the independent event. During a purple patch, Bindra won six gold medals at several international meets in the European Circuit in 2001. He was conferred the Rajiv Gandhi Khel Ratna Award for the year 2001. He freshly has won a gold medal in Beijing Olympics 2008. This was his biggest accomplishment.

Rajyavardhan Singh Rathore

The soft-spoken Rathore, born on January 29, 1970, brought the entire nation to its feet with that amazing performance in Men's Double Trap event. The event has already become a division of Indian sporting folklore for the absolute delight it brought to this nation of one billion people.

Olympic silver medal in the year 2004 Athens Games; won the gold in the individual and team events in Men's double trap at the Asian Clay Shooting championships held in 2005 in Bangkok; double trap team gold in 2005 Commonwealth Shooting Championships; Rajiv Gandhi Khel Ratna Award in 2004; Ati Vishisht Seva Medal. Rajyavardhan Singh Rathore has been the poster boy Indian shooting ever since he won the first individual Olympic silver medal for India in the 2004 Athens Games.

Rathore has not permitted success and adulation goes into his head and kept delivering his good performance at the international level. He won the gold in the individual and team events in Men's double trap at the 2005 Asian Clay shooting championships at Bangkok. In 2005 Commonwealth Shooting Championships in Melbourne, Rajyawardhan Rathore was the member of the winning Indian team in the double trap event.

A grateful nation has honoured Rathore with some of the most esteemed awards of the land. He was bestowed the Rajiv Gandhi Khel Ratna Award, the highest sporting honour in India, for the year 2004. A Lt. Col. in the Indian Army who fought terrorists in Kashmir, Rathore was bestowed the Ati Vishisht Seva Medal (AVSM), a gallantry award for service presented by the government.

Anjali Bhagwat

She won four gold medals at the 2002 Manchester Commonwealth Games; Rajiv Gandhi Khel Ratna Award in 2002. In a sport like shooting traditionally regarded the fiefdom of men, Anjali Bhagwat emerged as an ace shooter like a whiff of fresh air. Anjali's achievements have inspired many a young woman to take up the sport of shooting.

Anjali's first brush with shooting happened during her stint as a cadet in the National Cadet Corps (NCC). In 1990, under the guidance of Sanjay Chakravarthy, Anjali clinched her maiden national title and since then there has been no looking back.

In the 2000 Sydney Olympics, competing as a last-minute wildcard Anjali put up a spirited effort to become only the second Indian woman to reach the Olympic final and ended at seventh position. At the 2002 Manchester Commonwealth Games, Anjali grabbed four gold medals at the 10 meter Air Rifle and 50 meter Rifle 3-position events.

Jaspal Rana

Jaspal Rana is one of the most prominent shooters India has ever gave rise. Born on June 28, 1976, Jaspal lent a glamorous touch to the sober game of shooting both with his astonishing accomplishments and his good looks. Rana made his national debut at the age of 12 when he grabbed a silver medal at the 31st National Shooting Championship at Ahmedabad in 1988. Six years later Rana shot into national prominence when, contending in Standard Pistol, he won a gold at the 46th World Shooting Championship (Junior Section) with a world record score at Milan in Italy in 1994.

Since then Rana has won honours galore in domestic and international events, a lot of times rewriting record books. He twice equaled the world record score of 590 points in Centre Fire Pistol event, first at the National Shooting Championship in 1995 at Coimbatore and then at the National Games held at Bangalore in 1997 where he was declared the Best Sportsman.Although Centre Fire Pistol is Rana's pet event, he did well in Air Pistol, Standard Pistol, Free Pistol and Rapid Fire Pistol as well. He was bestowed the Arjuna Award in 1994.

REFERENCES

Antal, Dr. Laslo. *Competitive Pistol Shooting*. West Yorkshire: EP Publishing Ltd., 1983.

Chandler, John. *The Target Gun book of Pistol Coaching*. Worcs: Peterson Publishing Company Ltd., 1983.

Freeman, P.C. *Modern Pistol Shooting*. London: Faber and Faber, 1968.

Freeman, P.C. *Target Pistol Shooting: Eliminating the Variables*. London: Faber and Faber, 1981.

Herrigel, Eugen. *Zen in the Art of Archery*. New York: Vintage Books, 1999.

Kushner, Kenneth. *One Arrow, One Life: Zen, Archery, Enlightenment*. Boston: Tuttle Publishing, 2000.

Leathdale, Frank and Paul Leatherdale. *Successful Pistol Shooting*. Wiltshire: The Crowood Press, 1995.

Moran, Aidan P. *The Psychology of Concentration in Sports Performers: A Cognitive Analysis*. East Sussex, UK: Psychology Press, 1996.

18

Skiing

Snow skiing is a group of sports utilising skis as primary gear. Skis are employed in conjunction with boots that connect to the ski with use of a binding. Though snowboarding shares the usual characteristics of skiing sports, it evolved from surfing and skateboarding and so is not regarded a type of skiing. The posture assumed in snowboarding is a side on action whereas the skiing posture is chiefly front facing.

Skiing can be grouped into two usual categories. Nordic skiing is the oldest category and includes sport that evolved from skiing as done in Scandinavia. Nordic style bindings attach at the toes of the skier's boots, but not at the heels. Alpine skiing includes sports that developed from skiing as done in the Alps. Alpine bindings bind at both the toe and the heel of the skier's boots. As with many disciplines, such as Telemark skiing, there is few crossover. However, binding style and history tend to dictate whether a style is regarded Nordic or Alpine. Thus, in view of its lack of a locking heel, and its roots in Telemark, Norway, Telemark is usually regarded a Nordic discipline.

Types of Skiing

Alpine Skiing: The term "skiing" ordinarily refers to alpine skiing where one visits a ski resort, leverages a lift ticket, dons cold-weather clothing, skis, ski boots and often ski poles, and embarks on a chairlift, gondola lift, or other means of mechanical uphill transport. Upon reaching the summit, the skier disembarks from the ski lift and travels downhill, propelled by gravity, normally along a marked route known as a piste, "run," "trail," or "slope". Most ski resorts use mechanical gear to "groom," or pack down and smooth, the snow surface on certain ski trails. Alpine skiing evolved in the Alps starting in 1889. In Winterthur, Switzerland, Odd Kjelsberg may have been the first person in the Alps to try skiing. Previous to this time, the predominate Alpine winter sport had been tobogganing.

Alpine Freestyle: This kind of skiing could be known as acrobatics on skis. Alpine freestyle was pioneered by Stein Eriksen in 1962. It evolved in the 1970s into a style known as Hotdogging. More recently Alpine freestyle has evolved into the present style known as Jib skiing or freestyle skiing, a new style of skiing that began in the late 1990s. In this type of skiing, skiers use jumps also known as kickers, or rails to do urban style aerial tricks.

Downhill: This is conventionally the most esteemed and exhilarating of the alpine events. It comprises of a single downhill course which takes between ninety seconds and two minutes to complete. Gates are employed to help contenders maintain a straight line and a safe speed, as well as avoid any major obstacles. The chief goal is to maintain the highest speed throughout course, especially on the straights. However, negotiating the course without losing balance or line is also scored, which normally reflects the speed at which the whole course is finished. The high speeds mean that the smallest unregularities in the course can cause the skier to become airborne. This is not desirable as it can cause the skier to lose their line and balance, and landing exerts enormous force on the skis which brings down velocity. Riders therefore aim to stay as close to the ground as possible at all times to reduce the effect on their time.

Back Country Skiing: It is also known as Nordic touring. In the Alps where skiers can easily ski from area to area, Randonée and backcountry skiing are indistinguishable. In North America however, where chairlifts either aren't permited or are impractical for touring, skiers typically use Nordic style gear which is more suitable for skiing up-hill. The heels of the bindings invariably remain free, unlike Randonee bindings which can be locked down.

Cross-Country Skiing: Cross-country skiing takes its name from a type of ski race that is one third up, one third down, and one third flat. The name distinguishes it from other types of ski races and competition such as downhill racing, slalom racing, and Nordic jumping. Cross-country races can be either freestyle or classic. In freestyle racing, any technique is permited as long as it is human powered and on skis. In a classic race, skating methods are prohibited.

Ski Jumping: This is one of the straightforward types of competition, but one of the most daunting. Skiers descend a ramp and then effort to cover the longest distance possible without conceding points for style. Olympic events take place on a 90 or 120 metre hill, with a distance line set at 90 and 120 metres respectively from the point of take-off. Each contender gains 1.8 points for each metre they travel in the air beyond this point, and loses points if they do not cover this distance. Style points depend on steady flight, balance, control and the landing, which must be a telemark skiing position with one foot leading the other.

Technique and equipments have greatly changed magnitude the distances achieved over the last few decades. Most skiers adopt a V-Line with their skis in the air, the technique attributed to Sweden's Jan Boklov in 1985. Ski length must be exact to maximise aerodynamics; the optimal being 1.46 multiplied by the skier's height. Clothing is also designed to maximise upward lift and sustain the time in the air. This is attained by applying a spongy material that "inflates" while the skier is airborne.

Adaptive Skiing: It is done by individuals with physical disablements. Adaptations to standard ski gear or accompaniment by a non-disabled guide has enabled individuals with amputations, spinal injuries, TBI, deafness and visual impairments to ski, and in few cases, even race.

Telemark Skiing: Telemark skiers use flexible ski boots, either leather or plastic, and do not have their heels locked to the skis. Alpine skiers use stiffer plastic, non-flexible boots and have their heels locked to the skis with releaseable bindings. The venue, speed and technical difficulty associated with the sport can lead to collisions, accidents, hypothermia and other injury or illness, occasionally including death. Regional Ski Patrol organizations, such as the National Ski Patrol in the U.S., subsist as a voluntary organization to provide guidance, help, medical assistance and emergency rescue to those in need of it.

HISTORY

Pre-historic Nordic People invented skiing to assist hunting, military technique, and as a practical transportation for the Nordic people and the Samis. The oldest and most accurately documented proof of skiing origins is discovered in modern day Norway and Sweden. The most former primitive carving circa 5000 B.C. depicts a skier with one pole, situated in Rodoy, an island situated in the Nordland region of Norway. The first primitive ski was discovered in a peat bog in Hoting, Sweden which dates back to 2500 or 4500 B.C. Joel Berglund reported in 2004 the discovery of a primitive ski, or "85cm long piece of wood", carbon tested by researchers in 1997 while excavating a Norse settlement situated near Nanortalik, Greenland. The primitive ski dated back to 1010, and is thought to be Greenland's oldest ski brought by Norsemen circa 980 A.D.

Other accounts of ancient Nordic skiing are discovered with two modern cross-country endurance races in Norway and Sweden. These ski races were inspired by popular historical accounts of ancient medieval skiing in their respective countries. The oldest account involves the popular story from 1206 A.D. of the Birkebeiners throughout a civil war in medieval Norway. Regarded the underdog, the Birkebeiners were at war versus a rival faction known as the baglers. Following the death of the Birkenbeiner chief, the baglers feared a rival in his young son Haakon Haakonsson. In order to protect him, two of the most skillful Birkenbeiner skiers, with toddler in tow, skied through treacherous conditions over the mountains to safety in Lillehammer.

Since 1932, Norway's yearly Birkebeinerrennet runs a 54 km cross-country ski race which pays tribute to this historical account. Since 1922, Sweden has run their own ski marathon known as the Vasaloppet. With its longest race at 90 km, and ending up in Mora,Sweden, it is known as the world's longest cross-country ski race. This endurance race commemorates the memory of "freedom fighter" Gustav Vasa and subsequently Swedish independence. Pursued by the Danes in 1520 A.D. (under order from King Christian of Denmark who controlled Sweden at the time), Gustav Vasa attempted to raise an army versus the Danes, but was forced to flee by skis north west towards Norway. Tracked down by Mora's two best skiers, Gustav came back with them to Mora and lead an uprising which finally overthrew Danish decree.

Skiing is also registered in ancient literature. Icelandic saga author (circa 1200) Snorre Sturlason wrote of Ull "God of Skiing" and Skade "Goddess of Skiing and Hunting" in Norse mythology. One of the world's oldest references to skiing is by Egil Skallagrimsson's "950 AD saga describing King Haakon Adalsteinsfostre the Good's practice of sending his tax collectors out on skis" Another one of the oldest written accounts of skiing, is by Swedish writer Olaus Magnus in his writings A Description of the Northern Peoples in the year 1555.

His accounts record ancient primitive skiers (presumably the Sami People) and their "climbing skins" in Scricfinnia, a country or region at the top of modern day Norway. Sometime around 1800 A.D. Danish traveler Father Knut Leed made reference in Geographie to Norwegian kids "skiing just for the fun of it, being able to pick up a hat dropped on the slope while going at full speed." The word "ski" itself is one of a handful of words Norway has exported to the international community. It comes from the Old Norse word "skio" which means split piece of wood or firewood. Previously, English speakers regarded skiing to be a type of snowshoeing.

In parts where loose snow dominates, the indigenous population evolved snowshoes that did not slide across the snow, instead of skis which do. Today's forms of skiing are the advance extensions of ancient Nordic skiing. Whether it be the Nordic forms of Cross-country skiing (a kind of Telemark skiing) and Telemark skiing, Ski mountaineering or Alpine skiing, advance forms of skiing share common threads of origin from the Telemark region in Norway led by Norwegian ski innovator Sondre Norheim.

Norwegian Sondre Norheim is known as the "father of modern skiing" (meaning the originator of skiing as recreation and sport). From the Telemark district of Morgedal, Norway, which is also known as the "cradle of skiing", Norheim made the design templates from which all forms of advance skiing are derived. In 1850, woodcarvers from the Telemark region brought in lighter, thinner, cambered skis. These growths were accompanied by Norheim's creation of stiff bindings by fully securing the heel with a strong yet flexible strap built from birch roots.

This new bonding system enabled the skier to swing, jump and maneuver turns while skiing down the hills. These were known as "Osier" bindings. Morten Lund writes, in his piece outlining the growth of Alpine skiing, that "Telemark skiing marked the transition to dynamic control, altering the angle of the ski bottom on the snow and changing the direction of the ski to the line of descent—the basis of method even today", thus the necessity for Norheim's heel binding invention. And as a result, came the "flowering of the world's first "freestyle" contests climbing, running, making turns for the heck of it and flying off natural bumps on unready snow."

In 1868, along with a couple of fellow skiers, Norheim attended the "second annual Centralforeningen (Central Ski Association) open ski competition whose objective was to demonstrate skill at descending a specific slope in the city." At the competition, Norheim demonstrated groundbreaking methods which set the ideal benchmarks for skiing in Norway and the European Continent: the arc like sweep of "telemark turn" along with the slipped "stem" stop turn (or ordinarily known as the "parallel" stop turn), which was initially known as the "Christiania" turn (primitive name for modern day Oslo). The "Christiania" came to be known simply as the "Christi" turn with the formalization of ski conventions in 1901. Both turns, which initiated in Telemark, mark the distinction between Telemark and Alpine skiing.

Then in 1870, Norheim brought in his adaptive design of the Telemark or "narrow-waisted" ski - "the forerunner of the sidecuts employed on skis today." Skis were narrowed, shortened and sides curved inwards. These civilisations greatly eased easier ski turns and set "the standard for ski design over the next century." By the 1880s, as demand for Norwegian skis increased, alterations led to the growth of the first laminated skis which started to appear in 1881. These new fangled "hand-crafted" skis were built "with an ash sole and pine top" and first exported to Sweden in 1882. Also in 1882, the first hickory skis appeared in Norway providing for a thinner and more flexible ski. Ski growth was continued by Norwegian H.M. Christiansen who built the first two-layer laminated ski in 1893, persued by fellow Norwegian Bjorn Ullevoldsaeter's patented three-layer laminated ski.

Jointly, these innovative designs and methods laid the foundation for all forms of advance skiing and further growths, including one formed kind of skiing known as Slalom by Norheim and his contemporaries in the Telemark region. Slalom, or "slalåm" in Norwegian dialect, is a Norwegian word arising from Morgedal, Norway. "Sla" refers to slope, hill, or smooth surface while "låm" means "track down the slope".

The skiing techniques of 19th century Morgedal acknowledged as Telemark skiing or "telemarking" underwent a revival in the 1970s. This revival of Telemark skiing has been attributed by author Halvor Kleppen to five American skiers from Colorado: Doug Buzzell, Craig Hall, Greg Dalbey, Jack Marcial and Rick Borkovec, who were jointly inspired by Norwegian ski phenomenon and Olympic champion Stein Ericksen and his book Come Ski With Me.

Whereas Sondre Norheim had initially invented secure heeled bindings applying water-soaked, flexible birch roots, the next significant growth of binding came in 1894 from Fritz Huitfeldt who invented a binding with a secure toe iron which permited the heel to move freely. This turned the standard industry binding through the 1930s.

Section to possibly be arose here on the more significant binding growths: for instance 1933 Adolph Attenhofer - "complete fixed heel all-metal binding" and 1939 Hjalmar Hvam Saf-Ski binding.

Retired Austrian school teacher Mathias Zdarsky, like many others at the time, was intrigued by world-renowned Norwegian explorer and Telemark skier Fridtjof Nansen, and his "high-risk expedition" accounts, in the 1890 German translation of Nansen's book On Skis across Greenland. Inspired by Nansen's skiing exploits, Zdarsky took up the sport throughout his retirement by importing Norwegian skis and teaching himself to ski. Incorporating ski techniques from Norway, he evolved a ski technique system, known as the "Lilienfeld Method", which he outlined in his 1896 book Lillienfeld Skilaufer Technik. His key growth, which led to enthusiastic embrace of skiing in the Alps, was the "stem" technique, or what is ordinarily known is skiing as the "snowplow" technique. This new technique enabled beginners to experience the slopes in a "slow and controlled manner", beyond the more sophisticated and complicated Norwegian Telemark and Christiania techniques, which restricted the slopes to more advanced and skillful skiers. By 1896, he was teaching his new methods to large groups of "stem skiers" in Austria.

In 1908, flourishing on the growths of this fellow countryman Zdarsky, a young Austrian ski guide by the name of Johannes Schneider entered the scene. With respect to skiing, Johannes (also known as Hannes) is to Austrians as Sondre Norheim and Fridtjof Nansen is to Norwegians. By the 1920s, he had worked to refine Sondre Norheim's

"Christiania" stem christi turn, along with fellow countryman Mathias Zdarsky's "stem" or "snowplow" technique. He employed these Norwegian and Austrian methods to develop a logical system of ski instruction, a system which started with the easiest snowplow technique, then progressing through to more difficult ski skills. This system constituted the basis for Schneider's formalised Arlberg technique, which is named for his home region, and subsequently set a basis for professional ski instruction. This system also incorporated a set of ethical standards to the profession of teaching. With this, the Arlberg techniques disperse and helped make skiing a famous recreational activity.

History of Freestyle Skiing

Freestyle skiing started in the 1930s, when Norwegian skiers started performing acrobatics throughout alpine and cross-country training. Afterwards, non-competitive professional skiing exhibitions in the United States featured performances of what would afterwards be known as freestyle. Aerial skiing was evolved in approximately 1950 by Olympic gold medalist Stein Eriksen. Freestyle skiing started to develop further throughout the 1960s and into the 1970s, when it was often known as "hot-dogging." Bob Burns pioneered this style in Sun Valley, Idaho starting in 1965. In the late 1960s other followers of the style included Wayne Wong, John Clendenin, and Tom LeRoy. Few people thought that this style of skiing was too grievous and did not want it to be an Olympic sport. The free-form sport had few conventions and wasn't without danger; knee injuries turned a common phenomenon for professional freestylers.

The International Ski Federation (FIS) recognized freestyle as a sport in 1979 and brought in new rules concerning certification of athletes and jump techniques in an effort to curb the grievous components of the competitions. The first World Cup series was staged in 1980 and the first World Championships took place in 1986 in Tignes, France where skiers such as James Willingham contended. Freestyle skiing was a manifestation event at the Calgary Winter Olympics in 1988. Mogul skiing was added to the official programme of the Albertville Games in 1992, and aerials was added for the Lillehammer Games in 1994.

Hiostory of Cross-country Skiing

Cross-country skiing initiated in Fennoscandian countries in prehistoric times. It was still widely exercised in 19th century as a way of moving from place to place in winter. Elk, deer and other animals were hunted by skiing. Nowadays almost everyone in countries with strong cross-country skiing conventions like Norway, Sweden, Finland and Estonia have employed or regularly use skis.

By contrast, natives in North America were historically trappers and collecters, requiring free hands and the ability to walk through deep snow in forests, hence the common historical use of snowshoes. Skiing may have also been sparsely exercised by Natives for alike lengths of time as in Scandinavia, though the Norwegian emigrants Snowshoe Thompson is widely credited for bringing in the sport to California in the USA, and Jackrabbit Johannsen is widely credited for bringing in the sport to Canada.

THE GAME

Equipments

Ski: A ski is a long flat device worn on the feet designed to help the wearer slide smoothly over snow. Primitively intended as an aid to travel in snowy parts, they are now chiefly employed for recreational and sporting purposes. Also, a ski may denote a alike device employed for other purposes than skiing, for example, for steering snowmobiles.

Fig: Skiing

Snow skis glide on snow because downward pressure, as well as heat from surface friction, melts a thin layer of snow right away under the ski. This produces a very thin layer of water right away under the ski upon which the ski glides. Ski wax is employed to decrease drag by increasing the water resistant attributes of the base.

Poles: Pairs of carbon fibre or aluminium are employed. These have a spike to penetrate the hard ground and a ring (or basket) which prevents the pole from going too deep into the snow. Longer poles are employed for skating than classic cross-country skiing, but both should be long enough to reach as high as the user's armpit while standing.

Boots and Bindings: This is an incensing matter for skiers as there are three dissimilar types or binding employed in cross-country skiing; the New Nordic Norm, Salamon New Nordic System Profil and Salamoñ Nordic System Pilot.

All attach to the boot at the toe leaving the heel free to lift the ski without leaning it. The Pilot system is the most valuable and is employed at professional level, though any good ski shop should be able to advise you on which binding is best for you and your favoured type of cross-country skiing.

The Jury: The Jury is responsible for all technical aspects of the race and shall decide on all issues that arise throughout the competition. In general, the Jury makes decisions on all questions not clarified by the conventions. The Jury shall meet after each race in a assigned place. Notice of the Jury meeting shall be given if a protest or other emergency matters arising out of the race have to be regarded. Every member will be personally notified. No coach may serve on the jury if their athletes are taking part in the competition.

Referee

The TD shall be responsible for declaring or making known to the players before the meet begins any special conditions enforced by the Jury. In an Alpine event, the TD and/or the Referee must inspect the course immediately after it is set, and may direct the Course Setter (CS) to alter the course by taking out or adding gates as necessary. The TD can designate substitutions for officals or personnel who have failed to appear.

In an Alpine event, the Referee shall disqualify any contestant who does not pursue the racing conventions or refuses to pursue the conventions of the officials; the Referee shall inspect the gatekeeper cards and shall post on the unofficial results board the names and numbers of all players who have committed a fault. The start of the protest time will concur with the posting of the last run of the event and run for the needed time as said.

Techniques

Classic: Many cross-country trails have two parallel grooves cut into them and are known as pistes. The classic technique is adhered to on these tracks as it is what would have been employed when the practice started, when vast numbers of soldiers crossed terrains in single file, wearing tracks into the snow. There are four prime techniques; herringbone, double pole, double pole with kick and diagonal stride. All techniques require the weight to be shifted completely from one ski to the next.

Walking and gliding.

The side step.

Downhill schussing.

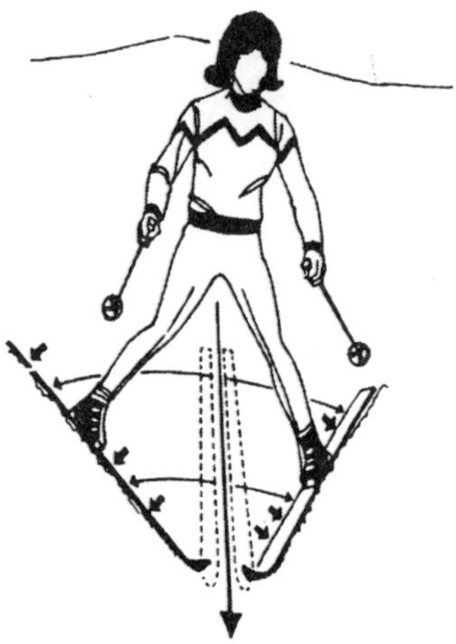

Snowplow braking technique.

Fig: Various Skiing Techniques

Telemark: This type of skiing has an image of indulgence and mystique generated by those who practice it. The technique varies from the other two types of cross country skiing in that it is only suitable for descents, as the technique is based on a type of turning instead of a method of propulsion.

It essentially arose due to the development of gear, specifically the free-heel boot. Telemark skiing was lost with the growth of alpine skiing and the fixed-heeled boot. It was re-invented by those wishing to explore back-country areas in the 1970s who discovered the narrow climbing skis unsuitable for unexplored descents.

It is revered as a very difficult method to master, but further alterations in technology have made it possible for those with an alpine skiing background to pick up telemark skiing in a matter of days.

MAJOR TOURNAMENTS

Alpine Skiing World Cup

The alpine skiing World Cup is a circuit of alpine skiing competitions established in 1966 by a group of ski racing friends and experts which included French journalist Serge Lang and the alpine ski team directors from France (Honore Bonnet) and the USA (Bob Beattie). It was soon supported by International Ski Federation (FIS) president Marc Hodler throughout the FIS Alpine World Ski Championships 1966 at Portillo, Chile, and turned a standard FIS event in the spring of 1967 after the FIS Congress at Beirut, Lebanon. The first World Cup ski race was held in Berchtesgaden, West Germany, on January 5, 1967. Jean-Claude Killy of France and Nancy Greene of Canada were the overall winners for the first 2 seasons.

Races are held chiefly at ski resorts in the Alps in Europe, with steady stops in Scandinavia, North America, and East Asia. Contenders attempt to attain the best time in four disciplines: slalom, giant slalom, Super G, and downhill. The fifth event, the combined, employs the downhill and slalom. The World Cup primitively included only slalom, giant slalom, and downhill races. Combined events (computed applying results from selected downhill and slalom races) were included commencing with the 1974–75 season, while the Super G was added for the 1982–83 season. The present scoring system was implemented in the 1991–92 season. For every race points are granted to the top 30 finishers: 100 points to the winner, 80 for second, 60 for third, winding down to 1 point for 30th place. The racer with the most points at the end of the season in mid-March wins the Cup, with the trophy comprising of a 9 kilogram crystal globe. Sub-prizes are also awarded in each individual race discipline, with a smaller 3.5 kg crystal globe.

Disabled Alpine Skiing World Championships

The Disabled Alpine Skiing World Championships, along with the Winter Paralympic Games are the most esteemed level of international competition in disabled ski racing. First held in 1974, the World Championships have been held every four years (even-numbered non-Paralympic years) from 198? To 2004; starting in 2009, they will be held every other year, in odd-numbered years. The alter from holding the World Championships every four years to every two was primitively set to happen in 2007. The 2007 edition was slated for Klosters, Switzerland, but organizers withdrew their bid in early 2006, citing a lack of funding. The IPC initially attempted to find a replacement host for the 2007 Championships but in April decided to cancel the event wholly.

FIS Nordic World Ski Championships

The FIS Nordic World Ski Championships have been held in several numbers and kinds of events since 1925 for men and since 1954 for women. Championship events include Nordic skiing's three disciplines: cross country skiing, ski jumping, and Nordic combined (the latter being a combination sport comprising of both cross-country skiing and ski jumping). From 1924 to 1939, the World Championships were held annually, including the Winter Olympics. After World War 2, the World Championships were held in even-numbered years from 1948 to 1982, including the Winter Olympics. Since 1985, the World Championships have been held in odd-numbered years.

FIS Freestyle World Ski Championships

The FIS Freestyle World Ski Championships is the world championship formed by the FIS for Freestyle Skiing. It was first organised in 1986 and is now held every odd year. Presently, the events included in the world championships are Moguls, Dual Moguls, Aerials, Skicross and Half-Pipe. Formally, Acroski (Ski Ballet) and a united event where held.

ADMINISTRATIVE BODIES

International Ski Federation

The International Ski Federation/Fédération Internationale de Ski (FIS) is the prime international organisation of ski sports. Established by 14 member nations in 1924 in Chamonix, France, today it has a membership of 101 national ski associations and is based in Oberhofen am Thunersee, Switzerland.

International Olympic Committee

The International Olympic Committee is an organisation based in Lausanne, Switzerland, made by Pierre de Coubertin and Demetrios Vikelas on June 23, 1894. Its membership comprises of the 205 National Olympic Committees. The IOC organises the modern Olympic Games held in summer and winter, every four years. The first Summer Olympics organised by the International Olympic Committee held in Athens, Greece, in 1896; the first Winter Olympics in Chamonix, France, in 1924. Until 1992, both summer and Winter Olympics were held in the same year. After that year, however, the IOC transferred the Winter Olympics to the even years between Summer Games, to help space the planning of the two events two years apart from one another.

U.S. Ski and Snowboard Association

The U.S. Ski and Snowboard Association (USSA) is the national regulating body for Olympic skiing and snowboarding. Established in 1905, the nearly century-old organisation provides leadership and direction for tens of thousands of young skiers and snowboarders from over 400 member clubs who share an Olympic dream.

The USSA and its local clubs coordinate nationwide programs in seven distinctly dissimilar Olympic sports — alpine, cross country, disabled, freestyle, ski jumping, nordic combined, and snowboarding. It is responsible for all aspects of competitive skiing and snowboarding from grassroots programs through elite international teams, including training and fielding the yearly U.S. Ski Team and U.S. Snowboarding, as well as the Olympic teams in skiing and snowboarding. The USSA is compiled of over 30,000 athletes, officials and coaches, with a network of over 100,000 parents, volunteers and supporters helping create chances for young athletes.

FAMOUS PLAYERS

Hermann Maier

Hermann Maier was born on December 7, 1972, in Altenmarkt im Pongau, is an Austrian skier who has won four overall World Cup titles (1998, 2000, 2001, 2004), two Olympic gold medals both won in the year 1998, three World Championship titles (1999: 2, 2005: 1) and 53 races in the World Cup. He ranks among the likes of Jean-Claude Killy, Ingemar Stenmark, Mark Girardelli, Pirmin Zurbriggen, Gustav Thoeni, Toni Sailer, Alberto Tomba, Kjetil André Aamodt and Franz Klammer as one of the best exponents of the sport.Taking part in local races, Maier turned a multiple regional champion in Salzburg and Tyrol, but still was not able to gain a place in the strong Austrian World Cup skiing team.

Putting that behind him, his outstanding talent was recognized for the first time by Austrian coaches in 1996, when he was timed with the 12th fastest time in a World Cup giant slalom in Flachau, though only commencing as a forerunner and not taking part in the actual competition. This would become the commencing point of his international career. In 1997 he won his first World Cup event - a super-G race in Garmisch-Partenkirchen, Germany. He quickly formed himself as an explosive and dynamic skier, well known for his strength, his willingness to take risks and the endless effort he put into his training sessions.

Bode Miller

Bode Miller was born on October 12, 1977,he is an American alpine skier. In 2008 Bode won his second overall Alpine Skiing World Cup title in four years, after also winning the title in 2005. This led the United States ski team to sweep the men's and women's overall World Cup titles for the first time in 25 years, as Lindsey Vonn won the woman's title. In 2005 Bode turned the first American in 22 years to win the overall title, subsequently Phil Mahre and Tamara McKinney in 1983.

Earlier throughout his championship season, with a victory on November 28, 2004, he turned only the fifth man to win World Cup races in all five disciplines: slalom, giant slalom, Super-G, downhill, and combined. With 31 World Cup victories, he is the most successful American alpine skier. He is also a four-time World Champion in four dissimilar disciplines and has a pair of silver medals from the 2002 Winter Olympics. On May 12, 2007, Miller announced that he would be leaving the US Ski Team. However, he still competes for the USA in international competitions.

Luc Alphand

Luc Alphand was born on August 6, 1965, he is a French former alpine skier, who is now a race car driver. Born in Briançon, Alphand made his World Cup skiing first appearance in 1984. In 1997 he won the World Cup. He retired in 1997 and began a career in auto racing.

First in the Nissan Micra Stars Cup (1997–1998), then in the European Le Mans Series (2001), the FIA GT Championship (2002), and the Lamborghini Supertrophy (2002). He won the 2006 Dakar Rally, in which he had finished up runner-up a year earlier. With this victory, he was the first ex ski driver who won the Paris-Dakar. He recently purchased two Corvette race cars from Pratt & Miller for use in the Le Mans Series and 24 Hours of Le Mans.

Verena Schneider

Verena ("Vreni") Schneider was born on November 26, 1964 in Elm, she is a former ski racer from Switzerland. She is the most successful alpine ski racer of her country, the second most successful female ski racer ever (after Annemarie Moser-Pröll) and was elected "Swiss Sportswoman of the Century".

She won the overall alpine skiing World Cup three times and eleven discipline World Cups in Slalom and Giant Slalom, along with 55 World Cup races (number two all-time among women to Moser-Pröll). She also won five medals at the Winter Olympics including 3 golds (Slalom and Giant Slalom at Calgary in 1988 and Slalom at Lillehammer in 1994), and six medals at the World Championships including 3 more golds (Giant Slalom at Crans-Montana in 1987 and Vail in 1989; Slalom at Saalbach in 1991). Throughout the 1988–89 season she won 14 World Cup races. Nobody had ever attained this before (the Swede Ingemar Stenmark once won 13 races), and her record has yet to be beaten since then.

Jan Ingemar Stenmark

Jan Ingemar Stenmark was born on March 18, 1956 in Joesjö, Storumans municipality, he is a former Swedish skier, active throughout the '70s and '80s. He is considered as one of the most prominent Swedish sportsmen, and as the greatest slalom and giant slalom specialist of all time. He contended for Fjällvinden Tärnaby. Stenmark was born in the province of Lappland. His family moved to Tärnaby when he was four years old, where he turned neighbours with Stig Strand, who would afterwards win the World Cup Slalom title. He started skiing at the age of five and won his first national competition at the age of eight.

REFERENCES

Alter, S.: *Science of Flexibility*, 2nd edn, Human Kinetics, Champaign, IL, 1996.

Alter, S.: *Sport Stretch*, Human Kinetics, Champaign, IL, 1998.

Dintiman, G. and Ward, R.: *Sport Speed*, Leisure Press, Champaign, IL, 1988.

Ellison, D.: *Performance Stretching*, Human Kinetics, Champaign, IL, 1999.

Micheli, L.J. (ed.): *Clinics in Sports Medicine: The Young Athlete*, W.B. Saunders, Philadelphia, PA, 1995.

Newsholme, E., Leech, T. and Duester, G.: *Keep on Running*, John Wiley & Sons, Chichester, UK, 1994.

Reaburn, P. and Jenkins, D.: *Training for Speed and Endurance*, Allen & Unwin, Sydney, 1996.

Rowland, T.W.: *Developmental Exercise Physiology*, Human Kinetics, Champaign, IL, 1996.

19

Softball

Softball is a team sport popular particularly in the United States. It is a direct descendant of baseball and the conventions of both sports are considerably alike; baseball is occasionally referred to as hardball to distinguish the two. Softball was invented by George Hancock in Chicago, Illinois. The first softball game was played employing a rolled up boxing glove as a ball and a broomstick as a bat.

Softball is a game which is often described as a cross between baseball and rounders. Although, of course, it is not quite that simple - why make things simple when it is so much more fun to confuse the bejesus out of everybody? It can be played single sex or mixed but we play the mixed slow-pitch version, which is so much more fun than single sex.

The ball is a little bigger than an orange but despite the name, it is NOT soft. In fact, it really hurts quite a lot if you get hit - which is why you wear a fielder's glove; a little larger than the ones baseball players wear but otherwise, identical. The bats tend to be aluminium although wooden bats can be used.

The sport is growing speedily in other regions of the country such as Birmingham, London, Bristol, Leeds, Scotland and God knows where else. It is played in Ireland, Jersey and all over Europe and America...It is speedily flourishing as a corporate sport so you could even look at it as an investment into your future and the first GB squad latterly came back from training in America and will be playing the GB men's baseball team at the Coor's Tournament in May.

Fastpitch softball is a form of softball played generally by girls, generally commencing at the age of 6 through college age, although male and co-ed fastpitch leagues also exist. The United States women's national softball team has won back-to-back-to-back gold medals at the 1996, 2000 and 2004 Summer Olympics. In the most recent Olympics, only one run was scored against the USA team.

The United States will field a team for the next Olympics in 2008. After that, the event is slated to be removed due to the number of players and the field space that has to be built. Pitchers throw the ball underhanded at speeds up to 76 mph from 40 or 43 feet away. This is the equal to being equivalent to that of a 90 mph baseball pitch.

The pitching style is entirely dissimilar from that of that of slowpitch softball. Fastpitch pitchers throw the ball in what is called a "windmill" type of pitch. This style of pitching involves bringing the ball in a circular movement, starting at the hip and then bringing it up over the head and finishing the circle back down at the hip.

The release is crucial in fastpitch. The pitcher must snap his/her wrist upwards at the accurate moment the ball is centered in the middle of his/her body. This release causes a spin motion on the ball, which thus contributes to a significant part of the speed.

HISTORY

Softball initiated in Chicago in 1887. A group of about twenty young men had accumulated in the gymnasium of the Farragut Boat Club in order to hear the consequence of the Harvard-Yale football game. After Yale's victory was declared and bets were paid off, a man picked up a stray boxing glove and threw it at someone, who hit it with a pole. George Hancock, usually regarded the inventor of softball, shouted, "Let's play ball!" He tied the boxing glove so that it resembled a ball, chalked out a diamond on the floor (smaller dimensions than those of a baseball field in order to fit the gym) and broke off a broom handle to serve as a bat. What carried on was an odd, smaller variant of baseball. That game is now, 111 years later, titled the first softball game. Softball may have seen its death on the day of its birth if Hancock hadn't been so enchanted by it. In one week, he made an oversized ball and an undersized rubber-tipped bat and went back to the gym to paint permanent white foul lines on the floor. After he wrote new conventions and named the sport indoor baseball, a more organised, yet still new, game was played. Its fame was fast.

Hancock's original game of indoor baseball rapidly caught on in fame, becoming international with the establishment of a league in Toronto. That year, 1897, was also the premiere publication of the Indoor

Baseball Guide. This was the first nationally distributed publication on the new game and it endured a decade. In the spring of 1888, Hancock's game moved outdoors. It was played on a small diamond and called indoor-outdoor. Due to the sport's mass appeal, Hancock published his first set of indoor-outdoor decrees in 1889.

While Chicago was unquestionably softball's birthplace, the game saw some alteration in Minneapolis. The year was 1895 when Lewis Rober, Sr., (a fire department officer) wanted an activity to keep his men engaged and in shape during their free time. He made his game to fit the confines of a vacant lot next to the firehouse and the result was straightaway appealing. Astonishingly, Rober was probably not familiar with Hancock's variant of the sport because it was still centered in Chicago at that time. The following year, 1896, Rober was moved to a new unit with a new team to manage. In honor of this group's name, the Kittens, the game was termed Kitten League Ball in 1900. The name was later shortened to kitten ball.

In order to reach the Olympics, the women's sport of softball apparently had to grow greatly from its commencements. The first women's softball team was conceived in 1895 at Chicago's West Division High School. They didn't obtain a coach for competitive play until 1899 and it was hard to produce interest among fans. However, only five years after, more attention was given to the women's game. The Spalding Indoor Baseball Guide 1904 issue fueled this attention by devoting a large division of the guide to the game of women's softball.

The Chicago National Tournament in 1933 also advanced the sport. At this competition, the male and female champions were honoured evenly. The International Softball World Championships in 1965 evolved women's softball by making it an global game, a step towards the Pan-American Games and the Olympics. Eleven years later, women softball players were given the closest equivalent to Major League Baseball with the 1976 constitution of the International Women's Professional Softball League. Player contracts ranged from $1,000 to $3,000 per year, but the leage disbanded in 1980 because of fiscal ruin. Vicki Schneider, a St. Louis Softball Hall of Famer and early professional player, recalls this league as being the high point of her career (Schneider).

The fame of women's fastpitch softball has grownup steadily since the professional league's end in 1980. In fact, once again, there is a different professional fastpitch league. The Amateur Softball Association reports that it "yearly registers over 260,000 teams aggregating to form a membership of more than 4.5 million" (About the ASA). These numbers don't all apply to fastpitch, yet it is consistently growing along with slowpitch. Vicki Schneider has seen a major growth in fame and intensity for the sport since she has been involved. She says it is also very obvious that girls are consistently getting more involved with and more competitive at an earlier age. Increased media coverage and the Olympics have greatly contributed to this development (Schneider). There is apparently some exceptional appeal of fastpitch softball that has permitted it to steadily grow in fame through the years.

THE GAME

Teams must be ready to play at scheduled time with a minimum of 8 players. Penalty: Forfeit. Home team is determined by a pre-game coin toss. Seven innings will constitute an official game, unless time limit, darkness, rain or run rule prevails. 5 innings (4 1/2 if the home team is ahead) is an official game. If a game is postponed while in progress, it will be resumed at the point from which it was stopped.

No new inning will be commenced after 60 minutes. Game time starts with the coin toss. At the end of the time limits (upon completion of inning started), the game will be called, unless darkness, rain, or run convention have been aroused. A team leading by 15+ runs after three innings or 10+ runs after five innings (4 1/2 innings if home team is ahead) or any complete inning thereafter will be announced the winner and the game complete. During the regular season, there will be no extra inning play.

A team may place a maximum of 11 (12 for coed) and minimum of 8 players in the batting order. There are no limitations regarding field substitution but, the batting order must persist the same. If a team begins with only 8 players they may add up players at the bottom of the batting order up until all players in the line-up have batted once. They will not be charged an out in 9th and 10th positions. Whenever a team is playing with only nine players, an out will be taken when the 10th position in the batting order seems.

When the batter enters the batter's box he/she will have the count of one ball and one strike. After the batter has obtained a count of two strikes, he/she will be declared out on the second foul (the first foul will be called a "courtesy foul").

All players in the field (maximum of 10, minimum of 8) must appear in the batting order Defensive alterations are unltimately provided that the game isn't unduly delayed. Any of the opening players may be substituted or replaced and re-entered once, provided players occupy the original positions whenever in the line-up. The opening player and his substitute may not be in the line-up at the same time. Non opening players may not re-enter.

Courtesy runners will be permitted for injured players. All courtesy runners must be the last player to have made an out. In coed play, the courtesy runner must be of the same gender. A pitch birthed lawfully with the proper arc demand that crosses the plate within the strike zone will be called a strike. The strike zone is that space over any part of home plate, between the batter's back shoulder and front knee, when s/he assumes a natural batting stance. The pitch, delivered with an underhand motion, must have a perceptible arc and reach a height of at least 6 feet from the ground, while not exceeding a maximum of 12 feet. If the catcher in any way obstructs the umpire's view, the pitch shall be announced a ball.

Ball

Despite the sport's name, softballs are not peculiarly soft. The size of the ball varies according to the categorisation of play; the allowed circumferences in international play are 12±0.125; in(30.5±0.3 cm), weight between 6.25 oz 178 g and 7.0 oz (198.4 g)in fast pitch; 11±0.125; in(29.7±0.3 cm), weight between 5.875 oz (166.5 g) and 6.125 oz (173.6 g) in slow pitch. Some balls have an elevated seam, and others don't. The ball is most often covered in white leather in two pieces approximately the shape of a figure 8 and sewn jointly with red thread, though other coatings are allowed. The core of the ball may be constructed of long fibre kapok, or a mixture of cork and rubber, or a polyurethane mixture, or another sanctioned material.

In 2002, high-visibility yellow "optic" covering, long-used for confined flight balls in co-ed recreational leagues, became criterion for competitive play. Yellow is the color of official NCAA and NAIA softballs. Yellow softballs are fast becoming the standard for all levels of play for girls' and women's play in particular. White balls are also permitted, but are much more common in slow pitch than in fast pitch.

In Chicago, where softball was invented, it remains conventional to play with a ball 16 inches in circumference. This larger ball is usually softer (occasionally called a mush ball). When using a 16-inch ball, the fielders don't wear gloves or mitts. A 16-inch ball is also used for wheelchair softball.

Bat

The bat used by the batter is made of metal, wood or composite materials (carbon fibre etc). It may be no more than 34 in (86.4 cm) long, 2.25 in (5.7 cm) in diameter, or 38 oz (1.08 kg) in weight. Also, in fastpitch a "drop" of no more than 12 is permitted. The drop is counted by taking the length of the bat in inches and deducting the weight in ounces.

Fig. Bat

Uniform

Each team wears distinctive uniforms. The uniform includes a cap, visor, a shirt, an undershirt, tight sliding undershorts, and shorts or pants; these are the components for which standards are set. Caps must be alike and are compulsory for male players. Caps, visors, and headbands are optional for female players, and do not have to be the same color. A fielder who chooses to wear a helmet (see below) is not needed to wear a cap.

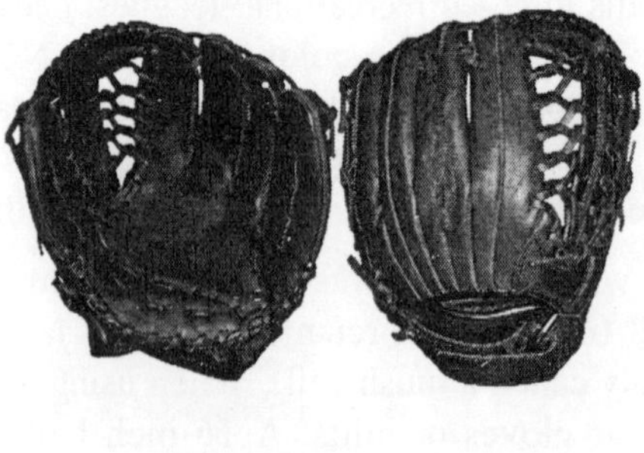

Fig. Softball Gloves

Umpires

Decisions about plays are made by umpires. They make the decisions like a referee in football. The number of umpires on a given game can range from a minimum of one to a maximum of seven. There is never more than one "plate umpire"; there can be up to three "base umpires", and up to a additional three umpires placed in the outfield. Most fast pitch games use a crew of two umpires (one plate umpire, one base umpire). Official umpires are often nicknamed "blue", because of their uniforms - in many jurisdictions, most importantly ISF, NCAA and ASA games; umpires wear navy blue slacks, a light powder blue shirt, and a navy baseball cap. Some umpires wear a variant of the uniform: some umpires in ASA wear heather gray slacks and may also wear a navy blue shirt; umpires from the USSSA wear red shirts with black shorts; NSA umpires usually wear either a cream- or black-colored shirt. Canadian umpires can wear either a light blue or red shirt. Regardless of what uniform is worn, all umpires in the same game are needed to have matching clothing.

Game Play

A softball game can last anywhere from 4 to 9 innings, depending on the league, conventions, and type of softball; however 7 innings is the most common. In each inning, each team bats until three batters have been put out. The teams take turns batting. Formally, which team bats first is settled by a coin toss, though a league may decide otherwise at its discretion. The most common convention is that the home team bats second. Batting second is beneficial.

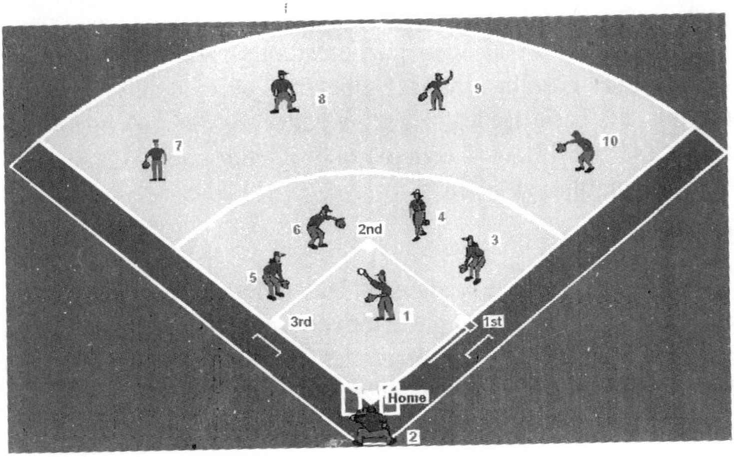

Fig. Field

In the event of a tie, extra innings are generally played until the tie is broken except in certain tournaments and championships. If the home team is leading and the road team has just completed its half of the seventh inning, the game ends because it is not necessary for the home team to bat again. In all variants of softball, the defensive team is the fielding team; the offensive team is at bat or batting and is trying to score runs.

Pitching

Play starts with the umpire saying "Play Ball". After the batter is ready and all fielders (except the catcher) are in fair territory, the pitcher stands at the pitching plate and tries to throw the ball past the batter to the catcher behind home plate. The throw, or pitch, must be made with an underhand often called "windmill" motion: the ball must be discharged below the hip when the hand is no farther from the hip than the elbow.

A windmill motion is done by expanding your throwing hand around your body backwards and ejecting the ball at about hip level at maximum speeds.

In girls' fastpitch, 12u pitchers generally throw in the high 30's (mph) to mid 40's, 14u is in the low to high 40's, 16u is when you will see girls throwing 50-60 mph; with the uncommon being high 60's to 70mph. However, speed isn't always the most important factor in fastpitch softball. Pitchers can throw balls that curve (in-Screw, out-curve), rise (straight rise, or rise screw), drop (straight drop or drop curve), as well as a change-up (slow) and fastball. –

A change of pace (off-speed) is also very important, good pitchers will be able to throw all their pitches at varying speeds and possibly even dissimilar pitching motions (submarine or windmill). Pitchers use deception as a basic tactic for getting batters out as the reaction times from 40' (43' for 18U and college) only provides approx.5 sec or less to react to the thrown pitch.

Batting

The abhorrent team sends one "batter" at a time to home plate to use the bat to try to hit the pitch forward into fair territory. The order the players bat is titled the "batting order", must stay the same throughout the game. Substitutes and replacings must bat in the same position as the player they are replacing. In co-ed, male and female batters must alternate.

The batter stands facing the pitcher inside a "batter's box" (there is one on each side of the plate). The bat is held with both hands, over the shoulder away from the pitcher. The ball is generally hit with a full swinging motion in which the bat may move through more than 360 degrees. The batter generally steps forward with the front foot and swings the bat.

Once the ball is hit into fair territory the runner must try to advance to first base or beyond. While running to first base, the batter is a "batter-runner". When she safely reached first she becomes a "base-runner" or "runner".

Scoring Runs

A "run" is scored when a player has touched all four bases in order, proceeding counterclockwise around them. They need not be touched on the same play; a batter may persist safely on a base while play carries on and attempt to advance on a later play.

A run isn't scored if the last out happens during the same play that the runner crosses home plate. For instance, if a runner gets on third base before a hit and they cross home plate before or after an out is made, either on the batter or another runner, the run is not counted.

Positions

There are nine players out on the field at one time. Though the pitcher and catcher have the ball the most, each person has a particular job. In the infield there is the pitcher, catcher, first baseman, second baseman, shortstop, and third baseman. In the outfield there is left fielder, center fielder, and right fielder. In slow pitch softball there is an extra fielder, who is assigned as a rover. Ordinarily, the defensive team will play with four outfielders, meaning there is a left fielder, left-center fielder, right-center fielder, and right fielder.

Field and Innings

Softball is played between 2 teams on a large field, compiled of a dirt or grass infield which bears the diamond and running regions, and a grass outfield. There are 4 bases on the infield (first base, second base, third base, and home plate); the bases are brought about in a square and are generally 45 to 65 feet apart. Near the center of this square is the pitcher's circle, and within the circle is the "rubber", a small flat rectangular area. The object of the game is to score more runs (points) than the other team by batting (hitting) a ball into play and running around the bases, touching each one in succession. The ball is a sphere of light material, coated with leather or synthetic. It is 10 to 12 inches (or rarely, 16 inches) (28 to 30.5 centimeters) in circumference. The game is officiated by one or more neutral umpires. Players and umpires are usually free to ask for a brief stoppage at any time when the ball isn't in play, or instantly following a play once its outcome is clear.

The game is played in a series of innings, generally seven. Youth leagues occasionally have 6 innings. An inning is one series of both teams playing offense and defense. Each inning is divided into a top half and a bottom half indicating which team is playing which role. The offense bats and attempts to score runs, while the defense occupies the field and attempts to record outs in a variety of ways. After the defense records 3 outs, the half inning is over and the teams switch roles.

MAJOR TOURNAMENTS

Canada Cup

The Canada Cup commenced in 1993 in South Surrey, British Columbia at the Softball City Complex. The registered gate for the entire 2005 tournament was over 105,000 fans. The first Canada Cup Champions were the Redding Rebels. This tournament enjoys strong local support with hundreds of community volunteers. Each team is allotted a bat girl from one of the local teams plus a family support liaison from the community. Other unusual part of this tournament is the concurrent co-ed Slow-Pitch Friendship Division tournament for developmentally disabled adults which is run at the same site as the premier International Women's Fast pitch tournament.

Laing Harrow Shield

The Laing Harrow Shield is a trophy symbolizing the Under 23 Men's Championship of the Australian Softball Federation. The Laing Harrow competition was first held in 1997 by the New South Wales Softball Association as an invitational tournament attended by all the east coast states, in 2004 ASF approved the championship in its own bid to bridge the gap between the Under 19 National Championships and Open National Championships, and increase the retention of elite players.

Hooters Championship Series

The Amateur Softball Association altered its tournament structure for Men's Class A, B, C and D Slow Pitch and Women's Class B, C and D Slow Pitch in 2001.

The Modern structure disunited the country into East and West National Championships with the winners of each advancing to Oklahoma City to decide the true National Champion in each division of play.

In 2002, Hooters of America became the official sponsor of the men's division of the event and received naming rights to the men's series and commenced assisting in promoting the event through a combination of nation wide in-store promotions and advertising campaigns.

In the past the Women's series had been titled the USA Softball National Championship Series but in 2003 the entire Championship Series was placed is under the HCS banner.In 2003, the Women's B classification became Women's Open and permitted teams from the upper divisions of play to contend for a shot at Oklahoma City.

ADMINISTRATIVE BODIES

International Softball Federation

The International Softball Federation is the international regulating body for the sport of softball. It is based in Plant City, Florida, USA. The ISF regards some dependent territories, such as the British Virgin Islands, to be "countries" for the purposes of international competition and regular territorial and world championship tournaments for men and women.. Those dependent territories compete separately from their "parent" country. There are members from every continent in the world, except Antarctica.

Amateur Softball Association

The Amateur Softball Association (ASA) is a volunteer, non-profit organization based in Oklahoma City, Oklahoma. It was founded in 1933.

The National Softball Hall of popularity and Museum is situated at 2801 NE 50th Street in Oklahoma City.

In 1978, the United States Olympic Committee named ASA the national regulating body of softball. ASA now runs competitions in every state through a network of 87 state associations. It has a membership of over 230,000 teams, with more than 3 million players and 60,000 umpires. Since 2005, they have run the World Cup of Softball. ASA Hall of Fame Stadium also hosts the NCAA Women's College World Series and the Big XII softball championship.

United States Peculiarity Sports Association

The USSSA (United States Specialty Sports Association) is a volunteer, sports regulating body, non-profit organization stationed in Kissimmee, Florida. It was established in 1968, originally in Petersburg, Virginia.

Primitively USSSA stood for United States Slow-pitch Softball Association. However, in 1998 USSSA flourished in other sports. Presently USSSA regulates 13 sports across the US, Puerto Rico, different US Military bases, and Canada and has a membership of over 3.2 million.

National Pro Fastpitch

National Pro Fastpitch (NPF), erstwhile the Women's Pro Softball League (WPSL), is the only professional women's softball league in the United States. The WPSL was established in 1997 and folded in 2001. The NPF revived the league in 2004 and presently features six teams: the Philadelphia Force, Washington Glory, Akron Racers, Chicago Bandits, New England Riptide, and the Rockford Thunder with possible expansion team Michigan Ice in 2008.

Independent Softball Association

In 1984 in Shelbyville, TN, the Independent Softball Association was established by a man named Larry Nash. First brought in to the sport of softball in 1967, Nash was hooked from his first game. "I played from early March until late October each year, averaging over two-hundred games a year, I loved it!" said Nash. After years of playing, Nash decided that though he may have lost a step or two in the game, he still had much to offer the game of softball in the form of coaching and organizing teams. He managed a local team for a while and also turned a director for one of Tennessee's existing softball organizations. Then after many years of enjoying the sport, Nash decided he had ideas to help make softball even more fun and enjoyable.

FAMOUS PLAYERS

Lisa Fernandez

Born on February 22, 1971, Lisa Fernandez was a good student at school with a natural genius for baseball. At an early age of eight, she started playing in the children's league and after moving to California, united her school's softball team. In 1994, she led her team in the

Women's College World Series Championship after which she was selected in the US Women's Olympic Softball Team. She is the proud winner of two Olympic gold medals. The first one came to her in the 2000 Sydney Olympics while the other came during the 2004 Athens Olympic Games, which were held in Greece. Presently, espoused and mother of Antonio, Lisa is the assistant softball coach for women's softball team at UCLA. She remains being in the list of internationally acclaimed softball players.

Jennie Finch

Born on September 3, 1980, this gifted softball player began playing softball since the age of five and began pitching since the age of eight. Receiving an early training from her father, she mastered the skills of softball and represented her college in softball tournaments. She has come out on TV for the promotion of softball and has always been inspiring young softball talents. In the Summer Olympics of 2004, Jennie Finch won the gold. She is the most renowned softball player of all time.

Michele Mary Smith

Born on June 21, 1967 is a two-time Gold medalist for the Olympic softball team. She has played in the Japanese Professional Softball League since 1992. She is an Ambassador of Softball and a Softball Analyst for ESPN. In 2006, Michele Smith welcomed the honour of being inducted to the ASA Softball Hall of Fame.

These were only some of the softball talents the world has seen. They have won medals and furthermore, won the hearts of their fans and the sports enthusiasts across the globe.

Cat Osterman

Born on April 16, 1983, Cat Osterman was a brilliant softball player since her years at school. She represented her school in softball and made it proud by setting several records in softball as a part of her school team. Her educative years in the University of Texas witnessed her outstanding performances in a lot of softball tournaments. She was the first player to be featured on the cover of Sports Illustrated. She was a division of the USA Women's softball team that won the gold at the 2004 Summer Olympics. She is also the gallant winner of the silver medal at the 2008 Summer Olympics. Cat Osterman has pitched 20 NCAA career no-hitters and 10 NCAA career perfect games. She carries on being one of the most acknowledged players of international baseball.

Crystl Bustos

Born on September 8, 1977, Crystl Bustos is a Mexican American softball player who bears the world record for home runs during an Olympic series. She is a member of the 2008 Olympic team. She has attained two World Cup Championships and is the winner of Three Pan American golds. Maybe Bustos will retire after the 2008 Olympic Games but will long be loved for her career.

REFERENCES

Alter, S.: *Science of Flexibility*, 2nd edn, Human Kinetics, Champaign, IL, 1996.

Alter, S.: *Sport Stretch*, Human Kinetics, Champaign, IL, 1998.

Dintiman, G. and Ward, R.: *Sport Speed*, Leisure Press, Champaign, IL, 1988.

Ellison, D.: *Performance Stretching*, Human Kinetics, Champaign, IL, 1999.

Newsholme, E., Leech, T. and Duester, G.: *Keep on Running*, John Wiley & Sons, Chichester, UK, 1994.

Reaburn, P. and Jenkins, D.: *Training for Speed and Endurance*, Allen & Unwin, Sydney, 1996.

Rowland, T.W.: *Developmental Exercise Physiology*, Human Kinetics, Champaign, IL, 1996.

20

Triathlon

Triathlon is an endurance event comprising of swimming, cycling and running back-to-back-to-back. Your race time comprises of your time of the total time from start-to-finish, including the time needed in between each 'leg' to switch your clothes and shoes. The first swim/bike/run triathlons were organised by members of the San Diego Track Club and held in San Diego's Mission Bay in 1974. The triathlons were held on summertime evenings and were signified as fun breaks in the normal grind of training for running races.

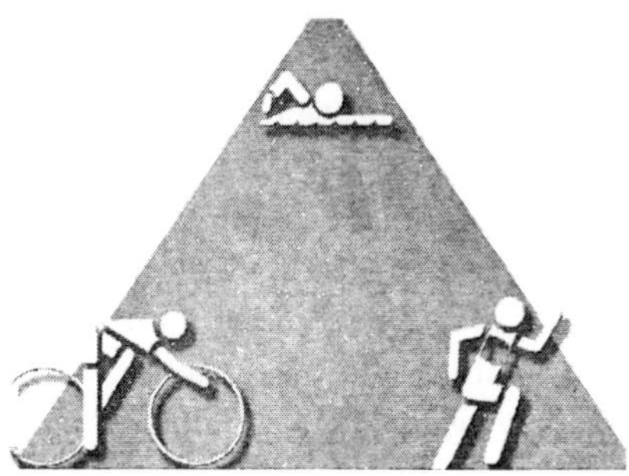

The first Ironman distance triathlon was held in1978 in Hawaii. Nowadays, there are four common triathlon distances: Sprint, Olympic, Half Ironman and Ironman. Most triathlons require players to register beforehand, and attend a pre-race briefing. Athletes are usually rendered with a race number, colored swim cap, and if the race is timed, an electronic timing chip. Typically, athletes are provided a rack to put their bike on the day before or the morning of the race. For most races, challengers have their race number marked on their arm, and their age marked on their calf during the morning of the race. Racers are usually categorised into various categories and age groups, which ascertains your beginning time.

Swimming

Triathletes will often use their legs less vigorously and more cautiously than other swimmers, preserving their leg muscles for the cycle and run to follow. A lot of triathletes use changed swim strokes to counterbalance for turbulent, aerated water and to preserves energy for a long swim. In summation, the majority of triathlons involve open-water (outdoor) swim stages, rather than pools with lane markers. As a result, triathletes in the swim stage must jockey for position, and can gain some advantage by drafting, following a challenger closely to swim in their slipstream. Triathletes will often use "dolphin kicking" and diving to make headway against waves and body surfing to use a wave's energy for a bit of speed at the end of the swim stage. Also, open-water swimmings necessitate "sighting": raising the head to look for landmarks or buoys that mark the course. An altered stroke permits the triathlete to lift the head above water to sight without interrupting the swim or wasting energy.

Because open water swimming areas are often cold and because wearing a wetsuit renders a competitive advantage, specialized triathlon wetsuits have been developed in a variety of styles to match the conditions of the water. The Springsuit, for instance, sleeveless and cut above the knee, was configured for warmer waters, while still rendering buoyancy. Wetsuits are only legal in approved events with a water temperature equal to or below 78 degrees Fahrenheit (25.5 degrees Celsius). A few events permit wetsuits regardless of water temperature, and occasionally they are required. Or, in a single event, wetsuits may be permitted for "age groupers" but not for professionals, as the temperature conventions differ slightly between the two groups.

Cycling

Triathlon cycling, with an exception of the Olympic triathlon and ITU World Cup races, is varied from most professional bicycle racing because it doesn't permit drafting, so racers do not cluster in a peloton. It closely resembles individual time trial racing. Triathlon bicycles are usually optimised for aerodynamics, having special handlebars called "aero-bars" or "tri-bars", aerodynamic wheels, and other parts.

Triathlon bikes use a specialised geometry, including a steep seat-tube angle both to improve aerodynamics and to spare muscle groups necessary for running (see also triathlon gear). At the end of the bike section, triathletes also often cycle with a higher "cadence" (revolutions per minute), which serves in part to keep the muscles loose and flexible for running. It is considered, although, that the elementary profit to cycling in a triathlon is that the strain of the effort is placed disproportionately on the slow twitch muscle fibers, preventing the athlete from accumulating an oxygen debt before the run.

Running

Running is a way for an animal to move on foot. It is defined in sporting terms as a gait in which at some point all feet are off the ground at the same time. Running is a complex and coordinated process that involves the entire body. Every human being runs differently, but certain general characteristics of running motion are common.

Running is performed as a sequence of strides, which alternate between the two legs. Each leg's stride can be approximately divided into three phases: support, drive, and recovery. Support and drive take place when the foot is in contact with the ground. Recovery occurs when the foot is off the ground. Since only one foot is on the ground at a time in running, one leg is always in retrieval, while the other goes through support and drive. Then, concisely, as the runner leaps through the air, both legs are in recovery. These phases are described in detail below.

The elementary differentiating characteristic of running in a triathlon is that it occurs after the athlete has already been exercising in two other disciplines for an extended period of time, so a lot of muscles are already tired. The effect of switching from cycling to running can be profound; first-time triathletes are often amazed at the bizarre, occasionally painful sensation in their thighs a few hundred yards into the run, and discover that they run at a much slower pace than they are accustomed to in training. Triathletes train for this phenomenon through transition workouts titled "bricks": consecutive workouts involving two disciplines, most ordinarily cycling and running.

Modern Triathlon

Early triathlons were held as off-beat training practices for runners. The first known swim/bike/run triathlons were held at San Diego's Mission Bay in 1974. Organised by members of the San Diego Track Club, the events were held on summer evenings and were intended as no more than light-hearted breaks in the standard grind of training for marathons and 10Ks. This happening is well-documented and wasn't based on the French events. Amongst them were runners, swimmers and cyclists and prior to long, training sessions inverted into informal races. Directed and formed by Jack Johnstone and Don Shanahan, the first Mission Bay Triathlon was held on September 25, 1974 and welcomed 46 athletes. This date is renowned as the day modern triathlon commenced.

Full Distance Triathlon

A Full Distance Triathlon (occasionally referred to improperly as an Iron Distance Triathlon) is a triathlon executed over the following distances:

- 3.8 km swimming
- 180 km bicycling
- 42.2 km running (the length of a standard marathon)

The historically first and most familiar instance is the Ironman Triathlon in Hawaii. The term "Ironman Triathlon" is trademarked by the World Triathlon Corporation (WTC), which runs a series of races subordinate to that name. The ITU organises a series of races addressed Long Distance Triathlons. The distances for these races are close to but somewhat dissimilar from the specifications for the Ironman Triathlon. Many autonomous (non-WTC approved) events are held each year throughout the world.

Various double, triple, quadruple, quintuple, and deca (10x) full distance events also held each year. In a deca full distance event, for instance, a 38 km swim is pursued by an 1800 km bike race and a 422 km run. Astrid Benöhr holds the women's world records over the triple quadruple and quintuple full distances.

In 1998, a double deca triathlon (20x full distance) was held in Monterrey, Mexico. The winner, Vidmantas Urbonas of Lithuania, accomplished the race in 437 hours 21 minute 40 second.

HISTORY

Early triathlons were held as off-beat training practices for runners. The first recognised swim/bike/run triathlons were held at San Diego's (California) Mission Bay in 1974. Organised by members of the San Diego Track Club, the events were held on summertime evenings and were intended as no more than cheerful breaks in the normal grind of training for marathons and 10Ks. This happening is well-documented and wasn't grounded on the French events. Among them were runners, swimmers and cyclists and before long training sessions inverted into informal races. Directed and formed by Jack Johnstone and Don Shanahan, the first Mission Bay Triathlon was held on September 25, 1974 and welcomed 46 athletes. This date is celebrated as the day advanced triathlon commenced.

The first advanced long-distance triathlon event (2.4-mile / 3.86-kilometer) swim, 112 mi (180.2 km) bike ride, and a 26.2 mi (42.2 km) run) was the Hawaiian Ironman Triathlon, which was formed during the awards ceremony for the 1977 Oahu Perimeter Relay (a running race for 5-person teams). Among the players were several representatives of both the Mid-Pacific Road Runners and the Waikiki Swim Club, whose members had long been arguing which athletes were more fit: runners or swimmers.

On this juncture, U.S. Navy Commander John Collins remarked that a recent article in Sports Illustrated magazine had announced that Eddy Merckx, the great Belgian cyclist, had the highest recorded "maximum oxygen uptake" of any athlete ever valuated, so perhaps cyclists were more fit than anybody. CDR Collins and his wife, Judy, had participated in the triathlons arranged in 1974 and 1975 by the San Diego Track Club in and around Mission Bay, California, as well as the Optimist Sports Fiesta Triathlon in Coronado, California in 1975. A number of the other military athletes in attendance were also familiar with the San Diego races, so they understood the concept when CDR Collins suggested that the argument ought be settled through a race merging the three surviving long-distance competitions already on the island: the Waikiki Roughwater Swim (2.4 mi./3.862 km), the Around-Oahu Bike Race (115 miles; primitively a two-day event) and the Honolulu Marathon (26.219 mi./42.195 km).

It is worth noting that no one present had ever done the bike race so didn't realise it was a two-day, not one-day, event; CDR Collins computed that, by shaving 3 miles off the course and riding counter-clockwise around the island, the bike leg could begin at the finish of the Waikiki Rough Water and end at the Aloha Tower, the conventional start of the Honolulu Marathon. Before racing, each athlete gets three sheets of paper listing a few decrees and a course description

With a nod to a local runner who was notorious for his needing workouts, Collins said, "Whoever ends up first, we will call him the

Ironman." Of the fifteen men to start off in the early morning on February 18, 1978, twelve accomplished the race and the world's first Ironman, Gordon Haller, accomplished it in 11 hours, 46 minutes, and 58 seconds

Today, a number of triathlon events over varying distances are accommodated around the world. The standard "Olympic Distance" of 1.5/40/10k was made by long time triathlon race director, Jim Curl in the mid-80's after he and partner Carl Thomas successfully created the U.S. Triathlon Series between 1982 and 1997. USTS, as it was known, did more to bring approachable triathlons to the masses than any other group. The Hawaii Ironman Triathlon now serves as the Ironman world championship, but the entity that owns the race, the World Triathlon Corporation, hosts other triathlons around the world that are also addressed Ironmans. Long-distance multi-sport events organised by groups other than the World Triathlon Corporation may not formally be called "Ironman" or "Iron" races. Such triathlons may be described as "Full distance" or "Half distance", but the "Ironman" and "Iron" labels are the official property of the World Triathlon Corporation.

The International Triathlon Union (ITU) was established in 1989 as the international regulating body of the sport, with the chief goal being to put triathlon on the Olympic program. The ITU has never formally approved the Ironman Triathlon. Some conceive that the Hawaii Ironman should be realised as the official world championship for the sport as a whole, and as such should be approved by the ITU. For its part, however, the ITU has expressed little interest in supporting longer distance triathlons, choosing to hold back its focus rather on the shorter races geared toward the Olympics.

The sport made its first appearance on the Olympic program at the Sydney Games in 2000 over the Olympic Distance (1500 m swim - 40 km bike - 10 km run).

According to triathlon historian and author Scott Tinley, the beginning of triathlon is anecdotally attributed to a race in France during the 1920s-1930s that was called diversely "Les trois sports", "La Course des Débrouillards", and "La course des Touche à Tout". At present this race is held every year in France near Joinville le Pont, in Meulan and Poissy. In 1920, the French newspaper "L´Auto" reported on a competition called "Les Trois Sports" with a 3 km run, 12 km bike, and a swim across the channel Marne. Those three parts were performed without any break. There were articles printed in French newspapers about a race in Marseille in 1927.

History of Swimming

Swimming has been renowned since prehistoric times; the most former record of swimming dates back to Stone Age paintings from around 7,000 years ago. Written references date from 2000 BC. Some of the earliest references include the Gilgamesh, the Iliad, the Odyssey, the Bible (Ezekiel 47:5, Acts 27:42, and Isaiah 25:11), Beowulf, and other sagas. In 1538, Nikolaus Wynmann, a German professor of languages, wrote the first swimming book, The Swimmer or A Dialogue on the Art of Swimming (Der Schwimmer Oder ein Zwiegespräch uber die Schwimmkunst). Competitive swimming in Europe began around 1800, lmainly using breaststroke.

John Arthur Trudgen in 1873 brought in the trudgen to Western swimming competitions, after imitating the front crawl employed by Native Americans. Due to a British disregard for splashing, Trudgen used a scissor kick rather of the front crawl's flutter kick. Swimming was part of the first advanced Olympic Games in 1896 in Athens. In 1902 Richard Cavill introduced the front crawl to the Western world. In 1908, the world swimming association, Fédération Internationale de Natation (FINA), was conceived. Butterfly stroke was evolved in the 1930s and was at first a variant of breaststroke, until it was accepted as a separate style in 1952.

History of Cycling

The first cycling race is popularly held to be a 1,200 metre race held on the 31 May 1868 at the Parc de Saint-Cloud, Paris. It was won by expatriate Englishman James Moore who rode a wooden bicycle with iron tyres. The machine is now on display at the museum in Ely, Cambridgeshire, England.

THE GAME

Gear and Equipment

For Swimming: Triathlon equipment comprises of all the equipment you need to swim, bike and run, plus a few other stuff. Most triathletes wear extraordinary 'triathlon shorts' that are alike to bike shorts, but have a thinner padding that does not absorb water so that they can be worn during the swim. Most triathlons permit swimmers to wear a wetsuit, which keeps your body warm in cold water and provides buoyancy, which makes you swim faster.

Specific triathlon wetsuits are designed specifically for swimming and changeovers. Most triathletes rub body glide, a waxy substance, on their neck to avoid chafing caused by the wetsuit rubbing against the body, while swimming. One may also want to put body glide or Vaseline on ones legs and arms to make it easier to remove your wetsuit after the swim.

For Cycling: For the bike portion of the race, in summation to your ones bike, shoes, helmet and shirt or singlet, you may prefer to use a pair of aero-bars, which is attached to bike to help make you more aerodynamic when you ride. Special triathlon bikes are optimised for aerodynamics and use a special geometry to spare muscle groups needed for the run, although most athletes ride on standard road bikes.

For Running: For the run, a good pair of running shoes is required and perhaps a visor whenever it is sunny out. Most likely wear your singlet or whatever shirt you wore on the bike. One may prefer to wear a race belt so you do not have to pin the race number to the shirt. Some racers also wear a belt where you can store water bottles and or gels, although most races have staffed aid posts every few miles along the run.

Timed: Triathlons are timed in five sections:

1. From the beginning of the swim to the beginning of the first transition (swim time);
2. From the beginning of the first transition to the end of the first transition (T1 time);
3. From the beginning of the cycling to the end of the cycling leg (cycling time);
4. From the beginning of the second transition to the end of the second transition (T2 time);
5. And ultimately from the beginning of the run to the end of the run, at which time the triathlon is finished.

Working of Triathlon

Major races need athletes to register and attend a race briefing the day before the real race. This race briefing details the course, the conventions, and any problems to look out for (road conditions, closures, traffic lights, aid stations). At registration the racers are rendered a race number, colored swim cap, and, if the event is being electronically timed, a timing band. Often racers are also given challenger wrist bands that permit them in and out of the changeover area or other athlete-only areas.

At a major event, such as an Ironman or a Long Course Championship, triathletes are needed to set up their bike in the changeover area the day before and leave it nightlong under guard.

For shorter distances the racers make it to the venue about an hour (or more) before the race is to commence. They register and receive their swim cap and number, then proceed to set up their spot in the changeover area. For most races, challengers have their race number tagged on their arms and legs, along with having their age group marked on their calf.

In the transition areas, athletes will usually be rendered with a rack to hold their bicycle and a small segment of ground space for shoes, clothing, etc. Usually, transition spots are allocated to racers by their competition number, although in some events, athletes choose their spot in the changeover area on a first-come, first-served basis. In some races, the bicycle stage does not finish in the same place it commences, so athletes set up two changeover areas: one for the swim-to-bike transition, and one for the bike-to-run transition.

Racers are usually categorised into separate professional and amateur classes. Amateurs, who make up the large majority of triathletes, are often referred to as "age groupers" since they are further classified by sex and age. One feature that has helped to boost the fame of such a complex, time-intensive sport is the chance to contend against others of one's own gender and age group. The age groups are specified in five or ten year intervals.

In some triathlons, amateur athletes may have the option to contend against other people in heavier-weight divisions. "Clydesdale" athletes are generally those men over 200 pounds, while "Athena" athletes are usually women over 150 pounds. These weight based divisions are not officially approved in any of the professional or Olympic events.

As in almost all marathons and other competitive endurance sport events, there is usually a lower age limit, although many races have been organised to permit children and teens to contend in their own categories.

After setting up their changeover areas, athletes don their swim gear and head to the swim area (generally a lake, river, or ocean) for the race begins. Depending on the water temperature, swimmers may be allowed to wear a wetsuit - triathlon special wetsuits are now common. Depending on the type and size of the race, there may be any of the following techniques applied to begin the race.

Mass begins, conventional in full distance events, see all the athletes enter the water at a single start signal. In wave start events, smaller groups of athletes begin the race every few minutes. An athlete's wave is usually determined either by age group or by predicted swim time. Wave commencements are more common in shorter races where a large number of amateur athletes are contending. Another option is individual time trial beginnings, where athletes enter the water one at a time, generally 3 to 5 seconds apart. The swim leg generally proceeds around a series of marked buoys and exits the water near the changeover area. Racers run out of the water, enter the transition area, and attempt to change from their swim gear into their cycling gear as quickly as possible. In some races, tents were rendered for changing clothes.

However, competition and pressure for time has led to the development of specialised triathlon clothing that is enough for both swimming and cycling, meaning many racers' transitions comprise of little more than removing wetsuit and goggles and pulling on a helmet and cycling shoes. In some cases, racers leave shoes attached to their bicycle pedals and slip their feet into them while riding. Some triathletes do not wear socks, decreasing their time in transition even more.

The cycling stage proceeds around a marked course, nearly always on public roads. In many cases, especially smaller triathlons, the roads are not closed to automobiles, although marshals are often present to help control traffic. Generally, the cycling stage finishes back at the same transition area. Racers enter the transition area, rack their bicycles, and quickly change into running shoes before heading out for the final stage. The running stage, also commonly held on public roads, generally ends at a separate finish line near the transition area. In most races, "aid stations" situated on the bike and run courses render water and energy drinks to the athletes as they pass by. Aid stations at longer events will often provide various types of food as well, including such items as energy bars, gels, fruit, cookies, and ice.

Once the triathletes have accomplished the event, there is typically another aid station for them to get water, fruit, cookies, and other post-race goodies. At the end of most larger or longer events, the provisions and post-race celebrations may be more elaborate - ranging from ice cream and professional massage tents to cookouts and barbecues.

MAJOR TOURNAMENTS

Ironman World Triathlon Championship

"Ironman" redirects here. For other uses, see Iron Man (disambiguation). The Ironman World Triathlon Championship or

Ironman Triathlon is a yearly triathlon race, made renowned by its grueling length, race circumstances, and sports television coverage.

Held every fall in the US city of Kailua-Kona, Hawaii, the race encompasses three endurance events: a 2.4 mile (3.8 km) ocean swim in Kailua-Kona Bay, a 112 mile (180 km) bicycle ride across the Hawaiian lava desert to Hawi and back, and a marathon (26.2 mile, 42 km) by the coast of the Big Island (from Keauhou to Keahole Point to Kailua-Kona); ending up on Ali'i Drive.

The present course record was set by Luc Van Lierde (Belgium) in 1996, whose winning time was 8 hrs 4 mins 8 sec. The next Ironman World Triathlon Championship will take place on October 11, 2008. Qualifying events for the Hawaii Ironman take place yearly around the world, in places such as Australia, Canada, the United States, the United Kingdom, Japan, the Canary Islands, South Africa and Europe.

Escape from Alcatraz

Escape from Alcatraz is the name given for two dissimilar triathlons held in the San Francisco Bay Area, on the West Coast of the United States. The Escape from Alcatraz initiated in 1981 as a private club event, beginning in San Francisco and ending in Marin County. The race split in 1983 with a distinct commercial event open to the public, which is now held on a shorter course entirely within San Francisco. The first Escape from Alcatraz was advised by Joe Oakes after the 1979 Ironman. The race was held in June 1981, with members of the Dolphin Club testing the course, beginning with a swim from Alcatraz to San Francisco, a bike ride to Mill Valley, and a Double Dipsea over Mount Tamalpais to Stinson Beach and back.

Wildflower Triathlon

The Wildflower Triathlon is a triathlon (swim-bike-run race) held at Lake San Antonio in Central California since 1983, the first winner being legendary Dean "The Machine" Harper. It is held the first weekend in May each year.

The original course was expanded to the standardised half-Ironman distance (1.2 mi / 56 mi / 13.1 mi) in the late 1980s, and is often adverted to as simply the long course. Two more races have afterwards been added to the event: an Olympic-distance (1.5 km / 40 km / 10 km) race and a short or "sprint" mountain-bike triathlon (0.25 mi / 10 mi / 2 mi).

Known for a specially hilly and gruelling course, it is among the largest triathlon events in the world, with 7,500 athletes and 30,000 spectators attending each year. Traditionally it is linked up with a Wildflower festival, although in recent years the festival has been eclipsed by the progressively large athletic event.

ADMINISTRATIVE BODIES

World Triathlon Corporation

The World Triathlon Corporation (WTC) is a for-profit corporation which organises, promotes and licenses the world-famous Ironman Triathlon series of triathlon races. WTC is also the owner of several "Ironman" and associated trademarks used both in connection with the Ironman race series and in conjunction with several commodity and services.

The Ironman race series culminates each year in the Hawaii Ironman Triathlon World Championships, held each year in Kailua-Kona on the Island of Hawai'i. WTC Ironman races are not approved by the International Triathlon Union (ITU) and are therefore not official triathlon world championships in the view of ITU. However, WTC and the Ironman Triathlon have been in beingness longer than the ITU, and the Hawaiian Ironman triathlon is regarded by most to be the most esteemed event on the yearly triathlon calendar. In 1990, Lew Friedland assisted Dr. James P. Gills in the acquisition and purchase of the World Triathlon Corporation. Friedland subsequently served as a member of the Board of Directors and as Vice President of WTC until his promotion to President in 1998.

Throughout his tenure, Friedland attended more than a dozen Ironman Triathlon World Championship races in Kona, Hawaii. After celebrating the successful 25th anniversary of the Ironman Triathlon in 2004, Friedland expressed interest in importantly reducing his role and amount of travel. Ben Fertic, formerly Vice President of Information Systems, followed Friedland as President of WTC in 2004. Fertic, an Ironman finisher joined WTC in 2000 and has been heavily engaged in the business operations and day-to-day decision making for WTC. During Fertic's tenure as VP, he was instrumental in making Ironman Live, the online presence of the Ironman Triathlon, which helped bring the race's online presence and the races themselves to a new level, including online video streaming of the events.

International Triathlon Union

The International Triathlon Union, headquartered in North Vancouver, British Columbia, Canada, was conceived in 1989, and organises official world championship series races for the sport of triathlon (swim-bike-run races). It was conceived in part to give the growing sport of triathlon an official organising body and in part to advocate for the entry of triathlon into the Olympic Games.

The main ITU race series is the short-course or Olympic Distance Triathlon world cup, which included thirteen races in 2004. The distances for the ITU world cup races are 1500m swim, 40km bike, and 10km run. They were selected from existing swim, bike, and run distances already in the Olympic Games.

This distance of triathlon has become one of the elementary standards in the world of triathlon. More freshly, the ITU has made a long distance race circuit with official world championships. Long Distance Triathlon races are very alike in length to Ironman Triathlon races owned and organised by the World Triathlon Corporation. The ITU also approves and organises official Aquathlon (swim-run) and Duathlon (bike-run) championships.

International Ultratriathlon Association

International Ultratriathlon Association (IUTA) is regrouping ultratriathlete and race organiser sharing the same goal of making Ultratriathlon a sport event recognise around the world. To explain what Ultratriathlon is, we should at the start mention that this sport is a sport extreme and it is addressed only to people that have a certain expertise in endurance sport and also to people who should prove their capacity before they could enter in that kind of event.

Ultratriathlon is a kind of race that applies the multiple of Ironman distance as bestowed in Hawaii. We multiply by a factor that will define the length of the race. The Ironman distance is a swim of 3.8 k, Bike ride of 180 k and finishing up by a run of one marathon which is 42.2 k. So in IUTA the distance are multiply by two, three, four or more depending of the race.

As an exempla if it is a double ultratriathlon the distance is 7.6 km of swim, 360 km of bike and 84.4 km of run and each of the distance are done non stop and the first finisher win the race. Up to know the records for that type of races are progressing on a steady basis. The IUTA is a recognise organisation in that field of activity and had already approved more than 50 races of that nature. Up to know there is no race requesting more endurance that those races made around the world. In the year 2007 there was six races approved by IUTA they where as follow:

FAMOUS PLAYERS

Jimmie Georgas

Born April 2, 1926, he is a Citizen of Canada. Gold medallist at six back-to-back ITU World Duathlon Championships: 1994-99 inclusive. Streak halted by flat tire at Calais in 2000. From a family of sports nuts and thespians. Father was partner in renowned Players Theatres. Brother Louis was member of Canada's 1940 Olympic team in downhill skiing. Eldest son Chris runs small hotel in southern France, remains top masters bike racer. Daughter Marilynn was top xc skier, now Canada's 50-54 champion in duathlon.

Paula Newby-Fraser

Paula Newby-Fraser was born on June 2, 1962, she is an Ironman triathlete. She was born in Rhodesia (now Zimbabwe) and raised in South Africa, where she was a nationally-ranked swimmer as a child.

She won the Ironman Triathlon World Championship in Hawaii an unprecedented 8 times in 1986, 1988-1989, 1991-1994, and 1996, four of them consecutively. She is also referred to as "The Queen of Kona". Newby-Fraser won 24 Ironman races overall between 1986 and 2002. Among several other awards, the United States Sports Academy named her as one of the top 5 professional women athletes of the last 25 years (1972-97). Newby-Fraser is the current holder of the Ironman Women's world record of 8:55:28.

Madonna Buder

Sister Madonna Buder was born on 24 July 1930, she is a Roman Catholic nun from Spokane, Washington. As a nun with the Sisters for Christian Community, Sister Madonna has the freedom to choose her own ministry and lifestyle.

She is well known in the Triathlon community for her accomplishments in age group races. She has accomplished over 200 triathlons including thirteen Ironman Triathlons. At the 2005 Hawaii Ironman, at age 75, she became the oldest woman ever to complete the race, finishing up 1 hour before the 17-hour midnight cut-off time. At the 2006 Hawaii Ironman, at age 76, she again became the oldest woman ever to finish the race, finishing with a time of 16:59:03.

Scott Eder

Scott Eder was born on October 7, 1957 in Brooklyn, New York, he is a sports executive, marathoner, triathlete, personal trainer and gym designer. He is the only child of Howard A. (1932-2002) and Diane G. Eder (b. 1934). Now a longtime resident of Dallas, Scott was an accomplished collegiate baseball player at Austin College. He later became an Ironman triathlete and presently a private coach/trainer to athletes of all sports.

In the past 23 years, Scott has completed more than 140 triathlons, qualified for and finished the Hawaiian Ironman Triathlon and The Boston Marathon. Scott has run a total of 18 marathons including a personal best of 2 hours 47 minutes in the 1983 Houston Tenneco Marathon.

Victor Andres Plata

Victor Andres Plata was born on April 10, 1973, he is a triathlete from the United States. He was born in Minneapolis, Minnesota; his hometown is Santa Cruz, California. Plata contended at the second Olympic triathlon at the 2004 Summer Olympics. He placed twenty-seventh with a total time of 1:57:09.09. Plata was the alternate for the U.S. Olympic Team in 2000. In 2005 Plata was ranked as high as 4th in the ITU World Rankings for triathlon.

In 1997 Plata graduated from California Polytechnic State University in San Luis Obispo with a degree in social sciences.

REFERENCES

Alter, S.: *Science of Flexibility*, 2nd edn, Human Kinetics, Champaign, IL, 1996.

Alter, S.: *Sport Stretch*, Human Kinetics, Champaign, IL, 1998.

Dintiman, G. and Ward, R.: *Sport Speed*, Leisure Press, Champaign, IL, 1988.

Ellison, D.: *Performance Stretching*, Human Kinetics, Champaign, IL, 1999.

Goldberg, B. (ed.): *Sports and Exercise for Children with Chronic Health Conditions*, Human Kinetics, Champaign, IL, 1995.

Newsholme, E., Leech, T. and Duester, G.: *Keep on Running*, John Wiley & Sons, Chichester, UK, 1994.

Reaburn, P. and Jenkins, D.: *Training for Speed and Endurance*, Allen & Unwin, Sydney, 1996.

Rowland, T.W.: *Developmental Exercise Physiology*, Human Kinetics, Champaign, IL, 1996.

21

Volleyball

Volleyball is an Olympic team sport in which two teams of six active players (five normal players and one 'libero'), are separated by a high net. Each team tries to score points versus one another by grounding a ball on the other team's court under organized conventions.

The complete conventions of volleyball are extensive, and points are awarded as follows: If the ball touches the ground outside the court area, the team which made contact with it last loses the point. If the ball touches the ground on team A's side of the net, team B is awarded a point, and vice-versa. The ball must be hit over the net to get a point. The team who wins the point then serves. The first team to reach 25 points wins the set and the first team to win three sets wins the match. Teams can contact the ball only three times before the ball crosses the net and consecutive contacts must be made by dissimilar players. The ball is normally played with the hands or arms, but players can legally strike or push (short contact) the ball with any part of the body.

Through time, volleyball has evolved to involve common methods of spiking, passing, blocking, and setting, as well as specialized player positions and offensive and defensive structures. Because many plays are made above the top of the net, vertical jumping is an athletic skill emphasised in volleyball. This article focuses on competitive indoor volleyball, which is carefully governed and played indoors. Several variations of volleyball have evolved for casual play, including the Olympic spin-off sport beach volleyball.

Women's Volleyball

The game of volleyball was primitively made for men, but women's volleyball quickly turned famous also. The games were very alike, but the women's volleyball games were shorter and much slower than the men's volleyball games– primarily because their playing style differed and throughout those times women still wore dresses, so they did not dive for the ball. Women's volleyball was viewed as a game to help girls improve their posture; many people did not expect women to play the game competitively or aggressively.

Most of the physical education teachers and experts did not regard athletics for females; they did not think that women should engage in those types of activities. Competitive women's volleyball did not start until after the first national volleyball championships were held in 1922.

The first women's volleyball teams were organized in 1923, and in 1924 the first conventions for women's volleyball were published. Another set of conventions was published for women's volleyball in 1926 by the National Section on Women's Athletics (NSWA). Those conventions set the women's volleyball court size at 30 by 60 feet and restricted ball contacts to no more than 3 per side. Additionally, the players could only touch the ball when it was above waist level.

Fig. Women Volleyball

Volleyball turned more and more famous among the women through the years. More women and girls wanted to play the sport, so dissimilar organizations set up teams and competitions. In the 1930's the NSWA changed its name to the National Section for Girls' and Women's Sports and they published decree books for high school volleyball and college volleyball. The sport was quickly growing, and many high schools and colleges tendered volleyball for both men and women.

Beach Volleyball

Beach volleyball, or sand volleyball, is an Olympic team sport played on sand. Like other variations of volleyball, two teams, separated by a high net, try to score points versus the other by grounding a ball on the other team's court. Competitive beach volleyball teams normally consist of two players, although recreational variations can contain any number of players. Originating in Hawai'i and popularized in Southern California, beach volleyball now enjoys worldwide fame, even in countries without conventional beaches, like Switzerland.

HISTORY

The history of volleyball has changed dramatically from it humble startings. As the fame has grown and the sport has dispersed around the world, the game has been adjusted into many dissimilar forms. Volleyball was made by the Young Men's Christian Instructors (YMCA) in Massachusetts, and more specifically by William G Morgan. At the time, basketball was also a new sport, and Morgan discovered that it was more strenuous then few of the men could play. Morgan saw that the physical contact of basketball and the fast pace tired the older businessmen that enjoyed playing sports. So, he made a sport known as "mintonette" which finally grew into the game of volleyball.

Morgan's game was played on a rectangular court with a net across the center of the court. The court was small enough so that the players would not need to run often over a large space. To reduce costs and permit more people to play the game, players could use their hands to bat the ball back and forth over the net instead of applying rackets or other gear. The net was positioned six feet six inches above the floor so that it was just above the average player's head. The ball was a lightweight ball built from an inflated basketball bladder. To eliminate the physical contact Morgan positioned each team on either side of the net. As the game started, players would use their hands to hit the ball back and forth until it went out of bounds or hit the floor. Morgan's game was designed to be playing in innings; each inning comprised of three serves by each team– just like baseball. Each team was permited to hit the ball as many times as they wanted in order to get the ball over the net to the opponents. If the ball hit the floor before returning over the net, then the other side won a point.

Morgan known as the game mintonette because it resembled badminton, and the game of mintonette quickly took off as men of all ages enjoyed it. Approximately a year after Morgan made mintonette, in 1896 Morgan presented it to a group of YMCA physical education directors. Dr. Alfred Halsted suggested to Morgan that he alter the name to "volley ball" subsequently the game comprised of volleying the ball back and forth over the net. The first standard volleyball game was playing on July 7, 1896 at Springfield College.

Volleyball was primitively designed for middle-aged men who were not vigorous sufficient to play basketball. But today, the sport of volleyball offers a wide range of competition for men, women, and children. As you look back through the history of volleyball, you will see how much alter has occurred over the years. The history of volleyball dates as far back as 1895 in Massachusetts. The game of volleyball was very tame compared to the sport that we play today.

You can find many dissimilar types of games in the history of volleyball it can be everything from a recreational activity, played for practice, and also amateur competitions and pro tournaments. It is played indoors, outdoors, on sand courts, on grassy fields, or even in a pool. People enjoy the sport of volleyball all over, no matter what their skill levels are. Volleyball through history has also grew into a sport that students enjoy.

Many high schools and colleges have teams that contend versus other high schools and colleges or on intramural or club teams. Volleyball has also been adapted so that people with disabilities can enjoy the sport. The outstanding thing about volleyball is that it can be adapted however the players would like, the net can be lowered, court dimensions can alter, and the game can be played just about anywhere.

Though there have been few varying conventions during the history of volleyball, today's competitive world of volleyball has strict conventions.

Regardless of the level of play, it is important to build both individual and teamwork skills. Building individual skills is important, but if the teamwork skills are not built it can be the difference between a defeat and victory. Teams should be able to communicate and work together to maximize each play.

The first standard ball employed in volleyball is disputed; few sources say that Spalding made the first standard ball in 1896, while others claim it was made in 1900. The conventions have evolved over time; by 1916, the skill and power of the set and spike had been brought in, and four years afterwards a "three hits" decree and back row hitting guidelines were formed. In 1917, the game was changed from 21 to 15 points. In 1919, approximately 16,000 volleyballs were distributed by the American Expeditionary Forces to their troops and allies, which sparked the growth of volleyball in new countries.

The first country outside the United States to adopt volleyball was Canada in 1900. An international federation, the Fédération Internationale de Volleyball (FIVB), was established in 1947, and the first World Championships were held in 1949 for men and 1952 for women.

The sport is now famous in Brazil, in Europe (where particularly Italy, the Netherlands, and countries from Eastern Europe have been major forces subsequently the late 1980s), in Russia, and in other countries including China and the rest of Asia, as well in as the United States. Beach volleyball, a variation of the game played on sand and with only two players per team, turned a FIVB-endorsed variation in 1987 and was added to the Olympic program at the 1996 Summer Olympics.

Volleyball moved across America as it dispersed from one YMCA to another. Within 10 years, volleyball dispersed to other countries through YMCA and the military. The history of volleyball shows that the Canadians started playing it in 1900, the Caribbean started playing it in 1906, and the Japanese started playing volleyball in 1908. It then moved onto other countries such as China, the Philippines, and South America.

The first Open Invitational Tournament was sponsored by YMCA and held in Germantown, Pennsylvania. Prevost Idell was the YMCA director in Germantown, and he was also one of the game's strongest supporters. The secretary of the YMCA War Office enjoyed the game of volleyball and decided that it should be integrated into the recreation and physical education programs for soldiers.

Because of this decision, soldiers started playing volleyball throughout their free time, particularly throughout World War 1. Eastern Europe caught onto the game while US soldiers were stationed there, and it quickly turned very famous because it could be played inside throughout the winter. The game also dispersed through US soldiers to Africa and Egypt.

History of Women's Volleyball

Women had been playing volleyball for a long time. However, they had to wait until 1949 for the U. S. Volleyball Association to start sponsoring actual competitions as they had already been doing for years for men. After the sport was added to the Olympics in 1964, it opened the door for women to make a name for themselves and gave them a dissimilar way to earn gold medals for their country.

Before they arrived at the Olympics, many women were already showcasing their volleyball skills for the world. Mary Jo Peppler was named "outstanding volleyball player" at Bulgaria's International Games in 1970. Just five years afterwards, she was named Coach of the Year by the International Volleyball Association. Eleven years afterwards the Women's Professional Volleyball Association starts and their first event is held in May in 1987 at Newport Beach in California.

In 1999, the Pan American games which were being held in Manitoba, Canada that year decided to include beach volleyball, as well as seven other sporting events for women. Women from the United States succeeded in landing a place at the Olympics for the third consecutive year in 2000.

Four years afterwards, player Holly McPeak breaks a record by scoring her 68th Professional Beach Volleyball title. She broke the record for the most tournament wins throughout a woman's sports career. That same year the U. S. volleyball team takes home the gold at the Olympics in Athens, Greece.

In 2005, a member of that gold medal winning Olympic team earned even greater honors by being named the NCAA's woman athlete of the year. Today, women like Kerri Walsh and Misty May-Treanor who have been named Sportswoman of the Year by the Woman's Sports Foundation for three back-to-back years continue to showcase all of the talent, hard work, and discipline women can bring to the table in competitive volleyball.

Without their and others' contribution to the sport, women would certainly have had a much harder time breaking through boundaries in the sports world. And that's incisively why understanding the history of women's volleyball is so important.

History of Beach Volleyball

Although popularised in Southern California, the first registered beach volleyball games took place on the beaches of Waikiki in Honolulu, Hawai'i at the Outrigger Canoe Club. Primitively designed to give bored surfers something to do when the surf was down, the game quickly evolved into more organized six-man matches. The most popular ancient player was legendary waterman, Duke Kahanamoku.

Beach volleyball started to appear in Europe in the 1930s. By the 1940s, doubles tournaments were being played on the beaches of Santa Monica for trophies. In the 1960s, an attempt to start a professional volleyball league was made in Santa Monica.

It failed, but a professional tournament was held in France for 30,000 French francs. The first Manhattan Beach Open was held in 1960. The tournament is now regarded the "Wimbledon of Beach Volleyball".

In the 1970s, a few professional tournaments in Santa Monica were sponsored by beer and cigarette companies. At the professional level, the sport persisted fairly obscure until the 1980s when beach volleyball experienced a surge in fame. Players like Karch Kiraly and Sinjin Smith turned household names. In 1987, the FIVB made the first World Beach Volleyball Championships, played in Rio de Janiero, Brazil. The FIVB started organizing worldwide professional tournaments, and laid the groundwork for the sport's Olympic first appearance in 1996.

THE GAME

The Court

The game is played on a volleyball court 18 meters long and 9 meters wide, split up into two 9 m × 9 m halves by a one-meter wide net placed so that the top of the net is 2.43 meters above the center of the court for men's competition, and 2.24 meters for women's competition (these heights are varied for veterans and junior competitions).

There is a line 3 meters from and parallel to the net in each team court which is regarded the "attack line". This "3 meter" (or 10 foot) line divides the court into "back row" and "front row" areas (also back court and front court).

These are in turn split up into 3 areas each: these are numbered as follows, commencing from area "1", which is the position of the serving player.After a team gains the serve (also known as siding out), its members must rotate in a clockwise direction, with the player previously in area "2" moving to area "1" and so on, with the player from area "1" moving to area "6".

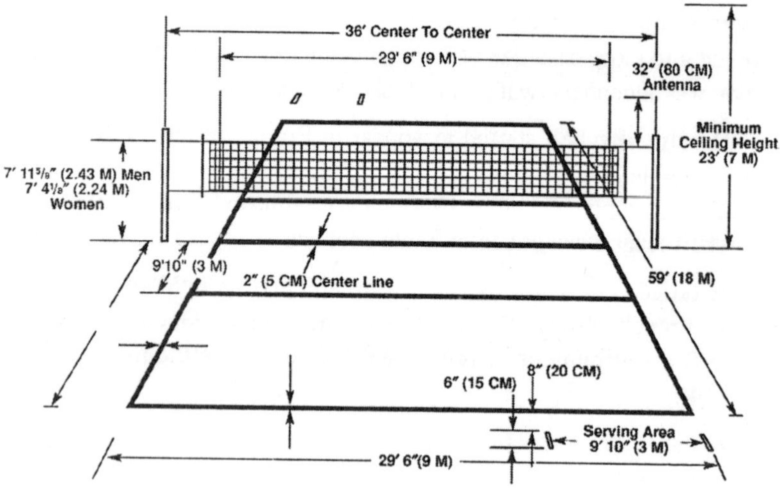

Fig. Court

The team courts are surrounded by an area known as the free zone which is a minimum of 3 meters wide and which the players may enter and play within after the service of the ball. All lines denoting the boundaries of the team court and the attack zone are drawn or painted within the dimensions of the area and are therefore a part of the court or zone. If a ball comes in contact with the line, the ball is regarded to be "in". An antenna is placed on each side of the net vertical to the sideline and is a vertical extension of the side boundary of the court. A ball passing over the net must pass completely between the antennae (or their theoretical extensions to the ceiling) without contacting them.

Ball

The volleyball is built of leather or synthetic leather and inflated according to FIVB rules:

- Its circumference is 65–67 cm and its weight is 260–280 g.
- Its inside pressure shall be 0.30–0.325 kg/cm2 (4.26–4.61 psi, 294.3–318.82 mbar or hPa).

Fig. Volleyball

Game Play

Each team comprises of six players. To get play commenced, a team is chosen to serve by coin toss. A player from the serving team (usually accepted to have the advantage inplay) throws the ball into the air and attempts to hit the ball so it passes over the net on a course such that it will land in the conflicting team's court (the serve).

Fig: Service

The conflicting team must use a combination of no more than three contacts with the volleyball to return the ball to the adversary's side of the net. These contacts normally consist first of the bump or pass so that the ball's trajectory is aimed towards the player assigned as the setter; second of the set (normally an over-hand pass applying wrists to push finger-tips at the ball) by the setter so that the ball's trajectory is aimed towards a place where one of the players assigned as an attacker can hit it, and third by the attacker who spikes (jumping, raising one arm above the head and hitting the ball so it will move quickly down to the ground on the adversary's court) to return the ball over the net.

The team with possession of the ball that is trying to attack the ball as described is said to be on offense. The team on defense attempts to prevent the attacker from directing the ball into their court: players at the net jump and reach above the top (and if possible, across the plane) of the net in order to block the attacked ball.

If the ball is hit around, above, or through the block, the defensive players arranged in the rest of the court attempt to control the ball with a dig (normally a fore-arm pass of a hard-driven ball). After a successful dig, the team transitions to offense. The game continues in this manner, rallying back and forth, until the ball touches the court within the boundaries or until an error is made.

Errors and Faults

- The ball lands out of the court, in the same court as the team that touched it last, under the net to the conflicting team's court, or the ball touches the net "antennas." The ball also may not pass over or outside the antennas even if it lands in the opponents' court.
- The ball is touched more than three times before being returned to the other team's court.
- The same player touches the ball twice in succession.
- A player "lifts" or "carries" the ball (the ball persists in contact with the player's body for too long).
- A player touches the net with any part of his or her body or clothing while making a play on the ball (with the exception of the hair).
- The players of one team do not manage to touch the ball before the ball lands in their half of the court.
- A back-row player spikes the ball while it is completely above the top of the net, unless he or she jumped from behind the attack line (the player is, however, permited to land in front of the attack line).
- A back-row player participates in a finished block of the conflicting team's attack (finished means at least one blocker touched the ball)

Scoring

When the ball hits the floor within the court boundaries or an error is made, the team that did not make the error is awarded a point, whether they served the ball or not. The team that won the point serves for the next point. If the team that won the point served in the former point, the same player serves again. If the team that won the point did not serve the former point, the players of the team revolve their position on the court in a clockwise manner. The game continues, with the first team to score 25 points (and be two points ahead) awarded the set. Matches are best-of-five sets and the fifth set (if necessary) is normally played to 15 points. (Scoring varies between leagues, tournaments, and levels; high schools occasionally play best-of-three to 30; in the NCAA games are played best-of-five to 25.)

Before 1999, points could be scored only when a team had the serve (side-out scoring) and all sets went up to only 15 points. The

FIVB changed the conventions in 1999 (with the alterations being compulsory in 2000) to use the present scoring system (formerly known as rally point system), primarily to make the length of the match more predictable and to make the game more spectator- and television-friendly.

The Libero

In 1998 the libero player was brought in internationally, the term means free in Italian, the NCAA brought in the libero in 2002. The libero is a player specialized in defensive skills: the libero must wear a contrasting jersey color from his or her teammates and cannot block or attack the ball when it is entirely above net height. When the ball is not in play, the libero can replace any back-row player, without prior notice to the officials.

This replacement does not count versus the substitution limit each team is permited per set, though the libero may be replaced only by the player whom they replaced. The libero may function as a setter only under certain limitations. If one makes an overhand set, one must be standing behind (and not stepping on) the 3-meter line; otherwise, the ball cannot be attacked above the net in front of the 3-meter line. An underhand pass is permited from any part of the court.

The libero is, usually, the most skilled defensive player on the team. There is also a libero tracking sheet, where the referees or officiating team must keep track of who the libero subs in and out for. There may only be one libero per set (game), though there may be a dissimilar libero in the starting of any new set.

MAJOR TOURNAMENTS

Volleyball World Championship

The Volleyball World Championship is a men's and women's indoor volleyball competition. It is the oldest and most important of all the international events organized by the FIVB and must not be confused with the Volleyball World Cup or the Volleyball World League.

The history of the World Championship goes back to the startings of volleyball as a professional, high level sport. One of the first concrete measures taken by the FIVB after its foundation in 1947 was the formation of an international competition involving teams from more than one continent. In 1949, the first edition was played in Prague, Czechoslovakia. At that point, the tournament was men's only and still restricted to Europe.

Three years later, a women's version was brought in; the events were synchronized and expanded to include nations from Asia, and started to be held in 4-year cycles. By the following edition, there were also teams from South, Central and North America.

Subsequently volleyball was to be added to the Olympic Program in 1964, the 4-cycles were advanced in 2 years after the fourth edition (1960), so that the World Championship may alternate with the Summer Olympics. As of 1970, teams from Africa also took part in the competition, and the primitive goal of having members from all five continental confederations in the games was attained.

The number of teams involved in the games has changed importantly over the years. Following volleyball's increase in fame, they raised steadily to over 20 in the 1970s and part of the 1980s, were then cut short to 16 in the 1990s, and eventually set up in 24 after 2002. Today, the World Championship is the most comprehensive of all events organized by the FIVB, and arguably the second most important, surpassed in prestige only by the Olympic Games.

World Grand Prix

FIVB World Grand Prix is a women's volleyball competition. Played every year since 1993, it is regarded the women's version of the World League. In 2004, it distributed US$ 1.295 million in prizes. World Grand Prix was made in 1993 as part of the FIVB's marketing strategy to raise the sport of volleyball by establishing yearly international competitions. It was modelled after the World League, a successful event for men that had been brought in three years before.

The Grand Prix made women's volleyball very famous in East Asia; the lack of concern on the part of the audience is nevertheless still significant throughout the world. Today (2004), the competition is maintained primarily with the support of Asian investors.

The budget for prize money has been growing steadily since 1993, but at a rather slow pace. The figures have arrived at $1.295 million dollars in 2004 - meager when compared to the World League's $13 million.

World League

The World League is a men's volleyball competition. Made in 1990, it is the longest and richest of all the international events organized by the FIVB. The tournament is yearly. In 2007, the final games took place on July 11–15 in Katowice, Poland. In 2006, $20 million dollars in prize money were distributed amidst 16 participating teams from 5 continents. This event should not be confused with the other international volleyball contests, the Volleyball World Cup and the Volleyball World Championships.

European Beach Volleyball Championship

The European Beach Volleyball Championship (or the Nestea European Championship Final) is a sport contest for national teams in the sport of beach volleyball. The championship combines events for men and women, and is held annually, organized by the CEV (the European volleyball federation). At the first European Championships held in 1993 just men contended. A year afterwards the women got their own championship. From 1995 it has been a combined event, for both men and women.

ADMINISTRATIVE BODIES

Association of Volleyball Professionals

The AVP (Association of Volleyball Professionals) was established in 1983 by Leonard Armato. The organization began its own American beach volleyball men's tour in 1984. By the late 80's, the tour was experiencing tremendous growth, in part through the promotion of the sport by successful players such as Sinjin Smith, Randy Stoklos, Mike Dodd, and Tim Hovland.

The early to mid 90's are seen by many as the "glory years" of the AVP as the tour corporate sponsorship, and thus, prize money, was at its peak. This period was largely reigned by the team of volleyball legend Karch Kiraly and Kent Steffes. The AVP also begun to hold women's events, contending with the WPVA tour.

By 1997, the tour was in decline under mounting fiscal problems as sponsors started to withdraw support for the sport. The organization entered Chapter 11 bankruptcy in 1998.

In 2001, Leonard Armato returned to revamp the AVP. The organization united the men's and women's beach volleyball tours under one umbrella. The AVP turned the focal point around which professional beach volleyball in the United States presently (2007) revolves. The international counterpart to the AVP is the FIVB.

The AVP represents professional beach volleyball via tours that are broadcast over television networks like NBC and versus.

Fédération Internationale de Volleyball

Fédération Internationale de Volleyball (FIVB) is the international regulating body for the sport of volleyball. Its headquarters are situated in Lausanne, Switzerland.

The FIVB was established in Paris, France in 1947. In the late 1940s, few of the European national federations started to address the issue of creating an international regulating body for the sport of volleyball. Initial discussions finally lead to the installation of a Constitutive Congress in 1947. Fourteen national federations representing five dissimilar continents attended the meetings where, between April 18 and 20, the entity was officially constituted, having Frenchman Mr. Paul Libaud as first president.

One of the prime goals of the 1947 Congress was attained two years afterwards with the formation of the first international major volleyball event, the World Championship. In 1952, a women's version of the tournament was also brought in. In 1964, the IOC endorsed the addition of volleyball to the Olympic program. By this time, the number of national federations affiliated to the FIVB had grown to 89. Afterwards in that year (1969), a new international event, the World Cup was brought in. It would grow into a qualifying event for the Olympic Games in 1991.

Following the retirement of Mr. Libaud and the election of Mexican Mr. Rubén Acosta Hernandez for the position of president in 1984, the FIVB moved its headquarters from Paris, France to Lausanne, Switzerland and intensified to an unprecedented level its policy of promoting volleyball on a worldwide basis. Measures taken in this direction include the formation of yearly competitions for men's and women's volleyball (the World League, in 1990, and the Grand Prix, in 1993), the indication of Beach volleyball as an Olympic event (1996) and a number of alterations in the conventions of the game with the purpose of raising public visibility.

Asian Volleyball Confederation

The Asian Volleyball Confederation (AVC) was formed on May 6th, 1952, and since then AVC has become one of the largest continental volleyball associations in the world, with its member federations increasing to 65 from only 12 at the time of its set-up.

The first concept of the AVC was launched by the initiative of the late Mr. Nishikawa of Japan on April 1952, and on May 6th of the same year, AVC was officially formed with 12 countries taking part. The major tasks of AVC at the time were the organization of volleyball championships and the Asian Games. In 1962, AVC was renamed the Asian Volleyball Federation (AVF) with 20 affiliated national federations after the FIVB Congress held in September 1961 decided to establish the continental zone committee.

NORCECA

The North, Central America and Caribbean Volleyball Confederation (NORCECA) is an incorporated, non-profit organization responsible for all volleyball activities that take place in its zone. NORCECA is the continental confederation that represents its thirty-five (35) member countries at the International Volleyball Federation (FIVB) level. The Confederation is responsible for, among other things, the staging of Olympic and World Championship zone qualification tournaments, as well as continental championships for both men and women in Indoor and Beach Volleyball. In 2003, NORCECA celebrated its thirty-fifth (35th) anniversary.Throughout the 1966 Caribbean and Central American Games held in San Juan, Puerto Rico, the idea of the NORCECA concept was born.

At that time it was known as the Caribbean and Central American Zone. The growth of the NORCECA Confederation came from the visionary mind of today's FIVB President, Dr. Rubén Acosta Hernández, in conjunction with various other sportsmen from Puerto Rico, Cuba, Dominican Republic and Haiti. NORCECA was formally made by the FIVB and its President, Mr. Paul Liband in 1968, when Canada and the United States of America brought together the Confederation. Its first Senior Championship was held in Mexico from Aug 4-9, 1969 and the inaugural game featured Haiti vs. Panama, with Haiti winning 3-0. NORCECA's first Junior Championship was staged in 1980.

FAMOUS PLAYERS

Dain Blanton

Dain Blanton was born on November 28, 1971 in Laguna Beach, California, he is an American beach volleyball player, who attended Pepperdine University where he was an All-American and guided The Waves to a National Volleyball Championship in 1992 as a sophomore.

He won the gold medal in Beach Volleyball in the 2000 Olympic Games, alongside partner Eric Fonoimoana. He came back to the 2004

Olympic Games in Athens, Greece with partner Jeff Nygaard, becoming the first and only two-time U.S. male Beach Volleyball Olympian. Blanton and Fonoimoana split after decree alterations went into effect in 2001. [(Rally or Point per Play scoring as opposed to having to conventional Serve to Score a point) (Court size changed from 30 by 30 feet per side to 8x8 meters)]. Height turned the deciding factor of the split subsequently new conventions cater to a full time tall blocker at the net at all times. They went different ways in search of Big Blockers.

Nicole Branagh

Nicole Branagh was born on January 31, 1979 in Orinda, California, she is an American volleyball player. She played internationally for the US National team in indoor play and is presently on the AVP tour playing beach volleyball professionally. Branagh played collegiately at the University of Minnesota. She was twice named to the All-America Second Team as an outside hitter. She also was the Big Ten's co-Player of the Year in her senior season. Following graduation, she played for the US National team from 2001 to 2003, ending up her national career after the 2003 Pan American Games, where she won a Bronze Medal.

After spending a season as an assistant coach at Cal-State Fullerton, Branagh joined the AVP tour. She has had relatively good success on the AVP tour: she was named the AVP Rookie of the Year in 2005 and it is Most Improved Player in 2006. She partnered with Olympian Holly McPeak for much of the 2006 season before partnering with Elaine Youngs, McPeak's partner in the 2004 Summer Olympics, for the remainder of the 2006 season and the 2007 season. She contended with Youngs at the 2008 Summer Olympics.

Elaine Youngs

Elaine Youngs was born on February 14, 1970 in El Toro, California; he is an American beach volleyball player. As of 2007, Youngs has won 38 professional beach volleyball tournaments in her career. In addition, she won a bronze medal at the 2004 Summer Olympics with teammate Holly McPeak. In 2002, she was named MVP of the AVP.

Youngs is a 1993 graduate of UCLA, where she majored in history. She played on the indoor womens team at the 1996 Olympics. She is also known for her intense nature which has led to a string of broken partnerships, occasionally even public disagreements with her partners.

She teamed with Rachel Wacholder for the 2005 and much of the 2006 season, but in August 2006, Wacholder left Youngs and partnered with Jennifer Kessy Boss. Youngs replaced Wacholder with Nicole Branagh for the 2007 AVP season. On September 8, 2007 Youngs won the Goddess of the Beach tournament for the first time in Las Vegas, Nevada.

Andrea Gardini

Andrea Gardini was born on October 1, 1965 in Bagnacavallo, he is an Italian former volleyball player. Standing at 202 cm, he played central blocker and totalled 418 caps for the Italian national volleyball team. He was three time world champion, in 1990, 1994 and 1998. One of the most effective and famous players of 1990s, he was also four times gold medal at the European Championship (1989, 1993, 1995 and 1999) and six times Italian champion.

REFERENCES

Alter, S.: *Science of Flexibility*, 2nd edn, Human Kinetics, Champaign, IL, 1996.

Alter, S.: *Sport Stretch*, Human Kinetics, Champaign, IL, 1998.

Dintiman, G. and Ward, R.: *Sport Speed*, Leisure Press, Champaign, IL, 1988.

Ellison, D.: *Performance Stretching*, Human Kinetics, Champaign, IL, 1999.

Goldberg, B. (ed.): *Sports and Exercise for Children with Chronic Health Conditions*, Human Kinetics, Champaign, IL, 1995.

Micheli, L.J. (ed.): *Clinics in Sports Medicine: The Young Athlete*, W.B. Saunders, Philadelphia, PA, 1995.

Newsholme, E., Leech, T. and Duester, G.: *Keep on Running*, John Wiley & Sons, Chichester, UK, 1994.

Reaburn, P. and Jenkins, D.: *Training for Speed and Endurance*, Allen & Unwin, Sydney, 1996.

Rowland, T.W.: *Developmental Exercise Physiology*, Human Kinetics, Champaign, IL, 1996.

Bibliography

Aahper. *Ideas for Tennis Instruction, Lifetime* Sports Education Project. Washington, D.C.: American Association for Health, Physical Education, and Recreation, 1966.

Allen Guttmann, *Games and Empires: modern sports and cultural imperialism* New York: Columbia University Press, 1994.

Allen, Kevin: *USA Hockey: A Celebration of A Great Tradition.* Chicago: Triumph Books, 1997.

Allen, Kevin: *Why is the Stanley Cup in Mario Lemieux's Swimming Pool?.* Chicago: Triumph Books, 2000.

Alter, S.: *Science of Flexibility*, 2nd edn, Human Kinetics, Champaign, IL, 1996.

Alter, S.: *Sport Stretch*, Human Kinetics, Champaign, IL, 1998.

Alwày, Leonore K.: "Indoor Group Golf Instruction". *Journal of Health and Physical Education*, 99: 1, January, 1938.

Andreson, C. W.: *Head Up, Heels Down.* New York, the Macmillan Company, 1944.

Ansell, M. P. (Lt. Col.): *Jumping*. London, The Naldrett Press, Ltd. 1954.

Antal, Dr. Laslo. *Competitive Pistol Shooting*. West Yorkshire: EP Publishing Ltd., 1983.

Antal, Laslo and Ragnar Skanaker. *Pistol Shooting*. Liverpool: Laslo Antal and Ragnar Skanaker, 1985.

anyway? London: Mainstream Publishing, 2000.

Archetti, E. P.: 'Hibridacion, diversidad y generalizacion en el mundo ideologico del futbol y el polo', *Prismas. Revista de historia intelectual,* 1997.

Arlt, R.: *Aguafuertesportenas: cultura ypolitica,* Buenos Aires: losada, 1994.

Armour, Tommy: *A Round of Golf with Tommy Armour*. New York, Simon and Schuster, 1959.

Armour, Tommy: *How to Play Your Best Golf All the Time*. New York, Simon and Schuster, 1953.

Armus, D.: Tja idea del verde en la ciudad moderna. Buenos Aires 1870–1940', *Entrepasados. Pevista de Historia,* 1996.

Arthurson: *Arko: My Game*, Ken Arthurson with Ian Heads,, Ironbark, Sydney, 1997.

Asociacion Argentina de Polo: *Canpeonato Argentine Abierto de Polo. Cien afios de historia 1893–1993,* Buenos Aires: Asociacion Argentina de Polo, 1993.

Barnaby, John M.: *Racket Work: the Key to Tennis*. Boston, Allyn and Bacon, Inc., 1969.

Barnett, John *Barnett's Manual: Analysis and Procedures for Bicycle Mechanics.* VeloPress, 2003.

Bassham, Lanny R. *With Winning in Mind.* Wilsonville, Oregon: BookPartners, Inc., 1995.

Baucher, F.: *Horsemanship, Including the Breaking and Trainirig of Horses.* 3rd American ed., Philadelphia, Parry and McMillan, 1856.

Baun, Bobby, with Anna Logan: *Lowering the Boom: The Bobby Baun Story.* Toronto : Stoddart Publishing Co. Limited, 2000.

Beardsley, Doug: *Country On Ice*. Canada : Polestar Press., 1987.

Benoist-Gironiere, Yves: *The Conquest of the Horse*. Warford, England, Mayflower Press, 1952.

Berg, Pattie, and Otis Dypwich: *Golf.* New York, A. S. Barnes & Co., 1941.

Beudant, E.: *Horse Training, Out-door and High School*. New York, Charles Scribner's Sons, 1950.

Bower, T.: *Broken Dreams: Vanity, Greed and the Souring of British Football.* London: Simon and Schuster, 2003.

Bradlee, Dick.: *Instant Tennis*. New York, Devin-Adair Company, 1962.

British Horse Society and the Pony Club: *Manual of Horsemanship*. London, 6th ed. reprint 1968.

British Show Jumping Association *Know the Game, Show Jumping*, London, Educational Productions, Ltd., 1954.

Broer, Marion R.: *Efficiency of human Movement*. Philadelphia, W. B. Saunders Company, 1966.

Broer, Marion R.: *Efficiency of Human Movement*. Second edition. Philadelphia, W. B. Saunders Company, 1966.

Bruce, Ben and Evelyn Davies: *Beginning Golf.* Belmont, California, Wadsworth Publishing Co., Inc., 1962.

Carlsöö, Sven: "A Kinetic Analysis of the Golf Swing". *The Journal of Sports Medicine and Physical Fitness*, 7:76-82, June, 1967.

Ceballos, F. (ed.): *El polo en la Argentina,* Buenos Aires: Ccmando en Jefe del Ejercito, 1969.

Chamberlain, Harry D.: *Riding and Schooling Horses.* Washington, D.C., Armoured Cavalry Journal, 1947.

Chandler, John. *The Target Gun book of Pistol Coaching.* Worcs: Peterson Publishing Company Ltd., 1983.

Christensen : *Rugby League Year Book 1974 Official Yearbook of the NSWRL,* E E Christensen, NSWRL, Sydney, 1974.

Christensen: *Rugby League Year Book 1973 Official Yearbook of the NSWRL,* E E Christensen, NSWRL, Sydney, 1973.

Coaching Association of Canada. *National Coaching Certification Program: Coaching Theory Level 1* Canada: Coaching Association of Canada, 1988.

Coaching Association of Canada. *National Coaching Certification Program: Coaching Theory Level 2* Canada: Coaching Association of Canada, 1988.

Cochran, Alastair and John Stobbs: *The Search for the Perfiect Swing.* New York, J. B. Lippincott Company, 1968.

Coleman : *Fatty The strife and times of Paul Vautin,* Mike Coleman, Ironbark Press, Randwick, 1992.

Conn, D.: *The Football Business: Fair Game in the 90s.* Edinburgh, 1997.

Corry, D., Williamson, P. and Moore, S,: *A game without vision: The crisis in English football,* 1993.

Crosman Corporation. *Airgun News, vol. 7: Shot Talk - Airguns Defined* Crosman Corporation, 1998.

Csikszentmihalyi, Mihaly and Susan A. Jackson. *Flow in Sports.* Windsor: Human Kinetics, 1999.

Cummings, Parke.: *American Tennis.* Boston, Little, Brown and Company, 1957.

Cuthbertson, Tom and Rick Morrall, *Bike Bag Book,* Ten Speed Press, 1981.

Cutler, Merrit.: *The Tennis Book.* New York, McGraw-Hill Book Company, 1967.

d'Endrody, A. L.: *Give Your Horse a Chance.* London, J. A. Allen & Co., reprint 1967.

Dante, Joe and Len Elliot: *Stop That Slice.* New York, McGraw-Hill Book Co., 1953.

David Underwood, *Start of Play: Cricket and Culture in Eighteenth Century England* London: Allen Lane, 2000.

Davies, Mike.: *Lawn Tennis*. New York, Arc Books, 1963.

Davis, Joe: "'Hit Down' for High Shots", *Golf Digest*, 17:5:63, May, 1966.

de Baretto Souze: *Advanced Equitation.* New York, E. P. Dutton & Co., Inc., 1926.

de Gregor Romaszkan: *Horse and Rider in Equilibrium.* Brattleboro, Vermont, The Stephan Green Press, 1967.

DeLong, Fred, *DeLong's Guide to Bicycles and Bicycling: The Art and Science.* Krause Pub, 1978.

DiCicco, Tony and Colleen Hacker, PhD. and Charles Salzberg *Catch Them Being Good.* London, England: Penguin Group, 2002.

Dintiman, G. and Ward, R.: *Sport Speed*, Leisure Press, Champaign, IL, 1988.

Domey, Richard L. *Mental Training for Shooting for Success, 2nd Ed.* Pullman, Washington: College Hill Communications, 1989.

Downs, Todd, *Bicycling Magazine's Complete Guide to Bicycle Maintenance and Repair: For Road and Mountain Bikes.* Rodale Press, 2005.

Ellison, D.: *Performance Stretching*, Human Kinetics, Champaign, IL, 1999.

Elmer, Robert P. and Nabih A. Faris: *Arab Archery.* Princeton, New Jersey, Princeton University Press, 1945.

Everett, Peter and Virginia Skillman: *Beginning Tennis.* Revised edition. Belmont, Wadsworth Publishing Company, Inc., 1968.

Filthy, ed. *Patrick Brown*, no. 1 Spring 2003.

Forbes, Thomas A.: *New Guide to Better Archery.* Harrisburg, Pennsylvania, The Stackpole Co., 1961.

Fossum, Bruce and Mary Dagraedt: *Golf.* Bostoll, Allyn and Bacon, Inc., 1969.

Fraley, Oscar: *Golf in Action.* New York, A. A. Wyn, Inc., 1952.

Frayne, Trent: *Famous Hockey Players.* New York: Dodd, Mead & Co., 1973.

Frayne, Trent: *The Mad Men of Hockey.* Toronto: McClelland & Stewart. 1974.

Freeman, P.C. *Modern Pistol Shooting.* London: Faber and Faber, 1968.

Freeman, P.C. *Target Pistol Shooting: Eliminating the Variables.* London: Faber and Faber, 1981.

Freeman, S.: *Own goal! How egotism and greed are destroying football.* London: Orion, 2000.

French : *100 Great Rugby League Players* , Ray French, Macmillan, Melbourne, 1989.

Fynn, A. and Guest, L.: *Out of time: Why football isn't working*. London: Simon and Schuster, 1994)

Fynn, A.: *Dream On: A year in the life of a Premier League club*. London: Simon and Schuster, 1996.

Garland, G., Malcolm, D. and Rowe, M.: *The future of football: challenges for the twenty-first century*. London: Frank Cass, 2000)

Gensemer, Robert: *Tennis*. Philadelphia, W. B. Saunders Company, 1969.

Goldberg, B. (ed.): *Sports and Exercise for Children with Chronic Health Conditions*, Human Kinetics, Champaign, IL, 1995.

Gould, Dick: *Tennis, Anyone*? Palo Alto, The National Press, 1965.

Hamil, S., Michie, J, and Oughton, C. (eds): *The changing face of the football business*. London: Frank Cass, 2001.

Harmon, Bob and Keith Monroe: *Use Your Head in Tennis*. New York, Macmillan Company, 1965.

Harris : *The Best of Both Worlds The Michael O'Connor Story*, Bret Harris, Pan Macmillan, Sydney, 1991.

Harvey, T. D.: "How Spin Controls Flight", *Golfing*, 18: 20-23, June, 1954.

Haugen, Arnold and Harlan Metcalf: *Field Archery and Bow Hunting*. New York, Ronald Press, 1963.

Heads : *The Kangaroos The saga of Rugby Leagues's great tours*, Ian Heads, Lester-Townsend, Sydney, 1990.

Heads : *True Blue The story of the NSW Rugby League*, Ian Heads, Ironbark Press, Randwick, 1992.

Henderson, Bob, and Stevenson, John, *Haynes Bicycle Book*. Haynes Pub., 2002.

Herrigel, Eugen. *Zen in the Art of Archery*. New York: Vintage Books, 1999.

Herrigel, Eugen: *Zen in the Art of Archery*. New York, Pantheon Books, Inc., 1963.

Hicks, Betty: *Fundainentals of Golf*. Chicago, J. A. Dubow Mfg. Co., 1948.

Hinchliffe, K.B. *Target Pistol Shooting*. London: David and Charles, 1981.

Hochman, Louis: *The Complete Archery Book*. Greenwich, Connecticut, Fawcett Publications, Inc., 1957.

Hoff, Feliks. *Kyodo: The Way of the Bow*. London: Shambhala Publishing Limited, 2002.

Hogan, Ben: *Power Golf.* New York, A. S. Barnes & Co., 1953. New York, Pocket Books, Inc., 1953.

Horton, E.: *Moving the goalposts: Football's Exploitation.* Edinburgh: Mainstream, 1997)

Institute for Public Policy Research: *Trust in Football.* London: IPPR, 2004.

Johnson, Joan and Paul Xanthos: *Tennis*. Dubuque, Wm. C. Brown Company Publishers, 1967.

Jolie Solomon, "*Baseball Is a Game of Hits, Runs, Errors and Lyric Poetry,*" Wall Street Journal, 4 February 1987.

Jones, C. M.: *Tennis: How to Become a Champion.* London, Faber and Faber, 1968.

Jones, Ernest, and Innis Brown: *Swinging Into Golf.* Revised ed. New York, Robert M. McBride and Co., 1946.

Jones, Robert T., Jr., and Howard E. Lowe: *Group Instruction in Golf.* New York, American Sports Publishing Co., 1939.

Jones, Robert Tyre (Bobby): *Golf is My Game*. Garden City, New York, Doubleday and Company, Inc., 1959.

Jorgensen, Theodore Jr.: "On the Dynamics of the Swing of a Golf Club", *American Journal of Physics*, 38:644-651, May, 1970.

Kelly, G.: *Sweet FA*. London: CollinsWillow, 1999.

Ken LaZebnick, "*Opinion," Minneapolis Review of Baseball* 1, no. 4 Fall 1981: 20-21.

Keneally : *The Uitility Player The Des Hasler Story*, Tom Keneally, Pan Macmillan, Sydney, 1993.

King, A.: *The End of the Terraces. The transformation of English football in the 1990s*. Leicester, Leicester University Press, 1998.

Kushner, Kenneth. *One Arrow, One Life: Zen, Archery, Enlightenment*. Boston: Tuttle Publishing, 2000.

Larsen, Marjorie: "Hockey and Archery Carts". *Journal of Health, Physical Education and Recreation*, 25:3:64, March, 1954.

Laver, Rod.: *How to Play Championship Tennis*. New York, Macmillan Company, 1965.

Leathdale, Frank and Paul Leatherdale. *Successful Pistol Shooting*. Wiltshire: The Crowood Press, 1995.

Leighton, Jim.: *Inside Tennis: Techniques of Winning*. Englewood Cliffs, Prentice-Hall, Inc., 1969.

Mangrum, Lloyd: *Golf, a New Approach.* New York, McGraw-Hill &Book Co., 1949.

Mark Schraf, *Cooperstown Verses* Jefferson NC: MacFarland, 2001.

Marr, Dave: "Get the Most out of What You've Got", *Golf Digest*, 17:5:29, May, 1966.

Masters : *Inside Out Rugby League Under Scrutiny*, Roy Masters, Ironbark, Sydney , 1997.

McDonald & Henderson : *The Manly Warringah Story* , Charles E McDonald & Captain C W T Henderson, Paul Hamlyn, Dee Why, 1975.

McFarlane, Brian: *One Hundred Years of Hockey.* Toronto: Deneau, 1989.

McFarlane, Brian: *The Youngest Goalie.* Toronto: Summerhill, 1989.

McGregor : *Simply the Best The 1990 Kangaroos*, Adrian McGregor, Queensland of University Press, St Lucia, 1991.

Metheny, Eleanor: *Movement and Meaning.* New York, McGraw-Hill, 1968.

Metz, Dick: *The Secret to Par Golf.* New York, The Macmillan Co., 1940.

Middlecoff, Cary: *Master Guide to Golf*. Englewood Cliffs, New Jersey, Prentice-Hall, Inc., 1960.

Middleton : *Rugby League 1987-88 Official Yearbook of the NSWRL*, David Middleton (Ed.), Lester-Townsend, Sydney, 1988.

Moorhouse : *At the George And Other essays on Rugby League*, Geoffrey Moorhouse, Hodder & Stoughton, London, 1989.

Morrison, Alex J.: *A New Way to Better Golf.* New York, Simon and Schuster, 1935.

Morrison, Alex J.: *Better Golf Without Practice.* New York, Simon and Schuster, 1940.

Mossop : *The Moose That Roared*, Rex Mossop with Larry Writer, Ironbark Press, Randwick, 1991.

Mosston, Muska.: *Teaching Physical Education from Command to Discovery.* Columbus, Ohio; Charles E. Merrill Publishing Co., 1966.

Mudville Diaries: *A Book of Baseball Memories, collected by Mike Schacht* New York: Avon Books, 1996.

Murphy, Bill and Chet Murphy: *Tennis for Beginners.* New York, Ronald Press Company, 1958.

National Golf Foundation: Golf in *Physical Education.* Chicago, 1941.

National Golf Foundation: *Golf Lessons; The Fundamentals as Taught by the Foremost Professional Instructors*. Chicago, 1952.

National Rifle Association. *The Basics of Pistol Shooting*. Fairfax: The National Rifle Association, 1991.

National Rifle Association. *Three Gun Bullseye Pistol Shooting*. Fairfax: The National Rifle Association, 1987.

Newsholme, E., Leech, T. and Duester, G.: *Keep on Running*, John Wiley & Sons, Chichester, UK, 1994.

Niemeyer, Roy: *Beginning Archery*. Belmont, California, Wadsworth, 1962.

Novak, Joe: *How to Put Power and Direction in Yonr Golf*. New York, Prentice-Hall, Inc., 1954.

Novak, Joe: *Par Golf in 8 Steps*. New York, PrenticeHall, Inc., 1950

O'Connell : *In Defence: The Wally O'Connell Story*, Wally O'Connell, Walter Patrick O'Connell OAM, Sydney, 2005.

Orlick, Terry. *In Pursuit of Excellence*. Windsor: Human Kinetics, 2000.

Pig Iron: *Baseball*, ed. Jim Villani and Rose Sayre, no. 9 1982.

Plante, Jacques: *Goaltending*. New York : Collier, 1972.

Player, Gary: "Square Your Stance to Groove Your Swing", *Golf Digest*, 17:5:34-37, May, 1966.

Pullum, Bill and Frank T. Hanenkrat. *Successful Shooting*. Washington: National Rifle Association of America, 1981.

Reichert, Natalie and Gilman Keasey: *Archery*. New York, Ronald Press, 1961.

Reilly: *Reilly a life in rugby league*, Malcolm Reilly with Ian Heads, Ironbark, Sydney, 1998.

Rotella, Dr. Bob, with Bob Cullen *The Golfer's Mind*. New York, New York: Free Press, 2004.

Runyan, Paul: "Magic Eye Golf". *Golf*, National Golf Review, Inc., 4:22, Nov., 1940.

Sharp, Archibald, *Bicycles and Tricycles: A Classic Treatise on Their Design and Construction*. Dover Press, 2003.

Slusher, Howard S.: *Man, Sport and Existence*. Philadelphia, Lea & Febiger, 1967.

Smith : *The Sea Eagle has Landed The Story of Manly Warringah Rugby League Club*, Robert Smith, Sea Eagle Marketing, Brookvale, 1991.

Snead, Sam: *How to Hit a Golf Ball from Any Sort of Lie*. Garden City, N. Y., Blue Ribbon Books, 1950.

Snead, Sam: *How to Play Golf and Professional Tips on Improving Your Score* New York, Garden City Publishing Co., 1946,

Snead, Sam: *Natural Golf*. New York, A. S. Barnes and (Co., 1953.

Snead, Sam: *Sam Snead on Golf*. Englewood Cliffs, New Jersey, Prentice-Hall, Inc., 1961.

Sogen, Omori. *An Introduction to Zen Training*. Boston: Tuttle Publishing, 2001.

Sports Illustrated Editors.: *Sports Illustrated Book of Tennis*. New York, J. B. Lippincott Company, 1961.

Standl, Hans. *Pistol Shooting as a Sport*. Translation by Anita Pennington. London: Kaye and Ward, 1979.

Talbert, William F. arld Bruce S. Old: *The Game of Doubles in Tennis*. Philadelphia, J. B. Lippincott Company, 1956.

The Best of Spitball: *The Literary Baseball Magazine*, ed. Mike Shannon New York: Pocket Books, 1988.

The Game of Singles in Tennis. Philadelphia, J. B. Lippincott Company, 1962.

Thompson, Maurice: *The Witchery of Archery*. Pinehurst, North Carolina, The Archers Co., 1928.

Training Hunters, Jumpers, and Hacks. New York-D. Van Nostrand Co., Inc., 1952.

Trengrove, Alan (ed.).: *How to Play Tennis the Professional Way*. New York, Simon and Schuster, 1964.

Video : *Munly the first 50 years*, Video, Sea Eagle Marketing, Brookvale, 1996.

W&H: Whiticker & Hudson : *The Encyclopedia of Australian Rugby League Players: Manly-Warringah Sea Eagles*, Alan Whiticker

Whiticker : *Captaining the Kangaroos: Rugby League Test and World Cup Captains*, Alan Whiticker, New Holland, Sydney, 2004.

Whiticker : *From the Bush to Brookvale The Cliff Lyons Story*, Alan Whiticker, Gary Allen Pty Ltd, Smithfield, 2000.

Whiticker : *Grand Finals of the NSW Rugby League*, Alan Whiticker, Gary Allen Pty Ltd, Smithfield, 1994.

Index

S

T